Literacies and Technologies

Literacies and Technologies

A Reader for Contemporary Writers

Robert P. Yagelski
State University of New York at Albany

New York   San Francisco   Boston
London   Toronto   Sydney   Tokyo   Singapore   Madrid
Mexico City   Munich   Paris   Cape Town   Hong Kong   Montreal

ACQUISITIONS EDITOR:	Lynn M. Huddon
DEVELOPMENT EDITOR:	David Cohen
MARKETING MANAGER:	Carlise Paulson
SUPPLEMENTS EDITOR:	Donna Campion
MEDIA SUPPLEMENTS EDITOR:	Nancy Garcia
PRODUCTION MANAGER:	Donna DeBenedictis
PROJECT COORDINATION, TEXT DESIGN, AND ELECTRONIC PAGE MAKEUP:	Elm Street Publishing Services, Inc.
COVER DESIGNER/MANAGER:	John Callahan
COVER ART:	José Ortega/Stock Illustration Source, Inc.
PHOTO RESEARCHER:	Caroline Gloodt
SENIOR MANUFACTURING BUYER:	Dennis J. Para
PRINTER AND BINDER:	The Maple-Vail Book Manufacturing Group
COVER PRINTER:	Phoenix Color Corp.

For permission to use copyrighted material, grateful acknowledgment is made to the copyright holders on pp. 587–589, which are hereby made part of this copyright page.

Library of Congress Cataloging-in-Publication Data

Literacies and technologies: a reader for contemporary writers / [compiled by] Robert Yagelski.
    p.   cm.
  Includes bibliographical references and index.
  ISBN 0-321-05118-1
    1. Readers–Technology. 2. English language–Rhetoric–Problems, exercises, etc. 3. Report writing–Problems, exercises, etc. 4. Technology–Problems, exercises, etc. 5. Literacy–Problems, exercises, etc. 6. Readers–Literacy. 7. College readers. I. Yagelski, Robert.

PE1127.T37 L58   2001
808'.0427–dc21   00-041957
                                   CIP

Please visit our website at **http://www.awl.com/yagelski**

ISBN 0-321-05118-1

1 2 3 4 5 6 7 8 9 10–MA–03 02 01 00

To Joe and Charlotte Hafich,
for their generous and constant support through these many years.

Contents

CHAPTER 7 *Futures* 538

Preface

Just a few years ago, teachers of writing could assume that many, perhaps most, of the students in their composition courses had little experience with the Internet. They could also assume that some of those students had probably not even used computers for basic word processing. Today, it is a rare student who has not surfed the World Wide Web, sent email, or used a word processing program to write a school paper. At a time when school officials no longer talk much about "getting wired" but worry instead about computer upgrades, students are surrounded by an astonishing array of powerful technologies for writing, reading, and communicating unimaginable even a decade ago.

In the midst of these rapid technological developments, the challenge for students to write effectively is greater than ever. The newest computer technologies and the virtual frontier of the World Wide Web represent exciting new possibilities for literacy learning. However, these technologies have complicated the challenge of learning to write well. It is no longer enough to compose clear sentences and coherent paragraphs. Now students must also learn to negotiate new contexts for writing and reading created by those technologies. The already challenging task of developing a critical perspective on the world and one's place in it is being redefined as new technologies reshape the ways in which we write and read and interact with each other.

Literacies and Technologies is designed to help students confront these challenges. Unlike other composition readers, *Literacies and Technologies* foregrounds literacy as a technology itself. It invites students to inquire into the nature of literacy and its function in their lives. And it challenges them to examine how technology, shapes their world. As they practice writing in a variety of forms, students are encouraged to examine not only what and how they write but also *why* they write as they do. *Literacies and Technologies* fosters the development of a *reflective literacy* that can help students negotiate the challenging writing and reading tasks they will confront in a world increasingly defined by new and ever more sophisticated technologies.

To foster reflective literacy among students, *Literacies and Technologies* includes several distinctive features:

- ▪ ***Carefully sequenced reading selections*** that demonstrate effective writing in a variety of genres, rhetorical situations, and voices. These reading selections encourage students to examine the nature of writing and reading. Students also explore the relationship between literacy and technology, and the implications of that relationship on their culture and lives. The texts include familiar pieces from well-known writers that have become classics as well as more contemporary writings, such as online "e-journals" and Websites. The readings are grouped into seven chapters, each highlighting an important theme related to students' ongoing inquiry into the nature of literacy and technology.

- *An innovative pedagogical apparatus that develops reflective literacy.* The questions and activities for each reading foster a reflective stance on reading and writing. Students are encouraged to place texts in various rhetorical and historical contexts and to examine the choices the writers made in those contexts. These questions and activities prompt students to engage in critical self-reflection by exploring the ways in which their writing and reading might grow out of their own experiences living in a modern, technological society.

- *A sustained attention to rhetorical issues* as those issues emerge in students' reading of the various texts in this book and in students' own writing. The chapter introductions and the headnotes for each reading focus students' attention on important ideas and issues addressed in the readings, and on the specific situations within which these texts were written and read. The questions and activities included with each reading selection, especially those under "Examining Rhetorical Strategies," encourage students to engage each text from the perspective of both the writer and the reader. Students examine the choices writers made—regarding style, content, structure, voice, and so on. They also examine their reactions to the readings in terms of their specific socio-cultural backgrounds and experiences.

These features make *Literacies and Technologies* an especially useful yet flexible resource at a time of change and challenge. *Literacies and Technologies* can supplement conventional writing and reading assignments in a variety of ways. It is well-suited for conventional composition courses. It can also be used in writing courses that focus on computer technologies. In either case, *Literacies and Technologies* is designed to encourage the same careful and sustained inquiry into the nature of literacy and technology and their role in our lives.

Literacies and Technologies includes an instructor's manual that provides a detailed explanation of the book's design along with a wealth of practical information and suggestions for using the book in a writing course. In addition, *Literacies and Technologies* has a Companion Website. It can be used by students and teachers as a supplemental resource. The Website includes links to relevant sites that relate to specific reading selections and to issues raised by the readings in the book. It also includes support for the questions and activities included in the book and provides a gateway for searching the Internet for more information related to the readings.

As the way we live and literacy itself is reshaped by new technologies, *Literacies and Technologies* can be an invaluable resource for students learning to write and read their ways into our complex and exciting world.

Acknowledgments

This book would not exist without the support, insight, and hard work of a number of people. Foremost among them are Anne Smith and Meg Botteon, formerly of Longman, whom I cannot thank enough. Anne's vision and persistence initially turned an idea into a proposal and then a project. Her confidence, support, and good humor helped give rise to the project and kept it going at critical times. Meg provided invaluable advice and direction, especially in the early stages of the project. Her savvy, insight, and sound ideas profoundly influenced the design and content of this book, and her keen understanding of composition enabled me to maintain a focus on teaching and writing. My sincerest thanks to both of them.

My thanks as well to the many other people at Longman who helped make this book possible, especially Arlene Bessenoff and Donna DeBenedictis. Special thanks to Erika Berg, who guided this project through difficult last-minute changes with enthusiasm and forward-looking advice. Thanks also to Caroline Gloodt, whose good work with permissions helped keep the project on track. Steven Pusztai of Elm Street Publishing Services provided solid editorial support in the project's latter stages, and Nancy Garcia provided guidance for the Companion Website.

Many reviewers offered careful and detailed feedback that helped make this a better book: Linda Adler-Kassner, University of Michigan–Dearborn; Maryam Barrie, Washtenaw Community College; Collin Brooke, Old Dominion University; Nick Carbone, Marlboro College; Wes Chapman, Illinois Wesleyan University; Debra Frank Dew, Texas A&M University, Corpus Christi; Keith Dorwick, The University of Illinois at Chicago; Timothy Flood, University of North Carolina, Greensboro; Jeffrey R. Galin, California State, San Bernardino; Vandana Gavaskar, Ohio State University; Susan-Marie Harrington, Indiana University–Purdue University, Indianapolis; Rich Haswell, Texas A&M University; Charles Hill, University of Wisconsin, Oshkosh; Charles Moran, University of Massachusetts, Amherst; Libby Roeger, Shawnee College; Rebecca Shapiro, Westminster College; Norinne J. Starna, University of California, Santa Barbara; Christian Weisser, University of Tampa; Joanna Wolfe, University of Texas, Austin; and Judith Wootten, Kent State. My thanks to all of them.

John Trimbur, of Worcester Polytechnic Institute, Victor Villanueva, of Washington State University, and Irwin Weiser, of Purdue University, provided helpful advice as I learned the nuances of developing a composition reader. I am grateful for their support. My thanks, too, to my students, especially those in English 494 at the State University of New York at Albany during spring semester, 2000, for helping me gain insights into teaching and writing that influenced this book in its latter stages.

Finally, my deepest thanks to my wife, Cheryl, for her unwavering support and patience. She provided the time, space, and comfort I needed to complete this book.

Robert P. Yagelski

GENERAL INTRODUCTION

Literacies and Technologies in Our Lives

You were probably using sophisticated computer technologies long before you entered your first college writing class. Word processing programs, Web authoring software, multimedia composers, browsers for surfing the Internet—most likely you routinely use one or more of these powerful technologies for writing and communicating. As you surely realize, it is becoming increasingly common for students at all levels of education not only to learn to use computers for writing and other tasks but also to explore new kinds of computer-based communication, such as Internet chat rooms or interactive Web sites. On television and movie screens, in classrooms, and in countless books and articles that invite you to "ride the information superhighway," you encounter images of the possibilities afforded you by these technologies—a seemingly constant barrage of images promising ever faster, ever more powerful, ever better technologies. But how often have you stopped to consider—carefully and with a skeptical but informed eye—the implications of these amazing new literacy technologies for your own writing and reading and communicating? How often have you thought about the subtle yet potentially problematic ways in which these technologies can affect how you see and understand the world and your place in it? How often have you considered the historical importance of the astounding technological changes that you are witnessing and participating in at the beginning of a new millennium?

This reader is intended to encourage you to do just that: to think carefully and in an informed and reflective way not only about how we use these new technologies as we write and read but also about literacy and technology in general and how they shape our worlds. You probably think of the computer as "technology," but you are surrounded by many other literacy technologies that you may use routinely without ever thinking about their impact on your life or the culture in which you live. The pen you use to jot down notes on a sheet of loose-leaf paper is, like the computer, a technology for writing and reading and communicating, as is the typewriter that sits on the desk in your room, as are the books in your backpack. Writing itself has been called a technology by some scholars, a tool of human design that systematizes human language and enables human beings to use that language in ways that are not possible through oral speech. Rarely do we think of writing in such grand terms, yet no other technology affects our lives as deeply.

By focusing your attention on writing and the technologies of literacy in ways that go beyond the *use* of those technologies, and by encouraging you to write and read in more critical ways not just *with* but also *about* those technologies, this book can help you become a more proficient and critical writer and reader and a more informed user of the new technologies that are increasingly available to you. This book can also help you understand how writing and reading and technology influence your life and the lives of those around you. In the reading selections presented to you and in the activities you are invited to do, this book will encourage you to think of technology as something more than the tools you use to complete certain tasks and will push you to understand literacy as something more than the basic skills of writing and reading words on a page or a screen. Ideally, this book will provoke you to examine your beliefs and attitudes about literacy and technology and will perhaps urge you to rethink your own views about these crucial matters.

The Changing Technologies of Literacy

Scholar Jay David Bolter, who has written extensively about the computer as a new technology for literacy, has argued that we have entered "the late age of print," an era in which the printing press, which has defined literacy for the past five hundred years, is giving way to the computer. Bolter has described the computer as "the fourth great technique of writing that will take its place beside the ancient papyrus role, the medieval codex, and the printed book" (*Writing Space,* p. 6). In short, Bolter announces, "The computer is restructuring our current economy of writing. It is changing the cultural status of writing as well as the method of producing books" (p. 3). (You can learn more about Bolter and his ideas about computers and writing in Chapter 2 of this book.) You don't have to look far to find a chorus of voices—in the academic world as well as in the popular media—echoing Bolter, and if you're like most students, you may already be an enthusiastic convert to this "fourth great technique of writing." With good reason: There can be no doubt that the computer is changing the ways in which we read and write, and in doing so, it profoundly influences how we conduct our daily lives and how we structure our communities. Computers as tools for communicating now pervade our lives. But we may not realize that as we use them to do everyday tasks; computers may be changing the very tasks themselves.

Consider, for instance, the use of the computer as a word processor. You have probably used a computer for writing school papers, letters, resumes, and the other kinds of documents that you need to create every day as a student or as an employee. If you're like most Americans, you probably take for granted that you can use a standard word processing program (such as Microsoft Word or WordPerfect) to write a document quickly and easily—adding, deleting, or changing words as you write. Without ever needing a sheet of paper, you can move paragraphs, delete entire pages, and even add charts or other graphics simply by clicking the mouse or typing in a few commands. You can also easily change the way your document looks: the size and shape of the letters, the margins, and even the color of the text. If you don't like something, a click of the mouse or tap of the keys will change it. (In fact, the newest word processing programs include special "macros" or "wizards": mini-programs that automatically format the piece of writing for you.) When you're satisfied with the way it looks on the screen, you can print it out so that it looks like a published document. All of these operations require the use of enormously sophisticated technology, yet they are almost as commonplace as picking up a copy of the morning newspaper from your local newsstand.

But some researchers believe that the operations you engage in as you write your letter on a computer are different in important ways from what you would have done if you had written your document on a typewriter or with a pencil and paper. For example, some studies show that writers do more revising and editing when they write with a computer than they do when writing with pencil and paper or a typewriter; these studies also show that writers pay more attention to things like the size of the letters and the margins of the page—things that affect the *appearance* of the document—when they use a computer for their writing. It is possible that these differences between word processing and pencil and paper are superficial and that in the end the document itself isn't really different. But some scholars are not so sure. They believe that using a technology like word processing for a common writing task may involve different kinds of *thinking*—that writing with a computer may alter what you are actually doing and thinking about as you write. In this sense, writing with a computer may be a profoundly different activity than writing with a pencil and paper or a typewriter.

But that isn't the whole story, either. Consider what happens when you leave the word processing program and connect the computer to the Internet in order to create a personal Web page. Once you do that—once you engage in purely *electronic* writing—everything potentially changes. With electronic writing, for example, a text is never permanent in the way a printed book or magazine makes a text permanent—that is, if the words are on the screen, you can manipulate them any way you like, whereas the words on the page of a book or a magazine can only be read—or ignored—not changed. Moreover, if you're creating a Web page, you're now using something different from conventional printed text; you're using *hypertext,* which enables you to link words, phrases, and images directly to other words, phrases, and images. Click a linked word on a Web page and you're instantly transported to another Web page. There may be more links on that page, which link to other pages or perhaps back to pages you've already visited. Many scholars believe that these capabilities of hypertext profoundly change the very nature of reading and writing. For instance, standard features of printed text such as indenting, paragraphing, and linear organization (that is, organizing your text from top to bottom and left to right), which we take for granted in a printed text, are either redefined or eliminated altogether in hypertext. Certain characteristics that we associate with "good" writing in print forms are changed or eliminated as well. In print, we usually call a "good" essay one that is clearly *focused* and well *organized,* with an effective *introduction* and *conclusion* and clear *transitions.* A Web page, however, may have a single image without words as its "introduction," and no "conclusion" at all, and the "transitions" on the page are the links that you click to go to other Web pages. All of this means that you have to read hypertext differently than you read a printed essay or book. And you write it differently as well. Hypertext may thus be redefining literacy.

This kind of change has happened before. Around 1450, a German merchant named Johannes Gutenberg developed a machine, which came to be known as the printing press, that allowed for rapid production and duplication of written materials such as fliers, journals, and books. Prior to the development of the printing press, the creation of a written document was a slow and laborious process. Copies of written documents had to be made by hand, which made books very time-consuming to produce as well as expensive. Hand copying also meant that errors were common, and, thus, copies might differ from one another. The printing press changed all that and more. According to historian Elizabeth Eisenstein, the printing press facilitated or influenced an amazing array of social, cultural, economic, and political developments throughout Europe within a few centuries of its invention (see *The Printing Revolution in Early Modern Europe,* 1983). For example, with the printing press scholars and scientists now had the possibility of obtaining *standardized* copies of important books and other documents (including charts, maps, and graphs) that previously were rare and sometimes unreliable (because of the mistakes that often occurred during hand copying). Legal practices began to change as laws were written down and distributed widely to the public. Written records of births, deaths, marriages, and business deals became common, influencing how people conducted their day-to-day activities. Inexpensive books soon became available, encouraging a dramatic increase in the numbers of people who could read and write. More interestingly, *how* people read and wrote was also changed by the printing press. Prior to the printing press, literacy rates were low, and often those few people who could read did so in a social setting rather than alone. It was not unusual, for instance, for a number of people to gather together to listen to someone read a poem or an announcement from the government. Individual silent reading was rare. After the printing press came into widespread use, however, printed materials became more widely available, and more people began learning to read. Individual silent reading became a common practice, and, by the time of the famous writer and scholar Samuel Johnson in the eighteenth century, it was one mark of an educated, literate person. These changes in literate activities and in attitudes toward literacy also shaped the potential social and political power of literacy. The printing press transformed the distribution of printed materials in European civilization and thus changed who had access to those materials. Social and political power could be wielded by those who controlled the distribution of print. In these and many other ways, the printing press dramatically changed how literacy was practiced and how it shaped people's lives.

Many observers believe that we are in the midst of similar profound changes in literacy practices as a result of the development of new computer technologies. In a hundred years, they believe, reading and writing—and how they are used in our culture—may be very different from how we know them today. If these observers are right, however, the changes they predict will not be brought about as a result of the computer alone. As the history of the printing press reveals, and as several of the writers in this book demonstrate, technology does not exist by itself; rather, it develops in the context of social, cultural, economic, legal, and political practices and beliefs. How we understand and use a specific technology can make all the difference in how that technology influences our lives. In fact, our attitudes about important aspects of our lives can profoundly shape how a particular technology is developed. For example, computer writing specialists Cynthia and Richard Selfe have examined how the *desktop*—that is, the way a particular operating system for the computer looks on the computer screen—for Microsoft Windows reflects the values of the American professional middle class. They point out that the very metaphor of a *desktop,* with images such as file folders, memos, and trashcans or recycling bins, which seems so natural to mainstream middle-class Americans, may be less familiar to people from nonmainstream groups who do not live in circumstances in which such items are commonplace. In such ways, the Selfes argue, software programs developed for computers reflect the values of certain segments of American culture and help determine how and by whom those technologies will be used (see Cynthia and Richard Selfe, "The Politics of the Interface," *College Composition and Communication,* vol. 45, 1994). Furthermore, economic and political circumstances will shape which technologies are developed and distributed and which are not. For instance, large corporations like Microsoft, which control much of the market for computer technologies, can play a huge role in influencing the development and distribution of computer hardware and software simply by deciding which products to market. In short, what we value as people and as communities will help determine to what extent technologies like the computer might affect how we read and write and communicate—and how we live.

An important purpose of this book is to encourage you to confront these complex connections and to think more carefully and critically about what might seem natural or commonplace about literacy and technology and the roles they play in your life. In doing so, this book will help you develop a kind of *reflective literacy* that can enable you to understand these important issues that affect your life and more effectively negotiate the writing and reading tasks that you face as a student and as a person in a technological and ever changing world.

Developing Reflective Literacy

When we think of literacy, we tend to think of it in a relatively simple and straightforward way as if it means one thing: the ability to read and write words on a page. But if you closely examine the activities of reading and writing, how they are done, and how they are valued, you begin to realize that "the ability to read and write" is a very complicated matter. Moreover, if you think carefully about the writing and reading that you do in your own life, it soon becomes clear that you engage in many kinds of writing and reading activities that might differ from each other in significant ways. Simply knowing how to form words with letters or to write correct sentences isn't enough to complete every writing task effectively. For instance, in order to write an effective research paper for your college psychology course, you need to know how to organize information and ideas appropriately in the paper, to refer properly to sources, to make appropriate transitions between sentences and paragraphs, to support your assertions with acceptable evidence, to sustain a viable analysis of the subject about which you're writing, and to draw relevant conclusions, among other tasks. And all of these tasks might be somewhat different if the research paper you are writing happens to be for a history course or a biology course, since each discipline requires you to have different knowledge and to understand different procedures and conventions for writing. Clearly, *literacy* means much more than simply knowing how to read and write words on a page.

Because of these complexities, it might be more accurate to speak of *literacies* when we are referring to the reading and writing activities we do. As a college student and as a person living in a technological and literate society, you develop several different literacies in order to be able to complete the writing and reading tasks that you confront in different situations in your life, each requiring the basic ability to understand letters and words but each also with its own conventions and purposes. And if you come from a background that differs in some way from mainstream American culture, then you may have developed other literacies as well. For instance, if you grew up in a home in which English was not your first language, you probably developed a literacy related to your primary language. People from particular geographic regions or people of specific religious or ethnic backgrounds may develop ways of writing and reading that differ from the mainstream literacy expected in schools and businesses. Thus, because literacy relates to specific social and cultural contexts, there is no such thing as a single literacy that is the same for everyone. Part of the challenge you face as a college student is learning new ways of writing and reading—engaging in different literacies—that may be unfamiliar to you.

In order to meet that challenge—and to meet the many other challenges you face as a literate person in our changing world—it may not be enough to learn how to read and write adequately in different situations; it may not be enough, in other words, to be able to write a "good" psychology research paper or business letter. Brazilian educator Paulo Freire, whose theories about literacy earned him international fame in the 1970's and 1980's, believed that literacy is related to how we understand the world and how we shape our roles in that world. For Freire, to be literate is to be "fully human," to be in control of your world. Freire believed that to be literate in that sense is to develop "critical consciousness" of how the world is shaped through language.* That is, a fully literate person not only can engage in reading and writing activities effectively but also understands how those activities are being used in a particular situation and the social, cultural, and political implications of those activities. That understanding enables that person to take greater control of his or her life through literacy.

The notion of *reflective literacy* in this book is based in part on Freire's ideas about critical consciousness. Reflective literacy is the ability to read and write critically and discerningly in order to understand the world more fully and to be able to participate in it effectively. You have probably heard teachers use the term *critical* in reference to thinking or reading. Usually, *critical* means to think more carefully and in more depth about something, to ask certain questions of a statement or a text, to try to place that statement or text in a larger context in order to understand it more fully. Reflective literacy encompasses that sort of critical thinking. To read and write *reflectively* is to develop a sophisticated stance toward texts from which you examine them and ask vital questions about them in order to understand not only what they might mean but also how they work in a specific context. To read and write reflectively is to ask the following kinds of questions about a text:

---

* Paulo Freire, *Pedagogy of the Oppressed,* 1970. (*Note:* All asterisk footnotes are added by the author of this volume.)

1. What do I know about this particular text?
   - What kind of text is it (for example, an academic essay, a newspaper editorial, a passage from an autobiography, a story)?
   - Where and when was it written?
   - Were there any special events or developments that gave rise to or influenced this text?
   - Does the text require familiarity with any specialized jargon or knowledge on my part?
   - Does it refer to other texts?
2. What do I know about who wrote this text?
   - Who is the author or authors?
   - What were his or her circumstances when he or she wrote this text?
   - What else might he or she have written?
   - What was his or her socioeconomic background?
   - What is his or her racial or ethnic background?
   - What kind of position in his or her community does he or she hold?
3. What do I know about why this text was written?
   - What seems to be the purpose of this text?
   - What particular circumstances seem to have led the author to write it?
   - How was the text used by the author or others?
   - What did it accomplish?
4. What do I know about the audience for this text?
   - For whom was the text first written?
   - Is the intended audience specialized or more general?
   - Does the intended audience have any special or unusual characteristics?
   - What is the author's relationship to that audience?
   - What other audiences might have influenced or been influenced by this text?

Asking such questions can help reveal how a text functions in a specific context: how it was put together by a particular person (or persons) for a particular purpose and for a particular audience, how it arises from circumstances related to that context, and how it does not exist separately from that context but must be understood within that context. In addressing such issues, you can begin to see how features of the text, such as its language and organization and the ideas or information it contains, might be related to the context in which it was written. You can begin to examine the choices the writer made in constructing this text and how those choices might reflect a variety of social, cultural, or ideological concerns beyond issues of style or structure. You can identify specific strategies the writer might have employed to accomplish his or her purpose with a particular audience. In other words, you can begin to see how that text represents a purposeful act of writing and reading.

But reflective literacy goes further than examining a text in this way. It also involves examining how a text is read and, most importantly, exploring how *you* read a text. In this sense, to develop reflective literacy is not just to read "critically" in order to examine a writer's strategies, arguments, and so on; it is also a process by which readers examine *their own* reading processes—their own ways of making meaning in a text—and try to identify how those reading processes relate to who they are as people. To read reflectively is to ask *why* you read as you do. It is to ask questions such as these:

- What do you notice about the texts you read or write? Why?
- What do you know about the subject matter of the text you are reading? What do you know about its author? How do these affect the way you read?
- What are your own beliefs about the topic of this text? Why do you have these beliefs? How might they affect your reaction to this text?
- What assumptions about reading and writing do you bring to this text? How do these assumptions influence the way you engage the text?
- How does your personal background influence the way you read and write? For instance, how does your gender, racial, or ethnic identity influence how you read this text?
- How might your social class background influence the way you read this text?
- How might your own experiences with the subject mater of the text shape your reaction to it?

Such questions rest on the belief that a reader always reads from a particular perspective related to his or her own background, experiences, identity, beliefs, and status. In other words, who you are and the experiences you have had help determine how you read and what a text means to you. In this sense, reading is a complex, *situated* activity—just as writing is—and to understand fully what a text might mean requires that you understand the perspective from which you are approaching that text. To be reflective in this way about your own reading can not only help you become a more aware, sophisticated reader with a fuller sense of who you are as a literate person, but also help you develop a better understanding of the complex nature of literacy itself.

You might reasonably wonder why it is necessary to develop such a *reflective literacy.* Isn't it enough simply to be able to read and write well enough to complete the assignments you are given in your college classes or the writing and reading tasks you have to do in your job? Perhaps. But if Paulo Freire is right that we make sense of the world through language, then to be fully literate is to control your world. Literacy is a primary means by which we understand and interact with the world and construct our own roles within it. From this perspective, literacy becomes a much more important matter than just being able to complete reading and writing tasks; it becomes a matter of acting in the world. The more fully you understand how literacy works, therefore, the more effectively you can use the power of literacy to shape your world.

In this sense, the technology of writing and the technologies used for writing and reading are at the center of your life. They constitute perhaps the most important power you have to control your life. But they are bewilderingly complex and always changing. And that complexity and change represent a great challenge for you, as a student and as a citizen, as you try to make sense of your world at the dawn of a new millennium.

Using This Reader

This reader is designed to help you develop the kind of reflective literacy described in the previous section. Accordingly, the reading selections represent a wide range of topics, writing styles, and textual forms that can help you explore the complexities of literacy and technology. The reading and writing activities that accompany each selection encourage you to examine some of the important issues raised by the readings and to try to connect those issues to your own experiences. The following sections of this introduction explain how the book is organized and how you might use it effectively as you work toward enhancing your understanding of literacy and technology and improving your own writing and reading abilities.

The Reading Selections

The reading selections included in this book are intended to encourage you to examine the relationship between literacy and technology and to consider the implications of that relationship for your culture and for your life. They are also intended to encourage you to examine your own beliefs about literacy and technology and the roles literacy and technology play in your life and in our society in general. These reading selections present you with a variety of perspectives on literacy and technology, some of which will be familiar to you and some of which will perhaps challenge you to think in unfamiliar ways about these issues. The readings also represent many different genres—personal narratives, magazine articles, research reports, and theoretical and scholarly essays—and various writing styles, and you will be encouraged to consider not only what each author is saying about literacy and/or technology but *how* he or she says it. As a whole, then, the reading selections are intended to highlight the many different ways in which questions and issues related to technology and literacy have been written about in different contexts for different audiences.

The reading selections are organized into seven chapters, each of which focuses on a specific theme related to literacy and technology. Although the readings in each chapter represent a variety of genres and perspectives on the chapter's theme, you will notice a pattern in the selections. Each chapter includes at least one first-person account of a writer's experiences with literacy and/or technology; these narratives are intended to provide portraits of how literacy and technology have helped shaped the lives of particular people in particular circumstances. In addition, each chapter includes one or more selections from popular publications such as newsmagazines or mass-market magazines about popular culture; some of these selections include articles or essays that appeared in publications available only on the Internet. These readings reflect the diversity of writing and represent provocative perspectives on literacy and technology that you might encounter in the popular press. Finally, each chapter includes several selections that are more academic and theoretical in nature. These selections are intended to push your thinking about literacy and technology by presenting challenging perspectives that may enable you to understand literacy and technology in new ways. By reading this variety of readings, ideally you will be encouraged to engage in more complex ways of thinking and to enhance your own sophistication as a reflective reader and writer.

The Reading and Writing Activities

Each reading in this book is accompanied by four different kinds of reading and writing activities that encourage you to read reflectively and to write in an informed, critical fashion. These activities are designed to help you actively explore the ways in which written language shapes your world and your interactions with your world. In addition, they are intended to provide you with carefully defined opportunities to practice various kinds of writing in various situations. There are four kinds of reading and writing activities: Reflecting Before Reading, Reflecting on the Reading, Examining Rhetorical Strategies, and Engaging the Issues. The first activity, Reflecting Before Reading, appears before each reading selection. The other activities follow each reading selection. These activities are arranged sequentially so that the questions listed under Examining Rhetorical Strategies and Engaging the Issues build upon questions listed under Reflecting on the Reading. Each type of activity is described below:

1. *Reflecting Before Reading.* These questions highlight important issues related to the reading selection to encourage you to think about those issues *while* you're reading. In doing so, these questions direct your attention to specific questions or problems that may influence the way you read the selection.

2. *Reflecting on the Reading.* These activities are intended to enhance your general understanding of the reading selection and to begin to raise important questions that might be pursued in subsequent activities. They are organized more or less from the beginning to the end of the reading selection, and they direct your attention to certain key concepts, issues, or arguments and highlight key aspects of the selection. Although these questions may sometimes seem relatively straightforward, they are a crucial part of learning what it means to read reflectively.

3. *Examining Rhetorical Strategies.* These questions focus your attention on the rhetorical situation of the reading selection—that is, the circumstances under which it was written, the audience for which the author originally wrote the piece, the author's apparent or stated purpose in writing the text, and so on. In focusing on the rhetorical situation of each reading selection, these questions can help you place the text in broader perspective and examine how and why it was written. They ask you to consider the specific circumstances and background of the author and to explore how these might have influenced the writing of the text. They also ask you to consider how *you* are reading these texts: how your own circumstances might influence your reactions to the texts. In this way, these questions direct your attention to the *activities* of writing and reading so that you might understand more fully the complexity of literacy in a variety of forms and situations.

4. *Engaging the Issues.* These activities invite you to read, write, and talk further about the issues that were raised in the previous questions. They provide you with opportunities to engage in a variety of reading and writing and group tasks that can help you deepen your understanding of the issues raised by the reading selections and to develop your own skills as a writer and a reader. The activities under this heading are often formal and include a variety of writing assignments that are intended to produce finished essays. Some of these assignments are relatively common writing activities that are typically expected of college students. Others ask you to engage in activities that extend beyond the classroom to the kinds of writing and reading that you might do in your community or job. Accordingly, you will be invited to write for audiences other than your classmates or your teacher, and you may be asked to write kinds of texts that you haven't written before. In addition, whenever appropriate, you will be invited to incorporate new computer technologies, especially the Internet, into these activities. It's important to note that for the formal essays you are asked to write in Engaging the Issues, you should work in drafts, with your teacher's guidance, and try to write finished, complete essays. In other words, engage in the process of writing as fully as you would for any formal writing assignment.

Using a Reflective Reading Journal

As the preceding sections of this introduction should make clear, reading is a complex and, above all, *active* process. The questions and activities in this book emphasize this complex and active nature of reading and invite you to roll up your sleeves and to read and write in a rigorous and reflective way. An effective way to take full advantage of these invitations to engage in the kind of active, reflective reading described here is to keep a *reflective reading journal.*

You have probably been asked by some of your high school or college teachers to keep some kind of reading log or journal or perhaps to submit regular written responses to assigned readings. Often, such assignments ask you to write your reactions to a reading passage, to form an opinion about an author's idea or argument, or to pose questions about something you find provocative or confusing in the reading. Writing about your reading in these ways encourages you to engage a reading selection in a fuller, more sustained way than might be possible by just thinking or talking informally about the reading. The reflective reading journal recommended for this book is intended to encourage just such a sustained and in-depth engagement with the readings and with the ideas and issues and questions about literacy and technology that they raise. But it goes beyond simple reactions to the readings: its primary purpose is to provide an informal but rigorous and systematic means for you to develop and practice reflective literacy.

To accomplish that purpose, you will need to use your reflective reading journal as a companion to this book—something you use whenever you read a selection from this book. You can organize and use your journal in a variety of ways, and you should try to make it comfortable, easy to use, and almost routine. But however you organize it, it is recommended that you *include four sections for each reading that coincide generally with the four kinds of questions and activities described previously in this introduction.* In each of these sections you will write responses to the questions listed under that heading for that reading selection. But each section of your reflective reading journal invites you to do more than just respond directly to the questions accompanying the readings; each section provides an opportunity to extend your thinking, to note questions or ideas, and to explore issues that arise from your reading.

If you organize and use your journal as recommended here, it can become a place where you engage in careful, critical, but sometimes messy, uncertain, and unfinished thinking about the issues raised by each reading selection in this book. In other words, your reading journal will not be a portfolio of finished, polished writing but a written forum in which to question, explore, wonder, examine, reconsider, puzzle, review, challenge, agree, disagree, and so on. How much you write in your journal will depend partly upon how fully you engage the reading and the issues raised by a specific question or an activity and partly upon how your instructor asks you to use this book in your class. Some of the questions accompanying the readings will obviously provoke much longer responses than others. Sometimes you may be excited or angered by something in a reading and will, as a result, write a lengthy response to a question about that reading. Other times you may simply jot down a few sentences in response to a question. Whatever the case, respond as fully and as honestly as you can, and don't worry about the length or quality of writing in your response.

Keep in mind that the purpose of the reflective reading journal and the other recommended activities in this book is to facilitate critical reflection about the readings and to be a vehicle for your development as a reflective reader and writer in a world defined by literacy and technology. Ideally, as you develop a more reflective literacy, you will also gain a deeper understanding of the role of literacy and technology in your life as a citizen in a democratic society, as a worker in a capitalist economy, and as a member of a diverse and complex culture. So engage the work in this reader as you engage in any reading and writing activity in your life: *as if it matters.*

CHAPTER 1

Technology, Literacy, and Progress

In the late 1960's the CBS television network aired a program called *The 21st Century*. Each week viewers of the program were informed about recent scientific and technological developments that were expected to lead to remarkable lifestyle changes in the industrialized society of the late twentieth century. One episode, for example, described new technologies that would enable manufacturers to build automobiles that could be programmed to travel to specific destinations without having to be operated by a driver. Other episodes portrayed advanced communications technologies like video telephones and high-tech homes in which computerized appliances prepared meals or washed laundry automatically so that inhabitants had fewer daily chores and more leisure time. The world of the twenty-first century, as depicted on this television program, would be filled with many such wondrous innovations that would make our lives easier, safer, more pleasant—and better.

The 21st Century aired on television at a time of stunning technological change in the United States and elsewhere in the world that perhaps made the predictions of that television program seem quite realistic to its viewers, especially to Americans. By the late 1960's, automobiles were sleeker, faster, and more plentiful than ever before; the telephone—which had once been an astonishing technological advance in its own right—was commonplace; and manufacturers were continually developing new kinds of household appliances, like dishwashers and refrigerators with automatic ice makers, that seemed to make life better. Medical advances, including powerful new drugs and amazing surgical procedures, seemed to promise a future free of previously life-threatening illnesses and terrible diseases that had plagued humankind for centuries. Television itself was a technological marvel, fast becoming a central facet of modern life. Color televisions began to replace old black-and-white sets in the 1960's, and live color pictures could be broadcast from anywhere in the world into American living rooms. Those same televisions displayed images of huge rockets launched by NASA on its quest to meet the challenge issued by President John F. Kennedy to land an astronaut on the moon by the end of the decade. When Neil Armstrong stepped onto the surface of the moon in 1969, millions of people watched the event on their television sets, and the achievement seemed to symbolize the stunning possibilities that technological progress held for human beings.

We live in a time of similarly remarkable technological developments. Consider, for instance, the cellular phone, which enables its users to talk to friends, family, or business partners from almost anywhere at any time. Or consider the desktop computer. In the 1950's, as the early computers were being developed, one of the developers commented that because the computer required so much space (the early prototypes actually filled a room the size of an average living room), it would never be a widespread technology, and he predicted that no more than a few hundred computers would ever be built. Today, small, portable, and astonishingly powerful computers are everywhere: in businesses of all kinds, in classrooms, on airplanes, in our homes. With sophisticated software programs, an individual student, using widely available computer hardware and "peripheral" equipment like a scanner or color printer, can publish a professional looking newsletter that a decade ago could have been produced only at great expense by a commercial printer using complex and expensive printing machinery. With another inexpensive piece of peripheral equipment, a modem, that same student can "publish" that newsletter on the World Wide Web, making its text and images instantly available to millions of people around the world. These technologies have become so commonplace that it is easy to forget that such technological capability was little more than a dream in the 1960's—indeed, it was unimaginable to many people even ten or fifteen years ago.

We tend to view such amazing technological developments as "progress," and we tend to think of "progress" as good. New technologies improve on old ones and make life better. We look back at the past and wonder how we lived without the technological innovations that we now take for granted. How did we manage with only pens and paper or typewriters? How did we manage without cellular telephones and electronic mail? But what we think of as technological progress does not come without its costs. The same technologies that enable us to watch live television images of events occurring on the other side of the world also help guide so-called "smart bombs" that destroy, maim, and kill with frightening accuracy and power. The latest automobiles containing conveniences that were unimaginable three decades ago also continue to pollute the atmosphere and consume gasoline made from oil that must be pumped out of the earth in ways that irreparably damage fragile ecosystems. In the 1980's, some Americans called for a boycott of the Exxon oil company after its oil tanker, the *Valdez,* ran aground off the Alaskan coast, spilling millions of gallons of crude oil along wild beaches with disastrous environmental results. But many of those same Americans were driving cars fueled by gasoline that might eventually have been made from the oil carried by the *Valdez.* Indeed, the same technologies that make our lives easier and more comfortable may directly or indirectly make the world less safe and less comfortable in ways that we see only when spectacular accidents such as the *Valdez* oil spill occur.

But the ramifications of technological progress are not always so obvious or clear-cut as the smog-filled air over a city or an oil-fouled coastline—especially for technologies we take for granted, such as pens or paper or printing presses. Literacy scholar Peter Mortensen has examined some of the environmental and social consequences of literacy and literacy technologies. He describes a small town in North Carolina whose primary employer is a large paper mill that supplies paper to printers and publishers, and he shows that the vast and increasing demand for paper—which is put to all kinds of uses in our society, including the publication of books like the one you are reading right now—can lead to the economic oppression of the workers in those mills, to terrible environmental destruction of local streams and forests, and to other social and economic ills that we typically do not associate with literacy. Mortensen reveals that the simple act of using a piece of paper to write an essay, for example, represents a choice that can have serious effects on people and places that are quite distant from that essay writer. At the same time, the paper produced by those mills is part of a complex process by which school children acquire books to help them learn to read, by which people in different parts of the world can share information and ideas through books, newspapers, and magazines, and by which physicians and researchers can record their experiments as they develop ways of combating horrifying diseases. The industrial process used to make paper at that North Carolina mill may degrade local streams and harm wildlife, but the paper made by that same process is used by environmental advocates to inform millions of people of the ways in which industry can destroy ecosystems: that same paper, manufactured in a way that can be environmentally harmful, can also be used to save the environment. Technology, literacy, and progress are complex and ambiguous matters indeed.

The readings in this chapter encourage you to consider that complexity and ambiguity. Although we as individuals and as a society may rarely question the benefits of technology, literacy, or progress, the authors of this chapter's readings ask you to do just that. They ask you to consider exactly what *progress* might mean in human terms, in environmental terms, in economic terms, in ethical terms. Does *progress* always mean a better life for all? What is lost and what is gained when technological advances are made and adopted by our society? Who benefits from such advances? Who doesn't? In what ways might technology improve *your* life? In what ways might it harm you and the world you live in? And how are literacy, technology, and progress linked? The example of the paper mill referred to earlier indicates that these links are many and complex and often not apparent to us as we use everyday technologies—like books and paper—that seem so harmless and indeed so "good." The readings in this chapter will encourage you to think carefully and perhaps in unfamiliar ways about these common technologies that we use in our daily lives; they will also encourage you to examine your own attitudes toward them.

Some of the writers in this chapter examine technological advances of the past century in human terms and encourage us to consider the value of technologies as a function of the quality of human life. They raise important questions about how technology and progress have affected our ability to connect with other human beings. Some of the writers in this chapter approach these questions of progress on a much grander scale. They see great promise in technology as well as potential harm in it. Some of these writers worry that the rush to embrace new computer technologies will result in changes that may be detrimental as traditional ways of reading and writing are abandoned for new hypertextual forms made available to us by powerful new computer technologies. And a few argue that we should reject those technologies if they don't serve what is valuable about literacy in our lives and if they don't enhance the quality of our lives. As a group, these writers raise difficult questions about literacy as a technology, about the new computer technologies that seem to be redefining literacy, and about what we think of as *progress* when it comes to reading and writing.

Some of the other authors in this chapter question the notion of *progress* more generally. They worry about the increasing dependence of humans on the machines they create, suggesting that technology and the progress it purportedly represents must ultimately be judged in terms of the kinds of lives and societies that we might wish to create for ourselves. These are old worries, as the selection by nineteenth-century philosopher Henry David Thoreau demonstrates. Perhaps the most famous skeptic of technological *progress,* Thoreau is often invoked as a kind of spiritual forefather of the modern environmental movement and the more recent "voluntary simplicity" movement, both of which place emphasis on quality of life over modern technology. Thoreau's incisive criticisms of his contemporaries' unexamined lifestyles and their apparent rush to embrace the latest technological developments of his day sound startlingly similar to the complaints of present-day critics in this chapter. It is worth thinking about that similarity, since Thoreau's criticisms were voiced a century and a half ago. Present-day writers force us to wonder whether 150 years of often astonishing technological developments have indeed resulted in what we would describe as *progress.* They ask us to look around at the many marvelous technologies that we use every day and consider whether our society is really better off as a result of those technologies. Perhaps more important, they ask you to consider whether your own way of understanding yourself and your world is a result of those very same technologies.

Such questions are more than academic debates, for they speak to the heart of how we make sense of ourselves and our world and thus how we conduct our day-to-day lives. The case of the notorious Unabomber makes it clear that for some people, these questions about technology and progress are truly matters of life and death. Although it may be easy to dismiss Ted Kaczynski, the Unabomber, as a criminal and a kind of "mad genius," as he was often portrayed in popular press reports after his capture in 1996, the views he expressed about technology and progress in his famous "manifesto" are shared by many others who are thoughtful and deeply concerned about the well-being of our culture and our planet. In his manifesto, Kaczynski railed against unchecked technological development that he claims leads to the oppression of citizens and to environmental destruction that harms all humans. It may be disconcerting to realize that some of Kaczynski's arguments are not very different from the concerns about technological progress expressed by Thoreau and other writers in this chapter. There is no question that the Unabomber case is disturbing and frightening, but it may offer some lessons that can be difficult for us to ignore as our world continues to be shaped by ever more sophisticated technologies. If nothing else, the authors in this chapter will encourage you to identify and question your own beliefs about technology, progress, and literacy.

Luddite vs. Fetishist

A Dialogue between Bill Henderson and Tim Barkow

INTRODUCTION Is technological development enhancing our lives or worsening them? That's the basic question posed by the editors of the online magazine *HotWired* to Bill Henderson and Tim Barkow, two well-known observers of technology in contemporary culture. The reference to the Luddites in the title of this text reveals that this question of the benefits and costs of "progress" is an old one, one that people return to whenever their lives are marked by rapid change that is brought on by technological developments. The Luddites were a group of textile workers in England in the early 1800's who engaged in vigorous and sometimes violent protest against the mechanization of British textile mills; they opposed the use of new textile manufacturing machinery, which they claimed led to reduced wages, poor working conditions, and unemployment. Since those protests in the 1800's, the term *Luddite* has acquired a pejorative, antitechnology connotation, but Bill Henderson openly embraces the label. For Henderson, skepticism about new technology—and even outright opposition to it—is well-founded, because technology, he believes, often leads to more problems than it can ever solve. Henderson's organization, the Lead Pencil Club, has even adopted the motto "Not so fast" when it comes to the latest computer technologies that seem to be reshaping how we read, write, and communicate. Tim Barkow, on the other hand, sees technological progress as not only beneficial but inevitable. For Barkow, refusing new technologies like computers is not only silly—it's also impossible. Barkow acknowledges that such new technologies do come with some costs, but he firmly believes that the benefits far outweigh those costs. He is enthusiastic about technology in general and about computers in particular and sees little reason to worry about their impact on human life as Henderson does.

In their dialogue, Henderson and Barkow address concerns about technological progress and stake out their respective positions about the costs and benefits of the many technological changes we are witnessing at the beginning of a new millennium. But their disagreements about specific changes or technologies may reveal a much more fundamental disagreement about quality of life, about social values, and about progress in general. How do we, as a society, assess the benefits and costs of technological change? When is such change detrimental to the quality of our lives? Should we resist such change—or perhaps evaluate it on the basis of certain human values? If so, who decides which values we should use? In many ways, these are the difficult questions that lie at the heart of the debate between Henderson and Barkow—and that our modern, technological society must address.

Bill Henderson, a writer and publisher, edited *The Minutes of the Lead Pencil Club* (1996), a collection of writings that present the beliefs of the antitechnology organization he founded, The Lead Pencil Club. He has become a well-known spokesperson for those who are skeptical about new computer technologies and about technological progress in general. Tim Barkow writes a column for *Wired* magazine, perhaps the best-known and most influential popular magazine devoted to computer technology and Internet culture. This exchange between the two writers was published over several days in 1997 in *HotWired*, an online version of *Wired*. It appeared in *HotWired* in the form of an email exchange, a form that could not have been used just a decade ago. In many ways, the editors of *HotWired* could not have chosen two writers more different in their views of the very medium (the Internet) in which their views were originally published. Their differences may help highlight some of the many questions surrounding the issue of technological progress that is the focus of this chapter.

REFLECTING BEFORE READING

1. In their exchange, Henderson and Barkow argue about specific technologies and the changes those technologies might cause. As you read their specific arguments, try to identify the basic values that each brings to this debate. Do their values match yours when it comes to progress?

2. The kind of dialogue in which Barkow and Henderson engage below has become increasingly common in online publications like *HotWired*. How do you feel about such dialogues? Do you think they are an effective way to address the kinds of complicated questions that Henderson and Barkow address in their dialogue? Does the dialogue enable them to address these issues in ways that they could not have addressed them in a more conventional form, such as an essay or editorial? As you read, consider how the form of the dialogue might shape the arguments that each participant advances. Consider, too, the usefulness of the dialogue for addressing important public issues.

I s the rising sea of gadgetry and technology actually decreasing our quality of life, or is there a limit to how much innovation can continue to enhance our lives?

Bill Henderson, editor of *Minutes of the Lead Pencil Club: Pulling the Plug on the Electronic Revolution,* says no, and that we now find ourselves with "a cure for which there was no disease." Henderson is also publisher of Pushcart Press in Wainscott, New York, which awards the Pushcart Prize series for fiction and poetry. Tim Barkow, who as an editor at *Wired* magazine fills three pages of Fetish each month with all things bright and beautiful and reeking of technolust, thinks our lives can, in the end, only be enhanced by a deluge of man-made creations.

Part I: Luddite vs. Fetishist

Wired Fetish editor Tim Barkow says technology does "not replace our humanity, but reminds us of our limitations and therefore helps make us more complete." Today Bill Henderson says his Lead Pencil Club suggests "that we may have lost our souls in a constant quest for speed, entertainment, and convenience." Is technology really enhancing our quality of living?

Monday, 27 January 1997
Post No. 1 of 8
by Bill Henderson

Let it be noted that I write this piece with a lead pencil on yellow lined paper, making good use, from time to time, of the handy eraser on the end of the pencil. The tablet of paper and the pencil cost me 95 cents. I didn't have to purchase a computer and printer, and assorted attachments and services. Nor did I need to use the electrical services of the nuclear power plant 20 miles across Long Island Sound in Connecticut.

I founded The Lead Pencil Club, with Doris Grumbach and Henry David Thoreau (emeritus), to point out the usefulness of simple tools like this pencil. I was concerned about the influence of computers and assorted electronic inventions. Our club insists on communication that is personal and thoughtful. "Not so fast." is our motto. The pencil is our symbol.

When I started this club—now 2,000 members strong, worldwide—I was laughing. Back in the winter of 1993-94, it seemed Rube Goldberg had been resurrected—all these complicated, expensive gizmos were being invented and celebrated, and bought, when often simple tools did the job better and cheaper. Very funny, I thought. But, as word of the club spread, my new members reminded me that, to many of them, the gizmos were serious, debilitating stuff. Gazing at a computer screen all day on the job was no fun. TVs and computer games were hypnotizing their children, etc. Their observations are detailed in the dozens of letters, essays, cartoons, and commentaries on "how and why to live contraption-free in a computer-crazed world" in our Minutes of the Lead Pencil Club, just published in paperback.

Most of our members see only an explosion of mad-hatter gadgetry, and not useful innovation, in the wildly hyped technological revolution. We suggest that we may have lost our souls in a constant quest for speed, entertainment, and convenience. We notice no gain in productivity, knowledge or wisdom—just an explosion of usually useless data zipping around the earth in a babble of Web sites and a cacophony of Internet chat and gossip.

As Thoreau said of the telegraph system—the miraculous invention of his time—"What if Maine and Texas have nothing to say to each other?"

As Leadite Neil Postman points out in our Minutes, the last thing any of us needs is more information. We are already stuffed like geese with "260,000 billboards, 11,520 newspapers, 11,556 periodicals, 27,500 outlets for video rentals, 500 million radios, 40,000 new books a year, and 30 million pieces of junk mail annually. Plus 98 percent of our homes have TVs."

The information age has spawned mostly sound-and-fury gadgetry—not useful innovation. We suffer from a plague of gizmos.

Part II

HotWired editors: Yesterday, luddite Bill Henderson claimed, "The information age has spawned mostly sound-and-fury gadgetry—not useful innovation. We suffer from a plague of gizmos." Today, *Wired* Fetish editor Tim Barkow says, "Email is a tool, and frankly, it's a smaller, cheaper, more efficient tool than the US Postal System. . . . So, where's the beef?" Has email only made users more scatterbrained?

Tuesday, 28 January 1997
Post No. 2 of 8
by Tim Barkow

Bill, geez, where do I start?

The pencil, which you so justly laud, is not the end of useful technology. How do you say that with a straight face? Technological innovation has always been ubiquitous—in our tools and the tools that make our tools. Always and in everything, even the bottle your maple syrup comes in. To some, the swiftly encroaching, yet nascent, and sometimes insensible, technology of the Net is overwhelming. But Bill, remember—speed doesn't kill, people kill.

Personally, I find email (not the Web) the most significant innovation of the digital age. It does so much more than a pencil ever could. The kvetching your members spit out is not a function of email technology, but of the people that use it. I unhappily find that letter writing is a dying art. But is that email's fault, or is it because people don't spend the time to elucidate their thoughts? Hmm. Well, let's go ahead and blame the technology—it's so scary.

Technological developments will always have their reactionaries, yet aren't all things—including the grass the monkey uses to draw termites from their nests—gizmos at their births? It's too easy to sit in some warm, converted farmhouse nestled among the woods of Vermont, scratching out pseudodeclarations of what's good and bad with the future. But can you honestly say the postal system is better than email? It just isn't. It's slow and extremely expensive. You may have that kind of time and money to waste—I don't. Email is a tool, and frankly, it's a smaller, cheaper, more efficient tool than the US Postal System. It fits all of Wendell Berry's requirements for technological innovation. So, where's the beef?

It's also interesting that while you decry the information explosion, you point out no gains in productivity. Well, where did all the information come from? One day, critics scream that technology is eliminating jobs. The next, they holler how computers don't increase productivity. Well, which is it? Truth is, work goes on as it always has. Just because you have a computer doesn't mean that one Thursday afternoon you're going to complete that spreadsheet and come to the horrifying realization that you're finished. It's a job, you're never done.

Bill, do me and America a favor, get down and figure out how to set the clock on your VCR. If you don't have one, find someone who does. But don't do it for me, Bill, do it for the children. They're counting on you to stop this madness.

Part III

HotWired editors: Yesterday, *Wired* Fetish editor Tim Barkow said to his luddite pen pal, "While you decry the information explosion, you point out no gains in productivity. Well, where did all the information come from?" Today, luddite Bill Henderson says, "Speed doesn't increase productivity," and insists we've lost respect for ourselves. "We run faster and faster—prodded by our technology—and we run to nowhere." How much is technology's all-consuming obsolescence cycle an unnecessary exercise?

Wednesday, 29 January 1997
Post No. 3 of 8
by Bill Henderson

The Lead Pencil Club was interested to hear from you, Tim, but you seem jumpy and confused about lots of things. Slow down.

You say you "unhappily find that letter writing is a dying art." Well, Tim, letter writing requires time and concern and caring and thought. A culture of speed at any cost—such as that encouraged by email—helps kill letter writing (and careful reading).

In your hurry to dash off a nifty reply to The Lead Pencil Club, you fabricate the idea that we think the pencil is "the end of useful technology." Ridiculous. The pencil is merely good technology. It's simple. It's cheap. It works. The computer is often none of the above.

Tim, you seem to have a case of the jitters. Info overload? Try to follow my argument, slowly.

The Lead Pencil Club doesn't decry the "information explosion"—just the fact that most of the info is of little use. As in any explosion, we have a big mess. This is not an increase in productivity. This is an increase in nonsense.

Calm down, Tim. Write a real letter to a real friend. Take a walk outside into the real world, to the post office maybe. You'll find people there, and maybe time to talk to them. You might even make a new friend.

"Not so fast," as we say at The Lead Pencil Club. Speed doesn't increase productivity. Remember "Haste makes waste"?

Speaking of waste. Why the contemporary frenzy for useless invention? What's driving the plague? Could it be something as simple as greed? There's a buck to be made in a wallet-sized Global Positioning System, so why not invent one and tell people they can't live without it? It worked for Gates, right? And that guy has waste-plus: a house big enough to need a GPS just to be able to walk through without getting lost, and enough money to stop starvation in an entire continent. (Not that he will.) So let's throw enough useless gimcracks up against the wall and see which one sticks. Now that consumers are so mind-wasted by their TVs and VCRs and Web surfing, they will buy almost anything new just to fend off the incredible boredom. You see, Tim, the terms we use give us away. Does "consumer" remind you of locusts in a field ruining the crops? "Word processor." Good grief, we have so little respect for words that we process them?

But who is it we really have lost respect for, Tim? Ourselves, of course. We run faster and faster—prodded by our technology—and we run to nowhere. We gobble facts, celebrity gossip, news, and data, and can never satisfy our hunger for what we really want: knowledge, wisdom, love.

Part IV

HotWired editors: Yesterday, luddite Bill Henderson ruminated on the invention of the word processor: "Good grief, we have so little respect for words that we process them?" Today, *Wired* Fetish editor Tim Barkow says, "To miss the point that 'word processors' put the power of Gutenberg in the hands of the people is to really have your head in the sand." How much would you say desktop publishing has increased your quality of life?

Thursday, 30 January 1997
Post No. 4 of 8
by Tim Barkow

Bummin' on Wal-Mart and CompUSA, Bill? What's the deal? Folks have been buying and selling since the dawn of time. Where's the value in a diamond-studded necklace? A gold-plated spear? These items are certainly useless. So it seems that innovative or not, people have been buying crap ever since barter was invented.

Innovation is man's forte. It's what we do as a species. Innovation involves adaptation, challenge, accretion of knowledge (both good and bad)—all this leads to wisdom. It does not guarantee wisdom, mind you—but neither does sitting on your ass in the woods. And no matter your take, innovation is a fact—a fact of nature, actually. Go talk to Darwin.

You make an interesting exception in your book: advances in medical tech. How then can you say GPS isn't useful for hikers? You like hikers, right Bill? Would you leave the tree-huggers stranded on a mountain to die? Should they spend the day worrying about getting back home, or soaking up that magical weave of animal, vegetable, mineral?

You picked a bad example, Bill. GPS is extremely useful. It's used in all kinds of geological and ecological research. The fact that a consumer can buy a GPS unit has no relevance to the technology's utility. And that's the point you seem to be missing. In a world that, especially in commerce, is shrinking, you cannot presuppose that someone won't find a particular tool extremely valuable. GPS is relatively silly in San Francisco, yet it can save your life on the African plains or in the Austrian Alps.

Innovation makes things different: new ideas, new terms. But words are only "processed" by the engineers who originally named the program. To miss the point that "word processors" put the power of Gutenberg in the hands of the people is to really have your head in the sand. That's what word processors are for, Bill.

I'm still waiting for some concrete examples. I doubt you can come up with a stumper. This technological gimcrack, as you call it, provides us with options. It's not about some final solution, Bill. It's about fitting the tool to the person. Now if the person doesn't understand the tool, what is more productive: blaming the tool or the person?

And money and greed have little to do with it. To simplify a market economy to the point where the only benefits gained are those in the CEO's bank account is to do a serious injustice to all of us, including yourself. Aren't you yourself cashing in on this innovation? Face it, Bill, you're at the craps table, same as everyone else. Only difference is, you bet against the thrower.

Part V

HotWired editors: *Wired* Fetish editor Tim Barkow said, "I'm still waiting for some concrete examples [against technology]. I doubt you can come up with a stumper." Today, luddite Bill Henderson pulls technology "turncoats" David Gelertner and Mark Slouka out of his Lead Pencil Club sheath to prove things have gotten bad. Have Gelertner and Slouka just been slumming it?

Friday, 31 January 1997
Post No. 5 of 8
by Bill Henderson

Tim, good to notice that you have slowed down a bit. Perhaps you took my advice and disconnected the email or briefly untangled yourself from the Web. I detect that you are less jangled and jumpy—characteristics of so many wired into the system. I'm thinking of Bill Gates and my Lead Pencil Club friend Cliff Stoll, who contributes a terrific chapter to our Minutes on how he rediscovered real life by pulling the plug on his computers and strolling to the neighborhood newsstand to buy an actual newspaper. He disconnected and learned to relax and enjoy again. You can too.

Seriously, Tim, enough about my sitting in the north woods longing for the old days. I live by the seashore, and I am surrounded by neighbors with all the gadgets you admire. I am constantly invited by to marvel at Web sites and online chat groups. I remain unmoved. These are "pretty toys," as Thoreau noted about the new telegraph devices of his time. They encourage us to yap ceaselessly. But we have less and less to say. The chatter is deafening. Those of us who have pulled the plug realize that knowledge often arrives with silence.

Very few of us in The Lead Pencil Club are as terrified about technology as you imagine. Check out the chapters in our Minutes by Russell Baker, David Gelertner, Mark Slouka, and Andrei Codrescu, for instance. Baker and Codrescu think much of computer innovation is merely silly. Slouka is astounded that the boys and girls at the MIT Media Lab take themselves so seriously that they imagine themselves to be theologians of a new quasi religion; and Gelertner, professor of computer science at Yale (for gosh sake), is rightfully concerned about the invasion of computers into our schools.

These are not off-the-wall old farts who don't recognize useful inventions when they see them, Tim, so relax. Unwire.

Think about what we agree on. "People have been buying crap ever since barter was invented," you offer. Right on, Tim. And we've never had so much crap to barter for as now, I offer.

You note that in the *Minutes* I praise some new technologies, such as medical innovations. Right on again. The list is certainly longer than that. But for now I will insist on reminding you of the value of the human mind—unfettered by electronic programs that, while promising to help us, merely detract by doing jobs we can do very well by ourselves—such as writing with our very own handwriting, balancing a checkbook, or meandering through a library of actual books to research a topic and, from time to time, coming up with an unprogrammed bit of knowledge all our own.

Part VI

HotWired editors: On Friday, luddite Bill Henderson asked how his tech-savvy, but weary, Lead Pencil Club members like Cliff Stoll, David Gelertner, Mark Slouka, and Andrei Codrescu could possibly be wrong. Today, *Wired* Fetish editor Tim Barkow replies: "Half of them are ignorant, the others have picked radically unrepresentative examples to illustrate their points. Their tales are distortions."

Monday, 3 February 1997
Post No. 6 of 8
by Tim Barkow

I'd like to clarify a point. When I say people have been buying "crap" for ages, and I did, I mean "stuff." The point you refuse to admit, Bill, is that individuals purchase for many different reasons. Some things are bought for their utility, others for their beauty, charm, or novelty—sometimes without the benefit of clear thinking. If people will buy it—for whatever reason—someone will make it. This is reality.

The beauty in all this gimcrack is where you find it. I can't go on the record and say everything I've bought has proved wonderful, but I enjoyed it nonetheless. I play my part as Fetishist.

Every day I'm inundated with products. Some are beautiful, some innovative—some are just cool. And people all over the world buy this stuff (crap). Every day. Frankly, I love it. It's just damn wonderful. I do so love my toys. But, you know, Bill, I love my tools even more. In my spare time, I draw and paint. So I consider myself schooled in your "lead" pencil. And what you'll find while drawing is that sometimes a pencil doesn't cut it. You might need charcoal. Maybe ink. And sometimes, you need a computer. Eek! The tool chosen is the one that suits the artist's needs.

As far as your contributor-members go, half of them are ignorant, the others have picked radically unrepresentative examples to illustrate their points. Their tales are distortions, as most are—but they are distortions. So I can't say I put much weight behind their expertise, such as it is: The argument was made on the first page—everything after that is watery propaganda.

If you've done your research, you know that Gelertner and his students are doing some interesting user-interface research at Yale. The project is called Lifestreams, and Gelertner is even helping to move Lifestreams into the marketplace. And sell it. For money. Eek!

This is what it's all about. Some people love the computer desktop. Some would be better served by Lifestreams' time-based metaphor. What works for one person is not necessarily appropriate for another. Sometimes, you've no recourse but to visit the library. Other times, the Web works faster—eek!—allowing you a leisurely, unfettered walk outside. More tools; more options. Innovation is good.

This goes out to all you fine folk in Web space—Señor Bill doesn't think you have anything worthwhile to say, as he invokes some odd rant of Thoreau's on the "pretty toy" telegraph. As far as Bill is concerned, you have nothing to add to life. And he won't know, couldn't know, because he refuses to explore your accomplishments before condemning them as ceaseless yapping.

Well Bill, I got news for you: Thoreau is dead. Looks like all us netizens got one up on Walden's bad boy.

Part VII

HotWired editors: Yesterday, *Wired* Fetish editor Tim Barkow claimed that the crux of innovation is "more tools; more options." Today, luddite Bill Henderson says, "Too much of today's electronic and digital inventing is just crap on a rock, and we don't need it." Is more really better?

Tuesday, 4 February 1997
Post No. 7 of 8
by Bill Henderson

Tim, thanks for your kind words about contributor-members to our Minutes: "half ignorant." Without the book in hand, "folks in Web space" won't have a clue about such silly attacks. I urge them to look for the book in their bookstore or library. It's worth a trip into the sunlight.

Most of the contributors to our book have come screaming out of Web space seeking solace. And most of our members have just trashed computers, or use them for planters.

Tim, this has been fun. I do hope our audience has learned something from this frolic, but I doubt it. Point is, Tim, you won't take the time to read what we say. Is it possible that, like Mr. Gates, you have difficulty in this regard?

To respect our audience, The Lead Pencil Club has no problem with true innovation. I too think useful innovation is one of the glories of our human experience. But you don't crap on a rock and call it useful innovation, and then go out and try to sell it to the world for a huge profit. Too much of today's electronic and digital inventing is just crap on a rock, and we don't need it. The stuff is not necessary for almost all of us. From giant TVs (with nothing worth watching), to Web sites (an electronic yellow pages and just a bit more fun than the phone book) to Internet sex and blab groups—this is not useful innovation. The old way, in most cases, was better, or at least just as good, for most of us.

The GPS and other new devices do have specialized uses, but not for most of us. It's hype, Tim, pure hype. You will not find wisdom, peace, love, friendship, or "A Life" in this stuff. You will be distracted endlessly by snake oil followed by brand new snake oil—all promising speed and convenience, followed by even more speed and convenience (for a profit to the person with the latest dump on the rock).

In signing off, I want to wish you well, Tim. (Remember, Tim with an "e" on the end is Time: Unplug and take time to read slowly and carefully, and think.)

And I want to thank *HotWired* (by the way, why is your magazine named as if it were a nervous breakdown?) for inviting me to endure your agitation. And to editor Roderick Simpson, my thanks for reading my pencil handwriting. It must make you long for that handwriting gizmo in 250 styles for US $39.50.

But thanks really to the members of The Lead Pencil Club worldwide. (You too can join us at Lead Pencil, Wainscott, NY, 11975. It's free!) Leadites unite! Power to the Pencil!

Part VIII

HotWired editors: After more than a week of hearing luddite Bill Henderson chant his Lead Pencil Club's motto of Not So Fast regarding technological innovation, *Wired* Fetish editor Tim Barkow has a reply for those like him railing against progress: "There's only one speed on this bus: full out. Which leaves only one option: Get in the driver's seat, grab the wheel, and hope you master driving before you master crashing."

Wednesday, 5 February 1997
Post No. 8 of 8
by Tim Barkow

Let's get a couple things clear, Bill. I did not call your members "half ignorant." I said that half of them were (totally) ignorant. There's a difference. And it is not a silly attack. I don't consider technophobes who can't get Windows 95 installed competent critics. You've got to get a little further than that before you can build a strong, defensible argument. Something, BTW, that you have been unable to do. So you don't like the Web, big deal. And GPS is just hype? Hype of what? We don't look for wisdom, peace, love, or a life "in" tech—but "through" it. We use and abuse technology for whatever purpose suits us. Same as I can take a pencil in my hand and with it compose a poem—or poke your eye out.

For the last time, Bill, I read your book. It sucked.

The reason it was so awful starts with the argument you chose.

As far as I can tell, there are three basic types of debates. First, there's the two intractable sides. With an issue like abortion, two sides come to the table already convinced. There's no discussion, only two foes hurling epithets. It's loud, but essentially pointless. Then you've got your healthcare-type arguments. These are the most interesting, since they focus on accomplishing a goal. They are also the most difficult, since everyone must work toward a single resolution. Then there's this "technology-out-of-control" argument—the worst of all, simply because it doesn't exist. You cannot stop, slow, or control technology. There's only one speed on this bus: full out. Which leaves only one option: Get in the driver's seat, grab the wheel, and hope you master driving before you master crashing.

Isn't it amazing the fuss that's grown out of something we can't even see. This whole revolution, if you want to call it that, is just electricity. That's all it is. But isn't it amazing what we can do by manipulating a pinch of electrons?

History is content with the triumphs and defeats concerning atoms. So why all the grumbling now that we're off to explore the possibilities of electronic, digital space? If you can't take the time to understand that a new frontier awaits, and why many people refuse status-quo "lead pencil" living, then you'd be best served by a history refresher class at your local community college.

And it looks like you've got the time for it as well. Adios, dear Bill, and thanks for the inscrutable attempts to defend your li'l club.

Remember, Bill with an "e" is—hmm, actually it's nothing.

Who woulda guessed?

REFLECTING ON THE READING

1. Notice how the editors of *HotWired* frame the debate between Henderson and Barkow. At the very beginning of the exchange, the editors write, "Is the rising sea of gadgetry and technology actually decreasing our quality of life, or is there a limit to how much innovation can continue to enhance our lives?" What exactly is the issue being addressed here, as suggested by the editors' question? Do you think that this question adequately sums up the central issue?

2. How does Henderson begin his first message in this exchange? Why do you think he begins in this way? What does he establish about himself right from the start? Compare his beginning to Barkow's. How is Barkow's different? What does he establish with his beginning?

3. Summarize Henderson's main position in this debate. Cite specific lines or statements from his messages in the exchange to indicate Henderson's position. What are his chief worries and/or complaints about technology?

4. Summarize Barkow's position in the debate. How does it differ from Henderson's? Why does he think Henderson's worries and complaints are not valid? Cite specific statements in your answer.

5. What does Henderson mean when he writes that "we may have lost our souls in a constant quest for speed, entertainment, and convenience"? What specific changes might he be referring to here? What does "soul" mean in this context? How does it fit into his position in general?

6. Barkow writes in his last message that Henderson has been unable to "build a strong, defensible argument." What does he mean specifically? He goes on to say that there are "three basic types of debates." What are they? Why does he tell us this?

7. Do the tone and content of this debate change as the exchange progresses? If so, in what ways? Why do you think the debate changes?

Examining Rhetorical Strategies

1. Describe the style and tone of Henderson and Barkow in this debate. What differences emerge in their styles and tones? How did you react to each? Were you drawn to one more than the other? Why? What might your answer to these questions reveal about you as a reader?

2. Examine the way each of these writers uses language. Look specifically at the words they use to describe each other and the positions they take. Are there specific words or phrases that stand out for you? What effect did they have on you as a reader—that is, on how you understood and felt about each writer?

3. How do you think Henderson and Barkow would define *progress,* based on what they write in this debate? Does each one hold the same assumptions about technology and progress? Does each one value the same things when it comes to technology and to life-style? Explain.

4. How do you think the medium in which this debate occurred (an online email exchange) affected the way each writer stated his position, the style and tone of

their writing, the language they used, and so on? Would these characteristics of their writing have been different if the debate had been published all at once in a print magazine? Explain.

5. How does each of these writers make his arguments in this debate? What sort of evidence does each provide for his assertions? Do you find one writer's arguments more effective than the other's? Why? Do you think Barkow is right when he says in his final message that Henderson has not made a "strong, defensible argument"? How do you think he would define such an argument, based on his own messages in this debate? Has Barkow himself made such an argument?

6. Examine the brief summaries written by the *HotWired* editors at the beginning of each message. How did these affect the way you read each section of the debate? Do you think their summaries are accurate and fair? Why or why not? Would you have written these summaries differently? Explain.

Engaging the Issues

1. In a group of your classmates, engage in a debate similar to the one Henderson and Barkow had. Address the question posed by the *HotWired* editors at the beginning of the debate. Allow each person in your group to make an initial statement, and then discuss (or argue about) the points raised, referring to Henderson and Barkow where appropriate. After the discussion is over, try to describe the main positions that were taken by the group members. Were there two, three, or more positions? Is it possible to describe each position simply? Based on these discussions, try to draw conclusions about the way these matters of technology and progress are discussed and debated in the media and elsewhere.

   Based on what you learned from this exercise, write an essay for an audience of your classmates in which you make your own argument about technology and progress. Draw on Henderson and Barkow's debate or on the discussions you had with your group. Try to support your position effectively using appropriate evidence.

2. Rewrite the dialogue between Henderson and Barkow as a conventional essay in which you summarize the arguments of each and identify the key differences between them. When you're finished, assess how your essay differs from the original online debate. How can you describe the differences between your essay and the debate? Which do you think is more effective in presenting the issues addressed in the debate? Why? What do the differences between the essay and the online debate indicate about these different forms of writing and how they are used?

3. Write an analysis of this debate in which you examine the strategies each writer uses in making his arguments as well as the style and tone of each writer. Draw conclusions about the general effectiveness of each writer in making his argument. In your analysis, refer to specific lines from the text to support your assertions.

4. Write an essay for a general audience in which you make your own argument about technology and progress. Use whatever material seems appropriate from this debate.

5. Compare the essays you wrote for Questions #1 and #4 above. How do they differ? How did considerations of audience affect the way you wrote each essay, if at all?

6. Follow the conversations on an online listserv or newsgroup for several days on a topic of interest to you. Keep notes on how participants in the discussion engage each other's points and make their arguments. Then write an analysis of this online discussion focusing on how people participated in it. Try to identify trends or characteristics of the discussion; determine whether there were common strategies for engaging in the online discussion.

   Now compare the online discussion with the dialogue between Henderson and Barkow. In what ways were the discussion you followed on the Internet and the dialogue between Henderson and Barkow similar or different? Can you draw any conclusions about how we make arguments and engage in discussions of complex issues using online media?

The Judgment of Thamus

NEIL POSTMAN

INTRODUCTION   In the introduction to his book *Technopoly,* from which the following passage is excerpted, Neil Postman writes that technology "is both friend and enemy." But Postman quickly makes it clear that in the latter days of the twentieth century, "technology has become a particularly dangerous enemy." This is so, Postman argues, because technology has so infused contemporary industrialized society that it has become an end in itself. Our society has now become a "technopoly," a self-perpetuating system in which technology not only meets and shapes even the most basic human needs but actually supersedes those needs. For Postman, the most pressing issue is not whether technology improves or degrades human life but whether or not it *controls* human life.

Some critics have charged that Postman's views about technology are too extreme, that he exaggerates the potential dangers of technology. Yet Postman's ideas have found wide support among his many readers, and it is worth investigating why. It is possible that Postman's concerns about technology are shared by many people, especially as the pace of technological change seems to have rapidly increased as the twentieth century became the twenty-first. Consider, for example, the amazingly rapid growth of cellular telephone networks, which were rare even as recently as the early 1990's, when Postman wrote the book from which the following excerpt is taken. Since that time, "cell phones" have become common and even essential for many kinds of businesses and professions. As their use has increased, some cities and towns often have found themselves debating whether or not to allow the construction of more cell phone towers within their boundaries. Sometimes, decisions to allow such construction are vigorously resisted by local residents, who claim that the towers adversely affect the quality of their lives—even as some people claim that the use of cell phones degrades daily life. Meanwhile, in 1999 a small town in Ohio passed a law making it illegal to use a cell phone while driving a car. The town leaders felt a need to pass such a law as more and more automobile accidents occurred as a result of drivers talking on their cell phones while driving. It is easy to identify similar examples of how a "new" technology develops into a "necessity" in ways that sometimes seem to take precedence over human needs: the television, the automobile, the Internet, the airplane. All these technologies can be seen as support for Postman's argument that technology can not only control but actually supersede basic human needs.

Neil Postman is a writer, cultural critic, and communications scholar who has written nearly twenty books, many of them addressing some of the most complex and difficult questions of our age. His writing is iconoclastic, often challenging conventional beliefs or attitudes in order to make arguments in favor of what he sees as fundamental human values. His book *Teaching as a Subversive Activity* (1978) became a minor classic among educators struggling to reform school systems that they believed no longer served their students' needs. Among his other books are *Amusing Ourselves to Death: Public Discourse in the Age of Show Business* (1985), *Conscientious Objections: Stirring Up Trouble About Language, Technology, and Education* (1991), *The Disappearance of Childhood* (1993), and *The End of Education: Redefining the Value of School* (1995). In 1987 he received an award from the National Council of Teachers of English for clarity in language, a recognition of the straightforward and incisive writing style in which he expresses his often controversial ideas. The following passage was originally published as a chapter in his book *Technopoly* (1992).

REFLECTING BEFORE READING

1. In the following passage, Postman makes several references to classical texts by figures such as Plato and Freud. What do you know about such figures and their ideas? What do Plato and Freud have to do with technology? How do Postman's references to their work affect you as a reader? What does it suggest to you about Postman's values?

2. Postman's writing style has often been noted by critics as distinctive. It has been described as irreverent, forceful, iconoclastic. Try to be aware of his writing style as you read. How would you describe his writing style? What specific features of it are most noticeable to you? Also, as you read, consider whether you think Postman's writing style reflects his beliefs about culture and technology and gives force to the arguments he makes.

You will find in Plato's *Phaedrus* a story about Thamus, the king of a great city of Upper Egypt. For people such as ourselves, who are inclined (in Thoreau's phrase) to be tools of our tools, few legends are more instructive than his. The story, as Socrates tells it to his friend Phaedrus, unfolds in the following way: Thamus once entertained the god Theuth, who was the inventor of many things, including number, calculation, geometry, astronomy, and writing. Theuth exhibited his inventions to King Thamus, claiming that they should be made widely known and available to Egyptians. Socrates continues:

Thamus inquired into the use of each of them, and as Theuth went through them expressed approval or disapproval, according as he judged Theuth's claims to be well or ill founded. It would take too long to go through all that Thamus is reported to have said for and against each of Theuth's inventions. But when it came to writing, Theuth declared, "Here is an accomplishment, my lord the King, which will improve both the wisdom and the memory of the Egyptians. I have discovered a sure receipt for memory and wisdom." To this, Thamus replied, "Theuth, my paragon of inventors, the discoverer of an art is not the best judge of the good or harm which will accrue to those who practice it. So it is in this; you, who are the father of writing, have out of fondness for your off-spring attributed to it quite the opposite of its real function. Those who acquire it will cease to exercise their memory and become forgetful; they will rely on writing to bring things to their remembrance by external signs instead of by their own internal resources. What you have discovered is a receipt for recollection, not for memory. And as for wisdom, your pupils will have the reputation for it without the reality: they will receive a quantity of information without proper instruction, and in consequence be thought very knowledgeable when they are for the most part quite ignorant. And because they are filled with the conceit of wisdom instead of real wisdom they will be a burden to society."[1]

I begin my book with this legend because in Thamus' response there are several sound principles from which we may begin to learn how to think with wise circumspection about a technological society. In fact, there is even one error in the judgment of Thamus, from which we may also learn something of importance. The error is not in his claim that writing will damage memory and create false wisdom. It is demonstrable that writing has had such an effect. Thamus' error is in his believing that writing will be a burden to society and *nothing but a burden.* For all his wisdom, he fails to imagine what writing's benefits might be, which, as we know, have been considerable. We may learn from this that it is a mistake to suppose that any technological innovation has a one-sided effect. Every technology is both a burden and a blessing; not either-or, but this and that.

Nothing could be more obvious, of course, especially to those who have given more than two minutes of thought to the matter. Nonetheless, we are currently surrounded by throngs of zealous Theuths, one-eyed prophets who see only what new technologies can do and are incapable of imagining what they will *undo.* We might call such people Technophiles. They gaze on technology as a lover does on his beloved, seeing it as without blemish and entertaining no apprehension for the future. They are therefore dangerous and are to be approached cautiously. On the other hand, some one-eyed prophets, such as I (or so I am accused), are inclined to speak only of burdens (in the manner of Thamus) and are silent about the opportunities that new technologies make possible. The Technophiles must speak for themselves, and do so all over the place. My defense is that a dissenting voice is sometimes needed to moderate the din made by the enthusiastic multitudes. If one is to err, it is better to err on the side of Thamusian skepticism. But it is an error nonetheless. And I might note that, with the exception of his judgment on writing, Thamus does not repeat this error. You might notice on rereading the legend that he gives arguments *for* and *against* each of Theuth's inventions. For it is inescapable that every culture must negotiate with technology, whether it does so intelligently or not. A bargain is struck in which technology giveth and technology taketh away. The wise know this well, and are rarely impressed by dramatic technological changes, and never over-joyed. Here, for example, is Freud on the matter, from his doleful *Civilization and Its Discontents:*

> One would like to ask: is there, then, no positive gain in pleasure, no unequivocal increase in my feeling of happiness, if I can, as often as I please, hear the voice of a child of mine who is living hundreds of miles away or if I can learn in the shortest possible time after a friend has reached his destination that he has come through the long and difficult voyage unharmed? Does it mean nothing that medicine has suc-ceeded in enormously reducing infant mortality and the danger of infection for women in childbirth, and, indeed, in considerably lengthening the average life of a civilized man?

Freud knew full well that technical and scientific advances are not to be taken lightly, which is why he begins this passage by acknowledging them. But he ends it by reminding us of what they have undone:

> If there had been no railway to conquer distances, my child would never have left his native town and I should need no telephone to hear his voice; if travelling across the ocean by ship had not been introduced, my friend would not have embarked on his sea-voyage and I should not need a cable to relieve my anxiety about him. What is the use of reducing infantile mortality when it is precisely that reduction which imposes the greatest restraint on us in the begetting of children, so that, taken all round, we nevertheless rear no more children than in the days before the reign of hygiene, while at the same time we have created difficult con-ditions for our sexual life in marriage…. And, finally, what good to us is a long life if it is difficult and barren of joys, and if it is so full of misery that we can only wel-come death as a deliverer?[2]

In tabulating the cost of technological progress, Freud takes a rather depressing line, that of a man who agrees with Thoreau's remark that our inventions are but improved means to an unimproved end. The Technophile would surely answer Freud by saying that life has always been barren of joys and full of misery but that the telephone, ocean liners, and especially the reign of hygiene have not only length-ened life but made it a more agreeable proposition. That is certainly an argument I would make (thus proving I am no one-eyed Technophobe), but it is not necessary at this point to pursue it. I have brought Freud into the conversation only to show that a wise man—even one of such a woeful countenance—must begin his critique of technology by acknowledging its successes. Had King Thamus been as wise as reputed, he would not have forgotten to include in his judgment a prophecy about the powers that writing would enlarge. There is a calculus of technological change that requires a measure of even-handedness.

So much for Thamus' error of omission. There is another omission worthy of note, but it is no error. Thamus simply takes for granted—and therefore does not feel it nec-essary to say—that writing is not a neutral technology whose good or harm depends on the uses made of it. He knows that the uses made of any technology are largely deter-mined by the structure of the technology itself—that is, that its functions follow from its form. This is why Thamus is concerned not with *what* people will write; he is concerned *that* people will write. It is absurd to imagine Thamus advising, in the manner of today's standard-brand Technophiles, that, if only writing would be used for the production of certain kinds of texts and not others (let us say, for dramatic literature but not for history or philosophy), its disruptions could be minimized. He would regard such counsel as extreme naïveté. He would allow, I imagine, that a technology may be barred entry to a culture. But we may learn from Thamus the following: once a technology is admitted, it plays out its hand; it does what it is designed to do. Our task is to understand what that design is—that is to say, when we admit a new technology to the culture, we must do so with our eyes wide open.

All of this we may infer from Thamus' silence. But we may learn even more from what he does say than from what he doesn't. He points out, for example, that writing will change what is meant by the words "memory" and "wisdom." He fears that memory will be confused with what he disdainfully calls "recollection," and he worries that wisdom will become indistinguishable from mere knowledge. This judgment we must take to heart, for it is a certainty that radical technologies create new definitions of old terms, and that this process takes place without our being fully conscious of it. Thus, it is insidious and dangerous, quite different from the process whereby new technologies introduce new terms to the language. In our own time, we have consciously added to our language thousands of new words and phrases having to do with new technologies—"VCR," "binary digit," "software," "front-wheel drive," "window of opportunity," "Walkman," etc. We are not taken by surprise at this. New things require new words. But new things also modify old words, words that have deep-rooted meanings. The telegraph and the penny press changed what we once meant by "information." Television changes what we once meant by the terms "political debate," "news," and "public opinion." The computer changes "information" once again. Writing changed what we once meant by "truth" and "law"; printing changed them again, and now television and the computer change them once more. Such changes occur quickly, surely, and, in a sense, silently. Lexicographers hold no plebiscites on the matter. No manuals are written to explain what is happening, and the schools are oblivious to it. The old words still look the same, are still used in the same kinds of sentences. But they do not have the same meanings; in some cases, they have opposite meanings. And this is what Thamus wishes to teach us—that technology imperiously commandeers our most important terminology. It redefines "freedom," "truth," "intelligence," "fact," "wisdom," "memory," "history"—all the words we live by. And it does not pause to tell us. And we do not pause to ask.

Here, there are several more principles to be mined from the judgment of Thamus that require mentioning because they presage all I will write about. For instance, Thamus warns that the pupils of Theuth will develop an undeserved reputation for wisdom. He means to say that those who cultivate competence in the use of a new technology become an elite group that are granted undeserved authority and prestige by those who have no such competence. There are different ways of expressing the interesting implications of this fact. Harold Innis, the father of modern communication studies, repeatedly spoke of the "knowledge monopolies" created by important technologies. He meant precisely what Thamus had in mind: those who have control over the workings of a particular technology accumulate power and inevitably form a kind of conspiracy against those who have no access to the specialized knowledge made available by the technology. In his book *The Bias of Communication,* Innis provides many historical examples of how a new technology "busted up" a traditional knowledge monopoly and created a new one presided over by a different group. Another way of saying this is that the benefits and deficits of a new technology are not distributed equally. There are, as it were, winners and losers. It is both puzzling and poignant that on many occasions the losers, out of ignorance, have actually cheered the winners, and some still do.

Let us take as an example the case of television. In the United States, where television has taken hold more deeply than anywhere else, many people find it a blessing, not least those who have achieved high-paying, gratifying careers in television as executives, technicians, newscasters, and entertainers. It should surprise no one that such people, forming as they do a new knowledge monopoly, should cheer themselves and defend and promote television technology. On the other hand and in the long run, television may bring a gradual end to the careers of schoolteachers, since school was an invention of the printing press and must stand or fall on the issue of how much importance the printed word has. For four hundred years, schoolteachers have been part of the knowledge monopoly created by printing, and they are now witnessing the breakup of that monopoly. It appears as if they can do little to prevent that breakup, but surely there is something perverse about schoolteachers' being enthusiastic about what is happening. Such enthusiasm always calls to my mind an image of some turn-of-the-century blacksmith who not only sings the praises of the automobile but also believes that his business will be enhanced by it. We know now that his business was not enhanced by it; it was rendered obsolete by it, as perhaps the clearheaded blacksmiths knew. What could they have done? Weep, if nothing else.

We have a similar situation in the development and spread of computer technology, for here too there are winners and losers. There can be no disputing that the computer has increased the power of large-scale organizations like the armed forces, or airline companies or banks or tax-collecting agencies. And it is equally clear that the computer is now indispensable to high-level researchers in physics and other natural sciences. But to what extent has computer technology been an advantage to the masses of people? To steelworkers, vegetable-store owners, teachers, garage mechanics, musicians, bricklayers, dentists, and most of the rest into whose lives the computer now intrudes? Their private matters have been made more accessible to powerful institutions. They are more easily tracked and controlled; are subjected to more examinations; are increasingly mystified by the decisions made about them; are often reduced to mere numerical objects. They are inundated by junk mail. They are easy targets for advertising agencies and political organizations. The schools teach their children to operate computerized systems instead of teaching things that are more valuable to children. In a word, almost nothing that they need happens to the losers. Which is why they are losers.

It is to be expected that the winners will encourage the losers to be enthusiastic about computer technology. That is the way of winners, and so they sometimes tell the losers that with personal computers the average person can balance a checkbook more neatly, keep better track of recipes, and make more logical shopping lists. They also tell them that their lives will be conducted more efficiently. But discreetly they neglect to say from whose point of view the efficiency is warranted or what might be its costs. Should the losers grow skeptical, the winners dazzle them with the wondrous feats of computers, almost all of which have only marginal relevance to the quality of the losers' lives but which are nonetheless impressive. Eventually, the losers succumb, in part because they believe, as Thamus prophesied, that the specialized knowledge of the masters of a new technology is a form of wisdom. The masters come to believe this as well, as Thamus also prophesied. The result is that certain questions do not arise. For example, to whom will the technology give greater power and freedom? And whose power and freedom will be reduced by it?

I have perhaps made all of this sound like a well-planned conspiracy, as if the winners know all too well what is being won and what lost. But this is not quite how it happens. For one thing, in cultures that have a democratic ethos, relatively weak traditions, and a high receptivity to new technologies, everyone is inclined to be enthusiastic about technological change, believing that its benefits will eventually spread evenly among the entire population. Especially in the United States, where the lust for what is new has no bounds, do we find this childlike conviction most widely held. Indeed, in America, social change of any kind is rarely seen as resulting in winners and losers, a condition that stems in part from Americans' much-documented optimism. As for change brought on by technology, this native optimism is exploited by entrepreneurs, who work hard to infuse the population with a unity of improbable hope, for they know that it is economically unwise to reveal the price to be paid for technological change. One might say, then, that, if there is a conspiracy of any kind, it is that of a culture conspiring against itself.

In addition to this, and more important, it is not always clear, at least in the early stages of a technology's intrusion into a culture, who will gain most by it and who will lose most. This is because the changes wrought by technology are subtle if not downright mysterious, one might even say wildly unpredictable. Among the most unpredictable are those that might be labeled ideological. This is the sort of change Thamus had in mind when he warned that writers will come to rely on external signs instead of their own internal resources, and that they will receive quantities of information without proper instruction. He meant that new technologies change what we mean by "knowing" and "truth"; they alter those deeply embedded habits of thought which give to a culture its sense of what the world is like—a sense of what is the natural order of things, of what is reasonable, of what is necessary, of what is inevitable, of what is real. Since such changes are expressed in changed meanings of old words, I will hold off until later discussing the massive ideological transformation now occurring in the United States. Here, I should like to give only one example of how technology creates new conceptions of what is real and, in the process, undermines older conceptions. I refer to the seemingly harmless practice of assigning marks or grades to the answers students give on examinations. This procedure seems so natural to most of us that we are hardly aware of its significance. We may even find it difficult to imagine that the number or letter is a tool or, if you will, a technology; still less that, when we use such a technology to judge someone's behavior, we have done something peculiar. In point of fact, the first instance of grading students' papers occurred at Cambridge University in 1792 at the suggestion of a tutor named William Farish.[3] No one knows much about William Farish; not more than a handful have ever heard of him. And yet his idea that a quantitative value should be assigned to human thoughts was a major step toward constructing a mathematical concept of reality. If a number can be given to the quality of a thought, then a number can be given to the qualities of mercy, love, hate, beauty, creativity, intelligence, even sanity itself. When Galileo said that the language of nature is written in mathematics, he did not mean to include human feeling or accomplishment or insight. But most of us are now inclined to make these inclusions. Our psychologists, sociologists, and educators find it quite impossible to do their work without numbers. They believe that without numbers they cannot acquire or express authentic knowledge.

I shall not argue here that this is a stupid or dangerous idea, only that it is peculiar. What is even more peculiar is that so many of us do not find the idea peculiar. To say that someone should be doing better work because he has an IQ of 134, or that someone is a 7.2 on a sensitivity scale, or that this man's essay on the rise of capitalism is an A– and that man's is a C+ would have sounded like gibberish to Galileo or Shakespeare or Thomas Jefferson. If it makes sense to us, that is because our minds have been conditioned by the technology of numbers so that we see the world differently than they did. Our understanding of what is real is different. Which is another way of saying that embedded in every tool is an ideological bias, a predisposition to construct the world as one thing rather than another, to value one thing over another, to amplify one sense or skill or attitude more loudly than another.

This is what Marshall McLuhan meant by his famous aphorism "The medium is the message." This is what Marx meant when he said, "Technology discloses man's mode of dealing with nature" and creates the "conditions of intercourse" by which we relate to each other. It is what Wittgenstein meant when, in referring to our most fundamental technology, he said that language is not merely a vehicle of thought but also the driver. And it is what Thamus wished the inventor Theuth to see. This is, in short, an ancient and persistent piece of wisdom, perhaps most simply expressed in the old adage that, to a man with a hammer, everything looks like a nail. Without being too literal, we may extend the truism: To a man with a pencil, everything looks like a list. To a man with a camera, everything looks like an image. To a man with a computer, everything looks like data. And to a man with a grade sheet, everything looks like a number.

But such prejudices are not always apparent at the start of a technology's journey, which is why no one can safely conspire to be a winner in technological change. Who would have imagined, for example, whose interests and what world-view would be ultimately advanced by the invention of the mechanical clock? The clock had its origin in the Benedictine monasteries of the twelfth and thirteenth centuries. The impetus behind the invention was to provide a more or less precise regularity to the routines of the monasteries, which required, among other things, seven periods of devotion during the course of the day. The bells of the monastery were to be rung to signal the canonical hours; the mechanical clock was the technology that could provide precision to these rituals of devotion. And indeed it did. But what the monks did not foresee was that the clock is a means not merely of keeping track of the hours but also of synchronizing and controlling the actions of men. And thus, by the middle of the fourteenth century, the clock had moved outside the walls of the monastery, and brought a new and precise regularity to the life of the workman and the merchant. "The mechanical clock," as Lewis Mumford wrote, "made possible the idea of regular production, regular working hours and a standardized product." In short, without the clock, capitalism would have been quite impossible.[4] The paradox, the surprise, and the wonder are that the clock was invented by men who wanted to devote themselves more rigorously to God; it ended as the technology of greatest use to men who wished to devote themselves to the accumulation of money. In the eternal struggle between God and Mammon, the clock quite unpredictably favored the latter.

Unforeseen consequences stand in the way of all those who think they see clearly the direction in which a new technology will take us. Not even those who invent a technology can be assumed to be reliable prophets, as Thamus warned. Gutenberg, for example, was by all accounts a devout Catholic who would have been horrified to hear that accursed heretic Luther described printing as "God's highest act of grace, whereby the business of the Gospel is driven forward." Luther understood, as Gutenberg did not, that the mass-produced book, by placing the Word of God on every kitchen table, makes each Christian his own theologian—one might even say his own priest, or, better, from Luther's point of view, his own pope. In the struggle between unity and diversity of religious belief, the press favored the latter, and we can assume that this possibility never occurred to Gutenberg.

Thamus understood well the limitations of inventors in grasping the social and psychological—that is, ideological—bias of their own inventions. We can imagine him addressing Gutenberg in the following way: "Gutenberg, my paragon of inventors, the discoverer of an art is not the best judge of the good or harm which will accrue to those who practice it. So it is in this; you, who are the father of printing, have out of fondness for your off-spring come to believe it will advance the cause of the Holy Roman See, whereas in fact it will sow discord among believers; it will damage the authenticity of your beloved Church and destroy its monopoly."

We can imagine that Thamus would also have pointed out to Gutenberg, as he did to Theuth, that the new invention would create a vast population of readers who "will receive a quantity of information without proper instruction . . . [who will be] filled with the conceit of wisdom instead of real wisdom"; that reading, in other words, will compete with older forms of learning. This is yet another principle of technological change we may infer from the judgment of Thamus: new technologies compete with old ones—for time, for attention, for money, for prestige, but mostly for dominance of their world-view. This competition is implicit once we acknowledge that a medium contains an ideological bias. And it is a fierce competition, as only ideological competitions can be. It is not merely a matter of tool against tool—the alphabet attacking ideographic writing, the printing press attacking the illuminated manuscript, the photograph attacking the art of painting, television attacking the printed word. When media make war against each other, it is a case of world-views in collision.

In the United States, we can see such collisions everywhere—in politics, in religion, in commerce—but we see them most clearly in the schools, where two great technologies confront each other in uncompromising aspect for the control of students' minds. On the one hand, there is the world of the printed word with its emphasis on logic, sequence, history, exposition, objectivity, detachment, and discipline. On the other, there is the world of television with its emphasis on imagery, narrative, presentness, simultaneity, intimacy, immediate gratification, and quick emotional response. Children come to school having been deeply conditioned by the biases of television. There, they encounter the world of the printed word. A sort of psychic battle takes place, and there are many casualties—children who can't learn to read or won't, children who cannot organize their thought into logical structure even in a simple paragraph, children who cannot attend to lectures or oral explanations for more than a few minutes at a time. They are failures, but not because they are stupid. They are failures because there is a media war going on, and they are on the wrong side—at least for the moment. Who knows what schools will be like twenty-five years from now? Or fifty? In time, the type of student who is currently a failure may be considered a success. The type who is now successful may be regarded as a handicapped learner—slow to respond, far too detached, lacking in emotion, inadequate in creating mental pictures of reality. Consider: what Thamus called the "conceit of wisdom"—the unreal knowledge acquired through the written word—eventually became the pre-eminent form of knowledge valued by the schools. There is no reason to suppose that such a form of knowledge must always remain so highly valued.

To take another example: In introducing the personal computer to the classroom, we shall be breaking a four-hundred-year-old truce between the gregariousness and openness fostered by orality and the introspection and isolation fostered by the printed word. Orality stresses group learning, cooperation, and a sense of social responsibility, which is the context within which Thamus believed proper instruction and real knowledge must be communicated. Print stresses individualized learning, competition, and personal autonomy. Over four centuries, teachers, while emphasizing print, have allowed orality its place in the classroom, and have therefore achieved a kind of pedagogical peace between these two forms of learning, so that what is valuable in each can be maximized. Now comes the computer, carrying anew the banner of private learning and individual problem-solving. Will the widespread use of computers in the classroom defeat once and for all the claims of communal speech? Will the computer raise egocentrism to the status of a virtue?

These are the kinds of questions that technological change brings to mind when one grasps, as Thamus did, that technological competition ignites total war, which means it is not possible to contain the effects of a new technology to a limited sphere of human activity. If this metaphor puts the matter too brutally, we may try a gentler, kinder one: Technological change is neither additive nor subtractive. It is ecological. I mean "ecological" in the same sense as the word is used by environmental scientists. One significant change generates total change. If you remove the caterpillars from a given habitat, you are not left with the same environment minus caterpillars: you have a new environment, and you have reconstituted the conditions of survival; the same is true if you add caterpillars to an environment that has had none. This is how the ecology of media works as well. A new technology does not add or subtract something. It changes everything. In the year 1500, fifty years after the printing press was invented, we did not have old Europe plus the printing press. We had a different Europe. After television, the United States was not America plus television; television gave a new coloration to every political campaign, to every home, to every school, to every church, to every industry. And that is why the competition among media is so fierce. Surrounding every technology are institutions whose organization—not to mention their reason for being—reflects the world-view promoted by the technology. Therefore, when an old technology is assaulted by a new one, institutions are threatened. When institutions are threatened, a culture finds itself in crisis. This is serious business, which is why we learn nothing when educators ask, Will students learn mathematics better by computers than by textbooks? Or when businessmen ask, Through which medium can we sell more products? Or when preachers ask, Can we reach more people through television than through radio? Or when politicians ask, How effective are messages sent through different media? Such questions have an immediate, practical value to those who ask them, but they are diversionary. They direct our attention away from the serious social, intellectual, and institutional crises that new media foster.

Perhaps an analogy here will help to underline the point. In speaking of the meaning of a poem, T. S. Eliot remarked that the chief use of the overt content of poetry is "to satisfy one habit of the reader, to keep his mind diverted and quiet, while the poem does its work upon him: much as the imaginary burglar is always provided with a bit of nice meat for the house-dog." In other words, in asking their practical questions, educators, entrepreneurs, preachers, and politicians are like the house-dog munching peacefully on the meat while the house is looted. Perhaps some of them know this and do not especially care. After all, a nice piece of meat, offered graciously, does take care of the problem of where the next meal will come from. But for the rest of us, it cannot be acceptable to have the house invaded without protest or at least awareness.

What we need to consider about the computer has nothing to do with its efficiency as a teaching tool. We need to know in what ways it is altering our conception of learning, and how, in conjunction with television, it undermines the old idea of school. Who cares how many boxes of cereal can be sold via television? We need to know if television changes our conception of reality, the relationship of the rich to the poor, the idea of happiness itself. A preacher who confines himself to considering how a medium can increase his audience will miss the significant question: In what sense do new media alter what is meant by religion, by church, even by God? And if the politician cannot think beyond the next election, then *we* must wonder about what new media do to the idea of political organization and to the conception of citizenship.

To help us do this, we have the judgment of Thamus, who, in the way of legends, teaches us what Harold Innis, in his way, tried to. New technologies alter the structure of our interests: the things we think *about*. They alter the character of our symbols: the things we think *with*. And they alter the nature of community: the arena in which thoughts develop. As Thamus spoke to Innis across the centuries, it is essential that we listen to their conversation, join in it, revitalize it. For something has happened in America that is strange and dangerous, and there is only a dull and even stupid awareness of what it is—in part because it has no name. I call it Technopoly.

Notes

1. Plato, *Phaedrus and Letters VII and VIII*. New York: Penguin Books, 1973, p. 96.

2. Freud, Sigmund, *Civilization and Its Discontents*. New York: W. W. Norton & Company, 1961, p. 38–39.

3. This fact is documented in Keith Hoskin's "The Examination, Disciplinary Power and Rational Schooling," in *History of Education,* vol. VIII, no. 2 (1979), pp. 135–46. Professor Hoskin provides the following story about Farish: Farish was a professor of engineering at Cambridge and designed and installed a movable partition wall in his Cambridge home. The wall moved on pulleys between downstairs and upstairs. One night, while working late

downstairs and feeling cold, Farish pulled down the partition. This is not much of a story, and history fails to disclose what happened next. All of which shows how little is known of William Farish.

4. For a detailed exposition of Mumford's position on the impact of the mechanical clock, see his *Technics and Civilization.*

REFLECTING ON THE READING

1. Postman begins this passage with a reference to the mythical story of Thamus, which he takes from the *Phaedrus* by Plato. Why does Postman tell us he begins in this way? What significance does Postman see in this story? What does Postman's reference to the "error" in the story reveal about his own attitude toward technology?

2. Near the beginning of the passage Postman writes that he has been accused of being a "one-eyed prophet" who opposes technology and that he is a "dissenting voice" that is necessary "to moderate the din made by the enthusiastic multitudes." Who has accused Postman of being a "one-eyed prophet"? Are they the same as the "Technophiles" he describes in the same paragraph? Why must he defend against such a charge?

3. Why does Postman quote Freud? What point does he make by quoting Freud?

4. Why, according to Postman, must we admit a new technology into our culture "with our eyes wide open"? What specifically does he mean by that statement? What is it about the nature of technology that he emphasizes here? Do you agree with him? Explain.

5. What does Postman mean when he writes that "technology imperiously commandeers our most important terminology"? In what sense can technology "commandeer" words and phrases? Do you think Postman is right about this? What does this statement tell us about Postman's view of technology? Is technology, in Postman's view, neutral? Explain.

6. What do the examples of television and the computer indicate about the nature of technology and how it tends to be used, according to Postman?

7. What does Postman mean by "ideological" changes brought on by technology? What example does he provide to illustrate this point?

8. What point about technology does Postman use the example of the invention of the mechanical clock to make?

9. What, according to Postman, are the differences between what he calls "the world of the printed word" and "the world of television"? Why are these differences important? Do you agree with Postman's description of these differences? Why or why not?

10. What does Postman mean when he describes technology as "ecological"? What examples does he offer to illustrate his point?

Examining Rhetorical Strategies

1. What do you think the beginning of this passage indicates about the kind of audience Postman imagined he was writing for? How did the reference to Plato and the story of Thamus affect you as a reader? Do you think you are among the audience Postman imagined for this text? Why or why not?

2. Why do you think Postman never specifically identifies those who he says have accused him of being a "one-eyed prophet" opposed to technology? Who do you think these accusers are? What effect does Postman's assertion that he must be a "dissenting voice" among the "enthusiastic multitudes" have on you as a reader? How does this assertion position Postman as the writer of this text? Did it make him more or less credible in your eyes? Explain.

3. Assess Postman's use of evidence in making his arguments. For example, what does he accomplish by using a quotation from Freud? Did you find that quotation effective? Why or why not? Further, examine his use of examples. Do you think his examples effectively illustrate his various points? For instance, how does his example of the mechanical clock help him make his point about the impact of technology on human life? What does this specific example indicate about Postman's own values regarding human existence? Identify other examples that might also reveal Postman's values.

4. Postman asserts that technological change is neither additive nor subtractive but "ecological." That assertion suggests that Postman thinks it would be impossible to return society to a state that existed prior to the introduction of a technology like the computer. Yet Postman seems to be arguing that the computer has been detrimental to education. Based on what he says in this passage, what kinds of changes do you think Postman wishes to make regarding technology? If we cannot eliminate a technology like the computer, what can we do? Does Postman provide options for addressing the problem of technology that seem reasonable to you? Explain.

5. How would you characterize Postman's tone in this passage? How does his tone relate to the argument he makes? Is his tone effective, in your view? Why or why not? What might your reaction to his tone indicate about you as a reader? Do you think Postman could have made his argument in a different tone without compromising his point? In what way?

Engaging the Issues

1. Write a response to Postman in which you make your own argument about technology and its impact on modern society. Where appropriate, refer to specific points that Postman makes.

2. Write a summary of Postman's argument and his concerns about technology for an audience who is likely to be enthusiastic in its support of technology (e.g., workers in a computer company, software developers, businesspeople for whom

cellular telephones have become indispensable equipment). How would you present Postman's argument to this apparently hostile audience?

3. Access the World Wide Web and identify several sites that show how recently developed computer technologies have enhanced the lives of human beings in ways that Postman might support. Write an essay in which you describe these sites in order to make an argument for the benefits of technology in human terms.

   Alternatively, construct a Web site that offers evidence for the benefits of technologies like the World Wide Web. Construct your site in a way that makes your purpose and point of view clear to a general audience of viewers who may not have a sophisticated understanding of the technologies you refer to.

4. Identify a technology that has had a significant impact on your own life. In an essay intended for an audience of your classmates, discuss the impact that technology has had on your life. Assess that impact and draw conclusions about it. Use this experience to evaluate the validity of Postman's concerns about technology.

5. Write an analysis of Postman's argument focusing on his use of language and his choice of examples and evidence to support his argument. Try to identify specific strategies Postman uses to make his points. What words and phrases does he choose in describing technology or the proponents of technology? What do these choices convey about his attitudes and beliefs? Similarly, what do his examples indicate about his attitudes and beliefs? Assess the fairness of his arguments.

6. In a group of your classmates, discuss Postman's position on technology. Do the members of your group generally agree or disagree with Postman? Why? What differences or similarities emerge among your group members in their ideas about technology? How might you account for those differences? For instance, do they have anything to do with your respective economic backgrounds, your previous experiences with technology, your gender, your age? Try to draw conclusions based on your discussion about the role of technology in contemporary society.

Counting Forward, Counting Back

ALAN CHEUSE

INTRODUCTION We tend to think of *progress* as a relatively straightforward and positive matter: We move forward; things improve. But as novelist Alan Cheuse reminds us in the following essay, this idea of progress seems to be a peculiarly Western one that grows out of a Judeo-Christian tradition. The ancient Greeks, he tells us, thought of life as moving in cycles. And anthropologists tell us that the same is true of many other cultures, including the Chinese, Australian Aboriginal peoples, and Native American communities. Moreover, our Western notion of progress seems to be intimately related to science and technology. We think of the "advance" of science, of technology making our lives better. Cheuse lists many of the developments in the twentieth century that we associate with progress: automobiles, telephones, heart pumps, email, laser discs. But Cheuse also reminds us of other such developments that seem less positive, such as the atomic bomb. Does the development of such a device represent progress? If so, is progress necessarily a good thing? And is such progress universal? Is the heart pump, for example, available to every patient who needs one? Does it represent progress only for those who are fortunate enough to be able to afford one?

Cheuse implicitly poses questions like these in his essay, reminding us that progress is really a very complicated idea whose meaning depends upon who you are and where you stand. And for many people, he admits, particularly those for whom the explosion of the atomic bomb was a central event in their lives, progress is no longer a source of hope and possibility. They see a world in which science can eradicate horrible diseases and help prolong life but also produce horrifying devices whose purpose is unimaginable destruction and death. And as we enter the new millennium, we see that developments such as the automobile, which seem to have made modern life so much easier and more convenient, can also result in environmental degradation and a host of social problems. In short, many people, like the friends Cheuse describes at the beginning of his essay, have begun to question our ideas about progress. Yet Cheuse remains hopeful and optimistic. Progress for him is still a compelling and positive idea, one that seems to fit in well with his own experiences as a writer and as a citizen of the twentieth century. Moreover, it is an idea that encompasses technology and literacy in ways that perhaps we don't usually consider. You may find that the connections he makes among these ideas—technology, literacy, and progress—surprise you and encourage you to reconsider your own understanding of them.

Alan Cheuse teaches writing at George Mason University. He is the author of two novels, *The Grandmother's Club* and *The Light Possessed,* as well as a collection of short stories and a memoir. He also hosts *The Sound of Writing,* a radio magazine devoted to fiction writing on National Public Radio, and regularly reviews books for National Public Radio's *All Things Considered.* The following essay was published in *How We Want to Live* (1998), a collection of essays about the meaning of progress, edited by Susan Richards Shreve and Porter Shreve.

REFLECTING BEFORE READING

1. Alan Cheuse begins his essay with a reference to the explosion of the first atomic bomb during a test by U.S. scientists in New Mexico in the 1940's. Cheuse suggests that that test was perhaps the most significant event for people who grew up in the twentieth century and forever changed the way they think about progress and about the world. What do you know about nuclear weapons and about the way they were developed and used in the twentieth century? Did you grow up with a fear of the bomb as Cheuse did? Consider how your own attitudes about nuclear weapons might affect your reading of Cheuse's essay.

2. In this essay, Cheuse shares some of his ideas about *progress* and how those ideas have changed during his life. As you read, pay attention to how he uses the term *progress*. What exactly does he mean by that term? What does *progress* mean to you?

Ten—
Nine—
Eight—
Seven—
Six—
Five—
Four—
Three—
Two—
One—
Ignition!

The blast, the fiery light, the cloud arises, unfolds, that huge white-and-grey mushroom on a stalk of flame. . . .

Dr. J. Robert Oppenheimer, one of the creators of this new and deadly fire, watched from the observation bunker as the first atomic cloud spilled upwards into the heavens and quoted from the *Bhagavad Gita*—"I am Death, Destroyer of Worlds. . . ."

And that was that, some people between the ages of twenty-five and forty were saying to me as we sat around a table and talked about the idea of progress one recent bright autumn day when the air was so warm and the sun so present that it seemed as though time and the season might be preserved forever in amber. Over the course of this conversation, most of them claimed that their notion of progress as a positive force in the world had disintegrated along with all of the New Mexico rocks and sand at Alamogordo, an event that most of them knew only from news reels and history books.

"Personal progress, that's all we have left," one of them said, a personable young woman in her late twenties with a bent for reading great literature and writing about it, a profession to which one can adhere, ironically enough, if one has only the greatest amount of optimism about the future of the job market.

"That's right," another student said, this fellow a family man, dark skinned, hard working, teaching public school by day and doing graduate work by night. "You can inch along, but you can't leap anymore. Those days are over."

They were convincing in that moment, so convincing that I sat there for a while at my end of the table wondering why my own sense of progress hadn't been destroyed in that blast. I had every reason to let it go. Wasn't I a first-generation child of the Atomic Age? My burgeoning sense of progress could easily have slipped away from me in the musty classrooms of School No. 7 in Perth Amboy, New Jersey, soon after that first poisonous mushroom cloud billowed up into the stratosphere. At the same time the teachers imbued me with my sense of American possibilities ("one nation, with liberty and justice for all"), they also taught us to duck beneath our desks at the sound of a siren or, if caught out in the dark hallways, to fold ourselves into fetal balls, one arm covering our faces, the other covering our heads. Death could descend on us in a pillar of fire at home while we ate or slept. But at school we were prepared.

Maybe this sense of false security helped me to fend off somehow that threat of instantaneous nuclear annihilation. Or maybe because of all of the propaganda and idealistic musings mixed with hype about the wonders of modern science, I never associated that explosion until much later with the dangers of science. Along with Stanley Kubrick's Dr. Strangelove we all, in some bizarre and disconcerting way, learned to love the Bomb.

It's easy to understand why that happened. The positive nature of progress was our creed as Americans ("one nation, indivisible . . .") and had been since the inception of our country. And in history classes at the university I learned that the twentieth century was the American century and that the idea of progress had become our anthem. All my living and reading after that confirmed for me that we were living in the age of the new, a century of marvelous new inventions, new medicine, new technology, new modes of painting, of writing—from *Ulysses* and cubism to the fax machine (actually predicted by Jules Verne in his novel *Life in the Twentieth Century,* written in 1861 though unpublished until 1996) to the probes of the far rim of the solar system. If fear of the atomic bomb was great, most of the time we repressed it, preferring to crow to ourselves about the great forward leaps in modern life.

We've all seen those movies, the assured voice-over about the inventions that are going to change the way we live, from self-cleaning houses to automobiles powered by solar panels. The moon landings. The Mars landing. Surveyor. Our eye on the outer planets. This is our world, this will be our future. We kept those voice-overs in our heads. News about the great advances in medicine, about battery-powered automobiles, portable telephones, faxes, beepers, miniature television sets, car phones, the compact disc, the laser, the laser disc, the heart pump, the hydraulic penis, the heart valve, the CD-ROM, the Mars Rover, the Jupiter probe, e-mail, synthetic insulin and the birth control pill, color printers, the pacemaker, the Net. . . . I believed all that. I believed that we could make great progress in communicating with one another across great distances. We ended totalitarianism in our time. We brought down the wall. Science played a role in this. Why else would the Communists have kept all their xerox machines under lock and key? Science and freedom go hand in hand. Science frees the word. Science frees the mind.

I had personal, if minor, testimony to give on this score. Three years ago I worked on an electronic typewriter and had been doing so for nearly ten years after the demise of my electric typewriter, mother of five books of my own and three of my ex-wife's, who gave the machine to me when she bought a computer (causing me to give up my manual machine). Then I began using a computer, and I haven't looked back.

"It's like going from a bicycle to a Mercedes," I heard myself saying to friends, amazed at my decision, for the first year or so that I was using it. How could I have ignored such a leap forward in useful technology? The same epoch that brought us the A-bomb made it easier for me to type and edit my work. This is technological progress at its most beneficent. Do I duck under my desk and place one arm across my face and the other over my neck before I begin to write each day? No, no, the A-bomb and global warming and all of the other horrors wrought by modern technological life seem too far away from my daily round for me to care much about them.

But lately we have seen technology, particularly modern medicine, falter and even fail us in ways far too close to home for us to ignore, mainly in the wake of the worldwide AIDS epidemic and in medicine's uphill battle against a plethora of mutated microbes—mean, nasty, disease-creating bugs for whom *progress* means rapidly making themselves immune to most of our so-called wonder drugs. And the cause of this problem? Medicine itself—too many doctors overprescribing or incorrectly prescribing the very antibiotics that modern chemistry has made it possible for the drug companies to produce.

The hitch in the stride of the great forward movement of conventional medicine reminded me that the idea of progress has not always been with us. Nothing like it obtained in preclassical antiquity. The Greeks knew cycles, not progressive incremental change. As the British philosopher-historian J. B. Bury pointed out in his 1932 book-length essay *Idea of Progress,* it was the Hebraic vision of a tribe singled out by a judgmental God as His primary agent for change in time that first introduced this paradigm into the world. With the idea of change in history suddenly apparent, things were ripe for the advent of Christianity, which put out the call that all people could change their situations in time by accepting Christ as their personal savior—do this and a better time, eternity as opposed to mere human time, looms in your future.

So the idea of an advance in time as an advance in quality comes to us from theology, from the quest to find a better world than this. The actual use of the verb *to progress* in association with this idea, however, is a rather late development. For many hundreds of years *to progress* meant only to move forward or advance in a physical fashion. From the Renaissance to the eighteenth century people used the word as a synonym for *parade.* I like that usage a lot. Worms make a progress through Polonius's guts, Hamlet tells us. Human progress made the picture in mind of row upon row of marchers, in the front ranks the latest human beings on earth; bringing up the rear, all of those who have come before.

The figurative use of the word as a way of describing an advance to a higher stage or better condition enters the language only in the seventeenth century. Look, for example, at the title of John Bunyan's famous allegory, published in 1678, about a Christian traveler in a world of despair: *The Pilgrim's Progress, from this world, to that which is to come.* Two hundred years pass and we find that science has appropriated the word in order to describe the betterment of the human condition. In the twentieth century left-wing politicians took up the word as well. What am I? I am a *progressive.* I believe in a political system that can make a better world.

I believed it. Almost all of it. A-bomb or no A-bomb, science could improve our lives beyond measure. I knew that. I celebrated it. In my house I have gadgets and services that make me in many ways richer than kings of old. And it's not just in the physical world of science that I can improve. I can undergo spiritual and psychological change. As the wonderfully naïve and optimistic Dale Carnegie system for self-betterment used to have its practitioners chant, "Every day, in every way, I am getting better and better."

Sort of.

My efforts as a writer, teacher, father, and husband have all, I think, improved over the days and years. (My work at being a friend, citizen, and enemy has probably deteriorated somewhat.) Overall, I may have made some progress as a human being. And as an artist.

And yet, as I've always been, I'm still parading toward the grave.

That's the tragic paradox lurking in the seemingly solid and attractive secular idea of progress. Having found its origins in the Christian conception of a place better than this, an afterworld toward which one can strive and hope some day to achieve, the notion of worldly progress presumes that we can all make this earth of ours better within the scope of human time—a paradise erenow. With one fatal catch. Anyone who works for it will only stick around for less than a hundred years, some considerably less.

So maybe what those folks were expressing in that autumnal conversation illuminated by that brilliant light was their disappointment that progress could not make them immortal. I'm quite disappointed in that, too, I have to admit.

But still remain a firm believer in the idea of progress, for all its complexity. What else can you believe if you try to write novels? The second draft must be better than the first draft, the third must improve upon the second, the fourth prove better than the third. The process reminds me of the labor of the gods in the creation myth at the beginning of the Quiche Maya creation story, the *Popul-Vuh.* The gods first make the world and populate it with creatures made of paper. Fire burns them up. Next they make people out of clay. But rain washes them away. After a while the gods get the hang of it and create human beings, fragile, yes, but not as fragile as paper or clay.

If it took the gods of Middle America four cycles of creation to get it right, why should a novelist believe that he can work any faster?

We find one, two, three, four, five, perhaps sometimes even ten drafts, in the writer's struggle to reach that moment of ignition in which the illusory world on the page sparks to life. This count forward seems to me to stand as a wonderful counterpoint to the numerical descent from ten to zero toward a world in which science and destruction go hand in hand.

So there are a number of different ways to understand the meaning of progress in a world in which a count forward also leads toward the end and euphemisms such as "senior citizen" (jargon from the realm of the "social services," that legacy of the progressive politics of our century) mask the deterioration and winnowing away of spirit, muscle, and bone. But metaphor sometimes can act as a valuable shield against the ironic forward tending of progress toward the grave. Flimsy poetry, mortal fiction, evanescent dance, delicate paintings—these are some of the only answers we have in the face of relentless forward motion in a world without a belief in immortality.

Poetry, as Frost once wrote, is a momentary stay against confusion. I think he used that word *confusion* in a deep, deep way, meaning chaos and whorl. Under the sway of impersonal technological progress, and moving toward a millennium in which we can only see more of the same, our feeble gestures at making art appear, in their very fragility, an immense and daring act. These flowers, these songs, we offer up amidst the countdown toward oblivion, and the best of them reveal themselves to be, in their own way, brighter than a thousand suns.

REFLECTING ON THE READING

1. Cheuse begins this essay with a countdown and refers to it near the end of the essay as well. What is the significance of this countdown? To what, specifically, does it refer? In what sense is counting important to the point Cheuse wishes to make in his essay?

2. Who are the people Cheuse is talking to in the beginning of the essay? Why are their ideas about progress so negative? Why is Cheuse's perspective on progress different?

3. Cheuse lists some of the many technological and scientific developments that he has witnessed in his life, and he describes his experience with two technologies that have been important in his own life: the typewriter and the computer. What significance does Cheuse see in the development of the computer for writing? Why does he call it "beneficent"?

4. Where, according to Cheuse, did the idea of progress as "progressive incremental change" come from? How has the use of the word *progress* changed over time? Why does Cheuse think this change is important?

5. What is the "tragic paradox" that Cheuse sees in "the idea of progress"? Why does Cheuse remain a "firm believer in the idea of progress" even in the face of this paradox? Does the paradox Cheuse describes worry you? Why or why not?

6. What does Cheuse mean when he writes that "metaphor sometimes can act as a valuable shield against the ironic forward tending of progress toward the grave"? What forms of "metaphor" does Cheuse cite? Do you agree with him about this role of "metaphor"? Explain.

Examining Rhetorical Strategies

1. Evaluate the way Cheuse begins this essay. How does he introduce the idea of progress? What images does his opening evoke for you? What reaction did you have to those images? Do you think other readers would have similar reactions? Explain. What might Cheuse's introduction suggest about his intended audience?

2. Explain what Cheuse means by *progress* in this essay. How does he understand that term? What assumptions does he have about progress and its relationship to technology? How does he build his idea of progress throughout his essay? Do you share his assumptions about progress? How might your own attitudes about progress and technology have influenced your reaction to Cheuse's essay?

3. This essay was originally part of a collection of essays by well-known writers that was published by a commercial publisher. Who do you think Cheuse imagined might read his essay? Do you think he imagined you among his audience? Explain. Cite specific passages from the essay in your answer.

4. How would you describe Cheuse's writing style? How did you react to that style? What might your reaction to his writing say about you and your own expectations as a reader? Point to specific examples in the essay to support your answer.

5. Notice the references Cheuse makes in his essay to books and movies. What might these references tell you about Cheuse as a writer—about his own values

and interests? What might they reveal about his beliefs about his audience? Did you recognize those references? How did they affect your reaction to Cheuse's essay? What might your reaction to these references reveal about you as a reader?

6. Examine Cheuse's use of anecdote and example in this essay. What kinds of anecdotes and examples does he include? What might they suggest about his own values as a writer and as a person interested in technology? Did you find these anecdotes and examples effective? Why or why not? Cite specific passages from his essay to support your answer.

Engaging the Issues

1. Write an essay for an audience of your classmates in which you describe the effects of one particular technological or scientific development on your own life. You can choose any kind of technological or scientific invention, procedure, or discovery: for example, a common technology such as a camera or telephone, or a special medical procedure that you might have benefited from. In your essay, tell the story of the role that technological or scientific development played in your life. How did it come into your life? How did it affect the way you live? How might it have affected your attitudes about yourself or about the world in general? Did it change your relationships with others? Try to explore the significance of that development to you and to others.

2. In a group of your classmates, share the essays you wrote for Question #1 above. Examine the roles played by the various technological or scientific developments that each of you wrote about. What was important about those developments in your lives? How might they have changed your lives? Discuss what these essays might say about your attitudes regarding *progress* and about technology. How might the different backgrounds of each of the members of your group have affected their attitudes about progress?

3. Cheuse reveals an optimistic view of *progress* in his essay, but he acknowledges a much less optimistic view on the part of other people he knows (such as those he is conversing with at the beginning of his essay). Write a letter to Cheuse in which you respond to his essay and especially to his ideas about progress. In your letter, summarize what you find most compelling or disturbing about his ideas regarding progress and offer your own view. Explain why you agree or disagree with him.

4. Rewrite the letter you wrote for Question #3 for the editorial page of your local newspaper. Focus your letter on the idea of progress and make your point for readers of your local newspaper. In your letter, you might find it appropriate to summarize Cheuse's essay and his ideas about progress, assuming that your readers may not be familiar with his essay.

   Now compare this letter to the letter you wrote for Question #3. How are they different? How are they similar? How did the audience affect your decisions about each letter? Did the fact that a letter to your newspaper would be read by hundreds or thousands of readers change the way you made your point? Explain.

5. Interview three or four people about their ideas regarding progress. If possible, try to find people who have very different backgrounds (age, race, gender, socioeconomic status, and so on). Ask them about how they understand progress, specifically regarding technology. You might share with them some of Cheuse's ideas about progress and ask for their reactions to those ideas. After completing your interviews, write a report for an audience of your classmates. In your report, describe each of the people you interviewed and list the kinds of questions you asked them. Then discuss their responses to your questions, looking for similarities and differences among them. Try to account for these similarities and differences. Finally, draw conclusions about attitudes toward progress on the basis of your research.

6. Search the World Wide Web for sites that specifically relate to technology. Try to find a variety of sites, including sites maintained by individuals, businesses, and professional organizations. For example, you might find a site that is maintained by an organization devoted to the uses of technology in schools. Or you might find a site for a business that develops specific kinds of communications software. Find several such sites and examine them to try to determine how they represent technology and progress. Do they present a positive view of technology? How? What do you think their sites indicate about their beliefs regarding progress? What assumptions about visitors to their sites do they make?

   Now write a brief analysis for your classmates in which you review the sites you visited. Be sure to provide the URL's of the sites and describe each one. In your analysis, discuss what you think are the attitudes about technology and progress that emerge from the sites you visited. Point to specific features or images or statements on the sites to support your analysis. Try to draw conclusions from your analysis about attitudes regarding technology and progress.

   Alternatively, build a Web site in which you present the results of your analysis, providing appropriate links to the Web sites you reviewed and offering your own assessment of each site.

Connections

DEBORAH TANNEN

INTRODUCTION   What does technological progress mean to individual human beings? We often hear about how technology has changed the world—how, for example, the television or the World Wide Web changed the way people learn about the world or communicate with each other. But how do such technologies affect the lives of a particular person and the important people in that person's life? Do these technologies influence the way this person or that person interacts with others? Do they change an individual life for the better?

   In the following essay, Deborah Tannen, an internationally known expert in interpersonal communications, addresses these questions by sharing stories about communicating—through technology—with the important people in her life. In doing so, she views the sweeping technological changes that occurred in the twentieth century through the lens of an individual life. As Tannen reminds us in her essay, the twentieth century brought us not only email but also the telephone, jet air travel, and television—technologies that have profoundly changed the way we communicate, congregate, and interact with each other. But such extensive change inevitably raises questions about what is gained and what might be lost when new technologies begin to reshape how we live together. Several writers in this chapter—and in other chapters in this book—wonder whether new technologies are truly beneficial, and some warn that we lose much more than we gain when we abandon old ways of communicating and interacting for technologies like the Internet. Such warnings remind us that change does not always bring improvement and that it affects different people in different ways. The *progress* that we associate with technological developments like the telephone or the Internet—which seem to make our lives easier and better—can thus be a complicated matter. For Tannen, assessing such progress is a matter of looking at individual lives. Only in that context, she suggests, can we begin to see clearly how technology affects us and whether it really changes—and improves—how we live with each other.

Deborah Tannen knows something about how individual human beings interact with each other. She is a professor of linguistics at Georgetown University, whose studies of cross-cultural communications, the relationship between written and spoken discourse, and similar topics have been supported by such organizations as the National Endowment for the Humanities and the National Science Foundation. But she is more widely known for her work on gender and communications. Her book *You Just Don't Understand: Women and Men in Conversation* (1990) was on the *New York Times* bestseller list for almost four years and has been translated into 24 languages; another of her books, *Talking from 9 to 5: Women and Men in the Workplace: Language, Sex, and Power* (1995), was also a best-seller. Her studies of gender and communication have made her a popular public speaker and a sought-after guest on television shows like *20/20, 48 Hours, Oprah, Good Morning America*, and *Larry King Live*. Tannen is also author of *That's Not What I Meant: How Conversational Style Makes or Breaks Relationships* (1990) and *The Argument Culture: Moving from Debate to Dialogue* (1998), her sixteenth book. The following essay was published in *How We Want to Live* (1998), a collection of essays about progress.

REFLECTING BEFORE READING

1. Tannen titled the following essay "Connections." Consider what that word means to you. What kinds of *connections* might you think of as you begin to read this essay? As you read, determine whether your sense of that word matches what you think Tannen means by it.

2. In her essay, Tannen refers to a variety of technologies by which people stay in touch with one another: telephones, radios, televisions, and email. As you read, consider how such technologies might affect the way you interact with others in your life. What significance do such technologies have in your relationships with people who are important to you?

M y father never knew his father. Until he was seven, he lived with his mother and sister in his grandparents' home: a Hasidic household in Warsaw. His grandfather was the closest he ever came to having a father.

In 1920, when my father was twelve, he left Poland to emigrate with his mother and sister to the United States, and he saw his grandfather for the last time. As my father tells it, his grandfather took him on his knee to say good-bye. Tears ran down the old man's face and into his long white beard. He knew he would never see his grandchild again. Even if the Holocaust had not taken his grandfather's life, my father would not have been able to return to Poland for a visit during his grandfather's lifetime. He wouldn't have been able to take the time off work to sail across the ocean, and he wouldn't have been able to afford the trip.

In 1966, I graduated from college, worked for six months, saved all the money I earned, and flew to Europe on a one-way ticket through Luxembourg on Icelandic Airlines. I ended up in Greece, where I lived for nearly two years, teaching English. I communicated with my parents by mail—but from time to time I would telephone them: I'd go to the main post office in downtown Athens, fill out a form, and wait until someone called my name and indicated in which booth my parents' voices would materialize. Sometimes I waited hours for the call to be put through—until the planned evening surprise had become a terrifying, sleep-destroying, wee-hours-of-the-morning alarm. "Do me a favor," my mother once said. "If it's after midnight, don't call." "But I've been waiting to put the call through for four hours," I said. "I didn't plan it to be after midnight." And there were not only telephones, but airplanes. During that year, my parents celebrated their thirty-fifth wedding anniversary, and they gave each of their children $1000. I used a portion of mine to fly home to New York City for their anniversary party.

In 1996, my oldest sister went to Israel for a year. Within a few weeks, she subscribed to Compuserve and hooked up her laptop computer to e-mail—and my other sister and my nieces all got on e-mail, too. Within a month, my sister was in daily communication with us all—much more frequent contact than our weekly (or biweekly or monthly) telephone calls had been when my sister was home in upstate New York.

And another surprise: my other sister, who generally is not eager to talk about her feelings, opened up on e-mail. One time I called her and we spoke on the phone; after we hung up, I checked my e-mail and found a message she had sent before we spoke, in which she revealed personal information that she hadn't mentioned on the phone. I asked her about this (on e-mail), and she explained, "The telephone is so impersonal." At first this seemed absurd: How could the actual voice of a person in conversation be more impersonal than on-screen little letters detached from the writer? But when I thought about it, it made sense: Writing e-mail is like writing in a journal; you're alone with your thoughts and your words, safe from the intrusive presence of another person.

I was the second person in my university department to get a computer. The first was my colleague Ralph. The year was 1980. Ralph got a Radio Shack TRS 80; I got a used Apple 2-Plus. He helped me get started, and before long helped me get on Bitnet, the precursor to the Internet. Though his office was next to mine, we rarely had extended conversations except about department business. Shy and soft-spoken, Ralph mumbled, so I could barely tell he was speaking. But when we were using e-mail, we started communicating daily in this (then) leisurely medium. We could send each other messages without fear of imposing, since the receiver determines when to log on and read and respond. Soon I was getting long self-revealing messages from Ralph. We moved effortlessly among discussions of department business, our work, and our lives. Through e-mail Ralph and I became friends.

Ralph recently forwarded to me a message he had received from his niece, a college freshman. "How nice," I commented, "that you have such a close relationship with your niece. Do you think you'd be in touch with her if it weren't for e-mail?" "No," he replied. "I can't imagine we'd write each other letters regularly or call on the phone. No way." E-mail makes possible connections with relatives, acquaintances, or strangers, that wouldn't otherwise exist. And it enables more frequent and different communication with people you're already close to. Parents are in daily contact with their children at college; people discover and reunite with long lost friends. One woman discovered that e-mail brought her closer to her father. He would never talk much on the phone (as her mother would), but they have become close since they both got on-line.

The Internet and the World Wide Web are creating networks of human connection unthinkable even a few years ago. But at the same time that technologically enhanced communication enables previously impossible loving contact, it also enhances hostile and distressing communication. Along with the voices of family members and friends, telephones bring into our homes the annoying voices of solicitors who want to sell something—at dinnertime. (My father-in-law startles a telephone solicitor by saying, "We're eating dinner, but I'll call you back. What's your home phone number?" To the nonplussed caller he explains, "Well, you're calling me at home; I thought I'd call you at home, too.") Even more unnerving, in the middle of the night come frightening obscene calls and stalkers.

The Internet ratchets up anonymity by homogenizing all messages into identical-appearing print and making it almost impossible to trace messages back to the computer that sent them. As the ease of using the Internet has resulted in more and more people logging on and sending messages to more and more others with whom they have a connection, it has also led to more communication with strangers, and this has led to "flaming": vituperative messages that verbally attack. Flaming results from the anonymity not only of the sender but also of the receiver. It is easier to feel and express hostility against someone far removed whom you do not know, like the rage that some drivers feel toward an anonymous car that cuts them off. If the driver to whom you've flipped the finger turns out to be someone you know, the rush of shame you feel is evidence that anonymity was essential for your expression—and experience—of rage.

Less and less of our communication is face to face, and more often with people we don't know. Technology that brings people closer also isolates us in a bubble. When I was a child, my family got the first television on our block, and the neighborhood children gathered in our dining room to watch *Howdy Doody*. Before long, every family had their own TV—just one, so that in order to watch it, families came together. Now many families have more than one television, so each family member can watch what they like—alone. The spread of radio has followed the same pattern. Early radios were like a piece of furniture around which a family had to gather in order to listen. Now radio listeners may have a radio in every room, one in the car, and another—equipped with headphones—for jogging. These technologies now exert a centrifugal force, pulling people apart—and increasing the likelihood that their encounters with each other will be anonymous and hostile.

Electronic communication is progress; it makes human relationships different. But it also makes human relationships more the same—there's more of what's good and more of what's bad. In the end, we graft the new possibilities onto what has always been there.

E-mail gave me the chance to be in touch with someone who was dying far away. College friends, Larry and I were not so close that we would make special trips to visit each other on opposite coasts, but we kept in touch through occasional notes, and we got together whenever we found ourselves in the same town. I learned from another college friend—on e-mail—that Larry was diagnosed with lung cancer. I didn't want to call Larry on the phone; that seemed too intrusive. I didn't know if he wanted to talk about his cancer with people like me; maybe he wanted to curl into his family. So I sent him an e-mail message, and he sent one in reply. Soon we were exchanging messages regularly. E-mail gave me a little path I could walk along. For two years, Larry kept me informed of how he was doing, and what the chemotherapy was doing to him—and asked me how my book was coming and whether I had managed to put up pictures in my new house yet. In April 1996 he was back to work and gaining weight. But then e-mail brought the bad news: new lesions were found, and the doctors held out no more hope.

On December 24, 1996, Larry wrote, "I will miss our e-mails, Deb. It was great being your friend, and I will always remain so." On December 27 I got messages—both on e-mail and on my telephone answering machine—telling me Larry had died the night before. I could not just sit at my desk that day and work. And e-mail was not immediate enough for the connection I wanted. I called friends who had been closer to Larry than I, to learn as much as I could about his last days. And I called friends who had been less close, to tell them. I spent much of that day talking with friends from our college circle. We told each other our memories of Larry's life, creating our own memorial to observe his passing from our lives.

My father never knew exactly when his grandfather died. When my friend Larry died, how much it meant that the telephone made it possible to spend the day talking to others who knew him. How much it meant that Larry said good-bye. This is a gift he gave me, and technology made it possible. That is progress. But the way we used technology—the telephone and e-mail—that was human emotion and experience as old as time.

REFLECTING ON THE READING

1. What is the significance of the brief story that Tannen tells about her father at the beginning of this essay? How does that story compare or contrast with the anecdotes Tannen tells about herself in the paragraphs that follow?

2. Tannen describes her use of several technologies in this essay: the telephone, airplanes, ships, television, and email. What purpose do these technologies serve in her life? How do they affect her relationships with the important people in her life? Do you think Tannen sees these technologies generally as positive? Explain.

3. In what sense does Tannen consider email to be less impersonal than the telephone as a technology for communicating with others? Do you agree with her? Why or why not?

4. According to Tannen, how have email and the Internet affected human communications in general? What does she mean when she writes that the Internet "ratchets up anonymity"? Does she see these changes as beneficial? Do you agree with her? Why or why not?

5. What does Tannen's experience with Larry reveal about how email can affect human relationships? How was Tannen's experience with Larry different from her father's experience with his father? What role did technology play in each case? What do these situations reveal about technology and human life, in Tannen's view? Do you think she's right? Explain.

Examining Rhetorical Strategies

1. Tannen mentions *progress* only twice in this essay: first, when she writes that "electronic communication is progress"; and again in the final paragraph, where she writes that technology made it possible for Larry to say good-bye before he died. What do you think she means by *progress* in these instances? Is the definition of the term the same in both cases? What do you think are Tannen's attitudes about technology and progress in general? How do those attitudes emerge in the anecdotes she tells in this essay?

2. At one point in her essay, Tannen describes her email conversations in the early 1980's with her university colleague Ralph, who, she says, was "shy and soft-spoken" and with whom she rarely had extended conversations. She writes, "But when we were using e-mail, we started communicating daily in this (then) leisurely medium." How does Tannen account for the fact that Ralph seemed much more willing to communicate with her via email than in face-to-face conversations? What might this anecdote indicate about technologies for communications, like email? What does it reveal about Tannen's own attitudes toward such technologies and toward communications in general? Also, what is the significance of the word *then,* which Tannen places in parentheses in this sentence? What does Tannen say about email and about personal communications with this one word? Why do you think she placed it in parentheses?

3. Evaluate Tannen's use of anecdotes in this essay. What important points does she make through the use of anecdotes? Do you think her use of anecdotes is effective? Explain. Do you think her essay would have been more or less effective if she had used other forms of evidence for her points, such as statistics about the uses of technologies like telephones or email? Why or why not?

4. Whom do you think Tannen imagines to be her audience for this essay? What does she assume they know about technology? How might someone who never used email react to this essay? Do you think the essay would be as effective for such a reader? Do you think you are a member of the audience for which Tannen wrote this essay? Explain. Use specific passages from her essay to support your answer.

5. Assess Tannen's voice in this essay. How would you describe it? Do you think it is appropriate for the point she makes in this essay? Did you find her voice effective? Why or why not? What might your reaction to her voice in this essay say about you as a reader?

Engaging the Issues

1. Write a narrative for an audience of your classmates about an experience you have had with email. Your narrative should focus on how email might have affected the way you communicate with others. Did it influence your relationships with others in any way? What might your experience reveal about technology and communications?

2. At one point in her essay, Tannen writes, "E-mail makes possible connections with relatives, acquaintances, or strangers, that wouldn't otherwise exist." Based on your own experiences with email and the Internet, write an essay for an audience of your classmates in which you discuss this idea. In your essay, examine this statement of Tannen's and assess its validity. Do you agree or disagree? Why? Describe some of your own experiences with email and other communications technologies to help support your position. Try to draw conclusions about how technology influences human communication.

3. Rewrite the essay you wrote for Question #2 for the opinion page of your local newspaper.
    Now compare the two essays. What are their similarities and differences? What changes did you make to address the newspaper audience? How did the different rhetorical situations affect your writing?

4. In a group of your classmates, share stories of your own experiences with email (or with other technologies that Tannen mentions in her essay). What similarities and differences do you see among the stories you and your classmates tell about email? How might your backgrounds have affected your experiences with email (or similar technologies)? How might your own attitudes toward technology in general have influenced your stories about your experiences with email? What might your stories reveal about technologies like email?

5. Write a research paper examining how email as a communications technology has affected human communications. For your paper, try to find some of the many studies that have been done on email and similar communications technologies. Use your library as well as the Internet for your research. You might also interview others who are experienced users of email, or perhaps you might interview a professor on your campus who has conducted research on email. In addition, you might participate in online conversations on a newsgroup or listserv to learn more about how others view this issue and how they conduct their discussions online. In your paper, explain how you did your research and why you think it is important. Discuss what you learned about email and its influences on human communications.

6. In light of the research you conducted for Question #5 above, assess the accuracy and validity of the points Tannen makes about email and technology in her

essay. Does she seem to be right about how email and technology in general affect human communications? Explain.

7. Write a letter to your local school board in which you draw on your knowledge of and experiences with technologies like email to argue for or against teaching students about such technologies. In your letter, justify your position by citing evidence you might have found in writing the research paper for Question #5. Also draw on essays like Tannen's to help support your points.

8. With a group of your classmates, construct a Web page that will serve as a resource about technologies of communication like email. On your web page, indicate its purpose and why you constructed it. Include notes about the links on your Web page.

Into the Electronic Millennium

Sven Birkerts

INTRODUCTION   What will happen to reading if the printed book is replaced by the computer? Will the act of reading remain the same even if readers see words on a computer screen rather than on the page of a printed book? And what difference would it make if people used computers instead of books for reading? Literary critic Sven Birkerts believes it makes a big difference. He is concerned that as more and more forms of print are replaced by electronic media, especially computer-based media such as the Internet, the activity we know as reading is profoundly changed—and not for the better. He is convinced that such a change does not bode well for the future of our society—that changing reading as we know it is not progress but the loss of something that lies at the heart of modern civilization.

Such a view might strike you as extreme. After all, whether you read words on a computer screen or on the page of a book, you're still reading; that is, you're still making sense of words and trying to understand a text. But Birkerts asks you to think of reading—and writing—in much broader terms. Reading is not just understanding a text but engaging in a sophisticated intellectual activity that is vital to human life and culture. And for Birkerts, reading is intimately linked to print forms, such as books, which have special characteristics that he believes shape how we think and how we understand our world. For instance, print is linear and static, requiring a reader's active engagement and sustained attention—characteristics that are lost in electronic forms of writing, according to Birkerts. In this sense, if you change from print forms to electronic forms, you change reading in ways that he believes are detrimental not only to individual readers themselves but to our very culture, which is founded on print literacy. Birkerts is so worried about these changes that he has coined a motto for those who share his concerns about using such technology: "Refuse it!" Perhaps his strident views about such changes may prompt you to reconsider your own attitudes toward technology and progress.

Birkerts has become well known for his warnings about the loss of print culture as a result of the rise of new forms of electronic media. His collection of essays, *The Gutenberg Elegies: The Fate of Reading in an Electronic Age* (1994), in which the following essay was originally published, provoked much debate among scholars, writers, critics, and educators about the implications of new electronic media for literacy and education. Birkerts has been accused of being a romantic when it comes to books, someone whose fears about new technologies rest on a desire to preserve the traditional forms of literacy that he himself engages in as a writer and literary critic. And, indeed, Birkerts has impressive credentials as a critic and writer. He is the author of three books of criticism—*An Artificial Wilderness: Essays on 20th-Century Literature* (1987), *The Electric Life: Essays on Modern Poetry* (1989), and *American Energies: Essays on Fiction* (1992)—and he has written essays and reviews for such publications as the *Atlantic Monthly, Harper's,* and the *New York Times Book Review.* He has also participated in many discussions about his ideas in online forums like the *Atlantic Unbound* and *FEED.* But it is his provocative warnings about the impact of new technologies on reading that have earned him the most praise and condemnation. The following essay may help you understand why, even as it provokes you to agreement or disagreement with him.

REFLECTING BEFORE READING

1. Birkerts rests much of his argument in the following essay on the changes he believes occur when reading is moved from a print form (such as a book) to an electronic form (such as a web page or hypertext). As you follow his argument, consider what happens when you read. Do Birkerts' descriptions of reading match your own experiences as a reader? If you have experienced reading in both print and electronic forms, consider whether Birkerts' comparisons of the two forms of reading ring true to you.

2. In his essay, Birkerts describes the changes he sees happening as new technologies for literacy become more widespread, and he discusses the potential effects of these changes. As you read his discussion, try to determine how Birkerts understands *progress*. What does progress mean to him? Is it connected to technological developments? Does it mean more than that? Is Birkerts opposed to change and nostalgic for a romantic past, as some of his critics have charged?

Some years ago, a friend and I comanaged a used and rare book shop in Ann Arbor, Michigan. We were often asked to appraise and purchase libraries—by retiring academics, widows, and disgruntled graduate students. One day we took a call from a professor of English at one of the community colleges outside Detroit. When he answered the buzzer I did a double take—he looked to be only a year or two older than we were. "I'm selling everything," he said, leading the way through a large apartment. As he opened the door of his study I felt a nudge from my partner. The room was wall-to-wall books and as neat as a chapel.

The professor had a remarkable collection. It reflected not only the needs of his vocation—he taught nineteenth- and twentieth-century literature—but a book lover's sensibility as well. The shelves were strictly arranged, and the books themselves were in superb condition. When he left the room we set to work inspecting, counting, and estimating. This is always a delicate procedure, for the buyer is at once anxious to avoid insult to the seller and eager to get the goods for the best price. We adopted our usual strategy, working out a lower offer and a more generous fallback price. But there was no need to worry. The professor took our first offer without batting an eye.

As we boxed up the books, we chatted. My partner asked the man if he was moving. "No," he said, "but I am getting out." We both looked up. "Out of the teaching business, I mean. Out of books." He then said that he wanted to show us something. And indeed, as soon as the books were packed and loaded, he led us back through the apartment and down a set of stairs. When we reached the basement, he flicked on the light. There, on a long table, displayed like an exhibit in the Space Museum, was a computer. I didn't know what kind it was then, nor could I tell you now, fifteen years later. But the professor was keen to explain and demonstrate.

While he and my partner hunched over the terminal, I roamed to and fro, inspecting the shelves. It was purely a reflex gesture, for they held nothing but thick binders and paperbound manuals. "I'm changing my life," the ex-professor was saying. "This is definitely where it's all going to happen." He told us that he already had several good job offers. And the books? I asked. Why was he selling them all? He paused for a few beats. "The whole profession represents a lot of pain to me," he said. "I don't want to see any of these books again."

The scene has stuck with me. It is now a kind of marker in my mental life. That afternoon I got my first serious inkling that all was not well in the world of print and letters. All sorts of corroborations followed. Our professor was by no means an isolated case. Over a period of two years we met with several others like him. New men and new women who had glimpsed the future and had decided to get out while the getting was good. The selling off of books was sometimes done for financial reasons, but the need to burn bridges was usually there as well. It was as if heading to the future also required the destruction of tokens from the past.

A change is upon us—nothing could be clearer. The printed word is part of a vestigial order that we are moving away from—by choice and by societal compulsion. I'm not just talking about disaffected academics, either. This shift is happening throughout our culture, away from the patterns and habits of the printed page and toward a new world distinguished by its reliance on electronic communications.

This is not, of course, the first such shift in our long history. In Greece, in the time of Socrates, several centuries after Homer, the dominant oral culture was overtaken by the writing technology. And in Europe another epochal transition was effected in the late fifteenth century after Gutenberg invented movable type. In both cases the long-term societal effects were overwhelming, as they will be for us in the years to come.

The evidence of the change is all around us, though possibly in the manner of the forest that we cannot see for the trees. The electronic media, while conspicuous in gadgetry, are very nearly invisible in their functioning. They have slipped deeply and irrevocably into our midst, creating sluices and circulating through them. I'm not referring to any one product or function in isolation, such as television or fax machines or the networks that make them possible. I mean the interdependent totality that has arisen from the conjoining of parts—the disk drives hooked to modems, transmissions linked to technologies of reception, recording, duplication, and storage.

Numbers and codes and frequencies. Buttons and signals. And this is no longer "the future," except for the poor or the self-consciously atavistic—it is now. Next to the new technologies, the scheme of things represented by print and the snailpaced linearity of the reading act looks stodgy and dull. Many educators say that our students are less and less able to read, or analyze, or write with clarity and purpose. Who can blame the students? Everything they meet with in the world around them gives the signal: That was then, and electronic communications are now.

Do I exaggerate? If all this is the case, why haven't we heard more about it? Why hasn't somebody stepped forward with a bow tie and a pointer stick to explain what is going on? Valid questions, but they also beg the question. They assume that we are all plugged into a total system—where else would that "somebody" appear if not on the screen at the communal hearth?

Media theorist Mark Crispin Miller has given one explanation for our situation in his discussions of television in *Boxed In: The Culture of TV.* The medium, he proposes, has long since diffused itself throughout the entire system. Through sheer omnipresence it has vanquished the possibility of comparative perspectives. We cannot see the role that television (or, for our purposes, all electronic communications) has assumed in our lives because there is no independent ledge where we might secure our footing. The medium has absorbed and eradicated the idea of a pretelevision past; in place of what used to be we get an ever-new and ever-renewable present. The only way we can hope to understand what is happening, or what has already happened, is by way of a severe and unnatural dissociation of sensibility.

To get a sense of the enormity of the change, you must force yourself to imagine—deeply and in nontelevisual terms—what the world was like a hundred, even fifty, years ago. If the feat is too difficult, spend some time with a novel from the period. Read between the lines and reconstruct. Move through the sequence of a character's day and then juxtapose the images and sensations you find with those in the life of the average urban or suburban dweller today.

Inevitably, one of the first realizations is that a communications net, a soft and pliable mesh woven from invisible threads, has fallen over everything. The so-called natural world, the place we used to live, which served us so long as the yardstick for all measurements, can now only be perceived through a scrim. Nature was then; this is now. Trees and rocks have receded. And the great geographical Other, the faraway rest of the world, has been transformed by the pure possibility of access. The numbers of distance and time no longer mean what they used to. Every place, once unique, itself, is strangely shot through with radiations from every other place. "There" was then; "here" is now.

Think of it. Fifty to a hundred million people (maybe a conservative estimate) form their ideas about what is going on in America and in the world from the same basic package of edited images—to the extent that the image itself has lost much of its once-fearsome power. Daily newspapers, with their long columns of print, struggle against declining sales. Fewer and fewer people under the age of fifty read them; computers will soon make packaged information a custom product. But if the printed sheet is heading for obsolescence, people are tuning in to the signals. The screen is where the information and entertainment wars will be fought. The communications conglomerates are waging bitter takeover battles in their zeal to establish global empires.

As Jonathan Crary has written in "The Eclipse of the Spectacle," "Telecommunications is the new arterial network, analogous in part to what railroads were for capitalism in the nineteenth century. And it is this electronic substitute for geography that corporate and national entities are now carving up." Maybe one reason why the news of the change is not part of the common currency is that such news can only sensibly be communicated through the more analytic sequences of print.

To underscore my point, I have been making it sound as if we were all abruptly walking out of one room and into another, leaving our books to the moths while we settle ourselves in front of our state-of-the-art terminals. The truth is that we are living through a period of overlap; one way of being is pushed athwart another. Antonio Gramsci's often-cited sentence comes inevitably to mind: "The crisis consists precisely in the fact that the old is dying and the new cannot be born; in this interregnum a great variety of morbid symptoms appears." The old surely is dying, but I'm not so sure that the new is having any great difficulty being born. As for the morbid symptoms, these we have in abundance.

The overlap in communications modes, and the ways of living that they are associated with, invites comparison with the transitional epoch in ancient Greek society, certainly in terms of the relative degree of disturbance. Historian Eric Havelock designated that period as one of "proto-literacy," of which his fellow scholar Oswyn Murray has written:

> To him [Havelock] the basic shift from oral to literate culture was a slow process; for centuries, despite the existence of writing, Greece remained essentially an oral culture. This culture was one which depended heavily on the encoding of information in poetic texts, to be learned by rote and to provide a cultural encyclopedia of conduct. It was not until the age of Plato in the fourth century that the dominance of poetry in an oral culture was challenged in the final triumph of literacy.

That challenge came in the form of philosophy, among other things, and poetry has never recovered its cultural primacy. What oral poetry was for the Greeks, printed books in general are for us. But our historical moment, which we might call "proto-electronic," will not require a transition period of two centuries. The very essence of electronic transmissions is to surmount impedances and to hasten transitions. Fifty years, I'm sure, will suffice. As for what the conversion will bring—and *mean*—to us, we might glean a few clues by looking to some of the "morbid symptoms" of the change. But to understand what these portend, we need to remark a few of the more obvious ways in which our various technologies condition our senses and sensibilities.

I won't tire my reader with an extended rehash of the differences between the print orientation and that of electronic systems. Media theorists from Marshall McLuhan to Walter Ong to Neil Postman have discoursed upon these at length. What's more, they are reasonably commonsensical. I therefore will abbreviate.

The order of print is linear, and is bound to logic by the imperatives of syntax. Syntax is the substructure of discourse, a mapping of the ways that the mind makes sense through language. Print communication requires the active engagement of the reader's attention, for reading is fundamentally an act of translation. Symbols are turned into their verbal referents and these are in turn interpreted. The print engagement is essentially private. While it does represent an act of communication, the contents pass from the privacy of the sender to the privacy of the receiver. Print also posits a time axis; the turning of pages, not to mention the vertical descent down the page, is a forward-moving succession, with earlier contents at every point serving as a ground for what follows. Moreover, the printed material is static—it is the reader, not the book, that moves forward. The physical arrangements of print are in accord with our traditional sense of history. Materials are layered; they lend themselves to rereading and to sustained attention. The pace of reading is variable, with progress determined by the reader's focus and comprehension.

The electronic order is in most ways opposite. Information and contents do not simply move from one private space to another, but they travel along a network. Engagement is intrinsically public, taking place within a circuit of larger connectedness. The vast resources of the network are always there, potential, even if they do not impinge on the immediate communication. Electronic communication can be passive, as with television watching, or interactive, as with computers. Contents, unless they are printed out (at which point they become part of the static order of print) are felt to be evanescent. They can be changed or deleted with the stroke of a key. With visual media (television, projected graphs, highlighted "bullets") impression and image take precedence over logic and concept, and detail and linear sequentiality are sacrificed. The pace is rapid, driven by jump-cut increments, and the basic movement is laterally associative rather than vertically cumulative. The presentation structures the reception and, in time, the expectation about how information is organized.

Further, the visual and nonvisual technology in every way encourages in the user a heightened and ever-changing awareness of the present. It works against historical perception, which must depend on the inimical notions of logic and sequential succession. If the print medium exalts the word, fixing it into permanence, the electronic counterpart reduces it to a signal, a means to an end.

Transitions like the one from print to electronic media do not take place without rippling or, more likely, *reweaving* the entire social and cultural web. The tendencies outlined above are already at work. We don't need to look far to find their effects. We can begin with the newspaper headlines and the millennial lamentations sounded in the op-ed pages: that our educational systems are in decline; that our students are less and less able to read and comprehend their required texts, and that their aptitude scores have leveled off well below those of previous generations. Tag-line communication, called "bite-speak" by some, is destroying the last remnants of political discourse; spin doctors and media consultants are our new shamans. As communications empires fight for control of all information outlets, including publishers, the latter have succumbed to the tyranny of the bottom line; they are less and less willing to publish work, however worthy, that will not make a tidy profit. And, on every front, funding for the arts is being cut while the arts themselves appear to be suffering a deep crisis of relevance. And so on.

Every one of these developments is, of course, overdetermined, but there can be no doubt that they are connected, perhaps profoundly, to the transition that is underway.

Certain other trends bear watching. One could argue, for instance, that the entire movement of postmodernism in the arts is a consequence of this same macroscopic shift. For what is postmodernism at root but an aesthetic that rebukes the idea of an historical time line, as well as previously uncontested assumptions of cultural hierarchy. The postmodern artifact manipulates its stylistic signatures like Lego blocks and makes free with combinations from the formerly sequestered spheres of high and popular art. Its combinatory momentum and relentless referencing of the surrounding culture mirror perfectly the associative dynamics of electronic media.

One might argue likewise, that the virulent debate within academia over the canon and multiculturalism may not be a simple struggle between the entrenched ideologies of white male elites and the forces of formerly disenfranchised gender, racial, and cultural groups. Many of those who would revise the canon (or end it altogether) are trying to outflank the assumption of historical tradition itself. The underlying question, avoided by many, may be not only whether the tradition is relevant, but whether it might not be too taxing a system for students to comprehend. Both the traditionalists and the progressives have valid arguments, and we must certainly have sympathy for those who would try to expose and eradicate the hidden assumptions of bias in the Western tradition. But it also seems clear that this debate could only have taken the form it has in a society that has begun to come loose from its textual moorings. To challenge repression is salutary. To challenge history itself, proclaiming it to be simply an archive of repressions and justifications, is idiotic.[1]

Then there are the more specific sorts of developments. Consider the multibillion-dollar initiative by Whittle Communications to bring commercially sponsored education packages into the classroom. The underlying premise is staggeringly simple: If electronic media are the one thing that the young are at ease with, why not exploit the fact? Why not stop bucking television and use it instead, with corporate America picking up the tab in exchange for a few minutes of valuable airtime for commercials? As the *Boston Globe* reports:

> Here's how it would work:
>
> Participating schools would receive, free of charge, $50,000 worth of electronic paraphernalia, including a satellite dish and classroom video monitors. In return, the schools would agree to air the show.
>
> The show would resemble a network news program, but with 18- to 24-year-old anchors.
>
> A prototype includes a report on a United Nations Security Council meeting on terrorism, a space shuttle update, a U2 music video tribute to Martin Luther King, a feature on the environment, a "fast fact" ('Arachibutyrophobia is the fear of peanut butter sticking to the roof of your mouth') and two minutes of commercial advertising.
>
> "You have to remember that the children of today have grown up with the visual media," said Robert Calabrese [Billerica School Superintendent]. "They know no other way and we're simply capitalizing on that to enhance learning."

---

[1] The outcry against the modification of the canon can be seen as a plea for old reflexes and routines. And the cry for multicultural representation may be a last-ditch bid for connection to the fading legacy of print. The logic is simple. When a resource is threatened—made scarce—people fight over it. In this case the struggle is over textual power in an increasingly nontextual age. The future of books and reading is what is at stake, and a dim intuition of this drives the contending factions.

As Katha Pollitt argued so shrewdly in her much-cited article in *The Nation:* If we were a nation of readers, there would be no issue. No one would be arguing about whether to put Toni Morrison on the syllabus because her work would be a staple of the reader's regular diet anyway. These lists are suddenly so important because they represent, very often, the only serious works that the student is ever likely to be exposed to. Whoever controls the lists comes out ahead in the struggle for the hearts and minds of the young.

Calabrese's observation on the preconditioning of a whole generation of students raises troubling questions: Should we suppose that American education will begin to tailor itself to the aptitudes of its students, presenting more and more of its materials in newly packaged forms? And what will happen when educators find that not very many of the old materials will "play"—that is, capture student enthusiasm? Is the *what* of learning to be determined by the *how?* And at what point do vicious cycles begin to reveal their viciousness?

A collective change of sensibility may already be upon us. We need to take seriously the possibility that the young truly "know no other way," that they are not made of the same stuff that their elders are. In her *Harper's* magazine debate with Neil Postman, Camille Paglia observed:

> Some people have more developed sensoriums than others. I've found that most people born before World War II are turned off by the modern media. They can't understand how we who were born after the war can read and watch TV at the same time. But we *can*. When I wrote my book, I had earphones on, blasting rock music or Puccini and Brahms. The soap operas—with the sound turned down —flickered on my TV. I'd be talking on the phone at the same time. Baby boomers have a multilayered, multitrack ability to deal with the world.

I don't know whether to be impressed or depressed by Paglia's ability to disperse her focus in so many directions. Nor can I say, not having read her book, in what ways her multitrack sensibility has informed her prose. But I'm baffled by what she means when she talks about an ability to "deal with the world." From the context, "dealing" sounds more like a matter of incessantly repositioning the self within a barrage of onrushing stimuli.

Paglia's is hardly the only testimony in this matter. A *New York Times* article on the cult success of Mark Leyner (author of *I Smell Esther Williams* and *My Cousin, My Gastroenterologist*) reports suggestively:

> His fans say, variously, that his writing is like MTV, or rap music, or rock music, or simply like everything in the world put together: fast and furious and intense, full of illusion and allusion and fantasy and science and excrement.
>
> Larry McCaffery, a professor of literature at San Diego State University and co-editor of Fiction International, a literary journal, said his students get excited about Mr. Leyner's writing, which he considers important and unique: "It speaks to them, somehow, about this weird milieu they're swimming through. It's this dissolving, discontinuous world." While older people might find Mr. Leyner's world bizarre or unreal, Professor McCaffery said, it doesn't seem so to people who grew up with Walkmen and computers and VCR's, with so many choices, so much bombardment, that they have never experienced a sensation singly.

The article continues:

> There is no traditional narrative, although the book is called a novel. And there is much use of facts, though it is called fiction. Seldom does the end of a sentence have any obvious relation to the beginning. "You don't know where you're going, but you don't mind taking the leap," said R. J. Cutler, the producer of "Heat," who invited Mr.

Leyner to be on the show after he picked up the galleys of his book and found it mesmerizing. "He taps into a specific cultural perspective where thoughtful literary world view meets pop culture and the TV generation."

My final exhibit—I don't know if it qualifies as a morbid symptom as such—is drawn from a *Washington Post Magazine* essay on the future of the Library of Congress, our national shrine to the printed word. One of the individuals interviewed in the piece is Robert Zich, so-called "special projects czar" of the institution. Zich, too, has seen the future, and he is surprisingly candid with his interlocutor. Before long, Zich maintains, people will be able to get what information they want directly off their terminals. The function of the Library of Congress (and perhaps libraries in general) will change. He envisions his library becoming more like a museum: "Just as you go to the National Gallery to see its Leonardo or go to the Smithsonian to see the Spirit of St. Louis and so on, you will want to go to libraries to see the Gutenberg or the original printing of Shakespeare's plays or to see Lincoln's hand-written version of the Gettysburg Address."

Zich is outspoken, voicing what other administrators must be thinking privately. The big research libraries, he says, "and the great national libraries and their buildings will go the way of the railroad stations and the movie palaces of an earlier era which were really vital institutions in their time . . . Somehow folks moved away from that when the technology changed."

And books? Zich expresses excitement about Sony's hand-held electronic book, and a miniature encyclopedia coming from Franklin Electronic Publishers. "Slip it in your pocket," he says. "Little keyboard, punch in your words and it will do the full text searching and all the rest of it. Its limitation, of course, is that it's devoted just to that one book." Zich is likewise interested in the possibility of memory cards. What he likes about the Sony product is the portability: one machine, a screen that will display the contents of whatever electronic card you feed it.

I cite Zich's views at some length here because he is not some Silicon Valley research and development visionary, but a highly placed executive at what might be called, in a very literal sense, our most conservative public institution. When men like Zich embrace the electronic future, we can be sure it's well on its way.

Others might argue that the technologies cited by Zich merely represent a modification in the "form" of reading, and that reading itself will be unaffected, as there is little difference between following words on a pocket screen or a printed page. Here I have to hold my line. The context cannot but condition the process. Screen and book may exhibit the same string of words, but the assumptions that underlie their significance are entirely different depending on whether we are staring at a book or a circuit-generated text. As the nature of looking—at the natural world, at paintings—changed with the arrival of photography and mechanical reproduction, so will the collective relation to language alter as new modes of dissemination prevail.

Whether all of this sounds dire or merely "different" will depend upon the reader's own values and priorities. I find these portents of change depressing, but also exhilarating—at least to speculate about. On the one hand, I have a great feeling of loss and a fear about what habitations will exist for self and soul in the future. But there is also a quickening, a sense that important things are on the line. As Heraclitus once observed, "The mixture that is not shaken soon stagnates." Well, the mixture is being shaken, no doubt about it. And here are some of the kinds of developments we might watch for as our "proto-electronic" era yields to an all-electronic future:

1. *Language erosion.* There is no question but that the transition from the culture of the book to the culture of electronic communication will radically alter the ways in which we use language on every societal level. The complexity and distinctiveness of spoken and written expression, which are deeply bound to traditions of print literacy, will gradually be replaced by a more telegraphic sort of "plainspeak." Syntactic masonry is already a dying art. Neil Postman and others have already suggested what losses have been incurred by the advent of telegraphy and television—how the complex discourse patterns of the nineteenth century were flattened by the requirements of communication over distances. That tendency runs riot as the layers of mediation thicken. Simple linguistic prefab is now the norm, while ambiguity, paradox, irony, subtlety, and wit are fast disappearing. In their place, the simple "vision thing" and myriad other "things." Verbal intelligence, which has long been viewed as suspect as the act of reading, will come to seem positively conspiratorial. The greater part of any articulate person's energy will be deployed in dumbing-down her discourse.

Language will grow increasingly impoverished through a series of vicious cycles. For, of course, the usages of literature and scholarship are connected in fundamental ways to the general speech of the tribe. We can expect that curricula will be further streamlined, and difficult texts in the humanities will be pruned and glossed. One need only compare a college textbook from twenty years ago to its contemporary version. A poem by Milton, a play by Shakespeare—one can hardly find the text among the explanatory notes nowadays. Fewer and fewer people will be able to contend with the so-called masterworks of literature or ideas. Joyce, Woolf, Soyinka, not to mention the masters who preceded them, will go unread, and the civilizing energies of their prose will circulate aimlessly between closed covers.

2. *Flattening of historical perspectives.* As the circuit supplants the printed page, and as more and more of our communications involve us in network processes—which of their nature plant us in a perpetual present—our perception of history will inevitably alter. Changes in information storage and access are bound to impinge on our historical memory. The depth of field that is our sense of the past is not only a linguistic construct, but is in some essential way represented by the book and the physical accumulation of books in library spaces. In the contemplation of the single volume, or mass of volumes, we form a picture of time past as a growing deposit of sediment; we capture a sense of its depth and dimensionality. Moreover, we meet the past as much in the presentation of words in books of specific vintage as we do in any isolated fact or statistic. The database, useful as it is, expunges this context, this sense of chronology, and admits us to a weightless order in which all information is equally accessible.

If we take the etymological tack, history (cognate with "story") is affiliated in complex ways with its texts. Once the materials of the past are unhoused from their pages, they will surely *mean* differently. The printed page is itself a link, at least along the imaginative continuum, and when that link is broken, the past can only start to recede. At the same time it will become a body of disjunct data available for retrieval and, in the hands of our canny dream merchants, a mythology. The more we grow rooted in the consciousness of the now, the more it will seem utterly extraordinary that things were ever any different. The idea of a farmer plowing a field—an historical constant for millennia—will be something for a theme park. For, naturally, the entertainment industry, which reads the collective unconscious unerringly, will seize the advantage. The past that has slipped away will be rendered ever more glorious, ever more a fantasy play with heroes, villains, and quaint settings and props. Small-town American life returns as "Andy of Mayberry"—at first enjoyed with recognition, later accepted as a faithful portrait of how things used to be.

3. *The waning of the private self.* We may even now be in the first stages of a process of social collectivization that will over time all but vanquish the ideal of the isolated individual. For some decades now we have been edging away from the perception of private life as something opaque, closed off to the world; we increasingly accept the transparency of a life lived within a set of systems, electronic or otherwise. Our technologies are not bound by season or light—it's always the same time in the circuit. And so long as time is money and money matters, those circuits will keep humming. The doors and walls of our habitations matter less and less—the world sweeps through the wires as it needs to, or as we need it to. The monitor light is always blinking; we are always potentially on-line.

I am not suggesting that we are all about to become mindless, soulless robots, or that personality will disappear altogether into an oceanic homogeneity. But certainly the idea of what it means to be a person living a life will be much changed. The figure-ground model, which has always featured a solitary self before a background that is the society of other selves, is romantic in the extreme. It is ever less tenable in the world as it is becoming. There are no more wildernesses, no more lonely homesteads, and, outside of cinema, no more emblems of the exalted individual.

The self must change as the nature of subjective space changes. And one of the many incremental transformations of our age has been the slow but steady destruction of subjective space. The physical and psychological distance between individuals has been shrinking for at least a century. In the process, the figure-ground image has begun to blur its boundary distinctions. One day we will conduct our public and private lives within networks so dense, among so many channels of instantaneous information, that it will make almost no sense to speak of the differentiations of subjective individualism.

We are already captive in our webs. Our slight solitudes are transected by codes, wires, and pulsations. We punch a number to check in with the answering machine, another to tape a show that we are too busy to watch. The strands of the web grow finer and finer—this is obvious. What is no less obvious is the fact that they will continue to proliferate, gaining in sophistication, merging functions so that one can bank by phone, shop via television, and so on. The natural tendency is toward streamlining: The smart dollar keeps finding ways to shorten the path, double-up the function. We might think in terms of a circuitboard model, picturing ourselves as the contact points. The expansion of electronic options is always at the cost of contractions in the private sphere. We will soon be navigating with ease among cataracts of organized pulsations, putting out and taking in signals. We will bring our terminals, our modems, and menus further and further into our former privacies; we will implicate ourselves by degrees in the unitary life, and there may come a day when we no longer remember that there was any other life.

While I was brewing these somewhat melancholy thoughts, I chanced to read in an old *New Republic* the text of Joseph Brodsky's 1987 Nobel Prize acceptance speech. I felt as though I had opened a door leading to the great vault of the nineteenth century. The poet's passionate plea on behalf of the book at once corroborated and countered everything I had been thinking. What he upheld in faith were the very ideals I was saying good-bye to. I greeted his words with an agitated skepticism, fashioning from them something more like a valediction. Here are four passages:

> If art teaches anything . . . it is the privateness of the human condition. Being the most ancient as well as the most literal form of private enterprise, it fosters in a man, knowingly or unwittingly, a sense of his uniqueness, of individuality, of separateness—thus turning him from a social animal into an autonomous "I."

> The great Baratynsky, speaking of his Muse, characterized her as possessing an "uncommon visage." It's in acquiring this "uncommon visage" that the meaning of human existence seems to lie, since for this uncommonness we are, as it were, prepared genetically.

> Aesthetic choice is a highly individual matter, and aesthetic experience is always a private one. Every new aesthetic reality makes one's experience even more private; and this kind of privacy, assuming at times the guise of literary (or some other) taste, can in itself turn out to be, if not a guarantee, then a form of defense, against enslavement.

> In the history of our species, in the history of Homo sapiens, the book is an anthropological development, similar essentially to the invention of the wheel. Having emerged in order to give us some idea not so much of our origins as of what that sapiens is capable of, a book constitutes a means of transportation through the space of experience, at the speed of a turning page. This movement, like every movement, becomes flight from the common denominator . . . This flight is the flight in the direction of "uncommon visage," in the direction of the numerator, in the direction of autonomy, in the direction of privacy.

Brodsky is addressing the relation between art and totalitarianism, and within that context his words make passionate sense. But I was reading from a different vantage. What I had in mind was not a vision of political totalitarianism, but rather of something that might be called "societal totalism"—that movement toward deindividuation, or electronic collectivization, that I discussed above. And from that perspective our era appears to be in a headlong flight *from* the "uncommon visage" named by the poet.

Trafficking with tendencies—extrapolating and projecting as I have been doing—must finally remain a kind of gambling. One bets high on the validity of a notion and low on the human capacity for resistance and for unpredictable initiatives. No one can really predict how we will adapt to the transformations taking place all around us. We may discover, too, that language is a hardier thing than I have allowed. It may flourish among the beep and the click and the monitor as readily as it ever did on the printed page. I hope so, for language is the soul's ozone layer and we thin it at our peril.

1. Birkerts begins this essay with a brief anecdote about a college professor who is selling his book collection. What does Birkerts suggest with this anecdote? What important issues does it raise for Birkerts?

2. What is the "shift" that is occurring in our culture that has Birkerts so concerned? Why is it an important "shift"? What evidence does Birkerts offer that we are experiencing this shift?

3. What changes does Birkerts say have occurred in contemporary society as a result of electronic media such as television? How is life different now than it was a century ago? Do you agree with Birkerts' descriptions of these changes? Is he exaggerating, in your view? Why, according to Birkerts, is it so difficult for us to perceive and understand these changes?

4. What are the primary differences between print and electronic media, as Birkerts describes them? Do these differences seem accurate to you? Does Birkerts omit or emphasize anything in ways that seem troublesome or inaccurate to you? Explain.

5. What are the developments in our culture that Birkerts claims indicate that we are entering an "all-electronic future"? Why should we be concerned about these developments? Are you concerned? Why or why not?

6. Why do you think Birkerts is so concerned about history in this essay? What does he believe is the value of understanding history? What does he mean by such phrases as "the great vault of the nineteenth century"? What does such a phrase suggest about his views of history and of the present day?

7. How would you summarize Birkerts' most important concerns about an "electronic future"? Do you share these concerns? Why or why not? Be as specific as you can in answering this question.

Examining Rhetorical Strategies

1. Look carefully at the opening few paragraphs of this essay in which Birkerts relates the anecdotes about the college professor. Examine how he describes that scene and the details he provides—or doesn't provide. How effectively do you think this anecdote introduces the main themes of Birkerts' essay? What do you think this beginning suggests about Birkerts as a writer and a reader? What does it reveal about his values regarding reading and literacy and technology? Do you share those values? How might your answer to that question affect your reaction to his introduction to this essay? Consider what your reaction to Birkerts' voice in this opening section might reveal about you as a reader.

2. Examine the evidence that Birkerts offers to support his contention that we are in the midst of a significant shift in the ways in which we communicate. What sort of evidence does he provide? What evidence does he leave out? Do you

find his evidence convincing? Are the trends and developments he describes "facts" or are they debatable? How does Birkerts use this evidence to support his arguments that this shift is detrimental to our culture? Do you think he "stacks the deck" with this evidence by providing only one kind of evidence for the perspective he wishes to support? Or do you think his description of the current situation regarding literacy and media is fair and accurate? Explain your answers.

3. How would you describe Birkerts' voice in this essay? How does he present himself to his readers? Do you think he presents himself as an expert, a concerned citizen, a scholar, or something else? Do you find his voice effective? Why or why not? Cite specific lines in the text to support your answers.

4. Birkerts seems to draw an important distinction between young people of today and older generations, especially in terms of what they know and how they respond to modern media like television. Do you find this distinction fair? What does it suggest about "young people"? About "older" people? What does it suggest about Birkerts' values and about his views of contemporary society? Do you agree with him? Are you one of the "young people" Birkerts describes in his essay? What might his description of these generations indicate about his conception of his audience?

5. How would you describe the audience that Birkerts seems to be addressing in this essay? Do you think he imagines a specialized or a general audience for this essay? Do you think he is effective in addressing this audience? Explain. Cite specific passages from the text to support your answer.

6. Birkerts spends a great deal of time describing what he sees as worrisome developments in our culture and expressing his concerns about what is happening with that culture. Do you think these concerns are shared by a wide variety of people today? Or is Birkerts speaking for a small group of people who have a special stake in books and print culture? Do you think Birkerts assumes that most of his readers share his concerns? Explain. Do you share his concerns? Why or why not? What might your answers to these questions indicate about your own position in our culture and your view of its future? Justify your answer.

7. Notice how Birkerts has structured his essay. How would you describe that structure? Is it effective, in your view, in presenting his case about electronic media? Does it make his arguments clearer and more convincing? Explain.

Engaging the Issues

1. Analyze Birkerts' essay in terms of how he builds his argument and the evidence he offers to support it. Summarize his main points and describe how he articulates and supports these points. Then assess the overall effectiveness of his argument. Be sure to refer to audience.

2. Write a response to Birkerts in which you take issue with his perspective and his arguments about electronic media and modern culture.

3. Birkerts seems especially concerned about what will happen to literature in a new electronic age. Access the World Wide Web and find Web sites that are

devoted to literature and literary study. Analyze these sites on the basis of Birkerts' arguments about electronic media. Do you think Birkerts' arguments are valid, based on what your research into literature on the Web has found? Draw conclusions about the validity of Birkerts' viewpoint.

4. Birkerts routinely refers to *culture* in this essay. What does he mean by that term? How does he use it in his essay? Why is it important to him? Write an analysis of his use of that term and what it means to him in this essay. Compare his sense of that term to other ways of using the term that you have found (such as how anthropologists use the term). Draw conclusions about how Birkerts understands culture and how his understanding of the term is central to the argument he makes in his essay about electronic media.

5. Using Birkerts' essay as a primary source of ideas, write a letter to your local school board in which you express your views about modern electronic media and how they are used in schools. In your letter you should make clear what you believe are the primary purposes of education and describe how you believe electronic media should be used (or not used) to achieve those purposes.

6. Locate some of the reviews that have been written of Birkerts' book, *The Gutenberg Elegies,* in which the above essay was originally published. (You can locate many of these reviews on the Internet.) Read through several of these reviews and try to identify the main objections to and criticisms of Birkerts' ideas that have been voiced by his critics. Then, in an essay intended for your classmates, summarize the criticisms of Birkerts' ideas. In your essay, offer your own view of the validity of these criticisms, based on your own reading of Birkerts.

7. Based on your work for Question #6 above, write an editorial essay for a general audience (such as readers of a large-circulation publication like *USA Today*) in which you assess Birkerts' ideas about literacy and technology. Offer your own views about these matters and draw conclusions about the importance or usefulness of Birkerts' ideas.

Economy

HENRY DAVID THOREAU

INTRODUCTION   Henry David Thoreau claimed that he wrote the book *Walden,* from which the following passage is taken, as a way to answer the questions people asked him about his solitary life at Walden Pond. If so, *Walden* may be the most important work ever written in answer to casual questions about how a person lived his daily life. First published in 1854, *Walden* is Thoreau's detailed, witty, irreverent, and often philosophical account of the two years he spent living in a cabin he built himself on the shore of a small lake a mile or so outside Concord, Massachusetts. Although it received some attention from intellectuals at the time it was published, it was not until long after Thoreau's death in 1862 that the book began to have wide influence. By the mid-twentieth century it was considered by many literary critics to be an American classic, but it achieved wider influence through the environmental movement in the 1960's and 1970's, whose supporters adopted it as a statement of principles for natural living. Today, nearly 150 years after it was written, readers continue to embrace it as a plain statement of self-reliance and individualism. As recently as 1992, a critic wrote that *Walden* and Thoreau's famous essay "Civil Disobedience" have become even more timely than when they were first written, because "they speak to a present condition instilled (occasionally drenched) with a daily aware-ness of the interdependence of all places and of the global consequences for better and worse of individual actions."

In light of such praise, it is worth remembering that in his day, Thoreau was considered by many to be an eccentric, out of step with his society and his times. And it is worth wondering why Thoreau's ideas about how to live eco-nomically and naturally (and how *not* to live) seem so profound and relevant to readers living so many years after he did in a world that is so drastically differ-ent from the one he knew. It may be that readers at the start of a new millen-nium find in Thoreau's writing descriptions of a kind of life-style that they believe is no longer possible, and so they engage his writing with a kind of nostalgia. But it may also be that his criticisms of the life-styles of his contem-poraries and his beliefs about how to live still ring true today—perhaps even more so as we face rapid social change and technological developments that were unimaginable in Thoreau's day. Indeed, many people who are skeptical of technological development (including Bill Henderson, the editor of *The Minutes of the Lead Pencil Club,* whose dialogue with Tim Barkow appears at the beginning of this chapter) consider Thoreau to be a kind of wise ancestor whose criticisms of progress in his time provide an historical foundation for their own views about progress at the start of the millennium. Not surprisingly, you'll notice Thoreau's name appearing in several of the readings in this chap-ter and in the next one.

Some of Thoreau's ideas that seem most compelling to readers today emerge in the passage below. In this passage, which is the opening section of *Walden,* Thoreau criticizes what he considers to be the misguidedness that characterizes the lives of most people, who, he says, "labor under a mistake." Their mistake, according to Thoreau, is that they waste their energies trying to acquire material goods that ultimately don't lead to a better life and, in fact, end up controlling their lives. He offers some ideas about an alternative to the common life-styles of the people of his culture.

Although Henry David Thoreau is best known today as the author of *Walden* and of the essay "Civil Disobedience," many of his other writings are also still read today, especially his accounts of wilderness travel, including *A Week on the Concord and Merrimack Rivers* (1849) and *The Maine Woods* (1964). During his life, Thoreau wrote often about his travels and about social issues for influential journals such the *Atlantic Monthly* and the *Dial,* which was founded by famed philosopher Ralph Waldo Emerson. Thoreau was associated with Emerson's philosophical movement known as transcendentalism, but his strident views about social, political, environmental, and economic issues earned him a reputation as an iconoclast. When invited to join the famous Brook Farm community, which was an experiment in communal living based on transcendentalist ideas, Thoreau declined, reportedly stating, "I had rather keep a bachelor's hall in hell than go board in heaven." He was briefly jailed for refusing to pay taxes that he claimed would be used to support the war against Mexico, which he opposed. In many ways, the following excerpt from *Walden,* his most famous work, reflects his iconoclasm and his heartfelt beliefs about living a moral and practical life.

1. As noted above, many people in Thoreau's time considered him to be an eccentric, even something of a crackpot. Yet today he is considered an important American author and thinker, and his ideas have been embraced by environmentalists and social critics of various political views. How can you explain this change in opinion about Thoreau and his ideas? What might it tell us about progress? What do you see in this passage that helps answer these questions?

2. As you read through this famous passage from Walden, consider whether you agree with the many people who believe that Thoreau's ideas truly are relevant to us today. Do his ideas make sense to you today, given your own experience in the world? Are his criticisms of popular culture and social fashion still valid today? Why or why not?

When I wrote the following pages, or rather the bulk of them, I lived alone, in the woods, a mile from any neighbor, in a house which I had built myself, on the shore of Walden Pond, in Concord, Massachusetts, and earned my living by the labor of my hands only. I lived there two years and two months. At present I am a sojourner in civilized life again.

I should not obtrude my affairs so much on the notice of my readers if very particular inquiries had not been made by my townsmen concerning my mode of life, which some would call impertinent, though they do not appear to me at all impertinent, but, considering the circumstances, very natural and pertinent. Some have asked what I got to eat; if I did not feel lonesome; if I was not afraid; and the like. Others have been curious to learn what portion of my income I devoted to charitable purposes; and some, who have large families, how many poor children I maintained. I will therefore ask those of my readers who feel no particular interest in me to pardon me if I undertake to answer some of these questions in this book. In most books, the *I*, or first person, is omitted; in this it will be retained; that, in respect to egotism, is the main difference. We commonly do not remember that it is, after all, always the first person that is speaking. I should not talk so much about myself if there were anybody else whom I knew as well. Unfortunately, I am confined to this theme by the narrowness of my experience. Moreover, I, on my side; require of every writer, first or last, a simple and sincere account of his own life, and not merely what he has heard of other men's lives; some such account as he would send to his kindred from a distant land; for if he has lived sincerely it must have been in a distant land to me. Perhaps these pages are more particularly addressed to poor students. As for the rest of my readers, they will accept such portions as apply to them. I trust that none will stretch the seams in putting on the coat, for it may do good service to him whom it fits.

I would fain say something, not so much concerning the Chinese and Sandwich Islanders as you who read these pages, who are said to live in New England; something about your condition, especially your outward condition or circumstances in this world, in this town, what it is, whether it is necessary that it be as bad as it is, whether it cannot be improved as well as not. I have travelled a good deal in Concord; and everywhere, in shops, and offices, and fields, the inhabitants have appeared to me to be doing penance in a thousand remarkable ways. What I have heard of Bramins sitting exposed to four fires and looking in the face of the sun; or hanging suspended, with their heads downwards, over flames; or looking at the heavens over their shoulders "until it becomes impossible for them to resume their natural position, while from the twist of the neck nothing but liquids can pass into the stomach;" or dwelling, chained for life, at the foot of a tree; or measuring with their bodies, like caterpillars, the breadth of vast empires; or standing on one leg on the tops of pillars, —even these forms of conscious penance are hardly more incredible and astonishing than the scenes which I daily witness. The twelve labors of Hercules were trifling in comparison with those which my neighbors have undertaken; for they were only twelve, and had an end; but I could never see that these men slew or captured any monster or finished any labor. They have no friend Iolaus to burn with a hot iron the root of the hydra's head, but as soon as one head is crushed, two spring up.

I see young men, my townsmen, whose misfortune it is to have inherited farms, houses, barns, cattle, and farming tools; for these are more easily acquired than got rid of. Better if they had been born in the open pasture and suckled by a wolf, that they might have seen with clearer eyes what field they were called to labor in. Who made them serfs of the soil? Why should they eat their sixty acres, when man is condemned to eat only his peck of dirt? Why should they begin digging their graves as soon as they are born? They have got to live a man's life, pushing all these things before them, and get on as well as they can. How many a poor immortal soul have I met well-nigh crushed and smothered under its load, creeping down the road of life, pushing before it a barn seventy-five feet by forty, its Augean stables never cleansed, and one hundred acres of land, tillage, mowing, pasture, and wood-lot. The portionless, who struggle with no such unnecessary inherited encumbrances, find it labor enough to subdue and cultivate a few cubic feet of flesh.

But men labor under a mistake. The better part of the man is soon plowed into the soil for compost. By a seeming fate, commonly called necessity, they are employed, as it says in an old book, laying up treasures which moth and rust will corrupt and thieves break through and steal. It is a fool's life, as they will find when they get to the end of it, if not before. It is said that Deucalion and Pyrrba created men by throwing stones over their heads behind them: —

Inde genus durum sumus, experiensque laborum,
Et documenta damus quâ sumus origine nati.

Or, as Raleigh rhymes it in his sonorous way, —

"From thence our kind hard-hearted is, enduring pain and care,
Approving that our bodies of a stony nature are."

So much for a blind obedience to a blundering oracle, throwing the stones over their heads behind them, and not seeing where they fell.

Most men, even in this comparatively free country, through mere ignorance and mistake, are so occupied with the factitious cares and superfluously coarse labors of life that its finer fruits cannot be plucked by them. Their fingers, from excessive toil, are too clumsy and tremble too much for that. Actually, the laboring man has not leisure for a true integrity day by day; he cannot afford to sustain the manliest relations to men; his labor would be depreciated in the market. He has no time to be anything but a machine. How can he remember well his ignorance—which his growth requires—who has so often to use his knowledge? We should feed and clothe him gratuitously sometimes, and recruit him with our cordials, before we judge of him. The finest qualities of our nature, like the bloom on fruits, can be preserved only by the most delicate handling. Yet we do not treat ourselves nor one another thus tenderly.

Some of you, we all know, are poor, find it hard to live, are sometimes, as it were, gasping for breath. I have no doubt that some of you who read this book are unable to pay for all the dinners which you have actually eaten, or for the coats and shoes which are fast wearing or are already worn out, and have come to this page to spend borrowed or stolen time, robbing your creditors of an hour. It is very evident what mean and sneaking lives many of you live, for my sight has been whetted by experience; always on the limits, trying to get into business and trying to get out of debt, a very ancient slough, called by the Latins *aes alienum,* another's brass, for some of their coins were made of brass; still living, and dying, and buried by this other's brass; always promising to pay, promising to pay, to-morrow, and dying to-day, insolvent; seeking to curry favor, to get custom, by how many modes, only not state-prison offenses; lying, flattering, voting, contracting yourselves into a nutshell of civility, or dilating into an atmosphere of thin and vaporous generosity, that you may persuade your neighbor to let you make his shoes, or his hat, or his coat, or his carriage, or import his groceries for him; making yourselves sick, that you may lay up something against a sick day, something to be tucked away in an old chest, or in a stocking behind the plastering, or, more safely, in the brick bank; no matter where, no matter how much or how little.

I sometimes wonder that we can be so frivolous, I may almost say, as to attend to the gross but somewhat foreign form of servitude called Negro Slavery, there are so many keen and subtle masters that enslave both North and South. It is hard to have a Southern overseer; it is worse to have a Northern one; but worst of all when you are the slave-driver of yourself. Talk of a divinity in man! Look at the teamster on the highway, wending to market by day or night; does any divinity stir within him? His highest duty to fodder and water his horses! What is his destiny to him compared wth the shipping interests? Does not he drive for Squire Make-a-stir? How godlike, how immortal, is he? See how he cowers and sneaks, how vaguely all the day he fears, not being immortal nor divine, but the slave and prisoner of his own opinion of himself, a fame won by his own deeds. Public opinion is a weak tyrant compared with our own private opinion. What a man thinks of himself, that it is which determines, or rather indicates, his fate. Self-emancipation even in the West Indian provinces of the fancy and imagination,—what Wilberforce is there to bring that about? Think, also, of the ladies of the land weaving toilet cushions against the last day, not to betray too green an interest in their fates! As if you could kill time without injuring eternity.

The mass of men lead lives of quiet desperation. What is called resignation is confirmed desperation. From the desperate city you go into the desperate country, and have to console yourself with the bravery of minks and muskrats. A stereotyped but unconscious despair is concealed even under what are called the games and amusements of mankind. There is no play in them, for this comes after work. But it is a characteristic of wisdom not to do desperate things.

When we consider what, to use the words of the catechism, is the chief end of man, and what are the true necessaries and means of life, it appears as if men had deliberately chosen the common mode of living because they preferred it to any other. Yet they honestly think there is no choice left. But alert and healthy natures remember that the sun rose clear. It is never too late to give up our prejudices. No way of thinking or doing, however ancient, can be trusted without proof. What everybody echoes or in silence passes by as true to-day may turn out to be falsehood to-morrow, mere smoke of opinion, which some had trusted for a cloud that would sprinkle fertilizing rain on their fields. What old people say you cannot do, you try and find that you can. Old deeds for old people, and new deeds for new. Old people did not know enough once, perchance, to fetch fresh fuel to keep the fire a-going; new people put a little dry wood under a pot, and are whirled round the globe with the speed of birds, in a way to kill old people, as the phrase is. Age is no better, hardly so well, qualified for an instructor as youth, for it has not profited so much as it has lost. One may almost doubt if the wisest man has learned anything of absolute value by living. Practically, the old have no very important advice to give the young, their own experience has been so partial, and their lives have been such miserable failures, for private reasons, as they must believe; and it may be that they have some faith left which belies that experience, and they are only less young than they were. I have lived some thirty years on this planet, and I have yet to hear the first syllable of valuable or even earnest advice from my seniors. They have told me nothing, and probably cannot tell me anything to the purpose. Here is life, an experiment to a great extent untried by me; but it does not avail me that they have tried it. If I have any experience which I think valuable, I am sure to reflect that this my Mentors said nothing about.

One farmer says to me, "You cannot live on vegetable food solely, for it furnishes nothing to make bones with;" and so he religiously devotes a part of his day to supplying his system with the raw material of bones; walking all the while he talks behind his oxen, which, with vegetable-made bones, jerk him and his lumbering plow along in spite of every obstacle. Some things are really necessaries of life in some circles, the most helpless and diseased, which in others are luxuries merely, and in others still are entirely unknown.

The whole ground of human life seems to some to have been gone over by their predecessors, both the heights and the valleys, and all things to have been cared for. According to Evelyn, "the wise Solomon prescribed ordinances for the very distance of trees; and the Roman prætors have decided how often you may go into your neighbor's land to gather the acorns which fall on it without trespass, and what share belongs to that neighbor." Hippocrates has even left directions how we should cut our nails; that is, even with the ends of the fingers neither shorter nor longer. Undoubtedly the very tedium and ennui which presume to have exhausted the variety and the joys of life are as old as Adam. But man's capacities have never been measured; nor are we to judge of what he can do by any precedents, so little has been tried. Whatever have been thy failures hitherto, "be not afflicted, my child, for who shall assign to thee what thou hast left undone?"

We might try our lives by a thousand simple tests; as, for instance, that the same sun that ripens my beans illumines at once a system of earths like ours. If I had remembered this it would have prevented some mistakes. This was not the light in which I hoed them. The stars are the apexes of what wonderful triangles! What distant and different beings in the various mansions of the universe are contemplating the same one at the same moment! Nature and human life are as various as our several constitutions. Who shall say what prospect life offers to another? Could a greater miracle take place than for us to look through each other's eyes for an instant? We should live in all the ages of the world in an hour; ay, in all the worlds of the ages. History, Poetry, Mythology!—I know of no reading of another's experience so startling and informing as this would be.

The greater part of what my neighbors call good I believe in my soul to be bad, and if I repent of anything, it is very likely to be my good behavior. What demon possessed me that I behaved so well? You may say the wisest thing you can, old man,—you who have lived seventy years, not without honor of a kind,—I hear an irresistible voice which invites me away from all that. One generation abandons the enterprises of another like stranded vessels.

I think that we may safely trust a good deal more than we do. We may waive just so much care of ourselves as we honestly bestow elsewhere. Nature is as well adapted to our weakness as to our strength. The incessant anxiety and strain of some is a well-nigh incurable form of disease. We are made to exaggerate the importance of what work we do; and yet how much is not done by us! or, what if we had been taken sick? How vigilant we are! determined not to live by faith if we can avoid it; all the day long on the alert, at night we unwillingly say our prayers and commit ourselves to uncertainties. So thoroughly and sincerely are we compelled to live, reverencing our life, and denying the possibility of change. This is the only way, we say; but there are as many ways as there can be drawn radii from one centre. All change is a miracle to contemplate; but it is a miracle which is taking place every instant. Confucius said, "To know that we know what we know, and that we do not know what we do not know, that is true knowledge." When one man has reduced a fact of the imagination to be a fact of his understanding, I foresee that all men will at length establish their lives on that basis.

Let us consider for a moment what most of the trouble and anxiety which I have referred to is about, and how much it is necessary that we be troubled, or at least careful. It would be some advantage to live a primitive and frontier life, though in the midst of an outward civilization, if only to learn what are the gross necessaries of life and what methods have been taken to obtain them; or even to look over the old day-books of the merchants, to see what it was that men most commonly bought at the stores, what they stored, that is, what are the grossest groceries. For the improvements of ages have had but little influence on the essential laws of man's existence; as our skeletons, probably, are not to be distinguished from those of our ancestors.

By the words, *necessary of life,* I mean whatever, of all that man obtains by his own exertions, has been from the first, or from long use has become, so important to human life that few, if any, whether from savageness, or poverty, or philosophy, ever attempt to do without it. To many creatures there is in this sense but one necessary of life, Food. To the bison of the prairie it is a few inches of palatable grass, with water to drink; unless he seeks the Shelter of the forest or the mountain's shadow. None of the brute creation requires more than Food and Shelter. The necessaries of life for man in this climate may, accurately enough, be distributed under the several heads of Food, Shelter, Clothing, and Fuel; for not till we have secured these are we prepared to entertain the true problems of life with freedom and a prospect of success. Man has invented, not only houses, but clothes and cooked food; and possibly from the accidental discovery of the warmth of fire, and the consequent use of it, at first a luxury, arose the present necessity to sit by it. We observe cats and dogs acquiring the same second nature. By proper Shelter and Clothing we legitimately retain our own internal heat; but with an excess of these, or of Fuel, that is, with an external heat greater than our own internal, may not cookery properly be said to begin? Darwin, the naturalist, says of the inhabitants of Tierra del Fuego, that while his own party, who were well clothed and sitting close to a fire, were far from too warm, these naked savages, who were farther off, were observed, to his great surprise, "to be streaming with perspiration at undergoing such a roasting." So, we are told, the New Hollander goes naked with impunity, while the European shivers in his clothes. Is it impossible to combine the hardiness of these savages with the intellectualness of the civilized man? According to Liebig, man's body is a stove, and food the fuel which keeps up the internal combustion in the lungs. In cold weather we eat more, in warm less. The animal heat is the result of a slow combustion, and disease and death take place when this is too rapid; or for want of fuel, or from some defect in the draught, the fire goes out. Of course the vital heat is not to be confounded with fire; but so much for analogy. It appears, therefore, from the above list, that the expression, *animal life,* is nearly synonymous with the expression, *animal heat;* for while Food may be regarded as the Fuel which keeps up the fire within us,—and Fuel serves only to prepare that Food or to increase the warmth of our bodies by addition from without,—Shelter and Clothing also serve only to retain the *heat* thus generated and absorbed.

The grand necessity, then, for our bodies, is to keep warm, to keep the vital heat in us. What pains we accordingly take, not only with our Food, and Clothing, and Shelter, but with our beds, which are our night-clothes, robbing the nests and breasts of birds to prepare this shelter within a shelter, as the mole has its bed of grass and leaves at the end of its burrow! The poor man is wont to complain that this is a cold world; and to cold, no less physical than social, we refer directly a great part of our ails. The summer, in some climates, makes possible to man a sort of Elysian life. Fuel, except to cook his Food, is then unnecessary; the sun is his fire, and many of the fruits are sufficiently cooked by its rays; while Food generally is more various, and more easily obtained, and Clothing and Shelter are wholly or half unnecessary. At the present day, and in this country, as I find by my own experience, a few implements, a knife, an axe, a spade, a wheelbarrow, etc., and for the studious, lamplight, stationery, and access to a few books, rank next to necessaries, and can all be obtained at a trifling cost. Yet some, not wise, go to the other side of the globe, to barbarous and unhealthy regions, and devote themselves to trade for ten or twenty years, in order that they may live,—that is, keep comfortably warm,—and die in New England at last. The luxuriously rich are not simply kept comfortably warm, but unnaturally hot; as I implied before, they are cooked, of course, *á la mode.*

Most of the luxuries, and many of the so-called comforts of life, are not only not indispensable, but positive hindrances to the elevation of mankind. With respect to luxuries and comforts, the wisest have ever lived a more simple and meagre life than the poor. The ancient philosophers, Chinese, Hindoo, Persian, and

Greek, were a class than which none has been poorer in outward riches, none so rich in inward. We know not much about them. It is remarkable that *we* know so much of them as we do. The same is true of the more modern reformers and benefactors of their race. None can be an impartial or wise observer of human life but from the vantage ground of what *we* should call voluntary poverty. Of a life of luxury the fruit is luxury, whether in agriculture, or commerce, or literature, or art. There are nowadays professors of philosophy, but not philosophers. Yet it is admirable to profess because it was once admirable to live. To be a philosopher is not merely to have subtle thoughts, nor even to found a school, but so to love wisdom as to live, according to its dictates, a life of simplicity, independence, magnanimity, and trust. It is to solve some of the problems of life, not only theoretically, but practically. The success of great scholars and thinkers is commonly a courtier-like success, not kingly, not manly. They make shift to live merely by conformity, practically as their fathers did, and are in no sense the progenitors of a nobler race of men. But why do men degenerate ever? What makes families run out? What is the nature of the luxury which enervates and destroys nations? Are we sure that there is none of it in our own lives? The philosopher is in advance of his age even in the outward form of his life. He is not fed, sheltered, clothed, warmed, like his contemporaries. How can a man be a philosopher and not maintain his vital heat by better methods than other men?

When a man is warmed by the several modes which I have described, what does he want next? Surely not more warmth of the same kind, as more and richer food, larger and more splendid houses, finer and more abundant clothing, more numerous, incessant, and hotter fires, and the like. When he has obtained those things which are necessary to life, there is another alternative than to obtain the superfluities; and that is, to adventure on life now, his vacation from humbler toil having commenced. The soil, it appears, is suited to the seed, for it has sent its radicle downward, and it may now send its shoot upward also with confidence. Why has man rooted himself thus firmly in the earth, but that he may rise in the same proportion into the heavens above?—for the nobler plants are valued for the fruit they bear at last in the air and light, far from the ground, and are not treated like the humbler esculents, which, though they may be biennials, are cultivated only till they have perfected their root, and often cut down at top for this purpose, so that most would not know them in their flowering season.

I do not mean to prescribe rules to strong and valiant natures, who will mind their own affairs whether in heaven or hell, and perchance build more magnificently and spend more lavishly than the richest, without ever impoverishing themselves, not knowing how they live,—if, indeed, there are any such, as has been dreamed; nor to those who find their encouragement and inspiration in precisely the present condition of things, and cherish it with the fondness and enthusiasm of lovers,—and, to some extent, I reckon myself in this number; I do not speak to those who are well employed, in whatever circumstances, and they know whether they are well employed or not;—but mainly to the mass of men who are discontented, and idly complaining of the hardness of their lot or of the times, when they might improve them. There are some who complain most energetically and inconsolably of any, because they are, as they say, doing their duty. I also have in my mind that seemingly wealthy, but most terribly impoverished class of all, who have accumulated dross, but know not how to use it, or get rid of it, and thus have forged their own golden or silver fetters.

1. What does Thoreau say prompted him to write the book from which this passage is taken? Do you believe him? Why or why not? Also, why does Thoreau say he will write in the first person? Why is it significant that he uses first person rather than the third person, which was more common at the time he was writing?

2. Thoreau tells us that he will write about inhabitants of New England (where he lived), who, he says, "have appeared to me to be doing penance in a thousand remarkable ways." What does he mean by this statement? In what sense does he consider his neighbors in New England to be "doing penance"? What does this statement suggest about the subject matter of his essay and about his own attitudes toward his subject matter?

3. Summarize Thoreau's criticisms of the life-styles that most people of his time led. What are his chief complaints about those life-styles? What problems result from those life-styles, as he sees them? Cite specific statements from the passage to support your answer.

4. Thoreau asserts at one point in this passage, "It is never too late to give up our prejudices" and "No way of thinking or doing, however ancient, can be trusted without proof." What do you think Thoreau means by these statements? What kind of "proof" is he referring to here? What do these statements tell you about Thoreau's own "prejudices"?

5. What does Thoreau think of the advice of his elders and others who claim to have wisdom about how to live? Why does he feel this way about such advice? How do his attitudes toward advice from others relate to his beliefs about "proof"?

6. What does Thoreau believe are the "necessaries of life"? What does he call "luxuries"? In what sense are these luxuries "hindrances to the elevation of mankind"?

7. What does Thoreau believe one should do with one's time once the "necessaries" of life are obtained? Do you agree with him? Explain.

Examining Rhetorical Strategies

1. Reread the opening five paragraphs of this excerpt from *Walden* and describe Thoreau's way of beginning the book. How does he introduce his subject? How does he establish his focus? What does he reveal about himself and his attitudes toward the people he describes here? Do you think he establishes himself as critical of them and unsympathetic to them? Did you find yourself engaged by his voice or resistant to it? Explain. What might your reaction to his voice suggest about you as a reader?

2. How would you describe Thoreau's own beliefs about technology, based on this passage? How do those beliefs relate to his ideas about the purpose of one's life and the nature of society? Identify specific statements in the passage to support your answer. Do you agree with Thoreau? Why or why not? How do you think these beliefs shape his perspective on the specific issues he addresses in this chapter (e.g., clothing fashion)?

3. Thoreau writes that most people spend the majority of their time engaged in what he describes as "superfluous" toil and thus are unable to enjoy the "finer fruits" of life. What are those "finer fruits," as Thoreau sees them? Cite specific words or phrases in the text to support your answer. What do these "fruits" suggest about what Thoreau values most? How do they influence Thoreau's criticisms of the life-styles of most people? Do these "fruits" apply to all people, in your view? Do you think Thoreau's ideas about what matters most in life are egalitarian, elitist, or pragmatic? Explain.

4. Thoreau's writing has been described as iconoclastic and provocative. Do you think he meant to be iconoclastic and provocative, based on this passage? Did he wish to provoke or offend his audience? Explain, citing specific passages from the text to support your answer. What might he accomplish as a writer by being intentionally provocative in his writing?

5. Thoreau writes that "no way of thinking or doing, however ancient, can be trusted without proof." What "proof" does he offer for his own ideas? How does he build his case for his criticisms? Do you find his "proof" convincing? Why or why not?

6. Describe Thoreau's writing style, paying particular attention to his use of words and phrases that are now outdated. Compare his writing to a more contemporary style. What differences and similarities do you see?

Engaging the Issues

1. Write a contemporary version of Thoreau's essay. Adapt Thoreau's arguments to the society in which you live, changing the references accordingly. For example, is Thoreau's list of the "necessaries of life" still relevant today, or does it need to be updated in any way? Similarly, what kind of example might you use in place of his example of the farmer and his oxen?

2. Write an argument in support of or in opposition to Thoreau's ideas about how to live. Try to identify specific points of Thoreau's that you think are central to his way of thinking and respond to those points from your point of view as someone living 150 years later.

3. Write an essay analyzing Thoreau's appeal to people today. Why do you think Thoreau's ideas are so popular 150 years after he published *Walden?* What accounts for the fact that so many people see his ideas as relevant to today's society? Draw your own conclusions about the usefulness of Thoreau's ideas. (For this assignment, you might consult other works that refer to Thoreau or discuss his ideas. Search for such works in your library or on the Internet.)

4. Using Thoreau's ideas, write an analysis of some common modern technology, such as the telephone, the television, the automobile, or the computer. What would Thoreau say about such a technology and how it is used? Draw conclusions about technology in general based on your analysis of the specific technology you chose.

5. Write an essay about Thoreau's ideas for an audience of people who have little direct access to the most advanced modern technologies (such as the computer). For example, how would you describe Thoreau's ideas about living to an audience of people who have no computers or access to the World Wide Web? What might Thoreau say to such an audience? What is important about Thoreau to them?

   Alternatively, write an essay about Thoreau's ideas regarding technology and progress for an audience of people who are directly involved with the development of new advanced technologies—for instance, a group of software developers at a company like Microsoft Corporation.

6. Compare the essays you wrote for Question #5. How do they differ? How are they similar? How did your sense of your audience influence the way you presented Thoreau's ideas in your essays?

7. With a group of classmates, discuss what you find most compelling or useful about Thoreau's ideas regarding progress and technology. Identify your agreements and disagreements about his ideas and try to arrive at a general consensus. Then construct a Web site based on your sense of the usefulness of Thoreau's ideas. On your site, include pages that summarize what you think are the most important of Thoreau's ideas (citing excerpts from his writing) and explain why you think these ideas are important for modern visitors to your site. Offer analyses or critiques of current practices, technologies, fashions, trends, and ideas based on your reading of Thoreau. Include relevant links to other Web sites that you think are useful.

Ballad of the Unabomber

David S. Bennahum

INTRODUCTION   In July 1995 the *New York Times* and the *Washington Post*, under an agreement with the FBI, published a 35,000-word document written by the notorious "Unabomber." The Unabomber, who at the time was suspected of committing sixteen bombing attacks between 1978 and 1995 that resulted in three deaths and nearly two dozen injured survivors, promised to cease his bombings if the *Times* and *Post* published his manifesto. It was a difficult decision for the editors of these two widely respected newspapers, who were concerned about setting a dangerous precedent by giving in to the Unabomber's threats of violence even as they worried about the victims he might target if his demands were not met. In deciding to publish the manifesto, they hoped to assist the FBI, who had been pursuing the bomber for seventeen years. It worked. The Unabomber's brother and sister-in-law, who were living in upstate New York, recognized the writing when they read the manifesto in the newspaper, and they eventually led the FBI to the suspect. Less than a year after the publication of the manifesto, Theodore Kaczynski, once a promising young professor at the University of California at Berkeley, was arrested and charged as the Unabomber. He was subsequently convicted and sentenced to life in prison.

The decision to publish the Unabomber's manifesto sparked a great deal of controversy. Some people applauded the effort to save the lives of potential bombing victims; however, critics claimed that the decision amounted to capitulating to violent extortion. In the months following the original publication, the controversy intensified as many people began to voice support for the Unabomber's ideas about progress and technology—even as those same people condemned the Unabomber for his horrible letter bombs. In his manifesto, Kaczynski argues that technology has resulted in myriad evils for humans and their environment; the only way to eliminate the social and environmental ills associated with technology, he believes, is to destroy modern society and rebuild it. Although many critics have described his manifesto as the ramblings of a madman bent on violence who is out of touch with the complexities of modern life, Kaczynski's views have unexpectedly found many supporters. Within just a few weeks of its original publication, the manifesto appeared on dozens of Web sites, many of which shared Kaczynski's concerns about technology. People also voiced support for his ideas in Internet discussion groups, on radio talk shows, and in letters to magazines and newspapers.

Some observers interpreted this support for Kaczynski's views as evidence that many people harbor a growing disaffection for the impact of modern technologies on the way we live and on the earth we inhabit. One such observer was David S. Bennahum, who has written extensively about technology. Bennahum believes that the reaction to the Unabomber's manifesto arose from the fact that it expressed basic fears that most Americans have about technology. He is concerned that developers of new technologies and those who support them have not been paying attention to Americans' fears. For Bennahum, the case of the Unabomber revealed worrisome divergences in the way Americans understand and feel about the technology in their lives. It may also reveal differences in how Americans understand *progress.* What does progress mean to us as a society? And how should we address the concerns that some segments of our society might have about the technologies that we associate with progress? Perhaps the horrifying methods that the Unabomber used to express his complaints forced Americans to address such questions, as Bennahum attempts to do here.

David S. Bennahum is a contributing editor at *Wired, Spin, Lingua Franca,* and *I.D.* and the founder of *MEME,* an email newsletter focusing on cultural, technological, and political issues, in which the following essay was originally published. He has written widely about computers and culture for such publications as the *New York Times,* the *Economist, Harper's Bazaar, Slate,* and *FEED.* He is also the author of *In Their Own Words: The Beatles After the Break-Up* (1991) and *Extra Life: Coming of Age in Cyberspace* (1998), an excerpt of which appears in Chapter 3 of this reader.

1. The publication of Kaczynski's manifesto and his subsequent arrest received massive publicity in the media. As you prepare to read Bennahum's article about the case, try to remember your own reaction to the case. Were you aware of the publication of the Unabomber's manifesto? Did you pay attention to it? Why or why not? What were your attitudes about it—and about Kaczynski? What might those attitudes reveal about your own views regarding technology and progress? How might those attitudes affect your reaction to Bennahum's article?

2. The following essay appeared in *MEME*, a newsletter available only through email. As you read, consider the audience Bennahum seems to be addressing in that newsletter. To whom is he writing? What does Bennahum assume about how his audience might feel about the Unabomber and about technology and progress?

I returned from France last Monday, intending to write about the Gallic reaction to the Internet and its impact on France's national computer network, Minitel. That will have to wait until the next *MEME*. This issue is dedicated to the Unabomber and this meme in his manifesto:

> As society and the problems that face it become more and more complex, and as machines become more and more intelligent, people will let machines make more and more of their decisions for them. Eventually a stage may be reached at which the decisions necessary to keep the system running will be so complex that human beings will be incapable of making them intelligently. At that stage machines will be in effective control. . . . If man is not adjusted to this new environment by being artificially reengineered, then he will be adapted to it through a long a painful process of natural selection. . .
>
> The technophiles are taking us all on an utterly reckless ride into the unknown.
>
> —*Unabomber, a.k.a. FC, from Tuesday, September 19, 1995, in a special supplement to the* Washington Post *titled "Industrial Society and Its Future."*

The Unabomber wants to get us out of this supposed mess by returning us to nature. ("That is WILD nature . . . free of human interference and control." Par. 183) What happens when 5.5 billion people go back to nature is that most of us die, because without technology the Earth cannot support all of us. This would be a very short, very brutal "painful process of natural selection" to say the least. It is also not going to happen. So, apart from the Unabomber's absurd prescription for saving the human race from mechanical enslavement, does he have a point?

The Unabomber's real importance, in the long-term, goes beyond the fact that he killed 3 people and injured 23 others in 16 attacks over 17 years. It goes beyond the fact that he essentially blackmailed the *New York Times* and *Washington Post* into reprinting his manifesto. The Unabomber is important because his argument against technology is destined to become the mainstream argument against our wired world in the next century. The fear that technology will erase something fundamental that defines us as human beings is old, as old as technology—see Prometheus or the tower of Babel. So if this is an old argument, why aren't we technophiles doing a better job of addressing it, as opposed to mocking it? Last Tuesday we got a sneak preview of the next decade's battle-lines.

The Global SuperOrganism

I've noticed that many of us technological sophisticates are also uncomfortable with some of the goals of our peers. I wince when I read in the latest issue of *Wired* that "by 2040 robots will be as smart as we are. Then they'll displace us as the dominant form of life on Earth." This isn't a problem though, it is presented as a form of human transcendence, the binary version of getting closer to the perfection of God. Should this be taken seriously? When I first saw that article I thought it was a joke, a sort of send-up on the cooks. Unfortunately it is dead-serious. It is also similar in logic to the Unabomber's conclusions about where technology is headed. The only difference is in their conclusions: one thinks it is cool, the other thinks it is not.

I was surprised how up-to-date the Unabomber is on the fusion of man and machines. He must have read such paragons of the genre as Bruce Mazlish's *The Fourth Discontinuity: The Co-Evolution of Humans and Machines,* (Yale University Press, 1993); *Metaman: The Merging of Humans and Machines into a Global Superorganism,* (Simon Schuster, 1993); and the seminal text *Out of Control: The Rise of Neo-Biological Civilization,* by Kevin Kelly (Addison Wesley, 1994). These are all serious books by serious writers published by serious publishers. Yet they all argue the same thing: we are merging with machines, becoming something more than human, and we should embrace it. The end of the individual is a blessing, the shedding of a tired meat-cocoon. What's troubling here is that we have two extremes coming from the same root — one calling for a return to wild nature, the other calling for the destruction of what it means to be a human being. Where is the alternative — a humanistic vision technology that bolsters both our individuality as humans and improves our ability to live together?

Technology with a Human Face

I got a computer at 12, went online then, and stayed online. I learned to program, learned to think the way a computer thinks. I made money writing programs for a while. I love science fiction and get a thrill from gadgets. More importantly, I think the combination of computers and communications can profoundly alter the nature of information by decentralizing it and getting it into the hands of people who otherwise would not be exposed to it. I relish the Internet and everything it stands for. But I am worried. I am worried that the folks writing these books about the joys of fusing with machines have lost all compassion for human beings. I am worried that what was once nutty is becoming conventional wisdom. Consequently I am worried that for many people the anger of the Unabomber will come to make sense. I am worried that, in our love of technology and gadgets and change we will at best ignore the silent majority that do not understand what is happening and want to; at worst we will mock them as hopelessly headed the way of the dodo bird.

Beware the Backlash

The initial euphoria of the digital revolution is over. We get the jargon. We get the possibilities. It's time to start translating what's possible for everyone else, or else we risk destroying the thing we're so proud of. So long as technology is associated with free enterprise those that fear technological change will be muffled. This association has insulated many technology firms from the rage out there in America—the rage behind credit reports, behind workplace automation, behind caller ID, bar codes and all those other points where data gathering meets human flesh. But the rage is there, simmering. The rage comes from confusion, from the fact that so little effort is made to explain how these technologies work. It comes from the arrogance of those who think most people are too stupid to understand.

If the changes before us in digital technology, nanotechnology and genetic technology are as huge as I think they are, then expect a resistance equal to the force behind these advances. To expect anything less would be foolish. If we are going to deal with this basic fact of human nature responsibly, then it is time to stop spouting jargon and start talking clearly about what is to be lost and what is to be gained as we digitize everything. That way at least we can try to influence what is happening, as opposed to believing it is an inevitable force of nature, unstoppable, unchangeable. If we can't have faith in our ability to define our future, then we really are worthy of our supposed role as nothing more than pollinating facilitators, nurturing some still-dormant machinic-species. In such a world I would resist too. To do otherwise would be insane.

Here is a quote from T.S. Eliot that I've had on my desk for awhile:

Where is the life we have lost in living?
Where is the wisdom we have lost in knowledge?
Where is the knowledge we have lost in information?

REFLECTING ON THE READING

1. Why does Bennahum wish to address a passage from the Unabomber's manifesto in this essay? Does he agree with the passage? Why or why not? Why does he think this passage and the manifesto in general are significant? Do you agree with him? Why or why not?

2. In what sense does Bennahum think that the reaction to the Unabomber's manifesto reflects an "old" fear? What fear is he referring to? Does he share that fear? Do you? Why or why not?

3. Early in this essay, Bennahum asks, "Why aren't we technophiles doing a better job of addressing it, as opposed to mocking it?" Whom do you think he is referring to in this passage? What is a "technophile"? Do you consider yourself one?

4. What concerns Bennahum about the issues of *Wired* magazine that he refers to in the section of his essay titled "The Global SuperOrganism"? Do you think his concern is valid? Explain.

5. Bennahum identifies two extremes in the views people have regarding technology: one extreme, represented by the Unabomber, fears technology and

wishes for a return to nature; the other extreme embraces technology and sees it as enhancing nature. What is the alternative to these views that Bennahum wishes for? Do you think his alternative is a valid one? Why or why not?

6. What worry does Bennahum confess regarding those who embrace technology and those who fear it? Why does Bennahum have this worry? What developments have given rise to it? Do you share this worry? Why or why not?

7. What is the rage that Bennahum believes is simmering in America? What is its source? How does he believe it can be addressed?

Examining Rhetorical Strategies

1. Bennahum begins his essay by saying he was originally planning to write about the French national computer network but will devote his attention to the Unabomber's manifesto instead. Why do you think he begins his essay in this way? What message does it send to you as reader? How did you react to it? Also, what does this introduction to the essay reveal about Bennahum as a writer and as a person? How might it establish his authority as someone who can speak knowledgeably about these issues?

2. Early in this essay, Bennahum refers to "we technophiles" and "us technological sophisticates." What kind of audience do these phrases indicate Bennahum was writing to? What assumptions do you think Bennahum makes about that audience? Do you consider yourself part of that audience? How might someone who is not a "technophile" react to this essay? Do you think Bennahum is concerned about such a reaction? Explain.

3. Based on this essay, how do you think Bennahum defines *progress*? What is the relationship between progress and technology, as he sees it? Do you think Bennahum's views about progress and technology are "mainstream"—that is, shared by most Americans? How do you think he addresses the concerns of those who might not share those views? Cite specific passages from the essay to support your answer.

4. How would you describe Bennahum's tone in this essay? Do you think it is effective? Do you think it is appropriate to the subject matter and to his arguments about technology? Explain.

5. Assess the conclusion to this essay. Why do you think Bennahum ended with an excerpt from T. S. Eliot's poetry? What might the use of such poetry reveal about Bennahum's own values as a writer and a reader? What effect did those lines of poetry have on you? What might your reaction to those lines indicate about you as a reader?

Engaging the Issues

1. Using the Internet or your library, find a copy of the Unabomber's manifesto and read through it. Then write your own reaction to it. What is the significance of the manifesto, in your view? What lessons can we learn from it? What might it reveal about us and about how we live? What might the reaction to it reveal

about our beliefs regarding technology and progress? Write your essay for the editorial page of your local newspaper or for a large-circulation general interest publication (such as *Newsweek* or *USA Today*).

2. Write a response to Bennahum in which you express agreement with or concerns about his views regarding technology and about the Unabomber case.

3. In a group of your classmates, discuss the appeal of Ted Kaczynski's ideas to people who otherwise were appalled by his violent acts. In the weeks following the publication of Kaczynski's manifesto and then, later, his arrest, dozens of Web sites appeared on the Internet voicing support for his ideas, and similar letters to the editor were published in newspapers around the country. How can you account for the appeal of Kaczynski's ideas? Try to identify what you think it is about his ideas that people found most compelling. (If possible, find some Kaczynski-related Web sites or newspaper accounts of his appeal as part of your research for this essay.)

   On the basis of your discussions, write an essay discussing the significance of the Unabomber case and what it might suggest about how people view technology and the idea of progress in contemporary society.

4. In a group of your classmates, play the role of editors at the *New York Times* or the *Washington Post* who are faced with the decision to print the Unabomber's manifesto. Consider the consequences of agreeing to publish it or denying the FBI's request that you publish it. Consider the violent acts the Unabomber had already committed and the fact that the FBI had not yet been able to apprehend him. Consider, too, the message that you might be sending about the effectiveness of violence as a means to an end if you publish the manifesto; consider what publishing the manifesto might imply about the role of a newspaper in a democratic society. Discuss the matter in your group and reach a decision about publishing the manifesto.

   Either individually or as a group, write an editorial for your school newspaper in which you justify your decision to your readers.

5. In their introduction to the Unabomber's manifesto on their Web site, the editors of *HotWired* wrote:

   The fact that the Unabomber demanded that his manifesto appear in the "respectable" organs of the pre-digital establishment, and the fact that these newspapers kept the text off-line for months, is an indication that the *New York Times,* the *Washington Post,* and Unabomber belong, in one sense at least, to the same party—the party of the past.

   Do you agree with this statement? Write a letter to the editors of *HotWired* in which you explain why you agree or disagree with this position regarding Kaczynski's use of the mainstream press and the decision of the *New York Times* and the *Washington Post* to publish the manifesto.

6. Visit the *MEME* or the *HotWired* site on the World Wide Web and read several other articles published there. How would you describe this publication? Its audience? Its focus? What issues is it most concerned about? How does it differ from traditional print magazines with which you are familiar? Write an analysis of

MEME or *HotWired,* using Bennahum's article and any others that seem appropriate. In your analysis, describe the key features of the publication and the audience it seems to target; assess its effectiveness in covering the issues it routinely publishes articles about and in addressing its audience.

7. Write a conventional academic essay in which you discuss Bennahum's ideas about technology and progress. In your essay, describe what you believe are Bennahum's assumptions about technology and about progress in general, citing specific passages from his essay as support for your analysis. Compare his assumptions about progress and technology to those of other authors whose work you read in this chapter. Evaluate his assumptions from your own perspective as someone familiar with technology.

8. For an audience of your classmates, write a critique of Bennahum's argument. How does he construct his argument? Does he offer sufficient support for his points, in your view? Is he convincing? How does he account for his audience? Draw conclusions about the effectiveness of his argument for his intended audience.

9. Write a letter to your local school board in which you propose that students should be asked to address some of the criticisms about progress and technology that Kaczynski voices in his manifesto. Justify your proposal as an important educational matter. Anticipate the criticisms and objections of those who would oppose your proposal on the grounds that students should not be exposed to a criminal's ideas.

   Alternatively, write a letter to your college or university president making a similar proposal.

FURTHERING YOUR INQUIRY

1. What do you think Henry David Thoreau and David S. Bennahum might say to one another about the future of literacy and technology? Imagine an exchange between these two, based on the passages from each included in this chapter (or other writing by them that you might have read). Consider what you believe are the primary issues for each of them: what seems to matter most to them about technology and literacy? Then write a dialogue between the two.

   Alternatively, write an essay in which you compare the ideas of each regarding the future of literacy.

2. Many of the authors in this chapter envision the future in light of recent technological developments. Some of these authors present hopeful and even enthusiastic visions of the future with respect to literacy and technology; others express concern and voice warnings about such a future. Drawing on several of the authors in this chapter whose ideas most engaged or interested you, write an essay in which you discuss your own vision for the future with respect to literacy and technology. What do you believe will happen? How might writing and reading and communications change as new technologies evolve? What concerns and hopes do you have? Try to make specific references in your essay to the authors whose ideas you find compelling or disturbing.

3. Write a conventional academic essay in which you discuss the idea of *progress.* Draw, where appropriate, on the authors in this chapter—and on any other authors whose work seems useful to you—in order to explain what *progress* is and how ideas about progress seem to influence the ways people make decisions about technology and literacy. Use examples from your own life to illustrate your points about progress.

4. Write an essay tracing the influence of Henry David Thoreau's *Walden* on one or more of the readings in this chapter.

5. Using any of the texts in this chapter that seem appropriate, write a letter to your local school board proposing changes in the high school curriculum that you think should be made in order to teach students effectively about technology and its effects on individuals and culture. You might, for example, propose a specific course about technology that would be required of all students. Or you might propose ways that technology education might be integrated into other subject areas in the curriculum. Or you might propose more drastic changes in the way your school district uses technology. Be sure to justify your proposed changes.

6. Write your own manifesto about technology and progress. Use whatever texts from this chapter would be appropriate. Your audience is your classmates.

   Alternatively, write a manifesto that might be published in your local newspaper.

7. In a group of your classmates, share the manifestos you wrote for Question #6 above. Discuss your respective views about technology and progress, identifying significant differences and similarities among your views. Try to account for those differences and similarities. What might your discussion reveal about how people view technology and progress?

8. Collaborating with a group of your classmates, construct a Web site that is a manifesto as described in question #6. With your group, discuss your respective views about technology and decide how to represent those views most effectively on your Web site.

   After finishing your Web site, review the sites constructed by other classmates and write an analysis of the sites in terms of audience, purpose, and technological medium.

9. Write a critical history of *progress* in the twentieth century for a general audience (for example, readers of a large-circulation newspaper like *USA Today*). In your history tell the story of technological progress in the twentieth century as you see it, focusing on what you believe were the key technological advances and describing their effects on human life, as you see them. Draw on writers in this chapter—and any other sources you deem appropriate.

CHAPTER 2

The Technologies
of Literacy

When you pick up your spoon to stir your morning cup of coffee or sprinkle sugar into your bowl of cereal, you probably don't think about the fact that you are using tools. Yet that spoon or cup or bowl, like dozens of other tools you use every day, profoundly shapes the way you live. And the fact that we rarely, if ever, think about these objects as tools suggests how extensively technology is integrated into our lives and our culture. Sociologist Peter Berger has discussed how the "logic" of tools shapes not only how we do things but also how we understand the things we do:

> Once produced, the tool has a being of its own that cannot be readily changed by those who employ it. Indeed, the tool (say, an agricultural implement) may even enforce the logic of its being on its users, sometimes in a way that might not be particularly agreeable to them. For instance, a plow, though obviously a human product, is an external object not only in the sense that its users may fall over it and hurt themselves as a result, just as they may [hurt themselves] by falling over a rock or a stump or any other natural object. More interestingly, the plow may compel its users to arrange their agricultural activity, and perhaps also other aspects of their lives, in a way that conforms to *its* own logic and that may have been neither intended nor foreseen by those who originally devised it.*

Berger suggests in this passage that a tool such as a plow may compel farmers to plant and grow their crops in a certain way—in straight rows, for instance—that they may not have done without that tool. If you were to visit the Native American cliff dweller ruins in Mesa Verde National Park in the southwestern part of the United States, you would encounter compelling evidence of Berger's point. The Native Americans who once lived in those ruins were farmers, but they raised and harvested their crops very differently from the white farmers who eventually settled in that region. The Native American farmers used no plows and did not plant in long, even rows as their white counterparts did; instead, they planted their fields almost

---

* Peter Berger, *The Sacred Canopy,* 1969, p. 9.

randomly, like natural meadows, and they gathered crops by hand. In short, the technology that each community of farmers used profoundly shaped their work and their lives—and, we might guess, how they understood their work and their lives. The use of the plow prompted white farmers to plant in rows, because rows made it easier to use the plow and thus facilitated the work of planting and maintaining their fields. Without the plow, however, it made little sense for Native American farmers to plant in rows; they employed a different strategy for planting and growing and harvesting crops that made sense for the tools they used: their hands and the baskets they carried for gathering crops.

Like those farmers, you also make decisions on the basis of the tools you use. For instance, consider how you might use a cordless telephone as compared to a conventional telephone with a cord. A conventional phone requires that you stay in one location when you make or receive a telephone call; a cordless phone allows you to move around your apartment or home or even wander outside the building where you live while you talk into the phone. That feature of the cordless phone may prompt you to make a call—to a friend, say—at a time when you would not be able to do so with a conventional phone. You might, for instance, be washing your bicycle in your driveway and decide to call your friend or a local bicycle shop to ask a question about greasing the bicycle's chain. With a cordless phone, you can make that call while you're in the driveway working on your bike. With a conventional phone, however, you would probably leave the bike and go inside to make the call. Because of that simple limitation of the conventional phone, you might decide not to call your friend at that particular moment, which might ultimately affect whether and maybe even *how* you will grease your bicycle chain. Or you might decide to call your friend later, when you're inside making other phone calls. The point is that seemingly minor characteristics of the tools you use every day can influence not only how you use those tools to perform a specific task but also the *kinds* of activities you engage in and the decisions you make about those activities.

We rarely stop to think in this way about the tools we use in our lives. And most of us have probably never considered that one of the most important of those tools—perhaps the most important human technology of all—is writing itself. We tend to think of writing, if we think of it at all, as a means of communication, a way to record and convey ideas, thoughts, or information. It's a common complaint among students that writing is often difficult, but we tend to overlook how complex it really is. And we don't often examine how deeply and extensively writing has affected virtually every aspect of our lives. You needn't look too far in your own life to get a glimpse of the extent of writing's effects on how you live. From the nutritional information on your cereal box to the sales receipt for your bicycle and the instruction booklet that came with it; from the signs on the bus that you might have taken to campus to the books you use for your classes; from the bills you received in the day's mail to the grocery list you made for your trip to the supermarket—few aspects of your life are untouched by writing.

But let's go a step further. Writing can shape your life—and the life of the society you live in—in ways that aren't as obvious but are much more profound than the bus signs or that grocery list. Did you happen to drive to work or school today? If so, you carried with you a driver's license, a small card containing written information about you that gives you legal permission to operate a car. Think of the many steps you took to obtain that card: filling out application forms, studying the driving manual in the state where you live, completing an examination about driving laws and procedures (laws that exist in written form), taking a vision test, taking the road test, sitting for a photograph, filing insurance forms, paying for all of it—and more. Think of the different technologies that might have been used in all these steps: pencils, pens, paper, typewriters, computers, copy machines, telephones, perhaps even the Internet. All of this to one degree or another involves writing; indeed, it becomes hard to imagine how all of this could be accomplished *without* writing (and that's not even considering how writing shaped the very development, production, delivery, and sale of the car you drive). Furthermore, just as the plow affected how farmers raised and harvested their crops and the cordless phone affects when and where you called your friend, writing affects how you *conduct* your life; in other words, writing as a technology can shape your behavior and how you interact with others. For example, you must go to a specific government office to obtain the proper forms to apply for a driving license (or you can write a letter to request the forms); you must acquire and study books or pamphlets about the various driving laws that you have to learn in order to pass your tests. And so on. You do all these things—you make certain choices about how to spend your time and what activities to engage in—in order to obtain a small card that represents legal permission to drive a car. And millions of other people do the same. If you are stopped by a police officer while driving your car, he or she will ask you for your driver's license and automobile registration—two written documents that will, in part, determine what the officer does next. In all these seemingly small ways, writing influences what you and others around you do every day.

We can go on to think about the many other ways in which writing is a part of this activity of obtaining permission to drive a car—for example, all the people whose jobs exist largely to manage the volumes of documents that are somehow related to you and the millions of people who drive cars, the production and distribution of those documents, and so on. In a sense, the lives of these people and the organizations for which they work are structured by the technologies of writing. The point is clear: when you look carefully at the role of writing in contemporary culture, you begin to understand why one eighteenth-century scholar called writing "the noblest invention that can possibly be conceived."* If the plow shaped the way farmers farm, writing has shaped much more.

The readings in this chapter ask you to think about writing as an *invention,* as a technology that has affected not only how we communicate but also how we interact with each other, how we organize and conduct our lives, and even how we *think.* Writing, according to scholar Walter Ong, restructures consciousness: "it transforms speech and thought as well." Such an assertion may seem extreme, and indeed some other scholars have challenged that assertion. But as the readings in this chapter suggest, there is a great deal of compelling evidence about the enormous impact that writing has had on human existence, and the great deal of scholarly debate about writing suggests not only its importance in human life but its complexity as well. We may take writing for granted, but the authors whose works appear in this chapter ask you to reexamine this technology that you use every day, that you are using right now as you read these words. These authors

---

*Roy Harris, *The Origins of Writing,* 1986.

raise complicated but important questions about the nature of writing and about the many different technologies of writing that we employ and that shape how we engage in literacy: pencil and paper, the printing press, the computer. As several of these authors suggest, the technologies we use to write and read can significantly affect how we write and read and, thus, how writing is used in our lives. To consider the ways in which this is true is to gain a fuller sense of the importance of literacy as a technology and of the technologies we use for writing and reading.

Each of the readings in this chapter addresses a particular set of issues or questions about the idea of writing *as* a technology and about the technologies *of* writing. As a group, the readings raise three major questions that you should keep in mind as you consider the specific points each author makes.

First, what exactly is writing? Scholars like Jay David Bolter suggest that writing is itself a specialized technology that goes well beyond simple communication. If indeed it is a technology, as they suggest, how does it function as such? What exactly does it mean to say that writing is a technology? Several writers in this chapter describe how the technologies they use shape their own writing. But others assert that writing is a technology for understanding ourselves and our worlds. If they are right, in what ways does writing shape our thinking and our ways of interacting with each other?

Second, why is this technology of writing so important? Some scholars have suggested that writing makes certain kinds of thinking possible; in that sense, writing is linked to how we understand ourselves and how we structure our culture and our social relationships. Such scholars see writing as a crucial *human* technology. But although some of the authors in this chapter address much more mundane aspects of the technologies of writing—such as pencils—all of them believe that writing is important. In what specific ways, they collectively ask, is writing a significant technology in our lives? What impact has it had on human existence—and what impact does it continue to have on our lives today?

Finally, the authors in this chapter pose the question, How might different technologies for writing affect literacy? That is, how do we engage in reading and writing; how do we understand reading and writing? Some writers claim that the computer profoundly changed how they write—and think—yet others ponder the implications of our uses of the computer as a tool for writing and for communication—implications that are not always comforting. Furthermore, some of the authors in this chapter examine how specific writing technologies—the pencil, the Inca *quipu,* and the computer—might shape the ways in which we actually define literacy. And several see significant changes in our uses of literacy as computers become ever more widespread. What will *literacy* be in a future in which computers—and perhaps other technologies that we cannot yet imagine—are the primary tools for writing and reading?

The answers to such questions may in some ways seem obvious. Considering how much emphasis writing is given in school and in other settings (such as the workplace or the courts), it may seem self-evident that writing is important; indeed, almost no one ever argues that writing is irrelevant or not worthy of sustained study by students. But the writers in this chapter urge you to go beyond the obvious, to ask why, to inquire into the complex nature of writing in order to gain a better understanding of the changes that are occurring in literacy and technology at the beginning of a new millennium. You are in the midst of those changes, from the rapid development of the Internet to portable email and the prospect of electronic books. What will they mean to you and to the society in which you live? These writers may help you begin to answer that question by illuminating some of the ways in which writing functions in your life and in the lives of others.

How the Computer Changed My Writing

Steven Johnson

INTRODUCTION   Steven Johnson is a writer and the editor in chief and copublisher of *FEED,* a provocative and respected online journal that addresses issues of technology and culture. In the following excerpt from his book *Interface Culture: How New Technology Transforms the Way We Create and Communicate* (1997), Johnson describes how his own writing was altered by his use of the computer. In some ways, Johnson's experience is typical of writers in the last decade or two of the twentieth century, when word processing became a standard technology in schools, homes, and businesses; and you may recognize your own experience with computers and writing in Johnson's description. But Johnson isn't just describing practical changes in the way he wrote that were brought on by his use of the computer: he also describes changes in *what* he wrote and how he thought about his writing. And in doing so, Johnson is raising some of the same complex questions about the connections between writing and thinking that other writers in this chapter, such as Jay David Bolter, address. His brief description of his own writing process as it changed with the use of computer technology thus helps open the door to the large, tricky issues that scholars, theorists, writers, and educators were wrestling with at the end of the twentieth century as computer technologies came into even more widespread use: What effects will computer technology have on *how* people write and read? Will such technology change not only how writing and reading are done but also what they look like and how they are used? Do we think in different ways when we write with different technologies? These complex questions have energized discussions about new technologies for literacy in recent decades. Johnson's description of his writing gives us one writer's distinctive angle on these important issues.

REFLECTING BEFORE READING

1. What technology do you use when you write? A computer? Pen and paper? Before reading Johnson's essay, jot down a brief description of how you do your own writing. For example, you might note whether you use a pen and paper or a computer for composing your first drafts of school assignments. Describe what steps you take and what technology you use for those steps. Then, as you read Johnson's description of his writing with computers, compare the changes he discusses to your own writing and consider whether they are really as profound as he says they are.

2. Johnson describes his experiences as a writer who uses a computer for writing. By the time he published the following essay in 1997, computers as writing tools were quite common in the United States. At the same time, statistics from the late 1990's reveal noticeable disparities in *who* had access to computers. For instance, African Americans were much less likely to own a computer than White Americans; also, people from low-income households were less likely to have access to computer technology. As you read, consider whether Johnson's discussion of writing and technology and his conclusions about the effects of technology on writing apply to all people who write. How might his account be different if he grew up in different socioeconomic circumstances? Do you think he needs to qualify his account in any way?

I was twelve when my parents shelled out for our first home PC—an Apple IIe souped up with an astonishing 32K of RAM—and while my recollections of the preceding years are not particularly vivid, I can still conjure up a little of the rhythm of life back then, in the dark ages before the digital revolution. Among my peers, this sometimes seems to be an unusual ability. I often hear friends wonder aloud: "How did we ever get along without e-mail and word processors?" And yet for the most part I can readily imagine how things happened in that world, the pace of that more settled and disconnected existence. It all seems rather obvious to me. We got along because we didn't know what we were missing. Folks have always griped about the postal service's sluggish performance, but the lag time only becomes intolerable once you have a taste of e-mail.

It's not life without computers that confounds me; it's life in the strange interregnum after the PC first appeared in our house. I lived within thirty feet of a fully functional computer from my twelfth to my eighteenth year, and yet the sad truth is, I used it almost exclusively as a presentation device for those six years, like a visit to Kinko's at the end of a term paper. Whatever I was writing—papers, poems, stories, plays—I dutifully etched out by hand on yellow legal pads, crossing out passages, scribbling new lines in the margins. Only when the language had reached a tolerable state did I bother typing it into the PC. The idea of composing on (and not transcribing into) the machine seemed somehow inauthentic to me. It was more like typing than writing, in Truman Capote's memorable phrase, somehow more mechanical, more mediated, a few steps removed from the whole books-on-tape phenomenon.

This continues to be a normal state of mind for the millions of people who still sense something menacing in the glare of the PC monitor, who find themselves more perplexed than enlightened by the digital revolution. But that fifteen-year-old version of me didn't belong to that demographic: I genuinely liked computers, and spent the requisite hours of my adolescence frittering away my allowance at the arcade. Like many kids of my generation, I dabbled with rudimentary programming languages (BASIC and Pascal) long enough to toss a few stray colored pixels up on the screen or scroll through the call-and-response formula of the medieval text adventures then in vogue. I wasn't even close to being what we would now call a "hacker," but I certainly felt confident enough with the PC to put a new word processor through its paces without spending much time with the manual. (In those days, you had to give the documentation at least a cursory glance before booting up the software.) I harbored no ill will toward the machine, no superstitions. But I could not bring myself to write on it.

Fast-forward a decade or two, and I can't imagine writing *without* a computer. Even jotting down a note with pen and paper feels strained, like a paraplegic suddenly granted the use of his legs. I have to *think* about writing, think about it consciously as my hand scratches out the words on the page, think about the act itself. There is none of the easy flow of the word processor, just a kind of drudgery, running against the thick grain of habit. Pen and paper feel profoundly different to me now—they have the air of an inferior technology about them, the sort of contraption well suited for jotting down a phone number, but not much beyond that. Writing an entire book by hand strikes me as being a little like filming *Citizen Kane* with a camcorder. You can make a go at it, of course, but on some fundamental level you've misjudged the appropriate scale of the technology you're using. It sounds appalling, I know, but there it is. I'm a typer, not a writer. Even my handwriting is disintegrating, becoming less and less *my* handwriting, and more the erratic, anonymous scrawl of someone learning to write for the first time.

I accept this condition gladly, and at the same time I can recall the predigital years of my childhood, writing stories by hand into loose-leaf notebooks, practicing my cursive strokes and then surveying the loops and descenders, seeing something there that looked like me, my sense of selfhood scrawled onto the page. On a certain level these two mental states are totally incompatible—bits versus atoms—but the truth is I have no trouble reconciling them. My "written" self has always fed back powerfully into my normal, walking-around-doing-more-or-less-nothing self. When I was young that circuit was completed by tools of ink and paper; today it belongs to the zeros and ones. The basic shape of the circuit is unchanged.

But what interests me now, looking back on it, is the *transition* from one to the other. That feeling of artificiality that undermined me as I typed into a word processor, the strangeness of the activity—all this is very difficult to bring back. How could I have resisted so long? Sure, the software was less powerful back then, but the basic components of word processing—the cutting and pasting, the experimentation, the speed of typing—were all very much in place. There were clear advantages to working on the computer, advantages I genuinely understood and appreciated. But they were not compelling enough to dissipate the aura of inauthenticity that surrounded the machine. My writing didn't seem real on the screen somehow. It felt like a bureaucratic parody of me, several steps removed, like a recycled Xerox image shuffled around the office one too many times.

So now I wonder: what force finally brought me over to the other side? After more than half a decade of tinkering with computers, what was it that finally allowed me to recognize myself in those bright pixels on the screen, to see those letterforms as real extensions of my thought? I wasn't totally aware of it at the time, of course, but I can now see that what drew me into the language-space on the screen was nothing less than interface design. The Mac's paper-on-desktop metaphor—the white backdrop, the typographic controls, Alan Kay's stacked windows—lured me away from real-world paper. The "user illusion" sucked me in, and I was hooked forever. I'd understood the benefits of using a word processor before I bought my Mac, but it took a fully realized graphic interface to make me feel comfortable enough to use one for honest-to-God *writing*. Everything before that twelve-point New York font first appeared on the screen, black pixels marching boldly across the whiteness—everything before that was just transcribing.

I suspect there are millions of people with similar stories to tell: the mind naturally resists the dull glare of the screen, feels ill at ease with it, unnatural. And then something in the user experience changes—the "direct manipulation" of the mouse, perhaps, or the resolution of the display—and suddenly you find yourself at home in front of the machine, so acclimated to the environment that you're no longer fighting the software. Before you know it, you're composing directly into the word processor, and the artifice, that original sense of mediation, is gone.

There are two lessons here, one relatively straightforward, the other more indirect. It's clear that the graphic interface played a crucial role in creating today's colossal market for word-processing applications, a market drawn not only to the functionality of the products but also to their look-and-feel. Plenty of us labored along with word processors in the days of the command-line interface, but the ease and fluidity of today's digital writing owe a great deal to the aesthetic innovations of the desktop metaphor. It's not just that the software has accumulated more features. It's also that the software has grown more seductive, more visually appealing over that period. For the creative mind, wrestling with language on the screen, that heightened visual sensibility can be enormously comforting.

But this is more than just a story about the sales records set by WordPerfect and Microsoft Word in the past decade. It also extends beyond the long-term trend of folks becoming more comfortable with their word processors as the user interface grows increasingly sophisticated. The truly interesting thing here is that using a word processor changes how we write—not just because we're relying on new tools to get the job done, but also because the computer fundamentally transforms the way we conjure up our sentences, the thought process that runs alongside the writing process. You can see this transformation at work on a number of levels. The most basic is one of sheer volume: the speed of digital composition—not to mention the undo commands and the spell checker—makes it a great deal easier to churn out ten pages where we might once have scratched out five using pen and paper (or a Smith-Corona). The perishability of certain digital formats—e-mail being the most obvious example—has also created a more casual, almost conversational writing style, a fusion of written letter and telephone-speak.

But for me, the most intriguing side effect of the word processor lies in the changed relationship between a sentence in its conceptual form and its physical translation onto the page or the screen. In the years when I still wrote using pen and paper or a typewriter, I almost invariably worked out each sentence in my head before I began transcribing it on the page. There was a clear before and after to the process: I would work out the subject and verb, modifiers, subsidiary clauses in advance; I would tinker with the arrangement for a minute or two; and when the mix seemed right, I'd turn back to the yellow legal pad. The method made sense, given the tools I was using—changing the sequence of words after you'd scrawled them out quickly made a mess of your document. (You could swap phrases in and out with arrows and cross-outs, of course, but it made reading over the text extremely unpleasant.) All this changed after the siren song of the Mac's interface lured me into writing directly at the computer. I began with my familiar start-and-stop routine, dutifully thinking up the sentence before typing it out, but it soon became clear that the word processor eliminated the penalty that revisions normally exacted. If the phrasing wasn't quite right, you could rearrange words with a few quick mouse gestures, and the magical "delete" key was always a split second away. After a few months, I noticed a qualitative shift in the way I worked with sentences: the thinking and the typing processes began to overlap. A phrase would come into my head—a sentence fragment, an opening clause, a parenthetical remark—and before I had time to mull it over, the words would be up on the screen. Only then would I start fishing around for a verb, or a prepositional phrase to close out the sentence. Most sentences would unfold through a kind of staggered trial and error—darting back and forth between several different iterations until I arrived at something that seemed to work.

It was a subtle change, but a profound one nonetheless. The fundamental units of my writing had mutated under the spell of the word processor: I had begun by working with blocks of complete sentences, but by the end I was thinking in smaller blocks, in units of discrete phrases. This, of course, had an enormous effect on the types of sentences I ended up writing. The older procedure imposed a kind of upward ceiling on the sentence's complexity: you had to be able to hold the entire sequence of words in your head, which meant that the mind naturally gravitated to simpler, more direct syntax. Too many subsidiary clauses and you lost track. But the word processor allowed me to zoom in on smaller clusters of words and build out from there—I could always add another aside, some more descriptive frippery, because the overall shape of the sentence was never in question. If I lost track of the subject-verb agreement, I could always go back and adjust it. And so my sentences swelled out enormously, like a small village besieged by new immigrants. They were ringed by countless peripheral thoughts and show-off allusions, paved by endless qualifications and false starts. It didn't help matters that I happened to be under the sway of French semiotic theory at the time, but I know those sentences would have been almost impossible to execute had I been scribbling them out on my old legal pads. The computer had not only made it easier for me to write; it had also changed the very substance of what I was writing, and in that sense, I suspect, it had an enormous effect on my thinking as well.

REFLECTING ON THE READING

1. Johnson writes in this passage that the computer "changed the very substance" of what he was writing. What does he mean by this statement? Identify specifically the changes that he describes in his writing as he used the computer more and more extensively. What was different about his writing as the computer became a routine part of his writing process? Were the differences really as substantive as he claims? Justify your answer with reference to specific elements in the passage.

2. Johnson tells us that it took approximately six years after his parents bought their first computer before any real changes began to occur in his writing. Why did it take so long? How does Johnson account for his reluctance to use the computer for writing?

3. Johnson claims that one result of his reliance on the computer as a writing tool is that his handwriting is "disintegrating." But he also says that he accepts this "gladly." Why? What are the benefits and disadvantages of writing with the computer, as Johnson sees them? Consider the implications of the tools Johnson uses for writing (and the tools *you* use for writing): how have they affected his life? How have they affected the decisions he makes about writing?

4. Johnson believes that the primary reason he eventually became comfortable with the computer is its "graphic interface"—that is, the ability to manipulate the icons and images on the screen instead of working only with text (as he did when he used pen and paper or a typewriter). What was it about the graphic interface that made the difference for Johnson and encouraged him to use the computer "for honest-to-God *writing*," as he puts it?

5. Do you think it's true that "the mind naturally resists the dull glare of the [computer] screen," as Johnson suggests? Does your own experience lend credence to this claim? If so, why do you think this is so? Do you think the mind also "naturally resisted" the use of typewriters, printing presses, mechanical pencils, copy machines, or telephones when they were new technologies? What is Johnson suggesting here about how humans communicate? What is he suggesting about what is "natural" and what is not when humans communicate?

6. What does Johnson mean when he says that the word processor changed the "relationship between a sentence in its conceptual form and its physical translation onto the page or screen"? Why was this change so important, in Johnson's view? Do you think he is right? Why or why not?

7. At the end of this excerpt, Johnson suggests that the changes in his writing brought on by the computer "had an enormous impact on my thinking as well." What sort of impact do you think Johnson is referring to here? What evidence does he provide that his thinking was changed?

Examining Rhetorical Strategies

1. Consider the tone of this passage. How would you characterize it? Why do you think Johnson effects such a tone? How do you think the tone of the passage relates to his point and his perspective on computer technology?

2. Given what you know about Johnson's background, about where this passage was originally published, and what you have read in this passage, what sort of audience do you think Johnson is addressing? Does Johnson assume that his audience has extensive knowledge of computers? Does he assume that they are generally favorable toward computer technologies? What does he assume about their socioeconomic status? For instance, he tells us that his parents bought a computer at a time when computers were relatively rare in private homes. Do you think he is knowingly addressing an audience of similar background who had the means to purchase a home computer when such machines were relatively expensive for most American households? In 1998, more than half of all American households still did not have a computer. How might readers from those households react to Johnson's arguments? Is he writing to them? Would

this passage be different if he were addressing them directly? If so, in what ways?

3. When Johnson suggests at the end of this passage that writing with the computer changed his "thinking," what exactly does he mean? How is *thinking* defined in this context? How is it different from—or similar to—the "thought process" that he refers to earlier when he writes that "the computer fundamentally transforms the way we conjure up our sentences, the thought process that runs alongside the writing process"?

4. Johnson writes that during the first six years that he had a computer, "the idea of composing on . . . the machine seemed somehow inauthentic." What does *inauthentic* mean here? Consult a dictionary for its meaning. How does Johnson use the term here? What does this term suggest that a synonym such as *strange* or *awkward* might not? If writing with a computer was "inauthentic," what was "authentic" writing? Why do you think Johnson uses this term here? What does it suggest about his perspective on writing as a technology? What does it indicate about his assumptions about what writing is? As you answer these questions, consider some of the other terms Johnson uses in describing his writing with computers: "the mind naturally resists the dull glare of the screen," which he calls "unnatural"; as he became "comfortable" with the computer, the "artifice" was gone; and so on.

5. What are the main strategies that Johnson uses to make his case in this passage? Summarize what you see as his main point and identify the ways in which he makes that point. What evidence does he provide for his assertions? How does he present that evidence? Do you find his argument convincing? Why or why not?

Engaging the Issues

1. For an audience of your classmates, write a brief description of your own writing process, discussing the technologies you use for writing. If you have changed from one technology to another (say, from pen and paper to word processor) as Johnson has, be sure to describe that change, how it came about, and how it seems to have affected your writing, if at all. In your passage, try to explain any changes you describe and refer specifically to the thinking you do when you write. When you're finished, compare your passage to Johnson's. Can you reach similar conclusions to Johnson's about the impact of technology on your writing? If not, how can you explain the differences?

2. If the description you wrote for the preceding question included discussion of the computer as a writing tool, rewrite your description for an audience of people who have never used a computer to write. When you're finished, compare the two descriptions: How did you use language differently? How did you change your discussion or alter your content in order to address each audience effectively?

3. After reflecting on Johnson's passage in light of the questions under Reflecting on the Reading above, write a response to Johnson based on your

own experiences with technologies for writing (such as the computer, type-writer, etc.). In your response, you should offer support for Johnson's argument about writing with computers or offer an alternative perspective. Draw on your own experiences as a writer—and those of other people you know, if possible—to help make your case.

4. Imagine that you have been asked to assess the implications of Johnson's passage for an audience of educators and parents of school-aged children. Write an essay to this audience in which you offer your analysis of Johnson's arguments and their implications for the education of children. What would you say to them about writing with computers and the impact of the new computer technologies on students' writing? What are the crucial points that Johnson makes that your audience should consider? How can you help them understand these issues? Write your essay as if it were to appear in a newsletter that will be sent to parents in the school district where you attended high school. Be sure to consider the specific background of your audience. For instance, if you came from a well-to-do suburban school district, your audience would likely have had different experiences with schools and technology than if you came from a rural or an urban school district.

5. If you have had the experience of writing with different technologies (for instance, pen and paper as opposed to word processor or typewriter), compare the experiences in the way that Johnson compares his writing with pen and paper to his writing with a computer. Describe what is different for you about writing with these different technologies, trying to be as specific as you can. Then discuss the implications of your experience for writers and especially for students who are learning to write. For instance, does your experience suggest that children should be taught to write with computers or with some other writing technology or a combination? Why?

6. In a group of your classmates, compare the essays you wrote for Question #1 above. What similarities and differences emerge? What impact does technology seem to have on how the members of your group write? What conclusions can you draw about writing as a process and about the influence of different technologies on how people write?

7. Based on your discussion for Question #5 above, write a letter to a designer or engineer at a company like IBM or Apple Computers (or a software company like Microsoft that makes word processing programs) with your ideas about the uses of computers as writing tools. In your letter, explain your concerns about computers as a technology for writing and offer suggestions for changes in how computers (or word processing software) are designed. Try to draw on your own experiences and those of others you know in explaining your concerns and suggestions. (You might also refer to Johnson's description of his writing with computers.)

8. Locate some other descriptions of how writers write. (These can sometimes be found in interviews with writers or on Web sites devoted to writing and writers.) Read several such descriptions and compare them with Johnson's description of his writing. What similarities and differences do you see in these descriptions? How might you account for these similarities and differences? Try to draw

conclusions about how writers write and how technology might influence their writing.

Why I Am Not Going to Buy a Computer

WENDELL BERRY

INTRODUCTION   We often tend to associate technology with progress so that whatever is new seems better, especially if it makes our work or lives easier. For many people, there are few better examples of such technological progress than the computer. Not for Wendell Berry.

Berry is a farmer and writer who has authored more than thirty books of essays, poems, short stories, and novels. He is the recipient of many awards for his writing and for his environmental advocacy. He has been called by one commentator "the unimpeachable Jeffersonian conscience of American public discourse";* a *New York Times* book reviewer called him "our foremost living literary exponent of the values of rural life and livelihood."** Those values inform Berry's attitudes about technology in general and about computers in particular.

In his writing, Berry focuses on the need for people to build a close relationship with the land, to construct life-styles that are not destructive to the environment and to themselves, and to work toward a sense of well-being and community. He is suspicious of technological progress, especially when that "progress" further estranges people from the land. In his collection of essays entitled *What Are People For?* (North Point Press, 1990), for example, Berry criticizes a variety of technologies—including television, chain saws, and computers—on the grounds that these technologies neither enhance our connection to the land nor make our work more fulfilling. You will hear the same theme echoed in the following selection, in which Berry explains in his characteristically blunt style why he will not use a computer to do his writing. His argument against using a computer is not narrowly practical but based on a wider philosophical view of one's relationship to the land. Following the essay itself, Berry responds to several people who criticized his essay after it was first published in the *New England Review and Bread Loaf Quarterly* and then reprinted in *Harper's* magazine. These letters and Berry's response to them extend the exploration of the issues of technology and progress—especially regarding literacy—that Berry begins in his essay. These are complex issues, but for Berry, the question of whether a computer is a good tool for writing cannot be separated from larger questions of life-style and environmental awareness.

---

* David Barber, *Poetry,* 1995. Quoted on Univ. of California, Santa Cruz, Library Web site: http://bob.ucsc.edu/library/exhibits/berry.html

** Charles E. Little, "No One Communes Anymore." *New York Times Book Review,* October 17, 1993.

REFLECTING BEFORE READING

1. For Wendell Berry, the decision to use a computer for his writing or to refuse it amounts to a moral choice. Do you think of technology in such overtly moral terms? Why or why not? As you read Berry's essay, consider whether his straightforward moral stance makes sense to you in these modern times.

2. Berry's writing has sometimes been described as provocative. As you read, pay attention to the tone Berry creates. Why do you think he creates such a tone? How might it serve his purposes in this essay? How do you think he wants his readers to respond to his tone?

L ike almost everybody else, I am hooked to the energy corporations which I do not admire. I hope to become less hooked to them. In my work, I try to be as little hooked to them as possible. As a farmer, I do almost all of my work with horses. As a writer, I work with a pencil or a pen and a piece of paper.

My wife types my work on a Royal standard typewriter bought new in 1956 and as good now as it was then. As she types, she sees things that are wrong and marks them with small checks in the margins. She is my best critic because she is the one most familiar with my habitual errors and weaknesses. She also understands, sometimes better than I do, what *ought* to be said. We have, I think, a literary cottage industry that works well and pleasantly. I do not see anything wrong with it.

A number of people, by now, have told me that I could greatly improve things by buying a computer. My answer is that I am not going to do it. I have several reasons, and they are good ones.

The first is the one I mentioned at the beginning. I would hate to think that my work as a writer could not be done without a direct dependence on strip-mined coal. How could I write conscientiously against the rape of nature if I were, in the act of writing, implicated in the rape? For the same reason, it matters to me that my writing is done in the daytime, without electric light.

I do not admire the computer manufacturers a great deal more than I admire the energy industries. I have seen their advertisements, attempting to seduce struggling or failing farmers into the belief that they can solve their problems by buying yet another piece of expensive equipment. I am familiar with their propaganda campaigns that have put computers into public schools in need of books. That computers are expected to become as common as TV sets in "the future" does not impress me or matter to me. I do not own a TV set. I do not see that computers are bringing us one step nearer to anything that does matter to me: peace, economic justice, ecological health, political honesty, family and community stability, good work.

What would a computer cost me? More money, for one thing, than I can afford, and more than I wish to pay to people whom I do not admire. But the cost would not be just monetary. It is well understood that technological innovation always requires the discarding of the "old model"—the "old model" in this case being not just our old Royal standard, but my wife, my critic, my closest reader, my fellow worker. Thus (and I think this is typical of present-day technological innovation), what would be superseded would be not only something, but somebody. In order to be technologically up-to-date as a writer, I would have to sacrifice an association that I am dependent upon and that I treasure.

My final and perhaps my best reason for not owning a computer is that I do not wish to fool myself. I disbelieve, and therefore strongly resent, the assertion that I or anybody else could write better or more easily with a computer than with a pencil. I do not see why I should not be as scientific about this as the next fellow: when somebody has used a computer to write work that is demonstrably better than Dante's, and when this better is demonstrably attributable to the use of a computer, then I will speak of computers with a more respectful tone of voice, though I still will not buy one.

To make myself as plain as I can, I should give my standards for technological innovation in my own work. They are as follows:

1. The new tool should be cheaper than the one it replaces.
2. It should be at least as small in scale as the one it replaces.
3. It should do work that is clearly and demonstrably better than the one it replaces.
4. It should use less energy than the one it replaces.
5. If possible, it should use some form of solar energy, such as that of the body.
6. It should be repairable by a person of ordinary intelligence, provided that he or she has the necessary tools.
7. It should be purchasable and repairable as near to home as possible.
8. It should come from a small, privately owned shop or store that will take it back for maintenance and repair.
9. It should not replace or disrupt anything good that already exists, and this includes family and community relationships.

1987

After the foregoing essay, first published in the *New England Review and Bread Loaf Quarterly,* was reprinted in *Harper's,* the *Harper's* editors published the following letters in response and permitted me a reply.

W.B.

Letters

Wendell Berry provides writers enslaved by the computer with a handy alternative: Wife—a low-tech energy-saving device. Drop a pile of handwritten notes on Wife and you get back a finished manuscript, edited while it was typed. What computer can do that? Wife meets all of Berry's uncompromising standards for technological innovation: she's cheap, repairable near home, and good for the family structure. Best of all, Wife is politically correct because she breaks a writer's "direct dependence on strip-mined coal."

History teaches us that Wife can also be used to beat rugs and wash clothes by hand, thus eliminating the need for the vacuum cleaner and washing machine, two more nasty machines that threaten the act of writing.

Gordon Inkeles
Miranda, Calif.

I have no quarrel with Berry because he prefers to write with pencil and paper; that is his choice. But he implies that I and others are somehow impure because we choose to write on a computer. I do not admire the energy corporations, either. Their shortcoming is not that they produce electricity but how they go about it. They are poorly managed because they are blind to long-term consequences. To solve this problem, wouldn't it make more sense to correct the precise error they are making rather than simply ignore their product? I would be happy to join Berry in a protest against strip mining, but I intend to keep plugging this computer into the wall with a clear conscience.

James Rhoads
Battle Creek, Mich.

I enjoyed reading Berry's declaration of intent never to buy a personal computer in the same way that I enjoy reading about the belief systems of unfamiliar tribal cultures. I tried to imagine a tool that would meet Berry's criteria for superiority to his old manual typewriter. The clear winner is the quill pen. It is cheaper, smaller, more energy-efficient, human-powered, easily repaired, and non-disruptive of existing relationships.

Berry also requires that this tool must be "clearly and demonstrably better" than the one it replaces. But surely we all recognize by now that "better" is in the mind of the beholder. To the quill pen aficionado, the benefits obtained from elegant calligraphy might well outweigh all others.

I have no particular desire to see Berry use a word processor; if he doesn't like computers, that's fine with me. However, I do object to his portrayal of this reluctance as a moral virtue. Many of us have found that computers can be an invaluable tool in the fight to protect our environment. In addition to helping me write, my personal computer gives me access to up-to-the-minute reports on the workings of the EPA and the nuclear industry. I participate in electronic bulletin boards on which environmental activists discuss strategy and warn each other about urgent legislative issues. Perhaps Berry feels that the Sierra Club should eschew modern printing technology, which is highly wasteful of energy, in favor of having its members hand-copy the club's magazines and other mailings each month?

Nathaniel S. Borenstein
Pittsburgh, Pa.

The value of a computer to a writer is that it is a tool not for generating ideas but for typing and editing words. It is cheaper than a secretary (or a wife!) and arguably more fuel-efficient. And it enables spouses who are not inclined to provide free labor more time to concentrate on *their* own work.

We should support alternatives both to coal-generated electricity and to IBM-style technocracy. But I am reluctant to entertain alternatives that presuppose the traditional subservence of one class to another. Let the PCs come and the wives and servants go seek more meaningful work.

Toby Koosman
Knoxville, Tenn.

Berry asks how he could write conscientiously against the rape of nature if in the act of writing on a computer he was implicated in the rape. I find it ironic that a writer who sees the underlying connectedness of things would allow his diatribe against computers to be published in a magazine that carries ads for the National Rural Electric Cooperative Association, Marlboro, Phillips Petroleum, McDonnell Douglas, and yes, even Smith-Corona. If Berry rests comfortably at night, he must be using sleeping pills.

Bradley C. Johnson
Grand Forks, N.D.

Wendell Berry Replies:

The foregoing letters surprised me with the intensity of the feelings they expressed. According to the writers' testimony, there is nothing wrong with their computers; they are utterly satisfied with them and all that they stand for. My correspondents are certain that I am wrong and that I am, moreover, on the losing side, a side already relegated to the dustbin of history. And yet they grow huffy and condescending over my tiny dissent. What are they so anxious about?

I can only conclude that I have scratched the skin of a technological fundamentalism that, like other fundamentalisms, wishes to monopolize a whole society and, therefore, cannot tolerate the smallest difference of opinion. At the slightest hint of a threat to their complacency, they repeat, like a chorus of toads, the notes sounded by their leaders in industry. The past was gloomy, drudgery-ridden, servile, meaningless, and slow. The present, thanks only to purchasable products, is meaningful, bright, lively, centralized, and fast. The future, thanks only to more purchasable products, is going to be even better. Thus consumers become salesmen, and the world is made safer for corporations.

I am also surprised by the meanness with which two of these writers refer to my wife. In order to imply that I am a tyrant, they suggest by both direct statement and innuendo that she is subservient, characterless, and stupid—a mere "device" easily forced to provide meaningless "free labor." I understand that it is impossible to make an adequate public defense of one's private life, and so I will only point out that there are a number of kinder possibilities that my critics have disdained to imagine: that my wife may do this work because she wants to and likes to; that she may find some use and some meaning in it; that she may not work for nothing. These gentlemen obviously think themselves feminists of the most correct and principled sort, and yet they do not hesitate to stereotype and insult, on the basis of one fact, a woman they do not know. They are audacious and irresponsible gossips.

In his letter, Bradley C. Johnson rushes past the possibility of sense in what I said in my essay by implying that I am or ought to be a fanatic. That I am a person of this century and am implicated in many practices that I regret is fully acknowledged at the beginning of my essay. I did not say that I proposed to end forthwith all my involvement in harmful technology, for I do not know how to do that. I said merely that I want to limit such involvement, and to a certain extent I do know how to do that. If some technology does damage to the world—as two of the above letters seem to agree that it does—then why is it not reasonable, and indeed moral, to try to limit one's use of that technology? *Of course,* I think that I am right to do this.

I would not think so, obviously, if I agreed with Nathaniel S. Borenstein that "'better' is in the mind of the beholder." But if he truly believes this, I do not see why he bothers with his personal computer's "up-to-the-minute reports on the workings of the EPA and the nuclear industry" or why he wishes to be warned about "urgent legislative issues." According to his system, the better in a bureaucratic, industrial, or legislative mind is as good as the "better" in his. His mind apparently is being subverted by an objective standard of some sort, and he had better look out.

Borenstein does not say what he does after his computer has drummed him awake. I assume from his letter that he must send donations to conservation organizations and letters to officials. Like James Rhoads, at any rate, he has a clear conscience. But this is what is wrong with the conservation movement. It has a clear conscience. The guilty are always other people, and the wrong is always somewhere else. That is why Borenstein finds his "electronic bulletin board" so handy. To the conservation movement, it is only production that causes environmental degradation; the consumption that supports the production is rarely acknowledged to be at fault. The ideal of the run-of-the-mill conservationist is to impose restraints upon production without limiting consumption or burdening the consciences of consumers.

But virtually all of our consumption now is extravagant, and virtually all of it consumes the world. It is not beside the point that most electrical power comes from strip-mined coal. The history of the exploitation of the Appalachian coal fields is long, and it is available to readers. I do not see how anyone can read it and plug in any appliance with a clear conscience. If Rhoads can do so, that does not mean that his conscience is clear; it means that his conscience is not working.

To the extent that we consume, in our present circumstances, we are guilty. To the extent that we guilty consumers are conservationists, we are absurd. But what can we do? Must we go on writing letters to politicians and donating to conservation organizations until the majority of our fellow citizens agree with us? Or can we do something directly to solve our share of the problem?

I am a conservationist. I believe wholeheartedly in putting pressure on the politicians and in maintaining the conservation organizations. But I wrote my little essay partly in distrust of centralization. I don't think that the government and the conservation organizations alone will ever make us a conserving society. Why do I need a centralized computer system to alert me to environmental crises? That I live every hour of every day in an environmental crisis I know from all my senses. Why then is not my first duty to reduce, so far as I can, my own consumption?

Finally, it seems to me that none of my correspondents recognizes the innovativeness of my essay. If the use of a computer is a new idea, then a newer idea is not to use one.

REFLECTING ON THE READING

1. Berry begins his brief essay by stating that he is "hooked to the energy corporations which I do not admire." What does he mean by this statement? In what

sense is he "hooked" to these corporations? What specific corporations do you think he might have in mind? And why does he not admire them?

2. Berry offers four main reasons why he will not buy a computer to do his writing. What are they? What connections do you see among these four main reasons? What do they suggest about Berry's values?

3. How does Berry characterize computer companies? Identify specific words or phrases that Berry uses to describe computer companies. How do these words and phrases compare to the words he uses in association with power companies?

4. What does Berry claim he will lose if he uses a computer for writing? Do you agree with him? What might your response to that question suggest about your own values regarding technology?

5. Berry ends his essay with a list of "standards for technological innovation." Only a tool that meets these standards, he suggests, will he use for his own work. What do the nine items in this list suggest about the kind of technology Berry might value and how it relates to his lifestyle? Can you think of other technologies that will meet Berry's standards?

6. In his response to the letters about his essay, Berry claims that the angry reaction on the part of the letter writers arose from their "technological fundamentalism." What does Berry mean by this phrase? What do you think he wishes to suggest about the letter writers and their attitudes about technology? Do you think he is right? Why or why not?

7. What new arguments to support his refusal to use computers does Berry offer in his response to the letters? How does Berry's response extend the arguments he makes in the original essay?

Examining Rhetorical Strategies

1. How would you describe the tone of this essay? Do you think Berry intends to provoke his readers in some way with his tone? Explain. What effect did his tone have on you as a reader? What might your reaction to his tone suggest about your own attitudes toward technology? Do you think Berry would be satisfied with the way his tone affected you as a reader? Why or why not?

2. Is Berry's tone in his response to the letters about his essay different from his tone in the original essay? If so, describe the differences. How can you account for these differences? Do you think these differences in tone are intentional on Berry's part? Why or why not? (Keep in mind that the original essay and Berry's response were published in different magazines for somewhat different reasons.)

3. At one point, Berry asserts that he will speak better of computers "when somebody has used a computer to write work that is demonstrably better than Dante's." Why do you think Berry invokes Dante here rather than another well-known writer? In what ways would his statement and what it implies be different if he had used a contemporary writer instead of Dante? What does this

reference to Dante tell you about Berry's attitudes about writing? What does it tell you about what he values in a piece of writing?

4. Berry ends the fifth paragraph of his essay with a list of things that he says matter to him: "peace, economic justice, ecological health, political honesty, family and community stability, good work." Do you as a reader oppose any of the things in this list—"peace" or "economic justice," for example? Do you think that Berry imagines that any of his readers, even those who use computers or manufacture them, genuinely believe that these things do *not* "matter"? What do you think this list is meant to suggest? How does it help Berry make his argument in favor of his position and against those who might choose to use a computer?

5. Compare the way Berry organizes his original essay to the way he organizes his response to the letters about his essay. How is the organization of each different? How can you account for these differences? Do you think they relate to Berry's purpose for each piece of writing? In what ways?

6. Do you find Berry's arguments for not using a computer convincing? Why or why not? What might your disagreement or agreement with Berry indicate about your own beliefs regarding technology and progress?

7. What, if anything, might be missing from Berry's arguments? Are *all* people in a position to refuse to use computers? Consider, for example, workers in places like fast-food restaurants, where just about every aspect of the operation is computerized. Can such workers refuse to use computers? What choices do they have, if they agree with Berry about computers? What might Berry say to them? How might Berry's arguments in his essay reflect his own circumstances as a rural resident and farmer and self-employed writer?

Engaging the Issues

1. Berry's essay was originally published in the *New England Review and Bread Loaf Quarterly* and was subsequently reprinted in *Harper's*. How might those publications have affected his writing?

    Using your library or the World Wide Web, learn what you can about these two publications; review copies of them, if possible. Then write an analysis of each magazine, considering its general focus, the subject matter it addresses, the writers whose work it publishes, the kind of audience it hopes to reach, and its "philosophy"—that is, its general view of the issues it focuses on. Offer specific examples from the magazines to support the conclusions you draw in your analysis.

    Now, given your analysis of these two publications, assess the effectiveness of Berry's argument for each publication. Do you find Berry's essay and response effective, given the audience he addresses in each? In your assessment, consider the reaction to Berry's original essay. For instance, do you think the readers of the *New England Review and Bread Loaf Quarterly* would have written letters similar to the letters written by the readers of *Harper's?* Do you think Berry might have written his piece differently if he had intended to publish it originally in

Harper's instead of the *New England Review and Bread Loaf Quarterly?* Also consider the tone and approach of Berry's response to the letters. How does his response "fit" *Harper's?* Draw conclusions about how well you think each piece—the essay and the response—"works."

2. For an audience of your classmates, write an essay about your use of technology in your own life. Like Berry, consider the fundamental reasons why you choose to use specific technologies—like a computer or perhaps a car—to do the work you need to do in your life. Offer your own justification for the choices you make.

3. Write an essay as described in Question #2 for a different audience (or rewrite the essay you wrote for Question #2). Choose an audience on the basis of a specific magazine or community (for example, residents of an urban neighborhood where you live or your coworkers at your workplace). Try to write your essay in a way that accounts for that audience's expectations and characteristics, as best you can determine from what you know of that audience. You need not write an essay that they will necessarily agree with; rather, write an essay that might make your argument most effectively with that particular audience.

4. Write a response to Berry's essay that might be published in a magazine like *Harper's.*

5. Write a letter to your school or town (or perhaps an organization you belong to or support) arguing for or against the use of computers or some other technology by that school or town (or organization). Address the specific needs of the school or town, and make your case in view of those needs. Try to convince that school or town why they should (or should not) use a specific technology in order to do their work.

6. Find a newsgroup or listserv that is devoted to the discussion of issues of technology and life-style. (You might search under "voluntary simplicity," a term that refers to a movement concerned with such matters.) Monitor the discussion on that newsgroup or listserv for a week or two to get a sense of how participants think about the kinds of issues Berry addresses in his essay. If appropriate, participate in the discussion yourself. Once you've followed the discussion for a week or two, write a report for your classmates about the experience. In your report, describe the newsgroup or listserv you monitored and the kinds of discussions you followed. Explain the ideas that participants shared and their views of issues concerning life-style and technology. Try to draw conclusions about these issues, based on your experiences with the newsgroup or listserv. In what ways might these experiences influence your reaction to Berry's arguments?

7. Write an essay in which you discuss Wendell Berry's arguments about writing with computers in light of Steven Johnson's experiences. How might Johnson's experiences validate, refute, or complicate Berry's arguments? What might Berry's stance on technology—and specifically on computers—mean for a writer like Johnson? What might they mean for other writers (perhaps including you) who rely on new technologies like computers?

The Writer a la Modem, Or, The Death of the Author on the Installment Plan

Julian Dibbell

INTRODUCTION   Does the technology a writer uses to write matter? According to writer Julian Dibbell, it matters a great deal. In fact, Dibbell believes that technology changes what a writer is. In other words, a *writer* in our mostly print culture may not necessarily be a *writer* in digital culture or cyberspace—and vice versa. For Dibbell, our ideas about writers are intimately related to the technology of print, in which writers' words are available to readers through published forms like books and magazines. But when we move into cyberspace—chat rooms and bulletin boards and MUDs—even though we're still using words, a writer becomes something new. The medium changes how a writer interacts with his or her audience and therefore redefines what a writer is. Technology, in short, is part of what makes a writer a writer.

Dibbell's ideas are not substantially different, in a sense, from the ideas of scholars like Jay David Bolter (whose essay appears elsewhere in this chapter) who believe that the new electronic technologies for writing and reading are profoundly changing how we read and write. But for Dibbell the matter is an intensely personal one, because he makes his living as a writer. As a result, the possibility that new computer technologies may be redefining what a writer does is more than an academic question for him. In the following essay, Dibbell describes his experiences as a newcomer to cyberspace and ponders the significance of his experiences for our understanding of writers and of each other. Although he does not believe that the Internet will necessarily eliminate writing as we know it, he does believe that the Internet is changing how we interact with each other through writing. On his Web site, he comments that the Internet is "a strange and challenging place for us to have wound up living in—and we forget that at the risk, I think, of our cultural soul." In exploring this idea in his writing, Dibbell encourages us to think about the role of technology in our social existence. And in the following essay he helps us examine how our understanding of writers and writing is intimately tied to the technologies we use for literacy. If those technologies change, then perhaps what literacy is changes as well.

Julian Dibbell is a free-lance writer who has written on technology and culture for the *Village Voice, Wired, Spin* magazine, *The New York Times*, and *Le Monde.* He has also been a contributing writer to *Time* magazine. In 1993 he published an article in the *Village Voice* called "A Rape in Cyberspace" that earned him the attention of critics and scholars interested in cyberculture. He eventually expanded that article into a book, titled *My Tiny Life: Crime and Passion in a Virtual World* (1999), about life in cyberspace. The following essay was originally published in the *Village Voice Literary Supplement* in 1993 and is available on Dibbell's Web site.

REFLECTING BEFORE READING

1. Dibbell's essay is concerned in large part with the idea of *writer*. As you prepare to read his essay, jot down your own thoughts about what you think a writer is. How would you define a writer? Where does such a definition come from? What makes a writer distinctive or different from others in our culture? Do you consider yourself a writer? Explain.

2. Dibbell's essay grew out of his experiences on the Internet, which led him to reconsider his understanding of what a writer is. If you have been on the Internet, consider how your own experiences there might have affected the way you think about writing, communication, and yourself. How might these experiences affect the way you read Dibbell's essay?

I became a writer the day I bought my first computer, and that, by no coincidence, was the last day I knew with any certainty what a writer was.

When I was four my father—nudging me toward a career he was well on his way to failing at—gave me a tot-sized typewriter for Christmas. From then on, I knew that to write was to claim a kind of patrimony, and in later years a host of cultural cues filled me in on the details of the inheritance. It was a title handed down from generation to generation of privileged latter-day artisans, a select few granted access to the costly medium of print by virtue of their ability to shape raw experience into language vivid enough or lucid enough to compel recognition by the inarticulate many. I wanted that title—wanted it with an increasingly anxious hunger the more conscious I grew of the possibility of failure—and spent much of my education preparing to receive it. I read hungrily, wrote dutifully, and by the time I left school had written volumes: poems, plays, stories, a ream or so of essays. I'd even been paid for a few of them.

But I knew what a writer was, and I didn't feel ready to call myself one. In retrospect, I suppose a little faith and a few more bylines was all I really needed to make the leap, but at the time, perhaps subconsciously reopening that primal Christmas present, I fixed on the means of production as the missing ingredient in my writerly self-image. I knew that the typewriter was ceding its role in textual manufacture to the personal computer, and that the computer demanded a far greater capital investment. But I was willing to make the sacrifice. Twelve hundred dollars for a piece of hardware might have seemed steep; but as the price of a professional identity it was peanuts. I forked the money over gladly, threw the machine in the back of a cab, and came home knowing, at last, that I was a writer.

What I didn't know was that the same invention that had just confirmed my entry into the writing class had also created a world in which the social and technological structures constituting that class were melting into air. It was a world in which modern definitions of the writer—of authorship, of publication, of intellectual property—were coming into question on a daily and practical basis; a world that continues to grow and to pose its questions while most writers remain only dimly aware of its existence; a world I stumbled into more or less by accident.

The accident was a modem, a $75 add-on that enabled my computer to pass data to and from other computers through a telephone line. I bought it for professional reasons—to file articles electronically with the newspapers and magazines I was starting to write for—and didn't imagine I'd find any other uses for it. But soon enough those other uses found me: word of modem-accessible message-bases known as bulletin boards reached my attention and piqued my curiosity. I dialed a Long Island number supplied by a friend, connected with a PC sitting in some hobbyist's basement, and saw on my screen a sight now transparently familiar but then tantalizingly new: a menu listing pages and pages of messages, posted by dozens of callers and grouped under topic headings ranging from the general (chat, politics) to the obsessively specific (bowling, Metallica) in a haphazard catalogue of contemporary human enthusiasms.

I plunged in, and as I moved aimlessly through the texts I felt my curiosity grow. I gradually realized that the messages themselves weren't what drew me in so much as the thrilling and unsettling novelty of their medium: this was public-access publishing, writings printed and disseminated with a single phone call. In tones pitched somewhere between the breezy intimacy of conversation and the measured advocacy of essays, people were writing publicly about their lives and about their cultures and about whatever else writers spin their products from—yet none of these people were writers as I had come to understand the term. Inside the social sphere of the bulletin board it was impossible to define a privileged class of writers, simply because everyone within that sphere was a writer by definition.

In the following months my fascination with this strange state of affairs led me from one bulletin board to another and showed no signs of flagging. In time, though, it came to mingle with a nagging frustration: my own attempts at participating in this new form of writership seemed to be missing the mark. Trained to write in competition for scarce access to publication, I couldn't help posting messages of futilely aggressive craft, messages that strove to rise above the surrounding dialogue, yet invariably failed to win the recognition I had to admit I was looking for. Suspecting I just hadn't found the right audience yet, I began to explore more sophisticated variations on the humble basement bulletin-board theme. But even in upscale electronic salons like the San Francisco-based WELL and New York's ECHO, where semifamously print-published writers could be found mixing with an emergent digital bohemia, I discovered that no amount of craft could generate the privileging aura that a writer enjoys in print. The problem was not in the audience after all, but in the medium. When finally I gained access to the mother of all bulletin boards—the "newsgroups" circulating like a global storm system of text through the thousands of computer networks linked together in the vast and rapidly expanding Usenet—it hardly surprised me that, even faced with a readership of millions spread through dozens of countries, my writerly instincts were no more appropriate than they had been on my local hobbyist's basement board.

It could be argued, of course, that my failure to get the hang of things arose not because of my professional background but because I had misconceptualized the very nature of online communication. After all, it does approach ludicrous understatement to think of the massively complex webwork of computers my modem had led me into as a glorified publishing industry—which is one reason it's become fashionable to speak instead of "cyberspace," a notion whose cosmic sweep in some ways better describes this new technology. The term migrated out of William Gibson's "Neuromancer," where it names a 21st century virtual dimension, entered into via a neuroelectronic interface, in which the world's data networks unfold before the user as a sensually vivid geography. Though Gibson himself knew squat about computers when he wrote the book, the aptness of his vision to existing networks is immediately apparent to anyone logging on for the first time—one senses, in the imaginary conversational present embodied by the bulletin board's array of messages, and in the computer's ease of mobility through remote chambers of information, that one has stepped into an alternate spacetime.

I sensed it, anyway, and recognized the pale incompleteness of traditional writing as a model for what happens online. Yet I sensed as well that Gibson in his fertile ignorance had gotten the picture only half right. Cyberspace is a place all right, but it is an insistently textual one—insistently and in fact traditionally, for cyberspace's grand illusion of alternate dimensionality represents not a departure from the nature of writing but a refinement of it. Writing, since its invention, has been a technology of virtual presence, simulating the here-and-nowness of both the writing subject and of whatever conceptual or sensual objects that subject cares to conjure. The technology of cyberspace may dazzle with its newness, but it really only extends the capabilities of an artificial-reality machine older than the Pyramids.

And if it extends the capabilities of that machine, it extends the perversities as well. For just as old as writing's power to fake presence is its tendency—the meal ticket of contemporary literary theory—to shatter the illusion in the act of creating it, to smear the transparency of communication with the opacity of its own mediating devices; and cyberspace bristles with instances of this tendency. Some are ornamental or playful, like the way the materiality of the signifier leaps forward in the skewed, subculturally assertive typography of young software pirates, who call themselves warez d00dz and wreak havoc on language and copyright laws from the safety of their "k-k00l uLtRa-eLyTe s00pEr SeKrEt" bulletin boards. Others are more pervasive and disturbing, like the constant threat of "flame wars"—arguments that rage out of hand when the powerful rhetorical weaponry afforded by the written word warps minor disagreements into escalating full-frontal assaults.

But nowhere does the textuality of cyberspace assert itself more forcefully than among the most ambitious online experiments in creating full-fledged virtual environments. Known as MUDs—short for multi-user dimensions—these online hang-outs recast the bulletin board as live theater, drawing on the venerable hacker tradition of computerized Dungeons & Dragons gaming: callers interact with one another in real-time through self-made personae, exploring together the nooks and crannies of textually constructed caverns, mansions, back alleys, forests. There's a lysergic lucidity to these spaces, a heightening of the illusion of presence to within a hair's breadth of the fully realized "consensual hallucination" that defines true cyberspace—and yet the stuff they're made of is the purest literary convention. Simple he-says-she-says dialogue cues organize the communication, environmentally evocative descriptions set the scenes, and the whole experience moves forward line by line in a balanced alternation between the two modes, just like any work of fiction.

Thus it's done me little good to recognize cyberspace as the proper metaphor for online communication, for rather than proving the irrelevance of my writerly anxieties to this strange new realm of interaction, cyberspace proves at every turn to be just another name for writing itself. Nor does it mean much to point out that the increasing capabilities of computer networks will sooner or later bring other media like sound and video encroaching on the present hegemony of text. Even if these other channels succeed in banishing text from the online universe (which seems unlikely given the unique fitness of the written word to vast realms of interpersonal communication), their digital form will endow them with writing's most significant properties as a medium: its ease of manipulation, of reproduction, and of dissemination. Thus, inevitably, the modemed world—a world you and I will be living in more and more as its current exponential growth pushes it well into the cultural mainstream—will remain in its fundamental logic a written one.

What will change just as inevitably, however, is the network of social relations that writing both defines and is defined by, and my own encounter with the online economy of textual production tells me this change will be as sweeping as what followed in the wake of Gutenberg's invention. I have seen the writing on the bulletin board, and it promises an irreversible diffusion of authorship throughout the social body, a blurring past all recognition of the line between reader and writer. The structure of written work grows more diffuse as well—the intense coherence of heroic individual efforts gives way to the drifting dialogue of message bases and the trippy collaborative fictions of MUDs. And good luck trying to cull any regulating canon from this woozy corpus. You'll find no center in the haze of ephemerae; even if you do, it will not hold.

That this set of changes conforms more or less precisely to the implicit prescriptions of the last two decades' most sophisticated and subversive literary theories will, in the eyes of many, be sufficient cause to celebrate it. But my own reasons are more personal. I am happy to have earned the title of writer; it will continue to provide my living and feed my sense of identity. But I don't think I will ever lose the fear that has partially motivated every public word I've written—the terror of exclusion, of the silence to which the traditional writer's audience is by definition consigned. And it gives me no small satisfaction to think that the system of centralized, limited-access publishing that instilled that fear in me will be dwarfed into irrelevance by a wide-open system that, via Usenet alone, already publishes the equivalent of 1,000 books a day.

My inability to find a voice appropriate to this system is of some concern to me, but I'm not sweating it. I imagine de Tocqueville felt the same way in his travels through young America—formed in an old regime, sympathetic to the new, confident he was seeing a better future but unsure of his place in it. And then I imagine too that my uncertainty itself may be enough to guarantee my place in a future where no one knows with any certainty what a writer is—only that everybody is one.

REFLECTING ON THE READING

1. Dibbell begins this essay by stating that he became a writer when he bought his first computer. What does he mean by "writer" here? Does his idea of a writer change in the course of this essay? If so, in what way? Is Dibbell's understanding of *writer* the same as yours? Explain. Why does Dibbell state that after buying his computer, he no longer was sure what a writer is?

2. Why did Dibbell believe he needed to purchase a computer in order to call himself a "writer"? Do you think he was right? Explain.

3. How did Dibbell's purchase of a computer change his understanding of what a writer is? What experiences did he have that challenged his previous understanding of *writer?* What might this change in Dibbell's understanding suggest about the relationship between writing and technology?

4. What did Dibbell find so compelling about the messages he read on the online bulletin boards? Why was the experience so unsettling for him? Why did he have such difficulty participating in these online conversations?

5. What does Dibbell mean when he writes that cyberspace is not a "departure from the nature of writing but a refinement of it"? Do you agree with him? Why or why not?

6. Dibbell asserts in this essay that cyberspace will not change writing, as some critics believe. But what does he think will change as a result of the increasing use of cyberspace? And why does he think such a change will be important? Do you agree? Why or why not?

7. What is the fear that Dibbell says motivates him as a writer? Why is that fear associated with print, rather than computer, technology, according to Dibbell?

Examining Rhetorical Strategies

1. What does Dibbell's conception of *writer* suggest about his background? Where does his idea of a writer come from? In what ways does it reflect his cultural values and his socioeconomic status? Do you think Dibbell's understanding of *writer* is common? Are you a writer by this definition? Explain.

2. This essay was first published in the *Village Voice Literary Supplement*, a respected publication whose audience is educated and professional. What features of this essay do you think might indicate its appropriateness for such an audience? Cite specific passages from the text in your answer. Ironically, Dibbell subsequently published this essay on his Web site. Do you think he should have changed anything in his essay for the broader and somewhat more diverse readers who might access it on the World Wide Web? Explain.

3. Given that Dibbell's original audience for this essay was the mostly educated, professional readers of the *Village Voice Literary Supplement,* do you think his essay would be appropriate for a very different audience—for instance, working-

class readers who did not attend college, or readers from very low-income backgrounds? Do you think Dibbell's discussion of how computer technology affects the idea of *writer* would be effective for such readers? Why or why not? How do you think readers from such backgrounds might react to Dibbell's essay? How did you react to it? What might your reaction say about you as a reader? Cite specific passages from the essay in your answer.

4. Assess Dibbell's voice in this essay. How would you describe his voice? Do you think it gives him credibility as the writer of the essay? Explain. How did you react to his voice? Did you find it effective or compelling? Why or why not?

5. Dibbell draws mostly on his own experiences as a writer and as a user of the Internet to support his comments about computers and writers. Do you find his discussion convincing? Do you think he offers adequate support for his conclusions about what will happen to writing as computer technology develops? Explain. What might your answer to these questions reveal about your expectations as a reader?

Engaging the Issues

1. Dibbell describes some of his experiences with Internet bulletin boards in this essay. If you have participated in online conversations in newsgroups, chat rooms, or listservs, write an essay in which you describe those experiences and how they might have affected you. Compare your reaction to those experiences to Dibbell's reaction. In your essay, try to draw conclusions about the effects of such technologies on how you understand such things as writing and communicating.

2. Visit several Internet newsgroups or chat rooms devoted to topics that interest you, and participate in online conversations for a week or two. As you do, make notes about your experiences: What struck you as interesting, surprising, or disturbing? What did you learn about such groups? What did you learn about others who participate in online conversations in such groups? What did you learn about yourself? For an audience of your classmates, write a report about your online experiences. In your essay, describe the newsgroups you visited and conversations you participated in; discuss some of the things you observed or learned. Try to draw conclusions about what occurs on these online groups and how it might be affecting the way people communicate with each other. (You might refer to the way Dibbell analyzes his own Internet experiences and the conclusions he draws from them.)

3. In a group of your classmates, share the reports you wrote for Question #2. Discuss similarities and differences in your respective experiences with online conversations. Try to account for those similarities and differences. Draw conclusions about online discussions and their role in our society.

4. Rewrite the report you wrote for Question #2 above as an essay for the editorial page of your local newspaper, focusing on what you learned about Internet

conversations and their importance in our society. In your editorial, discuss what you see as the advantages and potential problems of online activities such as those you have experienced, and examine their implications for our society.

5. Drawing on Dibbell's essay (and on any other essays in this reader that you think might be useful), write an academic essay for an audience of your class-mates in which you discuss the idea of *writer* and how that idea might be affected by technology. In your essay, try to analyze how you think we tend to understand what a writer is, and discuss the relationship of that idea to the technologies of writing. For example, is Dibbell right to suggest that people writing to one another on the Internet are not writers in the traditional sense? Why? What makes a writer? What is the role of technology in our understanding of *writer?* Try to draw conclusions about the way writers are understood in our society.

Alternatively, write an essay responding to Dibbell in which you take issue with his conclusions about writers and technology.

Pencils

GALE LAWRENCE

INTRODUCTION   Gale Lawrence is a naturalist and English teacher from Vermont whose books include *The Beginning Naturalist* (1980) and *A Field Guide to the Familiar* (1998). In his writing, he focuses attention on our every-day environment in an effort to expand our understanding of and appreciation for things that seem mundane. The brief essay on pencils included here illus-trates Lawrence's approach to writing about things familiar. In his essay, Lawrence muses about the physical nature and the history of this most common of writing implements. His curiosity about familiar objects and his attention to almost unnoticeable physical details lead to an unusual examina-tion of an object that most of us routinely use but never think about. He takes us into a surprisingly complex and rich history of the development of the pencil and suggests that there is much more to pencils than we might think. But this essay is also about the act of writing. Lawrence invites us to observe his own musings as he tries to foster what he calls "the right attitude" for writing, an attitude he incongruously associates with pencils.

This brief essay appeared in *The Minutes of the Lead Pencil Club*, a collec-tion of essays and other writings by a group of people who are suspicious of and even openly hostile to computer technology. (The essay by Wendell Berry that appears earlier in this chapter was also reprinted from *The Minutes of the Lead Pencil Club*.) Lawrence does not discuss computers directly in this essay, but his discussion of the pencil suggests an attitude about technology in general (and about writing) that may prompt us to raise questions about computers and about how we understand and use technology in our daily lives.

REFLECTING BEFORE READING

1. Do you use a pencil when you write? If so, do you *always* use a pencil, or do you use one for some writing tasks and not for others? Why? How does a pencil compare to other writing tools you might use? Do you write differently when using a pencil? How does it affect your writing, if at all? Consider what your answers to these questions might suggest about the role of different writing technologies—especially the pencil—in your life.

2. Lawrence's musings about the pencil arise from a broader perspective on the role of technology in our lives. As you read, pay attention to how Lawrence discusses technology and life-style and try to determine the values regarding each that he brings to his writing. What does he value about technology? About literacy? How does he measure the value of each?

I sharpened a lot of pencils while I was working on a recent book. A freshly sharpened pencil gave me the right attitude toward revising, and the act of sharpening offered me convenient breaks from my labor. I found myself not only sharpening my pencils but examining their lead, rubbing dirty smudges of it between my fingertips, and even looking at the different marks different pencils made through my hand lens. At one point I dropped the chapter I was revising and addressed my full attention to lead.

The first thing I learned is that pencil "lead" is not really lead. It is called "lead" only because until 1779 everyone thought it was merely a darker form of the familiar metal. In that year a Swedish chemist named Karl Wilhelm Scheele proved that the substance called pencil lead was actually a form of carbon. Eventually it was given a new name—graphite, from the Greek word *graphein,* meaning "to write."

Although graphite is technically a mineral, defined as an inorganic substance, it—like oil—was once living. It is derived from plant matter that has been metamorphosed by heat and pressure into almost pure carbon. It's related to both coal and diamonds, coal having been subjected to less heat and pressure, diamonds to more.

In graphite, the carbon atoms are arranged in layers, the atoms right beside each other closely linked but those above and below only loosely linked. This internal structure makes graphite tend to slip apart in thin, easily broken sheets. When you rub it, it will cover your fingers with dark little pieces of itself, which at the tip of a nicely sharpened pencil would form a dark line on a piece of paper.

Human beings had devised lots of implements to draw and write with before they discovered graphite. They used chalk, bits of burned wood, brushes made from plants or animal fur, reeds, and quills. The Egyptians, Greeks, and Romans used pieces of the metal lead to draw lines, and during the 1300s artists used thin rods of lead for artwork. But it wasn't until 1564, when a deposit of almost pure graphite, called *plumbago,* or "that which acts like lead," was unearthed in England, that pencils as we know them became a possibility.

At first people just used chunks of this pure graphite, but that got their fingers dirty. So someone decided to wrap twine around long, narrow pieces of graphite to create a primitive pencil. Next came the idea of encasing the graphite in wood, and the pencil began to take on its modern form. But these early pencils were still clumsy, messy tools that produced thick, dark, easily smeared lines. Finally, in 1795, a French inventor named Nicholas Jacques Conte, who was commissioned by Napoleon to come up with a French version of the pencil, thought of mixing moist clay with powdered graphite and baking this mixture into pencil leads. He discovered that he could create leads that would write lighter, thinner lines by adding more clay and darker, thicker lines by adding less clay.

If you'd like to explore some of the effects that are now possible with the varying proportions of clay offered by modern pencil manufacturers, buy yourself several pencils with different numbers on them. The standard number 2 is a mixture of about two-thirds graphite and one-third clay. If you like darker, broader lines, you can use a number 1, which includes less clay. For lighter, finer lines, try a number 3 or 4, which include more clay. You may also notice numbers $2^1/_2$, $2^5/_{10}$, and 2.5, all of which offer the same grade of lead. The numbers are different because when the Eagle Pencil Company came out with a number $2^1/_2$, the numerals became part of their trademark. Other pencil companies that wanted to produce the same intermediate grade of pencil, which consumers seemed to like, were prevented by law from calling their pencils $2^1/_2$, so they used $2^5/_{10}$ and 2.5 instead.

If you want to experiment with the extremes that are available today, buy some art and mechanical drawing pencils. Art pencils rated 4B or higher produce lines darker than the number 1 writing pencil. A 6B makes soft, bold lines that looked like black crayon through my hand lens. For the other extreme, look for mechanical drawing or drafting pencils rated 4H and higher. A 6H makes exceedingly fine lines that look like spider silk next to the strokes of the 6B.

Interestingly enough, none other than Henry David Thoreau was one of the early innovators who helped to develop the kinds of pencils that are now available in this country. His father was a pencil maker, and Thoreau went to work for him when he graduated from Harvard. Because young Thoreau was dissatisfied with the family pencil, he studied European pencil-making techniques to learn how other countries made their superior products. He discovered that the Germans were adding a very special clay from just one mine in Bavaria, found a supply of this clay, and added it to his family's formula. Then he decided that the graphite should be ground finer, and all the grinding that ensued, one scholar suggests, may have exacerbated the tuberculosis that killed both Thoreau and one of his sisters at an early age.

When I'm struggling with something as frustrating as revising what I've written, I'm easily distracted. Most of my distractions make me feel guilty, but my study of pencils—especially when I learned that Thoreau, too, had taken a serious interest in them—seemed legitimate respite. After all, if I'm going to continue to write, I need lots of pencils, and sharpening all those new pencils I bought gave me an excellent attitude toward getting back to work.

REFLECTING ON THE READING

1. What is the occasion that Lawrence claims gave rise to his exploration of pencils?

2. What does Lawrence mean when he describes graphite, the substance that we often call "lead" in a pencil, as "once living"?

3. What qualities of graphite does Lawrence tell us were most valued by those who developed pencils in the past? Why were these qualities important? How do they compare to the qualities that seem to be valued in pencils today? What might these differences suggest about technology and its role in a society?

4. What is Henry David Thoreau's importance in the history of pencils?

5. Why does Lawrence describe his distraction involving pencils as a "legitimate respite"? What does he mean by that phrase?

Examining Rhetorical Strategies

1. Lawrence informs us that graphite, the substance we commonly call "lead" in pencils, is an "organic substance" that was once "living." Why do you think he makes this point? Why did he define "organic" as "once living"? What purpose does that information—and his particular phrasing—serve in this context? What might this choice of language tell you about what Lawrence values?

2. What purpose do you think is served by the detailed information Lawrence provides about the nature of graphite and the various blends of graphite that are used in pencils? What was your reaction to this information? Do you think you reacted as Lawrence might have hoped? Why or why not?

3. Why does Lawrence invoke Henry David Thoreau in this brief essay? What does his reference to Thoreau suggest about Lawrence's values? What does it suggest about his assumptions about his audience? How did you react to the information about Thoreau? What does your reaction indicate about you as a reader? Do you think you are the kind of reader Lawrence hoped to address in this essay? Explain.

4. This essay appeared in a book that is described on its cover as a manual for "how and why to live contraption-free in a computer-crazed world." But the essay says nothing explicitly about computers. Why do you think that's the case? Further, what does the essay *imply* about computers? That is, what does this essay tell you about how Lawrence probably feels about computers? Does knowing that the essay appeared in a book that is critical of computers affect how you understand the essay? Do you think you would read the essay differently if it appeared elsewhere, say, as a separate essay on the editorial page of a newspaper? In what ways? Be specific.

5. What does Lawrence imply in this essay about the nature of writing as a process? Is his process of writing, as he implicitly describes it in this essay, similar to yours? Explain. What might his discussion suggest about the relationship between one's writing and the technologies a person uses to write?

Engaging the Issues

1. Choose some common technology that you use regularly (for example, the ink pen, the telephone, the fork) and write a brief essay about it in which you, like Lawrence, provide some background and/or historical information about that technology. Imagine a general audience for your essay—that is, an audience likely to read the essay if it appeared in a newspaper or general interest magazine. Have some idea of what you hope your essay might "say" about technology to this audience. In other words, your essay should have a larger point to make to your readers about technology and its uses in our lives.

2. Write (or rewrite) an essay as described in Question #1 above for a more specific audience. For example, imagine an audience who might have a specific and important relationship with the technology you are writing about (such as an audience of businesspeople who use cell phones for their work). After you've finished the essay, consider the ways in which your sense of your audience might have influenced your tone, choice of content, and language in your essay.

3. Write (or rewrite) the essay described in Question #1 above as a research report about the technology you have selected. In other words, consider the primary purpose of your essay not to make a point about technology but to inform readers about the construction and history of a technology.

4. Write an alternative version of Lawrence's essay about pencils that takes a more critical view of pencils as a technology. For example, consider some of the environmental implications of the graphite, clay, and wood that are used in pencils. Consider ways in which pencils may actually work against the values that Lawrence seems to hold about technology. Imagine an audience of readers who are sympathetic to technology and progress. (You may wish to consult some sources about the history of pencils for this exercise.)

5. Write an analysis of Lawrence's essay on the basis of the ideas of Jay David Bolter (whose essay appears elsewhere in this chapter). How do you think Bolter would react to Lawrence's views about the pencil and about writing? What beliefs about writing and writing technology does Lawrence convey in his essay? How might Bolter's ideas help us understand or question those beliefs?

6. Periodically, public advocacy groups will call for a daylong or weeklong moratorium on using a common technology. For example, every year several such groups call for families to go without television for a week. If you have ever had the experience of doing without a common technology on which you normally depend, describe that experience in an essay. Explain why you went without that technology and what the experience was like. Then try to identify implications of the experience for our society and its uses of technology. Try to avoid settling for easy conclusions, such as feeling closer to other people without the television to occupy your attention. Instead, try to look critically at what was really beneficial or problematic about the experience and what it might tell you about what you—and we—value in our lives.

   Alternatively, imagine living in a community that does not have access to a common communications or literacy technology that you use in your life (such as the telephone, computer, or television), and write a description of a typical day you might spend without that technology. How would your day be different from the way you live now? What would be the implications of eliminating that technology from your daily life? What might be the benefits or disadvantages of doing without such a technology?

Odyssey

MARCIA ASCHER AND ROBERT ASCHER

INTRODUCTION Scholars have long debated the question of how to define literacy: What kind of communication or record keeping system can legitimately be classified as *writing?* This is a much more complicated question than it might at first seem, for there are many different systems for communicating visually, only one of which is the alphabet that is so familiar to people in Western cultures. Among these systems are the Chinese system of writing, which is "logogrammatic"—that is, one symbol represents an entire word or phrase, as compared to the Western alphabet in which one symbol (a letter) represents a distinct speech sound. A well-known example of an earlier logogrammatic system is the ancient Egyptian hieroglyphic system. Such systems of written communication differ in obvious ways from the alphabetic literacy that characterizes Western cultures, but many linguists and other scholars nevertheless categorize them as *writing.* More difficult to categorize are systems in which a symbol or picture might represent an event or what would amount to several sentences or even paragraphs in an alphabetic system. For example, the pictographs and petroglyphs (often referred to as "cave paintings") common to many Native American cultures are often classified as *art,* even though most scholars agree that they were used for communicating or recording events. The Lakota people, for instance, sometimes depicted important events such as a special buffalo hunt, the death of a leader, or a significant battle in pictographs painted onto elk or buffalo hides. These hides were then carried by members of a band or tribe and presented to others as a way of recounting the event. Can such hides be classified as *writing?*

Perhaps the most intriguing example of such a communication system is the ancient Inca *quipu.* A quipu is a set of knotted and twisted cotton or wool strings or cords arrayed in a complex pattern that conveys information. The information in a quipu is "contained" in the size, color, texture, and placement of the strings and knots. Because quipus do not represent ideas in symbols and because they do not refer directly to words or sounds, most linguists do not categorize them as writing but describe them as similar to a kind of mathematical or scientific notation. However, some scholars argue that the complexity and effectiveness of quipus as a means of recording and communicating knowledge qualify them as writing, albeit writing of a very different kind than the alphabetic literacy with which we are so familiar. But however we classify the quipu, it is a fascinating example of a technology for communication that can encourage us to reconsider our notions about what writing is and how it functions in a society or a culture.

In the following passage from their book *Code of the Quipu* (1981), scholars Marcia Ascher and Robert Ascher provide historical and cultural background information to introduce us to the quipu and its role in the Inca culture in the sixteenth century. Their account is based on extensive scholarly research, but they acknowledge the difficulties of understanding a system of communication that has long since been abandoned and that no contemporary person knows how to use. They rely in large part on the writings of Spanish explorers and conquerors from that period who traveled through the South American lands inhabited by the Incas. For Ascher and Ascher, these writings offer modern researchers a window into the Inca culture that existed at the time; the Aschers draw especially on the writings of Pedro Cieza de León, a Spanish soldier who spent fifteen years among the Incas and who published an account of his journeys in South America. It is perhaps ironic that the alphabetic literacy of Cieza de León has become so important to modern researchers who are trying to understand the quipu, a nonalphabetic system of communication that was eliminated by the Spanish. The Aschers' account therefore offers us not only a glimpse of the unique communications technology of the quipu and its use in Incan society, but also suggests some ways in which literacies and technologies can be at the center of cultural and political conflict.

REFLECTING BEFORE READING

1. As noted above, scholars debate how to classify systems of communication and record keeping such as the quipu, and few of them tend to see the quipu as writing. What is your own conception of what counts as *writing*? Have you ever thought of writing as anything other than alphabetic literacy? As you read, pay attention to the references that the Aschers make to writing and to the quipu. Does their passage encourage you to reconsider your notions of what writing is?

2. The Aschers are scholars whose account of the quipu is based on extensive research from a variety of sources. But their account is unusual for this kind of academic research. As you read, pay attention to how they present their research on quipus in this passage. Do you find their writing to be *academic* as you understand that term? Why or why not? Consider your own expectations for *academic* writing. What are they? How are they fulfilled or not in the following passage?

One of the three brothers had a golden sling, and with it he could throw a stone up to the sky: it would almost touch the clouds.[1]

These are words from a story that the Incas told about their own origins. At first, it seemed a good way to start: what better way is there to begin to discuss the quipus of the Incas than by using an Inca story about their own beginnings. But right away we must pause; the story was spoken in Quechua, recorded in

---

[1] There are several versions of the Inca origin story. Parts of different versions appear in Harold Osborne, *South American Mythology*, (Feltham, Eng.: Hamlyn Publishing Group, 1968).

Spanish, and translated into American English. Once aware of this, we cannot go further until we answer the question, How do we know anything about the Incas?

The Spanish recorded the Inca origin story more than four and a half centuries ago. The Incas were a culture, a civilization, and a state. That is to say, the word Inca, as we use it, applies to particular forms of human association. The land that the Incas once occupied is today all of Peru and portions of Ecuador, Bolivia, Chile, and Argentina. When the Spanish arrived to conquer, the Inca state had existed for about one hundred years. Within thirty years—the number of years generally used to designate one human generation—Inca civilization was destroyed.

The Incas did not write as we usually understand that activity. For written accounts of Inca culture, we must turn to the sixteenth-century Spanish of soldiers, priests, and administrators. Yet, the culture of the Spaniards of that time is remote from our own. We do not share with them, for example, a real fear of the devil, even if we are part of the tradition that invented him. And the devil, together with many other cultural predispositions, figured largely in Spanish discussions of the Incas. To make matters worse, the Spanish got their information almost exclusively from deposed Inca bureaucrats. They were a special and numerically small part of a population estimated at somewhere between three and five million people. Whatever we may or may not have in common with sixteenth-century Spaniards, they shared close to nothing with the Incas. We can make sense out of Spanish accounts only on terms of our framework, and the Spanish, for their part, rendered what the Incas said from inside a Spanish framework. As a result, written accounts are distorted as they pass through this route: one culture (Inca) is interpreted via a second culture (Spanish), which is interpreted via a third culture (American), four hundred and fifty years later.

Luckily, there is a source of knowledge in addition to writing. Walking one day in the streets of Cuzco, once the capital of the Inca state, we saw an Inca wall, topped by a Spanish wall, on which was hung a Coca Cola sign. What we saw tells a great deal about the relationship between three cultures. But let us concentrate on the Inca wall. The Spanish could hear about the wall, and they could see it and touch it. We also can see it and touch it, but we cannot hear about it from the Incas. Nevertheless, the Inca wall, and other things that they made and that have survived, provide us with a direct way of knowing about the Incas.

Using material things as a source of knowledge does not, however, do away with distortion. Walls of some sort occur in every culture. This can lead us to think that wherever they occur they have the same meaning. They do not. Nevertheless, with due caution, it is reasonable to assume that walls, wherever they are found, serve a roughly similar purpose. But there is another more difficult problem in understanding material evidence. There are some things in one culture for which there are no counterparts elsewhere. When this happens, understanding becomes even more difficult for someone outside the culture. For example, native Australians had no counterpart of the airplane. It was at first difficult for them to understand that people flew through the air in metal containers. And the problem increases when an attempt is made to know about a culture that is remote in time as well as in space.

We wish to understand the quipus made by the Incas. But unlike walls, there were no counterparts of quipus in sixteenth-century Spanish culture and there are none in our own experience. A quipu is a collection of cords with knots tied in them. The cords were usually made of cotton, and they were often dyed one or more colors. When held in the hands, a quipu is unimpressive; surely, in our culture, it might be mistaken for a tangled old mop. For the Spanish, the Inca quipu was the equivalent of the Western airplane for native Australians. For us, the problem is compounded by a separation of four and a half centuries. Before rushing ahead to where touching, seeing, and thinking about quipus led us, a context for them must be provided. To do this, we call upon a Spanish witness.

Spanish writers shared a cultural framework, but there were very important individual differences. Today there is general agreement on which of the writers are relatively reliable. Cieza de León was perhaps the most reliable. He was a good observer and a careful listener, and he was the first person to write about quipus. Our knowledge of what the Spanish understood about quipus is increased only a little by going to other early writings, for Cieza understood more than his contemporaries, and many later writers simply copied from him.[2]

The writings of Cieza seized and held our attention from the start of our studies. There are minor reasons and one major reason for this. Cieza was in Inca territory only fifteen years after the conquest; this alone commends his work. He saw things that others who followed cannot have seen, and he spoke with people who were adults at the apogee of Inca power. In addition, Cieza is an able writer. His choice of vocabulary, his ability to put things concisely, his conscientious attempt to weigh evidence, and his respect for the intelligence of the reader, set him apart as much as does his being there before others.

But the major appeal of Cieza centers on what leads us to use the word odyssey to describe his work. At one level, an odyssey simply means a journey; that clearly applies to Cieza. In a broader sense, an odyssey is a quest or a search that may or

---

[2] The first part of the writings of Pedro Cieza de León was published in 1553, the second part in 1880, and the third part was published as late as 1946. The best English translation of the first two parts is by Harriet de Onís. It is in Victor Wolfgang von Hagen, ed., *The Incas of Pedro da Cieza de León* (Norman: University of Oklahoma Press, 1959). Our English citations from the works of Cieza derive largely from the Harriet de Onís translation, but Spanish versions have been consulted where there is a question of interpretation. There are two major sources on Cieza's life. They are: Marcos Jimenéz de la Espada, *Prologo de la Segunda Parte de la Cronica del Perú de Cieza de León,* vol. 5 (Madrid: Biblioteca Hispano-Ultramarina, 1880); and Miguel Maticorena Estrada, "Cieza de León en Sevilla y su Muerte en 1554," *Anuario de Estudios Americanos, 12* (1955): 615–73. In his editor's introduction to the Harriet de Onis translation, von Hagen provides a background of Cieza's times and a summary of his life. A study of the literary aspects of Cieza's writings is found in Pedro R. León, *Algunas Observaciones Sobre Pedro de Cieza de León y la Crónica del Peru* (Madrid: Biblioteca Románica Hispánica, 1973). This book also contains a rather complete bibliography on the work and life work of Cieza.

For English language readers who want to pursue what chroniclers other than Cieza had to say about quipus, the best place is the excerpts section at the back of Leland L. Locke, *The Ancient Quipu or Peruvian Knot Record* (New York: American Museum of Natural History, 1923). This section contains translations from about fifteen early Spanish sources. They vary in length from a few lines to several hundred lines of print. Some other sources have come to light since Locke wrote. See, for example, H. Trimborn, *Quellen zur Kulturgeschichte des Prâkolombischen Amerika* (Stuttgart: Strecker und Schroeder Verlag, 1936). John V. Murra, "An Aymara Kingdom in 1567," *Ethnohistory 15* (1968): 115–51, presents data that is said to have been originally recorded on a quipu; our discussion of this possible quipu is in "Numbers and Relations from Ancient Andean Quipus," *Archive for the History of Exact Sciences 8* (1972): 288–320.

may not involve travel through real space. It is important that the term odyssey in this second sense also applies to Cieza. In literature, the odyssey is often a self-conscious search for the self. Cieza's quest is different: he is not looking for himself, but rather for the substance of the victims of conquest. That Cieza thought of the Incas as victims is clear; as he says, "wherever the Spanish have passed, conquering and discovering, it is as though a fire had gone, destroying everything it passed." Although he was a party to conquest, the victor is of less interest to him than the vanquished.

In most odysseys, the route is selected by the traveler. Not in this case. Cieza was a common soldier, and as such he was more or less told when and where to move. The latter part of his journey interests us. It began in April, 1547, when he walked into the northern extreme of the area once ruled by the Incas. Cieza was then twenty-nine years old. He moved along good roads, ones which, he says, were superior to the Roman roads he knew as a boy in Spain. Day after day, however wearied, he paused and recorded some of the things he heard and saw. He stopped writing in September, 1550.

As we follow Cieza on his quest for the Incas, keep in mind that he lived over four centuries ago and that he describes something that was very different from what he knew. We convey the sense of his vision as we understand it. Even under the best circumstances, another culture is blurred as if seen through heavy gauze, Or, as Cieza put it, "Peru and the rest of the ladies are so many leagues from Spain and there are so seas between."

> And as the traveler trudges through all this sand, and glimpses the valley even though from afar, his heart rejoices especially if he is traveling on foot and the man is high and he is thirsty.

In the morning, Cieza set out from a place where he was soaking wet: by nightfall, he was in a region where it never rained. To do this, he traveled west and down from the mountains and then stopped when he reached the desert sands. In the late afternoon of another day he went south through the desert. Alternately, but still heading south, he stayed with mountains or the plains. The roads that he followed can be visualized as a ladder resting unevenly upon the ground. One side of the ladder runs through the mountains and is raised; the lower side goes through the desert at the edge of the Pacific Ocean. The crossbars of the ladder go down through the valleys connecting the mountains with the desert and the sea. At its greatest, a side of the ladder, as Cieza counted it, was 1,200 leagues (about 3,600 miles). The crossbars varied from as little as one hundred twenty miles to as long as three hundred miles of their rule.

> They observed the customs of their own people and dressed after the fashion of their own land, so that if there were a hundred thousand men, they could easily be recognized by the insignia they wore about their heads.

Cieza, the quester, was impressed by the diversity he found as he moved along the road. He noticed changes in animals, crops, weather, and landscape. Mostly, he was struck by the differences in groups of people. He might anticipate some of these: for example, people in rainy mountainous regions usually built houses of fieldstone; in the desert, clay bricks dried in the sun were used for the same purpose. There were also marked differences in customs, languages, myths, and sexual practices. Regarding the latter, Cieza often inquired about the diabolical sin of sodomy; he was very disturbed when he was told that it existed in one place or another. Beyond these observations, Cieza noted that people differed in the directness of their speech, their looks, and their attitudes. The quality was somehow different. For example, two groups living in the mountains might prefer wool for making clothing, but the bearing of the people, and hence the way their clothing fell about them, was not the same in both groups. Originally, the Incas were a group of people living in the mountains to the south. The ruling Inca family, the head of which we call Sapa Inca, started with three mythical brothers, whose thoughts, according to Cieza, soared high. The Incas differed from their neighbors just as their neighbors differed from others living close by. In our terms, the Incas were a culture, and each of the other groups were separate, more or less self-contained cultures.

> He sent messengers to these people with great gifts urging them not to fight him for he wanted only peace with honorable conditions and they would always find help in him as they had in his father and he wished to take nothing from them but to give them what he brought.

At almost every step along the way, Cieza noted the presence of one culture in the midst of all others. There was no puzzle in this. Going step by step, and increasing the pace in the three generations before Cieza, the Incas moved upon their neighbors. Doing this, they upset the solitude of the cultures in western South America. The Incas moved upon a group as if they were the bearers of important gifts. A deity bringing better times, or a method to make the land more fruitful, or food if the need for it existed, are examples of the gifts. If the gifts were accepted, there was no need for violence; if not, force was applied. In any case, the gifts were delivered, and thus, selected parts of Inca culture were everywhere superimposed. According to Cieza, the Incas did not want to destroy and replace the cultures already there. For example, an Inca deity was added to, not substituted for, the local gods. And locally important people continued to be important, even if they now had to take an interest in what the Incas wanted done.

> There were even provinces where, when the natives alleged that they were unable to pay their tribute, the Inca ordered that each inhabitant should be obliged to turn in every few months a larger quill full of live lice, which was the Incas way of teaching and accustoming them to pay tribute.

Cieza did not go far in any direction before he came upon compelling physical reminders of Inca rule. This took the form of a complex of buildings that were put up soon after the Incas took over. The components were mostly the same, regardless of region. There was a temple to the sun, storehouses, and lodgings. The buildings were now empty, their furnishings removed, and their elaborate decorations torn away. The bureaucratic officials, religious functionaries, and military personnel who peopled the buildings were gone, of course. When the buildings were in use, control had come from Cuzco, the principal Inca city, but it was hundreds of miles away, and particulars had to be administered locally. For example, tribute was fixed in Cuzco after an investigation to determine the form the tribute should take. The collection of tribute, however, was in the hands of local people. Another function of regional supervision was associated with the Inca policy of moving, en masse, thousands of people from one place to another. After the colonists arrived at their new place, it was the people in the Inca buildings who arranged the details of resettlement. Cieza thought that the tribute was levied fairly. He also thought well of the removal policy, pointing out that the colonists were often taught new trades.

> When the great dances were held the square of Cuzco was roped off with a cable of gold which he had ordered made of the stores of the metal which the regions paid as tribute, whose size I have already told, and on even greater display of statues and relics.

"I recall," writes Cieza, "that which I was in Cuzco last year, 1550, in the month of August, after they had harvested their crops, the Indians and their wives entered the city making a great noise, carrying their plows in their hands, and straw and corn, to hold a feast that was only singing and relating how in the past they used to celebrate festivals." In the past and during Cieza's visit, festivals were held in the central square of the city. Literally and figuratively, the four highways which partitioned the world of the Incas into four main divisions met at the center of the square. In the same square, the men who held leadership powers were confirmed in their authority amid theatrical displays of their inheritance rights. The remains of their ancestors were paraded about. The Incas founded Cuzco, resided in it, and ruled from it; yet, the people in the city included non-Incas. The crowd at festivals was made up of men from other cultures dressed in their traditional garb. They were there to keep up the connection between the Incas and the people whom they ruled. And they were there to learn the ways of the Incas. Cieza thought that Cuzco was a glorious place, with large buildings, wide streets, and lavish displays of wealth. It had, he says, "an air of nobility." He was just as certain that with so many different people in Cuzco, wizards, witches, and idolaters were plentiful, and the devil, having insinuated himself, held sway.

> Not a day went by that posts did not arrive, not one or a few but many, from Cuzco, the Colla, Chile, and all his kingdom.

The experienced traveler, and that Cieza was, is not gullible. He preferred to omit a story if it was not reinforced by the testimony of several people, or better yet, by his own observations. In the case of the communication system devised by the Incas for their own use, Cieza writes: "Nowhere in the world does one read that such an invention existed . . . "; so he was cautious. But he found corroboration for what he heard in the shape of small posthouses along the highways. The system was simple. A runner carried a message from the posthouse where he was stationed to the next posthouse up the road. As he approached, he called out for attention and then passed the message on; a new runner took the message the next few miles. This was repeated by successive runners until the message reached its destination. With a certainty unusual for him, Cieza says that the messenger system was superior to one dependent on horses and mules, animals he was familiar with. Only runners could negotiate the perilous mountain passes, suspension bridges, and rocky wastes overgrown with briars and thorns. Through this system, simple though it was, the Inca bureaucracy continuously monitored the areas under its control. The day of a Sapa Inca, according to Cieza, was taken up in large part with receiving messages and sending instructions. The Incas thought of something else to do about communication. They insisted that everyone learn Quechua, the Inca language, along with their native language. In time, many people could speak Quechua, and official business was carried on in that language.

> There have been occasions when I stopped beside one of the canals, and before I had time to pitch my tent, the ditch was dry and the water had been diverted elsewhere.

The lowly potato was first described in writing by Cieza. Potatoes are a basic food, akin to rice and wheat. For the benefit of his European readers, he explained that potatoes were like truffles, a food they knew. On his trip into the southern Andes, Cieza found that it was common practice to dry potatoes in the sun, put them away in that condition, and eat them the following year. In Cieza's time, the benefactors of this planning were often limited to the people who grew the potatoes. It was different under Inca rule. Recall that storehouses were part of the regional building complex. They held various items, including food. The Incas responded to a food shortage by taking food from a storehouse and sending it to where it was needed, regardless of who grew it. If food was in surplus, it was distributed to the poor and aged. The benefits of already existent planning schemes, such as stored, dried potatoes, were thus extended across ecological and cultural boundaries and reached those who were not party to the plan. The case of the dried potato can stand as a model for Inca planning and control. For example, the model fits the Inca solution to the water problem. As with dried potatoes, the problem was to move a resource from where it was abundant to where it was needed. The solution was irrigation and terracing. Irrigation, like the cultivation and storage of potatoes, predates the Inca expansion. The Incas redeveloped old systems and ordered the construction of new ones. In an agrarian society, nothing is as important as water, except perhaps the sun; and the Incas and the sun had a special relationship if the number of temples dedicated to that star is any guide. Cieza was struck by the beauty the irrigation systems brought: "All this irrigation," he says, "makes it a pleasure to cross the valleys, because it is as though one were walking amongst gardens and cool groves."

> And little boys, who if you saw them you would not think knew how to talk yet, understood how to do these things.

On the slope of a hill overlooking Cuzco, Cieza took the measure of an enormous stone and found that it was 270 hand spans in circumference. It was also very high. Quarry marks on the stone lent credence to the story that it was hauled up the hill to become part of a massive strong hold. The stone that Cieza measured had not reached the top of the hill, but others did, and were there to be seen, as they are today. Large numbers were needed to express the sizes of the stones, the years the project was underway, the dimensions of the overall structure, and the people needed to do the various jobs. Impressed as he was by the scale of Inca projects, Cieza did not neglect to write about the quality of the undertakings. In this instance, he dwelt on the craftsmanship of the masons who, with a few tools, cut and fit the stones so exactly that a coin could not be inserted between them. Skill in dealing with very large things also applied in the small. For example, Cieza wrote about goblets and candelabra made with the use of two or three stones and a few pieces of copper. He admired the cloth made by women using a simple loom. And he applied the term skill to undertakings other than making objects. In a show of statecraft, a Sapa Inca dressed himself in the native garb of each village he moved upon, and in this way, says Cieza, won the people over to his service.

In a word, it was once what no longer is, and by what it is, we can judge what it was.

If a word were chosen to condense the substance of the Incas as Cieza came toward an understanding of it, the word would have to be order. Cieza used the word in connection with almost everything, including the planting of crops, the behavior of armies, and the transfer of power. He went so far as to say that order saved the Incas from total destruction. He elaborated the point this way: when the Spanish went through a region their demands were met with goods from the Inca storehouses; those who paid out the most, and were therefore in trouble, were resupplied from the storehouses of the more fortunate. This response to Spanish plundering was possible, according to Cieza, because orderly records were kept of what goods had left which storehouses.

The records referred to by Cieza were on quipus. In earlier times, when the Incas moved in upon an area, a census was taken and the results were put on quipus. The output of gold mines, the composition of work forces, the amount and kinds of tribute, the contents of storehouses—down to the last sandal, says Cieza—were all recorded on quipus. At the time of the transfer of power from one Sapa Inca to the next, information stored on quipus was called upon to recount the accomplishments of the new leader's predecessors. Quipus probably predate the coming to power of the Incas. But under the Incas, they became a part of statecraft. Cieza, who attributed much to the action of kings, concluded his chapter on quipus this way: "Their orderly system in Peru is the work of the Lord-Incas who rule it and in every way brought it so high, as those of us here see from this and other greater things. With this, let us proceed."

His travels at an end, Cieza returned to Spain in 1551 at age thirty-three. A year later, the first part of his odyssey was in the hands of a printer. Another year went by, and after approval by the Holy Order of the Inquisition, the King's Council, and the Council of the Indies, it was finally issued in 500 copies. The next year, 1554, Cieza was dead.

From his last will and testament, we know that at the time of his death, Cieza had in his possession about half of the copies of the first printing of his book. In the portion of the will devoted to the saying of masses, he requests hundreds of them for himself, his family, and others. Included in the list of others are eight masses to be ~id for an Indian woman called Ana, and another ten for "... the souls of Indian ￼ and women in purgatory who came from the lands and places where I travelled ￼e Indies."

1. Why do the Aschers present the Inca story of their origin? Why is that story important to their goal of explaining the quipu? Where does the story come from? How was it recorded? How has it come down to modern readers? What might this information about the Inca origin story suggest about literacy?

2. In what ways was the Spanish culture of the sixteenth century different from our modern culture? Why are these differences important, according to the Aschers? What do these differences have to do with quipus?

3. Why do the Aschers rely on the writings of Cieza de León in providing an account of Inca life in the sixteenth century? What do we learn about Cieza in this passage? What, according to the Aschers, is special about him?

4. What are the key features of the way the Incas organized and ruled their society? In particular, how did the Incas typically communicate across long distances? What roles did language play in their rule? In what ways might these features of their society be important to our understanding of the quipu?

5. What was the primary use of the quipu in Inca society, according to the Aschers?

6. What did Cieza do with the copies of his book about his travels that he possessed at the time of his death? Why do you think this is an important fact in the story of the quipu?

Examining Rhetorical Strategies

1. From the very beginning of their account, the Aschers highlight the problem of reliability. In other words, they point out the difficulties of obtaining accurate and reliable information about Inca culture and about quipus. Why do you think they do so? What purpose is served by highlighting these difficulties? Do you think highlighting these difficulties calls into question the reliability of their own account? Why or why not? How did this strategy affect you as a reader? Did it make you more or less inclined to accept their account as reliable? Explain.

2. Notice the Aschers' reference to the Inca story of their origin, which is presented in the brief italicized passage at the beginning of the text. Why do you think the Aschers present the Inca origin story in this way? What purpose might they accomplish by doing so? How does the Inca story relate to their discussion of quipus? How does it relate to the story of Cieza de León? What might be lost if they did not set the story apart by italicizing it as they do? Did you find their use of the Inca origin story effective? Why or why not?

3. As noted in the introduction to this reading selection, the Aschers are scholars who base this account of the quipu on extensive academic research. Would you classify this passage as *academic* in its style and structure? Why or why not? Which features of the text would you describe as *academic?* What kinds of features that you typically associate with an academic text are missing from this passage? Why do you think the Aschers chose to write their account in this manner? Did you find the writing effective? Explain, citing specific passages from the text to support your answer.

4. In the preface to the book from which the above passage is taken, the Aschers explain that their book "does not assume any specialized knowledge. It is intended for anyone who is curious and willing to read participatively." Based on your reading of the passage, do you think the Aschers succeeded in writing to the audience described in this quotation? Explain.

5. Examine how the Aschers tell the story of Cieza. In what ways do you think they present his story as a conventional narrative? In what ways does their telling of his story differ from what you think of as a conventional story? Why do you think they present his story in this way? Do you think their use of his story is effective? Why or why not? What might your answer to this question suggest about you as a reader?

6. Examine the way the Aschers end this passage. Why do you think they end with this image of Cieza's will? What points or ideas do they emphasize or suggest through this ending? Did you find the ending effective? Why or why not?

Engaging the Issues

1. Write a conventional academic essay in which you present a rhetorical analysis of the Aschers' account of the quipu. In your analysis, examine the strategies the Aschers use to present information and ideas about the Incas and the quipu. Assess the effectiveness of their text on the basis of their intended audience and their stated purpose in writing the text. Cite specific passages from their text to illustrate your points.

2. Using your library, the Internet, or any other appropriate resource, investigate other systems of writing or written communication such as the Chinese system, Egyptian hieroglyphics, and similar systems that do not rely on an alphabet. Try to find out what linguists and other scholars say about what constitutes *writing* and how these systems function and compare to one another. Then write a conventional research paper based on your investigation for an audience of your classmates. In your paper, describe the various systems you investigated and explain how scholars understand and classify them. Try to convey a sense of the scholarly debates about writing that have taken place among linguists and other language experts. Keep in mind that your paper is intended for readers who are not linguists.

3. With a group of your classmates, try to identify the various ways in which we communicate, convey information, or record events or information without the use of alphabetic writing. For example, you might consider road signs as means of communication. Discuss how these various systems function in your life and

how they might relate to the use of writing in contemporary society. As a group try to draw conclusions about the ways in which we use different systems to communicate or record information.

4. On the basis of the discussions you participated in for Question #3 above, write a narrative in which you illustrate the various systems for communicating and recording information that you use in your own life.

5. Scholar Elizabeth Hill Boone has argued that Native American pictographs and petroglyphs that are usually categorized as "art" are essentially the same thing as writing. She asserts that "we have to think more broadly about visual and tactile systems of recording information, to reach a much broader definition of writing" (*Writing Without Words,* 1994, pp. 3–4). In a conventional academic essay, discuss Boone's argument, either supporting it or challenging it—or perhaps presenting a different perspective. In your essay, draw on the readings from this book and any other appropriate sources, as well as your own experiences, in making your argument.

The Late Age of Print

JAY DAVID BOLTER

INTRODUCTION As a scholar of classics at the University of North Carolina, Jay David Bolter may seem an unlikely enthusiast for the new computer technologies that he believes are profoundly changing how we read and write. But Bolter has emerged in academic circles as one of the most influential voices on technology and literacy and the future of writing and reading. Despite his classical training, Bolter does not share the concerns (or the nostalgia) of some of the other authors in this book who express skepticism or even outright hostility to the computer as a technology for writing and reading. Instead, he sees the computer as part of a long history of the development of literacy technologies. This latest technology, he believes, will not only replace print technology, which has dominated literacy for five hundred years, but will also lead to new ways of writing and reading that are already emerging in such forms as hypertext. These new ways of writing and reading, according to Bolter, will change what readers and writers do and will redefine the value of literacy in our culture.

In the following passage, Bolter explores a variety of characteristics of what he calls "electronic writing"—or writing done in the electronic medium of the computer—and examines how these characteristics make electronic writing fundamentally different from print-based writing. Specifically, Bolter argues that electronic writing is malleable and not "fixed" in the way print text is. This characteristic of electronic writing, he believes, radically changes the relationships among writer, reader, and text, giving the reader more control over a text and making the text itself "impermanent." For Bolter, these features of electronic writing have far-reaching implications for the ways in which we will use literacy in our lives. In his view, electronic writing affords us opportunities for using literacy that do not exist with traditional technologies like the printing press.

Bolter's vision is a hopeful and excited one, but his argument that we have now entered what he calls "the late age of print" worries many critics who believe that the new literacy technologies will result in loss as well as gain. Some critics have taken Bolter to task for being too enthusiastic about computer technologies and their impact on writing and reading. They argue that the changes in writing, reading, practices that he associates with electronic writing are overstated and not nearly as widespread as he claims, and they believe that print technology will not be superseded as rapidly or as completely as Bolter envisions. Nevertheless, Bolter's work urges us to examine carefully how a technology like the computer affects—or changes—the specific processes of writing, reading, and thinking that we engage in as we compose a text. He challenges us to consider how significant the impact of new technologies really is as the computer becomes an increasingly common technology for writing.

Jay David Bolter is author of several books and many articles on technology and literacy that have been widely influential in academic discussions about the implications of new computer technologies for writing. His book *Writing Space: The Computer, Hypertext, and the History of Writing* (1991), from which the following passage is taken, has become a minor classic among scholars and critics interested in writing and computers.

REFLECTING BEFORE READING

1. In the following passage, Jay David Bolter asserts that "electronic writing" of the kind that is possible with computers represents a radically new kind of literacy. As you read, pay attention to how Bolter describes "electronic writing." What does he emphasize? What do his descriptions of such writing—as well as of traditional print-based writing—suggest about his own values regarding literacy and technology? Do his descriptions of the nature of electronic writing correspond to your own experiences as a writer?

2. Bolter's writing has been influential in academic circles among scholars and researchers interested in technology and literacy. He is less well known outside those circles. As you read, consider how you think Bolter's ideas might be received by a more general audience (rather than a specialized academic audience). How might such readers react to his ideas? To his writing?

Opening the window of his cell, he pointed to the immense church of Notre Dame, which, with its twin towers, stone walls, and monstrous cupola forming a black silhouette against the starry sky, resembled an enormous two-headed sphinx seated in the middle of the city.

The archdeacon pondered the giant edifice for a few moments in silence, then with a sigh he stretched his right hand toward the printed book that lay open on his table and his left hand toward Notre Dame and turned a sad eye from the book to the church.

"Alas!" he said, "This will destroy that."

—*Hugo*, Notre-Dame de Paris, 1482, *1967, p. 197*

I n Victor Hugo's novel *Notre-Dame de Paris, 1482,* the priest remarked "Ceci tuera cela": this book will destroy that building. He meant not only that printing and literacy would undermine the authority of the church but also that "human thought … would change its mode of expression, that the principal idea of each generation would no longer write itself with the same material and in the same way, that the book of stone, so solid and durable, would give place to the book made of paper, yet more solid and durable" (p. 199). The medieval cathedral crowded with statues and stained glass was both a symbol of Christian authority and a repository of medieval knowledge (moral knowledge about the world and the human condition). The cathedral was a library to be read by the religious, who walked through its aisles looking up at the scenes of the Bible, the images of saints, allegorical figures of virtue and vice, visions of heaven and hell. (See *The Art of Memory* by Frances Yates, 1966, p. 124.) Of course, the printed book did not eradicate the encyclopedia in stone; it did not even eradicate the medieval art of writing by hand. People continued to contemplate their religious tradition in cathedrals, and they continued to communicate with pen and paper for many purposes. But printing did displace handwriting: the printed book became the most highly valued form of writing. And printing certainly helped to displace the medieval organization and expression of knowledge. As Elizabeth Eisenstein has shown, the printing press has been perhaps the most important tool of the modern scientist. (See *The Printing Press as an Agent of Change* by Elizabeth Eisenstein, 1979, especially vol. 2, pp. 520ff.)

Hugo himself lived in the heyday of printing, when the technology had just developed to allow mass publication of novels, newspapers, and journals. Hugo's own popularity in France (like Dickens' in England) was evidence that printed books were reaching and defining a new mass audience. Today we are living in the late age of print. The evidence of senescence, if not senility, is all around us. And as we look up from our computer keyboard to the books on our shelves, we must ask ourselves whether "this will destroy that." Computer technology (in the form of word processing, databases, electronic bulletin boards and mail) is beginning to displace the printed book. Until recently it was possible to believe that the computer could coexist with the printed book. Computers were for scientific analysis and business data processing. Pragmatic writing (business letters, technical reports, and stock prices) could migrate to the computer, but texts of lasting value—literature, history, scholarship—would remain in printed form. Now, however, this distinction between lasting texts and pragmatic communication is breaking down. Computers are being used for all kinds of writing, not just office memos and stock quotations. We shall see that the computer has even fostered a new genre of literature, one that can only be read at the computer screen. Major book publishers in the United States already translate their texts into computer-readable form for photocomposition; books pass through the computer on the way to the press. Many, perhaps most, of these texts will someday cease to be printed and will instead be distributed in electronic form.

The printed book, therefore, seems destined to move to the margin of our literate culture. The issue is not whether print technology will completely disappear; books may long continue to be printed for certain kinds of texts and for luxury consumption. But the idea and the ideal of the book will change: print will no longer define the organization and presentation of knowledge, as it has for the past five centuries. This shift from print to the computer does not mean the end of literacy. What will be lost is not literacy itself, but the literacy of print, for electronic technology offers us a new kind of book and new ways to write and read. The shift to the computer will make writing more flexible, but it will also threaten the definitions of good writing and careful reading that have been fostered by the technique of printing. The printing press encouraged us to think of a written text as an unchanging artifact, a monument to its author and its age. Hugo claimed that a printed book is more solid and durable than a stone cathedral; no one would make that claim, even metaphorically, for a computer diskette. Printing also tended to magnify the distance between the author and the reader, as the author became a monumental figure, the reader only a visitor in the author's cathedral. Electronic writing emphasizes the impermanence and changeability of text, and it tends to reduce the distance between author and reader by turning the reader into an author. The computer is restructuring our current economy of writing. It is changing the cultural status of writing as well as the method of producing books. It is changing the relationship of the author to the text and of both author and text to the reader.

Rewriting the Book

As early as the 1450s and 1460s, Gutenberg and his colleagues were able to achieve the mass production of books without sacrificing quality. Gutenberg's great book, the 42-line Bible, does not seem to us today to have been a radical experiment in a new technology. It is not poorly executed or uncertain in form. The earliest incunabula are already examples of a perfected technique; there remains little evidence from the period of experimentation that must have preceded the production of these books. Indeed, Gutenberg's Bible can hardly be distinguished from the work of a good scribe, except perhaps that the spacing and hyphenation are more regular than a scribe could achieve. The early printers tried to make their books identical to fine manuscripts: they used the same thick letter forms, the same ligatures and abbreviations, the same layout on the page. It took a few generations for printers to realize that their new technology made possible a different writing space, that the page could be more readable with thinner letters, fewer abbreviations, and less ink.

Today we find ourselves in a similar interim with the electronic book. We have begun by using word processors and electronic photocomposition to improve the production of printed books and typed documents. Yet it is already becoming clear that the computer provides a new writing surface that needs conventions different from those of the printed page. In fact, the page itself is not a meaningful unit of electronic writing. The electronic book must instead have a shape appropriate to the computer's capacity to structure and present text. Writers are in the process of discovering that shape, and the process may take decades, as it did with Gutenberg's invention. The task is nothing less than the remaking of the book.

Electronic technology remakes the book in two senses. It gives us a new kind of book by changing the surface on which we write and the rhythms with which we read. It also adds to our historical understanding of the book by providing us with a new form that we can compare to printed books, manuscripts, and earlier forms of writing. Electronic writing turns out to be both radical and traditional. It is mechanical and precise like printing, organic and evolutionary like handwriting, visually eclectic like hieroglyphics and picture writing. On the other hand, electronic writing is fluid and dynamic to a greater degree than any previous technique. The coming of the new electronic book helps us to understand the choices, the specializations, that the printed book entails. We see that, like the specializations on outer branches of an evolutionary tree, the printed book is an extreme form of writing, not the norm.

The Uses of Electronic Writing

Those who tell us that the computer will never replace the printed book point to the physical advantages: the printed book is portable, inexpensive, and easy to read, whereas the computer is hard to carry and expensive and needs a source of electricity. The computer screen is not as comfortable a reading surface as the page; reading for long periods promotes eyestrain. Finally—and this point is always included—you cannot read your computer screen in bed. But electronic technology continues to evolve: machines have diminished dramatically in size and in price during the past 40 years, and computer screens are becoming much more readable. It is not hard to imagine a portable computer with the bulk and weight of a large notebook and whose screen is as legible as a printed page. We can also envision an electronic writing system built into the top of a desk or lectern (like those used in the Middle Ages and the Renaissance), where the writer can work directly by applying a light pen instead of typing at a keyboard.

In any case, ease of use is only one measure of a writing technology. The great advantage of the first printed books was *not* that you could read them in bed. Gutenberg might well have been appalled at the thought of someone taking his beautiful folio-sized Bible to bed. For generations, most important printed books remained imposing volumes that had to be read on bookstands, so that people often read (and wrote) standing up. Mass production by printing did eventually make books cheaper and more plentiful, and this change was important. However, the fixity and permanence that printing gave to the written word were just as important in changing the nature of literacy. The book in whatever form is an intellectual tool rather than a means of relaxation. If the tool is powerful, writers and readers will put up with inconveniences to use it. In any technique of writing, structure matters more than appearance or convenience, and the electronic book, whether it is embodied in today's boxy microcomputer or in a slim electronic notebook of the future, gives text a new structure. In place of the static pages of the printed book, the electronic book maintains text as a fluid network of verbal elements.

Writers are only beginning to exploit the possibilities of this new structure; electronic writing in general is still in its infancy. The electronic incunabula include computer-controlled photocomposition, the word processor, the textual database, the electronic bulletin board and mail. As already mentioned, electronic texts are by no means rare: most of what we read today has passed through the computer on its way to our hands. In the United States it is common to produce newspapers, magazines, and printed books by means of electronic photocomposition. The texts are typed into the computer, revised and arranged by editors and typographers, and then output as camera-ready copy, photographic sheets or plates that the printer can use in his presses. However, computer-controlled photocomposition does not teach us how to write electronically. Publishers are simply using the computer to enhance the older technology, to make printing faster and less expensive.

The same is true of word processing. Word processors do demonstrate the flexibility of electronic writing in allowing writers to copy, compare, and discard text with the touch of a few buttons. Words in the computer are ultimately embodied in the collective behavior of billions of electrons, which fly around in the machine at unimaginable speeds. Change is the rule in the computer, stability the exception, and it is the rule of change that makes the word processor so useful. (See Mullins, 1988.)** On the other hand, the word processor has been enthusiastically accepted by so many writers precisely because it does not finally challenge their conventional notion of writing. The word processor is an aid for making perfect printed or typed copy: the goal is still ink on paper. Like programs for photocomposition, the word processor is not so much a tool for writing, as it is a tool for typography. With a sophisticated word processor and a laser printer, users can create their own camera-ready copy. The program allows small organizations and even individuals to bypass the publishing industry. This change is important, but it is not a revolution in writing. (On the interplay between fluidity and fixity in word processing, see Balestri, 1988.)**

The word processor treats text like a scroll, a roll of pages sewn together at the ends, and its visual structures are still typographic. A word processor stores its text as a simple sequence of letters, words, and lines. It remembers margins and pagination; it may remember which letters are to be printed in boldface, in Times Roman, or in 14-point type. But a conventional word processor does not treat the text as a network of verbal ideas. It does not contain a map of the ways in which the text may be read. It does not record or act on the semantic structure of the text. A true electronic text does all this, for a true electronic text is not a fixed sequence of letters, but is instead from the writer's point of view a network of verbal elements and from the reader's point of view a texture of possible readings.

An electronic text permits the reader to share in the dynamic process of writing. The text is realized by the reader in the act of reading. Electronic reading is already a feature of many current computerized texts. There are, for example, databases containing Supreme Court decisions for lawyers, newspaper articles for journalists, and even Greek or Shakespearean tragedies for scholars. Each such database constitutes a potential text of vast proportion and complexity: it offers millions of combinations of articles or passages that some reader might at some time request. No one reader examines every entry in such a database; instead the reader searches for appropriate phrases and retrieves only those passages that satisfy the search. The reader calls forth his or her own text out of the network, and each such text belongs to one reader and one particular act of reading.

The same principle of reader participation is embodied in computer-assisted instruction, commonly used in business and schools. Computer-assisted instruction is sometimes effective, often not, but in all cases it requires the dynamic reading of a multiply organized text. The computer presents the student with a question or problem. The student responds, and, based on that response, the computer may present another question, give the student a message, or take the student back to review

---

* Diane Balestri, "Soft copy and hard." *Academic Computing,* vol. 2, 1988, pp. 14–17, 41–45.
** Phil Mullins, "The Fluid Word." *Thought,* vol. 63, 1988, pp. 413–428.

material that he or she does not seem to understand. The teacher who wrote the program must anticipate and provide for a wide variety of responses from the student. The teacher is the writer whose text the machine juggles and displays to the student. The student also becomes a writer as he or she coaxes answers from the machine. The whole lesson is a composite of the two texts, one by the teacher and one by the student. Meanwhile, electronic bulletin boards take the principle of multiple authorship even further, allowing hundreds of participants from distant locations to exchange texts and questions. Each participant moves quickly and repeatedly between the roles of reader and writer.

All of these programs suggest what the computer can do as a technology of reading and writing. And yet they are all attempts to transfer previous techniques of writing into an electronicidiom. The word processor makes the computer into an electronic typewriter. A textual database makes it a file cabinet filled with copies of printed records. Computer-assisted instruction with its steady rhythm of question and answer is modeled on the exercises included in printed textbooks. And electronic bulletin boards are just what the name implies: a place for posting typed or written messages. But if we combine the dynamic writing of the word processor with the dynamic reading of the bulletin board or textual database and add the interactivity of computer-assisted instruction, then we do have a textual medium of a new order. This new medium is the fourth great technique of writing that will take its place beside the ancient papyrus roll, the medieval codex, and the printed book.

The New Voice of the Book

Writing in the classical and Western traditions is supposed to have a voice and therefore to speak to its reader. A printed book generally speaks with a single voice and assumes a consistent character, a persona, before its audience. A printed book in today's economy of writing must do more: it must speak to an economically viable or culturally important group of readers. Printing has helped to define and empower new groups of readers; particularly in the 19th and 20th centuries: for example, the middle-class audience for the 19th-century British novel. But this achievement is also a limitation. An author must either write for one of the existing groups or seek to forge a new one, and the task of forging a new readership requires great talent and good luck. And even a new readership, brought together by shared interests in the author's message, must be addressed with consistency. No publisher would accept a book that combined two vastly different subject matters: say, European history and the marine biology of the Pacific, or Eskimo folklore and the principles of actuarial science. It would be hard to publish a book that was part fiction and part non-fiction—not a historical novel, a genre that is popular and has a well-defined audience, but, let us say, a combination of essays and short stories that treat the same historical events. We might say that these hypothetical books lack unity and should not be published. Yet our definition of textual unity comes from the published work we have read or more generally from the current divisions of academic, literary, and scientific disciplines, which themselves both depend on and reinforce the economics of publishing. The material in a book must be homogeneous by the standard of some book-buying audience.

This strict requirement of unity and homogeneity is relatively recent, In the Middle Ages, unrelated texts were often bound together, and texts were often added in the available space in a volume years or decades later. Even in the early centuries of printing, it was not unusual to put unrelated works between two covers. On the other hand, it is natural to think of any book, written or printed, as a verbal unit. For the book is a physical unit; its pages are sewn or glued together and then bound into a portable whole. Should not all the words inside proceed from one unifying idea and stand in the same rhetorical relationship to the reader?

Because an electronic text is not a physical artifact, there is no reason to give it the same conceptual unity as the printed book, no reason not to include disparate materials in one electronic network. The writer or editor need not envision and address only one homogeneous readership; an electronic book may speak with different voices to different readers (and each reader is a different reader each time he or she approaches a text). Thus, an electronic encyclopedia may address both the educated novice and the expert: its articles may be written on several levels of expertise to suit the needs and background of various readers. Our traditional canon of unity no longer applies to the electronic book, whose shadowy existence in electronic storage does not convey the same sense of physical unity. The text may reside on a diskette or in the computer's internal memory, where it cannot be seen or directly touched by the reader. If the user is calling up a remote database, then the text may be hundreds or thousands of miles away and arrive only in convenient pieces through the telephone wires.

An electronic book can tailor itself to each reader's needs. As the reader moves quickly or deliberately through the textual network, he or she seldom feels the inertia that pulls a reader through the pages of a printed book. A reader who consults the *New York Times* Information Service does not want to read every article in the database; the student in computer-assisted instruction does not need or want to read every response the computer has to offer for every possible wrong answer. The reader exercises choice at every moment in the act of reading. Electronic reading is therefore a special instance of what economists now call "market segmentation." In the classic industrial age, economies of scale required that products be homogeneous: each factory produced one or a few kinds of toothbrushes, soft drinks, or deodorants in vast quantities. In today's more automated and flexible factories, goods are tailored to segments of the buying public. Before the invention of photocomposition, the printing press was a classic industrial machine, producing large quantities of identical texts. Marshall McLuhan called printing the first example of the assembly line and mass production (McLuhan, 1972, p. 124).* Photocomposition and then the computer as photocomposer have already made printing more flexible, allowing publishers to target books to well-defined markets. However, a true electronic book goes further still, changing for each reader and with each reading.

The vanishing of the fixed text alters the nature of an audience's shared experience in reading. All the readers of *Bleak House* could talk about the novel on the assumption that they had all read the same words. No two readers of an electronic book can make that assumption; they can only assume that they have traveled in the same textual network. Fixed printed texts can be made into a literary canon and

---

* Marshall McLuhan, *The Gutenberg Galaxy,* Univ. of Toronto Press, 1972.

therefore promote cultural unity. In the 19th and early 20th centuries, when the canon of literature was often taken as the definition of a liberal education, the goal was to give everyone the experience of reading the same texts—Shakespeare, Milton, Dickens, and so on. This ideal of cultural unity through a shared literary inheritance, which has received so many assaults in the 20th century, must now further suffer by the introduction of a new form of highly individualized writing and reading.

Critics accuse the computer of promoting homogeneity in our society, of producing uniformity through automation, but electronic reading and writing have just the opposite effect. The printing press was the great homogenizer of writing, whereas electronic technology makes texts particular and individual. An electronic book is a fragmentary and potential text, a series of self-contained units rather than an organic, developing whole. But fragmentation does not imply mere disintegration. Elements in the electronic writing space are not simply chaotic; they are instead in a perpetual state of reorganization. They form patterns, constellations, which are in constant danger of breaking down and combining into new patterns. This tension leads to a new definition of unity in writing, one that may replace or supplement our traditional notions of the unity of voice and of analytic argument. The unity or coherence of an electronic text derives from the perpetually shifting relationship among all its verbal elements.

Computing as Writing

So far we have been considering the computer as a vehicle for human (what computer specialists call "natural") language. But we cannot ignore the fact that the computer is used to manipulate numbers as well as words. The computer reminds us that any definition of writing must now include mathematics and symbolic logic along with verbal writing and graphics. And in all its various uses, the computer is best understood as a new technology for writing. Even computer programming is a kind of writing. Programming languages (like PASCAL or C) constitute a restricted and yet powerful mode of communication, a mode based on imperative sentences and the unambiguous use of symbols. Admittedly, their rigid syntax makes these computer languages unusual; natural language is far less precise. And unlike natural language, computer language is made to be written down: it belongs on the page or the computer screen. It is not easy to speak PASCAL or C, so that even a good programmer must see the lines of code in order to understand them. What the programmer sees is a network of symbols whose interaction defines the program's operation. Computer programs are by definition electronic texts, and a computer system is a sophisticated collection of programmed texts that act on and interact with each other—applications, system utilities, compilers, assemblers, and so on. All programs are texts that read texts and write other texts.

Computer programming is simply the newest version of the symbol manipulation that mathematicians and logicians have practiced for centuries. Programming is embodied logic: the establishment of logical relationships among symbols that are embodied in and empowered by the memory chips and processors of the digital computer. Mathematics has been a special kind of writing at least since the evolution of modern notation in the 17th century. The set of mathematical equations that defines a physical theory is a symbolic text of the highest order. And science itself has been a formal language since the time of Descartes and Leibniz, or indeed Galileo with his claim that the book of nature was written in the language of mathematics. In the 19th and 20th centuries, the desire to make language formal and rigorous has led to modern symbolic logic, to semiotics, to logical positivism, and ultimately to computer programming.

Formal language is, therefore, the natural language of computers. It is English, French, or Russian that poses problems when taken into the machine. Formal languages are operational: they direct the computer's actions. Human languages are merely stored in the machine, as texts to be divided, recombined, and presented to readers. Yet the computer can activate even these human texts in new and surprising ways. The computer as a writing technology invites us to recognize the similarities as well as the obvious differences between formal and natural language. It becomes easier to understand natural language too as a network of interconnecting signs.

In everything it does, the computer is called on to read and write either formal or natural language. Today the machine is indispensable in physics, chemistry, and biology, where it is a tool for reading and writing Galileo's language of nature. When the computer reads and writes numbers for scientists, it does so by executing a text of programmed instructions. It may print out its results in numbers and words, or it may display its results graphically, giving the user a map or a graph to read. It may be called on to simulate some aspect of nature or human technology and to present that simulation as a picture on the screen or as a graphic or numerical text. Even a graphics program does not draw: it writes. A computer graphic is a set of symbolically positioned bits: a texture of dots that our eyes convert to continuous lines on the screen. Even when the computer is controlling machinery in an automated factory, the controls are in fact a language of discrete commands that the computer constructs and sends to the machinery. The computer is performing a kind of writing on the world. All computing is reading and writing. The computer is therefore a technology for all writers—scientists and engineers as well as scholars, novelists, and poets. A text in the computer is always an interplay of signs, which may be mathematical and logical symbols, words in English, or graphics and video images treated symbolically.

Writing Spaces

Writing is the creative play of signs, and the computer offers us a new field for that play. It offers a new surface for recording and presenting text together with new techniques for organizing our writing. In other words, it offers us a new writing space. The computer's writing space resembles and differs from the space of its predecessors, particularly the papyrus roll, the codex, and the printed book.

By "writing space" I mean first of all the physical and visual field defined by a particular technology of writing. All forms of writing are spatial, for we can only see and understand written signs as extended in a space of at least two dimensions. Each technology gives us a different space. For early ancient writing, the space was the inner surface of a continuous roll, which the writer divided into columns. For medieval handwriting and modern printing, the space is the white surface of the page, particularly in a bound volume. For electronic writing, the space is the computer's videoscreen where text is displayed as well as the electronic memory in which text is stored. The computer's writing space is animated, visually complex, and to a surprising extent malleable in the hands of both writer and reader.

How the writer and the reader understand writing is conditioned by the physical and visual character of the books they use. Each physical writing space fosters a particular understanding both of the act of writing and of the product, the written text. In this late age of print, writers and readers still conceive of all texts, of text itself, as located in the space of a printed book. The conceptual space of a printed book is one in which writing is stable, monumental, and controlled exclusively by the author. It is the space defined by perfect printed volumes that exist in thousands of identical copies. The conceptual space of electronic writing, on the other hand, is characterized by fluidity and an interactive relationship between writer and reader. These different conceptual spaces foster different styles and genres of writing and different theories of literature.

In the act of writing, the writer externalizes his or her thoughts. The writer enters into a reflective and reflexive relationship with the written page, a relationship in which thoughts are bodied forth. It becomes difficult to say where thinking ends and writing begins, where the mind ends and the writing space begins. With any technique of writing—on stone or clay, papyrus or paper, and particularly on the computer screen—the writer comes to regard the mind itself as a writing space. The writing space becomes a metaphor, in fact literate culture's root metaphor, for the human mind.

REFLECTING ON THE READING

1. What point does Bolter make with his reference to a scene from Victor Hugo's novel *Notre-Dame de Paris, 1482* in the beginning of this passage? What might this reference suggest to you about Bolter's essay? About Bolter as writer?

2. What is the position about the future of the book and the future of the computer that Bolter establishes in the opening section of this passage? On what basis does he take this position? What does he say are the basic implications of this position regarding the future of literacy?

3. What are the important distinctions that Bolter makes between print and electronic writing?

4. What does Bolter mean when he says that we are now in the process of "remaking" the book? In what two ways does he believe the book is being remade? Do these ways sound reasonable to you? Why or why not?

5. Bolter makes a distinction between word processing and what he calls true electronic writing. Why? What is the difference between the two? Why is this difference important for Bolter? What exactly is electronic writing, according to Bolter? In what sense does it represent a "textual medium of a new order"? Do you think he is right? Explain.

6. What does Bolter mean when he says that a book has a "voice"? What are the key characteristics of the "voice" of the printed book? How is the "voice" of the book changing in electronic writing, according to Bolter?

7. How does Bolter believe the computer is changing the way we define writing? What does he mean by "writing space"? How does he see the computer as a writing space?

Examining Rhetorical Strategies

1. How would you characterize Bolter's voice and tone in this passage? Do you think they are appropriate for his subject matter? Are they effective? In what ways? Do you think he sounds credible as someone writing about these issues? Why or why not? What might your reaction to his voice indicate about you as a reader?

2. Whom do you think Bolter sees as his audience for this passage (which is the opening chapter of his book *Writing Space*)? Do you think he imagines a specialized audience? Explain, citing specific passages from his text in your answer. Are you part of that audience?

3. Bolter makes a series of assertions in this passage about the computer—specifically, electronic writing done with computers—and the changes it promises to foster in the way we read and write. On what basis does he make these assertions? What kinds of evidence does he cite in support of his assertions? Do his assertions sound convincing to you? Do they sound outlandish? Why or why not? What might your answer indicate about your own expectations regarding what counts as a valid argument?

4. Do you find that Bolter is generally optimistic or pessimistic about electronic writing and what it might mean for the future of the printed book? Why does he feel this way? Cite specific statements in his text to support your answer. Do you agree with him? Why or why not?

5. How does Bolter use history in this passage? Examine specific instances in which he refers to historical developments or events regarding writing technologies. Does he provide detailed information about these developments or events? Does the information he provides constitute effective support for his points, in your view? Explain.

6. Look closely at how Bolter describes writing and reading in the opening section and throughout this passage. Does he offer explicit definitions of writing and reading or literacy? Does he distinguish between different types of writing and reading? When Bolter refers to "electronic writing," do you think he is referring to *all* kinds of writing and reading? Why or why not? Does he leave anything out, in your view? What difference would it make to his argument if he were referring only to specific kinds of writing or reading?

Engaging the Issues

1. This passage from Bolter's book *Writing Space* was intended primarily for an academic audience concerned with understanding the nature of writing as a

technology (e.g., English professors, communications scholars, teachers of writing, technology experts). But his main points have been discussed in other circles that are not academic, such as in the popular press, in online discussions, and in business organizations. Identify what you think are the most important of Bolter's ideas and present them to a general audience in a brief essay that might be appropriate for a large-circulation publication such as *USA Today* or a local newspaper. How would you present these ideas to such an audience? How would you justify the importance of these issues? In other words, why should readers who are not technology or literacy experts care about what Bolter is saying here? Your essay should answer that question for your readers.

2. Drawing on your own experience with what Bolter calls "electronic writing," evaluate Bolter's assertions about how electronic writing will change literacy. Do you find his description of what electronic writing does accurate, based on your own experiences? Does he misrepresent the computer, in your view? Has he left anything out? Write a conventional academic essay in which you offer your evaluation of his view of electronic writing.

3. Use Bolter's passage as the basis for a letter to your local school board in which you argue for more emphasis on computer technology in your school's curriculum.

   Alternatively, write a letter to your local school board in which you warn against too much emphasis on computer technologies in the school curriculum.

4. Imagine an audience of people who have no access to computer technology for writing. What might Bolter say to them about the future of literacy? Write an essay analyzing Bolter's arguments for such an audience.

   Alternatively, write an essay responding to Bolter from the point of view of someone who has no access to computer technologies for writing.

5. Read a hypertext document (on a CD-ROM or on the World Wide Web), paying close attention to the process by which you read it. Then in an essay for an audience of your classmates, describe the experience, comparing it to the experience of reading print-based forms, such as books or newspaper articles. Assess Bolter's claims on the basis of your experience and draw conclusions of your own about the nature of electronic writing and its significance for the future of literacy.

   Alternatively, create a hypertext or Web site. Describe the process of creating that text and compare it to writing a conventional text. Assess Bolter's claims on the basis of that experience.

6. A study published in 1998 revealed that as of that year 44 percent of White households in the United States had a computer, whereas only 29 percent of Black households did. How might these numbers affect your reaction to Bolter's arguments in his passage? Look further into the access to computers in American culture to see who is actually using computers. Try to determine how widespread computer use is and how it is being used in various settings in American culture. Also try to find some reviews of Bolter's book in which critics have assessed his argument. Then write an analysis of Bolter's arguments in light of the information you have gathered.

The Future of Literacy

Umberto Eco

Introduction   Few writers demonstrate the breadth and depth that Umberto Eco exhibits in his extensive body of work. A professor in the faculty of letters and philosophy at the University of Bologna, Italy, Eco is the author, coauthor, or editor of more than twenty books, including popular novels, essays on popular culture, and scholarly books and essays on literature and language theory. His novel *The Name of the Rose* (1983) was an international best-seller (later adapted into a film of the same name), and for many years he has written columns on popular culture for the Italian magazine *L'Espresso*. To scholars and others interested in literacy, however, Eco is best known as an important theorist of *semiotics,* the study of sign systems in language, culture, and behavior. Eco is internationally respected among scholars for his many books and essays on semiotic theory, including *The Role of the Reader: Explorations in the Semiotics of Texts* (1984), *Semiotics and the Philosophy of Language* (1986), and *Limits of Interpretation (Advances in Semiotics)* (1990). Central to Eco's scholarly work has been the effort to explain how language works as a sign system and how it relates to other sign systems in human culture. For Eco, as for all semiotic theorists, the central task is to try to explain how signs—whether they be words and letters, visual symbols, gestures, or something else—carry meaning.

In the passage that follows, Eco does not discuss semiotic theory directly, but his training as a semiotician is evident as he offers examples of how new media influence literacy in contemporary society. He addresses the question of the future of literacy in view of recent worries about declining literacy rates and changing reading habits. Unlike some critics who follow such matters in our technological age, Eco is neither a vociferous opponent nor an enthusiastic supporter of new technologies for literacy, especially the computer. Rather, he presents himself as an interested observer of the contemporary scene who offers some insight into literacy and technology amidst the many loud voices registering opinions on these issues. In this essay, which was published in 1994 as part of a volume entitled *Apocalypse Postponed,* Eco attempts to place the discussions about literacy and technology in a broader context from his perspective as an academic, a writer, and an observer of contemporary culture. His predictions about the future of literacy may surprise you, for they focus not so much on what new technological developments we might expect as on a concern with the role of writing and reading in our lives. For Eco, the key question seems to be, Will reading and writing change in important ways as a result of the uses of new technologies? In raising such a question, this essay may encourage you to wonder about the impact that new technologies for literacy will have on your own life.

REFLECTING BEFORE READING

1. Eco refers in this essay to popular discussions of the "literacy crisis." What have you heard about the "literacy crisis"? What do you know about what scholars

and politicians and educators say about such a crisis? Do you believe such a crisis exists? On what do you base your belief? How might your answers to these questions influence the way you respond to Eco's essay?

2. Eco is a scholar who regularly writes for popular audiences. As you read his essay, consider whether it strikes you as scholarly, popular, or something else. How effectively does Eco address you as a reader?

According to Plato (in the *Phaedrus*) Thoth, or Hermes, the alleged inventor of writing, presents his invention to the Pharaoh Thamus, praising this new technique which will allow human beings to remember what they would otherwise forget. But the Pharaoh is not satisfied. My skilful Thoth, he says, memory is such a great gift that it ought to be kept alive by training it continuously. With your invention people will no longer be obliged to train memory. They will remember things not because of an internal effort, but by virtue merely of an external device.

We can understand the Pharaoh's concern. Writing, like any other new technological device, would have made sluggish the human power which it replaced and reinforced—just as cars have made us less able to walk. Writing was dangerous because it decreased the powers of the mind, by offering human beings a petrified soul, a caricature of mind, a machine memory.

Plato's text is, of course, ironic. Plato was writing his argument about writing. But he is putting it into the mouth of Socrates, who did not write. Therefore Plato was expressing a fear that still survived in his day. Thinking is an internal matter; the real thinker would not allow books to think in his place.

Nowadays nobody shares these concerns, for two very simple reasons. First of all, we know that books are not ways of making somebody else think in our place; on the contrary they are machines which provoke further thoughts. Secondly, if once upon a time people needed to train their memory in order to remember things, after the invention of writing they had also to train their memory in order to remember books. Books challenge and improve memory. They do not narcotize it. This old debate is worth reflecting on every time one meets a new communicational tool which pretends or appears to replace books.

During the last year some worried and worrying reports have been published in the United States on the decline of literacy. One of the reasons for the recent Wall Street crash, according to some observers, has been not only an exaggerated confidence in computers but also the fact that none of the yuppies who were controlling the stock market knew enough about the 1929 crisis. They were unable to face a crisis because of their lack of historical information. If they had read some books about Black Thursday they might have been able to make better decisions and avoid many well-known pitfalls.

I agree. But I wonder if books would have been the only reliable vehicle for acquiring information. Time was when the only way to acquire a foreign language (apart from travelling abroad) was to study the language from a book. Now kids frequently learn other languages by listening to records, watching movies or TV programmes in original versions, or deciphering the instructions on a drinks can.

The same happens with geographical information. In my childhood I got the best of my information about exotic countries not from textbooks but from adventure novels (Jules Verne, for example, or Emilio Salgari, or Karl May). My children at a very early age knew more than me on the same subject by watching movies and TV.

The illiteracy of the Wall Street yuppies was due not only to an insufficient exposure to books but also to a form of visual illiteracy. Books about the 1929 Black Thursday exist, and are still regularly published (the yuppies can be blamed for not being bookstore and library-goers), while television and cinema are largely unconcerned with any rigorous reconstruction of historical events. One could learn the history of the Roman Empire very well from the movies, if only those movies were historically accurate. The fault of Hollywood is not to have set up its films as an alternative to the books of Tacitus or Gibbon, but rather to have imposed a romantic, pulp version of both Tacitus and Gibbon. The yuppies' problem is not only that they watch TV instead of reading books; it is that in New York only on Channel 13 is there anyone who knows who Gibbon was.

I am not stressing these points in order to assert the possibility of a new literacy which would make books obsolete. God knows, every penny I ever made in my life—as publisher, as scholar, or as author—has come from books. My points are rather the following:

1. Today the concept of literacy comprises many media. An enlightened policy on literacy must take into account the possibilities of all these media. Educational concerns must be extended to the whole of the media. Responsibilities and tasks must be carefully balanced. If tapes are better than books for learning languages, look after cassettes. If a commentated presentation of Chopin on compact disc helps people to understand Chopin, don't worry if people don't buy a five-volume history of romantic music.

2. Do not fight against false enemies. Even if it were true that today visual communication has overwhelmed written communication, the problem is not one of opposing written to visual communication. The problem is rather how to improve both. In the Middle Ages visual communication was, for the masses, more important than writing. But Chartres Cathedral was not culturally inferior to the *Imago mundi* by Honorius of Autun.[1] Cathedrals were the TV of their times, and the difference with our TV was that the directors of the medieval TV read good books, had a lot of imagination and worked for the public good.

We are regularly misled by a 'mass media criticism of the mass media' which is superficial and almost always belated. The mass media are still repeating that our historical period is and will be more and more dominated by images. Mass media people have read McLuhan too late. The present and the forthcoming young generation is and will be a computer-oriented generation. The main feature of a computer screen is that it hosts and displays more alphabetic letters than images. The new generations will be alphabet and not image-oriented.

Moreover, the new generation is trained to read at an incredible speed. An old-fashioned university professor today cannot read a computer screen at the same speed as a teenager. These same teenagers, if they should happen to want to program their own home computer, must know, or learn, logical procedures and algorithms, and must type on a keyboard, at great speed, words and numbers.

I have said that we should not fight against false enemies. In the same vein let me say that we should not endorse false friends. To read a computer screen is not the same as to read a book. I do not know if you are familiar with the process of learning a new computer program. Usually the program is able to display on the screen all the instructions you need. But generally users who want to learn the program and to save their eyesight either print out the instructions and read them as if they were in book form, or buy a printed manual. It is possible to conceive of a visual program which explains very well how to print and bind a book, but in order to get instructions on how to write a computer program we need a book.

After spending a few hours at a computer console I feel the need to sit down comfortably in an armchair and read a newspaper, or maybe a good poem.

I think that computers are diffusing a new form of literacy but are unable to satisfy all the intellectual needs that they stimulate. I am an optimist twelve hours a day and a pessimist the remaining twelve. In my optimistic mood I dream of a computer generation which, obliged compulsively to read a computer screen, gets acquainted with reading but at a certain moment comes to feel dissatisfied and looks for a different form of reading, more relaxed and generating a different form of involvement. In Hugo's *Notre Dame de Paris,* Frollo, comparing a book with his old cathedral, says: 'Ceci tuera cela.' I think that today, speaking of computers and books, one could say: 'Ceci aidera cela.'

Do not fight against false enemies. One of the most common objections to the pseudo-literacy of computers is that young people get more and more accustomed to speaking through cryptic short formulas: dir, help, diskopy, error 67, and so on. Is that still literacy?

I am a collector of old books and I feel delighted when I read the seventeenth-century titles which take up a whole page and sometimes more. Introductions were several pages long, started with elaborate courtesy formulae praising the ideal addressee, usually an Emperor or a Pope, and went on for pages and pages explaining in a very baroque style the purposes and virtues of the text to follow.

If baroque writers were to read our modern scholarly books they would be horrified. Introductions are one page long, briefly outline the subject matter of the book, thank some National or International Endowment for a generous grant, briefly explain that the book has been made possible by the love and understanding of a wife or husband or children, credit a secretary for having patiently typed the manuscript. We understand perfectly all the human and academic ordeals suggested by those few lines, the hundreds of nights spent highlighting photocopies, the innumerable frozen hamburgers eaten on the go (no caviar for the scholar) ... I guess that in the near future three lines saying

TWO
SMITH
ROCKEFELLER
(to be read as: I thank my wife and my children, the book is due to the generous assistance of Professor Smith and was made possible by the Rockefeller Foundation)

would be as eloquent as a baroque introduction. It is a problem of rhetoric and of acquaintance with a given form of rhetoric. In years to come, I think, passionate love letters will be sent in the form of a short instruction.

There is a curious notion according to which in verbal language the more you say the more profound and perceptive you are. Mallarmé, however, told us that it is sufficient to spell out 'une fleur' to evoke a universe of perfumes, shapes and thoughts. Frequently, for poetry, the fewer the words the more things they imply. Three lines of Pascal say more than three hundred pages of a long and boring treatise on morals and metaphysics. The quest for a new and surviving literacy ought not to be the quest for a pre-computer verbal bulimia.

The enemies of literacy are hiding elsewhere.

Let us now reconsider the debate between Thoth and Thamus. Thamus assumed that the invention of writing would diminish the power of human memory. I objected that human memory has been improved by the continual exercise of remembering what books say. But to remember written words is not the same as to remember things. Probably the memory of the librarians of Alexandria was quantitatively greater than that of the illiterate savage, but the illiterate savage has a more specialised memory for things, shapes, smells, colours. In response to the invention of writing, Greek and Latin civilization invented the *artes memoriae* so that orators and teachers could survive as thinkers in times when books were in short supply.

The memory of Cicero or Aquinas was more flexible and powerful than ours. Though Thoth's invention may not have, Gutenberg's has certainly weakened the mnemonic capacity of our species. To counteract the negative effects of printing, the old school insisted on training young people to learn poems, dates and lists of historical figures by heart.

Our permissive society, relying on the abundance of tapes and other forms of recording, has further rendered memory as a mental ability somewhat obsolete. The use of computers will work in the same direction. You may recall a short story by Isaac Asimov where, in a future world dominated by intelligent machines, the last human being who still knows the multiplication tables by heart is wanted by the Pentagon and by various secret services because he represents the only calculator able to function in the event of power shortages. The way our present society tends to encourage well-trained memories is through TV quiz programmes and so-called trivia games.

Menaced by the growth of an image-oriented culture, our technological society has already spontaneously reacted in terms of free-market dynamics. After all, since the invention of TV the quantity of printed matter in the world has not decreased. On the contrary it has grown to an extent unprecedented in previous centuries—even though this increase has to be set against a corresponding increase in world population.

In simple terms, it seems that previously illiterate people, once exposed to television, at a certain moment start to read newspapers. I appreciate that such a merely quantitative evaluation is not very illuminating in terms of highbrow culture, since there are newspapers that are worse than TV programmes. But when speaking of literacy it is better to forget the shibboleths of highbrow culture. Speaking of literacy in the world today we are not only concerned with the happy few of Bloomsbury, but with the masses of the Third World.

The real question rather is how to confront a series of phenomena which are menacing the universe of books and the cultural heritage that books represent. I shall list some problems, without pretending to propose solutions. It is pretty late in the day and I have started my twelve hours of pessimism.

1. Books are menaced by books. Any excess of information produces silence. When I am in the USA I read the *New York Times* every day except on Sunday. Sunday's *Times* contains too much information and I do not have time enough to consume it. Bookstores are so crowded with books they can only afford to keep the most recent ones.

2. Books are still an expensive commodity, at least in comparison with other forms of communication such as TV. An international committee to oppose the taxation of books in the European Community has just been created and since I am its president I cannot but agree with its demands. But good ideas have unfortunate side effects. Lowering the price of books will encourage their publication and circulation but will at the same time increase their number—with all the dangers referred to under 1, above.

3. New technologies are competing with each other. Books are now more widely available than in any other period of human history, but all publishers know the extent to which photocopying technology is jeopardizing their interests.

   A photocopy of a paperback is still more expensive than the original, but publication in paperback is dependent on the success of the hardcover edition and for many important scientific books only hardcover publication is possible. I am a writer. I live on my royalties, and once my American publisher told me he was thinking of suing a professor who had told his thirty students to make photocopies of one of my books, too expensive for them to buy. I asked the publisher to refrain from any legal action, since in the professor's place I would have done the same.

   The main international scientific publishers have found a way to escape this predicament. They publish a very limited number of copies, they price the book at $300, and they take it for granted that copies will be bought only for major libraries and the rest will be piracy. So prices increase and the physical act of reading scientific material becomes more and more unpleasant, since everyone knows the difference between reading a crisp original page and a xerox. Moreover, the very act of photocopying a book tends to make me feel virtuous and up-to-date in my scholarship: I have the text, and afterwards I no longer feel the need to read it. Today scholars are accumulating enormous stocks of xeroxed material that they will never read. Ironically, the technology of photocopying makes it easier to have books, not easier to read them. Thus billions of trees are killed for the sake of unread photocopies.

4. Trees, alas. Every new book reduces the quantity of oxygen. We should start thinking of ecological books. When, in the last century, the book industry stopped making books from rags and started to make them from trees, it not only menaced our survival, it jeopardized the civilization of the book. A modern book cannot survive more than seventy years. I have books from the 50s that I can no longer open. In the next fifty years the modern section of my personal library will be a handful of

dust. We know that acid-free paper is expensive, and that chemical procedures for preserving already existing books can be reasonably applied only to a limited number of them. To microfilm all the books contained in a huge library will certainly save their content, but will limit the opportunity to consult them to a small number of professional students. A way to escape this danger is to republish books every few years. But decisions of this type are regulated by the market and by public demand. According to this criterion, a thousand years from now *Gone with the Wind* will survive, and *Ulysses* will not.

The only solution would be to appoint special committees to decide which books to save (by chemical rescue, by reprint, or by microfilm). The power of such committees would be enormous. Not even Torquemada, or Big Brother in *1984*, had such an authority to select.

I am an author. I want not to be saved by a special committee. I want not to be saved by mass demand. I want not to be saved in the form of a cryptic microfilm. I want to survive for centuries and centuries, unknown to everybody, in the secret of an old forgotten library, as happened to the classical authors during the Middle Ages. I cannot. I know for sure that I cannot. Should I sell myself to Gorbachev, to Reagan, to the Pope, to Khomeini, in order to have as a reward an acid-free edition?

5.   Finally, who will decide which books to give to the Third World? I recently attended a meeting at the Frankfurt Book Fair, organized by German publishers, about the need to send books to the young people of Nicaragua. I was sympathetic to the initiative, and I trust the group that invited me. But the problem is bigger than that. The whole of the Third World is escaping from illiteracy in the sense that the kids there will probably learn to read and write. But they will not have the economic possibility of having books. Who will choose the books for them? The American fundamentalist churches which are engaged in an economic push to spread their doctrines through Latin America? The Soviet Union? The Roman Church?

I suppose that three-quarters of the world population today cannot afford books. They can only accept some of them graciously. Who will decide for them? The immediate future offers the opportunity to make millions and millions of people think in one way or another, depending on the economic and organizational effort of those who decide to send them books. I feel worried by the power that somebody—I don't know who, but certainly not my university—will have in the next few decades.

Note

1. *Imago mundi:* a compendium of cosmology and geography popular throughout the Middle Ages and translated into various vernaculars.

REFLECTING ON THE READING

1. What recent events does Eco claim have given him occasion to write this essay? Why are these events important to a discussion of the future of literacy? What might they suggest about how our society views literacy?

2. Who are the "yuppies" Eco refers to early in this essay? Why are they important to his discussion of literacy? What is their "problem" regarding literacy, according to Eco? Do you think his assessment of them is accurate? Explain.

3. What are the two main points Eco says he wishes to make in this essay? What does he mean by an "enlightened policy on literacy"?

4. How does Eco describe today's teenagers as readers? Why is this description of teenagers as readers important to his point about literacy? Does his description seem accurate to you? Why or why not?

5. Why does Eco call the computer a "false friend"? How does he describe the computer as a reading tool? What does this description suggest about Eco's views regarding technology? Do you think his description is accurate? Does it match your own experience with reading and with computers? Explain.

6. What does Eco illustrate by his example of the short text "TWO SMITH ROCKEFELLER"? Is he being ironic in this instance? How do you know?

7. About halfway through his essay, Eco writes, "The enemies of literacy are hiding elsewhere." What does he mean by this statement? What does it tell you about his opinion of computers as tools for literacy?

8. What does Eco say about the effects of various literacy technologies (such as the printing press and the computer) on human memory? Is he concerned about these effects? Why or why not? Are you? Explain.

9. Eco writes at one point, "Speaking of literacy in the world today we are not only concerned with the happy few of Bloomsbury, but with the masses of the Third World." Who are "the happy few of Bloomsbury" and the "masses of the Third World"? Why, according to Eco, should we be concerned with both? Does he leave anybody out?

10. What are the phenomena that Eco believes are "menacing the universe of books and the cultural heritage that books represent"? Why are these phenomena of concern to Eco?

Examining Rhetorical Strategies

1. Eco begins this essay by referring to Plato's *Phaedrus* and specifically to Plato's retelling of the story of Thoth, the mythical inventor of writing in ancient Egypt. Plato uses that story to express concerns about the technology of writing. But Eco tells us, "Nowadays nobody shares these concerns." Why, then, does he refer to this old story? What purpose does it serve in this essay? What do you think Eco accomplishes by referring to Plato's *Phaedrus* as a way to begin this essay? Do you think this was an effective strategy for him to use in introducing the key points he wishes to make in this essay? How did you react to his reference to Plato? Were you familiar with Plato's *Phaedrus* or the story of Thoth? How do you think your familiarity with this reference or your lack of it affected your reaction to Eco's opening paragraphs? What might your reaction indicate about you as a reader?

2. Note the kinds of references Eco makes throughout his essay. For example, he refers to philosophers like Plato, Cicero, and Thomas Aquinas; to writers like Jules Verne, Karl May, Tacitus, Edward Gibbon, Marshall McLuhan, and Victor Hugo; to works like *Gone With the Wind, 1984,* and *Ulysses;* to historical events like "Black Thursday." What do these references tell you about Eco as a writer? What do they suggest about the audience he assumed for his essay? What sort of audience is it? Are you part of that audience? How did these references affect you? Could Eco have effectively made his points in this essay without making such references? How might the essay have been different without these references?

3. How would you characterize Eco's voice in this essay? Does he sound "scholarly" to you? Does he sound like a theorist? Do you think his voice is effective in this essay, given what he is writing about and the points he seems to make? Cite specific lines in the essay to justify your answer.

4. Eco argues that a "series of phenomena" (he offers five such phenomena) are "menacing the universe of books and the cultural heritage that books represent." What exactly is the "cultural heritage that books represent"? Whose heritage is this? Is it a heritage that you share? Is it one that everyone shares? What might this assertion indicate about Eco's assumptions regarding his readers?

5. How would you summarize Eco's overall point about literacy and technology in this essay? What, specifically, are his concerns? Given that this essay was originally published by a university press in a volume intended primarily for academic readers, do you think Eco's point is intended to worry or soothe his audience about the future of literacy? Does it worry or soothe you? Why or why not? How might your reaction differ from the reaction you think Eco wished to provoke in his readers?

6. In whose interest do you think Eco is expressing his concerns about the future of literacy? Do you think he is concerned with both "the happy few of Bloomsbury" and the "masses of the Third World," as he seems to suggest? Based on what he writes in the final few paragraphs of his essay about himself as an author, do you think he is primarily concerned with the literacy needs of a specific group? Are you part of the groups he mentions in this essay? Who might be left out of these groups?

Engaging the Issues

1. Write your own essay expressing your concerns, hopes, and/or expectations for the future of literacy in view of technological developments such as the World Wide Web and trends such as test scores or educational reforms that you see. Try to identify key problems you see regarding literacy and discuss what those problems might mean in years to come. Imagine an audience of your classmates—that is, an audience who shares some of the same knowledge and experience regarding literacy and technology that you have as a result of your reading and writing assignments for this writing course.

2. Write the essay described in Question #1 for a general audience of readers who may have little or no familiarity with the technology and "cultural heritage" that

Eco refers to in his essay. When you're finished, consider how your sense of your readers' experiences, knowledge, and socioeconomic status might have affected the way you wrote your essay.

3. Create an online version of the essay you wrote for Question #1 or #2 above. For example, construct a page for the World Wide Web or a multimedia hypertext that can be posted on the Web. When you're finished, compare your web site or hypertext to the essay you wrote. How do they differ in conveying their messages? How will readers respond to each? Will the audience be different for the Web site or hypertext than for the conventional essay? In what ways? How might those differences have affected the way you constructed your Web site or hypertext? Try to draw conclusions about what forms such as hypertext might mean for the future of literacy.

4. Write a rhetorical analysis of Eco's essay. In your analysis, consider specific aspects of his essay, such as its tone, content, structure, and use of examples and references, in view of his original audience for the essay (readers of an academic book published by a university press). Describe Eco's strategies in addressing his audience. Draw conclusions about the effectiveness of his essay for such an audience.

5. In a group of your classmates, compare your reactions to Eco's essay. Identify specific differences and similarities in the way you and the other members of your group responded to Eco's essay. Try to explain these differences in terms of your backgrounds, experiences as academic readers and writers, and/or knowledge of technology.

6. Using the Internet or your library, locate some other articles or books that examine the future of literacy. In your search, try to find academic discussions of the future of literacy as well as articles in the popular press that discuss new technologies. Compare the various predictions made by the writers you find. Then write a conventional academic essay in which you provide an overview of the various predictions made for the future of literacy. In your essay, describe some of the important technological developments that writers and scholars are most concerned about and discuss the implications they see for literacy. Draw conclusions about the validity of the various predictions that have been made about technology and literacy in the future.

FURTHERING YOUR INQUIRY

1. In a group of your classmates, compare your writing processes and consider how the technologies you use affect the way you all write. First, describe your own process of writing. What do you do first? Second? Third? Do you take notes? Brainstorm aloud or on paper? Talk to friends? Use an outline? Write in short sessions or complete an entire draft in one sitting? Revise as you go or wait until the draft is finished? Compare your process with your peers. In what ways are your various writing processes similar or different? How might you explain these differences and similarities? Now consider your use of technology. Do you write with a computer, with pen and paper, with a typewriter, or with some combination of these? How does the technology you use affect where, when,

and how you write? Would you write differently with different technologies? How? Discuss these matters with your peers. Finally, rethink your discussion about your writing process in light of the readings by some of the writers in this chapter, such as Steven Johnson, Wendell Berry, Julian Dibbell, and Jay David Bolter. Do their ideas about writing make sense given your own experience? Is your thinking really changed, as they suggest, by the way you write and the technologies you use? If so, in what ways? If not, explain the differences and similarities you see among you and your peers.

2. Compose a dialogue (or debate) between Steven Johnson and Wendell Berry. On the basis of their two essays, how do you think they might respond to each other? What issues would most vigorously engage them? Where might they most obviously disagree? Agree?

3. Compare the ways in which several of the authors of the selections in this chapter use language and construct their arguments. What similarities and differences do you see among them? How can you account for these similarities and differences? For example, how is Steven Johnson's approach different from that of Wendell Berry? How are those two different from Jay David Bolter or Umberto Eco? What specific differences do you see in the language they use, in the way they use evidence, and in the way they construct their respective arguments? Can you account for these differences by considering the audiences each was writing for? Focus your analysis on three or four of the authors in this chapter.

4. Write an essay in which you define *writing*. Draw as you see fit from the readings in this chapter as you try to explain to a general audience what writing is.

   Alternatively, working in a group of three or four of your classmates, write a brief essay that defines *writing* for a specific audience that differs from the audiences that each of the other members of your group is addressing. For example, you might write for a newspaper editorial page, while another group member writes for a class of high school students, another for parents of elementary school children, another for school board members, and another for a local business council. Compare your respective essays and discuss similarities and differences. Try to account for the role of audience in explaining these differences.

5. Construct a dialogue between Wendell Berry and Jay David Bolter on the merits of writing as a technology. Consider carefully what each might say about the benefits and risks associated with writing and the new technologies we use for writing. Be sure to consider the specific backgrounds of each person as you imagine what each might say to the other on this subject.

6. In the ongoing public discussions about education reform, critics and editorialists are fond of arguing about the merits of getting "back to basics" when it comes to teaching writing and reading. Typically, these commentators discuss—directly or indirectly—the importance of writing and reading, and they sometimes address the need for schools to incorporate more computer technology into the curriculum. Find an editorial from a newspaper (or similar popular publication) that addresses this issue of the importance of writing and reading. Consider how the author makes his or her case. Then examine the author's

arguments and assumptions about writing and reading in light of one or more of the readings in this chapter. In other words, how might the passage by Bolter or Berry or Dibbell provide you another way of understanding the issue that the editorial you're examining is addressing? Does it give you insight into this issue? Now write a response to the editorial in which you consider the author's argument from this new perspective.

7. Construct a site for the World Wide Web about literacy and technology. Using readings from this chapter, appropriate sites that you have found on the Web, and any other appropriate sources, construct your site so that it offers a particular perspective on literacy and technology. Construct your site with a specific audience in mind.

   Compare your site to the sites of other classmates or similar sites you have found on the Internet. Identify differences in similarities and assess how each site conveys its messages for the audience(s) it seems to address.

8. Each of the authors in this chapter writes from a perspective that implies various assumptions about writing, about literacy in general, and/or about technology. Write a conventional academic essay in which you identify and describe the main assumptions about literacy and technology that emerge from all or several of the readings in this chapter. Offer support from the readings themselves in your essay and draw conclusions about any problems you see with the assumptions you identify.

9. Identify an issue or problem concerning literacy and technology that emerges for you from several of the readings in this chapter and conduct an extended inquiry into that issue or problem. Frame the issue or problem as a question. For example, what impact are computers having on how people read? Use whatever sources of information you deem appropriate (including the World Wide Web, your classmates, the library, and teachers or professors) in order to try to answer that question. Then write a report on the issue or problem based on your inquiry. Imagine an audience of your classmates (or some other appropriate audience) for your report.

10. Investigate the history of a specific literacy technology, such as the typewriter or copy machine. Try to find out how that particular technology came to be developed and explore the economic, social, and cultural circumstances surrounding its development and use. Write a report for your classmates on the history of the technology you've chosen. If that technology is no longer in use, try to account for that as well.

CHAPTER 3

Literacy, Technology, and Identity

The great nineteenth-century American poet Walt Whitman began one of his poems with the line, "One's-Self I sing, a simple separate person." That line sums up one of the most enduring beliefs about writing in Western culture: that writing is fundamentally a means of self-expression, a way of proclaiming who you are and what you think—a way to "sing" your self. So deep is this belief in Western culture that we take it for granted that when we write, we are in effect putting on paper (or a computer screen) our own unique ideas or thoughts in our own words. To write is to "be yourself." And the desire to do that seems to be as basic as the desire to speak. But as anyone who has ever taken up a pen or punched the keys of a typewriter or computer knows all too well, expressing yourself in writing is no easy task. Indeed, to "be yourself" in writing is a far more complicated matter than it might seem at first glance. For when we write, we do not merely express ourselves: we also *create* ourselves.

Consider, for example, what is involved in the act of writing a resume and a letter of application for a job. That activity seems straightforward enough: you compile a resume that describes the previous jobs you have had and the skills and experience you possess; you compose a cover letter explaining your qualifications for the job. In effect, in your resume and cover letter you present yourself to your potential employer. Those two documents thus represent who you are to that employer. But in practical terms, those documents cannot possibly include everything there is to know about you—or even very much of what there is to know about you—as a potential employee and as a person. For instance, you will probably not include information about the way you dress, the bills you pay, the food you eat, the people you love, the places you've been, the things you've seen, the hopes and fears you have. Such information is not relevant to the task at hand, which is to obtain the job, so you exclude it from your resume. But that information nevertheless is an important part of who you are; it is part of your identity, your *self.* If it is not included in the resume and cover letter, can you then say that those documents really represent who you are? We might more accurately say they represent a *version* of you—a version that you create when you write those documents. In other words, you create a particular identity for yourself when you write your resume and cover letter, an identity that seems appropriate for the job for which you are applying. And that identity might be different in a variety of ways from the identity you create when you submit an application for admission to college or send a letter of complaint to your local school board or write a letter to a friend. In each of these instances, you express a slightly different *self.* In this very basic sense, writing is a way to construct your identity.

But many scholars believe that writing and reading are even more deeply implicated in our identities, in our sense of who we are as individuals and members of a particular culture. Indeed, some scholars believe that the very idea of a *self* is a function of literacy. These scholars argue that people in oral cultures—that is, cultures without a written literacy—do not possess a sense of themselves as thinking beings who exist separately from the physical world in the same way that people in literate cultures do. Philosopher David Abram, for example, has argued that the *psyche*—that is, the part of our minds that is capable of contemplating ideas—is "none other than the literate intellect, that part of the self that is born and strengthened in relation to the written letters [of the alphabet]" (*The Spell of the Sensuous,* p. 113). Abram compares how literate people from Western cultures understand their *selves* to how people from oral cultures—such as Australian aboriginal communities or Native American tribes—understand themselves, in order to show that people from oral cultures have a very different sense of their own beings as intimately related to the surroundings in which they live. For scholars like Abram, such comparisons are evidence of the powerful influence literacy has on each person's sense of self. Moreover, some scholars believe that the development of the technology of the printing press further encouraged the idea of a separate, thinking self by promoting literacy and making literacy a central feature of social existence. For example, Walter Ong writes:

> By removing words from the world of sound where they had first had their origin in active human interchange and relegating them definitely to visual surface [that is, on the page], . . . print encouraged human beings to think of their own interior conscious and unconscious resources as more and more thing-like, impersonal and religiously neutral. Print encouraged the mind to sense that its possessions were held in some sort of inert mental space. (*Orality and Literacy,* p. 132)

In other words, Ong believes that print literacy enabled humans to conceptualize the idea of themselves as thinking beings, each with an inner consciousness that exists separately from the world around him or her. For Ong, it isn't just literacy itself but the technology of the printing press that fostered these ideas of *self* among Western peoples. Although analyses such as Ong's have been disputed by some critics, most scholars who study literacy agree that literacy did have a significant influence on the ways in which we understand ourselves as individual beings.

It may seem difficult to accept the idea that the very concept of self—of identity—is a result of literacy, since we are so accustomed to thinking of ourselves as separate, thinking beings. But we need not look far to find examples of more obvious ways in which literacy and technology help shape how we understand who we are. Your signature, for example, is a particular kind of written expression of your identity that has different meanings in different contexts. In a personal letter to a friend, your signature perhaps expresses something of your social or emotional existence, your relationship with your friend, and your sense of yourself as a person. On a bank check, your signature represents your promise that you possess the amount of money written on the check, thus implicitly defining you as an economic being. On a petition opposing a law or supporting a cause, your signature presents you as a political being with a specific viewpoint. In other contexts, your signature might present you as a man or woman, as a person of a particular race, or as someone espousing particular religious views. In short, the seemingly simple act of writing your name can be a complex way of representing your various selves in relation to others and to the world.

As we noted earlier, technology can further complicate this already complicated matter. In a very practical sense, print technology makes it possible to disseminate your words—in a variety of forms—to a wide audience and to preserve your words over time in a way that is not possible in speech or with pen and paper. Books, pamphlets, newspapers, memos, petitions, fliers, and other documents are in one sense vehicles for distributing ideas, in the form of words and images, to readers; thus they enable you to present some version of yourself to many other selves. Recent advances in computer technologies make available to us different and even more powerful media by which we might express and construct ourselves in writing. The act of putting a personal Web page on the Internet, for instance, is a means of presenting a version of yourself instantly to millions of potential viewers. Compare the impact a Web page can have on those many potential viewers to the impact a resume and cover letter can have on a single prospective employer. In this sense, the technologies you use to create a Web page can be powerful tools in creating an identity and in determining the impact of that identity. But the use of such electronic media may mean even more. Theorist Jay David Bolter (whose writing appears in Chapter 2 of this book) believes that electronic technologies are changing our very definition of self in ways that are just as important as the changes that Ong believes were brought on by the printing press centuries ago. Radio, television, print, and computers, he argues, "are means of representation and self-presentation. They are media for presenting ourselves to ourselves and others, and as such they invite a definition and redefinition of the self" ("Virtual Reality," *Communication and Cyberspace,* p. 112). In cyberspace, he writes, "the self is no longer constructed as an autonomous, authorial voice; it becomes instead a wandering eye that occupies various perspectives, one after the other" (p. 106). According to Bolter, the very idea of the self as a separate, thinking, autonomous being—an idea so deeply ingrained in Western culture—is being challenged and even made obsolete by the new technologies of cyberspace.

Some of the authors in this chapter would not agree with Bolter's vision of the future, but they all agree that reading, writing, and technology are centrally implicated in our sense of ourselves and the ways in which we present ourselves to others. They offer a variety of perspectives from which we might examine how our understanding of ourselves is related to the writing and reading we do and to the technologies we use to communicate. For some of these authors, writing and reading are deeply personal ways in which to make sense of themselves, as people with a particular racial or gender identity, and the world. Others state that writing and reading—and how one learns to write and read—are intimately connected to one's cultural background and thus are a vital part of one's identity. And still others are directly concerned with how technology relates to one's sense of self. A few of these writers worry about the connection between technology and identity, suggesting that the increasing use of technologies like the Internet may signal serious problems for modern society. Together, the varied selections in this chapter present a complex picture of the ways in which literacy and technology are intimately wrapped up in our identities as individuals and as members of various communities. The writers whose work appears in this chapter may prompt you to think differently about the many common ways in which you use writing and reading in your own life. Those uses of writing and reading, from signing your name to writing a letter to completing a long report to logging onto an Internet chat room, may not only reveal a great deal about who you are and how you think of yourself but may also be the means by which you create your identity and use it in the world.

Becoming a Poet

Jimmy Santiago Baca

INTRODUCTION   "I never existed except through language," poet Jimmy Santiago Baca told an interviewer. In his compelling poetry and prose, Baca describes this process of creating himself through language in the midst of a difficult, sometimes terrifying and violent, life. As a young boy growing up in his native New Mexico, Baca became enmeshed in the violence of the *barrio* (or neighborhood) where he lived, and by his teenage years he was routinely in trouble with the law. At the age of eighteen, he was sent to prison on a narcotics charge stemming from his involvement in a gunfight between police and friends of his who were dealing drugs—a gunfight that left an officer dead. In prison he endured unspeakable abuse as he refused to cooperate with prison authorities, and he sank into a deep depression. Eventually, slowly and painfully, Baca pulled himself out of this state, which he has described as animal-like. He did so, he says, by discovering language: "I began to tie words together and knot words together, in such a way, where it voided me from this reality."

Baca describes this process in graphic and sometimes horrifying detail in his book *Working in the Dark: Reflections of a Poet of the Barrio* (1992), from which the following passage is excerpted. Baca was unable to read when he was first imprisoned, but he was exposed to reading by other prisoners who read to one another. The experience stirred in him a deep sense of the importance of language to his own sense of self. But it wasn't until he stole a book from a guard that Baca began to read and eventually to write and thus fully uncover this sense of himself through literacy. For Baca, the process was sometimes difficult but profound and life-changing. Writing and reading became the means by which he created himself. He described it to an interviewer in this way:

> I was all debris, but every single item in that cloud of debris had with it the sharp edges of a fragment of belonging to a whole somewhere. . . . And so language began for me as a tool by which I could put the fragments together. Once those

fragments were put together, not so much in a Chicano, not so much in a casi indio, detribalized Apache, but as a human being with a right to live on earth, a citizen of the earth. That's how I was formed primarily.*

Ultimately, Baca's early efforts to teach himself to read and write blossomed into a career as a critically acclaimed poet who speaks not only for Chicanos but for all of humanity. He has published several collections of poems including *Martin & Meditations on the South Valley* (1987) and *Black Mesa Poems* (1989), and is the author of *In the Way of the Sun* (1997). Among the many awards he has received for his writing are the Pushcart Prize and the American Book Award. He has also taught writing at Yale University, the University of California at Berkeley, and Colorado College.

REFLECTING BEFORE READING

1. In this passage, Baca refers often to language and its importance to him. Consider the ways in which he describes language. What exactly does he mean when he refers to language? Is there a connection between his spoken language and the poetry he eventually began to write?

2. Baca suggests in this passage that writing made him human. In what sense do you think writing can "make one human"? As you read, consider how Baca used writing to confront the terrible difficulties he describes in this passage.

O n weekend graveyard shifts at St. Joseph's Hospital I worked the emergency room, mopping up pools of blood and carting plastic bags stuffed with arms, legs, and hands to the outdoor incinerator. I enjoyed the quiet, away from the screams of shotgunned, knifed, and mangled kids writhing on gurneys outside the operating rooms. Ambulance sirens shrieked and squad car lights reddened the cool nights, flashing against the hospital walls: gray—red, gray—red. On slow nights I would lock the door of the administration office, search the reference library for a book on female anatomy and, with my feet propped on the desk, leaf through the illustrations, smoking my cigarette. I was seventeen.

One night my eye was caught by a familiar-looking word on the spine of a book. The title was *450 Years of Chicano History in Pictures.* On the cover were black-and-white photos: Padre Hidalgo exhorting Mexican peasants to revolt against the Spanish dictators; Anglo vigilantes hanging two Mexicans from a tree; a young Mexican woman with rifle and ammunition belts crisscrossing her breast; César Chávez and field workers marching for fair wages; Chicano railroad workers laying creosote ties; Chicanas laboring at machines in textile factories; Chicanas picketing and hoisting boycott signs.

From the time I was seven, teachers had been punishing me for not knowing my lessons by making me stick my nose in a circle chalked on the blackboard. Ashamed of not understanding and fearful of asking questions, I dropped out of school in the

---

* *Las Americas Journal,* vol. 19 (winter 1991): pp. 64–86.

ninth grade. At seventeen I still didn't know how to read, but those pictures confirmed my identity. I stole the book that night, stashing it for safety under the slop sink until I got off work. Back at my boardinghouse, I showed the book to friends. All of us were amazed; this book told us we were alive. We, too, had defended ourselves with our fists against hostile Anglos, gasping for breath in fights with the policemen who outnumbered us. The book reflected back to us our struggle in a way that made us proud.

Most of my life I felt like a target in the cross hairs of a hunter's rifle. When strangers and outsiders questioned me I felt the hang-rope tighten around my neck and the trapdoor creak beneath my feet. There was nothing so humiliating as being unable to express myself, and my inarticulateness increased my sense of jeopardy, of being endangered. I felt intimidated and vulnerable, ridiculed and scorned. Behind a mask of humility, I seethed with mute rebellion.

Before I was eighteen, I was arrested on suspicion of murder after refusing to explain a deep cut on my forearm. With shocking speed I found myself handcuffed to a chain gang of inmates and bused to a holding facility to await trial. There I met men, prisoners, who read aloud to each other the works of Neruda, Paz, Sabines, Nemerov, and Hemingway. Never had I felt such freedom as in that dormitory. Listening to the words of these writers, I felt that invisible threat from without lessen—my sense of teetering on a rotting plank over swamp water where famished alligators clapped their horny snouts for my blood. While I listened to the words of the poets, the alligators slumbered powerless in their lairs. Their language was the magic that could liberate me from myself, transform me into another person, transport me to other places far away.

And when they closed the books, these Chicanos, and went into their own Chicano language, they made barrio life come alive for me in the fullness of its vitality. I began to learn my own language, the bilingual words and phrases explaining to me my place in the universe. Every day I felt like the paper boy taking delivery of the latest news of the day.

Months later I was released, as I had suspected I would be. I had been guilty of nothing but shattering the windshield of my girlfriend's car in a fit of rage.

Two years passed. I was twenty now, and behind bars again. The federal marshals had failed to provide convincing evidence to extradite me to Arizona on a drug charge, but still I was being held. They had ninety days to prove I was guilty. The only evidence against me was that my girlfriend had been at the scene of the crime with my driver's license in her purse. They had to come up with something else. But there was nothing else. Eventually they negotiated a deal with the actual drug dealer, who took the stand against me. When the judge hit me with a million-dollar bail, I emptied my pockets on his booking desk: twenty-six cents.

One night in my third month in the county jail, I was mopping the floor in front of the booking desk. Some detectives had kneed an old drunk and handcuffed him to the booking bars. His shrill screams raked my nerves like a hacksaw on bone, the desperate protest of his dignity against their inhumanity. But the detectives just laughed as he tried to rise and kicked him to his knees. When they went to the bathroom to pee and the desk attendant walked to the file cabinet to pull the arrest record, I shot my arm through the bars, grabbed one of the attendant's university textbooks, and tucked it in my overalls. It was the only way I had of protesting.

It was late when I returned to my cell. Under my blanket I switched on a pen flashlight and opened the thick book at random, scanning the pages. I could hear the jailer making his rounds on the other tiers. The jangle of his keys and the sharp click of his boot heels intensified my solitude. Slowly I enunciated the words . . . p-o-n-d, ri-pple. It scared me that I had been reduced to this to find comfort. I always had thought reading a waste of time, that nothing could be gained by it. Only by action, by moving out into the world and confronting and challenging the obstacles, could one learn anything worth knowing.

Even as I tried to convince myself that I was merely curious, I became so absorbed in how the sounds created music in me and happiness, I forgot where I was. Memories began to quiver in me, glowing with a strange but familiar intimacy in which I found refuge. For a while, a deep sadness overcame me, as if I had chanced on a long-lost friend and mourned the years of separation. But soon the heartache of having missed so much of life, that had numbed me since I was a child, gave way, as if a grave illness lifted itself from me and I was cured, innocently believing in the beauty of life again. I stumblingly repeated the author's name as I fell asleep, saying it over and over in the dark: Words-worth, Words-worth.

Before long my sister came to visit me, and I joked about taking her to a place called Kubla Khan and getting her a blind date with this *vato* named Coleridge who lived on the seacoast and was *malías* on morphine. When I asked her to make a trip into enemy territory to buy me a grammar book, she said she couldn't. Bookstores intimidated her, because she, too, could neither read nor write.

Days later, with a stub pencil I whittled sharp with my teeth, I propped a Red Chief notebook on my knees and wrote my first words. From that moment, a hunger for poetry possessed me.

Until then, I had felt as if I had been born into a raging ocean where I swam relentlessly, flailing my arms in hope of rescue, of reaching a shoreline I never sighted. Never solid ground beneath me, never a resting place. I had lived with only the desperate hope to stay afloat; that and nothing more.

But when at last I wrote my first words on the page, I felt an island rising beneath my feet like the back of a whale. As more and more words emerged, I could finally rest: I had a place to stand for the first time in my life. The island grew, with each page, into a continent inhabited by people I knew and mapped with the life I lived.

I wrote about it all—about people I had loved or hated, about the brutalities and ecstasies of my life. And, for the first time, the child in me who had witnessed and endured unspeakable terrors cried out not just in impotent despair, but with the power of language. Suddenly, through language, through writing, my grief and my joy could be shared with anyone who would listen. And I could do this all alone; I could do it anywhere. I was no longer a captive of demons eating away at me, no longer a victim of other people's mockery and loathing, that had made me clench my fist white with rage and grit my teeth to silence. Words now pleaded back with the bleak lucidity of hurt. They were wrong, those others, and now I could say it.

Through language I was free. I could respond, escape, indulge; embrace or reject earth or the cosmos. I was launched on an endless journey without boundaries or rules, in which I could salvage the floating fragments of my past, or be born anew in the spontaneous ignition of understanding some heretofore concealed aspect of myself. Each word steamed with the hot lava juices of my primordial making, and I crawled out of stanzas dripping with birth-blood, reborn and freed from the chaos of my life. The child in the dark room of my heart, that had never been able to find or reach the light switch, flicked it on now; and I found in the room a stranger, myself, who had waited so many years to speak again. My words struck in me lightning crackles of elation and thunderhead storms of grief.

When I had been in the county jail longer than anyone else, I was made a trustee. One morning, after a fistfight, I went to the unlocked and unoccupied office used for lawyer-client meetings, to think. The bare white room with its fluorescent tube lighting seemed to expose and illuminate my dark and worthless life. And yet, for the first time, I had something to lose—my chance to read, to write; a way to live with dignity and meaning, that had opened for me when I stole that scuffed, sec- ondhand book about the Romantic poets. In prison, the abscess had been lanced.

"I will never do any work in this prison system as long as I am not allowed to get my G.E.D." That's what I told the reclassification panel. The captain flicked off the tape recorder. He looked at me hard and said, "You'll never walk outta here alive. Oh, you'll work, put a copper penny on that, you'll work."

After that interview I was confined to deadlock maximum security in a subter- ranean dungeon, with ground-level chicken-wired windows painted gray. Twenty- three hours a day I was in that cell. I kept sane by borrowing books from the other cons on the tier. Then, just before Christmas, I received a letter from Harry, a char- ity house samaritan who doled out hot soup to the homeless in Phoenix. He had picked my name from a list of cons who had no one to write to them. I wrote back asking for a grammar book, and a week later received one of Mary Baker Eddy's treatises on salvation and redemption, with Spanish and English on opposing pages. Pacing my cell all day and most of each night, I grappled with grammar until I was able to write a long true-romance confession for a con to send to his pen pal. He paid me with a pack of smokes. Soon I had a thriving barter business, exchanging my poems and letters for novels, commissary pencils, and writing tablets.

One day I tore two flaps from the cardboard box that held all my belongings and punctured holes along the edge of each flap and along the border of a ream of state- issue paper. After I had aligned them to form a spine, I threaded the holes with a shoestring, and sketched on the cover a hummingbird fluttering above a rose. This was my first journal.

Whole afternoons I wrote, unconscious of passing time or whether it was day or night. Sunbursts exploded from the lead tip of my pencil, words that grafted me into awareness of who I was; peeled back to a burning core of bleak terror, an embryo floating in the image of water, I cracked out of the shell wide-eyed and insane. Trees grew out of the palms of my hands, the threatening otherness of life dissolved, and I became one with the air and sky, the dirt and the iron and concrete. There was no longer any distinction between the other and I. Language made bridges of fire between me and everything I saw. I entered into the blade of grass, the basketball, the con's eye, and child's soul.

At night I flew. I conversed with floating heads in my cell, and visited strange houses where lonely women brewed tea and rocked in wicker rocking chairs listening to sad Joni Mitchell songs.

Before long I was frayed like a rope carrying too much weight, that suddenly snaps. I quit talking. Bars, walls, steel bunk, and floor bristled with millions of poem-making sparks. My face was no longer familiar to me. The only reality was the swirling cornucopia of images in my mind, the voices in the air. Mid-air a cactus blossom would appear, a snake-flame in blinding dance around it, stunning me like a guard's fist striking my neck from behind.

The prison administrators tried several tactics to get me to work. For six months, after the next monthly prison board review, they sent cons to my cell to hassle me. When the guard would open my cell door to let one of them in, I'd leap out and fight him—and get sent to thirty-day isolation. I did a lot of isolation time. But I honed my image-making talents in that sensory-deprived solitude. Finally they moved me to death row, and after that to "nut-run," the tier that housed the mentally disturbed.

As the months passed, I became more and more sluggish. My eyelids were heavy, I could no longer write or read. I slept all the time.

One day a guard took me out to the exercise field. For the first time in years I felt grass and earth under my feet. It was spring. The sun warmed my face as I sat on the bleachers watching the cons box and run, hit the handball, lift weights. Some of them stopped to ask how I was, but I found it impossible to utter a syllable. My tongue would not move, saliva drooled from the corners of my mouth. I had been so heavily medicated I could not summon the slightest gesture. Yet inside me a small voice cried out, I am fine! I am hurt now but I will come back! I am fine!

Back in my cell, for weeks I refused to eat. Styrofoam cups of urine and hot water were hurled at me. Other things happened. There were beatings, shock therapy, intimidation.

Later, I regained some clarity of mind. But there was a place in my heart where I had died. My life had compressed itself into an unbearable dread of being. The strain had been too much. I had stepped over that line where a human being has lost more than he can bear, where the pain is too intense, and he knows he is changed forever. I was now capable of killing, coldly and without feeling. I was empty, as I have never, before or since, known emptiness. I had no connection to this life.

But then, the encroaching darkness that began to envelop me forced me to re-form and give birth to myself again in the chaos. I withdrew even deeper into the world of language, cleaving the diamonds of verbs and nouns, plunging into the brilliant light of poetry's regenerative mystery. Words gave off rings of white energy, radar signals from powers beyond me that infused me with truth. I believed what I wrote, because I wrote what was true. My words did not come from books or textual formulas, but from a deep faith in the voice of my heart.

I had been steeped in self-loathing and rejected by everyone and everything—society, family, cons, God, and demons. But now I had become as the burning ember floating in darkness that descends on a dry leaf and sets flame to forests. The word was the ember and the forest was my life.

I was born a poet one noon, gazing at weeds and creosoted grass at the base of a telephone pole outside my grilled cell window. The words I wrote then sailed me out of myself, and I was transported and metamorphosed into the images they made. From the dirty brown blades of grass came bolts of electrical light that jolted loose my old self; through the top of my head that self was released and reshaped in the clump of scrawny grass. Through language I became the grass, speaking its language and feeling its green feelings and black root sensations. Earth was my mother and I bathed in sunshine. Minuscule speckles of sunlight passed through my green skin and metabolized in my blood.

Writing bridged my divided life of prisoner and free man. I wrote of the emotional butchery of prisons, and of my acute gratitude for poetry. Where my blind doubt and spontaneous trust in life met, I discovered empathy and compassion. The power to express myself was a welcome storm rasping at tendril roots, flooding my soul's cracked dirt. Writing was water that cleansed the wound and fed the parched root of my heart.

I wrote to sublimate my rage, from a place where all hope is gone, from a madness of having been damaged too much, from a silence of killing rage. I wrote to avenge the betrayals of a lifetime, to purge the bitterness of injustice. I wrote with a deep groan of doom in my blood, bewildered and dumbstruck; from an indestructible love of life, to affirm breath and laughter and the abiding innocence of things. I wrote the way I wept, and danced, and made love.

REFLECTING ON THE READING

1. What was the importance of the book *450 Years of Chicano History in Pictures* to Baca? What other books does Baca describe as important to him in this passage? How did these books figure into his development as a reader and a writer and, eventually, as a poet? What might the impact of these books on Baca suggest about literacy?

2. Why did Baca eventually try to teach himself to read while he was in prison? What led up to that decision? How do you think that decision might have been influenced by earlier incidents that he describes?

3. Baca writes in this passage, "Through language I was free." What does he mean? In what sense did language make him "free" even while he remained behind bars? Do you think he was writing and reading simply to escape his degrading situation? Or did his writing and reading mean more to him than simply escape? Explain.

4. Baca writes that he refused to work in prison unless he was allowed to earn his high school equivalency diploma (GED). Why do you think earning a GED was so important to him even though he was still able to read and write without it? Why would he endure the horrible physical abuse to which he was subjected as

a result of his refusal to work? What do you think that decision says about Baca as a person? About his attitudes toward writing and reading and education? Do you think his decision was a good one? Explain.

5. How did Baca change as a result of his writing? Do you think he could have experienced those changes without writing? Explain.

Examining Rhetorical Strategies

1. Describe Baca's voice in this passage. What textual features (e.g., word choice, sentence structure) help create this voice? Do you think his voice is appropriate for the kinds of experiences he describes in the passage? Explain.

2. Consider your own attitudes toward Baca as the narrator in this passage. Do you empathize with him as you read this passage? Why or why not? What aspects of the passage do you think affect you most as a reader? For instance, does the violent nature of the experiences he describes influence how you view him? Explain. What might your reaction to him suggest about you as a reader? What might it suggest about the role of our own background and experiences in your reading?

3. Assess Baca's writing style in this passage. How would you describe his style? Identify specific sentences or phrases that stand out for you. What do you find effective (or not effective) about these sentences and phrases? Note especially Baca's use of metaphor, particularly near the end of the passage where he uses images from nature. Do you find his use of metaphor effective? Do you think it helps Baca develop his themes in the passage? Why or why not?

4. Baca has been praised as a poet who speaks compellingly for Chicanos and people of color. Based on this passage, do you think that such praise is justified? In what ways do you think this passage indicates Baca's intention to speak for people of color? Do you feel that Baca speaks to you as a reader? Explain. How might your own racial background have affected the way you reacted to this passage? How might readers from different backgrounds react to his narrative?

5. In the introduction to this passage, Baca states that language was the means by which he gained an identity. Do you think this passage illustrates that idea effectively? How does Baca show that language was his means for creating himself? In your answer, consider the scenes he includes in the passage and the way he describes his experiences with writing and reading.

6. Note the importance of books in this passage. In several instances, Baca refers to books he obtained or books he actually constructed for himself. Why were books so important to Baca? What does his discussion of these books tell us about his attitudes toward books and literacy in general and what they mean to him? Do you agree with his beliefs about books and literacy? Explain. In your answer, make reference to specific passages in Baca's narrative.

7. Throughout this passage, Baca refers to a variety of writers and other historical figures, such as César Chávez, Pablo Neruda, Ernest Hemingway, and William

Wordsworth. Examine these references. Why do you think Baca refers to these particular people? What purposes might these references serve in this passage? Do you think the passage would have been less effective without these references? Explain. What do these references suggest about Baca's own values regarding writing? What do they suggest about Baca's assumptions about his readers? Were you familiar with the people to whom Baca referred? How did his references affect your reading of this passage? What might your reaction to these references suggest about you as a reader?

Engaging the Issues

1. Write a narrative describing your own literacy history. In your narrative, describe experiences you have had that might show the influence of writing and reading in your own life, as Baca does in this passage. You might focus your narrative on a specific experience or event, or you might describe several related experiences or events that occurred over time, as Baca does. Try to construct your narrative so that it provides your readers with a sense of the importance writing and reading might have had for you as a person.

2. In a group of your classmates, share the narratives you wrote for Question #1 above. Compare your respective experiences with literacy as they are described in your narratives. Are there any similarities? What are the most striking differences? How might you account for these similarities and differences? What might these narratives, taken together, tell us about literacy in our lives and our attitudes about literacy?

3. Write an analysis of Baca's passage focusing on his understanding of language and literacy and how that understanding shapes his narrative. What are his beliefs about language, about writing and reading? Where do you see those beliefs emerge in the passage? Does he offer a valid picture of what literacy is? Is that picture realistic? What might his narrative have to tell us about the role of language and literacy in our lives?

4. Write a conventional academic essay in which you describe and evaluate Baca's narrative style. How does he tell his story? What strategies does he use? What kind of language does he use to describe the experiences he has had? Are these aspects of his narrative effective, in your view? Try to provide appropriate evidence from the passage to support your conclusions about his writing.

5. In this passage, Baca refers to the GED, a high school equivalency diploma that many prisoners earn while serving their sentences. In some states, the opportunity to take classes toward a high school or college diploma while in prison has been cut back or eliminated in order to save money. With a partner or group of classmates, discuss whether such programs should be retained in prisons. Research the issue to find out what the situation is in your state. Then write a letter to the Department of Corrections in your state about these programs. In your letter, try to convince the department to maintain, expand, or eliminate such programs, according to your own view of the matter. You might make reference to Jimmy Baca's narrative or to similar narratives that you found in your research. Be sure to consider your audience as you construct your argument.

6. Rewrite the narrative you wrote for Question #1 above as a Web site on the Internet. Construct your Web site so that it tells your story of literacy for a general audience. Make use of any links to other Web sites you think might be appropriate, and try to use the visual capabilities of the Web to recount and enhance your narrative.

7. Compare the narrative you wrote for Question #1 above to the Web site you created for Question #6 above. In what ways do they differ? How are they similar? How did the technologies you used for each assignment influence the final product? Try to draw conclusions about the potential impact of technology on the way we construct our identities through writing.

Black Feminist Process

In the Midst of . . .

BARBARA CHRISTIAN

INTRODUCTION   In the past two or three decades, the identity of writers has become a central concern for professional literary critics like Barbara Christian. According to these critics, the specific cultural background of a writer—his or her race, gender, social class, and ethnic heritage—profoundly shapes who that writer is and how he or she writes. From this perspective, we cannot adequately understand a particular written work—a poem, novel, or essay—without accounting for the identity of the writer and the cultural context within which that writer lived. To account for identity and cultural context in this way involves much more than simply noting where a writer lived or when he or she wrote: it also involves exploring the complex ways in which writing is connected to one's own identity and how that connection affects not only what a writer has written but how others read that writer's work. In short, critics like Christian believe that writing can never be separated from the *identity* of the writer. For Christian, writing is a way to make one's voice heard, and that voice is always the voice of a specific person who writes from a specific racial, gender, and cultural perspective. In the same way, reading is always a matter of bringing one's own race and gender and culture to a particular text.

In the following essay, which is the introduction to a collection of academic essays that Christian edited called *Black Feminist Criticism: Perspectives on Black Women Writers* (1985), Christian explores the connections among writing, reading, race, and gender and makes an argument about the importance of a particular kind of reading: literary criticism. She makes that argument in the context of her own acclaimed work as a literary critic as well as from her perspective as the mother of a young daughter. Christian, who is a professor of African American studies at the University of California at Berkeley, has published many articles of criticism and several books including *Black Woman Novelists: The Development of a Tradition*, which received the Before Columbus American Book Award in 1993, the *Teaching Guide to Black Foremothers* (1980), and *Black Subjects in Black and White: Psychoanalysis,*

Race and Feminism (1997). Her work is devoted to exploring and celebrating the tradition of Black women writers, and in that work, she has been a pioneer. She was the first Black woman in the Ph.D. program in contemporary British and American literature at Columbia University and the first Black woman to receive tenure at the University of California at Berkeley. She has done ground-breaking work in helping bring Black women writers into the mainstream curriculum in English studies, and she is the contemporary editor of the first *Norton Anthology of African American Literature* (1996). The essay reprinted here provides some sense of the way she understands her work and why she has been so committed to it. It also offers a way to understand the relationship between literacy and identity.

REFLECTING BEFORE READING

1. For Barbara Christian, your race, gender, and social class are crucial elements in the way you write and read. Before you read Christian's essay, consider your own cultural background and the way it might affect you as a writer and a reader. In what sense can you say that you read as a man or a woman and as a person of a particular racial or ethnic background?

2. In her essay, Christian discusses what she believes is the importance of reading and writing to all people but especially to those people from specific groups that have been outside the mainstream. As you read, consider how Christian's arguments grow out of her own identity as a black woman, a mother, and a professional critic. How has that identity shaped the arguments she makes? How does she place that identity in the foreground in making her arguments? Do you think this an effective strategy for making her arguments?

I am sprawling at the low table I work at, surrounded by books and plants, a pad and pencil in front of me. Brow knit, sometimes muttering, sometimes reading or staring out the window, I am engrossed. My 10-year-old daughter touches me.

"Come play a game," she implores.

"I'm working," ending the discussion, I think. Her skeptical face bends down.

"You're not teaching," she retorts, "You're just reading a story."

I see an image from Foucault's "Fantasia of the Library," at the center of which is a European male reader, surrounded by books, which comment on books, his posture rapt. Not too long ago I'd read Marcelle Thiebaux's commentary on Foucault's "Fantasia," in which she proposed replacing the male reader with a woman reader. She reminds us that her reader would occupy a different space; her reading would be seen as time away from her main work. Interruptions would be normal and she would likely be reinterpreting the book she is reading without even being aware of it, reinventing herself in the midst of patriarchal discourse, as to who she is supposed to be.

Quite true, I think, but most of my black sisters *and* brothers would not even have gotten in the library, or if some of them did, like the parlour maid in *Jane Eyre,* they'd be dusting the books. *Their* libraries in Alexandria and elsewhere had been burnt long ago in the wake of conquest and slavery.

Not wishing to prolong the discussion by reminding my daughter that 100 years ago, I would not even have been conceived of as a reader, might in fact have been killed for trying, I notice the Nancy Drew book she has in her hand, her finger still tucked in her place. She's probably solved the mystery already.

"Why are you reading?" she presses.

I know the words that come to my mind—"If I don't save my own life, who will?"—are triggered by the Walker essay I'd been reading and the book under her arm. I dodge her question.

"That would involve a long discussion. I'm working."

But her comment has set my mind on a different track. She knows it, sees the shift, and pulls out her now-constant refrain.

"I'm old enough to know." As indeed she is.

I remember as a young girl in the Caribbean gobbling up Nancy Drew books, involved in the adventures of this intrepid white teenage girl, who solved mysteries, risked danger, was central to her world. I know their pull for a young girl—the need to see oneself as engaging the dangerous world in a fiction protective enough to imagine it, the need to figure out the world, the need to win. And I remember the privileges of Nancy's world—pretty, intelligent, well taken care of, white, American, she had winning allies. What girl actually lives in that universe? What black girl protagonist competed with her? My daughter has read about Harriet Tubman, Mary McLeod Bethune; she has even met Rosa Parks. Historical personages, they are still too awesome for her.

Alice Walker notes in her essay that when Toni Morrison was asked why she wrote the books she did, she replied because she wanted to read them. And Marcelle Thiebaux makes the same comment in the *lit crit* language of our day: "The only possible library for a woman is one invented by herself, writing herself or her own discourse into it."

My daughter is waiting for an answer. If I'd been reading a how-to manual, a history book, or even a cookbook, she'd have accepted the answer about work.

Leaving momentous questions aside, I respond: "I enjoy it."

Abandoned for the moment by her friends, having solved the Nancy Drew mystery, she sees a long boring afternoon ahead. She asks one of her whoppers:

"What good does it do?" Knowing that the reading will turn into writing, she looks at the low table, books, pen, and pencil: "What *are* you doing?"

A good question. I think. But she is not finished. Knowing she's got me in the grip of a conversation, she rallies:

"Why is it that you write mostly about black women's books? You read lots of other books. Is it because you like what they say best?"

Art is not flattery. I think, trying to remember if I'd read that in the Walker essay.

What my daughter was asking is not a new question. It's one I often ask myself. What is a literary critic, a black woman critic, a black feminist literary critic, a black feminist social literary critic? The adjectives mount up, defining, qualifying, the activity. How does one distinguish them? The need to articulate a theory, to categorize the activities is a good part of the activity itself to the point where I wonder how we ever get around to doing anything else. What do these categories tell anyone about my method? Do I do formalist criticism, operative or expressive criticism, mimetic or structuralist criticism (to use the categories I'd noted in a paper by a feminist colleague of mine)? I'm irked, weighed down by Foucault's library as tiers of books written on epistemology, ontology, and technique peer down at me. Can one theorize effectively about an evolving process? Are the labels informative or primarily a way of nipping the question in the bud? What are the philosophical assumptions behind my praxis? I think how the articulation of a theory is a gathering place, sometimes a point of rest as the process rushes on, insisting that you follow. I can see myself trying to explain those tiers of books to my daughter as her little foot taps the floor.

"Well, first of all." I say, having decided to be serious, "I'm a reader," stressing my activeness, as I try to turn her comment "You're just reading" on its head. As I state that simple fact, I think of the many analyses of the critic's role that bypass reading and move immediately to the critic's role as performer, as writer. I continue, "Reading is itself an involved activity. It's a response to some person's thoughts, and language, even possibly their heart."

When I read something that engages me, my reaction is visceral: I sweat, get excited, exalted or irritated, scribble on the edges of the paper, talk aloud to the unseen writer or to myself. Like the Ancient Mariner. I waylay every person in my path, "Have you read this? What about this, this, or this?" This reaction is no news to my daughter. She and her friends get that way about Michael Jackson, TV shows, stickers, possibly even Judy Blume. But that response, of course, is not so much the accepted critical mode, despite Barthes's *plaisir*. It's too suspect, too subjective, not grounded in reality.

Still, when I read much literary criticism today, I wonder if the critic has read the book, since so often the text is but an occasion for espousing his or her philosophical point of view—revolutionary black, feminist, or socialist program. The least we owe the writer, I think, is an acknowledgment of her labor. After all, writing is intentional, is at bottom, work.

I pause, trying to be as clear as possible to Najuma in my description of what I am doing.

"Right now," I say, "I'm listening to the voice, the many voices created by Alice Walker in this book and looking at the way she's using words to make these voices seem alive, so you believe them." (Aha, I think, formalist criticism, expressive criticism, operative criticism.) My daughter does not know these referents.

"Why," she inquires, "so you can write something?" She is now focused on the pencil and pad, which may take my attention away from her.

I try again, this time using a comparison. "Everybody wants to be understood by somebody. If you want somebody to know you, who you are, what you think and feel, you've got to say something. But if nobody indicates they heard you, then it's almost as if you never said anything at all. African people are wise when they say 'speech is knowledge.'"

My last sentence tells me my teaching instinct has been aroused. I'm now intent on her understanding of this point, the Nancy Drew book still in my mind.

"If black women don't say who they are, other people will and say it badly for them." I say, as I remember Audre Lorde's poem about the deadly consequences of silence. "Silence is hardly golden," I continue. "If other black women don't answer back, who will? When we speak and answer back we validate our experiences. We say we *are* important, if only to ourselves." Too hard for her, I think, but she's followed me.

"Like when you and your friends talk on the phone about how politicians don't understand what it means to be a mother?" she quips. "Then, why don't you just call Alice Walker on the phone and tell her what you think about her book?"

She has seen Alice. She's flesh and blood—a pretty brown-skinned woman with a soft voice. But I'm not finished.

"I am a black woman, which means that when I read I have a particular stance. Because it's clear to me that black people, black women, women, poor people, despite our marvelous resilience, are often prevented from being all they can be, I am also a black feminist critic."

I think of literary criticism as a head detaching itself from the rest of a body, claiming subjectivity only in one part of the brain. "Everybody has a point of view about life and about the world, whether they admit it or not," I continue.

"Then," she ventures, "why do you have all these other books around you?" (questioning my definite point of view). "And why can't you just tell Alice Walker what you think?"

While she's talking, she notices, on the low table, Paule Marshall's essay "Poets in the Kitchen." Seeing that our discussion is getting her nowhere, she changes the subject.

"Isn't it funny," she says, "that whenever your friends come over, whether you're cooking or not, you all end up in the kitchen?"

"That's what Paule is talking about." I shift back to our original conversation. "That's why I need all these other books. She's telling us how she learned about language and storytelling from her mother and her mother's friends talking in the kitchen" (rather than just in Foucault's library or Rochester's drawing room, I think).

"Are your friends poets too?" she smiles, amused by the thought. "They're in the kitchen because they're used to it," says Najuma as her face shows that she's begun thinking about the delights of food.

Yes, I think, but it's also because communities revolve around food and warmth, at least until they generate enough surplus to have women or blacks or some other group do it for them and they can retire to the library. (Ah, Marxist criticism?)

"That's true, Najuma, sometimes, we are forced to be there. But even then, human beings often make an opportunity out of a constraint. If we don't recognize what we're doing, the value of what we are doing . . . ? That's part of what a writer does. And as a critic (I now use the ponderous word), I call attention to the form, show how it comes out of a history, a tradition, how the writer uses it. If we and others don't understand Paule's form, that it *is* a form, we can't even hear what she's saying or how meaningful it is."

My being from the Caribbean helps me to recognize that people invent their own forms. I think of Ellison's discussion of the mask Afro-Americans use, of Elaine Showalter's analysis of the double-voiced discourse of women. But I've lost her—my daughter's face puckers. Wondering if interrupting me has been worth it, she looks out the window.

Of course, I think, following my own train of thought, it's even more complicated than that. For in illuminating her kitchen poets, Paule is also calling attention to the constraints imposed on them. In denying her expression as art, those who control the society can continue their cultural hegemony. What's published or seen as central has so much to do with the cultural reproduction of the powerful.

But Najuma has interrupted my thoughts. Intently she asks: "Why do you write it down, why not just tell Alice about her book?" Writing, she knows, is even more private than reading, which separates her from me and has many times landed her in bed before she wanted to go.

I smile. Barthes's comment "Writing is precisely that which exceeds speech" comes to mind. I pause. "Well," I say, again searching for a clear way out. "Writing is another way of ordering your thoughts. You write things differently from the way you say them, if only because you can look back at what you write, at what other people have written, and can look forward to what you may write. A blank piece of paper is an invitation to find out what you think, know, feel, to consciously make connection."

Medium criticism, I think. Is she going to ask about tape recorders or TV shows? No, I've lost her. But if she had asked, I'd remind her that tape recordings are transcribed and edited; even TV shows, as instant as they seem, are based on scripts.

Seeing her perplexity, I try again. "Sometimes," I say, "I haven't the slightest idea what I'm thinking. There's so much rushing through my mind. Don't you feel that way sometimes?" I ask as I look at her stare out the window. "Writing helps to form that chaos (I change the word), all that energy."

I can see she's heard me.

"But what good is it besides knowing a little better what you are thinking. Who cares?"

"Hmm," I mutter, "if you don't care, who will?" But I refrain from this flippant comment and decide to take a leap. "Najuma, do you know why you worry about your kinky hair? Why there are so many poor people in this rich country? Why your friends sometimes tease you about reading too much?"

She pauses, then surprises me: "For the same reason, my school wasn't sure that a jazz class, instead of classical music, would be good music training," she says, imitating a grown-up's voice.

She does notice things; I feel triumphant: "And that has to do with ideas," I continue, "and how they affect consciousness." Does she know the meaning of that word? I use it so often; do I know what it means? "People do things, one of which might be writing, to help themselves and other people ask questions about who they are, who they might be, what kind of world they want to create, to remind ourselves that we do create the world." (I am now being carried away by my own rhetoric.) "I teach too, go to conferences, support organizations I believe in, am a mother," I emphasize, as I begin to worry about whether I've exalted writing too much.

But the writing point holds her: "So," she says, "writers tell people what to do?"

My mind winces. "Well, not so much as they ask questions, try to express reality as they see it, feel it, push against what exists, imagine possibilities, see things that might not yet exist," I say, as I think of Wilson Harris's discourse on vision as a historical dimension.

"Anyway," she says, clearly wanting to end this too serious conversation, "I know what a critic is, because I saw it in the newspaper. You say what's good and what's bad," she says in triumph, knowing that I will finally agree with her.

"Literature is not a horse race," I mutter, as I remember Doris Lessing's response to such a statement. Foucault's library looms again.

Calmly I state: "First you've got to know what it *is* you're reading. What the writer, the person speaking, is doing, which may be unfamiliar since no two of us are, fortunately, alike. Remember how you told me that I didn't understand your way of dressing, that it had a way of its own?" (I see her combining colors I wouldn't even dream of, but when I calm down, they certainly do make their own statement.)

"Then, how do you judge what's good or bad," she says, "since everybody has their own way?"

From the past, I hear R. P. Blackmur's words, "the critic will impose the excellence of something he understands on something he doesn't understand." All those texts from Plato and Aristotle through Northrop Frye, the rationalist critics, the structuralists begin to fall on me. I relax by breathing deeply.

"You play the piano," I remind her. "Sometimes, something you're learning doesn't sound quite right at first, until you begin to see the way it's put together, how it works, what it's trying to do. Then you hear it, something new perhaps, something you just didn't know about before. It sounds beautiful. Writing is like that too. It's got its own workings. At least you need to understand the workings before you can say whether it's done well, which is not the same, I think, as whether you like it or not." I think of the Latin American writers whose work I find beautiful but whose tradition I know little about.

"There's no absolute way to tell what's good or bad," I continue, wondering how I got into this conversation. "I try to hear a writer's voice, or more precisely the one she's gotten on the page in comparison to the one she might have in her head. Then I try to situate that in a tradition that has evolved some approximate ways of how that gets written down best." My thoughts go faster than my speech. I think the best writers are often the ones that break the tradition to continue it. Baraka's comment on art, "hunting is not those heads on the wall," though male, is true.

"In any case," I emphasize, as she retreats to the kitchen, this conversation having become too heavy for her, "every critic knows one thing—writing is a complex activity. That's one of the reasons, I suppose, why we too must write." By now, I'm talking to myself. "And oh, how we write, as we invent our own vocabularies of mystification. Sometimes, things ought to be switched around and writers should get a chance to judge us."

Munching an apple, Najuma passes through the room, sweetly ending the conversation: "It sounds to me like too much work. Why don't you get involved with the airlines, so we can travel free." For her, traveling is the most pleasurable activity humankind has invented. "Or if that's too much, try gardening," she continues, compromising on my fetish for plants. "At least you'd look like you're having fun," she concludes as she turns to her collection of airline flyers.

"But I do have fun doing this," I respond, though, humbled again by the terror of the blank page in front of me, it's a mystery to me why.

REFLECTING ON THE READING

1. What does Christian mean when she writes early in this essay that the libraries of her black sisters and brothers in Alexandria "had been burnt long ago in the wake of conquest and slavery"? To what is she referring? Why is this reference

important to her in this essay? Why does she make this reference near the beginning of her essay?

2. Early in the essay, Christian's daughter asks her, "Why are you reading?" Why is this an important question for Christian? What answers does she give in this essay? Is reading "work," according to Christian? What is the importance of the idea of "work" in Christian's understanding of reading? Do you think she is right? Why or why not?

3. Christian is a professional literary critic, and in this essay she addresses what she sees as the role of such a critic. What is that role, according to Christian? What is the importance of literary criticism, in her view? How is literary criticism different from reading, according to Christian? What problems does she see with literary criticism?

4. Why does Christian engage in literary criticism about Black women writers? What are her reasons for being what she calls a "black feminist critic"? Why are her race and gender important to her work, according to her?

5. What does Christian mean when she says that she has a "particular stance" when she reads? What is your "stance" as a reader?

6. Christian makes several references to socioeconomic status, or social class, in this essay. Why is social class important to her discussion of reading?

7. Why, according to Christian, do people write? Why is it important for Black women to write? Why, according to Christian, should they write instead of just saying what they have to say, as her daughter suggests? What might her view of the importance of writing suggest about literacy?

Examining Rhetorical Strategies

1. Christian begins this passage with an image of her reading while her ten-year-old daughter plays near her. Why do you think she begins the passage in this way? What do these images suggest to you about reading and about gender?

2. In one sense, this essay is an extended answer to the question posed by Christian's daughter, "Why are you reading?" How does Christian organize her essay around that question? How does her answer to that question provide a structure for her essay? Why is the household scene in which she and her daughter are reading important to the points Christian makes in her essay?

3. In this essay, Christian argues that one reads and writes in certain ways because of one's race and gender. What do her views about the role of race and gender in writing and reading indicate about the importance of writing and reading in people's lives? Do you agree with her? Why or why not? Do you think your own race and gender influence how you responded to Christian's views? Explain.

4. In this essay, Christian presents her arguments in the form of answers to her daughter's questions or thoughts about what her daughter has asked her. Assess the effect of this approach on you as a reader. Did you find Christian's voice effective? Did you feel as though she was speaking to you as well as to her daughter? Do you think she intended for you to feel that way? Explain.

5. Do you find Christian's ending effective? Explain why or why not. What do you think Christian wishes to suggest by her ending? What points does she emphasize there? Do you think her ending effectively sums up the central points she has raised in this essay?

6. This essay was published as the introduction to a collection of essays by literary critics about black women writers. The essays in the collection are all scholarly and academic in nature and are intended for an audience of professional critics or students of literature. Why do you think Christian did not write a conventional academic introduction to this collection? Why do you think she included this brief narrative about her conversation with her daughter? What might she accomplish by using such a "nonacademic" essay as an introduction to a collection of academic essays? What might her introduction suggest about her identity as a writer, as she presents it in this essay? In what ways do you think Christian's essay about her conversation with her daughter makes a good introduction to such a collection?

Engaging the Issues

1. Write an essay of your own in which you answer the question, Why do you read? In your essay, try to explore the role of reading in your own life, as Christian does in her essay, and what that might say about the importance of reading in general.

2. In a group of three or four of your classmates, compare your reactions to Christian's views about the role of literacy criticism. Do you agree or disagree? What differences or similarities emerge in your group regarding this question? How do you and your classmates see the role of a literacy critic in American society? What value do you each assign to that role? How might you account for differences in your views about literary criticism?

3. In this essay, Christian makes a connection between writing and reading and one's race and gender. She asserts that when she reads or writes, her own identity as a Black woman shapes her writing and reading in specific ways. Write an essay for an audience of your classmates in which you consider how your own race, gender, and/or ethnicity influence the way you read and write.

4. Consider how your audience might have influenced the essay you wrote for Question #3. Did you explain the complicated matters of race or gender in certain ways that you think were appropriate for your classmates? Did you find it difficult to write about matters of race or gender? Explain. How might you have written your essay differently for a broader audience—for example, readers of a national newspaper?

5. Some critics have argued that literary criticism is an activity that has been reserved for members of an elite class, that it is not an egalitarian or democratic pursuit. In her essay, Christian suggests that women and people of color have traditionally been excluded from the library and drawing room. Yet Christian herself, who is a Black woman, is a literary critic, and she makes an argument for the importance of literary criticism to Black women writers. Write an essay in which you take up this issue of the relationship between literary criticism and

matters of race, class, and gender. How do you see that relationship? Is literary criticism a "universal" activity that is separate from race, class, and gender? Or are race, class, and gender always at the center of the way people write and read? In your essay, you might refer specifically to Christian's essay as you make your own arguments about this issue.

6. Rewrite the essay you wrote for Question #5 as an editorial for your local newspaper (or another general audience). In your editorial, offer your views about the study of literature and/or literary criticism in a way that you think would be effective for this audience.

7. In a conventional academic essay, compare Christian's ideas about the importance of race, class, and gender in writing and reading to Jimmy Santiago Baca's ideas about the importance of writing in his life as a Chicano. In what ways are their arguments about factors such as race and gender in writing similar? How are they different? In your essay, be sure to summarize the views of each writer and try to draw conclusions of your own about the influence of factors like race and gender on writing and reading.

Extra Life
Coming of Age in Cyberspace

DAVID S. BENNAHUM

INTRODUCTION For Jimmy Santiago Baca and Barbara Christian, whose essays appear earlier in this chapter, writing and reading are ways to establish identity; what they read and write is, in a sense, who they are as people. For writer David S. Bennahum, it is not writing and reading as much as technology that defines him. As a member of what he calls the "Atari generation," Bennahum identifies himself by the kinds of computers he has used and the significant role that computers have played in his life.

Bennahum is not unique in his notion that technology is more than the tools we use, that technology is related to how we understand who we are. As some of the readings in this book suggest, technology can profoundly change how we live as well as shape the way we think about ourselves. For instance, some technologies, such as the automobile, are often described as being part of what it means to be an American. For Bennahum, the computer is the central technology that defines his life and his sense of himself as a person. In the following passage, which is taken from his memoir, *Extra Life: Coming of Age in Cyberspace* (1998), he describes some of the experiences he had as a boy who grew up with the earliest desktop computers, and he presents a picture of how those experiences shaped him as a writer and a person. Bennahum's obsession with computers as a boy may be unusual, but his story reveals how technology can deeply influence a person's life; moreover, his story reveals the growing importance of computers and related technologies in American culture during the 1980's, when he was growing up. In this sense, Bennahum's story of his life is part of the story of technology in American culture in the late twentieth century. And his story may help raise questions about the benefits, costs, and broad implications of the development of technologies like computers.

David Bennahum, a contributing editor at *Wired, Spin, Lingua Franca,* and *I.D.,* has written widely on computers and culture for such publications as the *New York Times, The Economist, Harper's Bazaar, Slate,* and *FEED.* In addition to his memoir, he is the author of *In Their Own Words: The Beatles After the BreakUp* (1991) and *k.d. lang* (1994). In 1995 he launched *MEME,* a free email newsletter focusing on cultural, technological, and political issues that had reached twenty thousand subscribers by 1999.

REFLECTING BEFORE READING

1. One critic described David Bennahum's memoir *Extra Life: Coming of Age in Cyberspace,* as "*A Catcher in the Rye* for the Atari generation." Atari was a manufacturer of popular computers and computer games in the 1980's. As you read, consider what it means to identify oneself as a member of the "Atari generation." What does that say about the role of technology in one's life? What value does it place on technology? *A Catcher in the Rye,* a famous novel by J. D. Salinger, tells the story of an adolescent boy who is disaffected with American society after World War II yet struggles to find his own identity within that society. What might it suggest to say that Bennahum's book is like *A Catcher in the Rye?* What might that suggest about the book? About how the critic understood the book?

2. The following excerpt from Bennahum's memoir recalls his boyhood experiences with computers. As you read, consider the kind of environment Bennahum grew up in and how that environment might have played a role in the kinds of experiences he had with technology. Are his experiences representative of most Americans? Are they similar to your own?

T he first computer I ever owned sat in a brown box for ten years. In 1986, just before my high school graduation—after a test of wills that failed to end my mother's marriage—I walked out on her and my stepfather and went to live with my dad. When it became clear I wouldn't be coming back, my mom packed up all my possessions and placed them in a warehouse just about a mile from the Queens side of the 59th Street Bridge, creating a time capsule, a snapshot of my life. There they stayed, left to face the extremes of heat and cold, until one April morning in 1996 when I crossed the East River to reclaim them.

It was a clear day and the halls of the warehouse were dim. Silent rows of metal containers stood side by side, padlocked—a halfway house for cast-off treasures no longer a part of their owners' lives, yet with too much history to be consigned directly to the curb as worthless trash. It was a place frozen in time, where children come to find their parents' things and parents come to leave their children's things.

My computer should have been trash, thrown into the dustbin of technological history like any other electronic appliance unable to compete with the latest upgrade, but putting it out with the garbage would have been like putting an old pet to sleep. Yet I had done just this, abandoning my old companion to fate along with the rest of my belongings.

As my mom led me down the hall of the warehouse looking for container 10C4, I wondered, Will it still work? Will the floppy disks still be readable? Will the disk drives turn on, will the computer's silicon microprocessor carry electricity from one logic gate to the next? Or will the printed circuits and solder have degraded by now, destroyed by time and the vagaries of chance—of hot summers and cold winters expanding and contracting one vital part or another, pushing one piece beyond its limit and rendering the machine a useless heap of junk?

My mom stood before the metal door, key in hand, and unlocked the container. The door swung outward and weak light from the hallway crept in. I felt like an archaeologist poised at the edge of an ancient tomb. Motes of dust glittered in the air. I flipped on our old flashlight and an intimidating wall of boxes came into view. One by one we pulled them out, navigating among cast-off bed frames, tabletops, filing cabinets, and unidentifiable pieces of pieces, until finally we found the four boxes containing the components that formed my first computer system. As we dragged them into the hallway, cardboard scraping along the concrete floor, I had the sensation one gets seeing something long out of mind but never forgotten. A familiar smell wafted out of one box, and even before my eyes confirmed it I knew what it was. Here was my computer, still wrapped in its old dustcover, a cheap piece of vinyl dyed a walnut brown.

Out of another box came a hinged case made of black translucent plastic and decorated with an elephant head. The day I carefully glued on that sticker with the words *Elephant Memory Systems* was sharp as ever. As I lifted the case it swung open and dozens of floppy disks—large flat black things with donutlike holes in the center—broke loose and fell out, sliding onto the floor. Each was labeled in the blocky writing I recognized as my own: *Starcross, Astrochase, Sector Copier, Basic A+, Assembler, Amodem.*

As I bent down to collect the spill of memories I remembered a long-ago time when I'd carefully packed this same case into my bookbag to take to Roger's house at the outer edge of Queens, an hour's subway ride on a line I'd never traveled before. There we spent an entire Saturday afternoon—two twelve-year-olds pirating software, dual drives churning, cables connected, kilobytes of games traveling over telephone wires, through the modem and onto our disks, with Roger's mom occasionally picking up the phone, bewildered, hearing the warbling screeches and beeps of bits through the receiver and from our room, Roger's wailing "Mom!" and a whispered "fuck" from me. Redial and hope that the pirate board won't be busy, its four 300-baud modems jammed up by kids with speed dialers and a hunger for free software.

In the days when modems cost $600 and had to be hand-programmed I'd scored a 1,200-baud modem—four times faster than the usual modems—from my father's office in Manhattan (where he worked building tax shelters). Most of the pirate boards had nothing to match the speed of my modem, which forced me to slow it down to 300. This was the modem I brought to Roger's. His parents, both recent immigrants, were suspicious of what we were doing, but couldn't quite identify what it was or why it was wrong; all they could be sure of was that we were maddeningly intent over some nefarious enterprise, a quiet but clearly conspiratorial look about us.

Every time Roger's father came into the tiny room we leaned in toward the small television set, its blue screen and lines of code littered with the verbs PEEK and POKE—commands to examine the contents of the machine's dynamic memory (PEEK) or place a new value in the electric matrix that formed the abstract metaphor of machine memory (POKE). The states of these holes in memory controlled the modem and guided the incoming bits into the magnetic floppy drive, where a double rack of read-write heads were working overtime, grinding back and forth, making sounds like a cartoon kitchen appliance about to explode.

Scattered across the floor were plastic floppies, either blank (ready for formatting, the means by which the computer neatly metamorphoses the magnetic sheet at the heart of the floppy into a meaningful array of storage locations for incoming bits) or jammed with fresh copies of the latest games. Roger's father gazed at this chaos in dismay. There was his son, hunched over the computer he'd bought because he thought it would make his son smarter, a better student, a winner in America. Now he wondered if he had done the right thing sending Roger into uncharted waters. Was this what a computer was for, to turn his son into an unruly recluse?

The grown-ups couldn't get this any more than grown-ups of other generations could get rock 'n' roll or tongue piercing or pot. We were doing our thing, hacking, and the rest of the world didn't matter. Anyway, how could parents—or any grown-up for that matter—ever understand something that had not been invented in those ancient times when they were young?

That day I walked out of Roger's house fully loaded, two dozen double-sided disks neatly labeled, and headed for the F train, happy as hell. With floppy drives, disks, and modem snugly on my back, I was heading home to my computer to plug everything in and indulge. Here were days, maybe weeks, of new things to explore, a treasure trove courtesy of a nascent phenomenon, the Pirate Bulletin Board: usually one modem, one computer, and another kid with an extra phone line, his computer on twenty-four hours a day and a bank of disk drives ready to deal out the latest cracked software, copy protection broken—any program ripe for infinite duplication. We did it because it could be done, and we were among the few who knew how.

These bulletin boards popped up and disappeared from day to day while others sprung up in their place. Phone numbers passed from friend to friend were posted on other boards with names like Aladdin's, Rainbow, Pat100, Spider's Web, Pirate's Cove. These boards would last until parents figured out what was going on and shut them down, or until their operators got bored or distracted by the fresh call of puberty leading them to glossy magazines with centerfolds that told of a next stage of life.

Later that night I called Roger, wanting to know if he'd tried the software: What was good, what was sick, what hadn't been worth our time and trouble? Roger couldn't come to the phone, his father said. When I saw Roger in school on Monday, he told me his father had taken away his computer. It was distracting him from schoolwork. There was more. I couldn't ever come back, his father said. I never did.

As I stood next to my mom it was strange to think of that time after so many years. Holding the computer in my hands, it felt light, its design quaint—with big keys for a child's hands and color-coded buttons. Digital watches and pagers now have more memory, more processing power, than this machine. Yet I'd spent hundreds of nights exploring what seemed a wide world of bits; I'd lived a thousand lives, died a thousand deaths, had been both God and acolyte inside a 2-D world all my own, a 48K universe that exists today in $39 disposable gadgets. How huge that world had seemed! Cheap and omnipresent machines, so easy to slip into; they seduced us—me and so many of my friends. We just disappeared one day, stepped into the arcades and vanished, reemerging years later as adults.

In anticipation of my Bar Mitzvah in the spring of 1981 I studied the Torah and the back pages of the mail-order computer catalogues. Both evoked a strange new world of arcane symbols. Each offered the tantalizing possibility of uncovering knowledge buried behind a confusing new lexicon. Aleph, Bet, Gimmel. RAM, ROM, byte. The Torah is the heart of Judaism, our Hebrew teacher told our class of a dozen boys and girls as we slouched in our seats on a Sunday morning wishing we could be anywhere but here. It is the word of God, passed from generation to generation over several thousand years, that gave us our identity and religion. What is holy, above all, are the words, words that could be carried on paper or in our minds.

The Torah is our collective memory, the story of how Judaism came to be; it serves as shared software, booted up through study and reading. The Torah is an algorithm, code with specific instructions for living life. An operating system. So long as we copy the system uncorrupted, verbatim, and pass it forward through time we retain the core of Judaism. Studying the Torah, though, did not give me the same satisfaction as studying *Antic, A.N.A.L.O.G., Softside, Compute!, Joystik,* or *Electronic Games*—magazines I gathered after school and laid about my bed. I read and reread which home computer did what, gleaning from these pages the outlines of hardware, software, programming, and another fantastic symbolic world waiting for exploration. My printed copy of the Torah, a small bound volume, was a chore to retrieve, and my memorization of Hebrew vocabulary words a calvary best done in haste in the back of the school bus at the end of the week. Discerning the relative benefits of the Apple II, Atari 400, Atari 800, TRS-80, and Commodore 64, comparing hi-res monochrome to lo-res color and floppy drive to tape drive was a pleasure, a joy. At stake here was the ultimate question: Which computer would I choose?

In 1981 there was a swarm of competing home computers, each incompatible with the others. Of these brands only four companies succeeded in attracting substantial numbers of followers; like new religions, each vied for dominance. Each came with its own code, a particular philosophy of computing. For those who lusted after one, the machine's style and substance were embraced as a reflection of ourselves. Just as kids two generations earlier had lusted after particular cars, each with its own internal logic of cool that said "this is who I am and what I stand for," and just as the generation after that had followed different musicians and sounds, so we followed different computer makers.

The four companies with substance and verve were Apple, Atari, Commodore, and Radio Shack. Boys who came to computers through electronics wanted an Apple. Boys who came to computers through video games wanted an Atari. Boys whose parents wanted them to have a "serious" computer got a Radio Shack TRS-80. The Commodore 64 was a graphics machine too, but I didn't know anyone who bought one. In the far distance was a new computer, the IBM-PC, released in April 1981. That machine was not for kids. It was for grown-ups, and none of us ever dreamed of owning one. There was a purity to the market, driven foremost by the exuberant joy of hobbyists and children. It was untamed, undisciplined by serious uses such as accounting and word processing. These machines weren't for work, they were for play, for exploration, for adventure. What they were for was not up to marketing experts and advertising agencies to decide; it was up to us—the millions at home who took to programming, turning what once had been the arcane art of scientists and graduate students into a nationwide pastime.

By the end of seventh grade I'd made several new friends, kids whose sense of daring was winning at strategy and video games, or discussing the merits of different war movies, guns, and explosives. Most important, several of my new friends owned home computers. Kenny, Aaron, and Scott acquired machines in seventh grade. The TRS-80 for Kenny; the Apple II for Aaron, and an Atari 800 for Scott. As seventh grade waned I studied each machine judiciously, comparison shopping, feeling the energy, searching for the one that would match my own imagination.

The dream that lured me to computers was the fantasy of parallel universes, of an escape into a reality that could be animated and made real by a computer. I wanted one that could draw beautiful worlds, create vivid lands for me to explore. The ur-fantasy my friends and I shared came from science fiction: the scene in *Star Wars* when Luke Skywalker and Chewbacca play chess as their spaceship, the *Millennium Falcon,* races toward the hidden rebel base. The chessboard is circular and the pieces are miniature three-dimensional holograms of monsters, walking, alive. Luke moves a piece to take Chewbacca's and it hops over an ugly orc or troll, landing in an enemy square and killing its opponent with one hard blow, blood lust on its face. That moment evoked the rich, fantastic illusion we so desperately dreamed our computers could craft. No such machine existed then (or now); but the desire to weave realistic illusions remained, sated by what we could have: 8-bit graphics, 255-bit monsters built of tiny two-dimensional rectangles, pixels on a screen.

I was a graphics junkie. What I cared about most were pictures, drawn fast and beautiful. I wanted a machine with color, sound, and speed. I wanted a machine whose graphics mesmerized. Graphics, like a book or film, created the illusion of another world. Well-done graphics, like a well-done book or movie, suspended disbelief and brought us out of our bodies into a new place. This was why I sought out my first computer. Which could make the best worlds? Which would take me there fastest?

Kenny, short with neatly parted black hair and big brown glasses, lived (as most of us did) with one parent, his mother. His apartment was twenty blocks north of mine, near Aaron's, and there Kenny had his TRS-80—the Trash Eighty, as we called it. Kenny's mother bought it for him. The computer came with 16K of RAM, a tape drive that used audiocassettes to store programs as audible beeps and bleeps, and a built-in monochrome monitor. Kenny's Trash Eighty sat on his desk cattycorner to his bunk bed where sometimes I would sleep over. The Trash Eighty had its charms—cheaper than the rest, rugged, and easy to use. Built by Radio Shack, a division of Tandy, the TRS-80 was presented as the machine for adults who wanted a home computer for business or personal finance. A low-end TRS-80 could be had for $499.

Huddled together in front of Kenny's desk, we played games he'd bought for the Trash Eighty. The machine had no color, and the sound was lame; Kenny's games weren't impressive. Worse, his mother wouldn't buy him more games. She wanted him to use the computer for serious things like typing, math, and spelling. One afternoon when we were taking turns at a game Kenny's mom came into the room and said to Kenny, "How much longer are you going to sit in front of that thing? Why don't you go play outside?"

"Ma," Kenny said, "I'm busy."

"Oh!" his mom said, "too busy even to listen to your mother?"

Kenny kept playing.

"Look at me when I'm talking to you, young man! Too busy for your own mother?"

When Kenny's mom got mad her voice became very high, almost shouting. I started to squirm.

"I want you two to go outside and play. Now! Do you hear me?"

"Ma. LET ME FINISH MY GAME FIRST!"

Kenny's mom started to twitch like she was about to smack him. Uh-oh, I thought, starting to roll out of the way on my chair as his mom strode forward toward Kenny, and before I could duck she'd reached over and unplugged the computer.

"MAAAAA!"

"That's it," she said. "No more computer! You're grounded for a week."

"But Ma—"

"You want two weeks? You want me to call your father?"

That was it—the ultimate threat for most of us with separated parents: mom calling dad. Kenny slid off his chair, defeated. We went outside, walked to Radio Shack, and looked at more TRS-80 gear in the store, stuff that Kenny was even less likely to get now—rack after rack of audiocassettes in glassine packages, each containing an audio recording of bits and bytes, programs stored on acoustic tape. Kenny had an anemic collection of microcassettes neatly stacked in his desk drawer. Loading and saving games took a long time. The best games Kenny had were Space Invaders and Breakout, a Ponglike game whose object was bouncing a ball off a wall until all the bricks are destroyed and a new wall appears. Both games were designed by kids a few years older than us in Great Neck, Long Island, whose company was called Software Innovations. Their oldest executive was fifteen. The computer craze—unlike earlier crazes such as late-night radio, LP rock albums, or drag racing—could pay off with rich dividends. Earlier crazes were run by adults: record labels, film studios, General Motors, intrepid travelers bringing pot up from Mexico. Growing up with computers when computers were still young was different.

Here you could do more than just consume what adults passed down to you, cash registers *ka-chinging* in ecstasy. For every pocketful of quarters dumped into an arcade game and every preadolescent savings bond cashed in for a home computer, somewhere a kid programmer was writing code, making software, and passing it on to friends at school, or—if the product was good enough—getting it brokered through one of the grass-roots cooperatives formed to distribute software, later known as "shareware." An enterprising kid could write a program, give it to a co-op who would distribute it for free, and if so moved (as a kind of honor system) ask for $10 or $15 to be sent by mail. Two contradictory interpretations were made by the media, which looked at computer programming and video-game addiction with puzzlement. The first was one of initial protest—kids were rotting their brains on mental junk food and becoming video-game truants; arcades were swamps of iniquity, breeding grounds for vandalism and nihilism. The second was a tale of superbrains, *uber*kids with great round glasses, faces basking in the late-night glow of a monitor, coding. Both tropes were linked to the same root: these kids were amoral addicts. Videojunkie just wants a fix and cares little about anything else—except perhaps pizza. Superbrain's addiction is the thrill of power. Where Videojunkie thrives on a high score, Superbrain thrills at the idea of hacking into NORAD. He's unstoppable because grown-ups can't think like he does. We are at the mercy of his mood. Maybe he'll bring down the national telephone network today . . . or not. Such images bore little resemblance to what many of us experienced—the thrill of pioneering.

As computers entered our homes we were defining a new culture through gleeful experimentation, one that with the Internet in the 1990s would become dominant, capturing as much attention as did rebellion in the 1960s or jazz in the 1920s. Yet where the latter movements began from the top with supremely talented individuals and trickled down, digital culture began at the bottom and trickled up, starting in cramped bedrooms like Kenny's and moving upward from kid to kid until it colonized the outside world. Propelling its movement were two factors: the availability of new technology and our natural desire to grow up into men. For boys going through the transition from teenager to adult, we wanted what previous generations wanted—to be different from our parents, to have separate identities. In the computer we found a devoted accomplice. We could help define it while it helped define us. For a generation in which everything seemed to have been done before, what was there left to do? Drugs were done, music was done, street revolution was done. Everything seemed old. Except this. Together, computer and kid co-existed in a golden age, a time when the machine was available to us unconcealed, stripped to its component parts, when adults barely understood what we were doing and the outside world did little to interfere with our probings and pokings. For the Atari generation the evolution of the machine briefly matched that of our adolescent selves, becoming a vessel and partner, a co-conspirator in our mutual coming of age.

REFLECTING ON THE READING

1. What is the occasion for obtaining his old computer that Bennahum describes at the beginning of this passage? Why is it important to him?

2. Why were the parents of Bennahum's friends suspicious of their children's extensive use of computers? What reactions did they have to their children's use of computers? What do their reactions indicate about their attitudes toward computers, or toward technology in general?

3. Bennahum writes that computers "seduced" him and his friends. What does he mean? How does he depict this "seduction"? Why were computers so "seductive" to him and his friends? What might such a description suggest about Bennahum's attitude toward computers? Toward technology?

4. Bennahum describes the *Torah,* the most important sacred book of the Jewish religion, as a text that gave him and other Jews an identity. But he also writes that studying that text did not give him the same satisfaction as reading computer magazines. Why did he find such joy in studying computers? What was it that was so appealing to him about computers that he compares his study of them to studying religious texts? Do you think the comparison is an appropriate one? Why or why not? How might your own religious background influence your answer to that question?

5. At one point in his narrative, Bennahum writes, "Growing up with computers when computers were still young was different." What does he mean? What did he most value about that time?

6. At the end of this passage Bennahum writes, that "digital culture" was a "movement" in the 1990's. In what sense was it a "movement," according to Bennahum? What drove that movement, in his view? Do you agree with him? Explain.

Examining Rhetorical Strategies

1. What do you learn about Bennahum in the early paragraphs of this narrative? How does this information about him and his life influence your sense of him as a person and as a writer? Does it give him credibility in your eyes? Why or why not? Do you think he presents himself as someone with whom most readers can identify? Do you think he intends to do so? Explain.

2. Throughout this passage, Bennahum uses many relatively technical terms related to the computers he and his friends were using (for example, *baud, microprocessor, kilobytes*). Did you understand these terms? Do you think most readers would understand them? What does the use of these terms suggest about Bennahum's assumptions regarding his audience? Whom do you think he was writing his memoir for?

3. Bennahum's upbringing was obviously a middle-class one in which he had ready access to computer technologies that were, at the time he was growing up, not widely available to most Americans. How does his background as a middle-class boy influence his narrative? How do you think it shapes his attitudes toward technology? Do you think he intended to write a middle-class narrative? Explain. In what ways might his memoir have been different if he had grown up in a different setting—for example, in a poor, rural community—instead of in a middle-class home near New York City? How might the picture he presents of computers have been different? What was your own response to the kind of upbringing Bennahum describes? How might your own social class background affect your response to him?

4. Early in his essay, Bennahum writes that grown-ups couldn't understand his generation's use of computers any better than grown-ups of previous generations understood rock and roll music or marijuana. Why do you think Bennahum makes this comparison? What might this comparison suggest about his sense of himself as part of the "Atari generation"? Does this comparison make you more

or less inclined to view him favorably as the voice in this narrative? How might your response to him relate to your own sense of your generation?

5. Bennahum writes that by the time he was in seventh grade, he had several friends "whose sense of daring was winning at strategy and video games, or discussing the merits of different war movies, guns, and explosives. Most important, several of my new friends owned home computers." What might this brief description of his friends reveal about them as adolescent boys? Do you think he presents his friends in this passage as "typical" boys? Do you think he intends to? Why? What do you think this description reveals about Bennahum?

6. Some experts have suggested that gender is an important factor in science and technical professions—that women tend not to pursue careers in science and technical fields or are discouraged from doing so by social and cultural attitudes regarding gender. Evaluate Bennahum's narrative from the perspective of gender. How does gender seem to figure into his story? Do you think he is aware of gender or intends to address gender in any way in his essay? Explain. Would this essay be different in any ways if the narrator were a woman? Explain.

7. Late in this passage Bennahum writes that what he and his friends experienced with the early computers was "the thrill of pioneering." What might this suggest about how Bennahum saw himself and his friends who were interested in computers? Find some other words he uses to describe himself and his friends. What sort of identity is he constructing for himself and his friends? How does it relate specifically to other images of youth with which you are familiar?

Engaging the Issues

1. Write your own memoir of your childhood or adolescence, focusing on the role of technology, as Bennahum does.

2. In a group of your classmates, share the memoirs you wrote for Question #1. Identify differences and similarities in the experiences with technology that each of you describe. Can you explain some of the differences in terms of age, gender, race, class, religion, or geographic location? What might your collective experience indicate about technology in our lives and its role in shaping our identities?

3. Write an essay in which you examine the role of Bennahum's background in his memoir. Specifically, how does his upbringing as a White, middle-class boy shape the story he tells and his own attitudes about computers and technology? What might his story suggest about the identity of the "Atari generation"?

4. Bennahum suggests throughout his narrative that he and his friends shared a special kind of identity that differed from their parents'. This sense of identity was related to their knowledge of and interest in computers. He compares his generation and its connection to computers to earlier generations who used

other means (for example, rock and roll music) to establish their identity and separateness from their parents. Do you think Bennahum's characterization of his generation is accurate? Did computer technology define his generation in the way he indicates?

Write an essay for an audience of your classmates in which you address these questions. You might agree that Bennahum's characterization of his generation is accurate; if so, defend his characterization by showing how computers defined the age, perhaps drawing on your own experiences or on information that you gather from the Web (or other sources). Alternatively, you might challenge Bennahum's characterization of his generation, presenting arguments that show his perspective to be limited, narrow, or inaccurate.

5. Rewrite part of Bennahum's narrative as a historical account of the rise of personal computer use among young people in the 1980's. Write your essay in the third person (not as a first-person narrative), using Bennahum's narrative as a source along with any other relevant sources you might find in your library or on the World Wide Web. Your essay should be an "objective" account of the role of computers in American society in the 1980's and their influence on young people. It should be an account similar to what you might find in a high school history book or a similar kind of publication.

6. With a group of your classmates, compare the essays written for Question #5 with Bennahum's narrative and/or with the narratives written for Question #1. How do they differ in the ways they present information and depict technology? How can you account for these differences? Do you think one kind of essay is more effective than another? Explain.

7. Rewrite the essay you wrote for Question #1 as a Web site. Use the visual and audio capabilities of the Web in presenting your narrative to potential viewers of your site, and include appropriate links to other sites.

8. Compare the essays written in your class for Question #1 above and analyze them in terms of gender. Are there noticeable differences between the essays the men and women in your class wrote? What are they? What might these differences suggest about the role of gender in technology?

Alternatively, do a similar analysis of the Web sites constructed for Question #7 above.

9. Interview your parents or other people you know from a generation earlier than your own about the role of technology in their upbringings. Ask them about the specific technologies that were important in their early years (for example, telephones, televisions, automobiles, and so on). Try to get a sense of why these technologies were important to them and how these technologies might have influenced their lives and their ideas about who they are. Then write an essay for an audience of your classmates in which you discuss the role of technology in the lives of the people you interviewed. Try to draw conclusions about the connections between identity and technology. (For this essay, you may want to do some research on the specific technologies that the people you interviewed described as important.)

Becoming Literate

A Lesson from the Amish

ANDREA R. FISHMAN

INTRODUCTION   Does your ethnic or religious background matter when it comes to how you write and read? Furthermore, does literacy have anything to do with making you who you are as a member of a specific ethnic or religious group? In recent decades literacy researchers like Andrea R. Fishman have been trying to answer just such questions by exploring how literacy might be connected to a person's ethnic, religious, or cultural background. They examine the ways in which people from specific social or cultural groups write and read, and they try to understand how those ways of writing and reading might be related to the values and habits of members of those groups. This research indicates that how people learn to read and write in their homes and communities may differ in important ways from how schools teach reading and writing. If literacy is indeed somehow connected to how we define ourselves as people, then differences between literacy at home and literacy in schools can create problems for people from certain cultural backgrounds.

In the following essay about the writing and reading habits of an Amish family, Andrea R. Fishman explores the role of literacy in the way the Amish live their daily lives and in how they understand themselves as Amish people. As Fishman indicates in her essay, the Amish family she describes is part of a traditional Amish sect that rejects many aspects of mainstream American culture that most Americans accept as "normal." Because groups like the Amish tend to live separately from mainstream society, we often don't see how they use literacy and technology in their lives and perhaps assume that literacy and technology function for them in the same ways that they function for us. But Fishman's essay suggests that literacy and technology do not necessarily have universal value and can be understood and used very differently in different cultures. In the case of the Amish, learning to read and write is an integral part of learning how to *be* Amish. The way they teach and learn literacy and the way they use it in their daily lives serve the overt purpose of defining them as a culture and maintaining that cultural identity. Furthermore, the very decision about which technologies to use—for reading or writing or communicating or anything else—is, for the Amish, a statement about who they are and how they believe people should live. Fishman's descriptions of Amish literacy thus provide us with a compelling picture of how literacy and technology relate directly to cultural identity. In this sense, her essay presents us with the possibility that we must understand literacy and technology as they are used in "nonmainstream" groups if we are to understand adequately how literacy and technology help make us who we are.

Andrea R. Fishman is a professor of English at West Chester University in Pennsylvania, where she directs the Pennsylvania Writing and Literature Project, one of the oldest such projects in the country. She has studied literacy and culture extensively, and her research has been published in such scholarly publications as *English Journal, Phi Delta Kappan,* and *English Education.* She is also the author of *Amish Literacy: What and How It Means* (1988). The following essay was originally published in a volume of scholarly essays titled *The Right to Literacy* (1990).

REFLECTING BEFORE READING

1. Note Fishman's title for this essay. What do you understand her to mean by "literate"? What do you know about the Amish? What expectations does her subtitle, "A Lesson from the Amish," create for you? What is the "lesson" Fishman offers in this essay? Also, pay attention as you read to how Fishman presents the Amish. Is her presentation of them sympathetic, objective, critical?

2. As you read Fishman's descriptions of how the Fisher family writes and reads, compare their uses of literacy with those of your own family. What differences and similarities do you see between literacy in the Fisher household and literacy in your own? How might the way literacy is used in your home have helped make you who you are?

One clear, frost-edged January Sunday night, two families gathered for supper and an evening's entertainment. One family—mine—consisted of a lawyer, a teacher, and their twelve-year-old son; the other family—the Fishers—consisted of Eli and Anna, a dairy farmer and his wife, and their five children, ranging in age from six to seventeen. After supper in the Fisher's large farm kitchen—warmed by a wood stove and redolent of the fragrances of chicken corn soup, homemade bread, and freshly baked apples—the table was cleared and an additional smaller one set up to accommodate games of Scrabble, double Dutch solitaire, and dominoes. As most of us began to play, adults and children randomly mixed, Eli Fisher, Sr., settled into his brown leather recliner with the newspaper, while six-year-old Eli, Jr., plopped on the corner of the couch nearest his father with a book.

Fifteen or twenty minutes later, I heard Eli, Sr., ask his son, "Where are your new books?" referring to a set of outgrown Walt Disney books we had brought for little Eli and his seven-year-old brother, Amos. Eli, Jr., pointed to a stack of brightly colored volumes on the floor, from which his father chose *Lambert, the Sheepish Lion.* As Eli, Jr., climbed onto the arm of the recliner and snuggled against his father, Eli, Sr., began reading the book out loud in a voice so commandingly dramatic that soon everyone was listening to the story, instead of playing their separate games. Broadly portraying the roles of both Lambert and his lioness mother and laughing heartily at the antics of the cub who preferred cavorting with the sheep to stalking with the lions, Eli held his enlarged audience throughout the rest of the story.

As most of us returned to our games when he finished reading, Eli, Sr., asked of anyone and everyone, "Where's the *Dairy?*" Daniel, the Fishers' teenage son, left his game and walked toward his father. "It's in here," he said, rummaging through the newspapers and magazines in the rack beside the couch until he found a thick newsletter called *Dairy World,* published by the Independent Buyers Association, to which Eli belonged.

Eli leafed through the publication, standing and walking toward the wood stove as he did. Leaning against the wall, he began reading aloud without preface. All conversation stopped as everyone once again attended to Eli's loudly expressive reading voice, which said:

> A farmer was driving his wagon down the road. On the back was a sign which read: "Experimental Vehicle. Runs on oats and hay. Do not step in exhaust."

Everyone laughed, including Eli, Sr., who then read the remaining jokes on the humor page to his attentive audience. All our games forgotten, we shared the best and the worst riddles and jokes we could remember until it was time for bed.

Occasions like this one occur in many homes and have recently attracted the interest of family literacy researchers (Heath; Taylor; Wells). The scene at the Fishers could have been the scene in any home where parents value reading and writing and want their children to value them as well. It would not be surprising if Eli and Anna, like other literacy-oriented parents, read bedtime stories to their children, helped with their homework, and encouraged them to attain high school diplomas, if not college degrees. But Eli and Anna do none of these things: they read no bedtime stories, they are annoyed if their children bring schoolwork home, and they expect their children to go only as far in school as they did themselves, as far as the eighth grade.

So, although Eli and Anna appeared on that Sunday night to be ideal proliteracy parents, they may not be, according to commonly described standards, and one significant factor may account for their variations from the supposed ideal: Eli and Anna are not mainstream Americans but are Old Order Amish, raising their family according to Old Order tradition and belief. The Sunday night gathering I just described took place by the light of gas lamps in a house without radio, stereo, television, or any other electrical contrivance. Bedtime in that house is more often marked by singing or silence than by reading. Schoolwork rarely enters there because household, field, and barn chores matter more. And the Fisher children's studying is done in a one-room, eight-grade, Old Order school taught by an Old Order woman who attended the same kind of school herself. So while Eli, Jr., like his siblings, is learning the necessity and the value of literacy, what literacy means to him and the ways in which he learns it may differ in both obvious and subtle ways from what it means and how it's transmitted to many mainstream children, just as Eli's world differs from theirs, both obviously and subtly.

As suggested earlier. Eli, Jr., lives in a house replete with print, from the kitchen bulletin board to the built-in bookcases in the playroom to the tables and magazine rack in the living room. There are children's classics and children's magazines. There are local newspapers, shoppers' guides, and other adult periodicals. And there are books of children's Bible stories, copies of the King James Version of the Bible, and other inspirational volumes, none of which mark the Fishers' home as notably different from that of many other Christian Americans.

Yet there are differences, easily overlooked by a casual observer but central to the life of the family and to their definition of literacy. One almost invisible difference is the sources of these materials. Eli and Anna attempt to carefully control the reading material that enters their home. Anna buys books primarily from a local Christian bookstore and from an Amish-operated dry goods store, both of which she trusts not to stock objectionable material. When she sees potentially interesting books in other places—in the drugstore, in the book and card shop, or at a yard sale—she uses the publisher's name as a guide to acceptable content. Relatives and friends close to the family also supply appropriate titles both as gifts and as recommendations, which Anna trusts and often chooses to follow up.

Another, slightly more visible difference comes in the form of books and periodicals around the Fisher house that would not be found in many mainstream, farm, or Christian homes. Along with the local newspaper in the rack beside the couch are issues of *Die Botschaft,* which describes itself as "A Weekly Newspaper Serving Old Order Amish Communities Everywhere." On the desk is a copy of *The Amish Directory,* which alphabetically lists all the Amish living in Pennsylvania and Maryland by nuclear family groups, giving crucial address and other information, along with maps of the eighty-seven church districts included.

On top of the breakfront in the sitting area are copies of songbooks, all in German: some for children, some for adults, and one—the *Ausbund*—for everyone, for this is the church hymnal, a collection of hymns written by tortured and imprisoned sixteenth-century Anabaptists about their experiences and their faith. Kept with these songbooks is a German edition of the Bible and a copy of the *Martyrs Mirror,* an oversized, weighty tome full of graphic descriptions in English of the tortured deaths of early Anabaptists, each illustrated by a black-and-white woodcut print.

Despite what may seem to be the esoteric nature of these texts, none remain in their special places gathering dust, for all are used regularly, each reinforcing in a characteristic way the Amish definition of literacy and each facilitating the image Eli, Jr., has of himself as literate.

Because singing is central to Amish religious observance and expression, the songbooks are used frequently by all members of the family. Because singing requires knowing what is in the text and because Amish singing, which is unaccompanied and highly stylized, requires knowing how to interpret the text exactly as everyone else does, the songbooks represent a kind of reading particularly important to the community, a kind that must be mastered to be considered literate. Yet because singing may mean holding the text and following the words as they appear or it may mean holding the text and following the words from memory or from others' rendition, children of Eli's age and younger all participate, appearing and feeling as literate as anyone else.

Functioning similarly are the German Bible and the *Martyrs Mirror.* Though only the older Fishers read that Bible, they do so regularly and then share what they've read with their children. It is the older Fishers, too, who read the *Martyrs Mirror,* but that text Eli, Sr., usually reads aloud during family devotions, so that Anna and all the children, regardless of age, participate similarly through his oral presentations.

While it may seem easier to accept such variant definitions of reading in shared communal situations like these, the participation of Eli, Jr., was equally welcome and equally effective in shared individual reading. When individual oral reading was clearly text-bound, as it is during family devotions, Eli was always enabled to participate in ways similar to his brothers' and sisters', making him a reader like them. When all the Fishers took turns reading the Bible aloud, for example, someone would read Eli's verse aloud slowly, pausing every few words, so that he could repeat what was said and thereby take his turn in the rotation.

When the older children were assigned Bible verses or *Ausbund* hymn stanzas to memorize, Eli was assigned the same one as Amos, the sibling closest in age. Their assignment would be shorter and contain less complex vocabulary than the one the older children got, yet Amos and Eli would also practice their verse together, as the older children did, and would take their turns reciting, as the older children did, making Eli again able to participate along with everyone else.

Because oral reading as modeled by Eli, Sr., is often imitated by the others, Eli, Jr., always shared his books by telling what he saw or knew about them. No one ever told him that telling isn't the same as reading, even though they may look alike, so Eli always seemed like a reader to others and felt like a reader himself. When everyone else sat reading or playing reading-involved games in the living room after supper or on Sunday afternoons, Eli did the same, to no one's surprise, to everyone's delight, and with universal, though often tacit, welcome and approval. When the other children received books as birthday and Christmas presents, Eli received them too. And when he realized at age six that both of his brothers had magazine subscriptions of their own, Eli asked for and got one as well. Eli never saw his own reading as anything other than real; he did not see it as make-believe or bogus, and neither did anyone else. So, despite the fact that before he went to school Eli, Jr., could not read according to some definitions, he always could according to his family's and his own.

Just as all the Fishers read, so they all write, and just as Eli was enabled to define reading in a way that made him an Amish reader, so he could define writing in a way that made him an Amish writer. Letter writing has always been a primary family activity and one central to the Amish community. Anna writes weekly to *Die Botschaft,* acting as the scribe from her district. She, Eli, Sr., and sixteen-year-old Sarah all participate in circle letters, and the next three children all write with some regularity to cousins in other Amish settlements.

Yet, no matter who is writing to whom, their letters follow the same consistently modeled Amish format, beginning with "Greetings . . . ," moving to recent weather conditions, then to family and community news of note, and ending with a good-bye and often a philosophical or religious thought. I've never seen anyone in the community instructed to write this way, but in the Fisher family, letters received and even letters written are often read out loud, and though this oral sharing is done for informative rather than instructive purposes, it provides an implicit model for everyone to follow.

With all the other family members writing letters, reading them out loud, and orally sharing those they have received, Eli, Jr., wanted to write and receive letters, too, and no one said he couldn't. When he was very young, he dictated his messages to Sarah and drew pictures to accompany what she wrote down for him. Then, even before he started school, Eli began copying the dictated messages Sarah recorded, so that the letters would be in his own hand, as the drawings were.

Other forms of writing also occur in the Fisher household for everyone to see and use. Greeting cards, grocery lists, bulletin board reminders, and bedtime notes from children to absent parents were all part of Eli's life to some extent, and his preschool writing and drawing always adorned the refrigerator, along with the school papers of his brothers and sisters.

In addition, the Fishers played writing-involved games—including Scrabble and Boggle—in which everyone participated, as the family revised the rules to suit their cooperative social model and their definition of literacy. In any game at the Fishers, the oldest person or persons playing may assist the younger ones. No question of fairness arises unless only some players go unaided. Older players, too, may receive help from other players or from onlookers. Score is always kept, and, while some moves are ruled illegal, age or aid received neither bars nor assures a winner. Eli, Jr., therefore, has always played these games as well as anyone else.

Obviously, Eli, Jr., learned a great deal about literacy from all these preschool experiences, but what he learned went far beyond academic readiness lessons. More important, Eli learned that literacy is a force in the world—his world—and it is a force that imparts power to all who wield it. He could see for himself that reading and writing enable people as old as his parents and as young as his siblings to fully participate in the world in which they live. In fact, it might have seemed to him that, to be an Amish man, one must read and write, and to be a Fisher, one must read and write as well.

So, even before the age of six, Eli began to recognize and acquire the power of literacy, using it to affiliate himself with the larger Amish world and to identify himself as Amish, a Fisher, a boy, and Eli Fisher, Jr. However, what enabled Eli to recognize all these ways of defining and asserting himself through literacy was neither direct instruction nor insistence from someone else. Rather, it was the ability that all children have long before they can read and write print text, the ability, as Freire puts it, "to read the world." "It is possible," Freire asserts, "to view objects and experiences as texts, words, and letters, and to see the growing awareness of the world as a kind of reading, through which the self learns and changes" (6). Eli, Jr., clearly illustrates this understanding of how children perceive and comprehend the seemingly invisible text of their lives. What he came to understand and accept this way were the definition and the role of print literacy as his society and culture both consciously and tacitly transmit them.

When Eli, Jr., began school, therefore, he was both academically and socially ready to begin. To smooth the transition from home to school, Eli's teacher—like most in Old Order schools—held a "preschool day" in the spring preceding his entry to first grade. On that day, Eli and Mary, the two prospective first-graders in Meadow Brook School, came to be initiated as "scholars." Verna, their teacher, had moved the two current first-graders to other seats, clearing the two desks immediately in front of hers for the newcomers; all that day Mary and Eli sat in the first-grade seats, had "classes," and did seatwork like all the other children. They seemed to know they were expected to follow the rules, to do what they saw others doing, to practice being "scholars," and Verna reinforced that notion, treating those two almost as she would anyone else.

To begin one lesson, for example, "Let's talk about bunnies," she instructed, nodding her head toward the two littlest children, indicating that they should stand beside her desk. She then showed them pictures of rabbits, with the word *bunnies* and the number depicted indicated in word and numeral on each picture. After going through the pictures, saying, "three bunnies," "four bunnies," and having the children repeat after her, Verna asked three questions and got three choral answers.

"Do bunnies like carrots?" she asked.
"Yes," the two children answered together.
"Do they like lettuce?"
"Yes."
"Do they sometimes get in Mother's garden?"
"Yes."

Were it not for some enthusiastic head nodding, Eli, Jr., and Mary could have been fully matriculated students.

When she was ready to assign seatwork, Verna gave the preschoolers pictures of bunnies to color and asked, "What do we do first? Color or write our names?"

"Write our names," the pair chorused, having practiced that skill earlier in the day.

"Yes, we always write our names first. Go back to your desk, write your name, then color the picture. Do nothing on the back of the paper." And the children did exactly that, doing "what we do" precisely "the way we do it."

Verna also conducted what she called a reading class for the two preschoolers, during which they sat, and she held an open picture book facing them. Talking about the pictures, Verna made simple statements identifying different aspects of and actions in the illustrations. After each statement Verna paused, and the children repeated exactly what she had said. The oral text accompanying one picture said:

Sally is eating chips and watching TV.
Sally has a red fish.
Sally has spilled the chips.

After "reading" the text this way, the children answered questions about it.

"What does Sally have?" Verna asked.
"A fish," they replied.
"What color is her fish?"
"Red."
"Did Sally spill the chips?"
"Yes."
"Did the cat eat the chips?"
"Yes."

While the content of this lesson seems incongruous, I know, its form and conduct fit the Meadow Brook model perfectly. Precise recall and yeses are all that the questions demand. Even the last question, while not covered in the "reading," requires recognition of only what happens in the picture.

What happened in Meadow Brook School that day—and what would happen in the eight school years to follow—reinforced, extended, and rarely contradicted what Eli already knew about literacy. Reading and writing at school allowed him to further affiliate and identify himself with and within his social group. While his teacher occasionally gave direct instructions, those instructions tended to be for activities never before seen or experienced; otherwise, Eli and Mary knew to follow the behavioral and attitudinal lead of the older children and to look to them for assistance and support, just as they looked to the teacher. In other words, reading the school world came as naturally to these children as reading the world anywhere else, and the message in both texts was emphatically the same.

Most important here, however, may be the remarkable substantive coherence that Meadow Brook School provided, a coherence that precluded any conflict over what, how, or even whether to read and write. Eli's experience as a Fisher had taught him that reading comes in many forms—secular and religious, silent and oral, individual and communal—and they all count. Through his at-home experience, Eli had also learned which other, more specific, less obvious abilities count as reading in his world. He had learned to value at least four significant abilities: (1) the ability to select and manage texts, to be able to find his mother's letter in *Die Botschaft* or to find a particular verse in the Bible; (2) the ability to empathize with people in texts and to discern the implicit lessons their experiences teach: to empathize with Lambert the lion, who taught the possibility of peaceful coexistence, and to empathize with the Anabaptist martyrs, who taught the rightness of dying for one's faith; (3) the ability to accurately recall what was read, to remember stories, riddles, and jokes or to memorize Bible and hymn verses; and (4) the ability to synthesize what is read in a single text with what is already known or to synthesize information across texts in Amish-appropriate ways.

When Eli got to school, he found a similar definition of reading in operation. He and Mary were helped to select and manage text. Their attention was directed toward what mattered in the text and away from what did not. They were helped to discover the single right answer to every question. They had only to recall information without interpreting or extending it in any significant way. And they were expected to empathize with the people in Verna's lunchtime oral reading without questioning or hypothesizing about what had happened or what would happen next.

Similarly, before Eli went to school, he knew what counted as writing in his world, just as he knew what counted as reading. He learned at home that being able to write means being able to encode, to copy, to follow format, to choose content, and to list. And, when he arrived at school, this same definition, these same abilities, were all that mattered there, too.

While the dimensions of reading and writing that count at Meadow Brook and elsewhere in Eli's life seem little different from those that count in mainstream situations—a terrifying fact, I would suggest—it is important to recognize that several mainstream-valued skills are completely absent from the Amish world as I've experienced it. Critical reading—individual analysis and interpretation—of the sort considered particularly important by most people who are mainstream-educated or mainstream educators is not valued by the Amish because of its potentially divisive, counterproductive power.

Literary appreciation, too, is both irrelevant and absent because the study of text-as-object is moot. How a writer enables a reader to empathize with his characters doesn't matter; only the ability to empathize matters. Text, whether biblical or secular, is perceived not as an object but as a force acting in the world, and it is the impact of that force that counts.

When it comes to writing, the existing Amish definition also differs in what is absent, rather than what is present. While grammar, spelling, and punctuation do count for the Old Order, they do so only to the extent that word order, words, and punctuation must allow readers to read—that is, to recognize and make sense of their reading. If a reader readily understands the intention of an adjective used as an adverb, a singular verb following a plural noun, a sentence fragment, or a compound verb containing a misplaced comma, the Amish do not see these as errors warranting attention, despite the fact that an outside reader may.

Equally irrelevant in Old Order schools is the third-person formal essay—the ominous five-paragraph theme—so prevalent in mainstream classrooms. Amish children never learn to write this kind of composition, not because they are not college-bound but because the third-person-singular point of view assumed by an individual writer is foreign to this first-person-plural society; thesis statements, topic sentences, and concepts like coherence, unity, and emphasis are similarly alien.

One final distinction separates the Amish definition of literacy from that of many mainstream definitions: the absence of originality as a desirable feature. Not only do community constraints limit the number of appropriate topics and forms an Amish writer may use, but original approaches to or applications of those topics and forms is implicitly discouraged by the similarity of models and assignments and by the absence of fiction as an appropriate personal genre. All aspects of community life reward uniformity; while writing provides an outlet for individual expression and identification, singular creativity stays within community norms.

For Eli Fisher, Jr., then, the definition of literacy he learned at home was consistent with the one he found at school, though it differed in several important ways from those of most MLA members, for example. Yet for Eli, as for Freire, "deciphering the word flowed naturally from reading the immediate world" (7). From reading his world, this six-year-old derived a complete implicit definition that told him what literacy is and whether literacy matters. I can't help but wonder, however, what would have happened had Eli gone to school and been told, explicitly or through more powerful behaviors, that he really didn't know what counted as reading and writing, that his reading and writing were not real but other unknown or alien varieties were. What would have happened had his quiet imitative behavior made him invisible in the classroom or, worse yet, made his teacher assume that he was withdrawn, problematic, or less than bright? What if his work were devalued because it was obviously copied or just unoriginal? What if he had been called on to perform individually in front of the class, to stand up and stand out? Or what if he had been asked to discuss private issues in public? Or to evaluate what he read?

Had any of these things happened, I suspect that Eli would have had to make some difficult choices that would have amounted to choosing between what he had learned and learned to value at home and what he seemed expected to learn at school. To conform to his teacher's demands and values, he would have had to devalue or disavow those of his parents—a demand that public schools seem to make frequently of children from cultural or socioeconomic groups differing from those of their teachers or their schools, a demand that seems unfair, uncalled for, and unnecessary, not to mention counterproductive and destructive.

Eli Fisher's experience suggests, therefore, that those of us who deal with children unlike ourselves need to see our classrooms and our students differently from the way we may have seen them in the past. We need to realize that students, even first-graders, have been reading the world—if not the word—for at least five, six, or seven years; they come to school not devoid of knowledge and values but with a clear sense of what their world demands and requires, including what, whether, and how to read and write, though their understandings may differ significantly from our own. We need to realize that our role may not be to prepare our students to enter mainstream society but, rather, to help them see what mainstream society offers and what it takes away, what they may gain by assimilating and what they may lose in that process. Through understanding their worlds, their definitions of literacy, and their dilemmas, not only will we better help them make important literacy-related decisions, but we will better help ourselves to do the same.

Works Cited

Freire, Paulo. "The Importance of the Act of Reading." *Journal of Education* Winter 1983: 5–10.

Heath, Shirley Brice. *Ways with Words: Language, Life, and Work in Communities and Classrooms.* Cambridge: Cambridge UP, 1983.

Taylor, Denny. *Family Literacy.* Portsmouth: Heinemann, 1983.

Wells, Gordon. *The Meaning Makers.* Portsmouth: Heinemann, 1986.

REFLECTING ON THE READING

1. What is the scene that Fishman describes to begin this essay? What do we learn about the Amish in this opening scene? What is the contrast that Fishman sets up through the use of this opening scene? How does this contrast establish the focus of the essay?

2. In what ways are Amish children different from "mainstream" children in terms of literacy, according to Fishman? Why is this difference important? What does it tell us about literacy?

3. What are some of the characteristics of the books and periodicals found in the Fishers' home, as Fishman describes them? What do these books and periodicals tell us about literacy in the Fisher family?

4. How does Eli, Jr., learn to read, according to Fishman? What are the most important characteristics of the way he learns to read in the Fisher home? Why are these characteristics important, according to Fishman? What is the difference between "telling" and "reading" in Eli's case? Why does Fishman call attention to this difference?

5. How does Eli, Jr., learn to write? What are the central features of writing in the Fishers' home?

6. Fishman writes that by the time Eli, Jr., goes to school, he has learned that "literacy is a force in the world." In what sense is literacy a "force," according to Fishman? What does this mean in the case of an Amish child like Eli, Jr.?

7. According to Fishman, what are the four significant abilities in reading and writing that Eli, Jr., learns at home? How do those abilities compare with what he learns about reading and writing in school? In what ways do these abilities differ

from what Fishman calls "mainstream literacy"? Why are these differences important?

8. What lessons does Fishman draw from her description of Eli's experiences with writing and reading at home and at school? Do you think these are valuable lessons? Why or why not?

Examining Rhetorical Strategies

1. Notice the details Fishman provides in her description of the Amish family in the opening scene of this essay. How does she describe the family? How does she describe the setting? What image of *family* does Fishman present in this scene? How does this image affect you as a reader? Do you feel drawn to the scene Fishman describes? Why or why not? Is this a "typical" family, according to Fishman? What do you think Fishman hopes to accomplish by describing the scene in this way? Does she succeed, in your view? Explain. What might your answers to these questions suggest about your own attitudes about *family?*

2. Fishman never explicitly explains her relationship to the Fisher family, yet she uses the first person ("us") in the opening scene. Based on what you know about Fishman from the introduction to this reading selection, what do you think her relationship to the Fisher family is? How does that relationship shape her essay about them? Do you think she presents an "objective" picture of the Fishers? Do you think she intends to be "objective" in this essay? Why or why not?

3. What kinds of "evidence" does Fishman provide as she describes literacy in the Fisher home? How do you think she gathered this "evidence"? Do you find her description of literacy in this home complete and believable? Explain. What questions do you have about the picture of literacy that Fishman presents in this essay?

4. Fishman wrote this essay for a book intended for an audience of professional educators interested in literacy. What features of Fishman's essay (such as her writing style, the language she uses in her descriptions, the way she organizes her essay, and so on) seem to imply that audience? In what specific ways does Fishman address that audience? Do you think her essay is appropriate for audiences who are not educators or literacy researchers? Explain, citing specific passages from her text to support your answer.

5. Examine Fishman's descriptions of the reading and writing activities of the Fishers both at home and at school. How does she construct these descriptions? What specific kinds of information and details does she give? What does she leave out? How effectively do you think these descriptions present a picture of literacy and of the Fishers as literate people?

6. Based on this essay, what do you think are Fishman's views about how literacy should be taught in schools? Do you think she presents a favorable description of the Fisher family as a way to put forth her own views about literacy? Explain, citing specific passages from her essay to support your answer.

Engaging the Issues

1. Write a third-person description of literacy in your own home. In your essay, try to describe the characteristics of writing and reading in your home, as Fishman does of the Fisher home. For this essay, you may need to be an observer in your home for several days, noting the kinds of reading and writing materials there and the literacy activities that your family regularly engages in. Try to be thorough in your description of your family's literacy and draw conclusions about the role of literacy in your family's life.

   When you have finished this essay, compare your account to Fishman's essay. What similarities and differences do you see between your account and hers? What might these differences and similarities suggest about literacy and the role of writing and reading in people's lives? What might they suggest about the role of cultural factors (such as ethnicity and religious beliefs) in literacy and literacy learning? Also, what did you learn about writing an account such as this? Does you experience raise any questions for you about Fishman's essay and how she wrote it?

2. Write an essay as described in Question #1, but this time describe the literacy of a family you do not know personally, such as the family of a classmate. (To complete this exercise, you will need to obtain permission from a family—perhaps a neighbor's or the family of someone you have met through a friend—to interview them and perhaps observe their writing and reading at home for a day or two.)

3. Fishman's essay about Amish family literacy suggests that literacy is not the same for all people, even if those people live in the same region or country. Moreover, Fishman suggests that the *ways* in which parents teach their children to read and write can be related to their religious views and their ethnic or cultural identity. Consider the implications of such a view of literacy. If literacy can differ from one group of people to the next, what might that suggest about how writing and reading are taught in schools? What might that suggest about standardized tests that evaluate how well children read and write? Do we need to try to account for these differences in the way literacy is taught to children from different backgrounds? Should all children, regardless of their backgrounds, be taught to write and read in the same ways?

   Discuss these questions with a group of your classmates, noting the differences and similarities in their views. Try to come to some conclusions of your own about how you think writing and reading should be understood and taught in schools in order to address the needs of children from different backgrounds. Then write an essay for an audience of your classmates in which you discuss these issues and present your own views on these questions.

4. Based on the same inquiry and discussions you participated in for Question #3 above, write a letter to the editor of your local newspaper explaining your views about the issue of confronting ethnic, religious, and cultural diversity in literacy education in schools. In your letter, you might refer to Fishman's essay as a way to support your views.

Alternatively, address your letter to the superintendent of your local school district.

5. Fishman describes the kinds of reading and writing instruction that Eli, Jr., receives at home and at school, suggesting that in many ways the two are similar but also different. Write an essay in which you compare the ways in which you learned to write and read at home to how you were taught at school to read and write. Identify similarities and differences, and discuss what you believe are the effects of these experiences on you as a writer and a reader. Identify any cultural factors (such as race, ethnicity, gender, religious belief, and so on) that seem to have influenced how you learned to read and write at home. Try to draw conclusions about the relationship between your literacy learning at home and your literacy instruction at school and how each might have influenced your identity.

6. Compare your essay for Question #5 to the essays written by your classmates. What similarities and differences are evident in your experiences? In a group of your classmates discuss how those similarities and differences might be related to such factors as your age, race, gender, ethnic background, religion, and so on. What conclusions can you draw about literacy from these discussions?

Entering Adolescence
Literacy and Allegiance in Junior High

MARGARET FINDERS

INTRODUCTION   For many people, adolescence is a time significantly shaped by school and friends. Most of us probably have memories of the times we spent with our friends at school dances or athletic events, and perhaps we tell stories of a favorite class or a teacher we feared. When we tell these stories of adolescence, we may remember ourselves—or others—as part of particular groups ("jocks" or "preps") that seem to be common in American adolescent culture. For many adolescents, the groups with whom they associate and socialize are an important part of their sense of identity. Literacy researcher Margaret Finders tells a story of adolescence that involves these typical elements. But her story suggests that literacy, as much as anything else, plays a vital role in how adolescents understand themselves and how they interact with each other. Literacy, Finders writes in the introduction to her book *Just Girls: Hidden Literacies and Life in Junior High* (1997, p. 4), "provided a tangible means by which to claim status, challenge authority, and document social allegiances."

Finders conducted an extensive study of a group of seventh-grade girls in a junior high school in the Midwest. She spent a year observing the girls and interviewing them, their parents, and their teachers in order to explore the kinds of writing and reading the girls engaged in and the role that literacy played in their social and academic lives. The girls she studied fell into two social groups, which Finders called "the Social Queens" and "the Tough

Cookies" (names that were suggested in interviews by the girls' parents). The social queens were the popular girls in their class at school and generally came from comfortable, middle-class families. Tiffany and Angie were members of this group. The tough cookies were girls at the margins of the school's social life; they lived in trailer parks, which Finders describes as a sign of lower socioeconomic status. Cleo and Dottie were tough cookies. As she observed these girls during the year she spent at their school, Finders came to see that they used "literate practices . . . to present a particular kind of self." For Finders, who these girls were was determined in part by how and what they read and wrote. In the following passage, Finders focuses on the school year-book, which she describes as "the biggest school-sanctioned literacy event of the year," examining how the yearbook was not just a reflection of the identi-ties and social roles of the students but also was used to help establish and maintain those identities.

Margaret Finders is an associate professor of English and education at Purdue University, where she teaches language and literacy courses and works closely with teachers to improve literacy instruction in schools. She taught lan-guage arts in a middle school for thirteen years before pursuing a career as a professor and researcher. In addition to *Just Girls: Hidden Literacies and Life in Junior High* (1997), from which the following passage is taken, she is the author of a number of articles on literacy and literacy education.

REFLECTING BEFORE READING

1. Finders' study of literacy among adolescent girls focuses a great deal on the social lives of the junior high school girls she observed. She describes the importance of social groups to these girls and examines how those groups influenced the reading and writing the girls did. As you prepare to read the fol-lowing excerpt from Finders' study, consider your own experiences as a middle school or junior high school student. Who were your friends? To what extent were your relationships with them and with other students important in your life? Did these relationships affect your academic work, especially your reading and writing, in any way? As you read, consider how your experiences compare to the experiences of the girls Finders' describes.

2. In this passage, Finders focuses on the yearbook as an important "literacy event" that was part of how the girls she studied established and maintained their identities and relationships. As you read, consider whether your own experiences with yearbooks in middle or high school match the descriptions Finders offers here. What other "literacy events" were important in your life as a student? What might these events suggest about the role of literacy in your own identity?

I turn now to the end of a story: The last weeks in May at a junior high school. I begin here because I believe that an examination of one culminating event reveals the themes and tensions that permeated my year at Northern Hills Junior High School. The distribution of the junior high yearbook serves as a window onto the complex processes that create and constrain, within the school context, social roles that are informed by socioeconomic status, gender, and social-group alle-giances. As school years draw to a close, students across the nation anticipate the biggest school-sanctioned literacy event of the year: the sale and distribution of the school yearbook. Like students elsewhere, Northern Hills Junior High students anxiously awaited its arrival.

"A Sense of Belonging": Social Roles and the Yearbook "Event"

At Northern Hills, seventh grade marked the year in which students first produced and published a school yearbook, providing, it seems, a signpost of students' entrance into the adolescent arena. Many of these seventh graders bought their first yearbook, a symbol of distinction that separated them from elementary students. As elementary students, they had heard from older siblings and friends about *the junior high yearbook,* and its significance had been made clear since early October, when they were warned by way of intercom announcements to "Order now. Don't wait. Yearbooks will sell out fast."

With yearbook photographers occasionally popping into classrooms and disruptions from the intercom regularly announcing that band members or the volleyball team or the drama club should report to the gym for yearbook photographs, the presence of the yearbook was felt not just in May but throughout the year.

Produced by 65 students working together with the help of two staff advisors, the yearbook, a 48-page soft-bound document, captured the year through photographs, student-produced artwork, and captions. Sports held a prominent place in the pages of the yearbook: Photos of football, track, basketball, and wrestling events for the boys and track, tennis, volleyball, and basketball for the girls filled the pages. The book also contained photos of Soda—a drug and alcohol awareness club—and drama club.

I believe that most teachers would agree with one of the yearbook's faculty advisors, the media specialist, who described the importance of the yearbook this way:

> If you can find your mug in here [yearbook], it gives you a tremendous sense of belonging. We tried to cover all of the major events, and it's important to find yourself. We took a lot of pictures. If you and your mom can find yourself in here, then everything is just A-OK.

Here, the media specialist pointed out the importance of belonging, describing how belonging is documented by a photo in the yearbook. Similarly, Smith (1986) describes the necessity of belonging in regard to literacy learning. Using the metaphor of a "literacy club," he writes:

> And once again, membership in the literacy club adds to the individual's sense of personal identity, of who he or she is. "Hi, kid, you're one of us," say the members of the literacy club. (p. 38)[1]

Borrowing Smith's metaphor, Meyers (1992)[2] examines how students' social relations and thinking processes impinge on each other by categorizing students' uses of literacy within different social contexts as follows: to share membership, to contest

---

[1] Smith, F. *Insult to Intelligence: The Bureaucratic Invasion of Our Classrooms.* Portsmouth, NH: Heinemann, 1986.

[2] Meyers, J. "The Social Contexts of School and Personal Literacy." *Reading Research Quarterly,* vol. 27 (1992): 297–333.

membership, to fake membership, and to maintain membership. At Northern Hills, the junior high yearbook served similar functions, documenting membership in what might be considered an adolescent club. I use the term "club" to describe a set of discursive practices that shape and create social roles. As it is used here, a club provides an opportunity to examine the institutional conception of membership, of belonging. Giroux (1992)[3] argues that "student experience will have to be analyzed as part of a wider relationship between culture and power" (p. 16). What implicit cultural attributes encompass becoming "one of us"? What is valued? What roles are made available? How is the organization structured? What privileges and rewards are conferred by such a membership? What are the duties and obligations?

Photographs of after-school club and team activities dominated the book, revealing implicit values: Clearly, high value was placed on extracurricular participation, team membership, and competition.

Teachers, administrators, and many parents perceived extracurricular involvement as the key to both enjoyment and academic success. The faculty and student handbooks referred to sports, drama, and club activities as "cocurricular" rather than as "extracurricular." While carried on outside the designated school day, these activities were perceived by teachers, administrators, and many parents as central to the school's academic program. When asked what was most beneficial for her daughter during the school year, one mother explained, "After-school sports. I really like them. They keep her involved." This parent, like many others, believed that involvement in after-school activities would have a positive academic impact.

I contend that an examination of the school as a club makes visible disparate positions of status and power. Infused with the discourse of adolescence, the junior high school filters attention toward one particular group of students and, as you will see, renders others invisible.

Social Boundaries: The Queens and the Cookies

Just a few days before the sale of yearbooks, intercom announcements and rumors of the exact date of arrival revved students up. During second period, Mr. Anson, the building principal, announced, "The yearbooks are not here yet, but we will let you know the moment they get here." "The moment" was enunciated with such clarity that students in Mrs. Zmoleck's language arts class began buzzing with excitement. Mrs. Zmoleck attempted to distract them from the coming attraction. "Okay, it's free-reading time," she announced to counterbalance Mr. Anson on the intercom. For several days, Mr. Anson's morning announcements continued to remind students of the sale of yearbooks—as if any of them could not be keenly aware of the impending arrival.

Teachers' conversations, too, were laced with references to the arrival of the yearbook as they planned for the event. At Northern Hills Junior High, the yearbook had become a central part of the end-of-the-year curriculum. The distribution date seemed to be the only negative concern mentioned by teachers, who feared

---

[3] Giroux, H. "Critical Literacy and Student Experience: Donald Graves' Approach to Literacy." In Patrick Shannon, ed., *Becoming Political: Reading and Writing in the Politics of Literacy Education.* Portsmouth, NH: Heinemann, 1992. 15–20.

that an early release date might sabotage their scheduled plans for "signing time" in class during the last week of school. They talked to each other about the need to save the yearbook for the last week so it would fit within their curricular calendar. For the most part, teachers described the yearbook as a celebration and a well-earned reward for a year of hard work. They allocated class time for signing and sharing yearbooks. Perceived as a way to control the behavior of the 531 seventh and eighth graders who in late May might not be eager to participate in discussions or complete end-of-semester projects, signing time was a tool for negotiating with students, often appearing as a bribe. Teachers told students: "If we get all our work done . . . ," "If you are all good . . . ," "If you cooperate, and we can hurry through this . . ." The following teacher comment received several nods and "me toos" from staff in the teacher's lounge: "I give them the last five to ten minutes to write depending on how the class goes. It's a reward. It's a privilege. It's their reward for good behavior."

When the book was sold one full week before the last day of the school year, several teachers expressed frustration: "What are we going to do with them the last week? Students won't have anything to do"; "It gives them something to do at the end of school." Teachers explained that all the students looked forward to receiving the book, and that this sense of urgency might have forced the early sales.

The yearbook played such a large part in the end-of-school activities because the teachers and administrators all believed, as the media specialist articulated, that it gave a tremendous sense of belonging. The discourse of adolescence that privileges peer-group allegiances constructed filters, it seems, that prevented school personnel from seeing the yearbook as exclusionary. Although the yearbook was viewed as a symbol of solidarity for all students, only a particular population of students was made to feel as if they belonged to this club. Other students remained outsiders.

Having provided insight into the role of the yearbook from the institutional perspective, I turn now to the focal students themselves, describing the day of arrival of the yearbook from their perspective.

The Arrival of the Yearbook: Tiffany's Scene

It was lunch time, but students crowded the hallway outside the cafeteria. Crouched down in bunches, girls giggled, shrieked, and tipped one another over as they huddled together to sign each other's books. Boys and girls leaned against lockers or used a friend's back to steady a book for signing. Yearbooks flew across the corridor with a verbal "Hey, sign mine," tagged onto them.

It was easy to hear Tiffany's voice above the loud chatter. She leaped up from a crowd of girls, her long red hair flying back as she cackled loudly and ran full speed to the end of the hall, sloshing small amounts of her chocolate malt across the tan carpet as she went. She slammed into a group of friends and yanked a yearbook from one boy's hand, screaming, "Whose's this? You want me to sign it, don't you?" She looked over her shoulder at me, shouting, "I just have to keep writing until they'll let me stop. Everybody wants me to sign their book." She grinned and plopped herself down in the middle of the group. Like a pile of puppies, her friends pushed up against each other as she elbowed them over and wriggled her way in.

The Arrival of the Yearbook: Cleo's Scene

Inside, the cafeteria was much less crowded on that day. The large room was nearly empty and particularly quiet. I scanned the room and found Cleo and her friends in their usual seats in the middle of the front section, "the woof-woof tables," as Tiffany's friends described the area. Without difficulty, because there were so few students in the area, I made my way to them and stuffed my backpack under the table. Beth, Pat, Cleo, and Dottie were eating in silence. Not one yearbook was visible at their table. Sensing the awkwardness of the silence, I did not ask about it. Instead, I mentioned the rainy weather, and Dottie complained that she and her mother had worked late the night before, trimming all the tall, wet grass from around their trailer so they wouldn't be charged a penalty fee by the trailer-park management. Lunch continued with talk about rain, cookies, and favorite flavors of malts.

After lunch, I asked Cleo privately about the yearbooks. "Oh, I'm not very interested in them," she reported. When I reminded her that she had told me a week before that she thought she'd get one, she just shrugged her shoulders and repeated that she wasn't interested: "I don't know why I would want one. None of my friends are in there anyway."

The literacy event surrounding the arrival of the yearbook appears very different when one looks through the eyes of Tiffany and Cleo. These two scenes illustrate sharp contrasts between the two groups of girlfriends.

The yearbook was one mechanism that created tangible boundaries between groups. Students used photos and messages to assess status and document allegiances. One powerful position within the school was that of yearbook staff member. Many considered it an honor to be a member of the yearbook staff and especially to be one of the eighth-grade photographers, who were allowed to leave study halls throughout the year to snap candid shots of the student body. This position held power because it carried the privilege of added mobility around the school and access to other classrooms. Most important, individuals who held this position acted as gatekeepers, controlling who populated the pages of the yearbook.

The queens literally counted the number of photos each had in the yearbook, using the number as a measurement of popularity. When the yearbook arrived, these girls quickly flipped through the pages looking for themselves and their friends as proof of their belonging. On the other hand, Cleo's remark, "None of my friends are in there anyway," makes it clear that the cookies were aware of their absence.

Tiffany's and Cleo's networks of friends seemed to have very little in common. Tiffany loved to socialize. Her friends were active in athletic events, attended school activities and dances, and spent much of their leisure time together with same-age peers. In contrast, Cleo, like her friends, spent most of her leisure time with her family. She did not participate in any extracurricular activities and preferred to spend her time at home.

Constant comments from Northern Hills staff that "Everybody gets one" and "Everyone loves them" reveal that Cleo and Dottie and many others were invisible to school personnel. Current enrollment was 531; 425 books were ordered. Eight were sold to adults, 10 were distributed as complimentary copies, 10 were mailed to students who no longer lived in the district, and 5 remained unsold. In all, 397 copies were sold to students, which left 134 students without yearbooks. That figure represents 25% of the total student population. While students may not have purchased a yearbook for a variety of reasons, the socioeconomic status of families may have been a critical issue. For whatever reason, when teachers rewarded students with "signing time," one out of four students was not able to participate.

Economic constraints prevented some students from fully participating in the culture of the school and from participating in the biggest school-sanctioned literacy event of the year. This lack of a sense of belonging, of shared culture, was a constant tension in the conversations of Cleo, her family, and her friends. Cleo and Dottie lived in trailer parks, which in the Midwest carries a stigma that spills over into the school context, where some teachers and some administrators perceive that such living arrangements lead to school problems.

At times, it was not simply a matter of economics that interfered with the institution's construction of full participation in school activities, but the perceptions of economic status that others brought to the school context. This attitude was more fully illustrated by the principal's comments about students who come from trailer parks, which he described as "places that are too closely knit. They live too closely together. They know each other's problems and that causes problems at school." Likewise, constructions of the social dimension of schooling created obstacles for some students. At Northern Hills, I often heard the category "trailer-park kids" used to connote a lack of appropriate social skills in particular students. Some teachers described their class makeup in terms of numbers of students from trailer parks. A teacher's comment such as "I've got seven trailer-park kids" conveyed to other teachers the implicit yet clearly understood assumption of impending trouble for that teacher.

While economic resources played a major part in determining who would participate more fully in ways that the school had constructed participation, there was much evidence to suggest that an equal if not greater factor was the circulation of what Bourdieu (1977)[4] calls cultural capital: the attitudes, beliefs, cultural background, knowledge, and skills that are passed from one generation to the next. In order to understand the cultural capital that each girl carried to school, I turn now to their homes.

Perspectives from the Homes of the Social Queens

Tiffany and Angie were prominent members of this school's "club," clearly evidenced by the fact that each had four pictures in the yearbook. Besides her "mug shot," Tiffany appeared in team pictures with the volleyball team and the basketball team. She also appeared on the collage pages with her arms thrown around Lauren at the fall school dance. All of her best friends appeared throughout the book in candid shots and in volleyball, basketball, and track pictures.

While Tiffany's parents were concerned when her social life interfered with academics, they both explained that it was the cocurricular activities, especially sports, that were helping to shape her in a positive way. They attributed Tiffany's success in school to a great extent to her participation in extracurricular activities, and they

---

[4] Bourdieu, P. *Outline of a Theory of Practice.* Cambridge, England: Cambridge University Press, 1977.

encouraged her to undertake every opportunity that was available to her. "She's a very social person. With sports and friends and all," her mother told me. Later in the year, her father attributed her school-year success to this fact:

> I think overall it's been successful because of participating in extracurricular activities. That's been good for her, not only physically but mentally. But I personally didn't think I'd survive this year with her, from the standpoint of the constantly, about every other week, getting a letter from the school about this or that, incomplete assignments or whatever just due to her social butterfly attitude she had throughout the year, you know.

Notice the values placed on the benefits of extracurricular activities, "not only physically but mentally." While her father acknowledged that her "social butterfly attitude" caused some difficulties at home due to the demands it entailed (making driving arrangements, attending sporting events and social functions, and occasionally dealing with incomplete assignments), he accepted them as healthy signs of this developmental period. The discourse of adolescence reverberates in Tiffany's father's words. Letters from school, incomplete assignments, along with the social butterfly attitude, signaled to him that Tiffany was a normal adolescent.

Like Tiffany, Angie was actively involved in the school's social life. She participated in volleyball, basketball, and track as well as chorus and weight-lifting. Angie's mother described her, too, as social:

> A big part of her life's her social life. She's involved in a lot of things. It's an important part of school, in terms of learning because if you've got a happy child, all around happy child, she's going to do better at everything. Probably doesn't need to be quite as involved as she is, but she needs it. I think it's important to have extracurricular activities to keep her happy.

Parents of the queens expressed concern that there simply wasn't as much time for reading or family now that they were in junior high, but they strongly supported the importance of extracurricular activities as a direct route to school success: physically, socially, and academically.

Perspectives from the Homes of the Tough Cookies

Missing from the yearbook were any pictures other than the official "mug shots" of Cleo, Dottie, or their friends. Tough cookies did not participate in any extracurricular activities and were invisible to the eighth-grade photographers who were busy throughout the year taking candid shots around school.

Even purchasing a yearbook created tension. Consider Cleo's mother's frustration with her inability to send $8.00 to school so her daughter could have a yearbook to sign like all the other girls. Torn between the pressures of stretching a tight budget and wanting her daughter to belong, she said:

> I do not understand. I do not understand why they assume that everybody has tons of money, and every time I turn around it's more money for this and more money for that. Where do they get the idea that we've got all this money?

Like Cleo, Dottie had a picture only in the mug-shot section. Like Cleo's mother, Dottie's mother did not have the economic resources to allow Dottie to participate fully in school in ways the school might have envisioned. For instance, after Dottie's language arts teacher encouraged her to try out for the fall play, her mother explained to me why she did not "choose" to participate: "I think Dottie told you that we don't have a car right now. She's embarrassed and doesn't want her teachers to know."

Understanding the social dimensions of this condition go far beyond any economic factors. While Cleo's mother may have regretted that Cleo did not get a yearbook and Dottie's mother might have liked Dottie to try out for the play, both women regularly expressed values that conflicted with the sense of belonging that permeated the messages surrounding the sale of the yearbook. Cleo's mother explained her anxiety and worries in the move to junior high:

> The biggest thing for me is the social stuff. I'm not ready for her to move outside the family, and it's hard for me to say, "yeah, you can do it," because I don't feel comfortable yet.

Later in the same interview, she told me that she planned for her daughter to attend a nearby college so she can remain at home. She explained the importance of family in this way:

> Like the Orientals and even the Indian people, [I think] families are most important. And everybody works together to get wherever they're going. And I really don't think that us, as White people or whatever, I don't think we do that. I think we just start cutting off, saying you're on your own, you know. And I really do think that families should always stick together as long as possible. I mean you give them a boost up. I don't like that boot-out stuff.

In opposition to the discourse of adolescence, which privileges allegiance with same-age peers, this quote reveals a continued emphasis on close ties with significant adults. Unlike parents of the social queens, who regarded severing ties with adults as a sign of normal progression into adolescence, the parents of the cookies regarded maintaining allegiances with family as central. Emphasis on maintaining family ties in working-class families during adolescence is documented elsewhere (Schlegel & Barry, 1991;[5] Weiss, 1993[6]). McRobbie's (1978)[7] study documents the centrality of home and family life for working-class girls. I argue that one must account for marked differential role constructions that accompany the move into adolescence. In the school setting, it seems that adolescence as a life stage may have constructed filters that deny diversity.

Cleo's mother regularly made sharp contrasts between academic and social aspects of schooling. She explained, "I want Cleo to be educated. I don't want her to be social." Like Cleo's mother, Dottie's mother discouraged her daughter from

---

[5] Schlegel, A., and H. Barry, III. *Adolescence: An Anthropological Inquiry.* New York: The Free Press, 1991.

[6] Weiss, L. "Disempowering White Working-Class Females: The Role of the High School." In L. Weiss and M. Fine, eds., *Beyond Silenced Voices: Class, Race, and Gender in the United States Schools.* Albany, NY: State University of New York Press, 1993. 95–121.

[7] McRobbie, A. "Working Class Girls and the Culture of Femininity." In Women's Studies Group, eds., *Women Take Issue: Aspects of Women's Subordination.* London, Hutchinson, 1978. 96–108.

participating in any cocurricular activities: "Maybe when she is in high school, 16 or 17, then she can do track or something. *Not now!*"

Both women expressed a strong distrust of the social side of schooling and presented a set of values that conflicted with Northern Hills teachers' thinking about appropriate pedagogy for the language arts classroom. (Note the importance of peer response and collaborative groups in reading and writing workshops in the work of Atwell, 1987,[8] and Graves, 1983.[9]) Both women deemphasized the importance of peer groups. Both mothers strongly resisted the notion that social activities were a part of the educational process or a sign of progression into the developmental stage of adolescence.

"Sign Mine": Constructing Identity and Claiming Allegiance

Time to write in the school yearbook was perceived as a reward by teachers, and students often announced that this sanctioned writing time was their right, demanding time to scrawl their messages across the face of another student.

Literacies—both sanctioned literacies and literate underlife—served to maintain particular social roles and document particular allegiances. At Northern Hills, writing in the yearbook provides a unique opportunity to examine the dimensions of sanctioned literacies (those that are recognized and circulated by adults in authority) and literate underlife (those literate practices that are out of sight and out of control of those in authority, practices in opposition to the institution). Within the pages of the yearbook, literate practices marked membership and measured status within social groups. Messages were borrowed, erased, and scribbled over to present a particular kind of self as well as to document and deny allegiances. Six pages were included at the back for just such writing practices. Clearly, writing in the yearbook privileged those who matched the dominant image of the adolescent, both economically and culturally. The cookies are absent from the remaining discussion.

Presenting a particular self through their literate choices, boys' inscriptions centered on action while girls' messages focused on relationships. Messages such as "Your [*sic*] a total babe," "Yo, The spirit 40 lives on," and "Stay sweet and sexy, NOT" found their way onto these pages. Just as the sixth-grade girls in Cherland's (1994)[10] study used dress, demeanor, and leisure-time activities (including reading) as a way to "do gender," signing the yearbook was a means of marking gender. Drawing on West and Zimmerman (1987),[11] Cherland writes that "doing gender involves a complex of socially guided perceptual, interactional, and micropolitical activities that cast particular pursuits as expressions of masculine and feminine 'natures'" (p. 12). Of the messages printed above, "Your [*sic*] a total babe" and "Yo, The spirit 40 lives on" were written by males, while "Stay sweet and sexy, NOT" was written by seventh-

---

[8] Atwell, N. *In the Middle: Writing, Reading, and Learning With Adolescents.* Portsmouth, NH: Heinemann, 1987.

[9] Graves, D. *Writing: Teachers and Children at Work.* Portsmouth, NH: Heinemann, 1983.

[10] Cherland, M. *Private Practices: Girls Reading Fiction and Constructing Identity.* London: Taylor and Francis, 1994.

[11] West, C., and D. H. Zimmerman. "Doing Gender." *Gender and Society,* vol. 1 & 2 (1987): 125–151.

grade girls. The boys often inscribed their basketball jersey number into their messages: "The spirit 40 lives on." Although many girls participated in basketball, no reference to sports was evident in their yearbook inscriptions.

Both boys and girls sought to affix a kind of permanence to their messages. Yearbook inscriptions served, it seems, to secure one's role and relationships in print. "Forever" and "lives on" appeared in an overwhelming majority of messages. Girls most often signed their inscriptions with B.F.F. (Best Friends Forever) while boys secured their social position by such comments as "Yo, #15 Forever" and "We're #1 forever." In these attempts to attach permanence to a presentation of self, such signatures were clearly declarations of cultural masculine and feminine identification: Boys sought to present a competitive self while girls sought attachment with others.

Romance marked the signatures of the seventh-grade girls. They often searched for red and pink pens with which to write and dotted their I's with hearts. The girls often drew hearts around boys' pictures and wrote "Love," carefully turning the letter O into a small red heart near a particular boy's picture.

Boys' inscriptions focused on action and on power, presenting the male self as a powerful competitor at the top of the social hierarchy. Girls, in contrast, presented the self through the male gaze, finding a place in the social order through one's ability to attract male attention: "Stay sweet and sexy" was the most common inscription for girls.

Some yearbooks were considered to be "ruined" by boys who wrote comments that girls feared would result in punishment at home. Comments such as "Hey, Boobs, I hope I see ALOT of you this summer" created bursts of muffled anger in groups of girls, yet the girls refused to tell adults about such practices and quickly hushed each other up so a teacher would not approach them. Similar to the Oak Town girls in Cherland's 1994 study, the Northern Hills girls never reported such acts. Cherland writes of similar acts of sexual harassment:

> Instead of telling the child what she must do, the culture tells her what she is (Bourdieu, 1991).[12] MTV, the television news, novels, fashion advertisements, older relatives and the boys at school all told Oak Town girls what they were: powerless people whose bodies were "naturally" the object of others' desires. It is not surprising, therefore, that most accepted the practice of sexual harassment. Bourdieu suggests that people come to accept these violent suggestions inscribed in the practices of everyday life, no matter what their status or class, and no matter what the effect on them, because cultural discourses position them as people who must accept the warning, while they in turn come to interpret themselves as those who must submit. In this way, domination is sustained through interpersonal relations, and symbolic violence is accepted as legitimate. (p. 42)

While Northern Hills girls expressed outrage about certain boys' writing practices, they continued to ask Stevie, "the one who ruined that yearbook," to "sign mine" and granted status to the girl who was the victim of the message. Clearly, this comment can be read as a way boys exert control over girls. But trained by the larger culture, the Northern Hills girls received it as a mark of distinction, accepting their position as powerless people defined through their body images.

---

[12] Bourdieu, P. *Language and Symbolic Power.* Cambridge, MA: Harvard University Press, 1991.

Gossip about the comment carried much currency for several days. While the Northern Hills male presented the self as a powerful actor, he represented the female as object of desire. The early adolescent girl accepts his representation of her as an object, more specifically as an anatomical commodity.

Although this particular comment was made invisible, by blocking it out with a thick black marker, the seventh graders continued to regard its presence. Under the black ink was the secret sexual message that was revealed to those deemed an appropriate audience. Girls led each other by the hand to the yearbook, "See, this is where it is." The phrase was repeated in present tense: "where it is," not "where it was." The sexual message remained present under the black marker. As children, these girls accepted sexuality as taboo; yet, as early adolescents, they sought to enact a sexual self through their literate practices. Although hidden from adults, the message was not erased. It was not erased from the yearbook or from the construction of identity that these girls were internalizing.

Patrolling the Borders: Literacy as Ritual of Exclusion

KATIE: Can I sign your yearbook?
BARB: No.

A quick glance at the yearbook shows row after row of white faces ordered by alphabetical arrangement. The seeming homogeneity conceals diversity: Invisible barriers such as attitudes, beliefs, economics, and experiences separate these young people into at least two camps. The girls created markers to maintain the borders between them. Allegiances became visible in both the act of writing and in the messages themselves. What is written and to whom is controlled by one's social status. Yearbooks circulated across social boundaries, yet those with the greatest social status stood in judgment of those less powerful. Students carefully monitored who could sign their yearbooks. To allow one of lesser status to mark one's book appeared to lower the status of the book owner. Students often asked for and were denied signing privileges. The cookies did not participate in signing, and within the queens' friendship network, a hierarchy was clearly visible. Some students were in fact told "No," after asking, "Can I sign your yearbook?" In the same way, some students refused to sign yearbooks of those perceived to be outside the circle of significance. Who had the right to write was clearly an issue of entitlement defined by Shuman (1986)[13] as "the rights of both addressors and addressees, as well as to the onlookers, witnesses, eavesdroppers and third-party listeners to a message, as well as the characters in the message" (p. 18). If one was perceived as an outsider, then one was not entitled to write. Likewise, one might or might not be entitled to even view the message. Students guarded their written texts and controlled who had the right to see them.

The issue of entitlement, according to Shuman (1993),[14] concerns one's rights to "appropriate another's voice as a means of borrowing authority, whether in an act

---

[13] Shuman, A. *Storytelling Rights: The Uses of Oral and Written Texts by Urban Adolescents.* Cambridge, England: Cambridge University Press, 1986.

[14] Shuman, A. "'Get Outa My Face': Entitlement and Authoritative Discourse." In S. Hill and J. Irvine, eds., *Responsibility and Evidence in Oral Discourse.* New York: Cambridge University Press, 1993. 135–160.

of complicity or resistance to that authority" (p. 136). Messages inscribed in the year-book illustrate positions of both compliance and resistance—most often compliance to peers deemed higher in social status and resistance to adults. Layers of authority become visible when one examines these written texts. For example, as an act of resistance, one student parodied Mr. Tibidioux, her language arts teacher, taking that teacher's own words to mock his authority: "It is clear that . . ." Borrowing these words from his recurring instruction for writing appropriate responses, she wrote them in a yearbook and then, to claim publicly that she knew that he was leaving the school system at the close of the year, she added, "It is clear that Scooby-doo [rhymes with Tibidioux] is leaving," spoofing his name and his practice. Standing in judgment, the queens erased some teachers' pictures altogether. To exercise their authority over others, they drew over and scribbled on teachers' images and those of other students.

Students with the greatest status were freed from judgment, and their written comments became models for others to copy. As I watched, one student carefully moved her finger across the page, working cautiously to transfer a phrase exactly from one yearbook to another. Because a particular phrase was perceived as carry-ing more currency in this arena, this teen appropriated the words of another student as her own in order for her own voice to contain that power. Students shared texts and at times took another person's message for their own, copying the same phrase from one yearbook to the next to the next. In such borrowing of texts, one, in a sense, borrowed the social status of another. In taking another's message as her own, each girl had to be careful not to overstep her boundaries, and, as Shuman (1986)[15] sug-gests, write what she was not entitled to write.

In the act of writing, students inadvertently may mark themselves as outsiders by writing a message judged inappropriate by others. If one was not savvy enough to create an appropriate text or powerful enough to forgo judgment, often, out of fear of marking oneself as outsider, one just scribbled safe messages such as "Have a good summer" or "See ya next year."

Some students, in order to preserve their social position, asked a friend, "What should I write? What do you want me to say?" Students took this opportunity to exert their position of authority and made such playful comments as "Say I'm 'just too cool'" or "Say 'she's always got a taco'" (a current description for shorts or jeans that were considered too tight across the seat of the pants) or "Write, 'BFF ASS'" (a code for <u>b</u>est <u>f</u>riends <u>f</u>orever and <u>a</u>lways <u>s</u>tay <u>s</u>weet or <u>s</u>exy). Many comments were so highly coded that only those few insiders could translate them.

In order for students to demonstrate that they were with it, comments carrying the current pop jargon taken from movies, television, or local sources become etched into this school-sanctioned document, creating an unusual juxtaposition of sanc-tioned and out-of-bounds literacies. Dark, graffiti-like messages boldly cut across the white-bordered layout and quite literally "defaced" students and teachers alike. With big pink erasers, students rubbed out the faces of outsiders.

Constructing a dual set of standards as a way to separate themselves from adults and from children, the queens at times judged their yearbook writing as appropriate for their friends but too obscene to share with parents, teachers, or those outside their social network. Adhering to the adolescent code, the queens sought to present a

---

[15] Shuman, A. *Storytelling Rights: The Uses of Oral and Written Texts by Urban Adolescents.* Cambridge, England: Cambridge University Press, 1986.

sexual self, lacing romance and sexual innuendo into their messages. They reported to me that such topics were appropriate for them as teenagers and continued to hide them from parents and teachers.

In all of this writing, the queens demonstrated a tremendous sense of play. Signing yearbooks had the feeling of recess, providing playtime away from the institutional demands of schooling, away from adult supervision. Similar to the playground, who could play was controlled by the peer dynamic. The yearbook was used to stake out territory and control social interactions. Yearbook messages regulated relationships and interests. In these ways, yearbook writing served two purposes: to construct a border around particular adolescents and to measure growth into adulthood.

Embracing Adolescence: The Yearbook as Process and Object

The yearbook provided a pictorial history, freezing moments of friendship, of athletic prowess, of academic endeavors. It provided, too, a unique opportunity to blur the boundaries between school-sanctioned literacies and literate underlife; sanctioned time in the school context given over to leisure, words written publicly yet secretly and quite literally written across the faces of authority while under the watchful gaze of those in authority. For seventh graders here, it was their first yearbook, a symbol of membership in the junior high school and entry into an adolescent arena: photos published as proof of sanctioned membership in the junior high, words scribbled across those pages as proof of the unsanctioned resistance that marks one as adolescent.

As a member of any club, one accepts the rules and obligations of the organization in order to enjoy the rights and benefits that accompany such a membership. Membership in the junior high "club" carried dues; competition and cocurricular participation were a central part of such obligations. In other words, one must embrace or at least comply with the roles that such a membership enlists.

Belonging to the Northern Hills district is a privilege that few parents or teachers would refute. With top standardized test scores and a near zero dropout rate, Northern Hills is looked on as a highly successful, fully functioning district. A full array of cocurricular opportunities, well-kept grounds and facilities, abundant instructional materials, and low student-teacher ratios serve as markers of school success that carry across state lines and distinguish the Northern Hills Community School District as one of the finest in the nation. Northern Hills, fully entitled to call itself a place of pride, closely matches an idealized school. Yet, do we fully understand the implications of this match? Terry Eagleton (1991)[16] writes:

> In the field of education, for example, symbolic violence operates not so much by the teacher speaking "ideologically" to the students, but by the teacher being perceived as in possession of an amount of "cultural capital" which the student needs to acquire. The educational system thus contributes to reproducing the dominant social order not so much by the viewpoint it fosters, but by this regulated distribution of cultural capital . . . those who lack the "correct" taste are unobtrusively excluded, relegated to shame and silence. (pp. 157–58)

---

[16] Eagleton, T. *Ideology: An Introduction*. New York: Verso, 1991.

I contend that it is not the teacher alone but the entire institution and larger community that distribute a pervasive cultural capital. As a "Place of Pride," Northern Hills articulates a progressivism that characterizes its curriculum; yet such an insistent argument masks the traditional remnants that persist under the surface. When we examine school as a symbol of membership in a larger culture, we uncover a powerful ideology that continues to privilege the dominant class and insists on maintaining the status quo. The junior high comes equipped with one way of being in the world. The junior high school arena requires the strong sense of competition and team membership that permeated the pages of the yearbook. To resist the demands of this adolescent organization marks one as less than a fully functioning member.

I would argue that the characteristics of adolescence as a developmental stage are not so much a part of this stage because they are biologically wired or psychologically triggered. They emerge because they are ideological constructs that are fostered by the schedule and structure of the junior high school. Beyond economics, the emphasis at Northern Hills on cocurricular activities that fill up after-school, evening, and weekend hours requires children to realign their positions within their family structure. A focus on winning both in the classroom and on the athletic field nurtured a keen focus on the self. Thus, to fully participate in this club, earning the privileges that it entails, demanded strong same-age social networks, severing or at least distancing from parental ties, and placing emphasis on a competitive self, all highly prized by Northern Hills standards. Members in good standing met such demands. Anyone who was unwilling or unable to meet them was marginalized.

The junior high yearbook packed the ideology of the school district and the larger culture into its 48 pages, translating a set of values into images and texts that were carried through the halls and through the community. Looking back at the yearbook as literacy event, looking through the eyes of Cleo and Tiffany, the yearbook takes on significance both as process (ideological inculcation) and object (cultural capital).

Throughout this examination of the yearbook as event, it becomes clear that while the discourse of adolescence denies diversity, those complexities, however subtle, do exist, creating invisible obstacles. A vast tangle of competing expectations and allegiances shapes the school context, which in turn shapes social roles. As an actual event and as a larger symbol, the school yearbook illustrates how one's membership constricts and enables particular literate practices that in turn constrict and enable particular roles available to group members.

Conceived of as an opportunity for all to celebrate the completion of another successful academic year, the yearbook provided much more. It served as a marker. For Tiffany and the other social queens it reaffirmed their position in the school arena and in the larger community. They measured their status by the number and size of their pictures and by the number of requests to sign books: "Everybody wants me to sign their book." For Cleo and her friends, it also reaffirmed their position: "None of my friends are in there anyway."

The role of the yearbook within the institutional context remains central to the closing of the school year. The yearbook stands as an icon. Unknowingly, some are allowed to speak while others are silenced, some to write while others are written upon.

REFLECTING ON THE READING

1. Finders focuses her essay (which was one chapter of her book about adolescent literacy) on the school yearbook. Why does she choose this event as her focus? What does she offer as justification for examining how yearbooks were perceived and used in the school where she conducted her research? Is her justification valid, in your view? Why or why not?

2. Finders uses the metaphor of an "adolescent club" to describe the activities surrounding the yearbook at Northern Hills Junior High School. What does she mean? In what sense did the yearbook represent a "club"? She also calls the yearbook "exclusionary." What does she mean by that term in this context? In what ways does she believe the yearbook excluded students? From what were they excluded?

3. Why, according to Finders, was a position on the yearbook staff one of "power"? What kind of power did such a position provide? In what sense does Finders use the term *power* here? What does the "power" of the yearbook editor suggest about literacy and its role in adolescent life?

4. What does Finders mean by "cultural capital"? How does she use this concept to help explain how different groups of students functioned in different ways at Northern Hills Junior High School?

5. Finders describes differences in the economic status of the girls in her study. How did those differences affect the girls' participation in school activities? How did it influence their writing and reading? How did it shape their attitudes toward school and toward each other? What might the example of these girls suggest about the role of socioeconomic status in school? In literacy?

6. What is the difference between "sanctioned literacies" and "literate underlife," according to Finders? Why is this distinction important in her explanation of the writing and reading done by the girls in her study? What might this distinction suggest about how literacy functions in our lives?

7. How did signing and writing in the yearbook establish identity and membership in social groups, according to Finders? How did it exclude some groups of students? What might the example of the yearbook at Northern Hills Junior High School suggest about how writing and reading affect social relationships?

Examining Rhetorical Strategies

1. This essay is taken from a book in which Finders reports on her study of literacy among adolescent girls in a middle school in Iowa. It was intended primarily for teachers and researchers interested in literacy. Accordingly, throughout her essay she refers to other studies of literacy as she discusses her observations of the girls she studied. This practice of citing other research is common among researchers and scholars. Examine Finders' use of references. How does she use them in her essay? What purpose do they serve? How do they help her make her point about the reading and writing practices of the girls in her study? Do you find these references effective? Why or why not? Do you think Finders imagined someone like you as a reader of her book? Explain.

2. Finders devotes a great deal of attention in this essay to describing the various activities and interactions she observed at Northern Hills Junior High School. Why does she provide so much detail about these activities and interactions? What purpose do these descriptions serve in her analysis of the literacy of the students she studied? Did you find these descriptions effective? Why or why not? Do the activities and interactions she described resemble your own experiences in junior high or middle school? Explain. How might your own experiences influence the way you respond to Finders' descriptions?

3. As a researcher, Finders strives to take an "objective" stance on the students she studies. Her description is intended to be a picture of what she observed while she conducted her study at Northern Hills Junior High School. Do you think she takes an objective stance on the students in her study? Does she seem more favorable or sympathetic to one group of girls over another? How do you think her own presence as an observer might have influenced what she observed? Explain, citing specific instances from the text to support your answer.

4. Finders presents her observations of the activities of the girls at Northern Hills Junior High School as "evidence" for her conclusions about how literacy helped shape and maintain their identities and social relationships. Assess the effectiveness of Finders' use of this evidence. Does she make a strong case for her conclusions, in your view? Why or why not? What does she emphasize in her use of evidence? What does she leave out? What might her use of evidence suggest about her own views about adolescence and schools and literacy?

5. Evaluate Finders' prose in this essay, especially her use of specialized words and phrases such as "discursive practices," "discourse," and "cultural capital." How do these terms function in her essay? Do they help make her essay more effective? Explain. These terms are obviously familiar to scholars, for whom Finders wrote her study. Do you think they are understandable to other readers who might not be familiar with scholarly research on literacy? How did these terms affect you as a reader? Did they make the essay seem more believable or authoritative to you? Did they help you understand the points Finders makes in the essay? Do you think readers must have knowledge of these terms in order adequately to understand an essay like this?

6. The publisher of the book from which this passage was taken described the book as "essential reading for teachers, teacher educators, parents, and anyone else interested in literacy learning and the social lives of adolescent girls." Based on your reading of this passage, do you think this is an accurate description of the audience for Finders' study? Do you think Finders wrote with such a broad audience in mind? Explain, citing specific passages from her text in your answer.

Engaging the Issues

1. Find your yearbook from your high school or middle school years (if you have one) or borrow one from a friend and analyze what it might say about the social roles and relationships at your old school. Do the photos and text reveal anything about those roles and relationships? Who put together the yearbook? What did they seem to want to achieve with that book? What is the image of

school and students that emerges from the book? If there are signatures or other writings in the book, what might they reveal about how the book was used by you (or its owner) or about your roles and relationships at your school? Now write an essay for an audience of your classmates in which you present your analysis, focusing on how the yearbook might have been an important factor in the social life of your school, as Finders suggests the yearbook was at Northern Hills Junior High School.

2. Finders' study suggests that certain literacy practices, such as producing, distributing, and signing yearbooks, can be ways of establishing and maintaining identity and exerting social power. In a group of your classmates, discuss the ways in which the yearbook functioned as a means of exerting power at Northern Hills Junior High School, according to Finders' description, and compare it to your respective experiences in your own schools. Together, identify some other writing or reading practices that might function as vehicles for "power" in the way that the yearbook functioned as a vehicle for power at Northern Hills Junior High School. Assess Finders' conclusions about these "powerful" literacy practices, and try to draw your own conclusions about how literacy can function as a vehicle for social power.

3. Based on your discussions for Question #2, explore a specific writing or reading activity that seems to have an important influence on the identities and social relationships of those involved, as the yearbooks did for the students at Northern Hills Junior High School. Conduct research of your own into this activity, perhaps observing the activity, as Finders did. Then write a report of your study for your classmates. In your report, be sure to describe the literacy activity that you are analyzing so that your readers will understand how it happened. Draw on Finders' study or any other appropriate resources in explaining this activity.

4. Finders' study suggests that parents and educators may have cause to worry about the ways in which students engage in activities like signing yearbooks in school. Write a letter to the superintendent of your school district in which you express concerns about such activities, drawing on your own experiences and on Finders' study as support for your concerns. Propose measures that the school system might take to address your concerns. Be sure to consider the audience for whom you're writing as you compose your letter.

5. In a group of your classmates, compare the letters written for Question #4. First, compare the specific concerns each of you has raised. Discuss these, considering pros and cons of each. Next, assess the effectiveness of the letters you have each written. Are they well written? Do they present their arguments convincingly? Do they address their audience's concerns appropriately? How might they be made more effective? When you're finished with this exercise, make appropriate changes to your letter.

6. In a group of your classmates, discuss the role of gender in the kinds of school-related literacy activities (such as the yearbook or the school newspaper) that Finders describes in her study. Were there differences in the ways in which boys and girls engaged in these activities? If so, what were they? How might you account for them? Share your own experiences with such activities with your

group members, and compare your respective experiences. Try to draw conclusions about the relationship between literacy and gender.

7. Based on your discussions for Question #6 above, write a conventional academic essay about the role of gender in school-related literacy events.

In a Chat Room, You Can Be NE1

Constructing a Teen-age Self On Line

CAMILLE SWEENEY

INTRODUCTION   In the latter part of the 1990's, the increase in the number of people using the Internet as a means of communication was remarkable. Among the growing number of Internet users, young people—especially teenagers—embraced the Net more completely than any other demographic group. As journalist Camille Sweeney informs us in the following article, research indicated that by 1999 almost 70 percent of all teenagers were spending time online. For many of those teenagers, that time was largely devoted to visiting Internet "chat rooms," where they were able to converse, socialize, and even develop relationships with other teenagers exclusively through the use of their computers. In one sense, these activities are nothing new: teenagers routinely spend much of their time socializing with each other and have been doing so since long before the development of the Internet. But this online version of teen social life raises interesting questions about the role of technology and literacy in the formation of identity, a matter that lies at the center of teen life. For instance, does the technology of the Internet influence the way teens understand who they are and how they relate to others? Are online chat rooms just the high-tech equivalent of hanging out with friends at the movies or on neighborhood street corners? Or do these chat rooms actually change how teens establish their identities? And does a teen's online identity differ from his or her "real-life" identity? Is there, as Sweeney puts it, something we can call a "cyberself"?

Such questions are important if only because so many teens spend time online and because online chat rooms have become such an established part of American youth culture. For today's teenagers, chatting online with other teenagers is as commonplace as attending a high school sporting event or taking a standardized test. Accordingly, understanding how adolescents see themselves and how they interact with one another would seem to require an understanding of the role of chat rooms and similar online communications technologies in contemporary youth culture. Part of Sweeney's interest in online chat rooms lies in exploring that role, and she casts a journalist's eye toward the phenomenon so that her readers might get a better sense of what these chat rooms are all about and what they might mean for teens and for our society. But as Sweeney takes us into these chat rooms, posing as a teen herself, she encourages us to confront a host of more complex issues. For instance, the capability that users have in Internet chat rooms to create online identities might lead us to wonder about the relationship of these online identities to the "real" teens who create them. In what ways might these online selves differ from "real-life" selves? And why do teens feel they need to have "different" selves online? Further, if Internet chat rooms are really just online versions of teen socializing, are they replacing the traditional face-to-face socializing at the movies or on the street corner or at a friend's home? If so, why?

Sweeney offers some potential answers to such questions. In doing so she explores the role of technology and literacy in the formation of identity in a broader sense. Internet chat rooms are textual environments in which users create identities exclusively through the words they use. In this sense, literacy becomes a powerful medium through which we create who we are—or who we wish to be. (Other authors in this chapter explore this process in different contexts—for example, Andrea R. Fishman examines how reading and writing help establish the cultural identity of members of Amish communities.) But the technology of the Internet, which allows for such rapid and far-reaching communication, may magnify or perhaps even alter the power of literacy as a means of establishing identity. If so, then we might wonder how the online experiences of today's young people will shape the adults they will eventually become and the understanding those adults will have of literacy and technology—and themselves. In this sense, Sweeney may be giving us a glimpse of the future of teen life and how it may be shaped by literacy and technology.

Camille Sweeney is a journalist who has written about popular culture for such publications as *Newsday* and the *New York Times.* She also served as project editor for a special series of articles devoted to the millennium in the *New York Times Magazine,* in which the following article originally appeared in 1999.

REFLECTING BEFORE READING

1. As she tells us in the following article, Camille Sweeney is a journalist who posed as a teenager in Internet chat rooms. As you read, pay attention to how she presents herself as the narrator of the article. What kind of narrator is she? Why might she have presented herself in this way? Do you find her voice credible in the article? Why or why not?

2. If you're like most American students, you have probably spent some time visiting Internet chat rooms. What kinds of experiences have you had in such chat rooms? Do you have a generally favorable view of these chat rooms? How might that view influence the way you read Sweeney's descriptions? If you have never experienced an Internet chat room, what do you know about them? What impression do you have of them? As you read, pay attention to whether or not Sweeney fulfills your own impressions of online chat rooms.

" **Y**o yo yo, what's up what's up?" The lines scroll up my screen. Different fonts, different colors, the words whiz by, everyone's screen name sounding vaguely pornographic. I'm on America Online, in a chat room for young adults. There are hundreds of such chat rooms on AOL, and it has taken a lot of Net navigating simply to find one that has room enough to let me in.

For all the crowds and clamoring, there's not much being said in this chat room, or rather, not much that's being paid attention to. A 16-year-old girl is talking about her baby due in two months. A grumpy 15-year-old guy reluctantly wishes her well. Another girl, 17, asks, "Are your parents cool with it?" The lines continue to scroll, a word here, a phrase there, live text that reads much like a flow of conversation you might overhear in a crowded high-school hallway or parking lot between classes in old-fashioned meat space (that is, anyplace not in the cyberworld).

I've been on line, off and on, for months trying to determine if there is such a thing as a cyberself and, if so, what goes into the making of this most modern of personality constructs. Teen-agers especially are fitting specimens for this experiment because they are the first generation saturated in this new medium. In any given week, according to Teenage Research Unlimited, nearly 70 percent of all 12- to 19-year-olds go on line. The Internet has shaped them—just as television shaped their parents, and radio their grandparents. Once a generation saw itself grow up on TV; now a generation is watching itself grow up on line. It would follow then that the 31 million teen-agers of Gen Y or Generation Why or Echo Boomers or Millennials, as this group is variously called, would have completely new ways of perceiving one another and themselves. I went undercover as a cyberteen to find out.

Teen-age years—at least in my memory—are reserved largely for trying out different personas. As the psychoanalyst Erik Erikson contended, adolescence is a period "during which the individual through free role experimentation may find a niche in some section of his society, a niche which is firmly defined and yet seems to be uniquely made for him."

Herein lies the thrill of the on-line self: its malleability, its plasticity, the fact that it can be made up entirely of your own imagination. You can take your old self, or don a fresh one, and hang out in a group of jocks for a postgame chat, argue the banality of Britney Spears with an international posse of pop connoisseurs, post a note to a cool-sounding guy from Detroit—all without ever having to leave your bedroom. Maybe this is the Internet's greatest asset to teendom: access, and the confidence to slip in and out of personalities, the ability to try on identities, the adolescent equivalent of playing dress-up in the attic, standing before the mirror in heels and lipstick long before you own your own.

March 1999

I'm on line as Red720720, a cumbersome screen name that I believe, nonetheless, sounds teen-age blunt and allows me gender flexibility. I've been slow to get started. In fact, I really haven't said much beyond commiserating with the pregnant girl, telling her that when my sister was pregnant she found cocoa butter helpful, that it helped her skin feel "not as stretchy." I'm trying to talk in their language, although I worry that I'm not. For all the identify shifting that occurs on line, teen-agers tend to talk in a uniform way that leaves me scrambling. Not only is it teen talk—it's 90's teen talk. I have to think to remember "girl" not "woman." I have to think to remember "cool" not "very cool."

A crew of teen-agers suddenly bursts into the room crying out to get it on: "Want 2 cyber? Want 2 cyber?" They beg for "pics" (pictures) and often stop chatters in their tracks for what amounts to an all-room booty call. "Everybody, give me age, sex and favorite position," one guy writes; "everybody" is written in capital letters, the on-line version of shouting. The crew is ignored, washing over the room like a tide, before heading back out to sea. I chat with a Croatian teen-ager about obscure Scandinavian death-metal bands. He says he is 18. A lot of people post their ages and sex at the outset—"18/m." I find this frankness a little startling. I write "16/f" and ask him if his screen name, Flock82, was inspired by the 80's synth-pop band A Flock of Seagulls. He writes that he has never heard of them. I struggle to remember their big hit but realize I'm dating myself in doing so. "I can't remember their biggest hit," I write, "maybe I'll ask my older brother." Perhaps sensing a fraud, Flock82 moves on. I suddenly feel out of place, as if I'm wearing a thick turtleneck at a summer rave. Someone new has just entered the room, looking for love. "Watch out," he writes, in a flashy robin's-egg-blue font, "I'm coming in. . . ."

May 1999

The Internet has been compared to a fun house, a free-for-all, a place where you might be robbed or cheated or deceived, a place where you can be promised a rainbow but given a mouthful of ashes. I spend a lot of time cruising E-zine sites for teen-agers and connecting to the ever-multiplying number of hyperlinks a lot of the Web pages offer. The randomness makes me dizzy. But in fact, I manage my first cyber-romance with a guy I meet a series of links away from a surfing site. He calls himself Brian_the_Hawaiian. He has something like a million screen names on a million different sites. He tells me he is 16, from Honolulu, but wants to get out of there soon to come to the continental U.S. We chat a few times, about waves and about whether the volcanoes in Hawaii are cool. (I have to think to remember not "very cool.") We become pals, going as far as to search for each other in a variety of spots if a couple of days go by without contact.

Then one night, out of nowhere, he asks me if I want to cyber. (He actually sounds serious!) I say no, but agree to send him a kiss, which I do. I write something like "peck." Actually, I write "peck peck," and, yes, I'm still mortified about it. Even though this is an experiment, and even though he says he's "crazy 4 older women" (this time I've said I'm 18), it still feels weird. He tells me his favorite movie star is Austin Powers, though I don't have the heart to mention to him that Austin Powers isn't real. He also says that maybe he wants to be an actor someday, or a professional surfer. I tell him "2 go 4 it." And I don't start getting worried until he wonders exactly how far I live from the Brooklyn Bridge. (I've told him I can see the bridge from my window.)

This feels a little too real. I tell him I have a boyfriend and say, "my boyfriend n i are planning 2 b 2gether 4 ever," and after I log off I begin to wonder if "Brian" isn't actually some 11-year-old boy living two floors above me. This kind of access is new to me. Are teen-agers all over the globe meeting up with their on-line pals in real life—at concerts, in the second-class compartments of European trains? Are they surfing the waves together off Waikiki? I never hear from Brian again.

August 1999

The measure of a successful site, an Internet entrepreneur tells me, is its "stickiness." This is the number of hits a site receives, people checking it out, multiplied by the amount of time they spend on it. Bolt.com is sticky, a cyber-friend says, definitely a place where a lot of teen-agers go to hang and mostly talk about stuff teen-agers talk about—romance being No. 1. I log on to the friendly blue-and-orange home page, with features and bulletins, a quote of the day and a daily poll: "Would you date someone of different ethnicity?" "Would you date someone your parents don't approve of?" "Where would you say you get your style from?" Unlike so many dismally designed sites for teen-agers. Bolt seems like a breezy, busy, cool community. I choose "camarules" as my screen name, ditching my letter-digit combo. Dan Pelson, cofounder of the site, is right—if being on AOL is like driving your father's Oldsmobile on the Interstate, being on Bolt.com is like riding a Day-Glo mountain bike with a beefy shock absorber and no particular place to go.

Though there are plenty of other places for teen-agers to hang out on line, I spend most of my time on Bolt's bulletin boards. There are many to choose from, with topics ranging from Activism and Jobs and Money to Style and Sex and Dating. This is where you can post a message that either attracts a response or goes completely unheeded. The success of a message depends on a lot of factors: the catchiness of the subject line, the popularity of the board and, most important, the general level of boredom of those on line. If people are bored, they'll check out just about anything.

And judging from my time on line, people are bored. "I'm so bored," writes a 16-year-old guy who refers to himself as Baron Vampire. Unlike a lot of the Boltsters, but like a lot of teen-agers, Baron Vampire doesn't really follow the topic being discussed on the board; instead, he turns the conversation back to himself. And he seems to attract attention—maybe because he's a bored vampire, maybe because the icon he uses with his screen name is a tiny bat, hanging upside down, blinking. I feel a maternal tug to respond, but I hold back, letting some of the girls on the board jump in to console him—it would be like getting in the way of a tribal dance.

Before long a group of female Boltsters have virtually surrounded the wounded vampire. "Why are you bored V?" they ask, firing him note after note. Doubtless some are even using a private note system that only he can see. He responds with an emoticon —:*(— that evokes both childhood pathos and "Rebel Without a Cause." "Crying on the net strange," one girl writes without punctuation. After several messages of concern, the vampire seems to perk up. "So how is everyone else?" he writes. "I don't want to hear if you're bored." I skate away.

A girl who calls herself Cool_P2 is giving a party in an area marked Miscellaneous. It's got the feel of a younger girls' party—too much soda, no boys. I look up the personal profile Cool_P2 filled out for Bolt: it includes things like date of birth, favorite movies, music. She has written that she's 11. Unlike many adult boards on the Net where everyone claims to be a teen-ager (even when no one is), the registered members of Bolt, now approaching 1.5 million worldwide, are mostly actual teen-agers. Even if Cool_P2 is lying about her (or his) age, I think a party's a great idea. Imagine letting your kids go to a party and not having to worry what time they come home. Cool_P2 kicks off using the asterisks code, which means that anything written between asterisks is considered action as opposed to dialogue. It's like a scene from a screenplay or a little theater piece, written, starring and directed by teen-agers, each line added onto by someone else.

9:05:51   *puts on music and shakes her thang*
9:07:02   Oh, so we're going to try this party thing again? Good luck!
9:07:03   Oh god . . . *shakes her head and walks away*
9:07:14   *busts a move*
9:07:52   Yumphf humphf! You people are weiiiiiiird!

It gets later. I go to the Sex Questions board. A 15-year-old girl wants to know if cybering with a guy she met on line is cheating on her boyfriend. There's a frenzy of response. One guy writes, "You're so stupid!!" I consider writing something about lust in the heart, but decide to let them work it out on their own and scroll to the next posting. A real problem is being discussed. A 14-year-old girl writes: "My bf doesn't like taking off his hat when we make out. I like to rub my fingers threw [sic] his hair but I can't with his hat!!?? How do I get it off??? Help." A 15-year-old girl from Australia replies, "I bet he has some nasty, nasty hat hair." A guy of the same age writes that she should start playing the national anthem so he'll be forced to take it off. "I know that wasn't funny," he writes. "I'm bored." A younger girl writes that she should just tell him that "it's hard for u 2 make out when he's got his hat on." A 16-year-old girl calling herself Lollypop writes, "Let him kiss your ears if he lets you fondle his hair." That seems fair.

A few days later, I meet Stifbizkit. His screen name's a rip of Limp Bizkit, a popular hip-hop rock band out of Florida. Stif says he is 16 and posts a message on the Girl Trouble board; "popping the question" is his subject. He wants to know the sweetest way to do it: should he play a song, give her a letter or play a song and give her a letter. He writes that he is open to suggestions. I write asking him exactly what question he wants to pop. He jets me a note saying he wants to ask her to go out with him. We have several back-and-forths over the next couple of days. I'm happy to give him "girl" advice, and he is happy to report that in the interim he has spent a non-cyber evening with her and another couple. The girl from the other couple has told him that the girl he's after likes him. "She thinks I'm really hot," he writes, but also reports that despite a long night spent on top of a mountain, in his parent's hot tub and on a beach, all they did was talk. I tell him that sounds like cool progress and to keep it up.

No sooner have we finished than the board becomes transfixed with the plight of Fourtraxman, a 14-year-old whose girlfriend, he says, broke up with him two hours ago and has already got back together with her ex. He says "she's one of those girls that's hard to get over." In the short time since the breakup, Fourtraxman has solicited a lot of advice. I watch as guys and girls from all over the world weigh in with remedies, consolation and just pure commiseration.

The on-line immediacy is astounding. This is not something that has to wait until first period Monday morning. Gold_Angel, an 18-year-old girl, writes that what that girl's done to him is just plain mean. "To ditch your current man for an ex is just wrong!" she writes, adding, "write me if you need to talk more!"

Where was this when I was their age? Where was this when Wade turned me down for the junior prom? In my teenage world, to get that rapid-fire attention would have taken several phone calls and lots of jockeying for phone time with my sisters, and maybe because of it my predicament would have gone undiscussed, at least through an entire evening. It's difficult to know just what has changed for teen-agers today. Much of it is a general overexposure to the adult world, but the new teen-age cyberself is demanding to be acknowledged and won't go away. The new teen-ager says: Here's what I'm thinking about. Here's what's happening to me right now. What am I going to do?

Maybe this isn't all that new. After all, speaking from my own increasingly distant experience, teen-agers have never been free from self-absorption. What is different is that, like everything in this cyberworld, kids are moving through their teen-age years at a lightning pace. The songs of teen-age life remain the same, but they're being remixed, played at a faster speed and at a much higher volume.

Once on line, you can get the definitive word on the date you left an hour ago, a review of a concert that just ended, advice on the right sling-pack to carry, a report on the latest come-on line. But you also get something else, something no other generation has ever had: the ability to leave your teen-age body behind and take advantage of the almost limitless freedom to explore your personal identity. Today's teen-agers can discover themselves (or the many parts of themselves) by roaming the boards and the chat rooms, connecting, disconnecting, shooting questions out into the universe—and maybe, just maybe, receiving answers.

REFLECTING ON THE READING

1. What does Sweeney say is her purpose for going online and posing as a teenager in Internet chat rooms? What justification does she offer for doing so? Do you think presenting herself as a teenager was acceptable? Explain.

2. What, according to Sweeney, is the appeal of having an online identity, of what Sweeney calls a "cyberself"? In what sense does Sweeney believe such a self is "the Internet's greatest asset to Teendom"? Do you agree with her? Why or why not?

3. What kinds of experiences does Sweeney have in Internet chat rooms? What do these experiences in chat rooms indicate to her about the concerns of the teenagers who visit them? What do her experiences suggest about the appeal of the Internet to teens? Cite specific passages from her article to support your answer.

4. What differences does Sweeney encounter among the various teen Internet sites and chat rooms that she visits? Do these differences have any significance, in Sweeney's view? Explain.

5. In what ways does Sweeney encounter what she calls the "immediacy" of the online experience? What examples of this feature of chat rooms does she provide? Why is this such an important feature of the Internet experience for teens, according to Sweeney? Do you think she's right? Why or why not?

6. What conclusions does Sweeney reach regarding the Internet and teen life? Does she leave her readers with a positive sense of today's teenagers and their online lives? Do you agree with her conclusions? Why or why not?

Examining Rhetorical Strategies

1. Sweeney tells us that one of her interests in the Internet is the way it enables teens to create identities online, and she describes how she creates various teen identities when she visits Internet chat rooms. What sort of "writerly" identity does she create in this article? Or, to put it another way, how would you describe her voice in this article? How does this voice relate to the online teen identities that she creates when she goes online? Do you find her voice in this article effective? Explain.

2. Some critics worry about the ethical issues surrounding the creation of online identities that are not "real" or "true." For example, such critics might charge that Sweeney's online teen identities amount to lies because she hides her "real" adult identity when she visits online chat rooms. In this sense, they would argue, her use of these "false" teen identities is unethical. Does Sweeney herself address this problem? If so, in what ways? Cite specific passages in which you think she addresses the ethical issues associated with her online research. Why might Sweeney avoid or ignore these ethical problems? Do you think that her use of the online teen identities she creates is unethical? Why or why not? What might your answer to that question suggest about your own ethical principles?

3. In this article, Sweeney shares several anecdotes of the experiences she has when she visits online chat rooms. Examine her use of anecdote in this article. How does she characterize the experiences she had in chat rooms? Does she present them in a way that you find positive, critical, objective? Explain, citing specific passages from the text to support your answer. What do you think she hopes to illustrate or argue through the use of these anecdotes? Do you think she succeeds? Why or why not?

4. Assess Sweeney's characterization of teenagers in this article. Do you think she presents teens in a way that is sympathetic, critical, objective? Do you think she *intends* to present teens in this way? Why or why not? Do you think her characterization of teens is fair or accurate? Explain, citing specific passages from the text in your answer.

5. This article was initially published in the *New York Times Magazine,* a respected and widely circulated publication. Based on your reading of this article, what assumptions do you think Sweeney makes about her readers in terms of their age and their attitudes regarding technology and adolescence? Do you think you are the kind of reader Sweeney imagined for this article? Why or why not? Cite specific passages from the article to illustrate your answer.

Engaging the Issues

1. Visit an online chat room (or several) of a kind that interests you. Spend a week or two visiting the chat room and participating in conversations there. Then write a first-person account of your experiences for an audience of your class-mates. In your account, describe your experiences, try to explain them, and draw conclusions about what those experiences might indicate about literacy, technology, and identity.

2. Rewrite the essay you wrote for Question #1 for a different audience—for example, for readers of your local newspaper. Then compare the two essays. In what ways do your essays differ? How did your sense of your audience influence your revisions?

3. Interview several teenagers about their experiences in Internet chat rooms. Ask them about the kinds of chat rooms they visit, how often they chat online, and why they do so. Try to identify patterns in their responses. Are there any similarities or differences in those responses? Then write a report for an audience of your classmates about your interviews. In your report, explain whom you interviewed and what you asked them, and then discuss what you learned from the interviews. Try to draw conclusions about how and why teens visit online chat rooms.

4. On the basis of the research you conducted for Question #3 above, write a response to Sweeney in which you express support for her perspective on teen use of Internet chat rooms or in which you disagree with her characterization of teen use of the Internet.

   Alternatively, write a letter to the editor of the *New York Times* in which you express your agreement or disagreement with Sweeney's article. In your letter, be sure to provide support for your position.

5. In a conventional academic essay, discuss the relationship between the issue of literacy and technology and the issue of identity formation in teenagers. In your essay, draw on Sweeney and any other appropriate sources as well as on your own experiences in analyzing and explaining this relationship.

6. Create a Web site devoted to issues relating to teen use of the Internet. Before designing your site, decide on its purpose and focus. For example, you might intend your site as a guide for teens who wish to visit Internet chat sites. Or you might wish to create a site devoted to critical reviews of chat rooms. Design your site accordingly, so that it effectively fulfills your intent. Be sure your purpose is clear to potential visitors, and include any links to other sites that you think would be appropriate.

7. Visit several popular sites on the Internet devoted to teens. Examine these sites not only for what they contain but also for how they present themselves to teens and what they seem to have as their purpose. Then write a review of teen Internet sites for a local newspaper.

8. Rewrite the review you wrote for Question #7 above for a teen magazine (such as *Teen*).

Technology's Strange, Familiar Voices

JANET CAREY ELDRED

INTRODUCTION   *Voice* is a term that writers and teachers sometimes use to describe a particular—and hard-to-define—quality of a piece of writing. A piece of writing is said to have a distinctive voice if it "sounds" a certain way, exhibits a particular kind of tone, or conveys a certain kind of "feel." Similarly, a writer is said to have a strong or distinctive voice if his or her writing exhibits those same qualities. Despite the difficulty of precisely defining *voice*, most of us claim to "hear" it in a piece of writing. And most of us tend to assume that it has something to do with the kind of writing a writer is doing and with the way a writer chooses his or her words, constructs sentences, and addresses an audience. Janet Carey Eldred suggests that there's something else that helps determine a writer's voice: the technology he or she uses for writing. In this age of Internet communication, Eldred asserts that a writer's voice might emerge differently in one medium—email, for example—than in another.

In the following essay, Eldred suggests that the voice in one's writing is intimately related to who that person is—to that person's identity and state of mind. For Eldred, writing can be a powerful means of personal expression: it can be a way both to understand and to express one's identity. But it can also be complex and painful. In describing her own writing experiences in her relationship with her mother, Eldred explores the ways in which writing became a central vehicle by which she and her mother were able to relate to one another as mother and daughter; paradoxically, writing was also, at times, an obstacle in their relationship. Both their identities were somehow wrapped up in the writing they did for themselves and for each other, and in telling her story, Eldred encourages us to examine the complicated and sometimes problematic role that writing can play in our identities and in the relationships we develop with others. Eldred also explores the role that technology can play in influencing one's ability to use writing as personal expression. For Eldred's mother, various technologies—including computers—became the means by which she could overcome some of the debilitating limitations of her illness to write and communicate with others. In this sense, technology became the only means by which her voice could be heard. Eldred's experience might prompt us to consider the complex ways in which technology and writing might influence and shape our personal relationships—and our identities—at a time when new technologies provide new capabilities and possibilities for written communication that never before existed.

Janet Carey Eldred is associate professor of English at the University of Kentucky. Her writing, which focuses on technology and literacy, has been published in a number of professional journals. She serves on the editorial board of *Computers and Composition,* a professional journal devoted to the study of computer technology in the teaching of writing. The following essay was published in *Passions, Pedagogies, and 21st Century Technologies,* a collection of essays for writing teachers and scholars interested in the use of technology in teaching and writing. A slightly different version originally appeared in 1997 in *College Composition and Communication,* a professional journal about writing and writing instruction for college-level teachers and scholars.

REFLECTING BEFORE READING

1. As you prepare to read Eldred's essay, think about your understanding of *voice* in writing. What does it refer to? How have your teachers used the term to describe a quality of writing? How have you heard others use that term in reference to writing? What do *you* mean by the term?
2. Eldred's essay is focused on deeply personal issues in her life in which writing figured prominently. As you read, consider the role that writing played in Eldred's relationship with her mother. Have you had experiences in which writing played a role in an important relationship in your life? Do you think the experiences Eldred describes are unique or unusual in any way?

> Although they have no words or language,
> and their voices are not heard
>
> Their sound has gone out into all lands
> and their message
> to the ends of the world

These days I check my email with some anticipation: I'm waiting, not for the news from an academic colleague, not for the latest conference notice, not for an announcement of a new online archive, not even for the news from the wheaten terrier fanciers. I'm waiting instead, for the "senior special"; words from either my mother or my uncle, ages 66 and 71 respectively, and both wired.

My uncle's voice online is strange—he doesn't use paragraphs for one thing, and so all his thoughts flow into one long list. But he sounds particularly strange because I've never before seen his written voice. His wife is a prolific and disciplined letter writer and has long served as the family correspondent. My uncle has always been the handwritten brief postscript at the end of a letter or the voice on the other phone, the one somewhere in the basement that never seems to come in quite clearly. "She can't hear you," my aunt calls out. "Move away from the television, turn off your modem, hang up the other phone," all in that search to find some elusive, magical technological act that turns a faint sound into an AT&T's true voice. I'm beginning to understand that in any discussion of voice, we necessarily hear technology's inflections.

Even when she's on the wrong channel of her cordless phone, I recognize my mother's voice. I'm more familiar with it in all its incarnations because we've had a long history of spoken and written correspondence. When I was in fourth grade, I wrote a completely unmemorable story that impressed a heroin addict who was brought to our parochial school to give one of those "Don't end up like me" testimonials. When the woman asked me to send more of my stories to keep her entertained during the rest of her jail term, I was a writer born. With audience found and purpose worthy, I penned a story, "The Purple Poodle," which my mother stubbornly refused to send. Censored, and indignantly so, I stopped writing. I had no way of seeing what I do now: that it wasn't the story-writing my mother objected to, nor the failure of this particular story (although a story about a purple poodle could hardly have been riveting reading for inmates). It was simply that as a mother, she didn't want me deeply involved in the life of a deeply troubled woman. And, more importantly, she herself wanted to and was to become my audience.

At age 13, I started writing again, this time long, impassioned letters to my mother, mostly trying to persuade her to persuade my father to let me date an 18-year old young man who, I was convinced, was the only one who could possibly understand someone as mature and sensitive and deep as I was. My mother was never persuaded, so I eventually dropped the letter-writing campaign, but not before we had discussed many an issue dear to my teenage heart. It was for both of us a reminder of a childhood lesson: we heard each other when we wrote.

But not when we spoke. It was the early 1970s and the time of the infamous P.E.T. voice. From what I could tell, Parent Effectiveness Training relied on one phrase—"Let's talk about it"—offered up in every circumstance, no matter how varied the occasion, emotion, or motive. I was caught smoking in the bathroom. "Let's talk about it," my mother said. I was caught sneaking out to meet my somewhat older boyfriend. "Let's talk about it," my newly effective parent suggested.

"Let's not," I said, shooting her a look, an exact copy of her angry or impatient one: left brow cocked like a loaded bow, right one arrow straight. Two people in the world can create such a look, and I—through the wonders of genetics—am one of them.

P.E.T., as its cute name suggested, was indeed pet training, and I resented it, more so because it was bad pet training. Even dogs can choose to disobey and are punished for the choice. No trainer makes them bark or whine or otherwise repeatedly give voice to the error. Still, P.E.T. was an even further cruelty because it fed on my mother's natural affection for talk and her faith in the power of language. It transformed her into a psycho-voiced horror.

Thankfully, my mother is a woman of many words with a range of emotions and a slow-boiling temper. P.E.T., though she never admitted it, tired her as well. She needed to use words badly—a wide range of them. So, somewhat newly-widowed and about to be empty-nested, she enrolled in composition, literature, and fiction writing courses at the local community college and wrote intensely for a space of three or four years, the same time that I was finishing an undergraduate degree in English. During these years, my mother was as generous with her prose as I was with my juvenilia and teenage outpourings, while I, with my new college writing, was stingy and safe. She gave me drafts of her literary analysis of D.H. Lawrence's *Women in Love*, a piece in which she tried to come to terms with something completely foreign and frightening to her. The final version contained this instructor comment, "Good revisions, Chris. No philosophizing in this version!" I recognized the academic "don't get too close" rule. It was something I proved my mastery and love of when I gave her, in return for her disturbing, disturbed feeling drafts, a carefully constructed analysis of the same novel.

Undaunted, she gave me letters she wrote to my father—angry, unromantic letters to a partner who had in death deserted her. In return, I shared a class assignment analyzing the nineteenth-century narrative poem, "The Haystack in the Floods"—and, as I headed off to graduate school, my cat named after Morris's heroine.

Finally, my mother showed me part of her in-progress autobiography:

> All of my childhood and young adult years, I lived in a New England city of 100,000 people. The homes were old, close together, close to the street and drab. Unlike my other relatives who lived in the Portuguese ghetto, we lived in a fairly nice area of town. Still, it was cramped and old and colorless—even to the black automobile my father drove—"the only way to drive." Our home was furnished with mahogany furniture, which had to be polished, always. There were starched white curtains at the windows. Any piece of silver or brass that was around had to be polished to gleaming. Beds were always made-tight and straight, hospital-cornered.
>
> I wanted to live in a small town, with front lawns. I wanted a house not so scrubbed and shined that there was no time for living.

I did not give her one of my struggling attempts at autobiographical poetry (nor indeed, anything else with which I struggled):

FIRST COMMUNION

The first grade choir sang as we, their superiors, processed
white shoes
white lace
white veils
white prayer books with Corpus Christi embossed in gold.

But once seated, they disappeared
And it was just me
in white, sitting near the altar,
looking up at the gold stars on the blue-sky dome,
hearing not the priest
but a choir of angels chanting the processional hymn.

At home in the living room
family voices conflicted and rose in Jesuit mock debate
brought out on special occasions with the silver.

I left the living room to find my mother who had pinned and repinned lace,
caressed my hair into shape
in rooms without brothers and sisters.

I found her in the kitchen washing dishes.
"I'll never forget this," I whispered passionately.
But she had transformed, forgotten.

And I thought it was the dirty dishes, her aloneness in the kitchen.
I thought she must have heard and felt it just as I had.
But now I know

She heard the discordant voices of a first grade choir.
I wore white and heard angels.

This passion-play poem I kept hidden (and keep hidden still). Instead, I mailed her a *published* paper, which had a chilling effect on our writing swaps.

Or perhaps I'm reading too much in and it was simply life. My mother stopped writing and started living again: the new town became familiar, the new job creative but demanding, her new friends rooted. "Write," I would urge her. But it was difficult for her to find the time—or the pain; she knew no other way to write. And while the P.E.T. voice never returned, an older voice did return with more intensity: her church voice.

As a small girl, I remember the passion of my mother's Catholicism. Having survived Vatican II, she now was a passionate new Catholic, singing loudly to the wheat-and-honey guitar hymns, participating in the new liturgy

First Communion

and life of the church. She even worked there. And thus it happened that when I returned home from graduate school for visits, I found congregation members who knew intimately my life details. "This is my daughter who lives in Illinois," she'd say. And then I'd stiffen, waiting for their very physical embrace and the usual refrain, "I feel as if I know you." Still more annoying, I sensed that they never knew the intimate details of her life. I was the post-Vatican II sacrificial lamb, and I knew where she learned the ritual: those writing classes at the community college with the Ken Macrorie textbook. As a Master Catechist (lay people now held impressive titles with their low salaries), she had brought writing to her church work.

What was worse, she too now had a professional voice, and it was mimicking the one I was apprenticing. "I always begin my catechist training sessions with journaling," she told me proudly on one of my visits home.

"You do what?" I say in a tone that should make her rethink this accomplishment. It does not.

"I have them journal," she repeats, pride still there.

"Journal," I say in my best old-fashioned English teacher voice, "is *not* a verb."

But for her it was. As I realized on my last visit home, she had been journaling since the time she was empty-nested in 1980 until just this year, filling on a fairly regular basis a decorative, hardback notebook a year, working at the discipline of it.

September 1980: Read my journal. Too many words. Like weeds in a garden. Choking-hindering-covering up the beauty. Is this what I do with my life too?

May 1985: Mea culpa, mea culpa! So long, so long—two weeks—since I took pen in hand, wrote in my journal.

April 1995: I am reminded of the importance of telling your story—how we tell it over again and again until it is right.

After I earned my degrees and began my probationary period for tenure, I longed for the exchange of our written voices. But she wasn't writing (or so I thought) and I was writing pieces I no longer reproduced for her. Secretly, I rewrote the ending for a short story she had sent to me some years back. She was dissatisfied with the conclusion, and I thought I might fix it and repair our writing relationship. But I realized almost immediately that editing and writing aren't the same. (It didn't help that the ending I wrote was also bad.) Instead, I asked her to begin a memoir for me, assigned it, so to speak. For a few years she was stymied. Then one day, while cleaning closets, she found some old photographs and began writing about them prolifically, with ease. When I returned for my biannual trips to California, she'd read sections aloud to me as I looked at photographs and listened. It was the relationship we had been practicing for.

Then I married and she remarried and our memoir project halted. For the past eight years, we haven't really shared writing at all. Instead, we've talked by phone about once a week. Superficial stuff, neighbor voice mostly, nothing like those moments when we were each other's private audience. Still, sometimes we spoke seriously—about my marriage, about her marriage, about pregnancies and miscarriages, about adoptions, about health, about distance.

And then her voice began to break, slowly at first. A word slurred here or there. A year later, the slurring grew more pronounced. Entire phrases tripped her up. In mid-sentence, she changed directions so she wouldn't enter the unspeakable. We tried to pretend like her words were all there. But they weren't, and they were leaving quickly. While she could somewhat mask the slurs in person, the phone lines were unforgiving.

Wedding

Soon, the game was up anyway as the slurring was followed by coughing and then choking. "Allergies," she would say. But by now, we all knew it was more than pollen. *Testing 1-2-3. Modern medicine, can you hear me?*

After the diagnosis (A.L.S.), there was one entire month of silence in which I heard about my mother only through my brother's or uncle's online postings. The phone, which feeds on true clear voices, became obsolete. Enter new technology: my mother was persuaded to go online. Through email I can now hear her written voice again. Sometimes, she writes in a casual phone way, neighbor-speak: so-and-so called, your sister did this, we drove here. But other times I hear the voice of the letters to my father and her photo-memoir. Back we are, I think, to the old times. But these aren't the old times.

It's not pen and paper, it's keyboard and modem. And of course, there's the crucial distinction: I'm grown now, a mother myself, and she's dying. Which is why, I'm sure, my mother still prefers, indeed insists on, old technology.

And there is no technology like a visit, which the distance between Kentucky and California frustrates, but an airplane or two and some rental cars make possible. This summer, I see her for the first time since speech left her. Although she has a hand-held Crespeaker, she takes it out mainly for show and for the grandchildren to play with. She does a little demo for me and my son: we hear a male voice, with mechanical inflection. It mispronounces the names of family members unless she misspells them. Instead of the "ee" sound in "Kira," it gives voice to a long "i." Instead of the "oo" sound in "Kuka" (my son's Americanized shorthand for "babushka"), it sounds out the first "u" in "cucumber." The technological voice provided by the Crespeaker is strange and slow—she must pick out each letter one by one with a stick. I look at her thumbs, A.L.S.-crooked now, and realize that typing and writing will soon end. The Crespeaker will provide her future voice, however foreign.

But for now, through a combination of pantomime and writing, my mother converses, electing out of some talk, initiating some, and inserting herself into some. I'm surprised at how easy it is to enter the rhythm:

"What's this wet spot on the floor?" I ask as my bare feet find a cold spot on the carpet. My mother is staying at my sister's: one child (mine), one toddler, one dog, one cat—the wet spot could be anything.

My mother fills her cheeks, and as she does, moves her top hand in an arch over her bottom one, which rests in her lap.

"Ah, the giant bubble-making machine," I nod instantly, smiling because the wet spot is really only soap and glycerin, but most of all, because we're in sync.

My son and I come to the visit, of course, bearing gifts. We buy her a Discman and some compact discs. I choose something light and whimsical—MGM musical hits. She listens to the first track, moves her head as if dancing, and then begins crying, all the time still dancing with her upper body. She tries to move to the next track but, thankfully, does not yet know where the right buttons are and hits the stop. We take the chance to give her the music my four-year old son has chosen: the soundtrack from one of his favorite movies. *The Secret of Roan Inish,* a film about a lost child, and about a seal, who transforms herself into a woman, a wife, a mother, but all the time longs to be free of her body. Eventually, she is freed as she gives into her longing, shedding her human skin and slipping back to the sea. After my plot summary, my mother listens to the music intently, thoughtfully. Her hands form a "'T'"

"That means thank you," my sisters tell us. Mom nods affirmatively.

"Make a "T" for grandma," I instruct my son.

"No," he says with the confidence I lack, "I say, 'You're welcome.'"

He has no trouble remembering that she can hear, no inclination to pass over her in a conversation. He does not speak about her in the third person. His two-year old cousin cries when grandma claps, points a finger, and shakes her head; she hates to be scolded.

As my mother eats her lunch, she puts on the *Roan Inish* music to drown out the noise and distractions. And though I don't hear the music, I see distinctly two images: the woman from the film, looking out to sea, longing to shed her human skin, and my mother, concentrating on bringing the blended food from bowl to lips, collecting the extra with napkins, clearing with faint noises the minute grains which, despite their pureed smoothness, deposit in the folds of her throat.

"Look at my shirt," she writes in her notebook when she's finished. She hands the message to my sisters who keep close and quiet watch during meals. "I think I need a bib."

But she doesn't need a bib; she just needs my sisters to share the joke, which they do with both light and heavy hearts.

During this visit, because I am thinking a lot about my mother's writing, I also bring along as a gift a May Sarton journal with an inscription: "From one journal writer to another." She finishes reading most of it while I'm there. Several months earlier when my mother could still speak, she told me she had begun a journal about her illness, thought then to be a stroke. It was to be her recovery journal. I'm not sure if she continued the journal when progress clearly became regress. I haven't read—or been shown—a single entry. Still, she is not going unrecorded. Quite the contrary. When pantomime fails, my mother grabs for her pen and notebook. It sits, like her walker and the notebook personal computer, within arm's reach. In it, she lends us her voices: practical ("Where's the TV control?"), trivial ("That dog's a pain"), thoughtful ("Here I am sitting a death sentence and your cousin is dead at 43. It makes no sense. At least I am not in pain. I live in fear of choking or suffocating, but I am not in pain"). At the end of each day, she has a record of everything she has said. At least theoretically.

"Do you need me to refresh your notebook," my sister asks, tearing out the notebook pages and wadding them for the trash.

All those words, I think, But, of course, my sister is right. No one has their every word recorded. It is only right that the everyday be weeded. And then, of course, there's the issue of privacy, which in my family, is not only a virtue, but a miracle. I know that I myself read several entries back on the page. Anything within view without flipping a notebook page is fair game. And if she naps, even a page flip or two is within limits. When my sisters enter the room, they check the notebook to catch up on anything they've missed. It saves having to recap.

"Oh, I see she didn't like lunch," one sister says to the other. "Next time I'll blend it with yogurt instead of cottage cheese." My mother nods her assent vigorously. Sometimes, my mother herself goes back a few pages and underscores or draws an arrow to save the effort of rewriting.

After lunch, my mother and son rest, she in my sister's guest bedroom, he in my mother's old room. I go with my son, ostensibly to rest, but instead of closing my eyes, I open them, wider than ever before. I do what I love best—archival research— scanning her bookshelf for clues, for words I might before have missed. And I find them—an assortment of her journals. I see her first journal, begun the year my brother, the last of her children, left home. She was preparing to move to a new city and take a new job, which she did, dutifully recording the change—the 1980 journal she devoted to looking back over her life; the 1981 journal she reserved for life unfolding. Then there are three missing years—years in which I know she wrote, the years we exchanged writing. I peruse the journals out of chronological order, as they appear on the shelf. I notice especially the references to me:

A nice end to a 12-hour day. I talked with Janet and she passed her M.A. competencies. But the joy was not limited to that alone. Someone asked her, "What are you going to do now?" and without thinking she said, "Call my mother!" After the blank stare, she realized that that wasn't what the speaker meant—they meant long term. But who cares? To still be #1 in her mind—to want to share her joy with me.

YIPPEE!! JANET IS COMING HOME!!

It's hard to not see your child for over a year—to touch her—to embrace her. The others can't take her place. Each is important—each loved but I can't love her by loving another.—The woman with the lost coin. The shepherd who loses one sheep. My God—the prodigal son.

Graduation

This entry, I discover after placing them all in order, is from a period during which she centers her journals on her spiritual struggles. My mother, never one to miss a cultural movement, is heavy into meditation and for over a year records her efforts.

Meditating went well. I entered quickly and stayed with it. After some sensory exercises, I moved into painful memories to make sure that I wouldn't run or evade this important part of my meditation journey. I went to Bud's death and memories of the few days preceding. In retrospect, I realized he was dying then and going through the process and I didn't recognize it. He was abnormally upset because there wasn't enough taco sauce for Charles's birthday dinner, he was upset because Janet had Paul over and he wanted him to leave, for the first time ever in our married life we couldn't make love. I stayed with the pain—went through the guilt, felt the loss and asked for help.

In 1985, she began recording and analyzing the spiritual significance of her dreams, a practice she continued for a full year. A few of the entries catch me:

4/2/86

I awoke (in my dream) to see myself in a mirror. I was amazed that as I slept, my hair grew. I was brushing my hair. The sun shone through it from behind. It was the color of gold. Somebody was watching me and we talked about my hair and how it shone in the sunlight.

Hair. My mother loves to have her hair brushed. It remains a pleasure untouched by A.L.S., one outside the disease's far reach. During my visit, I brush her hair frequently, following the strokes with my hands. Her hair is still thick. It still shines in the sunlight of her recorded dreams.

In her journals, I find her pleasures again and again, but it is the 1984 record of spiritual struggles that surprises me most. My mother has always struck me as someone who had faith, though now, A.L.S. has greatly shaken it. It is difficult to chant *lauds* and *vespers* with no voice, difficult to commune when host can't be swallowed, difficult to sway with a folk guitar when legs buckle beneath body, difficult to mingle with people when A.L.S. tears refuse to recognize restraint, difficult to find peace when A.L.S. ushers in anxiety. With no voice heard crying in the wilderness, the church congregation which enjoyed her labor, her words, for 15 years, has allowed her to lapse into silence. Instead of home visits, they dedicate a service to her. It is one of life's little ironies that her hairdresser continues to minister freely to her failing body with regular manicures, pedicures, salon cuts, daily massages; meanwhile, her spirit is left sparsely, sporadically attended.

So faith is collapsing, understandably. But the journals showed that she had struggled all along. I consider slipping the two volumes in my suitcase. No one besides me, I think, is interested in her as a writer. And then I look to the front of the 1984 journal—a year that might have been the one in which our exchanges ended, certainly one before our memoir project began. The 1984 journal is inscribed to my sister, Gerianne, who along with my oldest sister, daily feeds her, administers her medications, arranges her medical visits, sponge bathes her, moves her: "Dedicated to Gerianne in thanks for the gift of this book—and the gift of herself." I put the book back on the shelf. There is so much I don't do and don't know. I can barely pronounce the names of the medications my sisters refer to with ease. I pack my suitcases, leaving all the journals in place. Instead, I take what I am certain my siblings don't want: a 10-volume set of short stories (at my mother's urging), and her underscored copies of Macrorie's *Telling Writing,* and Lyons's *Autobiography.* As an afterthought, I take her tattered *Morning Praise and Evensong.* One evening, home in Kentucky, I open the book, and two holy cards fall out, carrying with them the old order, the old sounds. I recite and chant vespers for her, singing the praises for August 15th, the (now unfashionable) feast of The Assumption.

V: Let my prayer come before You like incense.
R: The lifting up of my hands like an evening sacrifice.
1ANT: Like a cedar of Lebanon I am ráised aloft, / like a rosebush in Jericho.
2ANT: Fairer is she thán the sun / surpassing every starry cónstellation.
3ANT: The king's daughter enters all glórious / her róbes of spun gold.
READING: I grew to my full stature as cedar grows on Lebanon, as cypress on Sion's hill; or a palm tree in Cades, or a rose bush in Jericho; grew like some fair olive in the valley, some plane-tree in a well-watered street. Cinnamon and odorous balm have no scent like mine; the choicest myrrh has no such fragrance. Perfumed is all my dwelling-place with storax, and galbamum, and onycha, and stacte, and frankincense uncrushed; the smell of me like pure balm.
ANT. ZACH: Who is this that comes forth like the dawn, beautiful as the moon, as resplendent as she sun, / as awe-inspiring as bannered troops.

As promised, my words, the very words I remember her chanting when I was a child, rise like incense, assumed, body and soul, syllables carrying meaning, intention.

I couldn't have imagined chanting *lauds* and *vespers* as I packed away *Morning Praise and Evensong* on the last day of my summer visit. Instead I was thinking about her journals, about how I am not the prodigal son, but a married daughter, a college professor with classes about to begin, about how this is not a return, but a visit. And about how visits must end.

"I'll email you," I say upon leaving.

My mother nods affirmatively and moves her hand as if typing on a keyboard. And then she makes the other gesture, hand grasping imaginary phone to ear. She wants me to remember to call, as agreed on, once a week. It is the old technology she prefers, and the old gesture she uses. But it is a new form we must rely on.

Illness

"California Relay Operator #335, Please hold one second while I connect you to your party."

And then I hear a sound, a keyboard clicking. I picture her on the other end with a headset, typing intently. I wait until the sound stops. A stranger's voice, sometimes female, sometimes male, says "It's mom. Go ahead."

"Hi mom," I say, trying not to sound as if I'm talking in the presence of a third party, "How are you feeling? How was your visit at the specialist's? Go ahead." But we are speaking in the presence of a third person and all the family rules apply: no incriminating information, no emotion, just flat speech, facts, med-speak. Above all else, no tears, not in the presence of a third person—not when tears trigger choking.

My mother responds, but in the stranger's voice again: "I'm O.K. The home nurse will bring a respirator. They want to tubefeed me. Go ahead."

And so we continue, she through the strange operator, me estranged. "Go ahead," I say. "Go ahead," the mother/operator says. A treadmill of words, hard to get off.

"Well, I'm going to go now." A pause, "And your party has hung up. Thank you for using California Relay."

"Thank you," I say to the operator, and somewhat mean it.

I feel relieved. For a week, I know, my mother will be happy communicating with me by email and I will be happy to hear my mother's voice—the old one, the written one. But I know too, that after a week, she will request the T.D.D. phone, "Please call me this week. I want to hear your voice."

And I know that she means it. Because I want the impossible too: I want to hear her sing too loudly in church. I want to hear her neighbor voice. I'd even accept P.E.T. For the first time in my life, I want her to have the last word.

Before she died on December 17, 1996, my mother finished writing her memoirs. She left me her journals; she left me a better writing teacher.

REFLECTING ON THE READING

1. What does Eldred mean by "voice" in this essay? How does she see *voice* as related to technology? Does *voice* have different meanings in this essay? Explain, citing specific passages from the essay in your answer.

2. Early in this essay, Eldred writes that as a professional she resisted "personal writing." What does she mean by "personal writing"? Why did she resist it? Why was it so difficult for her? In what way is it "aesthetic," as she describes it? Do you agree with her? Explain.

3. Why is writing important in Eldred's relationship with her mother? In what ways do they use writing in their relationship? What role does writing play in that relationship? How does the role of writing change during the course of their relationship? What might this example suggest about the role of writing in personal relationships?

4. At one point in her essay, Eldred refers to her mother's use of journals and writes that her mother "now had a professional voice . . . [that] was mimicking the one I was apprenticing." What does Eldred mean by "professional voice" here? In what sense had her mother developed such a voice? And in what sense was she "mimicking" Eldred's own professional voice? Why do you think Eldred seems upset by her mother's use of a term like "journaling"?

5. How does technology provide a way for Eldred's mother to reclaim her voice after her illness sets in? What changes occur as a result of her use of this new technology? What does Eldred learn about technology as a result of these experiences? How do different technologies affect her mother's voice and her own? What might these differences suggest about the role of technology in one's personal life?

6. What purpose do you think Eldred's mother's journals serve—for her mother and for Eldred? What does she learn by reading her mother's journals?

7. Why do you think Eldred wants her mother to "have the last word," as she writes at the end of this essay? What do you think Eldred has learned from her experiences with writing in her relationship with her mother? How do you think those experiences have left Eldred a "better writing teacher," as she writes in the essay's final sentence? What do you think the experiences she describes in this essay suggest about writing? Do you agree with her? Why or why not?

Examining Rhetorical Strategies

1. Examine the way Eldred describes her relationship with her mother in this essay. How would you describe that relationship? How does Eldred convey to her readers the nature of that relationship? What details or comments or descriptions does she provide that help paint a picture of the relationship she has with her mother and how the relationship might have changed over time? Cite specific passages from her essay to illustrate your answer. Do you think Eldred is effective in conveying the nature of her relationship with her mother to her readers? Explain.

2. Assess Eldred's descriptions of her family. What image of her family does she present? In what ways might this family be labeled "typical"? Do you think she wishes to present a sympathetic picture of them? For what purpose? How did you respond to these images? What might your responses to her descriptions of her family indicate about your own attitudes regarding family?

3. Eldred's family seems very middle class. As such, they have access to relatively sophisticated technologies—such as computers and the Crespeaker—that are not universally available. How do you think Eldred's background influences her experiences with and attitudes toward technology? Toward writing? Do you think the ideas she expresses in this essay about voice and technology apply to people from different socioeconomic backgrounds than Eldred's? Explain. Do you think Eldred thinks so? Explain, citing specific passages from her essay to support your answer.

4. How would you characterize Eldred's views about technology in this essay? What does she see as positive about the kinds of technologies she describes? What concerns does she have about those technologies? How might those concerns be related to her own position as a professor who studies technology and writing? Do you agree with her views? Why or why not?

5. Why do you think Eldred includes excerpts from other writing by her and by her mother—for example, her poem and passages from her mother's journal? What purposes do these excerpts serve in her essay? How might they have influenced your impression of Eldred and of her mother? Do you think Eldred hoped to encourage such a reaction in her readers? Explain.

6. Assess Eldred's own voice in this essay. How would you describe it? What textual features (such as her word choice, sentence structure, and so on) help create this voice? Do you think her voice is appropriate for her topic? Explain. Do you think readers of the journal in which her essay was originally published would find it appropriate? Why or why not? Did you find her voice effective? What might your response to that question suggest about your expectations as a reader?

7. This essay was originally published in a professional journal intended for college-level scholars and teachers of writing and then was reprinted in a book intended for a similar audience. Such journals or books do not often publish personal narrative essays such as Eldred's. Although most of the narrative describes Eldred's experiences with her family and with writing, in what ways do you think it would be appropriate for the professional journal in which it was originally published? What features of the essay suggest that it was published in a professional academic journal? What do you think it lacks that you would expect to see in a scholarly article? Do you think the essay is accessible to readers who might not be scholars or teachers of writing? Explain.

8. When this essay was originally published in the journal *College Composition and Communication* in 1997, it included no photographs. However, when the version included in this reader was published in 1999, it included the photographs of Eldred and her mother. Why do you think Eldred included those photographs when her essay was reprinted? What purpose do you think they

serve? Do you think Eldred hoped that the photographs would influence her readers in a particular way? Explain. How did they influence your reading of this essay? Do you think the essay would be less effective without the photographs? Why or why not?

Engaging the Issues

1. Write a personal narrative describing an experience you had in which writing played a significant role in your personal life.

2. Write an essay for an audience of your classmates in which you analyze the role of technology in Eldred's experiences. How did technology figure into her relationship with her mother? How did technology affect her mother's "voice"? What implications did technology have for Eldred and for her mother as her mother became ill? Try to draw conclusions about how technology can figure into one's personal life. Be sure to cite relevant passages from Eldred's article in your essay.

3. In a group of your classmates, try to define *voice* in writing. Discuss how voice might relate to technologies that are used for writing (e.g., email or word processing). When you have finished your discussion, write a brief definition of *voice,* making reference to how technology might relate to voice in writing.

4. Write a personal letter to a relative or friend about some recent event or experience in your life. Then write an email message to the same person about the same event or experience. When you have finished both, compare the two. How do they differ in terms of the writing style and in terms of voice? How are they similar? Write a brief analysis of these similarities and differences.

5. Go onto the World Wide Web and visit several personal Web pages. Describe the "voice" of each page. Then write a brief definition of *voice* as it pertains to Web sites. How might such a definition differ from the definition you wrote for Question #3 above? What might the differences say about the role of technology in shaping the "voice" of a text?

6. Have several classmates read examples of your writing. Then ask them to write a paragraph describing your voice as a writer. What do they say about your voice? Do they agree, or do they seem to "hear" more than one voice? Do their descriptions of your voice match your own sense of your voice as a writer?

7. Write a conventional academic essay in which you compare the voices of Eldred and one or two other writers in this chapter. In your essay, try to describe the voice of each writer, using passages from his or her writing to illustrate your descriptions. Try to explain how each writer creates his or her voice, again citing specific passages from their writing. Then analyze the effects of each writer's voice and try to draw conclusions about *voice* in writing.

8. Deborah Tannen, whose essay "Connections" appears in Chapter 1 of this reader, addresses some of the same issues that Eldred addresses in her essay on *voice.* Write an essay in which you compare the approaches of each of these writers to the issue of the role of technology and writing in one's personal relationships. Describe the approach each writer takes to this issue, and

identify similarities and differences in their approaches. Cite specific passages from their essays to support your analysis. Try to draw conclusions about the effectiveness of each writer in addressing these issues.

FURTHERING YOUR INQUIRY

1. Based on several of the readings in this chapter and drawing on your own experiences as a literate person, write an essay for an audience of your classmates in which you discuss what you believe are the most important implications of new technologies (like the Internet) for the ways in which we use writing and reading in our lives. In your essay, address some of the issues of identity that are discussed in some of the selections in this chapter.

   Alternatively, write this essay for a general audience, such as readers of a large-circulation newspaper like the *New York Times.*

2. Several of the authors in this chapter address issues of identity and technology. Among these authors, Camille Sweeney and Janet Carey Eldred write specifically about our sense of identity and its relationship to technology. Write an essay in which you analyze the views of these two authors regarding this issue of identity and technology. Specifically, compare their views on identity creation online and its potential implications for social interactions among people. What view of technology in general does each of these authors have? How are their views similar or different? What insights does each author present? Do you find one author's stance more compelling than the other's? Address questions such as these in your essay and draw conclusions from your analysis about the implications of cyberspace for our understanding of identity and technology.

   Alternatively, write an imaginary dialogue between Sweeney and Eldred in which they discuss the issue of identity and technology. What might each say? What disagreements might they have? Use your understanding of their essays to construct your dialogue. (You might consider writing the dialogue as an exchange of email messages. If so, how might that differ from a face-to-face dialogue?)

3. Go onto the World Wide Web and visit a number of personal Web sites. Try to locate as many different kinds of sites as you can. Examine how these sites are constructed and the purposes they have. Try to draw conclusions about the identity that the author of the site is constructing for himself or herself on that site. What kinds of statements, images, or links does the author use on the site? What might these say about the author? What information is presented? How does that information help establish an identity for the site's author? Compare the sites you have visited, describing key features of each. Draw conclusions about how identity can be constructed on the World Wide Web, referring to the reading selections in this chapter where appropriate. Write a report for your classmates in which you present the results of your analysis.

   Alternatively, examine professional sites on the World Wide Web and conduct the same kind of analysis described above.

4. Based on the readings in this chapter and on your own experiences, write a letter to the superintendent of your school district (or to the president of your

university or college) proposing changes in the curriculum that would address your own concerns about literacy education and technology. What problems or concerns about literacy and technology emerge for you from the readings in this chapter? Why should we be concerned about these problems? How do they affect the way we teach students to read and write and to use technologies like computers?

5. Write a conventional academic essay defining *identity* and how it is related to literacy and technology. Draw on the readings in this chapter and on any other appropriate sources.

6. Select a common activity involving writing and reading. For example, you might consider activities like taking an essay test in school, writing a college application essay, sending a letter of complaint to a company, applying for a job, taking a written test for a driver's license, or writing a memo at work. Examine that activity carefully, and in a conventional academic essay discuss how a person creates or uses his or her identity through writing or reading in doing that activity. Draw on any readings in this chapter that you think might help in your analysis.

7. Create a personal Web site. Use whatever materials you deem appropriate for your site. When you're finished, write an explanation of your site, discussing what you included and how you made decisions about what to include. Consider such matters as the information you presented, the images or photos you used, the colors you selected, how you designed the page layout, and so on.

   In a group of several classmates or friends, compare your web sites and the explanations each of you wrote for those Web sites. What differences or similarities emerge? How did each of you make decisions about your sites? What questions or concerns emerged? Discuss these issues, trying to draw conclusions about how Web sites might be used to create an identity and about how readers might use a Web site to draw conclusions about its author's identity.

8. Many critics have expressed grave concerns about literacy and technology and their implications for modern society. Some of these critics have discussed how popular media and the development of technologies like the Internet may contribute to serious social ills. Do you share such concerns? Write an essay intended for an editorial page of a publication like the *New York Times* or *Newsweek* magazine in which you offer your own views or concerns about an issue or problem that relates to literacy or technology. You might want to find examples of such criticisms of technology for your essay. You might also wish to cite the work of writers in this chapter (such as Bennahum, Sweeney, or Eldred) who write about technology.

9. Select one of the readings from this chapter and discuss the identity that the author presents in that selection. Who is the author? How does he or she present him- or herself in the selection? What conclusions can you draw about the author, based on this selection? What might your analysis suggest about how we construct identities when we write?

CHAPTER 4

Reading, Writing, Computing, and Schooling

Perhaps nothing is as deeply associated with literacy as schooling. Reading and writing seem to be fundamental to our conception of school as the central activities that we associate with academic work. That isn't surprising, of course, since reading and writing are not limited to English or "language arts" classes but occur in every subject in the school curriculum, and it's hard to imagine a school curriculum that is not structured around literacy. Moreover, reading and writing are integral to the way schools function, both in and outside the classroom. Consider how many different documents are somehow involved in keeping schools operating: grade reports, examinations, letters to students and parents, enrollment forms, curriculum guidelines, schedules, the minutes of committee meetings, and more. Scholar Eli Goldblatt of Temple University has described writing as the "work" of schools, and he calls attention to the great volume of writing that students and professors do at universities like the one where he teaches. "Take away the buildings," he states, "and you have a university in search of a home; take away the writing and a university is unimaginable" (*Round My Way,* 1995, p. 30). The same seems true of schooling at all levels.

Few of us would argue with Goldblatt's point, since our own experiences in schools clearly indicate how extensive a role writing and reading play in education. But the place of literacy in education goes well beyond the fact that schools generate so much text and operate largely through writing and reading. As scholar Harvey Graff has pointed out, literacy is a form of social and cultural regulation, and its role in schools is a complicated one that involves not just the skills associated with writing and reading but with ideology as well. In his book *The Legacies of Literacy* (1987), Graff demonstrates that how literacy is taught in schools reflects larger cultural values and beliefs. He argues that in Western cultures, the teaching of reading and writing historically has been closely associated with morality and with efforts to create a certain kind of society:

> Although literacy as a skill was often important and highly valued, its moral bases have been historically more dominant. The inculcation of values, habits, norms, and attitudes to transform the masses, rather than skills alone or per se, was the developing task of schooling and its legitimating theme. Literacy properly was to serve as

an instrument for training in a close and mutually reinforcing relationship with morality. . . . (*Legacies of Literacy*, p. 12)

In other words, reading and writing have been taught in schools in ways that are intended to produce people who will become certain kinds of citizens, with certain beliefs about themselves, their society, and their roles in that society. Graff offers voluminous evidence to support his argument, analyzing demographic data, literacy rates, and many other kinds of documents to show that the teaching of literacy in schools is as much about values as about skills. If we are to understand the effects of literacy, Graff believes, we must understand how literacy reflects values. We must understand, that is, the connection between literacy and ideology.

Such arguments may seem to be the province of scholars interested in theorizing about literacy—far removed from the concerns of a student struggling through an essay assignment or a teacher grading that assignment. But it is precisely in those common school activities of writing and reading and grading that we can perhaps begin to see the complex nature of literacy and how the teaching of literacy reflects our values as a society. For instance, think about the kinds of assignments you have typically been given in school. If you're like most students who have attended conventional schools, you almost certainly have been assigned to write "book reports" or essays in classes such as social studies. Most likely you had little choice in determining which books to read or which questions to respond to in your reports or essays—or, if you did have a choice, you were probably given a list, compiled by your teacher, from which to choose. You were probably also given specific instructions about the form your report or essay should take, with guidelines or requirements for matters like length, thesis statements, organization, supporting evidence, and so on. And you may even have been required to use specific vocabulary words or to follow a specific paragraph format. In one sense, all these requirements can be seen as part of an effort to help you learn how to put together effective reports and essays—to develop the *skills* you need to be a successful writer in school. But these common and seemingly straightforward assignments teach other lessons as well. For instance, if you have been asked to write a report on a specific book, who chose that book and why? What might that choice say about who controls knowledge, about who has authority for determining what counts as valid knowledge? Why are you being asked to read that particular book? What are you supposed to learn by reading it? And why can't you read different books (for instance, a popular romance novel or a biography of a hip-hop star)? Moreover why are you asked to write a specific kind of "report" on that book? What does such a writing activity say about the purpose of books and how you should read them? What are you supposed to learn through such a highly constrained assignment? What is left out of such reading and writing assignments and why? The same sorts of questions might in fact be raised about the writing and reading assignments you are given in any course, not just English or language arts.

These are large and complex questions to which there are many answers and about which there are conflicting opinions. But such questions highlight the complexity of literacy as it is taught in schools and the connections between literacy and the values that shape school curricula. Education researcher Jean Anyon has addressed these questions in her studies of what she calls the "hidden curriculum" of schools. Anyon believes that conventional school assignments and routine practices such as classroom discussions and "seatwork" carry powerful messages about work, authority, knowledge, and behavior. Based on her research, she argues that schools teach students how to behave and how to understand who they are as people; furthermore, such messages are related to the social class of the students and the communities where their schools are located. For example, students from lower socioeconomic backgrounds, she asserts, generally learn to be complacent workers, while students from privileged socioeconomic backgrounds learn to take the initiative for solving problems in ways that enable them to succeed as corporate managers. This process is extremely complicated, encompassing many social, political, and economic factors, and some critics argue that the kinds of messages about knowledge and authority that Anyon associates with the "hidden curriculum" are precisely the kinds of messages students *should* be learning in our schools. Whatever your own perspective about such matters, the point is that how you are taught to read and write in school involves much more than developing basic literacy skills.

Perhaps because literacy and its teaching are connected to deeply held values, literacy is often at the center of public controversies about education that have arisen in recent years. During the 1990's, many states moved toward more stringent and widespread standardized testing for students in kindergarten through twelfth grade. The trend toward more standardized testing, especially for reading and writing, suggests the importance Americans place on literacy instruction in their schools. But standardized tests also reflect certain beliefs about literacy itself—similar, in some ways, to the kinds of values implicit in the typical school essay assignment that we saw above. Critics of such tests charge that they reduce writing and reading to rote skills and thus don't adequately prepare students for the writing and reading they'll have to do outside school. Others charge that such tests can be culturally biased, placing students from certain sociocultural backgrounds at a disadvantage because those students learn to read and write in their communities differently than children from mainstream communities, who tend to do better on such tests. There are no clear-cut solutions to these problems, but such controversies about reading and writing tests highlight the connections among literacy, schooling, and values.

Those connections seem even more evident in the controversies that regularly occur over the reading materials that students are given in schools. Each year students, parents, and teachers in communities throughout the country struggle in censorship battles, often when parents or students object to specific books that the students are assigned to read in their English classes. (Indeed, it is likely that you have been asked to read a book that has been the focus of such censorship fights; *The Adventures of Huckleberry Finn, The Diary of Anne Frank,* and *The Catcher in the Rye* are among the most commonly targeted books.) Sometimes these conflicts involve religious or racial issues, and they can quickly turn schools into political battlefields. But these same conflicts suggest that schools can also be places that reflect hope for the resolution of some of the difficult ideological conflicts that generally plague society. Americans seem to expect schools to address and perhaps even eliminate a whole host of social ills, including racism, religious intolerance, and economic inequalities. English and language arts classes in particular often seem to be viewed as sites of social change. The kinds of reading and writing students are asked to do in such classes often relate directly to important social issues such as race relations, and thus they reflect this sense of the social mission of literacy education. For example, Maya Angelou's *I Know Why the Caged Bird Sings,* which describes her experiences as a

Black girl and then a young woman growing up in a segregated community, is now routinely assigned to middle and high school students. Such a book would never have found its way into the classroom in many (and probably most) American schools forty or fifty years ago, and its popularity today leads to questions about *why* such books are assigned. Does a book like Angelou's enable students to learn to read more effectively? If so, why weren't such books assigned in schools in the 1950's or 1960's? It may be that the inclusion of such books reflects changes in American society in general regarding racial and social issues. It may also be that curricular changes in English classes reflect the expectation Americans have that schools can help change our society for the better. If so, then learning to read and write in school is part of the process of learning to "be" a member of American society.

This complex process is further complicated by the technologies of literacy. In recent years the development of powerful computer-based technologies and multimedia capabilities has begun to influence not only how students are taught but also how educators understand literacy education. As we saw in Chapters 1 and 2 of this book, literacy is itself a technology for using language, and the various technologies used for writing and reading—such as the printing press and the word processor—can shape how we write and read and, indeed, the very nature of writing and reading. The changes brought about by the recent developments of computer-based technologies such as hypertext and the World Wide Web, which are challenging our ways of thinking about literacy, are also encouraging some educators to re-imagine the teaching of writing and reading, while other educators resist new technologies in favor of traditional methods of instruction that they believe better serve students' needs. In either case, educators cannot ignore the vast changes that have occurred in the past few decades as new technologies have become common tools for communication. Consider, for instance, how widespread email has become. Just a decade ago, only a small group of researchers, corporate workers, and a few others had access to email; today, it is fast becoming as common as the telephone. The same might be said of the World Wide Web, whose growth in business and personal use exploded in the 1990's. As these technologies change the way people write and read and communicate, they force educators to wonder whether conventional ways of teaching literacy in schools will suffice. Does learning to write a book report, for example, help prepare students for the kinds of writing and reading they will be asked to do in this increasingly technological world?

The authors of the readings in this chapter address these and other questions about schools and literacy at a time of remarkable social and technological changes in American society and, indeed, in the world. Some of the authors in this chapter examine those changes directly and explore their implications for literacy and education. Their essays thus provide a glimpse of what education might be like in the future and suggest a pressing need for schools to help students acquire the technological skills they'll need in a future shaped by new technologies. But such a task raises concerns, too, about what students will actually learn about writing and reading in the midst of these extensive and far-reaching technological changes. Together, these reading selections highlight the great faith Americans seem to place in technology as a tool for making a better society. But there is a need for skepticism and vigilance as well, for, as several of the authors in this chapter remind us, the technology we use to improve education can carry serious risks.

There is a sense of urgency in some of these readings, which speaks to the importance we as a society tend to place on literacy and education. And there is also a sense of the familiar here. Despite important changes in education, schools have not changed very much in the past century. They are still organized and run in much the same way that they were organized and run at the beginning of the twentieth century. Classrooms function in more or less the same way, the school day is organized similarly, and the curriculum is structured around the same general subject areas—reading, writing, and arithmetic along with science, social studies, and the arts—that defined the curriculum one hundred years ago. In this sense, the arguments made by some of the authors in this chapter are really new versions of old arguments. Perhaps our great faith in schools—and in literacy—as a means to creating a better society makes us less willing to change them.

Despite their seemingly conservative nature as social institutions, however, schools have always been places of great *personal* change. Accordingly, several of the readings in this chapter include familiar stories of personal transformation through education. Such stories help us see again how central schools can be to our sense of personal and cultural identity and how deeply education is associated with American values of hard work and individual initiative. While these values may seem commonsensical to us, several authors in the chapter remind us that we now live in a multicultural society that may require us to adjust those traditional values—or at least reexamine them—as American society continues to define and redefine itself. There seems to be little question, however, that literacy and education will continue to be central to that process of redefinition.

Open Admissions and the Inward I

PETER J. RONDINONE

INTRODUCTION   For the vast majority of us, school is the central experience of our youth and, for many people, of adulthood as well. Mandatory school attendance laws, the huge amounts of money spent on education, and the intensity of the many public controversies about education all indicate the important place schooling has in American society. For Americans, school seems to represent not just a rite of passage but also a place of possibility and opportunity. As a nation, we place great faith in our schools to help us create the kind of society we aspire to have and to provide opportunities for each student to achieve his or her potential. And perhaps it is schooling more than any other aspect of American life that shapes our collective beliefs about individual self-determination.

In the following essay, writer and teacher Peter J. Rondinone offers his version of the common American story about overcoming daunting obstacles to achieve personal goals through education. It is a story of transformation: a troubled young man from a tough working-class neighborhood struggling to create a better future for himself through hard work in school. In telling this story, Rondinone reveals how important his belief in himself was to his eventual success as a student and a writer. He reveals, too, the sense of possibility that pervades our cultural attitudes about school as a place where futures can be made—or remade. Indeed, the open-admissions policy that enabled Rondinone to attend college in the first place reflects this deep American faith in education as a site of possibility. Such open-admissions policies, which began to be implemented in the late 1960's amidst growing concerns about the lack of access to higher education among students from disadvantaged backgrounds, were intended to provide such students the opportunity to transform their lives as Rondinone transformed his. And the familiar triumphant ending to his story is a compelling statement that such policies can work.

But Rondinone's story also raises complex and perhaps troubling questions about schooling and our beliefs about it. His own experiences in school, which he presents as his path to success, are mixed, conflicted, sometimes contradictory, and even painful. His description of the way his teachers in effect ignored him as he stumbled through high school strikes a familiar chord, as we often hear stories of ineffective schools and students who fall through the cracks. He describes, too, the criticisms he endures from friends, family, and faculty members as he struggles to succeed in college as an open-admissions student. If schools represent places of opportunity, we might ask, why should Rondinone have had to confront such obstacles to his academic success? Indeed, his experiences may perhaps lead us to wonder about the less obvious effects of school on our ideas about who we are as individuals and as a society. Rondinone speaks with a triumphant and almost defiant voice at the end of his essay, but as a reader you may wonder whether the story he tells about schools is as happy as it may at first seem. Whether you agree or not with his views about education, his story can help us examine the role of education in our individual lives and the place of school in American society.

Peter J. Rondinone is an English professor and the director of the journalism program at LaGuardia Community College in New York. He is also a writer whose essays, stories, and screenplays have won various awards, including a Pushcart Prize for short fiction in 1997. He has written articles and essays for the *New York Times* and *Omni* magazine, a writing textbook, and *The Digital Hood*, a collection of short fiction (1998). The following essay has been reprinted in a number of college readers and textbooks.

REFLECTING BEFORE READING

1. In this essay, Rondinone describes his experiences as an "open-admissions" student at the City College of New York in the early 1970's. Such policies were controversial when they were first implemented, and in some cases they remain controversial today. In the 1990's, for example, Ohio State University eliminated its long-standing open admissions policy in response to public concerns about low standards in higher education. What do you know about open-admissions policies? As you read, examine how Rondinone describes those policies, and consider your own attitudes about them. How might your attitudes influence the way you react to Rondinone's story?

2. In a sense, Rondinone's essay is about the relationship between one's social background (family life, ethnic heritage, social class) and school. As you read, consider how this relationship is depicted in Rondinone's essay. How does his social background affect his experiences in school, for example? Consider,

too, what beliefs about this relationship Rondinone reveals. Do you think Rondinone wishes to present his social background in a sympathetic way? Why or why not?

T he fact is, I didn't learn much in high school. I spent my time on the front steps of the building smoking grass with the dudes from the dean's squad. For kicks we'd grab a freshman, tell him we were undercover cops, handcuff him to a banister, and take his money. Then we'd go to the back of the building, cop some "downs," and nod away the day behind the steps in the lobby. The classrooms were overcrowded anyhow, and the teachers knew it. They also knew where to find me when they wanted to make weird deals: If I agreed to read a book and do an oral report, they'd pass me. So I did it and graduated with a "general" diploma. I was a New York City public school kid.

I hung out on a Bronx streetcorner with a group of guys who called themselves "The Davidson Boys" and sang songs like "Daddy-lo-lo." Everything we did could be summed up with the word "snap." That's a "snap." She's a "snap." We had a "snap." Friday nights we'd paint ourselves green and run through the streets swinging baseball bats. Or we'd get into a little rap in the park. It was all very perilous. Even though I'd seen a friend stabbed for wearing the wrong colors and another blown away with a shotgun for "messin'" with some dude's woman, I was too young to realize that my life too might be headed toward a violent end.

Then one night I swallowed a dozen Tuminols and downed two quarts of beer at a bar in Manhattan. I passed out in the gutter. I puked and rolled under a parked car. Two girlfriends found me and carried me home. My overprotective brother answered the door. When he saw me—eyes rolling toward the back of my skull like rubber—he pushed me down a flight of stairs. My skull hit the edge of a marble step with a thud. The girls screamed. My parents came to the door and there I was: a high school graduate, a failure, curled in a ball in a pool of blood.

The next day I woke up with dried blood on my face. I had no idea what had happened. My sister told me. I couldn't believe it. Crying, my mother confirmed the story. I had almost died! That scared [the] hell out of me. I knew I had to do something. I didn't know what. But pills and violence didn't promise much of a future.

I went back to a high school counselor for advice. He suggested I go to college.

I wasn't aware of it, but it seems that in May 1969 a group of dissident students from the black and Puerto Rican communities took over the south campus of the City College of New York (CCNY). They demanded that the Board of Higher Education and the City of New York adopt an open-admission policy that would make it possible for anybody to go to CCNY without the existing requirements: SATs and a high school average of 85. This demand was justified on the premise that college had always been for the privileged few and excluded minorities. As it turned out, in the fall of 1970 the City University's 18 campuses admitted massive numbers of students—15,000—with high school averages below 85. By 1972, I was one of them.

On the day I received my letter of acceptance, I waited until dinner to tell my folks. I was proud.

"Check out where I'm going," I said. I passed the letter to my father. He looked at it.

"You jerk!" he said. "You wanna sell ties?" My mother grabbed the letter.

"God," she said. "Why don't you go to work already? Like other people."

"Later for that," I said. "You should be proud."

At the time, of course, I didn't understand where my parents were coming from. They were immigrants. They believed college was for rich kids, not the ones who dropped downs and sang songs on streetcorners.

My mother had emigrated from Russia after World War II. She came to the United States with a bundle of clothes, her mother and father, a few dollars, and a baby from a failed marriage. Her first job was on an assembly line in a pen factory where she met my father, the production manager.

My father, a second-generation Italian, was brought up on the Lower East Side of Manhattan. He never completed high school. And when he wasn't working in a factory, he peddled Christmas lights door to door or sold frankfurters in Times Square.

My family grew up in the south Bronx. There were six children, and we slept in one room on cots. We ate spaghetti three times a week and were on welfare because for a number of years my father was sick, in and out of the hospital.

Anyhow, I wasn't about to listen to my parents and go to work; for a dude like me, this was a big deal. So I left the dinner table and went to tell my friends about my decision.

The Davidson Boys hung out in a rented storefront. They were sitting around the pool table on milk boxes and broken pinball machines, spare tires and dead batteries. I made my announcement. They stood up and circled me like I was the star of a cockfight. Sucio stepped to the table with a can of beer in one hand and a pool stick in the other.

"Wha' you think you gonna get out of college?" he said.

"I don't know, but I bet it beats this," I said. I shoved one of the pool balls across the table. That was a mistake. The others banged their sticks on the wood floor and chanted, "Oooh-ooh—snap, snap." Sucio put his beer on the table.

"Bull!" he yelled. "I wash dishes with college dudes. You're like us—nuttin', man." He pointed the stick at my nose.

Silence.

I couldn't respond. If I let the crowd know I thought their gig was uncool, that I wanted out of the club, they would have taken it personally. And they would have taken me outside and kicked my ass. So I lowered my head. "Aw, hell, gimme a hit of beer," I said, as if it were all a joke. But I left the corner and didn't go back.

I spent that summer alone, reading books like *How to Succeed in College* and *30 Days to a More Powerful Vocabulary*. My vocabulary was limited to a few choice phrases like, "Move over, Rover, and let Petey take over." When my friends did call for me I hid behind the curtains. I knew that if I was going to make it, I'd have to push these guys out of my consciousness as if I were doing the breaststroke in a sea of logs. I had work to do, and people were time consuming. As it happened, all my heavy preparations didn't amount to much.

On the day of the placement exams I went paranoid. Somehow I got the idea that my admission to college was some ugly practical joke that I wasn't prepared for. So I copped some downs and took the test nodding. The words floated on the page like flies on a crock of cream.

That made freshman year difficult. The administration had placed me in all three remedial programs: basic writing, college skills, and math. I was shocked. I had always thought of myself as smart. I was the only one in the neighborhood who read books. So I gave up the pills and pushed aside another log.

The night before the first day of school, my brother walked into my room and threw a briefcase on my desk. "Good luck, Joe College," he said. He smacked me in the back of the head. Surprised, I went to bed early.

I arrived on campus ahead of time with a map in my pocket. I wanted enough time, in case I got lost, to get to my first class. But after wandering around the corridors of one building for what seemed like a long time and hearing the sounds of classes in session, the scrape of chalk and muted discussions, I suddenly wondered if I was in the right place. So I stopped a student and pointed to a dot on my map.

"Look." He pointed to the dot. "Now look." He pointed to an inscription on the front of the building. I was in the right place. "Can't you read?" he said. Then he joined some friends. As he walked off I heard someone say, "What do you expect from open admissions?"

I had no idea that there were a lot of students who resented people like me, who felt I was jeopardizing standards, destroying their institution. I had no idea. I just wanted to go to class.

In Basic Writing I the instructor, Regina Sackmary, chalked her name in bold letters on the blackboard. I sat in the front row and reviewed my *How to Succeed* lessons: Sit in front/don't let eyes wander to cracks on ceilings/take notes on a legal pad/make note of all unfamiliar words and books/listen for key phrases like "remember this," they are a professor's signals. The other students held pens over pads in anticipation. Like me, they didn't know what to expect. We were public school kids from lousy neighborhoods and we knew that some of us didn't have a chance; but we were ready to work hard.

Before class we had rapped about our reasons for going to college. Some said they wanted to be the first in the history of their families to have a college education—they said their parents never went to college because they couldn't afford it, or because their parents' parents were too poor—and they said open admissions and free tuition ($65 per semester) was a chance to change that history. Others said they wanted to be educated so they could return to their neighborhoods to help "the people"; they were the idealists. Some foreigners said they wanted to return to their own countries and start schools. And I said I wanted to escape the boredom and the pain I had known as a kid on the streets. But none of them said they expected a job. Or if they did they were reminded that there were no jobs.

Ms. Sackmary told us that Basic Writing I was part of a three-part program. Part one would instruct us in the fundamentals of composition: sentence structure, grammar, and paragraphing; part two, the outline and essay; and part three, the term paper. She also explained that we weren't in basic writing because there was something wrong with us—we just needed to learn the basics, she said, Somehow I didn't believe her. After class I went to her office. She gave me a quick test. I couldn't write a coherent sentence or construct a paragraph. So we made an agreement: I'd write an essay a day in addition to my regular classwork. Also, I'd do a few term papers. She had this idea that learning to write was like learning to play a musical instrument—it takes practice, everyday practice.

In math I was in this remedial program for algebra, geometry, and trigonometry. But unlike high school math, which I thought was devised to boggle the mind for the sake of boggling, in this course I found I could make a connection between different mathematical principles and my life. For instance, there were certain basics I had to learn—call them 1, 2, and 3—and unless they added up to 6 I'd probably be a failure. I also got a sense of how math related to the world at large: Unless the sum of the parts of a society equaled the whole there would be chaos. And these insights jammed my head and made me feel like a kid on a ferris wheel looking at the world for the first time. Everything amazed me!

Like biology. In high school I associated this science with stabbing pins in the hearts of frogs for fun. Or getting high snorting small doses of the chloroform used for experiments on fruit flies. But in college biology I began to learn and appreciate not only how my own life processes functioned but how there were thousands of other life processes I'd never known existed. And this gave me a sense of power, because I could deal with questions like, Why do plants grow? not as I had before, with a simple spill of words: "'Cause of the sun' man." I could actually explain that there was a plant cycle and cycles within the plant cycle. You know how the saying goes—a little knowledge is dangerous. Well, the more I learned the more I ran my mouth off, especially with people who didn't know as much as I did.

I remember the day Ms. Sackmary tossed Sartre's *No Exit* in my lap and said, "Find the existential motif." I didn't know what to look for. What was she talking about? I never studied philosophy. I turned to the table of contents, but there was nothing under E. So I went to the library and after much research I discovered the notion of the absurd. I couldn't believe it. I told as many people as I could. I told them they were absurd, their lives were absurd, everything was absurd. I became obsessed with existentialism. I read Kafka, Camus, Dostoyevski, and others in my spare time. Then one day I found a line in a book that I believed summed up my unusual admittance to the college and my determination to work hard. I pasted it to the headboard of my bed. It said: "Everything is possible."

To deal with the heavy workload from all my classes, I needed a study schedule, so I referred to my *How to Succeed* book. I gave myself an hour for lunch and reserved the rest of the time between classes and evenings for homework and research. All this left me very little time for friendships. But I stuck to my schedule and by the middle of that first year I was getting straight A's: Nothing else mattered. Not even my family.

One night my sister pulled me from my desk by the collar. She sat me on the edge of the bed. "Mom and Dad bust their ass to keep you in school. They feed you. Give you a roof. And this is how you pay them back?" She was referring to my habit of locking myself in my room.

"What am I supposed to do?" I said.

"Little things. Like take down the garbage."

"Come on. Mom and Dad need me for that?"

"You know Dad has arthritis. His feet hurt. You want *him* to take it down?" My sister can be melodramatic.

"Let Mom do it," I said. "Or do her feet hurt too?"

"You bastard," she said. "You selfish bastard. The only thing you care about is your books."

She was right. I *was* selfish. But she couldn't understand that in many ways college had become a substitute for my family because what I needed I couldn't get at home. Nobody's fault. She cried.

When I entered my second year my family began to ask, "What do you want to do?" And I got one of those cards from the registrar that has to be filled out in a week or you're dropped from classes. It asked me to declare my major. I had to make a quick decision. So I checked off *BS* degree, dentistry, though I didn't enroll in a single science course.

One course I did take that semester was The Writer and the City. The professor, Ross Alexander, asked the class to keep a daily journal. He said it should be as creative as possible and reflect some aspect of city life. So I wrote about different experiences I had with my friends. For example, I wrote "Miracle on 183rd Street" about the night "Raunchy" Rick jumped a guy in the park and took his portable radio. When the guy tried to fight back Rick slapped him in the face with the radio; then, using the batteries that spilled out, he pounded this guy in the head until the blood began to puddle on the ground. Those of us on the sidelines dragged Rick away. Ross attached notes to my papers that said things like: "You really have a great hit of talent and ought to take courses in creative writing and sharpen your craft! Hang on to it all for dear life."

In my junior year I forgot dentistry and registered as a creative writing major. I also joined a college newspaper, *The Campus.* Though I knew nothing about journalism, I was advised that writing news was a good way to learn the business. And as Ross once pointed out to me, "As a writer you will need an audience."

I was given my first assignment. I collected piles of quotes and facts and scattered the mess on a desk. I remember typing the story under deadline pressure with one finger while the editors watched me struggle, probably thinking back to their own first stories. When I finished, they passed the copy around. The editor-in-chief looked at it last and said, "This isn't even English." Yet, they turned it over to a rewrite man and the story appeared with my by-line. Seeing my name in print was like seeing it in lights—flashbulbs popped in my head and I walked into the school cafeteria that day expecting to be recognized by everyone. My mother informed the relatives: "My son is a writer!"

Six months later I quit *The Campus.* A course in New Journalism had made me realize that reporting can be creative. For the first time I read writers like Tom Wolfe and Hunter S. Thompson, and my own news stories began to turn into first-person accounts that read like short stories. *The Campus* refused to publish my stuff, so I joined *The Observation Post,* the only paper on campus that printed first-person material. I wanted to get published.

My first *Post* feature article (a first-person news story on a proposed beer hall at CCNY) was published on the front page. The staff was impressed enough to elect me assistant features editor. However, what they didn't know was that the article had been completely rewritten by the features editor. And the features editor had faith in me, so he never told. He did my share of the work and I kept the title. As he put it: "You'll learn by hanging around and watching. You show talent. You might even get published professionally in 25 years!" Another thing they didn't know—I still hadn't passed my basic English proficiency exam.

Get into this: When people hear me tell this story about how I struggled without friends and closed myself off from most things, they often wonder: "Well, what did you do for . . . uh, you know, GIRLS!" And so I tell them: The only girlfriend I had, in my junior year, left me after 10 months. She got tired of watching television every weekend while I occupied myself with reading and studying, and she got tired of my pulling English usage books from under the pillow after we'd made love. But I did pass the English proficiency exam at the end of my junior year.

During my four years at CCNY I have learned something else—that an awful lot of people were put off by open-admission students. And some of them were City College professors. Take a book I reviewed a few months ago in *The Observation Post—The End of Education* by Geoffrey Wagner, a CCNY English professor. Wagner refers repeatedly to open-admission students as "Joe Blows," "dunces," and "sleeping beauties." And he also clearly detests blacks ("Leroi" he calls them) and others who wear afros, whom he describes in a cruel and absurd fashion: "I would find myself telling some charming child whose only visible sign of imminent anarchy was an afro so wide she had difficulty navigating my door, 'See, you've used "imperialist" four times.'"

Shortly after my review appeared, protesting that the book "is so full of inaccuracies that people at the college are calling it a great work of fiction," I received a copy of a letter attached to another, favorable review of *The End of Education* by Wagner's colleague Robert K. Morris. The letter said:

> Perhaps you would be so kind as to pass this one on to the ineffable (& unlovely) RONDINONE, with my compliments—if he can read!
>
> Best, Geoffrey

Though Wagner questions my ability to read (me, this open-admission "dummy"), he should in fact remember that I was once a student in his Writing for Humanities course—and he gave me an A!

Not all the detractors of open admissions were insiders. I once watched a network television crew interview a campus newspaper staff for a documentary on open admissions. An interviewer from "60 Minutes," notebook on his lap, sat like he had a box of Cracker Jacks, opposite three campus editors who looked as if they were waiting for the prize. I stood in a corner. He passed a remark: "I was down at the Writing Center today. Those kids are animals. They can't write." The editors, who were a conservative bunch, shook their heads as if they understood this to be their terrible legacy. I wanted to spit.

"Hey you!" I said. "Do I look like an animal?"

He closed his notebook and looked down his long nose at me. I felt like an ant at the mercy of an aardvark. The editors got puffy. "Who is this kid?" they mumbled. "Who do you think you are?" I yelled back. "Those kids you are talking about are not only willing to learn, but they are learning. They've written some beautiful essays and stories. You stupid jerk!"

God, those early days were painful. Professors would tear up my papers the day they were due and tell me to start over again, with a piece of advice—"Try to say what you really mean." Papers I had spent weeks writing. And I knew I lacked the basic college skills: I was a man reporting to work without his tools. So I smiled when I didn't understand. But sometimes it showed and I paid the price: A professor once told me the only reason I'd pass his course was that I had a nice smile. Yes, those were painful days.

And there were nights I was alone with piles of notebooks and textbooks. I wanted to throw the whole mess out the window; I wanted to give up. Nights the sounds of my friends singing on the corner drifted into my room like a fog over a graveyard and I was afraid I would be swept away. And nights I was filled with questions but the answers were like moon shadows on my curtains: I could see them but I could not grasp them.

Yet I had learned a vital lesson from these countless hours of work in isolation: My whole experience from the day I received my letter of acceptance enabled me to understand how in high school my sense of self-importance came from being one of the boys, a member of the pack, while in college the opposite was true. In order to survive, I had to curb my herd instinct.

Nobody, nobody could give me what I needed to overcome my sense of inadequacy. That was a struggle I had to work at on my own. It could never be a group project. In the end, though people could point out what I had to learn and where to learn it, I was always the one who did the work; and what I learned I earned. And that made me feel as good as being one of the boys. In short, college taught me to appreciate the importance of being alone. I found it was the only way I could get any serious work done.

But those days of trial and uncertainty are over, and the open-admission policy has been eliminated. Anybody who enters the City University's senior colleges must now have an 80 percent high school average. And I am one of those fortunate individuals who in a unique period of American education was given a chance to attend college. But I wonder what will happen to those people who can learn but whose potential doesn't show in their high school average; who might get into street crime if not given a chance to do something constructive? I wonder, because if it weren't for open admissions, the likelihood is I would still be swinging baseball bats on the streets on Friday nights.

REFLECTING ON THE READING

1. Why does Rondinone initially decide to apply to college? Why are the circumstances of his decision important in this essay? How do they affect the way you responded to the experiences he describes later in the essay, especially his earliest college experiences?

2. What do we learn about Rondinone's family in this essay? What kind of relationship does he have with them? What reactions do they have about his attending college? What importance do their attitudes about college have in his

decision to attend college and remain there? How does his attending college affect his relationship with his family? Do you think he sees the impact of school on his family life as a benefit? Explain. What might his experiences suggest about the relationship between schooling and social background?

3. What was the "open-admissions policy" under which Rondinone attended City College of New York, as he describes it? What effect did that policy have on City College, according to Rondinone? Why did many people criticize the policy? What importance did that policy have to students like Rondinone, in his view? Do you think he is right? Why or why not?

4. What effect does attending college have on Rondinone's relationship with his friends? Why does Rondinone believe that in order to succeed in college, he would have to "push his [friends] out of my consciousness"? Do you think he is right? Explain. What might his belief about his friends indicate about his views regarding educational success? Do you think his views are common ones? Explain.

5. What role did writing play in Rondinone's college experience? What problems did he experience as a student writer? What was the source of those problems? What was it about writing that eventually led Rondinone to pursue it further? What importance does he attach to writing? What is the relationship between writing and his identity? Do you think his experiences as a student writer influenced his attitudes about school? Explain.

6. What "vital lesson" does Rondinone learn from his college experience? Do you agree with him? Why or why not? What might your answer suggest about your own values regarding school?

7. Why does Rondinone say he had to "curb my herd instinct" in order to succeed in college? What does that statement reveal about his attitudes about school and learning? Do you think he is right? Explain.

Examining Rhetorical Strategies

1. Rondinone ends the opening scene of his essay by telling us that after he almost died as a result of a night of drinking, he consulted his school guidance counselor for advice regarding his future. The guidance counselor, Rondinone writes, "suggested I go to college." What effect did that line have on you as a reader? Do you think Rondinone meant that line to be ironic? In what sense might that line call upon common beliefs and attitudes about college to achieve its effect? How does it set up the college experiences that Rondinone describes later in the essay?

2. Describe Rondinone's voice in this essay. What impression does his voice create for you as a reader? Do you think his voice is appropriate for the points he raises about school? Explain. How did you respond to his voice? Did you find it appealing? Why or why not? What might your response suggest about you as a reader?

3. Examine how Rondinone describes his family in this essay. Why do you think he describes them in this way? How might his description of his family relate to

the points he wishes to raise about school? How might his descriptions of his family help present a picture of who he is as a person? What reaction did you have to his descriptions of his family and his relationship with them? How might your reaction relate to your experiences with your own family?

4. Notice how Rondinone structures his essay. What is the time frame within which these experiences take place? How does he represent the passing of time in the essay? What moments does he highlight? Do you think he leaves anything out? Explain. How might the structure influence your reaction to the experiences he describes?

5. Rondinone presents himself in this essay as coming from an ethnic, working-class background. What picture of his social class background does he present? Did it strike you as flattering? Critical? Realistic? Sympathetic? Explain. What attitudes about social class do you think Rondinone reveals in this essay? Does he believe social class was an important factor in his own educational experience? Does he wish to emphasize it as a factor, in your view? Cite specific passages from his essay to support your answer. Consider your own reactions to his descriptions of his background. Did you find yourself critical of or sympathetic to his background? Explain. How might your reactions to these descriptions relate to your own social class?

6. What picture of school and of teachers does Rondinone present in this essay? Do his depictions of school seem accurate to you? In what ways? Do you think he is critical of school and teachers? Do you think he intends to be? What attitudes about education and teachers do you think he reveals in this essay? Do you think these attitudes are common ones in American culture? Explain.

7. Rondinone's story is about his experiences as an open-admissions student, but it is also about how he became a writer. Examine his descriptions of his experiences as a student and then as a professional writer, and identify what you think are his fundamental beliefs about writing and about who writers are. What characteristics does he associate with writers? What image of the writer does he present? Do you find this image compelling or attractive or valid? Explain. What might your response to these questions reveal about your own beliefs about writing and writers?

8. In a sense, Rondinone's story is a classic American tale of hard work, determination, and belief in oneself. Identify the scenes in the essay that you think most clearly reveal his sense of his individual struggle to succeed. How does Rondinone present himself in those scenes? How does he present others? Does he identify himself with any specific groups? Explain, citing specific passages in your answer. Do you think it is accurate for Rondinone to portray his struggle as a lonely one? Explain.

Engaging the Issues

1. Write an essay for an audience of your classmates about an important school-related experience you have had. You might write about a specific event (such as transferring to a new school, winning a special award, or encountering some kind of problem), or you might write about a period of time in your education

that was especially important to you, as Rondinone does in his essay. In your essay, tell the story of that event or period in a way that enables your readers to understand why that experience was important to you.

2. In a group of your classmates, share the essays you wrote for Question #1 above. Compare the school-related experiences you each wrote about. What kinds of experiences are they? What similarities and differences emerge? What common themes emerge as important in these essays? Discuss what your essays, taken together, might suggest about schools. Try to account for differences or similarities in your respective views about the impact of schooling on your lives.

3. Investigate open-admissions policies using the World Wide Web, your library, and any other resources available to you. Try to find a person (or several) who might have attended college under such a policy. Or try to find someone who might have been a teacher or administrator in an open-admissions institution. If possible, interview these people about such policies. If you yourself have attended college under an open-admissions policy, draw on your own experience as such a student. Now, write a research paper for an academic audience examining open-admissions policies and their effects on higher education. Explain these policies and how they came to be, providing examples of such policies, if possible. Discuss the effects they have had on higher education. Examine the evidence you have gathered and try to draw conclusions about the usefulness or disadvantages of such policies.

4. Write an academic essay in which you compare the papers you wrote for Questions #1 and #3 above. What differences and similarities can you identify in terms of style, format, organization, tone, and your use of evidence? How might those similarities and differences relate to the audience and purpose of each paper? Address these questions and draw conclusions about the relationship between the audience and specific features of your texts.

5. In the 1990's, open-admissions policies came under attack by many critics and political leaders. Some well-known open-admissions policies (including the one that enabled Peter Rondinone to attend college in New York City) were discontinued or drastically reduced. Using the same research described in Question #3 above, write an editorial for a major newspaper, such as the *New York Times* or *Washington Post,* in favor of or against open-admissions policies. Use whatever sources you have gathered in making your argument. (Also consider using Rondinone's essay as a source in your editorial.)

6. Rewrite the editorial you wrote for Question #5 above as a letter to an educational institution in which open admissions does not exist or has recently been discontinued. In your letter, which you should address to the president of the school or some other high-level administrator, express your support for or opposition to open-admissions policies. Support your view by drawing on any appropriate sources or on your own experiences.

7. Write a conventional essay for an audience of your classmates in which you analyze Rondinone's attitudes about education. In your analysis, describe what you believe are his most basic beliefs about education and schooling. Cite specific passages from his essay in your analysis. Discuss whether you think his

beliefs about education are common. Try to draw conclusions about the implications of his beliefs in terms of what people think about such important educational matters as school reform or college loan programs.

Reflections of an Online Graduate

EMILY WEINER

INTRODUCTION   Most students today have had some experience with online education, usually as part of an assignment that requires them to do research on the Internet or to participate in a class discussion in a chat room or on an electronic bulletin board. But despite the rapid growth of online technologies in education, few students have completed an entire course of study—earned an entire college degree—online. Writer Emily Weiner is one of the few of a growing number of people who have done so. Her essay is the story of an "online pioneer," as she calls herself.

The degree program Weiner enrolled in (in 1993) was offered exclusively online. There were no class meetings, no visits to a faculty member's office, no strolls along tree-lined campus walkways. Instead, Weiner "attended" class by sitting down at her computer a few times each week, logging onto the Internet, and accessing the computer network maintained by Empire State College. Using her computer and the postal service, she received and submitted assignments; when necessary, she communicated with her faculty mentor and other students via the Internet. In this fashion she worked independently to complete all the requirements to earn her degree. Such "guided independent study" programs, which are sometimes called "correspondence courses," have been available to students for many years as an alternative to conventional classroom-based schooling. They have been popular with students whose situations make attending a conventional school difficult or impossible. What has changed in such programs in recent years is the medium through which they are offered. Instead of sending the materials through the mail, such programs now deliver their courses via the Internet. Students like Weiner study independently, but the new online technologies enable them to keep in direct contact with their teachers and to interact with other students—something that was previously very difficult or even impossible to do in independent study programs. Partly for that reason, perhaps, programs like the one Weiner completed are increasing in number as the Internet continues to grow and as new online capabilities—including multimedia technologies—become more widely available. In addition to exclusively online programs like the one Weiner completed, many traditional colleges and universities are offering online courses and programs to supplement their conventional courses and programs. Near the end of the 1990's, more than half of all four-year colleges and universities were offering "distance education" courses online, and that number was growing rapidly. The story Weiner tells in her essay is thus an increasingly common one.

But Weiner's essay is not just a story of what it is like to be an online student. It is also a story about how we think about education and about the changes that technology might bring to schooling. For many people, education is a community undertaking, and the experience of coming together physically with other students is sometimes cited as a crucial part of the learning. Indeed, Weiner discusses in her essay the importance of the relationship she developed with her faculty mentor as she worked through the program, and her description of that relationship will probably sound familiar to those of us who can recall a special teacher who helped guide us through a course or a program. But Weiner's essay also presents new images of teachers and students and of schooling itself. In this sense, her essay raises questions about the role of teachers in education and about the importance of the relationships teachers develop with their students. For instance, if teachers are central to a student's learning, as Weiner suggests, can that relationship be adequately maintained online? How might the technologies that Weiner used to complete her degree change the way students and teachers develop relationships and learn from each other? For some readers, the images Weiner presents may be unsettling, since they differ dramatically from the traditional images we have of schools and teachers. But the images she provides may also be glimpses of new possibilities for education—possibilities fostered by new technologies and new ways of using those technologies to enhance teaching and learning.

REFLECTING BEFORE READING

1. As you prepare to read Weiner's essay, consider any online educational experiences you may have had. For example, you might have been required to complete a school assignment by using the World Wide Web. Or perhaps you engaged in online discussions via email with students from other states or countries. Or maybe your teacher set up online email discussions that took place after your regular classroom meetings. Whatever your experience, think about how it might have affected you. What were the advantages and disadvantages of the online components of your education? How did they seem to affect your learning or help facilitate the assignments you completed? As you read Weiner's essay, think about how your own online experiences might influence your reaction to her descriptions of her own online experiences.

2. We tend to think of schools as communities, as places where we come together to learn and interact as students and teachers. In this sense, education is a social activity. Weiner describes an alternative to conventional schooling in which students for the most part learn independently. How do you feel about independent study? Do you think it can replace conventional schooling? Why or why not? What might your answer to these questions reveal about your beliefs about education? As you read, consider how those beliefs might influence your response to Weiner's essay.

I saw my college for the first time on June 12, 1995, five hours before I graduated. My campus until that day had been my computer. I live in Bellingham, Washington, and for a year and a half I had been hooking up by modem to the State University of New York's Empire State College.

In 1993 I realized I needed a degree fast. I was teaching news graphics through the continuing education program at Western Washington University, but was told that, though I had two decades of professional experience, I couldn't be hired as an adjunct instructor of journalism without a bachelor's degree. I had about two years of college credits, accumulated from three different schools from 1968 to 1971.

I was an online pioneer. By the end of this decade, cyberspace diplomas may be common. Innovative electronic teaching materials that will prepare students for work revolving around computers will free educational institutions from the limits of geography. Courses that teach students to work online won't be bound by classroom walls. Journalism students are already editing electronic newspapers. In my online experience, I merely talked via e-mail with the mentor assigned to me by Empire State, used the Internet for research, and participated in a computer course that was like a private chat room with a goal, a time frame and a leader.

How well will students be served by these new forms of teaching? In June [1996] the governors of ten Western states announced the establishment of a virtual university. One of its key goals is to lower the cost of education. I worry about this because their plan so far is silent on the value of personal contact between students and teachers.

My experience was terrific because my relationship with my mentor thrived over the computer network. The guided independent study model that Empire State College developed twenty-five years ago provided an effective alternative to conventional college for adults who wanted to pursue individually structured programs. This is why it survives so well even in the isolation of cyberspace, where you are connected to the school only by a telephone line.

I was a perfect fit with Empire State's teaching design. I wanted a program that would grant enough credits for prior learnings so I would have to register for the full-time equivalent of only one academic year. I didn't want to lose momentum in my teaching and freelance writing; I needed a school that would let me incorporate work projects into my study program. I also needed to fit my schoolwork into the time constraints of caring for my two sons, 10 and 3.

When I enrolled, Professor Diana Worby was assigned as my mentor. Instead of meeting every week or so in her office in Nyack, N.Y., we sent e-mail messages every few days. We used ordinary mail for packages of manuscripts and other material. Diana guided me through the process of developing a personal degree program, organizing my prior knowledge into academic equivalents that could be granted college credits, setting up and completing learning contracts for independent study, registering for one college class locally and one computer conference course and arranging an internship at a public radio station. And she was with me while I did the work.

It can be lonely going to school sitting at your own desk. We exchanged photographs so Diana could picture me with my husband and kids and I could see her broad supportive smile as I wrote. As we got to know each other, Diana's commitment to my successful completion of my degree was as palpable as if I had been in Nyack with her. In fact, our meeting the afternoon of my graduation was in some ways a letdown. I had expected fireworks. Our e-mail conversations had felt so intimate, that, after a long-awaited hug, there wasn't a new closeness to experience.

Looking back into the file folders stuffed with printouts of our e-mail correspondence, I find lots of necessary details like, "I wrote up the evaluation of your first contract." But these were usually sandwiched inside descriptions of what we were doing and thinking about on particular days: my son bicycling off to his first day of fifth grade; Diana's grown daughter's search for record albums they'd listened to together many years before; leads I was pursuing for part-time work and books and articles we recommended to each other.

While some students might find it a burden to have to accomplish almost everything with the written word, for me it was an extra opportunity to improve my writing. What appears on the surface to be primarily an old-fashioned (although high-tech) correspondence between two thoughtful friends was also the vehicle for an experienced critic of literature to let me know when she was particularly informed, moved or challenged by my writing.

My computer conference with a tutor used an independent study structure that had been developed for correspondence courses. We still read assignments and mailed in papers, but instead of scheduling individual phone conferences, the teacher of our section met online with me and the other student in the class.

The biggest difference I noticed from typical classroom discussions was that, with time to edit our contributions and without other people waiting their turn to speak, we developed our thoughts fully and addressed the complexity of topics instead of making a single point at a time. Every so often, the teacher suggested a different way to think about something or added relevant assignments to those in the printed course guide.

I enjoyed finally meeting another Empire State College student. We chatted about his Greenwich Village neighborhood where I had once lived, and joked about his e-mailing me a loaf of Zito's whole wheat bread. (My mouth watered.)

The online world is changing so fast that, if I were enrolled today, I would use Writer's Complex, Empire State's new interactive tutorial on writing and researching. I could follow links to screens about punctuation, style and how to write a research paper, read sample student papers in different disciplines, practice writing exercises, hang out with other writers in the virtual student lounge and contact tutors for help. (It's at http://coord_notes.esc.edu/admin/complex.nsf/complexhome?openform.)

Despite my excitement about new electronic educational opportunities, I'm concerned that others seeking convenient online degrees won't have the opportunities to find programs that nurture them intellectually and emotionally. Individual course requirements can certainly be completed by exhibiting competence on tests or by sending in papers or by using new interactive computer programs. But will there be a person on the other end of the line who is watching to see that students are stretching themselves, choosing appropriate courses, struggling with new ideas, overcoming personal obstacles, getting smarter?

I'm concerned that feedback will be limited to course work itself, and that the fuller relationships that develop between students and teachers on a college campus will be missing. I'm concerned that part-time instructors will be hired course-by-course but won't be paid enough or be on staff long enough to be available to guide students through the full process. Every student needs someone to say, "You're doing fine, just keep at it," or "Whoops, you're not going to make it unless you try another approach." Whether it's a mentor or faculty adviser, it has to be someone who knows what's ahead in a field of concentration better than the student.

There are probably other models that will work as well for online students as Empire State's, but only if "the virtual university" aims to be more than a collection of courses. Teachers need structures that give them a stake in their students' success. I hope that the shift of education into cyberspace represents a continuation of the drive for excellence and not a retreat.

REFLECTING ON THE READING

1. What campus did Weiner "attend" to earn her college degree? Why did she choose this particular campus? In what sense was she a "pioneer" by attending this campus? What images does the term *pioneer* conjure up for you? In what ways might those images be appropriate for a discussion of new technologies in education?

2. What specific advantages does Weiner see in the program she completed? Why does she describe her own experience in such a program as "terrific"? In what ways was she a "perfect fit" for such a program? Do you agree with her about the advantages of this kind of degree program? Why or why not? What might your answer suggest about your own views regarding education and technology?

3. Why was Weiner's face-to-face meeting with her mentor a "letdown"? What might this scene indicate about student-teacher relationships in online or conventional classrooms?

4. What differences does Weiner identify between her online "classroom" experiences and conventional classroom experiences? Do you see any other important differences? Explain.

5. What concerns does Weiner express about online education? Do you share those concerns? Why or why not? What might her concerns reveal about her assumptions regarding what is most important in formal education?

Examining Rhetorical Strategies

1. How would you characterize Weiner's voice in this article? Identify specific passages that you think exemplify that voice. In what ways do you think her voice is appropriate to her topic and to the points she makes about online education? Did you find her voice effective? Why or why not? How might your reaction to her voice in this essay have been influenced by your own views about education and technology?

2. Weiner describes her face-to-face meeting with her mentor as a "letdown" after the two had developed what she calls an "intimate" relationship online. In what ways does this brief scene reinforce one of Weiner's main praises of—and concerns about—online education? What does it reveal about Weiner's beliefs about education and about her own values as a person? Do you think Weiner intended to convey these beliefs and values in this scene? Explain.

3. This essay was originally published in the *New York Times*, a widely circulated newspaper read by a large and diverse audience. In what ways do you think Weiner's writing is appropriate for such an audience? Do you think her discussions of her educational experience and her descriptions of her online studies

are effective for such a large audience? Do you think she discusses technology in a way that is suitable for such an audience? Explain. What does she seem to assume about her readers' views regarding education and technology? Cite specific passages from her essay to support your answer.

4. Examine the way Weiner organizes this essay. She is essentially telling the story of her experiences as a student in an online college degree program. How does she structure this story? Does she tell it chronologically? What do you think she accomplishes by organizing her essay in the way she does? Do you think she might have organized it more effectively? Explain.

5. How would you characterize Weiner in terms of her social class and cultural background? Does she describe herself in ways that might reveal something about her social class and racial or ethnic identity? Do you think those factors in any way shape her discussions of education and technology? Explain. How might her discussions be different if she were from a very different social background—for example, if she lived in a low-income urban neighborhood rather than in upscale Bellingham, Washington?

Engaging the Issues

1. Write an essay for a general audience (such as the audience for which Weiner originally wrote her essay) in which you offer a different perspective on the matter of online education. In your essay, identify problems (or potential problems) that you see with online degree programs. Explain why you are concerned about such programs. Make suggestions about how such programs ought to be managed or supervised, based on your own beliefs about the purposes of education and your experiences with technologies like those Weiner used.

   Alternatively, write an essay in support of the kind of online program that Weiner completed. In your essay, explain what you see as the benefits of such programs. Draw on Weiner's essay to help support your view, if appropriate.

2. In her essay, Weiner predicts that "cyberspace diplomas" may be common by the end of the 1990's. Using the World Wide Web and any other appropriate sources, look into programs like the one Weiner describes. Are such programs common? Has the number of online programs continued to grow since they began to appear in the early 1990's? How many "online graduates" like Weiner receive their "cyberspace diplomas" each year? If possible, interview (by email, phone, or in person) someone directly involved in online degree programs (such as an administrator at Empire State College or at a similar institution). Get that person's perspective on online degree programs. Once you've finished your research, write a report for your classmates describing what you learned about such programs. Describe the current state of such programs and examine the nature of them, citing specific examples to illustrate your points. Draw conclusions about the effectiveness of such programs and their prospects for the future.

3. In her essay, Weiner refers to the differences between online education and the conventional classroom experience. Investigate these differences. What are they? How does online education differ from conventional classroom education

in terms of student learning, student-teacher interactions, assignments, etc.? Use the library and the World Wide Web to locate some studies of online education, and draw on your own experiences as well; in addition, interview people you know who have had such experiences (or visit a listserv or newsgroup to locate such people). Write a report based on your findings. In your report, use different resources to identify what you see as the most important characteristics of online education and conventional classroom education. Draw conclusions about the advantages and disadvantages of each form of education.

4. If you have had experience with online education (either in a program like Weiner's that was exclusively online or in a conventional program that had some online components), write an essay for your classmates in which you describe that experience. What was the experience like? How did it differ from your experiences in conventional classrooms? What advantages or disadvantages to the program did you see? Like Weiner, try to draw conclusions from that experience about online education and technology in general.

5. With a group of your classmates, share the essays you wrote for Question #4 above. What similarities and differences can you identify among your various experiences with online education? Compare the conclusions you all drew from your experiences. Were members of your group generally favorable toward or skeptical about online education? Try to account for the differences and similarities in the conclusions about online education. How did your respective experiences influence your conclusions? How did your general attitudes about technology and education influence your conclusions? How might social class and cultural backgrounds have influenced your group's conclusions?

6. Visit several sites for online education programs like the one Weiner was enrolled in. Examine the kinds of programs these sites describe. What kinds of activities and experiences are available to students who enroll in such programs? Try to contact students who have enrolled in such programs to ask them about their experiences. Then construct an informational Web site about such programs for prospective students—a guide to online education. On your Web site, include descriptions of the kinds of programs you have found on the Web. Also include advice about online education.

7. Visit the Web sites of online educational programs (as described in Question #6 above). Carefully examine these sites, the services they provide, and their apparent assumptions about learning and education. Then write an essay in which you analyze these Web sites. In your essay, describe the sites you visited and the most important services and features of those sites. Examine how the sites seem to represent learning and what they seem to value most about education. For example, what kinds of images are included in the sites? How interactive are they? How are students described or addressed? Discuss what you believe are the assumptions that seem to inform the kind of education provided by these online degree programs. Draw conclusions about online education based on your analysis of these sites.

8. Investigate the economic aspects of online education. For example, is it less expensive or more expensive than conventional schooling? Is it available to students of all social classes? Or is it limited in any way to students of upper

socioeconomic status? Do schools make or lose money by offering such programs? Use the World Wide Web, your library, and any other resources to explore these and related questions. Then write a report on your findings for your classmates. In your report, try to draw conclusions about the accessibility and equality (or lack thereof) of online education.

9. On the basis of your research for Question #8 above, write a letter to an administrator of an online education service in which you express your concerns or offer your support for the kind of services provided by that administrator's online program.

The Classroom and the Wider Culture

Identity as a Key to Learning English Composition

FAN SHEN

INTRODUCTION Some scholars believe that language is the primary means by which we create our identities. On the surface, such a view seems sensible enough, since so much of what we do and who we are is shaped by our use of language. But language is not simply a way of speaking or writing: it is also intimately related to culture, which encompasses traditions, beliefs, rituals, and behaviors—all of which somehow figures into our identities as individuals and as members of particular groups. To speak or write in a particular language, then, is to *be* part of a particular culture and, therefore, to have an identity as part of that culture. But there is no one-to-one correspondence between a language and a culture. In other words, a person can speak Spanish or Japanese and "be" American; conversely, a person can speak English and not "be" American. In our deeply multicultural society, English may be the dominant language, but it surely isn't the only language. For many Americans, their identities encompass more than one language, yet they still somehow identify themselves as "American."

This complicated set of connections among language, culture, and identity can emerge starkly in schools, where cultural norms and expectations can become rules that govern teaching and learning. These rules, which are often implicit, present particularly difficult challenges for people who grow up speaking a language other than English or who grow up in a different culture and then come to live in the United States. For Fan Shen, who came to the United States after growing up in China, the central challenge was not to learn to speak English but to understand how to "be" English in order to write and read successfully in American schools. Shen found that learning to write and read in ways that teachers valued in American schools meant "unlearning" the ways he wrote and read in Chinese schools. And that process, he says, ultimately challenged his own sense of identity.

Shen's essay about the difficulties he encountered as he learned how to write and read according to expectations in an American university classroom reveals the ideological nature of American education that students raised in the United States may not see. American students accept as "normal" or perhaps commonsensical such unstated rules as "be yourself"—rules that, according to Shen, govern how students are expected to write in American schools. Such rules carry important messages about how Americans understand themselves as individuals and as members of the society in which they live. But for Shen, who was raised in a nation where *individualism* was denigrated and discouraged, rules such as "be yourself" made little sense. And in learning how to write according to such rules, what Shen really learned was how to think as an American. His story of his struggles to write as an American student is thus a story about the ideological nature of literacy education. In this sense, his essay, which was originally published in a professional journal for teachers of writing called *College Composition and Communication*, provides a picture of the complicated relationships among literacy, identity, culture, and schooling.

REFLECTING BEFORE READING

1. Fan Shen writes in this essay that the primary rule in English composition is "Be yourself." Do you agree? Does your own experience with writing in schools support Shen's contention that students must learn to "be themselves" when they write? As you read, consider how your own experiences either support or challenge Shen's views. Consider, too, whether his essay provokes you to see your own education differently, especially when it comes to writing and reading.

2. Shen's essay suggests that how we write is intimately related to how we are taught to think about ourselves within the culture in which we grow up. In a sense, his essay reveals an important aspect of how Americans think of themselves. As you read, pay particular attention to what Shen says about Americans and American schools. What specifically does he say about "being" an American? Is he right? Why or why not? Do you think American schools teach students how to "be Americans"? Explain.

One day in June 1975, when I walked into the aircraft factory where I was working as an electrician, I saw many large-letter posters on the walls and many people parading around the workshops shouting slogans like "Down with the word 'I'!" and "Trust in masses and the Party!" I then remembered that a new political campaign called "Against Individualism" was scheduled to begin that day. Ten years later, I got back my first English composition paper at the University of Nebraska-Lincoln. The professor's first comments were: "Why did you always use 'we' instead of 'I'?" and "Your paper would be stronger if you eliminated some sentences in the passive voice." The clashes between my Chinese background and the requirements of English composition had begun. At the center of this mental struggle, which has lasted several years and is still not completely over, is the prolonged, uphill battle to recapture "myself."

In this paper I will try to describe and explore this experience of reconciling my Chinese identity with an English identity dictated by the rules of English composition.

I want to show how my cultural background shaped—and shapes—my approaches to my writing in English and how writing in English redefined—and redefines—my *ideological* and *logical* identities. By "ideological identity" I mean the system of values that I acquired (consciously and unconsciously) from my social and cultural background. And by "logical identity" I mean the natural (or Oriental) way I organize and express my thoughts in writing. Both had to be modified or redefined in learning English composition. Becoming aware of the process of redefinition of these different identities is a mode of learning that has helped me in my efforts to write in English, and, I hope, will be of help to teachers of English composition in this country. In presenting my case for this view, I will use examples from both my composition courses and literature courses, for I believe that writing papers for both kinds of courses contributed to the development of my "English identity." Although what I will describe is based on personal experience, many Chinese students whom I talked to said that they had had the same or similar experiences in their initial stages of learning to write in English.

Identity of the Self: Ideological and Cultural

Starting with the first English paper I wrote, I found that learning to compose in English is not an isolated classroom activity, but a social and cultural experience. The rules of English composition encapsulate values that are absent in, or sometimes contradictory to, the values of other societies (in my case, China). Therefore, learning the rules of English composition is, to a certain extent, learning the values of Anglo-American society. In writing classes in the United States I found that I had to reprogram my mind, to redefine some of the basic concepts and values that I had about myself, about society, and about the universe, values that had been imprinted and reinforced in my mind by my cultural background, and that had been part of me all my life.

Rule number one in English composition is: Be yourself. (More than one composition instructor has told me, "Just write what *you* think.") The values behind this rule, it seems to me, are based on the principle of protecting and promoting individuality (and private property) in this country. The instruction was probably crystal clear to students raised on these values, but, as a guideline of composition, it was not very clear or useful to me when I first heard it. First of all, the image or meaning that I attached to the word "I" or "myself" was, as I found out, different from that of my English teacher. In China, "I" is always subordinated to "We"—be it the working class, the Party, the country, or some other collective body. Both political pressure and literary tradition require that "I" be somewhat hidden or buried in writings and speeches; presenting the "self" too obviously would give people the impression of being disrespectful of the Communist Party in political writings and boastful in scholarly writings. The word "I" has often been identified with another "bad" word, "individualism," which has become a synonym for selfishness in China. For a long time the words "self" and "individualism" have had negative connotations in my mind, and the negative force of the words that naturally extended to the field of literary studies. As a result, even if I had brilliant ideas, the "I" in my papers always had to show some modesty by not competing with or trying to stand above the names of ancient and modern authoritative figures. Appealing to Mao or other Marxist authorities became the required way (as well as the most "forceful" or "persuasive" way) to prove one's point in written discourse. I remember that in China I had even committed what I can call "reversed plagiarism"—here, I suppose it would be called "forgery"—when I was in middle school: willfully attributing some of my thoughts to "experts" when I needed some arguments but could not find a suitable quotation from a literary or politial "giant."

Now, in America, I had to learn to accept the words "I" and "Self" as something glorious (as Whitman did), or at least something not to be ashamed of or embarrassed about. It was the first and probably biggest step I took into English composition and critical writing. Acting upon my professor's suggestion, I intentionally tried to show my "individuality" and to "glorify" "I" in my papers by using as many "I's" as possible—"I think," "I believe," "I see"—and deliberately cut out quotations from authorities. It was rather painful to hand in such "pompous" (I mean immodest) papers to my instructors. But to an extent it worked. After a while I became more comfortable with only "the shadow of myself." I felt more at ease to put down *my* thoughts without looking over my shoulder to worry about the attitudes of my teachers or the reactions of the Party secretaries, and to speak out as "bluntly" and "immodestly" as my American instructors demanded.

But writing many "I's" was only the beginning of the process of redefining myself. Speaking of redefining myself is, in an important sense, speaking of redefining the word "I." By such a redefinition I mean not only the change in how I envisioned myself, but also the change in how I perceived the world. The old "I" used to embody only one set of values, but now it had to embody multiple sets of values. To be truly "myself," which I knew was a key to my success in learning English composition, meant *not to be my Chinese self* at all. That is to say, when I write in English I have to wrestle with and abandon (at least temporarily) the whole system of ideology which previously defined me in myself. I had to forget Marxist doctrines (even though I do not see myself as a Marxist by choice) and the Party lines imprinted in my mind and familiarize myself with a system of capitalist/bourgeois values. I had to put aside an ideology of collectivism and adopt the values of individualism. In composition as well as in literature classes, I had to make a fundamental adjustment: if I used to examine society and literary materials through the microscopes of Marxist dialectical materialism and historical materialism, I now had to learn to look through the microscopes the other way around, i.e., to learn to look at and understand the world from the point of view of "idealism." (I must add here that there are American professors who use a Marxist approach in their teaching.)

The word "idealism," which affects my view of both myself and the universe, is loaded with social connotations, and can serve as a good example of how redefining a key word can be a pivotal part of redefining my ideological identity as a whole.

To me, idealism is the philosophical foundation of the dictum of English composition: "Be yourself." In order to write good English, I knew that I had to be myself, which actually meant not to be my Chinese self. It meant that I had to create an English self and be *that* self. And to be that English self, I felt, I had to understand and accept idealism the way a Westerner does. That is to say, I had to accept the way a Westerner sees himself in relation to the universe and society. On the one hand, I knew a lot about idealism. But on the other hand, I knew nothing about it. I mean I knew a lot about idealism through the propaganda and objections of its opponent, Marxism, but I knew little about it from its own point of view. When I thought of the word "materialism"—which is a major part of Marxism and in China has reputedly been "shown" to be the absolute truth—there were always positive connotations, and words like "right," "true," etc., flashed in my mind. On the other hand, the word "idealism" always came to me with the dark connotations that surround words like "absurd," "illogical," "wrong," etc. In China "idealism" is depicted as a ferocious and ridiculous enemy of Marxist philosophy. Idealism, as the simplified definition imprinted in my mind had it, is the view that the material world does not exist; that all that exists is the mind and its ideas. It is just the opposite of Marxist dialectical materialism which sees the mind as a product of the material world. It is not too difficult to see that idealism, with its idea that mind is of primary importance, provides a philosophical foundation for the Western emphasis on the value of individual human minds, and hence individual human beings. Therefore, my final acceptance of myself as of primary importance—an importance that overshadowed that of authority figures in English composition—was, I decided, dependent on an acceptance of idealism.

My struggle with idealism came mainly from my efforts to understand and to write about works such as Coleridge's *Literaria Biographia* and Emerson's "Over-Soul." For a long time I was frustrated and puzzled by the idealism expressed by Coleridge and Emerson—given their ideas, such as "I think, therefore I am" (Coleridge obviously borrowed from Descartes) and "the transparent eyeball" (Emerson's view of himself)—because in my mind, drenched as it was in dialectical materialism, there was always a little voice whispering in my ear "You are, therefore you think." I could not see how human consciousness, which is not material, could create apples and trees. My intellectual conscience refused to let me believe that the human mind is the primary world and the material world secondary. Finally, I had to imagine that I was looking at a world with my head upside down. When I imagined that I was in a new body (born with the head upside down) it was easier to forget biases imprinted in my subconsciousness about idealism, the mind, and my former self. Starting from scratch, the new inverted self—which I called my "English Self" and into which I have transformed myself—could understand and *accept,* with ease, idealism as "the truth" and "himself" (i.e., my English Self) as the "creator" of the world.

Here is how I created my new "English Self." I played a "game" similar to ones played by mental therapists. First I made a list of (simplified) features about writing associated with my old identity (the Chinese Self), both ideological and logical, and then beside the first list I added a column of features about writing associated with my new identity (the English Self). After that I pictured myself getting out of my old identity, the timid, humble, modest Chinese "I," and creeping into my new identity (often in the form of a new skin or a mask), the confident, assertive, and aggressive English "I." The new "Self" helped me to remember and accept the different rules of Chinese and English composition and the values that underpin these rules. In a sense, creating an English Self is a way of reconciling my old cultural values with the new values required by English writing, without losing the former.

An interesting structural but not material parallel to my experiences in this regard has been well described by Min-zhan Lu in her important article, "From Silence to Words: Writing as Struggle" (*College English* 49 [April 1987]: 437–48). Min-zhan Lu talks about struggles between two selves, an open self and a secret self, and between two discourses, a mainstream Marxist discourse and a bourgeois discourse her parents wanted her to learn. But her struggle was different from mine. Her Chinese self was severely constrained and suppressed by mainstream cultural discourse, but never interfused with it. Her experiences, then, were not representative of those of the majority of the younger generation who, like me, were brought up on only one discourse. I came to English composition as a Chinese person, in the fullest sense of the term, with a Chinese identity already fully formed.

Identity of the Mind: Illogical and Alogical

In learning to write in English, besides wrestling with a different ideological system, I found that I had to wrestle with a logical system very different from the blueprint of logic at the back of my mind. By "logical system" I mean two things: the Chinese way of thinking I used to approach my theme or topic in written discourse, and the Chinese critical/logical way to develop a theme or topic. By English rules, the first is illogical, for it is the opposite of the English way of approaching a topic; the second is alogical (non-logical), for it mainly uses mental pictures instead of words as a critical vehicle.

The Illogical Pattern

In English composition, an essential rule for the logical organization of a piece of writing is the use of a "topic sentence." In Chinese composition, "from surface to core" is an essential rule, a rule which means that one ought to reach a topic gradually and "systematically" instead of "abruptly."

The concept of a topic sentence, it seems to me, is symbolic of the values of a busy people in an industrialized society, rushing to get things done, hoping to attract and satisfy the busy reader very quickly. Thinking back, I realized that I did not fully understand the virtue of the concept until my life began to rush at the speed of everyone else's in this country. Chinese composition, on the other hand, seems to embody the values of a leisurely paced rural society whose inhabitants have the time to chew and taste a topic slowly. In Chinese composition, an introduction explaining how and why one chooses this topic is not only acceptable, but often regarded as necessary. It arouses the reader's interest in the topic little by little (and this is seen as a virtue of composition) and gives him/her a sense of refinement. The famous Robert B. Kaplan "noodles" contrasting a spiral Oriental thought process with a straight-line Western approach ("Cultural Thought Patterns in Inter-Cultural Education," *Readings on English as a Second Language,* Ed. Kenneth Croft, 2nd ed., Winthrop, 1980, 403–10) may be too simplistic to capture the preferred pattern of writing in English, but I think they still express some truth about Oriental writing. A Chinese writer often clears the surrounding bushes before attacking the real target. This bush-clearing pattern in Chinese writing goes back two thousand years to Kong Fuzi (Confucius). Before doing anything, Kong says in his *Luen Yu (Analects),* one first needs to call things by their proper names (expressed by his phrase "Zheng Ming" 正名. In other words, before touching one's main thesis, one should first state the "conditions" of composition: how, why, and when the piece is being composed. All of this will serve as a proper foundation on which to build the "house" of the piece. In the two thousand years after Kong, this principle of composition was gradually formalized (especially through the formal essays required by imperial examinations) and became known as "Ba Gu," or the eight-legged essay. The logic of Chinese composition, exemplified by the eight-legged essay, is like the peeling of an onion: layer after layer is removed until the reader finally arrives at the central point, the core.

Ba Gu still influences modern Chinese writing. Carolyn Matalene has an excellent discussion of this logical (or illogical) structure and its influence on her Chinese students' efforts to write in English ("Contrastive Rhetoric: An American Writing Teacher in China," *College English* 47 [November 1985]: 789–808). A recent Chinese textbook for composition lists six essential steps (factors) for writing a narrative essay, steps to be taken in this order: time, place, character, event, cause, and consequence *(Yuwen Jichu Zhishi Liushi Jiang [Sixty Lessons on the Basics of the Chinese Language],* Ed. Beijing Research Institute of Education, Beijing Publishing House, 1981, 525–609). Most Chinese students (including me) are taught to follow this sequence in composition.

The straightforward approach to composition in English seemed to me, at first, illogical. One could not jump to the topic. One had to walk step by step to reach the topic. In several of my early papers I found that the Chinese approach—the bush-clearing approach—persisted, and I had considerable difficulty writing (and in fact understanding) topic sentences. In what I deemed to be topic sentences, I grudgingly gave out themes. Today, those papers look to me like Chinese papers with forced or false English openings. For example, in a narrative paper on a trip to New York, I wrote the forced/false topic sentence, "A trip to New York in winter is boring." In the next few paragraphs, I talked about the weather, the people who went with me, and so on, before I talked about what I learned from the trip. My real thesis was that one could always learn something even on a boring trip.

The Alogical Pattern

In learning English composition, I found that there was yet another cultural blueprint affecting my logical thinking. I found from my early papers that very often I was unconsciously under the influence of a Chinese critical approach called the creation of "yijing," which is totally nonWestern. The direct translation of the word "yijing" is: yi, "mind or consciousness," and jing, "environment." An ancient approach which has existed in China for many centuries and is still the subject of much discussion, yijing is a complicated concept that defies a universal definition. But most critics in China nowadays seem to agree on one point, that yijing is the critical approach that separates Chinese literature and criticism from Western literature and criticism. Roughly speaking, yijing is the process of creating a pictorial environment while reading a piece of literature. Many critics in China believe that yijing is a creative process of inducing oneself, while reading a piece of literature or looking at a piece of art, to create mental pictures, in order to reach a unity of nature, the author, and the reader. Therefore, it is by its very nature both creative and critical. According to the theory, this nonverbal, pictorial process leads directly to a higher ground of beauty and morality. Almost all critics in China agree that yijing is not a process of logical thinking—it is not a process of moving from the premises of an argument to its conclusion, which is the foundation of Western criticism. According to yijing, the process of criticizing a piece of art or literary work has to involve the process of creation on the reader's part. In yijing, verbal thoughts and pictorial thoughts are one. Thinking is conducted largely in pictures and then "transcribed" into words. (Ezra Pound once tried to capture the creative aspect of yijing in poems such as "In a Station of the Metro." He also tried to capture the critical aspect of it in his theory of imagism and vorticism, even though he did not now the term "yijing.") One characteristic of the yijing approach to criticism, therefore, is that it often includes a description of the created mental pictures on the part of the reader/critic and his/her mental attempt to bridge (unite) the literary work, the pictures, with ultimate beauty and peace.

In looking back at my critical papers for various classes, I discovered that I unconsciously used the approach of yijing, especially in some of my earlier papers when I seemed not yet to have been in the grip of Western logical critical approaches. I wrote, for instance, an essay entitled "Wordsworth's Sound and Imagination: The Snowdon Episode." In the major part of the essay I described the pictures that flashed in my mind while I was reading passages in Wordsworth's long poem, *The Prelude.*

> I saw three climbers (myself among them) winding up the mountain in silence "at the dead of night," absorbed in their "private thoughts." The sky was full of blocks of clouds of different colors, freely changing their shapes, like oily pigments disturbed in a bucket of water. All of a sudden, the moonlight broke the darkness "like a flash lighting up the mountain tops." Under the "naked moon," the band saw a vast sea of mist and vaper, a silent ocean. Then the silence was abruptly broken, and we heard the "roaring of waters, torrents, streams/Innumerable, roaring with one voice" from a "blue chasm," a fracture in the vapor of the sea. It was a joyful revelation of divine truth to the human mind: the bright, "naked" moon sheds the light of "higher reasons" and "spiritual love" upon us; the vast ocean of mist looked like a thin curtain through which we vaguely saw the infinity of nature beyond; and the sounds of roaring waters coming out of the chasm of vapor cast us into the boundless spring of imagination from the depth of the human heart. Evoked by the divine light from above, the human spring of imagination is joined by the natural spring and becomes a sustaining source of energy, feeding "upon infinity" while transcending infinity at the same time. . . .

Here I was describing my own experience more than Wordsworth's. The picture described by the poet is taken over and developed by the reader. The imagination of the author and the imagination of the reader are thus joined together. There was no "because" or "therefore" in the paper. There was little *logic.* And I thought it was (and it is) criticism. This seems to me a typical (but simplified) example of the yijing approach. (Incidentally, the instructor, a kind professor, found the paper interesting, though a bit "strange.")

In another paper of mine, "The Note of Life: Williams's 'The Orchestra',," I found myself describing my experiences of pictures of nature while reading William Carlos Williams's poem "The Orchestra," I "painted" these fleeting pictures and described the feelings that seemed to lead me to an understanding of a harmony, a "common tone," between man and nature. A paragraph from that paper reads:

> The poem first struck me as a musical fairy tale. With rich musical sounds in my ear, I seemed to be walking in a solitary, dense forest on a spring morning. No sound from human society could be heard. I was now sitting under a giant pine tree, ready to hear the grand concert of Nature. With the sun slowly rising from the east, the cello (the creeping creek) and the clarinet (the rustling pine trees) started with a slow overture. Enthusiastically the violinists (the twittering birds) and the French horn (the mumbling cow) "interpose[d] their voices," and the bass (bears) got in at the wrong

time. The orchestra did not stop, they continued to play. The musicians of Nature do not always play in harmony. "Together, unattuned," they have to seek "a common tone" as they play along. The symphony of Nature is like the symphony of human life: both consist of random notes seeking a "common tone." For the symphony of life

> Love is that common tone
>   shall raise his fiery head
>   and sound his note.

Again, the logical pattern of this paper, the "pictorial criticism," is illogical to Western minds but "logical" to those acquainted with yijing. (Perhaps I should not even use the words "logical" and "think" because they are so conceptually tied up with "words" and with culturally-based conceptions, and therefore very misleading if not useless in a discussion of yijing. Maybe I should simply say that yijing is neither illogical nor logical, but alogical.)

I am not saying that such a pattern of "alogical" thinking is wrong—in fact some English instructors find it interesting and acceptable—but it is very non-Western. Since I was in this country to learn the English language and English literature, I had to abandon Chinese "pictorial logic," and to learn Western "verbal logic."

If I Had to Start Again

The change is profound: through my understanding of new meanings of words like "individualism," "idealism," and "I," I began to accept the underlying concepts and values of American writing, and by learning to use "topic sentences" I began to accept a new logic. Thus, when I write papers in English, I am able to obey all the general rules of English composition. In doing this I feel that I am writing through, with, and because of a new identity. I welcome the change, for it has added a new dimension to me and to my view of the world. I am not saying that I have entirely lost my Chinese identity. In fact I feel that I will never lose it. Any time I write in Chinese, I resume my old identity, and obey the rules of Chinese composition such as "Make the 'I' modest," and "Beat around the bush before attacking the central topic." It is necessary for me to have such a Chinese identity in order to write authentic Chinese. (I have seen people who, after learning to write in English, use English logic and sentence patterning to write Chinese. They produce very awkward Chinese texts.) But when I write in English, I imagine myself slipping into a new "skin," and I let the "I" behave much more aggressively and knock the topic right on the head. Being conscious of these different identities has helped me to reconcile different systems of values and logic, and has played a pivotal role in my learning to compose in English.

Looking back, I realize that the process of learning to write in English is in fact a process of creating and defining a new identity and balancing it with the old identity. The process of learning English composition would have been easier if I had realized this earlier and consciously sought to compare the two different identities required by the two writing systems from two different cultures. It is fine and perhaps even necessary for American composition teachers to teach about topic sentences, paragraphs, the use of punctuation, documentation, and so on, but can anyone design exercises sensitive to the ideological and logical differences that students like me experience—and design them so they can be introduced at an early stage of an English composition class? As I pointed out earlier, the traditional advice "Just be yourself" is not clear and helpful to students from Korea, China, Vietnam, or India. From "Be yourself" we are likely to hear either "Forget your cultural habit of writing" or "Write as you would write in your own language." But neither of the two is what the instructor meant or what we want to do. It would be helpful if he or she pointed out the different cultural/ideological connotations of the word "I," the connotations that exist in a group-centered culture and an individual-centered culture. To sharpen the contrast, it might be useful to design papers on topics like "The Individual vs. The Group: China vs. America" or "Different 'I's' in Different Cultures."

Carolyn Matalene mentioned in her article (789) an incident concerning American businessmen who presented their Chinese hosts with gifts of cheddar cheese, not knowing that the Chinese generally do not like cheese. Liking cheddar cheese may not be essential to writing English prose, but being truly accustomed to the social norms that stand behind ideas such as the English "I" and the logical pattern of English composition—call it "compositional cheddar cheese"—is essential to writing in English. Matalene does not provide an "elixir" to help her Chinese students like English "compositional cheese," but rather recommends, as do I, that composition teachers not be afraid to give foreign students English "cheese," but to make sure to hand it out slowly, sympathetically, and fully realizing that it tastes very peculiar in the mouths of those used to a very different cuisine.

REFLECTING ON THE READING

1. What is the "mental struggle" that Shen refers to in the beginning of this essay? How does he introduce this struggle?

2. What is the difference between Shen's "logical" identity and his "ideological" identity? Why is this distinction important?

3. Why was it so difficult for Shen to follow the rule to "be yourself" in his composition classes? Why does he believe this rule was so important? Do you agree with him? Have you had to "be yourself" in your own writing in school? Explain.

4. What does Shen mean by "idealism" and "materialism"? Why were these ideas so important for him as he learned to write in his composition classes?

5. How did Shen create his new "English Self"? Why was it so difficult for him to create such a self? Do you think it was necessary? Why or why not?

6. What are the two patterns of writing and thinking that Shen says he learned in China? Why does he describe these two patterns? What do they tell us about his experience in coming from China to the United States? What do they suggest about the relationship between how we learn to write and our cultural background?

7. What lessons does Shen draw from his experience? Does he suggest changes in the way American students are taught to write? Explain. Do you think he has any regrets about his experiences? Does he express a sense of loss about coming to the United States? What impression does he leave at the conclusion of his essay?

Examining Rhetorical Strategies

1. How would you characterize Shen's voice in this essay? Identify specific features of this essay that you think contribute to his voice. Did you find him credible in this essay? Were you sympathetic to him as you read? How might your own racial or ethnic background have influenced the way you responded to Shen in this essay? Explain.

2. Shen wrote this essay for an American professional journal that is read by scholars and teachers of writing. Identify features of his essay that you think indicate that it was written for a scholarly journal. In what ways do you think he addressed an audience of teachers and scholars? Do you think his essay is suitable for readers who might not be teachers of writing? Explain, citing specific passages in his essay to support your answer.

3. In this essay, Shen describes his experiences under the Marxist education system in China and under the American education system. How does he describe each system and his experiences in each? What purpose do his descriptions of each system serve in his essay? Do you think he intends to condemn one system and praise the other? Explain, citing specific passages from the essay to support your answer.

4. As the United States becomes increasingly diverse and its schools enroll more students from other cultures, it is likely that many more students will have the same kinds of difficulties that Shen describes. At the end of his essay, Shen suggests that American teachers should be more sensitive to these difficulties that students from Asian countries might have in their English classes. But he does not propose that American teachers change the way they teach writing, despite the difficulties he experienced. Why not? Do you think his ending is more or less effective without a call for specific changes that address the kind of difficulties he experienced as a student in an American university? Explain. What do you think his ending suggests about Shen's views regarding culture and education? Do you think he believes that all immigrants should adapt to the ways of American culture? Do you agree with him? Explain.

5. Notice how Shen structures his essay. What major sections does he organize his essay into? What is the focus of each of those sections? What purpose might be served in organizing the essay in this way? Does the essay's structure relate in any way to the conventions of professional academic writing, such as is published in the journal where Shen's essay originally appeared? Explain. How might the essay be structured differently if it appeared in a publication with a more general audience, such as the *New York Times* or *Time* magazine?

Engaging the Issues

1. Write an essay in which you describe how your own experiences with writing and reading in school might have helped you learn how to "be American."

   Alternatively, write an essay in which you describe experiences you had attending school in another country. In your essay, focus on how attending school in that country might have challenged your sense of yourself as an American or encouraged you to become more like a member of that other culture.

2. Shen's essay raises some complicated questions about culture and schooling. His essay describes how he was able to learn to "be English" after coming to the United States—to be assimilated into the mainstream American culture. Some critics might complain that Shen is too quick to place the burden on the new-comer; in other words, they might argue that American culture is a product of immigrants just like Shen and, therefore, changes as new immigrants arrive with their own cultural backgrounds and languages and traditions. Others argue that immigrants come here precisely because American culture is the way it is and, therefore, they should adapt themselves to it—that American schools and institutions should not change in order to accommodate each new culture but that immigrants must become part of the mainstream culture. Education is a cen-tral part of this ongoing debate in American society, since schools are, as Shen suggests in this essay, places where students learn how to "be Americans."

   In a group of your classmates, discuss these questions, using Shen's essay as a starting point. Do you agree with his recommendations at the end of his essay? Why or why not? Try to account for the views of each member of your group. Then consider what your viewpoints might say about the role of educa-tion—and especially English education—in American culture.

3. Based on your discussions for Question #2, write an essay in which you offer your own views about how American schools should address the challenges of a culturally diverse student population.

4. Compare Shen's views about writing and schooling to the views expressed by one or more other writers in this chapter (for example, Rondinone, Hirsch, or Freire). In your essay, explain how each writer understands the role of literacy in education and the relationship between individual identity and the purpose of education. Discuss similarities and differences among their views. Try to draw conclusions about literacy education and its relationship to culture and identity.

5. With a group of your classmates, create a pamphlet or brochure intended to help students from other countries or cultures learn how to "survive" English courses in America. As you construct your pamphlet, you might conduct some research about students from other cultures or students who speak languages other than English to see what challenges they face in American schools. You might also find other accounts like Shen's to help you compile advice for your pamphlet.

6. At one point in his essay, Shen refers directly to an essay by Min-zhan Lu, "From Silence to Words: Writing as Struggle," which appears in Chapter 6 of this

reader. Shen asserts that Lu's struggle is different from his and not representative of the majority of Chinese students who come to the United States. Write a conventional academic essay in which you discuss these two essays, addressing Shen's assertion that his struggle differs from Lu's. Do you think he is right? Why or why not? What similarities do you see in their respective experiences? What differences? What might their respective experiences enable you to say about the relationship between literacy and cultural identity?

7. Find someone who came from another country to attend school in the United States, and interview that person about his or her experiences with writing and reading in American schools—and with American education in general. Ask this person about similarities and differences between American schools and schools in his or her native country. Try to get a sense of the specific challenges that person has had with writing and reading in school or with other aspects of American education—such as the hidden "rules" to which Shen refers in his essay. Then write a report about your interview for an audience of your classmates. In your report, describe the person you interviewed and his or her cultural background. Discuss differences between education in the United States and education in his or her home country, especially regarding literacy instruction. On the basis of your interview, try to draw conclusions about the relationship between schooling and culture .

Cultural Literacy

E. D. HIRSCH

INTRODUCTION   What is the relationship between knowledge and literacy? Or, to put it another way, what do you need to know in order to read and write effectively? According to scholar E. D. Hirsch, Jr., this question of the relationship between literacy and knowledge is a crucial one, because how that relationship is understood ultimately determines how a school's curriculum is structured. Hirsch believes that contemporary education is based on a problematic understanding of the relationship between literacy and knowledge. And he has devoted much of his career as an educator to addressing that problem.

If you are like most students who attend American schools, you almost certainly have taken classes in reading and "language arts," especially in elementary and middle school. In most schools, those classes are distinct from "content area" classes such as math, science, and social studies. In reading and language arts classes, students do not learn content the way they learn content in those other classes; instead, they practice the reading and writing skills needed to understand words on a page. E. D. Hirsch believes that this way of organizing the school curriculum reflects the central problem in American education: a separation between literacy and content knowledge. In fact, Hirsch believes that schools generally devalue the importance of specific kinds of knowledge about the world and about American culture in favor of teaching literacy and thinking *skills*. And that, he says, is at the heart of what he believes is a literacy crisis and a general crisis in American education.

Hirsch's solution to this crisis is to structure the school curriculum around a body of general and cultural knowledge that he believes all students must have not only to develop into effective readers and writers but also to become active, engaged citizens in American society. The school reform organization that Hirsch founded to help achieve these goals, the Core Knowledge Foundation, has constructed its own model curriculum on the belief that "literacy depends on shared knowledge. To be literate means, in part, to be familiar with a broad range of knowledge taken for granted by speakers and writers." What is included in that "broad range of knowledge" is described in detail in Hirsch's book *Cultural Literacy: What Every American Needs to Know* (1987). Hirsch's list of essential knowledge encompasses information and ideas about American history, government, and politics; popular culture (including television shows, movies, and music); science and technology; and so on—all of it knowledge that Hirsch considers necessary for Americans to understand and participate in society. This "cultural literacy" approach to education, he believes, produces students who are effective readers and writers and informed citizens.

When it was first published, *Cultural Literacy* quickly became a bestseller and seemed to strike a chord with Americans concerned about the problems in their schools. But Hirsch's argument about how to reform education also provoked a strong, angry reaction from critics who saw his proposals as a challenge to diversity and a way to exclude nonmainstream cultures and communities from American schools. Such critics raised difficult questions about Hirsch's proposals: Who determines what counts as important "shared knowledge"? Doesn't such a curriculum teach students to be passive learners rather than active thinkers? Isn't such a curriculum really just the traditional approach in disguise? Would this approach exclude other kinds of literacies that are practiced in nonmainstream cultures? There are no easy answers to such questions, and Hirsch openly acknowledges in the following essay that literacy is "a political decision." The vigorous reactions—positive as well as negative—to his ideas about literacy and education seem to reinforce that point.

E. D. Hirsch, Jr., is Linden Kent Memorial Professor of English at the University of Virginia, where he has taught since 1966. In addition to *Cultural Literacy*, he has written a number of other books including *The Schools We Need and Why We Don't Have Them* (1996), *The Philosophy of Composition* (1977), *The Aims of Interpretation* (1976), and several volumes in the "core knowledge" series for students in kindergarten through sixth grade. For his scholarly work and his educational reform efforts he has received many awards including the Biennial QuEST Award for Outstanding Contribution to Education from the American Federation of Teachers (1997) and fellowships from the Guggenheim and Fulbright foundations. The following article, which originally appeared in 1983 in *The American Scholar*, a journal of the Phi Beta Kappa organization, is an early statement of the beliefs that Hirsch eventually developed into his book *Cultural Literacy*.

REFLECTING BEFORE READING

1. Hirsch bases the arguments he makes about literacy and education in the following essay in part on problems he sees with a specific theory of education

and on his own highly technical educational research. Some or all of the theories and principles he discusses may be unfamiliar to readers who are not educators or researchers. As you read, be aware of the specific theories and principles that Hirsch discusses as he makes his argument. How much do you know about these theories and principles? Do you understand his discussions even if you are unfamiliar with the theories he refers to? In what ways might your own familiarity—or lack of familiarity—influence your reaction to his arguments?

2. Hirsch's ideas have been influential as well as controversial in the ongoing public discussions about school reform. As you read, consider how his ideas challenge or reinforce what you believe about education in American society. Why do you think Hirsch has been so controversial? What is it about his ideas that have generated such a strong reaction? What might that strong reaction indicate about American attitudes toward education? Do you find yourself agreeing or disagreeing with him? Why?

F or the past twelve years I have been pursuing technical research in the teaching of reading and writing. I now wish to emerge from my closet to declare that technical research is not going to remedy the national decline in our literacy that is documented in the decline of verbal SAT scores. We already know enough about methodology to do a good job of teaching reading and writing. Of course we would profit from knowing still more about teaching methods, but better teaching techniques alone would produce only a marginal improvement in the literacy of our students. Raising their reading and writing levels will depend far less on our methods of instruction (there are many acceptable methods) than on the specific contents of our school curricula. Commonsensical as this proposition might seem to the man in the street, it is regarded as heresy by many (I hope by ever fewer) professional educators. The received and dominant view of educational specialists is that the specific materials of reading and writing instruction are interchangeable so long as they are "appropriate," and of "high quality."

But consider this historical fact. The national decline in our literacy has accompanied a decline in our use of common, nationwide materials in the subject most closely connected with literacy, "English." From the 1890s to 1900 we taught in English courses what amounted to a national core curriculum. As Arthur Applebee observes in his excellent book *Tradition and Reform in the Teaching of English*, the following texts were used in those days in more than 25 percent of our schools: *The Merchant of Venice, Julius Caesar,* "First Bunker Hill Oration," *The Sketch Book, Evangeline,* "The Vision of Sir Launfal," "Snow-Bound," *Macbeth,* "The Lady of the Lake," *Hamlet,* "The Deserted Village," Gray's "Elegy," "Thanatopsis," *As You Like It.* Other widely used works will strike a resonance in those who are over fifty: "The Courtship of Miles Standish," "Il Penseroso," *Paradise Lost,* "L'Allegro," "Lycidas," *Ivanhoe, David Copperfield, Silas Marner,* etc., etc. Then in 1901 the College Entrance Examination Board issued its first "uniform lists" of texts required to be known by students in applying to colleges. This core curriculum, though narrower, became even more widespread than the earlier canon. Lest anyone assume that I shall urge a return to those particular texts, let me at once deny it. By way of introducing my subject, I simply want to claim that the decline in our literacy and the decline in the commonly shared knowledge that we acquire in school are causally related facts. Why this should be so and what we might do about it are my twin subjects.

That a decline in our national level of literacy has occurred few will seriously doubt. The chief and decisive piece of evidence for it is the decline in verbal SAT scores among the white middle class. (This takes into account the still greater lowering of scores caused by an increased proportion of poor and minority students taking the tests.) Now scores on the verbal SAT show a high correlation with reading and writing skills that have been tested independently by other means. So, as a rough index to the literacy levels of our students, the verbal SAT is a reliable guide. That is unsurprising if we accept the point made by John Carroll and others that the verbal SAT is chiefly a vocabulary test, for no one is surprised by a correlation between a rich vocabulary and a high level of literacy. A rich vocabulary is not a purely technical or rote-learnable skill. Knowledge of words is an adjunct to knowledge of cultural realities signified by words, and to whole domains of experience to which words refer. Specific words go with specific knowledge. And when we begin to contemplate how to teach specific knowledge, we are led back inexorably to the contents of the school curriculum, whether or not those contents are linked, as they used to be, to specific texts.

From the start of our national life, the school curriculum has been an especially important formative element of our national culture. In the schools we not only tried to harmonize the various traditions of our parent cultures, we also wanted to strike out on our own within the dominant British heritage. Being rebellious children, we produced our own dictionary, and were destined, according to Melville, to produce our own Shakespeare. In this self-conscious job of culture making, the schools played a necessary role. That was especially true in the teaching of history and English, the two subjects central to culture making. In the nineteenth century we held national conferences on school curricula. We formed the College Board, which created the "uniform lists" already referred to. The dominant symbol for the role of the school was the symbol of the melting pot.

But from early times we have also resisted this narrow uniformity in our culture. The symbol of the melting pot was opposed by the symbol of the stew pot, where our national ingredients kept their individual characteristics and contributed to the flavor and vitality of the whole. That is the doctrine of pluralism. It has now become the dominant doctrine in our schools, especially in those subjects, English and history, that are closest to culture making. In math and science, by contrast, there is wide agreement about the contents of a common curriculum. But in English courses, diversity and pluralism now reign without challenge. I am persuaded that if we want to achieve a more literate culture than we now have, we shall need to restore the balance between these two equally American traditions of unity and diversity. We shall need to restore certain common contents to the humanistic side of the school curriculum. But before we can make much headway in that direction, we shall also need to modify the now-dominant educational principle that holds that any suitable materials of instruction can be used to teach the skills of reading and writing. I call this the doctrine of educational formalism.

The current curriculum guide to the study of English in the state of California is a remarkable document. In its several pages of advice to teachers I do not find the title of a single recommended work. Such "curricular guides" are produced on the theory that the actual contents of English courses are simply vehicles for inculcating formal skills, and that contents can be left to local choice. But wouldn't even a dyed-in-the-wool formalist concede that teachers might be saved time if some merely illustrative, non-compulsory titles were listed? Of course; but another doctrine, in alliance with formalism, conspires against even that concession to content—the doctrine of pluralism. An illustrative list put out by the state would imply official sanction of the cultural and ideological values expressed by the works on the list. The California Education Department is not in the business of imposing cultures and ideologies. Its business is to inculcate "skills" and "positive self-concepts," regardless of the students' cultural backgrounds. The contents of English should be left to local communities.

This is an attractive theory to educators in those places where spokesmen for minority cultures are especially vocal in their attack on the melting-pot idea. That concept, they say, is nothing but cultural imperialism (true), which submerges cultural identities (true) and gives minority children a sense of inferiority (often true). In recent years such attitudes have led to attacks on teaching school courses exclusively in standard English; in the bilingual movement (really a monolingual movement) it has led to attacks on an exclusive use of the English language for instruction. This kind of political pressure has encouraged a retreat to the extreme and untenable educational formalism reflected in the California curriculum guide.

What the current controversies have really demonstrated is a truth that is quite contrary to the spirit of neutrality implied by educational formalism. Literacy is not just a formal skill; it is also a political decision. The decision to *want* a literate society is a value-laden one that carries costs as well as advantages. English teachers by profession are committed to the ideology of literacy. They cannot successfully avoid the political implications of that ideology by hiding behind the skirts of methodology and research. Literacy implies specific contents as well as formal skills. Extreme formalism is misleading and evasive. But allow me to illustrate that point with some specific examples.

During most of the time that I was pursuing research in literacy I was, like others in the field, a confirmed formalist. In 1977 I came out with a book on the subject, *The Philosophy of Composition,* that was entirely formalistic in outlook. One of my arguments, for instance, was that the effectiveness of English prose as an instrument of communication gradually increased, after the invention of printing, through a trial-and-error process that slowly uncovered some of the psycholinguistic principles of efficient communication in prose. I suggested that freshmen could learn in a semester what earlier writers had taken centuries to achieve, if they were directly taught those underlying psycholinguistic principles. (With respect to certain formal structures of clauses, this idea still seems valid.) I predicted further that we could learn how to teach those formal principles still more effectively if we pursued appropriately controlled pedagogical research.

So intent was I upon this idea that I undertook some arduous research into one of the most important aspects of writing pedagogy—evaluation. After all, in order to decide upon the best methods of inculcating the skills of writing, it was essential to evaluate the results of using the different teaching methods. For that we needed non-arbitrary, reliable techniques for evaluating student writing. In my book I had made some suggestions about how we might do this, and those ideas seemed cogent enough to a National Endowment for the Humanities panel to get me a grant to go forward with the research. For about two years I was deeply engaged in this work. It was this detailed engagement with the realities of reading and writing under controlled conditions that caused me finally to abandon my formalistic assumptions. (Later I discovered that experimentation on a much bigger scale had brought Richard C. Anderson, the premier scholar in reading research, to similar conclusions.)

The experiments that changed my mind were, briefly, these: To get a non-arbitrary evaluation of writing, we decided to base our evaluations on actual audience effects. We devised a way of comparing the effects of well-written and badly written versions of the same paper. Our method was to pair off two large groups of readers (about a hundred in each group), each of which, when given the *same* piece of writing, would read it collectively with the same speed and comprehension. In other words, we matched the reading skills of these two large groups. Then, when one group was given a good version and the other given a degraded version, we measured the overall effect of these stylistic differences on speed and accuracy of comprehension. To our delight, we discovered that good style did make an appreciable difference, and that the degree of difference was replicable and predictable. So far so good. But what became very disconcerting about these results was that they came out properly only when the subjects of the papers were highly familiar to our audiences. When, later in the experiments, we introduced unfamiliar materials, the results were not only messy, they were "counterintuitive," the term of art for results that go against one's expectations. (Real scientists generally like to get counterintuitive results, but we were not altogether disinterested onlookers and were dismayed.) For what we discovered was that good writing makes very little difference when the subject is unfamiliar. We English teachers tend to believe that a good style is all the more helpful when the content is difficult, but it turns out that we are wrong. The reasons for this unexpected result are complex, and I will not pause to discuss them at length, since the important issues lie elsewhere.

Briefly, good style contributes little to our reading of unfamiliar material because we must continually backtrack to test out different hypotheses about what is being meant or referred to. Thus, a reader of a text about Grant and Lee who is unsure just who Grant and Lee are would have to get clues from later parts of the text, and then go back to re-read earlier parts in the light of surer conjectures. This trial-and-error backtracking with unfamiliar material is so much more time-consuming than the delays caused by a bad style alone that style begins to lose its importance as a factor in reading unfamiliar material. The contribution of style in such cases can no longer be measured with statistical confidence.

The significance of this result is, first of all, that one cannot, even in principle, base writing evaluations on audience effects—the only non-arbitrary principle that makes any sense. The reading skill of an audience is not a constant against which prose can be reliably measured. Audience reading skills vary unpredictably with the subject matter of the text. Although we were trying to measure our prose samples with the yardstick of paired audiences, the contrary had, in effect, occurred; our carefully contrived prose samples were measuring the background knowledge of our audiences. For instance, if the subject of a text was "Friendship," all audience pairs, everywhere we gave the trials, exhibited the same differentials. Also, for all audiences, if the subject was "Hegel's Metaphysics," the differential between good and bad writing tended to disappear. Also, so long as we used university audiences, a text on Grant and Lee gave the same sort of appropriate results as did a text on friendship. But for one community college audience (in, no less, Richmond, Virginia) "Grant and Lee" turned out to be as unfamiliar as "Hegel's Metaphysics"—a complacency-shattering result.

While the variability of reading skills within the same person was making itself disconcertingly known to me, I learned that similar variability was showing up in formal writing skills—and for the same reasons. Researchers at the City University of New York were finding that when a topic is unfamiliar, writing skill declines in all of its dimensions—including grammar and spelling—not to mention sentence structure, parallelism, unity, focus, and other skills taught in writing courses. One part of the explanation for such results is that we all have limited attention space, and cannot pay much heed to form when we are devoting a lot of our attention to unfamiliar content. But another part of the explanation is more interesting. Part of our skill in reading and in writing is skill not just with linguistic structures but with words. Words are not purely formal counters of language; they represent large underlying domains of content. Part of language skill is content skill. As Apeneck Sweeney profoundly observed: "I gotta use words when I talk to you."

When I therefore assert that reading and writing skills are contentbound, I mean also to make the corollary assertion that important aspects of reading and writing skills are *not* transferable. Of course some skills *are* carried over from task to task; we know that broad strategies of reading and writing can become second nature, and thereby facilitate literary skills at all levels. But the content-indifferent, how-to approach to literacy skills is enormously oversimplified. As my final example of this, I shall mention an ingenious experiment conducted by Richard C. Anderson and his colleagues at the University of Illinois. It, too, was an experiment with paired audiences and paired texts. The texts were two letters, each describing a wedding, each of similar length, word-familiarity, sentence complexity, and number of idea units. Each audience group was similarly paired according to age, educational level, marital status, sex, professional specialty, etc. Structurally speaking, the texts were similar and the audiences were similar. The crucial variables were these: one letter described a wedding in America, the other a wedding in India. One audience was American, the other Indian. Both audiences read both letters. The results were that the reading skills of the two groups—their speed and accuracy of comprehension—were very different in reading the two linguistically similar letters. The Americans read about an American wedding skillfully, accurately, and with good recall. They did poorly with the letter about the Indian wedding. The reverse was the case with the group of Indian readers. Anderson and his colleagues concluded that reading is not just a linguistic skill, but involves translinguistic knowledge beyond the abstract sense of words. They suggested that reading involves both "linguistic-schemata" (systems of expectation) and "content-schemata" as well. In short, the assumptions of educational formalism are incorrect.

Every writer is aware that the subtlety and complexity of what can be conveyed in writing depends on the amount of relevant tacit knowledge that can be assumed in readers. As psycholinguists have shown, the explicitly stated words on the page often represent the smaller part of the literary transaction. Some of this assumed knowledge involves such matters as generic conventions, that is, what to expect in a business letter, a technical report, a detective story, etc. An equally significant part of the assumed knowledge—often a more significant part—concerns tacit knowledge of the experiential realities embraced by the discourse. Not only have I gotta use words to talk to you, I gotta assume you know *something* about what I am saying. If I had to start from scratch, I couldn't start at all.

We adjust for this in the most casual talk. It has been shown that we always explain ourselves more fully to strangers than to intimates. But, when the strangers being addressed are some unknown collectivity to whom we are writing, how much shall we then need to explain? This was one of the most difficult authorial problems that arose with the advent of printing and mass literacy. Later on, in the eighteenth century, Dr. Johnson confidently assumed he could predict the knowledge possessed by a personage whom he called "the common reader." Some such construct is a necessary fiction for every writer in every literate culture and subculture. Even a writer for an astrophysics journal must assume a "common reader" for the subculture being addressed. A newspaper writer must also assume a "common reader" but for a much bigger part of the culture, perhaps for the literate culture as a whole. In our own culture, Jefferson wanted to create a highly informed "common reader," and he must have assumed the real existence of such a personage when he said he would prefer newspapers without government to government without newspapers. But, without appropriate, tacitly shared background knowledge, people cannot understand newspapers. A certain extent of shared, canonical knowledge is inherently necessary to a literate democracy.

For this canonical information I have proposed the term "cultural literacy." It is the translinguistic knowledge on which linguistic literacy depends. You cannot have the one without the other. Teachers of foreign languages are aware of this interdependency between linguistic proficiency and translinguistic, cultural knowledge. To get very far in reading or writing French, a student must come to know facets of French culture quite different from his own. By the same token, American children learning to read and write English get instruction in aspects of their own national culture that are as foreign to them as French. National culture always has this "foreignness" with respect to family culture alone. School materials contain unfamiliar materials that promote the "acculturation" that is a universal part of growing up in any tribe or nation. Acculturation into a national literate culture might be defined as learning what the "common reader" of a newspaper in a literate culture could be expected to know. That would include knowledge of certain values (whether or not one accepted them), and knowledge of such things as (for example) the First Amendment, Grant and Lee, and DNA. In our own culture, what should these contents be? Surely our answer to that should partly define our school curriculum. Acculturation into a literate culture (the minimal aim of schooling; we should aim still higher) could be defined as the gaining of cultural literacy.

Such canonical knowledge could not be fixed once and for all. "Grant and Lee" could not have been part of it in 1840, or "DNA" in 1940. The canon changeth. And in our media-paced era, it might change from month to month—faster at the edges, more slowly at the center, and some of its contents would be connected to events beyond our control. But much of it is within our control and is part of our traditional task of culture making. One reassuring feature of our responsibilities as makers of culture is the implicit and automatic character of most canonical cultural knowledge; we get it through the pores. Another reassuring aspect is its vagueness. How much do I really have to know about DNA in order to comprehend a newspaper text directed to the common reader? Not much. Such vagueness in our background knowledge is a feature of cultural literacy that Hilary Putnam has analyzed brilliantly as "the division of linguistic labor." An immensely literate person, Putnam claims that he does not know the difference between a beech tree and an elm. Still, when reading those words he gets along acceptably well because he knows that under the division of linguistic labor somebody in the culture could supply more precise knowledge if it should be needed. Putnam's observation suggests that the school curriculum can be vague enough to leave plenty of room for local choice regarding what things shall be studied in detail, and what things shall be touched on just far enough to get us by. This vagueness in cultural literacy permits a reasonable compromise between lockstep, Napoleonic prescription of texts on the one side, and extreme laissez-faire pluralism on the other. Between these two extremes we have a national responsibility to take stock of the contents of schooling.

Although I have argued that a literate society depends upon shared information, I have said little about what that information should be. That is chiefly a political question. Estimable cultures exist that are ignorant of Shakespeare and the First Amendment. Indeed, estimable cultures exist that are entirely ignorant of reading and writing. On the other hand, no culture exists that is ignorant of its own traditions. In a literate society, culture and cultural literacy are nearly synonymous terms. American culture, always large and heterogeneous, and increasingly lacking a common acculturative curriculum, is perhaps getting fragmented enough to lose its coherence as a culture. Television is perhaps our only national curriculum, despite the justified complaints against it as a partial cause of the literacy decline. My hunch is that this complaint is overstated. The decline in literacy skills, I have suggested, is mainly a result of cultural fragmentation. Within black culture, for instance, blacks are more literate than whites, a point that was demonstrated by Robert L. Williams, as I learned from a recent article on the SAT by Jay Amberg (*The American Scholar,* Autumn 1982). The big political question that has to be decided first of all is whether we *want* a broadly literate culture that unites our cultural fragments enough to allow us to write to one another and read what our fellow citizens have written. Our traditional, Jeffersonian answer has been yes. But even if that political decision remains the dominant one, as I very much hope, we still face the much more difficult political decision of choosing the contents of cultural literacy.

The answer to this question is not going to be supplied by theoretical speculation and educational research. It will be worked out, if at all, by discussion, argument, and compromise. Professional educators have understandably avoided this political arena. Indeed, educators should *not* be left to decide so momentous an issue as the canonical contents of our culture. Within a democracy, educational technicians do not want and should not be awarded the function that Plato reserved for philosopher kings. But who is making such decisions at a national level? Nobody, I fear, because we are transfixed by the twin doctrines of pluralism and formalism.

Having made this technical point where I have some expertise, I must now leave any pretense of authority, except as a parent and citizen. The question of guidance for our national school curriculum is a political question on which I have only a citizen's opinion. For my own part, I wish we could have a National Board of Education on the pattern of the New York State Board of Regents—our most successful and admirable body for educational leadership. This imposing body of practical idealists is insulated by law from short-term demagogic pressures. It is a pluralistic group, too, with representation for minority as well as majority cultures. Its influence for good may be gauged by comparing the patterns of SAT scores in New York with those in California, two otherwise comparable states. To give just one example of the Regents' leadership in the field of writing, they have instituted a requirement that no New Yorker can receive a high school diploma before passing a statewide writing test that requires three types of prose composition.

Of course I am aware that the New York Regents have powers that no National Board in this country could possibly gain. But what a National Board could hope to achieve would be the respect of the country, a respect that could give it genuine influence over our schools. Such influence, based on leadership rather than compulsion, would be quite consistent with our federalist and pluralist principles. The Board, for instance, could present broad lists of suggested literary works for the different grades, lists broad enough to yield local freedom but also to yield a measure of commonality in our literary heritage. The teachers whom I know, while valuing their independence, are eager for intelligent guidance in such matters.

But I doubt that such a Curriculum Board would ever be established in this country. So strong is our suspicion of anything like a central "ministry of culture," that the Board is probably not a politically feasible idea. But perhaps a consortium of universities, or of national associations, or of foundations could make ongoing recommendations that arise from broadly based discussions of the national curriculum. In any case, we need leadership at the national level, and we need specific guidance.

It would be useful, for instance, to have guidance about the *words* that high school graduates ought to know—a lexicon of cultural literacy. I am thinking of a special sort of lexicon that would include not just ordinary dictionary words, but also include proper names, important phrases, and conventions. Nobody likes word lists as objects of instruction; for one thing, they don't work. But I am not thinking of such a lexicon as an object of instruction. I am thinking of it rather as a guide to objects of instruction. Take the phrase "First Amendment," for instance. That is a lexical item that can hardly be used without bringing in a lot of associated information. Just what are the words and phrases that our school graduates should know? Right now, this seems to be decided by the makers of the SAT, which is, as I have mentioned, chiefly a vocabulary test. The educational technicians who choose the words that appear on the SAT are already the implicit makers of our national curriculum. Is then the Educational Testing Service our hidden National Board of Education? Does it sponsor our hidden national curriculum? If so, the ETS is rather to be praised than blamed. For if we wish to raise our national level of literacy, a hidden national curriculum is far better than no curriculum at all.

Where does this leave us? What issues are raised? If I am right in my interpretation of the evidence—and I have seen no alternative interpretation in the literature—then we can only raise our reading and writing skills significantly by consciously redefining and extending our cultural literacy. And yet our current national effort in the schools is largely run on the premise that the best way to proceed is through a culturally neutral, skills-approach to reading and writing. But if skill in writing and in reading comes about chiefly through what I have termed cultural literacy, then radical consequences follow. These consequences are not merely educational but social and political in their scope—and that scope is vast. I shall not attempt to set out these consequences here, but it will be obvious that acting upon them would involve our dismantling and casting aside the leading educational assumptions of the past half century.

REFLECTING ON THE READING

1. What does Hirsch believe is the cause of what he calls "the national decline in our literacy"? How does he establish that such a decline has occurred?

2. In what ways, according to Hirsch, has the school curriculum been an important part of the formation of American culture? What specific roles have schools served? Why is an understanding of the role of schools in American culture important to Hirsch's argument about literacy?

3. What is "educational formalism"? How has this principle influenced schools and their curricula, according to Hirsch? Why is educational formalism misleading and evasive, in his view? How has it led to the problems in literacy that he describes? Have you experienced this approach to education? Do you think Hirsch's criticisms of this approach to education are valid? Why or why not?

4. How did Hirsch's own research on writing evaluation convince him that his earlier support for educational formalism was a mistake? What specifically did his own research reveal about literacy and knowledge?

5. What does Hirsch mean by the term *cultural literacy?* Why is such literacy important to democracy? Do you think Hirsch is right? Why or why not?

6. In what sense does Hirsch believe that literacy and education are political decisions? Do you agree with him? Why or why not? What might your answer suggest about your beliefs regarding literacy and education?

7. What specific suggestion does Hirsch make for creating the kind of curriculum he would like to see in all American schools? Do you think his suggestion is feasible? Why or why not? Does Hirsch think such a suggestion is realistic? Why? What effects do you think his suggestion might have on schools?

Examining Rhetorical Strategies

1. Notice how Hirsch begins this essay. He immediately identifies himself as an experienced education researcher. Why do you think he begins his essay in this way? What impression did this introduction have on you as a reader? Do you think it helps establish Hirsch's credibility as an expert on his subject? How might that have influenced the way you read his essay and responded to his argument? Do you think Hirsch intended such an effect? Explain. What might your response to his presentation of himself indicate about your expectations of a writer and your own attitudes regarding a writer's credibility?

2. Hirsch claims that "few will seriously doubt" that "a decline in our national level of literacy has occurred." Assess the specific evidence he offers to support this point. Do you think this evidence is adequate or convincing? What does it suggest about how Hirsch defines literacy?

3. Hirsch devotes a great deal of attention in this essay to discussing problems he sees with a theory of education that he calls *educational formalism* and to describing his own specialized research on literacy. Assess the way Hirsch presents these highly technical discussions. *The American Scholar,* the journal in which this article first appeared, is devoted to educational issues but is not necessarily a specialized journal intended exclusively for education researchers. Do you think Hirsch is speaking primarily to educational specialists in this essay? Explain. Do you think he discusses technical matters in this article in ways that are understandable to a wide audience? Cite specific passages from the article in your answer.

4. Hirsch's ideas about school reform have generated a great deal of criticism, much of it from advocates for nonmainstream communities. Identify elements of his argument that you think might be particularly worrisome for readers from nonmainstream backgrounds. Does he attempt to anticipate criticisms of his arguments in any way? How does Hirsch seem to understand *diversity?* In what ways might his understanding of diversity concern nonmainstream readers? Cite specific passages from the article in your answer.

5. Examine the way Hirsch organized his essay. How does he establish the problem he wishes to address? How does he present his main argument? What key points does he offer in support of his main argument? How does he support those points? How does he move to his conclusion? Why do you think he organized his essay in this way? What advantages can you see to the way he does so? Do you find the way he organized this argument effective? Why or why not?

6. At one point in his essay, Hirsch explains in detail how his own views about literacy changed as a result of the research he conducted on reading and writing style. Examine that section of his essay. How does Hirsch explain his research? Do you think he wishes to present his research as credible and useful? Explain. Why do you think he details this research and its eventual effect on his attitudes about literacy? What does he accomplish by telling us this? Do you think he uses this account effectively in his essay? Why or why not?

Engaging the Issues

1. Write a rebuttal to Hirsch.

    Alternatively, write an essay explaining why you support the arguments Hirsch makes in his essay.

2. In a group of your classmates discuss Hirsch's essay and the essays you wrote in response to it for Question #1 above. Identify key similarities and differences in your reactions to Hirsch's ideas. Discuss what your agreements or disagreements about Hirsch's ideas might suggest about your beliefs regarding education and literacy. Focus your discussion in part on the reforms that Hirsch proposes and whether you think such reforms might improve American education.

3. Using your library, the World Wide Web, or any other sources available to you, find reviews or articles discussing Hirsch's work (especially his book *Cultural Literacy*). Read several such reviews or articles, and then write a report for your classmates in which you summarize the major criticisms of Hirsch's work and the support for it as well. In your report, try to draw conclusions about what the reactions to Hirsch's work might indicate about Americans' beliefs regarding education.

4. Visit the Web site of the Core Knowledge Foundation, which Hirsch founded. How does the Web site present the Foundation? How is the foundation's purpose expressed? Does it seem politically oriented in any obvious way? Does it seem to reflect the ideas about literacy and education that Hirsch discusses in this essay? Who does its audience seem to be? How does it address that audience? After analyzing the Web site, write a report for your classmates, describing the site and offering your analysis of how it presents itself and its ideas about education.

5. Conduct a search on the World Wide Web and find the Web sites of other organizations devoted to educational reform. Analyze those sites as described in Question #4 above. Then compare the sites in terms of the way they are designed and the way they present the organizations they represent. Draw conclusions from your analysis about effective strategies for designing Web sites for interest groups.

6. Ask several classmates to visit the Web sites you analyzed for Question #5 above. Ask them to describe their reactions to each of those Web sites, and then compare their reactions to your own. Did their reactions change your analysis or conclusions in any way about Web design for interest groups? Explain.

7. Examine the curriculum described on the Web site of the Core Knowledge Foundation. What sort of curriculum is it? How does it differ from the curriculum you experienced in your school? What advantages or disadvantages to the foundation's curriculum do you see? How do Hirsch's ideas look in practice? Now write an essay for your classmates in which you compare the Core Knowledge Foundation curriculum to your own (or to what you consider to be the typical curriculum in American schools). Draw conclusions about the effectiveness of each.

8. Write a letter to your local school board proposing curriculum reforms that you believe should be implemented in your school district. In your letter, draw on Hirsch's ideas or on any other sources you deem appropriate in order to make a convincing case for your proposed changes.

9. Write an essay in which you analyze your own educational experiences on the basis of Hirsch's ideas. In your essay, describe the kinds of activities, assignments, reading materials, and ideas to which you were exposed in your high school curriculum or are exposed in your college curriculum. Using Hirsch's concept of educational formalism, discuss how your experiences reflect or do not reflect the problems that Hirsch associates with conventional schooling. Pay particular attention to your literacy activities. Draw conclusions about the nature of your own education on the basis of Hirsch's ideas.

The Banking Concept of Education

PAULO FREIRE

INTRODUCTION   The importance of education might be reflected in the staggering amount of money spent on it: billions of dollars each year in the United States alone. In 1998, for example, more than $30 billion was allocated for the U.S. Department of Education, representing nearly 2 percent of the total federal budget; states and local governments typically devote a much higher percentage of their budgets to education. This money, in part, supports an enormous education bureaucracy, from the federal government down to local school boards, an extensive and complex system by which education is conducted and controlled. In most states, children are required by law to attend school into their teenage years (usually to age sixteen), ensuring that most Americans will be educated within this vast bureaucratic system of public and private schools. Most of us probably take this situation for granted. Even if we are actively involved in education or genuinely concerned about schools and school reform, we probably don't often think about *why* so much effort, money, and time are devoted to managing the education of our children. We probably don't often think about the *purpose* of education because it seems self-evident.

Paulo Freire may be an exception. He spent his long and active adult life writing and talking about what education is and what it should be and working toward realizing his vision of education as a means to freedom. For Freire, questions about the purpose of education are not simply professional concerns but matters that go directly to the heart of what it means to be human. In Freire's view, to be "fully human" means to understand that the reality we inhabit is a *process* in which we as individual human beings participate; in other words, we don't simply inhabit the world: we construct it. But conventional education, according to Freire, is not based on such a view; rather, it rests on a view of reality as static and unchanging, as a *status quo*, and it defines students as passive components of that status quo. It thus "dehumanizes" them. This conventional, or "banking concept," of education, Freire argues, helps maintain the status quo, with all of its inequalities and injustices. In this sense, conventional education inhibits human efforts to build free and fair societies.

According to Freire, literacy is crucial to building free and fair societies because language—and especially written language—is the primary means by which we interact with and construct our world. In a book he coauthored with Donald Macedo, Freire writes that "the act of learning to read and write . . . is a creative act that involves the critical comprehension of reality" (*Literacy: Reading the Word and the World*, p. 157). Because literacy is a "creative act" of comprehending reality, it shapes how we understand ourselves and our relationship to that reality. In a sense, in learning to read and write, we learn a way of understanding and acting in the world.

These views about literacy and education are not as abstract as they may seem, for Freire developed his ideas while teaching reading and writing to nonliterate rural peasants in Brazil in the 1960's. In 1964, after a military coup

there, he was jailed and then exiled for his "subversive" work in literacy programs—which is perhaps a compelling vindication of Freire's belief in the political importance of literacy. After being exiled, Freire continued his work in
Chile, where he ran rural literacy programs for five years. In the late 1960's, he
was invited to become a Visiting Professor at Harvard University, a position that
enabled him to share his ideas about literacy education with many other educators and scholars. During this time he published his most influential work,
Pedagogy of the Oppressed (1970). Freire left Harvard in the early 1970's to
assist educational programs of newly independent countries in Asia and Africa,
such as Tanzania, as Assistant Secretary of Education for the World Council of
Churches in Switzerland. By the time he returned to Brazil in the 1980's, he had
become an internationally prominent voice for education reform, and in 1988,
with Brazil once again under civilian rule, he became Minister of Education for
the City of Sao Paulo. He remained in Brazil, developing and implementing his
ideas about literacy education, until his death in 1997.

As Freire's reputation grew in the 1980's, educators around the world began
trying to implement the methods for teaching literacy that he described in
Pedagogy of the Oppressed. In the United States, several projects in schools
and community literacy programs were based on Freire's ideas, and in some
cases they were met with resistance and controversy. Some critics charged
Freire's programs with being too political, amounting to indoctrinating students with leftist ideology. Others complained that his programs couldn't work
in places like the United States, where the government is not a military one and
where the schools function very differently than those in Brazil. Despite such
criticisms, Freire's ideas continue to have wide influence among educators—in
the United States and elsewhere—who believe that literacy education is a crucial element in helping to foster freedom and social justice. The intense
debates about Freire's work and the brutal resistance to his programs by his
own government in the 1960's underscore not only the significance of his work
but also the political nature of literacy education in general.

In addition to *Pedagogy of the Oppressed*, Freire wrote a number of books
about literacy and education including *Pedagogy of Hope* (1994), *A Pedagogy
for Liberation: Dialogues on Transforming Education* (coauthored with Ira Shor,
1987), and *Letters to Cristina: Reflections on My Life and Work* (1996). The following essay originally appeared as Chapter 2 of *Pedagogy of the Oppressed*
and has become a widely read and oft-reprinted statement of Freire's basic
views about education.

REFLECTING BEFORE READING

1. Freire's writing has sometimes been described as abstract and difficult to read.
   Part of the reason for such complaints is that Freire discusses theoretical or
   abstract concepts that are important to his understanding of how education
   works. Some of these concepts relate to such matters as the relationship
   between reality and human consciousness. Understanding these concepts can
   be central to understanding Freire's ideas about education. As you read, jot
   down these concepts as you encounter them, and define them as best you
   can—as you think Freire defines them. It might be useful to compare your
   notes with those of other classmates.

2. Freire's ideas about education grow out of fundamental beliefs about human
   existence. For Freire, education is really about becoming "fully human." Before

you begin reading, examine your own beliefs about the basic purposes of education. What are those purposes, as you see them? As you read, consider how your views about the purposes of education might differ from or converge with Freire's.

A careful analysis of the teacher-student relationship at any level, inside or outside the school, reveals its fundamentally *narrative* character. This relationship involves a narrating Subject (the teacher) and patient, listening objects (the students). The contents, whether values or empirical dimensions of reality, tend in the process of being narrated to become lifeless and petrified. Education is suffering from narration sickness.

The teacher talks about reality as if it were motionless, static, compartmentalized, and predictable. Or else he expounds on a topic completely alien to the existential experience of the students. His task is to "fill" the students with the contents of his narration—contents which are detached from reality, disconnected from the totality that engendered them and could give them significance. Words are emptied of their concreteness and become a hollow, alienated, and alienating verbosity.

The outstanding characteristic of this narrative education, then, is the sonority of words, not their transforming power. "Four times four is sixteen; the capital of Pará is Belém." The student records, memorizes, and repeats these phrases without perceiving what four times four really means, or realizing the true significance of "capital" in the affirmation "the capital of Pará is Belém," that is, what Belém means for Pará and what Pará means for Brazil.

Narration (with the teacher as narrator) leads the students to memorize mechanically the narrated content. Worse yet, it turns them into "containers," into "receptacles" to be "filled" by the teacher. The more completely he fills the receptacles, the better a teacher he is. The more meekly the receptacles permit themselves to be filled, the better students they are.

Education thus becomes an act of depositing, in which the students are the depositories and the teacher is the depositor. Instead of communicating, the teacher issues communiqués and makes deposits which the students patiently receive, memorize, and repeat. This is the "banking" concept of education, in which the scope of action allowed to the students extends only as far as receiving, filing, and storing the deposits. They do, it is true, have the opportunity to become collectors or cataloguers of the things they store. But in the last analysis, it is men themselves who are filed away through the lack of creativity, transformation, and knowledge in this (at best) misguided system. For apart from inquiry, apart from the praxis, men cannot be truly human. Knowledge emerges only through invention and re-invention, through the restless, impatient, continuing, hopeful inquiry men pursue in the world, with the world, and with each other.

In the banking concept of education, knowledge is a gift bestowed by those who consider themselves knowledgeable upon those whom they consider to know nothing. Projecting an absolute ignorance onto others, a characteristic of the ideology of oppression, negates education and knowledge as processes of inquiry. The teacher presents himself to his students as their necessary opposite; by considering their ignorance absolute, he justifies his own existence. The students, alienated like the slave in the Hegelian dialectic, accept their ignorance as justifying the teacher's existence—but, unlike the slave, they never discover that they educate the teacher.

The *raison d'être* of libertarian education, on the other hand, lies in its drive towards reconciliation. Education must begin with the solution of the teacher-student contradiction, by reconciling the poles of the contradiction so that both are simultaneously teachers and students.

This solution is not (nor can it be) found in the banking concept. On the contrary, banking education maintains and even stimulates the contradiction through the following attitudes and practices, which mirror oppressive society as a whole:

(a)   the teacher teaches and the students are taught;

(b)   the teacher knows everything and the students know nothing;

(c)   the teacher thinks and the students are thought about;

(d)   the teacher talks and the students listen—meekly;

(e)   the teacher disciplines and the students are disciplined;

(f)   the teacher chooses and enforces his choice, and the students comply;

(g)   the teacher acts and the students have the illusion of acting through the action of the teacher;

(h)   the teacher chooses the program content, and the students (who were not consulted) adapt to it;

(i)   the teacher confuses the authority of knowledge with his own professional authority, which he sets in opposition to the freedom of the students;

(j)   the teacher is the Subject of the learning process, while the pupils are mere objects.

It is not surprising that the banking concept of education regards men as adaptable, manageable beings. The more students work at storing the deposits entrusted to them, the less they develop the critical consciousness which would result from their intervention in the world as transformers of that world. The more completely they accept the passive role imposed on them, the more they tend simply to adapt to the world as it is and to the fragmented view of reality deposited in them.

The capability of banking education to minimize or annul the students' creative power and to stimulate their credulity serves the interests of the oppressors, who care neither to have the world revealed nor to see it transformed. The oppressors use their "humanitarianism" to preserve a profitable situation. Thus they react almost instinctively against any experiment in education which stimulates the critical faculties and is not content with a partial view of reality but always seeks out the ties which link one point to another and one problem to another.

Indeed, the interests of the oppressors lie in "changing the consciousness of the oppressed, not the situation which oppresses them";[1] for the more the oppressed can be led to adapt to that situation, the more easily they can be dominated. To achieve this end, the oppressors use the banking concept of education in conjunction with a

---

[1] Simone de Beauvoir, *La Pensée de Drolte, Aujord'hui* (Paris); ST, *El Pensamliento político de la Derecha* (Buenos Aires, 1963), p. 34.

paternalistic social action apparatus, within which the oppressed receive the euphemistic title of "welfare recipients." They are treated as individual cases, as marginal men who deviate from the general configuration of a "good, organized, and just" society. The oppressed are regarded as the pathology of the healthy society, which must therefore adjust these "incompetent and lazy" folk to its own patterns by changing their mentality. These marginals need to be "integrated," "incorporated" into the healthy society that they have "forsaken."

The truth is, however, that the oppressed are not "marginals," are not men living "outside" society. They have always been "inside"—inside the structure which made them "beings for others." The solution is not to "integrate" them into the structure of oppression, but to transform that structure so that they can become "beings for themselves." Such transformation, of course, would undermine the oppressors' purposes; hence their utilization of the banking concept of education to avoid the threat of student *conscientização*.

The banking approach to adult education, for example, will never propose to students that they critically consider reality. It will deal instead with such vital questions as whether Roger gave green grass to the goat, and insist upon the importance of learning that, on the contrary, *R*oger gave green grass to the *r*abbit. The "humanism" of the banking approach masks the effort to turn men into automatons—the very negation of their ontological vocation to be more fully human.

Those who use the banking approach, knowingly or unknowingly (for there are innumerable well-intentioned bank-clerk teachers who do not realize that they are serving only to dehumanize), fail to perceive that the deposits themselves contain contradictions about reality. But, sooner or later, these contradictions may lead formerly passive students to turn against their domestication and the attempt to domesticate reality. They may discover through existential experience that their present way of life is irreconcilable with their vocation to become fully human. They may perceive through their relations with reality that reality is really a *process,* undergoing constant transformation. If men are searchers and their ontological vocation is humanization, sooner or later they may perceive the contradiction in which banking education seeks to maintain them, and then engage themselves in the struggle for their liberation.

But the humanist, revolutionary educator cannot wait for this possibility to materialize. From the outset, his efforts must coincide with those of the students to engage in critical thinking and the quest for mutual humanization. His efforts must be imbued with a profound trust in men and their creative power. To achieve this, he must be a partner of the students in his relations with them.

The banking concept does not admit to such partnership—and necessarily so. To resolve the teacher-student contradiction, to exchange the role of depositor, prescriber, domesticator, for the role of student among students would be to undermine the power of oppression and serve the cause of liberation.

Implicit in the banking concept is the assumption of a dichotomy between man and the world: man is merely *in* the world, not *with* the world or with others; man is spectator, not re-creator. In this view, man is not a conscious being (*corpo consciente*); he is rather the possessor of *a* consciousness: an empty "mind" passively open to the reception of deposits of reality from the world outside. For example, my desk, my books, my coffee cup, all the objects before me—as bits of the world which surrounds me—would be "inside" me, exactly as I am inside my study right now. This view makes no distinction between being accessible to consciousness and entering consciousness. The distinction, however, is essential: the objects which surround me are simply accessible to my consciousness, not located within it. I am aware of them, but they are not inside me.

It follows logically from the banking notion of consciousness that the educator's role is to regulate the way the world "enters into" the students. His task is to organize a process which already occurs spontaneously, to "fill" the students by making deposits of information which he considers to constitute true knowledge.[2] And since men "receive" the world as passive entities, education should make them more passive still, and adapt them to the world. The educated man is the adapted man, because he is better "fit" for the world. Translated into practice, this concept is well suited to the purposes of the oppressors, whose tranquility rests on how well men fit the world the oppressors have created, and how little they question it.

The more completely the majority adapt to the purposes which the dominant minority prescribe for them (thereby depriving them of the right to their own purposes), the more easily the minority can continue to prescribe. The theory and practice of banking education serve this end quite efficiently. Verbalistic lessons, reading requirements,[3] the methods for evaluating "knowledge," the distance between the teacher and the taught, the criteria for promotion: everything in this ready-to-wear approach serves to obviate thinking.

The bank-clerk educator does not realize that there is no true security in his hypertrophied role, that one must seek to live *with* others in solidarity. One cannot impose oneself, nor even merely co-exist with one's students. Solidarity requires true communication, and the concept by which such an educator is guided fears and proscribes communication.

Yet only through communication can human life hold meaning. The teacher's thinking is authenticated only by the authenticity of the students' thinking. The teacher cannot think for his students, nor can he impose his thought on them. Authentic thinking, thinking that is concerned about *reality,* does not take place in ivory tower isolation, but only in communication. If it is true that thought has meaning only when generated by action upon the world, the subordination of students to teachers becomes impossible.

Because banking education begins with a false understanding of men as objects, it cannot promote the development of what Fromm calls "biophily," but instead produces its opposite: "necrophily."

> While life is characterized by growth in a structured, functional manner, the necrophilous person loves all that does not grow, all that is mechanical. The necrophilous person is driven by the desire to transform the organic into the inorganic, to approach life mechanically, as if all living persons were things. . . . Memory, rather than experience; having, rather than being, is what counts. The necrophilous person can relate to an object—a flower or a person—only if he possesses it; hence a

---

[2] This concept corresponds to what Sartre calls the "digestive" or "nutritive" concept of education, in which knowledge is "fed" by the teacher to the students to "fill them out." See Jean-Paul Sartre, "Une idée fundamentale de la phénoménologie de Husserl: L'intentionalité," *Situations 1* (Paris, 1947).

[3] For example, some professors specify in their reading lists that a book should be read from pages 10 to 15—and do this to "help" their students!

threat to his possession is a threat to himself; if he loses possession he loses contact with the world. . . . He loves control, and in the act of controlling he kills life.[4]

Oppression—overwhelming control—is necrophilic; it is nourished by love of death, not life. The banking concept of education, which serves the interests of oppression, is also necrophilic. Based on a mechanistic, static, naturalistic, spatialized view of consciousness, it transforms students into receiving objects. It attempts to control thinking and action, leads men to adjust to the world, and inhibits their creative power.

When their efforts to act responsibly are frustrated, when they find themselves unable to use their faculties, men suffer. "This suffering due to impotence is rooted in the very fact that the human equilibrium has been disturbed."[5] But the inability to act which causes men's anguish also causes them to reject their impotence, by attempting

> . . . to restore [their] capacity to act. But can [they], and how? One way is to submit to and identify with a person or group having power. By this symbolic participation in another person's life, [men have] the illusion of acting, when in reality [they] only submit to and become a part of those who act.[6]

Populist manifestations perhaps best exemplify this type of behavior by the oppressed, who, by identifying with charismatic leaders, come to feel that they themselves are active and effective. The rebellion they express as they emerge in the historical process is motivated by that desire to act effectively. The dominant elites consider the remedy to be more domination and repression, carried out in the name of freedom, order, and social peace (that is, the peace of the elites). Thus they can condemn—logically, from their point of view—"the violence of a strike by workers and [can] call upon the state in the same breath to use violence in putting down the strike."[7]

Education as the exercise of domination stimulates the credulity of students, with the ideological intent (often not perceived by educators) of indoctrinating them to adapt to the world of oppression. This accusation is not made in the naïve hope that the dominant elites will thereby simply abandon the practice. Its objective is to call the attention of true humanists to the fact that they cannot use banking educational methods in the pursuit of liberation, for they would only negate that very pursuit. Nor may a revolutionary society inherit these methods from an oppressor society. The revolutionary society which practices banking education is either misguided or mistrusting of men. In either event, it is threatened by the specter of reaction.

Unfortunately, those who espouse the cause of liberation are themselves surrounded and influenced by the climate which generates the banking concept, and often do not perceive its true significance or its dehumanizing power. Paradoxically, then, they utilize this same instrument of alienation in what they consider an effort to liberate. Indeed, some "revolutionaries" brand as "innocents," "dreamers," or even "reactionaries" those who would challenge this educational practice. But one does not

---

[4] Fromm, *op. cit., The Heart of Man,* 1966, p. 41.
[5] *Ibid.,* p. 31.
[6] *Ibid.*
[7] Reinhold Niebuhr, *Moral Man and Immoral Society* (New York, 1960), p. 130.

liberate men by alienating them. Authentic liberation—the process of humanization—is not another deposit to be made in men. Liberation is a praxis: the action and
reflection of men upon their world in order to transform it. Those truly committed
to the cause of liberation can accept neither the mechanistic concept of consciousness
as an empty vessel to be filled, nor the use of banking methods of domination (propaganda, slogans—deposits) in the name of liberation.

Those truly committed to liberation must reject the banking concept in its
entirety, adopting instead a concept of men as conscious beings, and consciousness
as consciousness intent upon the world. They must abandon the educational goal of
deposit-making and replace it with the posing of the problems of men in their relations with the world. "Problem-posing" education, responding to the essence of consciousness—*intentionality*—rejects communiqués and embodies communication. It
epitomizes the special characteristic of consciousness: being *conscious of,* not only as
intent on objects but as turned in upon itself in a Jasperian "split"—consciousness as
consciousness *of* consciousness.

Liberating education consists in acts of cognition, not transferrals of information.
It is a learning situation in which the cognizable object (far from being the end of the
cognitive act) intermediates the cognitive actors—teacher on the one hand and students on the other. Accordingly, the practice of problem-posing education entails at
the outset that the teacher-student contradiction be resolved. Dialogical relations—
indispensable to the capacity of cognitive actors to cooperate in perceiving the same
cognizable object—are otherwise impossible.

Indeed, problem-posing education, which breaks with the vertical patterns characteristic of banking education, can fulfill its function as the practice of freedom only
if it can overcome the above contradiction. Through dialogue, the teacher-of-the-stu-
dents and the students-of-the-teacher cease to exist and a new term emerges: teacher-
student with students-teachers. The teacher is no longer merely the-one-who-teaches,
but one who is himself taught in dialogue with the students, who in turn while
being taught also teach. They become jointly responsible for a process in which all
grow. In this process, arguments based on "authority" are no longer valid; in order
to function, authority must be *on the side of* freedom, not *against* it. Here, no one
teaches another, nor is anyone self-taught. Men teach each other, mediated by the
world, by the cognizable objects which in banking education are "owned" by the
teacher.

The banking concept (with its tendency to dichotomize everything) distinguishes
two stages in the action of the educator. During the first, he cognizes a cognizable
object while he prepares his lessons in his study or his laboratory; during the second,
he expounds to his students about that object. The students are not called upon to
know, but to memorize the contents narrated by the teacher. Nor do the students
practice any act of cognition, since the object towards which that act should be
directed is the property of the teacher rather than a medium evoking the critical
reflection of both teacher and students. Hence in the name of the "preservation of
culture and knowledge" we have a system which achieves neither true knowledge
nor true culture.

The problem-posing method does not dichotomize the activity of the teacher-student: he is not "cognitive" at one point and "narrative" at another. He is always "cognitive," whether preparing a project or engaging in dialogue with the students. He

does not regard cognizable objects as his private property, but as the object of reflection by himself and the students. In this way, the problem-posing educator constantly re-forms his reflections in the reflection of the students. The students—no longer docile listeners—are now critical co-investigators in dialogue with the teacher. The teacher presents the material to the students for their consideration, and re-considers his earlier considerations as the students express their own. The role of the problem-posing educator is to create, together with the students, the conditions under which knowledge at the level of the *doxa* is superseded by true knowledge, at the level of the *logos*.

Whereas banking education anesthetizes and inhibits creative power, problem-posing education involves a constant unveiling of reality. The former attempts to maintain the *submersion* of consciousness; the latter strives for the *emergence* of consciousness and *critical intervention* in reality.

Students, as they are increasingly posed with problems relating to themselves in the world and with the world, will feel increasingly challenged and obliged to respond to that challenge. Because they apprehend the challenge as interrelated to other problems within a total context, not as a theoretical question, the resulting comprehension tends to be increasingly critical and thus constantly less alienated. Their response to the challenge evokes new challenges, followed by new understandings; and gradually the students come to regard themselves as committed.

Education as the practice of freedom—as opposed to education as the practice of domination—denies that man is abstract, isolated, independent, and unattached to the world; it also denies that the world exists as a reality apart from men. Authentic reflection considers neither abstract man nor the world without men, but men in their relations with the world. In these relations consciousness and world are simultaneous; consciousness neither precedes the world nor follows it.

> La conscience et le monde sont dormés d'un même coup: extérieur par essence á la conscience, le monde est, par essence relatif à elle.[8]

In one of our culture circles in Chile, the group was discussing (based on a codification[9]) the anthropological concept of culture. In the midst of the discussion, a peasant who by banking standards was completely ignorant said: "Now I see that without man there is no world." When the educator responded: "Let's say, for the sake of argument, that all the men on earth were to die, but that the earth itself remained, together with trees, birds, animals, rivers, seas, the stars . . . wouldn't all this be a world?" "Oh no," the peasant replied emphatically. "There would be no one to say: 'This is a world'."

The peasant wished to express the idea that there would be lacking the consciousness of the world which necessarily implies the world of consciousness. *I* cannot exist without a *not-I*. In turn, the *not-I* depends on that existence. The world which brings consciousness into existence becomes the world *of* that consciousness. Hence, the previously cited affirmation of Sartre: *"La conscience et le monde sont dormés d'un même coup."*

---

[8] Sartre, *op. cit.*, p. 32.
[9] See Chapter 3. —Translator's note. "Codification" refers to sketches, photographs, or word phrases that literacy teachers, following Freire's approach, use to help students analyze their life situations.

As men, simultaneously reflecting on themselves and on the world, increase the scope of their perception, they begin to direct their observations towards previously inconspicuous phenomena:

> In perception properly so-called, as an explicit awareness [*Gewahren*], I am turned towards the object, to the paper, for instance. I apprehend it as being this here and now. The apprehension is a singling out, every object having a background in experience. Around and about the paper lie books, pencils, ink-well, and so forth, and these in a certain sense are also "perceived", perceptually there, in the "field of intuition"; but whilst I was turned towards the paper there was no turning in their direction, nor any apprehending of them, not even in a secondary sense. They appeared and yet were not singled out, were not posited on their own account. Every perception of a thing has such a zone of background intuitions or background awareness, if "intuiting" already includes the state of being turned towards, and this also is a "conscious experience", or more briefly a "consciousness of" all indeed that in point of fact lies in the co-perceived objective background.[10]

That which had existed objectively but had not been perceived in its deeper implications (if indeed it was perceived at all) begins to "stand out," assuming the character of a problem and therefore of challenge. Thus, men begin to single out elements from their "background awarenesses" and to reflect upon them. These elements are now objects of men's consideration, and, as such, objects of their action and cognition.

In problem-posing education, men develop their power to perceive critically *the way they exist* in the world *with which* and *in which* they find themselves; they come to see the world not as a static reality, but as a reality in process, in transformation. Although the dialectical relations of men with the world exist independently of how these relations are perceived (or whether or not they are perceived at all), it is also true that the form of action men adopt is to a large extent a function of how they perceive themselves in the world. Hence, the teacher-student and the students-teachers reflect simultaneously on themselves and the world without dichotomizing this reflection from action, and thus establish an authentic form of thought and action.

Once again, the two educational concepts and practices under analysis come into conflict. Banking education (for obvious reasons) attempts, by mythicizing reality, to conceal certain facts which explain the way men exist in the world; problem-posing education sets itself the task of demythologizing. Banking education resists dialogue; problem-posing education regards dialogue as indispensable to the act of cognition which unveils reality. Banking education treats students as objects of assistance; problem-posing education makes them critical thinkers. Banking education inhibits creativity and domesticates (although it cannot completely destroy) the *intentionality* of consciousness by isolating consciousness from the world, thereby denying men their ontological and historical vocation of becoming more fully human. Problem-posing education bases itself on creativity and stimulates true reflection and action upon reality, thereby responding to the vocation of men as beings who are authentic only when engaged in inquiry and creative transformation. In sum: banking theory and practice, as immobilizing and fixating forces, fail to acknowledge men as

---

[10] Edmund Husserl, *Ideas—General Introduction to Pure Phenomenology* (London, 1969), pp. 105–106.

historical beings; problem-posing theory and practice take man's historicity as their starting point.

Problem-posing education affirms men as beings in the process of *becoming*—as unfinished, uncompleted beings in and with a likewise unfinished reality. Indeed, in contrast to other animals who are unfinished, but not historical, men know themselves to be unfinished; they are aware of their incompletion. In this incompletion and this awareness lie the very roots of education as an exclusively human manifestation. The unfinished character of men and the transformational character of reality necessitate that education be an ongoing activity.

Education is thus constantly remade in the praxis. In order to *be,* it must *become.* Its "duration" (in the Bergsonian meaning of the word) is found in the interplay of the opposites *permanence* and *change.* The banking method emphasizes permanence and becomes reactionary; problem-posing education—which accepts neither a "well-behaved" present nor a predetermined future—roots itself in the dynamic present and becomes revolutionary.

Problem-posing education is revolutionary futurity. Hence it is prophetic (and, as such, hopeful). Hence, it corresponds to the historical nature of man. Hence, it affirms men as beings who transcend themselves, who move forward and look ahead, for whom immobility represents a fatal threat, for whom looking at the past must only be a means of understanding more clearly what and who they are so that they can more wisely build the future. Hence, it identifies with the movement which engages men as beings aware of their incompletion—an historical movement which has its point of departure, its Subjects and its objective.

The point of departure of the movement lies in men themselves. But since men do not exist apart from the world, apart from reality, the movement must begin with the men-world relationship. Accordingly, the point of departure must always be with men in the "here and now," which constitutes the situation within which they are submerged, from which they emerge, and in which they intervene. Only by starting from this situation—which determines their perception of it—can they begin to move. To do this authentically they must perceive their state not as fated and unalterable, but merely as limiting—and therefore challenging.

Whereas the banking method directly or indirectly reinforces men's fatalistic perception of their situation, the problem-posing method presents this very situation to them as a problem. As the situation becomes the object of their cognition, the naïve or magical perception which produced their fatalism gives way to perception which is able to perceive itself even as it perceives reality, and can thus be critically objective about that reality.

A deepened consciousness of their situation leads men to apprehend that situation as an historical reality susceptible of transformation. Resignation gives way to the drive for transformation and inquiry, over which men feel themselves to be in control. If men, as historical beings necessarily engaged with other men in a movement of inquiry, did not control that movement, it would be (and is) a violation of men's humanity. Any situation in which some men prevent others from engaging in the process of inquiry is one of violence. The means used are not important; to alienate men from their own decision-making is to change them into objects.

This movement of inquiry must be directed towards humanization—man's historical vocation. The pursuit of full humanity, however, cannot be carried out in isolation or individualism, but only in fellowship and solidarity; therefore it cannot unfold in the antagonistic relations between oppressors and oppressed. No one can be authentically human while he prevents others from being so. Attempting *to be more* human, individualistically, leads to *having more,* egotistically: a form of dehumanization. Not that it is not fundamental *to have* in order *to be* human. Precisely because it *is* necessary, some men's *having* must not be allowed to constitute an obstacle to others' having, must not consolidate the power of the former to crush the latter.

Problem-posing education, as a humanist and liberating praxis, posits as fundamental that men subjected to domination must fight for their emancipation. To that end, it enables teachers and students to become Subjects of the educational process by overcoming authoritarianism and an alienating intellectualism; it also enables men to overcome their false perception of reality. The world—no longer something to be described with deceptive words—becomes the object of that transforming action by men which results in their humanization.

Problem-posing education does not and cannot serve the interests of the oppressor. No oppressive order could permit the oppressed to begin to question: Why? While only a revolutionary society can carry out this education in systematic terms, the revolutionary leaders need not take full power before they can employ the method. In the revolutionary process, the leaders cannot utilize the banking method as an interim measure, justified on grounds of expediency, with the intention of *later* behaving in a genuinely revolutionary fashion. They must be revolutionary—that is to say, dialogical—from the outset.

REFLECTING ON THE READING

1. What does Freire mean when he writes, "Education is suffering from narration sickness"? Why is this a problem, in his view? Have you experienced what Freire calls the "narrative character" of education? Explain. Does your own experience support Freire's views about the problems with such an approach to education?

2. What are the primary characteristics of "the banking concept of education," as Freire describes them? Why is this approach to education so worrisome to Freire? Do you think his worries are justified? Do you think he overstates the problem? Why or why not?

3. What does Freire mean by the "teacher-student contradiction"? What does this contradiction reveal about how students are understood in the banking concept of education? What does it reveal about how teachers are understood? What does it say about what knowledge is and who controls it? Why is it something to be changed, in Freire's view? Do your own experiences as a student support Freire's ideas about the "student-teacher contradiction"? Explain.

4. In what specific ways does Freire believe the banking concept of education can serve the interests of those who hold political or economic power, whom Freire calls "oppressors"? Cite specific passages from the text to support your answer.

5. What does Freire mean when he describes reality as a *process?* What is the relationship of humans to this process? How does that view differ from how reality

is conceived under the banking concept of education? How does the view of reality as a process challenge the control exercised by oppressors under the banking concept of education, according to Freire?

6. What does Freire mean when he writes, "Liberation is a praxis"? How does that statement reflect his view of reality as a process?

7. What are the characteristics of Freire's "problem-posing" method of education? In what fundamental ways does it differ from the banking concept of education? How can it achieve liberation, according to Freire? How does it overcome the "teacher-student contradiction"? Do you think such an approach would work in the schools you attended? Explain.

8. Why does Freire believe it is so important for educators to help students who have been educated under the banking concept to change how they view themselves and their relationship to the world? How does his problem-posing method help accomplish this change?

Examining Rhetorical Strategies

1. Freire's writing style has been described as dense, abstract, and overly theoretical. Do you agree with that assessment? Why or why not? Do you think his style is appropriate to his subject matter? Could he have adequately discussed such subject matter in less abstract language, in your view? If so, why do you think he wrote in this style? What advantages or disadvantages might his writing style have, given his subject matter? How might it relate to his circumstances as a writer, educator, and exile (which he was at the time he wrote the book from which this essay is taken)?

2. Freire's theories about education and literacy grew out of his experiences as a literacy educator in South American countries that endured military rule. Some critics have charged that his ideas about literacy education and his approach to teaching literacy are valid only in that specific context and may not apply to different contexts, such as American schools. In what ways do you think Freire's ideas are specific to the experiences he had as an educator in Brazil and Chile under military regimes? Do you think his ideas are applicable to very different settings, such as the schools you attended? Do you think Freire was mindful of these differences in writing this essay? Explain. Do you think his critics are correct in pointing out that his approach to literacy education cannot work in places like American schools, where circumstances are so different from the classes he taught in Brazil and Chile? Explain, citing specific passages from his essay in your answer.

3. Freire's ideas about education and literacy have been widely influential around the world, including in countries like the United States that have very different political systems from the ones Freire experienced in his native South America. Based on your reading of this essay, why do you think his work has been so compelling and controversial? Why has it had such wide appeal outside his own country? Do you think Freire intended to write in ways that would provoke such vigorous reactions? Explain.

4. Based on this essay and on what you know about Paulo Freire, what audience do you think Freire was addressing in this essay? Point to specific passages in the essay to support your answer. Do you think his writing addresses this audience effectively? Why or why not?

5. Assess the way Freire makes his arguments against the "banking concept" of education and in favor of his "problem-posing" method. What kinds of support or evidence does he offer in his criticisms of the banking concept? How does he establish the need for his problem-posing method? Do you find his method of argumentation convincing? Why or why not? Do you think your response to that question relates to your own background in any way? Explain.

6. Describe your own overall reaction to Freire's ideas. Did you find yourself sympathetic to his arguments about education or resistant or indifferent to them? Why? Explain your reaction. In what ways can you account for your reaction to his ideas? How might your reaction relate to your own experiences as a student? To your own ideas about education and its purposes?

Engaging the Issues

1. Write an essay in which you summarize and explain Freire's ideas about education for a general audience of American readers who may not be familiar with him or his work. In your essay, summarize his criticisms of the banking concept of education and describe the key elements of his problem-posing method. Try to explain his basic assumptions about reality and the relationship of human beings to the world we live in. Explain why you think Freire's ideas have been so important and influential to some educators but so threatening to others.

2. Using Freire's ideas about education, write a critique of your own school (either the one you now attend or the high school you previously attended). In your critique, offer a summary of Freire's key ideas, and then describe your school in terms of Freire's ideas. Try to use your experiences in your school to illustrate what Freire means by ideas such as the banking concept of education, the student-teacher contradiction, and so on.

3. Compare the essay you wrote for Question #2 above with the essays written by several of your classmates. What similar or different problems in the schools you attended do your essays describe? On the basis of your discussion, try to draw conclusions about the usefulness of Freire's ideas about education or about the problems you see with his ideas.

4. Write a letter to the Paulo Freire Institute, an international organization devoted to education reform based on Freire's work, in which you offer your concerns or complaints about Freire's ideas or in which you express support for his work.

5. With a group of your classmates, construct a Web site based on Freire's ideas about education. Design the Web site not as a resource but as a tool to be used by students (either high school or college) to become the kind of critical thinkers that Freire hoped for. As part of your research for this project, visit instructional Web sites that are designed for student use in order to get some ideas for your

own site. What kinds of information, activities, and characteristics do these sites have? In designing your own site, try to base it on what you see as Freire's most important ideas about who students are and how they should be understood and treated. Include an explanation of your project for visitors to your site.

6. Using your library and the World Wide Web, find some examples of schools or classrooms in the United States in which Freire's ideas have been implemented. Review these programs to learn how Freire's ideas were adapted to American classrooms and how effective (or ineffective) the programs seem to be. If possible, visit such a classroom or school and talk to the teacher and students about their curriculum. Based on this research, write a report for your classmates about what you learned. In your report, describe what you learned about how Freire's ideas have been implemented in U.S. schools and identify problems or successes you've discovered. Draw conclusions about the usefulness of Freire's ideas in American schools.

7. Based on your research for Question #6 above, write a letter to your local school board in which you discuss the importance of Freire's ideas for American students. Propose changes to the schools in your area based on those ideas.

On the Road to Cultural Bias
A Critique of The Oregon Trail *CD-ROM*

BILL BIGELOW

INTRODUCTION   In the 1980's, as desktop computers became more affordable, more versatile, and more widely available, computer software companies began to develop a variety of "educational" programs that were designed to help students learn everything from the alphabet to zoology. If you attended elementary, middle, or high school during that time, you probably used such programs as part of your math, English, or social studies classes. Many educators saw exciting possibilities in such programs, which they believed could become powerful learning tools that might engage students' interest and foster in-depth thinking in ways that more traditional methods of instruction could not. Although these computer technologies were new and in many ways unprecedented, technology itself has always been an integral part of schooling. Consider, for instance, that the blackboard itself is an important technology that allows students and teachers to do certain kinds of tasks that they cannot do as easily with pencil and paper. But computers seemed to promise something more than just helping students and teachers accomplish practical tasks in their classrooms. Computers, many believed, could help foster critical thinking in students and perhaps deepen students' intellectual engagement with the material in the school curriculum.

It is precisely this potential of computers to shape thinking that teacher and writer Bill Bigelow addresses in the following article. Bigelow recognizes the potential power of computer programs to help students engage certain kinds of material in new and perhaps useful ways. In this case, he examines a popular computer program called *Oregon Trail II* that was widely praised by educators, parents, and others for the effective way it could help students understand the experience of settlers who traveled that famous trail in the 1800's. Bigelow acknowledges that this program can teach students a great deal about what it was like to journey to Oregon on that trail in the nineteenth century and to try to make a new home in unfamiliar territory. But he also believes that the game—along with similar educational games—carries less obvious but more powerful and perhaps damaging messages about issues of race, class, gender, violence, and the environment. Because educational computer games are programmed by human beings, he believes the games will inevitably be shaped by the biases of the programmers. Thus, playing a game like *Oregon Trail II* is not just a potential learning experience: it is an *ideological* experience as well.

Bigelow is not the only educator to express such concerns about the uses of technology in education. In the past few decades, as computers have become such an integral a part of contemporary life and as they have begun to influence education, critics of all ideological views have warned about some of the potentially damaging implications of technology in schools. Programs like *Oregon Trail II* may communicate values to students that teachers and parents would rather the students not learn, as Bigelow argues, but the influence of technology in schools extends well beyond the use of educational software. Some critics worry that students might have access to inappropriate ideas and information by using the Internet to do their schoolwork; others worry that some teachers rely too heavily on computers to teach rote skills rather than the critical thinking students will eventually need to secure desirable employment. Still others point out that computers have the potential to enable administrators to exert greater control over students and teachers. Such concerns may grow as computers and related technologies become ever more common in schools. Or perhaps these concerns will diminish as students and teachers become more and more familiar with technology and, thus, less sensitive to the kinds of troubling messages that Bigelow believes are hidden in computer games like *Oregon Trail II*. Whatever the case, his critique of *Oregon Trail II* may help call attention to the subtle but powerful ways in which technology can influence what and how we learn. And perhaps it may prompt you to reconsider your own views about the role of such technology in education.

Bill Bigelow is a teacher in Portland, Oregon, who has been active in promoting progressive educational ideas and pedagogies. He has taught history at the high school level in Portland and has also taught in the Graduate Teacher Education Program at Portland State University. He has coedited two books about progressive education, *Rethinking Columbus: The Next 500 Years* (1998) and *Rethinking Our Classrooms: Teaching for Equity and Justice* (1994), and has written a number of articles about teaching, many of them published in *Rethinking Schools,* a journal about urban educational issues for which he has served as an editorial associate. The following article originally appeared in *Rethinking Schools* in 1995; the version included here appeared in *Language Arts,* a journal for literacy educators, in 1997.

1. If you have played and are familiar with *Oregon Trail II,* take a moment to recall the game. If you haven't played the game and have the opportunity to do so, play it. Or play a similar educational game. How did you like the game? What features of the game strike you? What was most enjoyable or troublesome about the game for you? Keep your reaction to the game in mind as you begin reading Bigelow's critique of it.

2. *Oregon Trail II,* the computer game that Bigelow discusses in the following article, is about a period in American history in which the American West was settled by people from the eastern part of the United States, most of whom were White. One of the focal points of Bigelow's critique of the game is the way the game seems to depict that period and the attitudes it seems to communicate about the settlement of the American West. As you prepare to read this essay, examine your own attitudes about the settlement of the American West during the 1800's. What do you know about that period and about the events and conflicts that occurred as White Americans moved west? Do you view that period in a favorable way? Do you associate it with problems in the way the United States was settled? As you read, consider how your own views about that period might influence your reaction to Bigelow's critique.

T he critics all agree: *The Oregon Trail* (1993) is one of the greatest educational computer games ever produced. *Prides' Guide to Educational Software* awarded it five stars for being "a wholesome, absorbing historical simulation," and "multiethnic," to boot (Pride & Pride, 1992, p. 419). The new version, *The Oregon Trail II* (1994), is the "best history simulation we've seen to date," according to Warren Buckleitner, editor of *Children's Software Review Newsletter* (*The Oregon Trail II,* 1994). Susan Schilling, a key developer of *The Oregon Trail II* and recently hired by *Star Wars* film maker George Lucas to head Lucas Learning Ltd., promises new interactive CD-ROMs targeted at children 6 to 15 years old and concentrated in math and language arts (Armstrong, 1996).

Because interactive CD-ROMs like *The Oregon Trail* are encyclopedic in the amount of information they offer, and because they allow students a seemingly endless number of choices, the new software may appear educationally progressive. CD-ROMs seem tailor-made for the classrooms of tomorrow. They are hands-on and "student-centered." They are generally interdisciplinary—for example, *The Oregon Trail II* blends reading, writing, history, geography, math, science, and health. And they are useful in multi-age classrooms because they allow students of various knowledge levels to "play" and learn. But like the walls of a maze, the choices built into interactive CD-ROMs also channel participants in very definite directions. The CD-ROMs are programmed by people—people with particular cultural biases—and children who play the new computer games encounter the biases of the programmers (Bowers, 1988). Just as we would not invite a stranger into our classrooms and then leave the room, we as teachers need to become aware of the political perspectives of CD-ROMs and to equip our students to "read" them critically.

At one level, this article is a critical review of *The Oregon Trail!* CD-ROMs. I ask what knowledge is highlighted, what is hidden, and what values are imparted as students play the games. But I also reflect on the nature of the new electronic curricula, and suggest some questions teachers can ask before choosing to use these materials with their students. Finally, I offer some classroom activities that might begin to develop students' critical computer literacy.

Playing the Game

In both *The Oregon Trail* and *The Oregon Trail II,* students become members of families and wagon trains crossing the Plains in the 1840s or 1850s on the way to the Oregon Territory. A player's objective, according to the game guidebook, is to safely reach the Oregon Territory with one's family, thereby "increasing one's options for economic success" (*The Oregon Trail II*, 1994).

The enormous number of choices offered in any one session—what to buy for the journey; the kind of wagon to take; whether to use horses, oxen, or mules; the size of the wagon train with which to travel; whom to "talk" to along the way; when and where to hunt; when to rest; and how fast to travel—is a kind of gentle seduction to students. It invites them to "try on this world view and see how it fits." In an interactive CD-ROM, students don't merely identify with a particular character, they actually adopt his or her frame of reference and act as if they were that character (Provenzo, 1991). In *The Oregon Trail,* a player quickly bonds with the "pioneer" maneuvering through the "wilderness."

In preparation for this article, I played *The Oregon Trail II* until my eyes became blurry. I can see its attraction to teachers. One can't play the game without learning a lot about the geography between Missouri and Oregon. (However, I hope I never have to ford another virtual river again.) Reading the trail guide as one plays teaches much about the ailments confronted on the Oregon Trail and some of the treatments. Students can learn a tremendous amount about the details of life for the trekkers to Oregon, including the kinds of wagons required, the supplies needed, the vegetation encountered along the route, and so forth. And the game has a certain multicultural and gender-fair veneer that, however limited, contrasts favorably with the white male-dominated texts of yesteryear. But as much as the game teaches, it *mis*-teaches more. In fundamental respects, *The Oregon Trail* is sexist, racist, culturally insensitive, and contemptuous of the earth. It imparts bad values and wrong history.

They Look Like Women, But . . .

To its credit, *The Oregon Trail II* includes large numbers of women. Although I didn't count, women appear to make up roughly half the people students encounter as they play. But this surface equity is misleading. Women may be present, but gender is not acknowledged as an issue in *The Oregon Trail.* For example, in the opening sequences, the game requires students to select a profession, any special skills they will possess, the kind of wagon to take, and the city from which to depart. Class is recognized as an issue—bankers begin with more money than saddle makers, for example—but not gender or race. A player cannot choose to be a female or African American.

Without acknowledging it, *The Oregon Trail* maneuvers students into thinking and acting as if they were all males. The game highlights a male lifestyle and poses problems that historically fell within the male domain, such as whether and where to hunt, which route to take, whether and what to trade, and whether to caulk a wagon or ford a river. However, as I began to read feminist scholarship on the Oregon Trail (e.g., Faragher & Stansell, 1992; Kesselman, 1976; Schlissel, 1992), I realized that women and men experienced the Trail differently. It's clear from reading women's diaries of the period that women played little or no role in deciding whether to embark on the trip, where to camp, which routes to take, and the like. In real life, women's decisions revolved around how to maintain a semblance of community under great stress, how "to preserve the home in transit" (Faragher & Stansell, 1992, p. 190). Women decided where to look for firewood or buffalo chips, how and what to cook using hot rocks, how to care for the children, and how to resolve conflicts between travelers, especially between the men.

These were real-life decisions, but, with the exception of treating illness, they're missing from *The Oregon Trail.* Students are rarely required to think about the intricacies of preserving "the home in transit" for 2000 miles. An *Oregon Trail II* information box on the screen informs a player when "morale" is high or low, but other than making better male-oriented decisions, what's a player to do? *The Oregon Trail* offers no opportunities to encounter the choices of the Trail as women of the time would have encountered them and to make decisions that might enhance community and thus "morale." As Lillian Schlissel (1992) concludes in her study, *Women's Diaries of the Westward Journey:*

> If ever there was a time when men and women turned their psychic energies toward opposite visions, the overland journey was that time. Sitting side by side on a wagon seat, a man and a woman felt different needs as they stared at the endless road that led into the New Country. (p. 15)

Similarly, *The Oregon Trail* fails to represent the texture of community life on the Trail. Students confront a seemingly endless stream of problems posed by *The Oregon Trail* programmers, but rarely encounter the details of life, especially that of women's lives. By contrast, in an article in the book, *America's Working Women,* Amy Kesselman (1976) includes this passage from the diary of one female trekker, Catherine Haun, in 1849:

> We women folk visited from wagon to wagon or congenial friends spent an hour walking ever westward, and talking over our home life "back in the states" telling of the loved ones left behind; voicing our hopes for the future in the far west and even whispering, a little friendly gossip of pioneer life. High teas were not popular but tatting, knitting, crocheting, exchanging receipts for cooking beans or dried apples or swopping food for the sake of variety kept us in practice of feminine occupations and diversions. (p. 71)

The male orientation of *The Oregon Trail* is brought into sharp relief in the game's handling of Independence Day commemoration. Students-as-pioneers are asked if they wish to "Celebrate the Fourth!" If so, they click on this option and hear loud "Yahoos" and guns firing. Compare this image to the communal preparations described in Enoch Conyers' 1852 diary:

> A little further on is a group of young ladies seated on the grass talking over the prob-lem of manufacturing "Old Glory" to wave over our festivities. The question arose as to where we are to obtain the material for the flag. One lady brought forth a sheet. This gave the ladies an idea. Quick as thought another brought a skirt for the red stripes. . . . Another lady ran to her tent and brought forth a blue jacket, saying: "Here, take this; it will do for the field." Needles and thread were soon secured and the ladies went at their task with a will, one lady remarking that "Necessity is the mother of invention," and the answer came back, "Yes, and the ladies of our com-pany are equal to the task." (Hill, 1989, p. 58)

The contrast of the "Yahoos" and gunfire of *The Oregon Trail* to the collective female exhilaration described in the diary excerpt is striking. This contrast alerted me to something so obvious that it took me a while to recognize. In *The Oregon Trail,* people don't talk to *each other,* they all talk to you, the player. Everyone in *The Oregon Trail*-constructed world directs her or his conversation to you, underscoring the sim-ulation's individualistic ideology that all the world exists for *you,* the controller of the mouse. An *Oregon Trail* more alert to feminist insights and women's experiences would highlight relationships between people, would focus on how the experience affects our feelings for each other, and would feature how women worked with one another to create and maintain a community, as women's diary entries clearly reveal.

As I indicated, large numbers of women appear throughout *The Oregon Trail* simulation, and they often give good advice, perhaps better advice than the men we encounter. But *The Oregon Trail*'s abundance of women, and its apparent effort to be gender-fair, masks an essential problem: The choice-structure of the simulation privileges men's experience and virtually erases women's experience.

African Americans as Tokens

From the game's beginning, when a player starts off in Independence or St. Joseph's, Missouri, African Americans dot *The Oregon Trail* landscape. By and large, however, they are no more than black-colored white people. Although Missouri was a slave state throughout the Oregon Trail period, I never encountered the term "slavery" while playing the game. I found race explicitly acknowledged in only one exchange, when I "talked" to an African American woman along the trail. She said: "I'm Isabella. I'm traveling with the Raleighs and their people. My job is to keep after the cows and watch the children. My husband Fred is the ox-driver—best there is." I won-dered if they were free or enslaved, and if we are to assume the Raleighs are white. I asked to know more, and Isabella said: "I was born in Delaware. My father used to tell me stories of Africa and promised one day we'd find ourselves going home. But I don't know if I'm getting closer or farther away with all this walking." The end. Like Missouri, Delaware was a slave state in antebellum days, but this is not shared with students. Isabella offers provocative details, but they hide more than they reveal about her identity and culture.

The Oregon Trail's treatment of African Americans reflects a superficial multiculturalism. Black people are present, but their lives aren't. Attending to matters of race requires more than including lots of black faces or having little girls "talk black": "I think it's time we be moving on now." (This little girl reappears from time to time to repeat these same words. A man who looks Mexican, likewise, shows up frequently to say, with a heavy accent: "Time is a-wasting. Let's head out!")

Although one's life prospects and world view in the 1840s and 1850s—as today—were dramatically shaped by one's race, this factor is invisible in *The Oregon Trail*. *The Oregon Trail* players know their occupations but not their racial identities, even though these identities were vital to the decisions the Oregon Trail travelers made before leaving on their journeys and along the way.

For example, many of the constitutions of societies that sponsored wagon trains specifically excluded blacks from making the trip west. Nonetheless, as Elizabeth McLagan (1980) points out in her history of blacks in Oregon, *A Peculiar Paradise*, blacks did travel the Oregon Trail, some as slaves, some as servants, and even some, like George Bush, as well-to-do pioneers. Race may not have seemed important to *The Oregon Trail* programmers but race mattered a great deal to Bush: Along the Trail, he confided to another emigrant that if he experienced too much prejudice in Oregon, he would travel south to California or New Mexico and seek the protection of the Mexican government (McLagan, 1980).

And Bush had reason to be apprehensive: African Americans arriving in Oregon Territory during the 1840s and 1850s were greeted by laws barring them from residency. Two black exclusion laws were passed in the Oregon Territory in the 1840s, and a clause in the Oregon state constitution barring black residency was ratified in 1857 by a margin of eight to one—a clause, incidentally, not repealed until 1926.

Upon completion of one of my simulated Oregon Trail journeys, I clicked to see how my life turned out: "In 1855, Bill built a home on 463 acres of land in the Rogue River Valley of Oregon," experienced only "moderate success" and later moved to Medford, "establishing a small business that proved more stable and satisfying." Although *The Oregon Trail* simulation never acknowledges it, "Bill" must have been white because in 1850 the U.S. Congress passed the Oregon Donation Land Act granting 640 acres to free white males and their wives. It is unlikely that a black man, and much less a black woman, would have been granted land in 1855 or have been allowed to start a business in Medford some years later.

Why were whites so insistent that blacks not live in Oregon? The preamble of one black exclusion bill explained that "situated as the people of Oregon are, in the midst of an Indian population, it would be highly dangerous to allow free negroes and mulattoes to reside in the territory or to intermix with the Indians, instilling in their minds feelings of hostility against the white race . . . " (McLagan, 1980, p. 26). And Samuel Thurston, a delegate to Congress from the Oregon Territory, explained in 1850 why blacks should not be entitled to homestead in Oregon:

> The negroes associate with the Indians and intermarry, and, if their free ingress is encouraged or allowed, there would a relationship spring up between them and the different tribes, and a mixed race would ensue inimical to the whites; and the Indians being led on by the negro who is better acquainted with the customs, language, and manners of the whites, than the Indian, these savages would become

much more formidable than they otherwise would, and long and bloody wars would be the fruits of the commingling of the races. It is the principle of self preservation that justifies the action of the Oregon legislature. (McLagan, 1980, pp. 30–31)

Thurston's argument carried the day. But *The Oregon Trail* programmers have framed the issues so that race seems irrelevant. Thus, once students-as-pioneers arrive in Oregon, most of them will live happily ever after—never considering the impact that race would have on living conditions.

Just Passing Through?

The Oregon Trail programmers are careful not to portray Indians as the "enemy" of westward trekkers. However, the simulation's superficial sympathy for Native groups masks a profound insensitivity to Indian cultures and to the earth that sustained these cultures. The simulation guidebook lists numerous Indian nations by name—and respectfully *calls* them "nations." *The Oregon Trail* guidebook explains that emigrants' fear of Indians is "greatly exaggerated."

> Some travelers have been known to cross the entire breadth of the continent from the Missouri River to the Sierra Nevadas without ever laying eye on an Indian, except perhaps for occasional brief sightings from a distance. This is all well and good, for it is probably best for all parties concerned for emigrants and Indians to avoid contact with each other. Such meetings are often the source of misunderstandings, sometimes with regrettable consequences.

Emigrants often spread disease, according to the guidebook, which made the Indians "distrust and dislike" them. The guidebook further warns *The Oregon Trail* players not to over-hunt game in any one place as "few things will incur the wrath of the Indian peoples more than an overstayed welcome accompanied by the egregious waste of the natural resources upon which they depend."

The ideology embedded in *The Oregon Trail* and *The Oregon Trail II* is selfish and goal-driven: Emigrants should care about indigenous people only insofar as they need to avoid "misunderstanding" and incurring the wrath of potentially hostile natives. *The Oregon Trail* promotes an anthropocentric earth-as-natural resource outlook. Nature is a *thing* to be consumed or overcome as people traverse the country in search for success in a faraway land. The simulation's structure coerces children into identifying with white settlers and dismissing non-white others. It also contributes to the broader curricular racialization of identity that students absorb—learning who constitutes the normalized "we" and who is excluded.

The Oregon Trail players need not take into account the lives of others unless it's necessary to do so in order to accomplish their personal objectives. Thus, the cultures of Plains Indians are backgrounded. The game marginalizes their view of the earth. Contrast, for example, the Indians' term "mother earth" with *The Oregon Trail* term "natural resource." The metaphor of earth as mother suggests humans in a reciprocal relationship with a natural world that is alive, that nourishes us, and that sustains us. On the other hand, a resource is a thing to be used. It exists *for* us, outside of us, and we have no obligations in return.

The consequences of the Oregon Trail for the Plains Indians, the Indians of the Northwest, and for the earth were devastating. In fairness to *The Oregon Trail,* students may hear some of the details of this upheaval as they play. For example, on one trip I encountered a "Pawnee Village." Had I paid attention to the warning in the guidebook to "avoid contact" I would have ignored it and continued on my trip. But I entered and "talked" to the people I encountered there. A Pawnee women said: "Why do you bother me? I don't want to trade. The things that we get from the white travelers don't make up for all that we lose." I clicked to hear more. "We didn't know the whooping cough, measles, or the smallpox until your people brought them to us. Our medicine cannot cure these strange diseases, and our children are dying." I clicked on "Do you have any advice?" Angrily, she said, "No. I just want you to leave us alone." The implication is that if I just "leave [them] alone" and continue on the trail I can pursue my dream without hurting the Indians.

However, this interpretation hides the fact that the Oregon Trail itself, not just contact with the so-called pioneers, devastated Indian cultures and the ecology of which those cultures were an integral part. Johansen and Maestas' (1979) description of the Lakota language for talking about these pioneers helps us see how they were regarded by the Indians:

> (The Lakota) used a metaphor to describe the newcomers. It was *Wasi'chu,* which means "takes the fat," or "greedy person." Within the modern Indian movement, *Wasi'chu* has come to mean those corporations and individuals, with their governmental accomplices, which continue to covet Indian lives, land, and resources for private profit. *Wasi'chu* does not describe a race; it describes a state of mind. (p. 6)

The *Wasi'chu* cut down all the cottonwood trees found along the rich bottom lands of plains rivers—trees which "offered crucial protection during winter blizzards as well as concealing a village's smoke from its enemies. In lean seasons, horses fed on its bark, which was surprisingly nourishing" (Davidson & Lytle, 1992, p. 114).

The Oregon Trail created serious wood shortages, which even the *Wasi'chu* acknowledged. "By the Mormon guide we here expected to find the last timber," wrote overlander A. W. Harlan in describing the Platte River, "but all had been used up by others ahead of us so we must go about 200 miles without any provisions cooked up." A few weeks later, in sight of the Black Hills, Harlan wrote: "[W]e have passed many cottonwood stumps but no timber . . ." (Davidson & Lytle, 1992, p. 115).

Wasi'chu rifles also killed tremendous numbers of buffalo that Plains Indians depended upon for survival. One traveler in the 1850s wrote that, "The valley of the Platte for 200 miles presents the aspect of the vicinity of a slaughter yard, dotted all over with skeletons of buffaloes" (Davidson & Lytle, 1992, p. 117). Very soon after the beginning of the Oregon Trail the buffalo learned to avoid the Trail, their herds migrating both south and north. Edward Lazarus (1991) points out in *Black Hills/White Justice: The Sioux Nation Versus the United States—1775 to the Present* that "the Oregon Trail did more than move the buffalo; it destroyed the hunting pattern of the Sioux, forcing them to follow the herds to the fringes of their domain and to expose themselves to the raids of their enemies" (p. 14).

However, wrapped in their cocoons of self-interest, *The Oregon Trail* players push on, oblivious to the mayhem and misery they cause in their westward drive. This is surely an unintended, and yet intrinsic, part of the game's message: Pursue your goal as an autonomous individual, ignore the social and ecological consequences: "look out for number one."

No Violence Here

The Oregon Trail never suggests to its simulated pioneers that they should seek permission of Indian nations to travel through their territory. And from this key omission flow other omissions. The simulation doesn't inform players that, because of the disruptions wrought by the daily intrusions of the westward migration, Plains Indians regularly demanded tribute from the trekkers. As John Unruh, Jr. (1993), writes in *The Plains Across:*

> The natives explicitly emphasized that the throngs of overlanders were killing and scaring away buffalo and other wild game, overgrazing prairie grasses, exhausting the small quantity of available timber, and depleting water resources. The tribute payments . . . were demanded mainly by the Sac and Fox, Kickapoo, Pawnee, and Sioux Indians—the tribes closest to the Missouri River frontier and therefore those feeling most keenly the pressures of white men increasingly impinging upon their domains. (p. 169)

Wasi'chu travelers resented this Indian-imposed taxation and their resentment frequently turned to hostility and violence, especially in the later years of the Trail. The Pawnee were "hateful wretches," wrote Dr. Thomas Wolfe in 1852, for demanding a 25 cent toll at a bridge across Shell Creek near the North Platte River (Unruh, 1993, p. 171). Shell Creek and other crossings became flashpoints that escalated into violent skirmishes resulting in the deaths of settlers and Indians.

Despite the increasing violence along the Oregon Trail, one choice *The Oregon Trail* programmers don't offer students-as-trekkers is the choice to harm Indians. Doubtlessly MECC, the publisher of *The Oregon Trail,* is not anxious to promote racism toward Native peoples. However, because simulation players can't hurt or even speak ill of Indians, the game fails to alert students that white hostility was one feature of the westward migration. The omission is significant because the sanitized non-violent *The Oregon Trail* fails to equip students to reflect on the origins of conflicts between whites and Indians. Nor does it offer students any insights into the racial antagonism that fueled this violence. In all my play of *The Oregon Trail,* I can't recall any blatant racism directed at Indians. But as Unruh (1993) points out, "The callous attitude of cultural and racial superiority so many overlanders exemplified was of considerable significance in producing the volatile milieu in which more and more tragedies occurred" (p. 186).

The End of the Trail

> Soon there will come from the rising sun a different kind of man from any you have yet seen, who will bring with them a book and will teach you everything, after that the world will fall to pieces.
>
> *—Spokan Prophet, 1790 (Limerick, 1987, p. 39)*

A person can spend two or three hours—or more—playing one game of *The Oregon Trail* before finally reaching Oregon Territory. Upon arrival, a player is awarded points and told how his or her life in Oregon turned out. Yet the game fails to raise vital questions about one's right to be there in the first place and what happened to the people who were there first.

In its section on the "Destination," the guidebook offers students its wisdom on how they should view life in a new land. It's a passage that underscores the messages students absorb while engaged in the simulation. These comforting words of advice and social vision are worth quoting at length:

> Once you reach the end of your journey, you should go to the nearest large town to establish your land claim. If there are no large towns in the area, simply find an unclaimed tract of land and settle down. . . . As they say, possession is nine-tenths of the law, and if you have settled and worked land that hasn't yet been claimed by anyone else, you should have little or no trouble legally establishing your claim at a later time. As more and more Americans move into the region, more cities and towns will spring up, further increasing one's options for economic success. Rest assured in the facts that men and women who are willing to work hard will find their labors richly rewarded, and that you, by going west, are helping to spread American civilization from ocean to ocean across this great continent, building a glorious future for generations to come! (*The Oregon Trail II,* 1994)

The Lakota scholar and activist Vine Deloria, Jr. (1977), in his book, *Indians of The Pacific Northwest,* offers a less sanguine perspective than that included in the CD-ROM guidebook. People coming in on the Oregon Trail "simply arrived on the scene and started building. If there were Indians or previous settlers on the spot they were promptly run off under one pretext or another. Lawlessness and thievery dominated the area" (p. 53). From 1850 on, using provisions of the Oregon Donation Act, thousands of "settlers" invaded "with impunity."

As Deloria points out, there were some in Congress who were aware that they were encouraging settlers to steal Indian land, and so Congress passed the Indian Treaty Act requiring the United States to get formal agreements from Indian tribes. Anson Dart, appointed to secure land concessions, pursued this objective in a despicable fashion. For example, he refused to have the treaties translated into the Indians' languages, instead favoring "Chinook jargon," a non-language of fewer than 300 words good for trading, giving orders, and little else. Dart's mandate was to move all the Indians east of the Cascades, but he decided some tribes, like the Tillamooks and Chinooks, should keep small amounts of land as cheap labor reserves:

> Almost without exception, I have found [the Indians] anxious to work at employment at common labor and willing too, to work at prices much below that demanded by the whites. The Indians make all the rails used in fencing, and at this time do the boating upon the rivers: In consideration, therefore, of the usefulness as labourers in the settlements, it was believed to be far better for the Country that they should not be removed from the settled portion [sic] of Oregon if it were possible to do so. (Deloria, 1977, p. 51)

Meanwhile, in southwestern Oregon white vigilantes didn't wait for treaty niceties to be consummated. Between 1852 and 1856 self-proclaimed Volunteers attacked Indians for alleged misdeeds or simply because they were Indians. In August of 1853, one Martin Angel rode into the Rogue River Valley gold mining town of Jacksonville shouting, "Nits breed lice. We have been killing Indians in the valley all day," and "Exterminate the whole race" (Beckham, 1991, p. 103). Minutes later a mob of about 800 white men hanged a 7-year-old Indian boy. In October 1855, a group of whites massacred 23 Indian men, women, and children. This incident began the Rogue Indian war, which lasted until June 1856 (Beckham, 1991). Recall that this is the same region and the same year in one Oregon Trail session where "Bill" built a home and experienced "moderate success," but, thanks to *The Oregon Trail* programmers, he learned nothing of the social conflicts swirling around him.

Nor did Bill learn that, even as a white person, he could protest the outrages committed against the Rogue River Valley Indians, as did one anonymous "Volunteer" in a passionate 1853 letter to the *Oregon Statesman* newspaper:

> A few years since the whole valley was theirs [the Indians'] alone. No white man's foot had ever trod it. They believed it theirs forever. But the gold digger come, with his pan and his pick and shovel, and hundreds followed. And they saw in astonishment their streams muddied, towns built, their valley fenced and taken. And where their squaws dug camus, their winter food, and their children were wont to gambol, they saw dug and plowed, and their own food sown by the hand of nature, rooted out forever, and the ground it occupied appropriated to the rearing of vegetables for the white man. Perhaps no malice yet entered the Indian breast. But when he was weary of hunting in the mountains without success, and was hungry, and approached the white man's tent for bread; where instead of bread he received curses and kicks, ye treaty kicking men—ye Indian exterminators think of these things.
>
> — *A Soldier (Applegate & O'Donnell, 1994, p. 34)*

The Oregon Trail hides the nature of the Euro-American invasion in at least two ways. In the first place, it simply fails to inform simulation participants what happened between settlers and Indians. To *The Oregon Trail* player, it doesn't feel like an invasion; it doesn't feel wrong. After one of my arrivals, in 1848, "Life in the new land turned out to be happy and successful for Bill, who always cherished bittersweet but proud memories of the months spent on the Oregon Trail." (This struck me as a rather odd account given that I had lost all 3 of my children on the trip.) The only person that matters is the simulation player. I was never told whether life turned out equally "happy and successful" for the Klamaths, Yakimas, Cayuses, Nez Percés, Wallawallas, and all the others who occupied this land generations before the *Wasi'chu* arrived. The second way the nature of the white invasion is hidden has to do with the structure of the simulation. For a couple hours or more the player endures substantial doses of frustration, tedium, and difficulty. By the time the Willamette or Rogue River Valleys come up on the screen we, the simulated trekkers, feel we *deserve* the land, that our labors in transit should be "richly rewarded" with the best land we can find.

Data Deception and Thoughts on What to Do About It

In the Beatles' song, all you need is love; in *The Oregon Trail,* all you need are data. *The Oregon Trail* offers students gobs of information: snake bite remedies, river locations and depths, wagon specifications, ferry costs, and daily climate reports. Loaded with facts, it feels comprehensive. Loaded with people voicing contrasting opinions, it feels balanced. Loaded with choices, it feels democratic. But the simulation begins from no moral or ethical standpoint beyond individual material success; it contains no vision of social or ecological justice, and, hence, promotes a full litany of sexist, racist, and imperialist perspectives, as well as exploitive perspectives of the earth. And simultaneously, it hides these biases. The combination is insidious, and makes interactive CD-ROMs like this one more difficult to critique than traditional textbooks or films. The forced identification of player with simulation protagonist leaves the student no option but to follow the ideological map laid out by the programmers.

Nonetheless, my critique is not a call to boycott the new "edutainment" resources. But we need to remember that these CD-ROMs are not teacher substitutes. The teacher's role in analyzing and presenting these devices in a broader ethical context is absolutely vital. Thus, teachers across the country must begin a dialogue toward developing a critical computer literacy. We need to figure out ways to equip students with the ability to recognize and evaluate the deep moral and political messages imparted by these CD-ROMs as they maneuver among the various computer software programs.

Before choosing to use CD-ROMs that involve people and places, like *The Oregon Trail*—or, for example, its newer siblings *The Yukon Trail, The Amazon Trail,* and *Africa Trail*—teachers should consider the following questions.

- *Which social groups are students not invited to identify with in the simulation?* For example, Native Americans, African Americans, women, and Latinos are superficially represented in *The Oregon Trail,* but the "stuff" of their lives is missing.

- *How might these social groups frame problems differently than the simulation?* As we saw in the foregoing critique of *The Oregon Trail,* women tended to focus more on maintaining community than on hunting. Native Americans had a profoundly different relationship to the earth than did the Euro-American "tamers of the wilderness."

- *What decisions do simulation participants make that may have consequences for social groups not highlighted in the simulation?* And what are these consequences? Although the very existence of the Oregon Trail contributed to the decimation of Plains and Northwest Indians, simulation participants are never asked to consider the broader effects of their decision-making. What may be an ethical individual choice may be unethical when multiplied several hundred thousand times. In this respect, CD-ROM choice-making both reflects and reinforces conventional notions of freedom that justify disastrous social and ecological practices.

- *What decisions do simulation participants make that may have consequences for the earth and non-human life?* Similarly, a simulation participant's choice to cut down trees for firewood may be rational for that individual, but may also have deleterious effects on the ecological balance of a particular bio-region.

- *If the simulation is time-specific, as in the case of* The Oregon Trail, *what were the social and environmental consequences for the time period following the time represented in the simulation?* The wars between Indians and the U.S. Cavalry in the latter decades of the nineteenth century are inexplicable without the Oregon Trail as prologue.

- *Can we name the ideological orientation of a particular CD-ROM?* The question is included here simply to remind us that all computer materials—indeed, all curricula—have an ideology. Our first step is to become aware of that ideology.

These questions are hardly exhaustive, but may suggest a useful direction to begin thinking about CD-ROMs as they become increasingly available and begin to cover more and more subjects.

Finally, let me use the example of *The Oregon Trail* to introduce some ways teachers can begin to foster a critical computer literacy. Once we have identified some of the social groups that are substantially missing in a CD-ROM activity like *The Oregon Trail,* we can try to locate excerpts from diaries, speeches, or other communications of members of these groups. We can then engage students in role play where, as a class, students face a number of Oregon Trail problems. For example, class members could portray women on the Oregon Trail and decide how they would attempt to maintain a community in transit. Or they might role play a possible discussion of Oglala people as they confront the increasingly disruptive presence of *Wasi'chu* crossing their lands. Students might be asked to list all the ways African Americans would experience the Oregon Trail differently than Euro-Americans—from the planning of the trip to the trip itself. (It's unlikely, for example, that every white person on the streets of Independence, Missouri, said a friendly "Howdy," to the blacks he encountered, as each of them does to the implied but unacknowledged white male *Oregon Trail* simulation player.) Students also could assume a particular racial, cultural, or gender identity, and note whether the choices or experiences described in the simulation make sense from the standpoint of a member of their group. For example, would a typical African American in Missouri in 1850 be allowed to choose from which city to begin the trek west?

As we share with students the social and ecological costs of the Oregon Trail, we could ask them to write critical letters to each of the "pioneers" they portrayed in the simulation. Some could represent Rogue River Valley Indians, Shoshoni people, or even Mother Earth. For instance, how does Mother Earth respond to the casual felling of every Cottonwood tree along the Platte River? A Native American elder or activist could be invited into the classroom to speak about the concerns important to his or her people and about the history of white-Indian relations.

We could encourage students to think about the politics of naming in the simulation. They could suggest alternative names for the Oregon Trail itself. For example, the historian of the American West, Frederick Merk (1978), aptly calls the Oregon Trail a "path of empire." Writer Dan Georgakas (1973) names it a "march of death." Other names might be "invasion of the West," or "The 20-year trespass." Just as with Columbus's "discovery" of America, naming shapes understanding, and we need classroom activities to uncover this process.

Students could write and illustrate children's books describing the Oregon Trail from the standpoint of women, African Americans, Native Americans, or the earth.

After doing activities like these, students could "play" *The Oregon Trail* again. What do they see this time that they didn't see before? Whose world view is highlighted and whose is hidden? If they choose, they might present their findings to other classes or to teachers who may be considering the use of CD-ROMs.

The Oregon Trail is no more morally obnoxious than other CD-ROMs or curricular materials with similar ideological biases. My aim here is broader than merely shaking a scolding finger at MECC, publisher of *The Oregon Trail* series. I've tried to demonstrate why teachers and students must develop a critical computer literacy. Some of the new CD-ROMs seem more socially aware than the blatantly culturally insensitive materials that still fill school libraries and book rooms. And the flashy new computer packages also invoke terms long sacred to educators: student empowerment, individual choice, creativity, and high interest. It's vital that we remember that coincident with the arrival of these new educational toys is a deepening social and ecological crisis. Global and national inequality between haves and have-nots is increasing. Violence of all kinds is endemic. And the earth is being consumed at a ferocious pace. Computer programs are not politically neutral in the big moral contests of our time. Inevitably, they take sides. Thus, a critical computer literacy, one with a social and ecological conscience, is more than just a good idea—it's a basic skill.

References

Applegate, S., & O'Donnell, T. (1994). *Talking on paper: An anthology of Oregon letters and diaries.* Corvallis, OR: Oregon State University Press.

Armstrong, D. (1996, February 23). Lucas getting into education via CD-ROM. *The San Francisco Examiner,* pp. E-1–E-2.

Beckham, S. D. (1991). Federal-Indian relations. *The First Oregonians.* Portland, OR: Oregon Council for the Humanities.

Bowers, C. A. (1988). *The cultural dimensions of educational computing: Understanding the non-neutrality of technology.* New York: Teachers College Press.

Davidson, J. W., & Lytle, M. H. (1992). *After the fact: The art of historical detection.* New York: McGraw-Hill.

Deloria, Jr., V. (1977). *Indians of the Pacific Northwest.* Garden City, NY: Doubleday.

Faragher, J., & Stansell, C. (1992). Women and their families on the overland trail to California and Oregon, 1842–1867. In F. Binder & D. Reimer (Eds.), *The way we lived: Essays and documents in American social history, Vol. I* (pp. 188–195). Lexington, MA: Heath.

Georgakas, D. (1973). *Red shadows: The history of Native Americans from 1600 to 1900, from the desert to the Pacific Coast.* Garden City, NY: Zenith.

Hill, W. E. (1989). *The Oregon Trail: Yesterday and today.* Caldwell, ID: Caxton Printers.

Johansen, B., & Maestas, R. (1979). *Wasi'chu: The continuing Indian wars.* New York: Monthly Review.

Kesselman, A. (1976). Diaries and reminiscences of women on the Oregon Trail: A study in consciousness. In R. Baxandall, L. Gordon, & S. Reverby (Eds.), *America's working women: A documentary history—1600 to the present* (pp. 69–72). New York: Vintage.

Lazarus, E. (1991). *Black Hills/White justice: The Sioux Nation versus the United States—1775 to the present.* New York: HarperCollins.

Limerick, P. N. (1987). *The legacy of conquest: The unbroken past of the American west.* New York: W. W. Norton.

McLagan, E. (1980). *A peculiar paradise: A history of Blacks in Oregon, 1788–1940.* Portland, OR: The Georgian Press.

Merk, F. (1978). *History of the westward movement.* New York: Knopf.

The Oregon Trail [Computer software]. (1993). Minneapolis, MN: Minnesota Educational Computer Company.

The Oregon Trail II [Computer software]. (1994). Minneapolis, MN: Minnesota Educational Computer Company.

Pride, B., & Pride, M. (1992). *Prides' guide to educational software.* Wheaton, IL: Crossway Books.

Provenzo, Jr., E. F. (1991). *Video kids: Making sense of Nintendo.* Cambridge, MA: Harvard University Press.

Schlissel, L. (1992). *Women's diaries of the westward journey.* New York: Schocken.

Unruh, Jr., J. D. (1993). *The plains across: The overland emigrants and the trans-Mississippi west, 1840–1860.* Urbana, IL: University of Illinois Press.

REFLECTING ON THE READING

1. Summarize Bigelow's main complaints about the game *Oregon Trail II.* Why are these complaints important for teachers to know about, according to Bigelow? Do you agree with him? Why or why not? What might your answer suggest about your own views of the purposes of education?

2. What are some of the characteristics of the game that make it appealing to educators and to children, according to Bigelow? Why might the popularity of the game worry educators like Bigelow?

3. In what ways, according to Bigelow, does the game privilege a male perspective? What evidence does Bigelow offer to show that the role of women along the Oregon Trail is misrepresented in the game?

4. What problems does Bigelow see with the way race is represented in *Oregon Trail II?* Why does he call the game's treatment of African Americans "a superficial multiculturalism"? How is the game insensitive to Native Americans, according to Bigelow? Cite specific passages from the article in your answer.

5. What does Bigelow mean when he charges that the game "promotes an anthropocentric earth-as-natural resource outlook"? In what specific ways does the game promote such a view? Why is this a problem for students and teachers, in Bigelow's view? Do you agree with him? Why or why not?

6. How is the game programmed to emphasize self-interest, according to Bigelow? What are the implications of such a programming emphasis? Why is this emphasis a problem?

7. In what two main ways, in Bigelow's view, does the game *Oregon Trail II* "hide the nature of the Euro-American invasion" of the territory of Oregon? What were the real characteristics and effects of that "invasion," according to Bigelow's reading of history?

8. What does Bigelow believe are a teacher's responsibilities when he or she is deciding whether to use computer games like *Oregon Trail II* in a class? What

questions should teachers raise about computer programs like *Oregon Trail II* as they decide whether to use them in schools? How will posing such questions help teachers foster a "critical computer literacy"? Do you think he is right? Explain.

Examining Rhetorical Strategies

1. Examine the kinds of evidence Bigelow uses to support his complaints about the game *Oregon Trail II.* What specific kinds of evidence does he present? How does he use that evidence? What does his use of evidence suggest about his own assumptions about what counts as valid or trustworthy information? Did you find his use of evidence effective? Why or why not? What might your reaction to his arguments indicate about your ideas regarding what counts as valid or trustworthy information?

2. Bigelow criticizes the way that the game *Oregon Trail II* represents African Americans and Native Americans. How does *he* represent them? Assess his own assumptions about these peoples. Does he present an unbiased view of African Americans and Native Americans, in your estimation? Explain. How does he represent the white settlers who are depicted in the game? Why does he use the term *Wasi'chu* to refer to them? How might that term affect readers? What might his use of that term reveal about his views regarding the settling of the American West by white Americans? What might his presentation of African Americans and Native Americans reveal about his own beliefs regarding race and ethnicity? Cite specific passages from the text in your answer.

3. Based on this article, how would you describe Bigelow's beliefs about teaching and the purposes of education? What does he see as the primary goals a teacher should pursue in a history class? How does he reveal these beliefs? How do you think his beliefs about the purpose of education shape his critique of *Oregon Trail II*? Cite specific statements and language that Bigelow uses in his article to support your answer.

4. Examine the way Bigelow ends his article. How does his emphasis at the end of the article on what he calls a "deepening social and ecological crisis" influence your reaction to his critique of the game *Oregon Trail II?* Do you think your reaction was one Bigelow hoped he might provoke in readers? Why or why not?

5. This article was originally published in *Rethinking Schools,* an urban educational journal whose readers are likely to be teachers who share some of Bigelow's views about education and related social and political issues. In what ways do you think Bigelow addresses such an audience? Do you think he makes a convincing case about the game *Oregon Trail II* for such an audience? Explain. How might this article be received by a more general audience (for example, an audience of readers of a large-circulation newsmagazine such as *Time* or *Newsweek*), in your view? Cite specific passages from the text to support your answer.

6. Assess Bigelow's use in this article of first-person accounts of playing *Oregon Trail II.* Do you think his use of his own experiences in playing the game is an effective way to make his argument? Explain. How do you think his use of the

first person affects your reading of his critique? What effect does it have on your impression of Bigelow as a writer and/or a teacher? Do you think it makes his critique more effective? Explain.

Engaging the Issues

1. If possible, play *Oregon Trail II* (or another version of the same game) and write your own critique of the game. Assume that your audience is familiar with games of this type. In your critique, describe the game and your experience playing it, and assess the way it seems to address the issues of race, class, gender, and so on, that Bigelow addresses in his critique. Draw your own conclusions about the potential effects (positive, negative, or otherwise) of the game on users.

   Alternatively, play a different computer-based educational game and write a critique of it as described above.

2. Find several reviews of educational computer games, and in order to identify any biases that the authors of the reviews might have, examine the ways the reviews present the games. For instance, how does the author of a particular review seem to feel about such games in general? How does he or she seem to feel about their usefulness or educational purpose? Try to draw conclusions about how to analyze such reviews. (In order to find such reviews, you may have to search some education journals or library-related publications like *Booklist;* you might also search technology-oriented publications like *Technology Review.*)

3. Construct a guide of selected educational computer software for teachers or students. For example, you might focus your guide on computer games designed to teach reading or writing or games focused on history or math, or you might focus on the most popular educational programs. For your guide, use the World Wide Web, the library, local bookstores, teachers, and any other appropriate resources to identify and review various educational software programs. Try to play as many of the games you review as possible. In your guide, explain your purpose to your audience and organize the guide to make it as accessible to that audience as possible. Consider how the format and design of your guide might help you achieve your purposes with it.

4. In a group of your classmates, share the guides you constructed for Question #3 above. Examine the focus, content, and design of each guide, and identify what you see as the strengths and weaknesses of each on the basis of the intended audience. Draw conclusions about how best to design such documents.

   Alternatively, examine the guides each of you has constructed and discuss what they reveal about technology in education. How are such computer games used to teach concepts, skills, and ideas? Do they serve as substitutes for other ways of teaching the same material? Do they rely on technology in ways that are inappropriate, in your view?

5. Write a pamphlet for middle or high school students about using educational games like *Oregon Trail II.* In your pamphlet, describe several of the more popular or available educational computer games. Also, discuss what you see as the potential problems of each, especially regarding the issues of gender, race, and

class that Bigelow addresses in his critique. Be sure to write your pamphlet in a way that you think is appropriate for readers of middle school or high school age. If you have access to desktop publishing software, you might "publish" a finished version of your pamphlet and ask several middle or high school students to read and comment on it.

6. Read the instructions and related material that come with *Oregon Trail II* or another educational computer game. Examine how these materials present the game: what they highlight, what they omit, what assumptions they seem to make about who will play the game and why. Then write an essay in which you analyze these materials. In your essay, describe the game and the materials that come with it. Then discuss the way these materials present the game and the assumptions they seem to make about who will play it and why. Draw conclusions about the purposes of these materials and their reliability.

7. Arrange to interview several teachers in your local schools (ideally, from two or more different school districts) about their uses of educational computer software like *Oregon Trail II.* Ask them how they use such technology and what they believe are the benefits and the disadvantages of such technology. Share Bigelow's critique of the *Oregon Trail II* CD-ROM with them and ask for their reactions to his critique. Try to get a sense of their views of the uses of such technology in education in general. If possible, also interview students about the uses of such programs in their schools. Then write a report for your classmates in which you summarize and discuss the results of your interviews with these teachers and students. Draw conclusions on the basis of your research about the implications of the uses of technology—and specifically educational computer games—in education.

8. Write a letter to the superintendent of your local school district in which you express your views about the use of educational software programs like *Oregon Trail II* in your local schools. In your letter, you might refer to Bigelow's article or to any other sources you deem appropriate. You might also refer to the research you did for Question #7 above. Suggest steps the superintendent might take to address your concerns.

Seeing Through Computers
Education in a Culture of Simulation

SHERRY TURKLE

INTRODUCTION   In the past two decades, "computer literacy" has become associated with schooling almost as closely as the "three R's" of Reading, 'Riting, and 'Rithmetic. Educators no longer debate *whether* to teach computer literacy but *how*. As scholar Sherry Turkle writes at the beginning of the follow-ing essay, "Today nearly everyone is certain that schools and universities should teach students about computers, but exactly what they should teach isn't so clear." Indeed, the question of what students should be taught about computers is the subject of often intense debate among educators as com-puter technologies become more powerful and more widespread. For many educators, government officials, and business leaders, computer literacy is cru-cial if students are to become competitive in a world economy that is increas-ingly driven by computer technologies. They argue that students need to learn the computer skills necessary to function effectively in that world economy. Some educators, however, see the computer as a powerful learning tool in its own right, a tool that can profoundly enhance student learning and encourage problem solving, and they want to do more with computers than simply teach students how to use certain programs.

Sherry Turkle understands both these views, but she is less concerned about which computer skills students should learn in school than she is about how they are taught to understand computers and computers' role in how we inter-act with the world. Turkle points out that how we understand and use comput-ers has changed dramatically in the past two decades. The powerful graphical programs, such as Microsoft Windows, that we now use enable us to complete extraordinarily complex tasks without having to know how the computer actu-ally works. What we see on the computer screen as we use a program like Windows is a *simulation* of the operations we are commanding the computer to do. And that worries Turkle, because simulations necessarily distort the world; moreover, working with simulations encourages certain ways of thinking that she believes may compromise students' abilities to understand and control that world. For Turkle, it isn't enough to teach students how to use computers effectively: they must also learn how computers simulate our world and how to "read" those simulations. In effect, she advocates teaching a new kind of liter-acy.

In raising her concerns about what we teach students about computers, Turkle also raises broader questions about the purpose of schooling. Do we teach students skills to enable them to perform certain kinds of jobs? Do we teach them how to critically evaluate the world? Do we teach them how to understand the world in order to have greater control over it? These are the same difficult questions that other authors (such as Paulo Freire) address in this chapter—questions that American society has wrestled with since the advent of public education more than a century ago. Turkle also raises questions about the nature of literacy and the influence of technology on how we read and write. How *should* we read in a culture so deeply influenced by computer tech-nologies? What should literacy become in "a culture of simulation"? These questions speak to the heart of what it means to be human in a changing world shaped by technology. And the rapid pace of technological change in that world may give even greater weight to Turkle's concerns.

Sherry Turkle has devoted much of her impressive career to understanding the connections between technology and human existence. She is a professor of the sociology of science at the Massachusetts Institute of Technology and a licensed clinical psychologist who has written extensively about computers and human identity. Her books include *The Second Self: Computers and the Human Spirit* (1984) and *Life on the Screen: Identity in the Age of the Internet* (1995), which have been widely influential and have earned her much acclaim.

She was selected as one of the fifty "Most Influential People to Watch in Cyberspace" by *Newsweek* magazine in 1995 and included in "America's New Leadership Class" by *Esquire* magazine in 1985; in 1984 *MS.* magazine named her Woman of the Year. The following article, which was published in *The American Prospect* in 1997, was named one of the top twenty articles of the year by the American Library Association's Library Instruction Round Table.

REFLECTING BEFORE READING

1. Computer education has become widespread in American schools and is now an integral part of the curriculum of many schools. As you prepare to read Turkle's article, consider your own experiences with computer instruction or computer-based assignments in the schools you've attended. What kinds of computer education did you have? What kinds of assignments were you given? How were computers presented to you? What assumptions about technology—and about the purpose of computer education—were communicated to you? Did you find your computer education useful? Why or why not? Keep your experiences with computer education in mind as you read Turkle's article.

2. Much of Turkle's argument in the following article rests on her concerns about what she calls the "culture of simulation." What do you think she might mean by that phrase? As you read, be aware of how she defines and uses that term. Try to understand its importance to her argument.

Today nearly everyone is certain that schools and universities should teach students about computers, but exactly what they should teach isn't so clear. The ideal of computer literacy, of an empowering relationship with the computer, has changed dramatically since educators and their critics first began worrying about making Americans computer literate two decades ago. Originally, the goal was teaching students how computers worked and how to write programs; if students could understand what was going on "inside" the computer, they would have mastery over it. Now the goal is to teach students how to use computer applications, on the premise that if they can work with the computer, they can forget what's inside and still be masters of the technology. But is that enough? And might it be too much in some fields of education where using computers is almost too easy a substitute for hands-on learning?

The uncertainty about what students (and the rest of us) need to know reflects a more general cultural change in the understanding of computers. When I first studied programming at Harvard in 1978, the professor introduced the computer to the class by calling it a giant calculator. No matter how complicated a computer might seem, what happened inside it could be mechanically unpacked. Programming, the professor reassured us, was a cut-and-dried technical activity whose rules were crystal clear.

These reassurances captured the essence of the computer in a culture of calculation. Computers were thought to be "transparent" when the users could look beyond the magic to the mechanism. The first personal computers of the 1970s and early 1980s, like the mainframes and minicomputers, required users to know how to issue exact instructions. Someone who knew programming could handle the challenge more easily. By the mid-1980s, increased processing power made it possible to build graphical user interfaces, commonly known by the acronym GUI, which hid the bare machine from its user. The new opaque interfaces—the first popular one on the mass market was the 1984 Macintosh—represented more than a technical change. The Macintosh "desktop" introduced a way of thinking about the computer that put a premium on the manipulation of a surface simulation. The desktop's interactive objects, its dialogue boxes in which the computer "spoke" to its user, pointed toward new kinds of experience in which people did not so much command machines as enter into conversations with them. In personal relationships, we often interact without understanding what is going on within the other person; similarly, when we take things at (inter)face value in the culture of simulation, if a system performs for us, it has all the reality it needs.

In 1980, most computer users who spoke of transparency were referring to a transparency analogous to that of traditional machines, an ability to "open the hood" and poke around. But when users of the Macintosh talked about its transparency, they were talking about seeing their documents and programs represented by attractive and easy-to-interpret icons. They were referring to an ability to make things work without needing to go below the screen surface. Today, the word "transparency" has taken on its Macintosh meaning in both computer talk and colloquial language. In a culture of simulation, when people say that something is transparent, they mean that they can see how to make it work, not that they know how it works.

Most people over 30 years old (and even many younger ones) have had an introduction to computers similar to the one I received in my first programming course. But children growing up with computers today are dealing with objects that suggest that the fundamental lessons of computing that I was taught are wrong. The lessons of computing today have little to do with calculation and rules; instead they concern simulation, navigation, and interaction. The very image of the computer as a giant calculator has become quaint. Of course, there is still "calculation" going on within the computer, but it is no longer widely considered to be the important or interesting level to focus on. But then, what is the interesting and important level?

What's in an Algorithm?

Through the mid-1980s, when educators wanted to make the mechanism transparent, they taught about the logical processes of the computer's inner workings, typically beginning with an introduction to binary numbers, and instructed children in programming languages that would make computational processes transparent to them. In the highly influential *Mindstorms: Children, Computers, and Powerful Ideas,* published in 1980, Seymour Papert of the Massachusetts Institute of Technology wrote that learning about the computer should mean learning about the powerful ideas that the computer carries. In the Logo programming language he developed, children were taught to give explicit commands to a screen cursor known as a Turtle: FORWARD 100; RIGHT TURN 90. The commands cause the Turtle to trace geometric patterns that could be defined as programs. The idea behind the exercise went beyond the actual programs; Papert hoped that the process of writing these programs would teach children how to "think like a computer." The goal of the exercise was to experience procedural thinking and to understand how simple programs could be used as building blocks for more complex ones.

Although Logo is still in use, educators now most often think of computer literacy as the ability to use the computer as an information appliance for such purposes as running simulations, accessing CD-ROMs, and navigating the Internet. There is certainly nothing wrong and much that is right with students having those skills. But many teachers question whether mastery of those skills should be the goal of "computer education" or "computer literacy."

"It's not my job to instruct children in the use of an appliance and then to leave it at that," says an unhappy seventh-grade teacher at a June 1996 meeting of the Massachusetts chapter of an organization of "Computer Using Educators," a group known as MassCUE. Most of the 80 or so teachers present have been in computer education for over a decade. In the 1980s, many of them saw their primary job as teaching the Logo programming language because they believed that it communicated important thinking skills. One teacher describes those days: "Logo was not about relating to the hardware of the computer, so it wasn't about how the computer 'worked' in any literal sense, but its claim was that it could teach about procedural thinking. It could teach about transparency at its level."

Another adds, reflecting on Logo: "The point was not that children needed to understand things about the simplest level of how the hardware worked, but that things needed to be translated down to an appropriate level, I mean, a relevant level." Someone asks how she knows what is relevant. She stumbles, and looks around to her fellow teachers questioningly. A colleague tries to offer some help: "You have to offer children some model of how a computer works because the computer needs to be demystified. Children need to know that it is a mechanism, a mechanism that they control."

By now, the conversation is animated. Several teachers disagree, arguing that teaching that the computer is a controllable mechanism is not enough. One says: "Children know that the telephone is a mechanism and that they control it. But it's not enough to have that kind of understanding about the computer. You have to know how a simulation works. You have to know what an algorithm is." The problem, however, may be that a new generation no longer believes they have to know what an algorithm is.

Walking Through the Machine

The changing exhibits at Boston's Computer Museum illustrate the evolution of ideas about how to present computers and the dilemmas that educators now face. Oliver Strimpel, the museum's current director, proposed the idea for a "Walk-Through Computer" exhibit in 1987 when he was director of exhibits. Strimpel describes his original idea in the language of a computer transparent to its users: "I wanted to blow up the computer so that its invisible processes could be made visible. I wanted people to understand the computer from the bottom up." The exhibit opened in 1990, its trademark a room-size computer keyboard, a keyboard kids could play on.

At that time, the exhibit began by introducing the visitor to a computer program that charted the shortest route between two cities, *World Traveller*. All that followed was designed to help the visitor trace how a keyboard command to *World Traveller* was translated to lower and lower levels in the machine—all the way down to the changing patterns of electrons on a computer chip. "The key to my thinking," says Strimpel, "was the idea of levels, of layers. We worked very hard to show several levels of how a computer worked, trying to take visitors along the long conceptual path from the behavior of a program to the anatomy of the hardware and low-level software that made it all work. We built 'viewports' that attempted to give people a look inside key components such as the CPU, disk, and RAM."

By 1995, it was time to update the exhibit. The museum's studies of visitor reaction to the original exhibit had shown that many people went through the exhibit without understanding the notion of layering or the message of the viewports. In focus groups conducted by the staff, children said they wanted to know what "happened" when you touched a key on a computer. Their question encouraged Strimpel to go into the first planning meetings committed to a new exhibit that would show the translation of a keyboard stroke into a meaningful signal—the connection between the user's action and the computer's response. He imagined that with improved technology and more exhibit experience, a new version of the walk-through computer could communicate layering in a more sophisticated way.

But Strimpel, in his forties, a member of the "culture of calculation," did not prevail. The people on his staff, mostly in their twenties, were products of the culture of simulation. "What seemed important to them when we went to our second version," says Strimpel wistfully, "was explaining the functionalities—what a disk drive does, what a CD-ROM player does, not how the chip worked. The revised exhibit does not attempt to give explanations at different levels." In the culture of simulation one does not dwell on how the computer solves "its" problems. What is important is that it solves your problems. Strimpel had insisted that the original walk-through computer stress the notion of algorithm. "You could look into a blow-up of how information was passed from one part of the program to another as it attacked the problem of finding the shortest distance between two points," says Strimpel. "In the second exhibit, the idea of algorithm dropped out."

In the revised exhibit, the presentation of a giant, walk-through machine was maintained, updated now to look more like a modern desktop PC. The walk-through computer had quickly become the museum's trademark. But its function was now purely iconic. As Strimpel puts it, "The giant keyboard became a piece of sculpture."

Boston-area schoolteachers regularly take their students to the Computer Museum. They praise the richness of its special exhibits, the many chances it offers for students to try out computer applications to which they would not otherwise have access. Students learn how buildings and cars and turnpikes are designed. They play with voice recognition and artificial intelligence. Teachers praise the museum's Internet exhibits; their students can go online at speeds and with display technology that they cannot even demonstrate in their schools.

But at the MassCUE meeting, the very mention of the walk-through computer provokes heated debate. Several teachers remark that children get excited by the exhibit, but other teachers are skeptical. One comments: "Sometimes, the fifth graders go through that and ask, 'What were we supposed to learn?' But what's worse is that lots of them don't even ask what they were supposed to learn.

They're used to the computer as a black box, something you take 'as-is.'" Another teacher says: "When you look in a microscope at a cell and the cell gets bigger and bigger, you are learning that you can see more structure when you change the scale. With the walk-through computer, you get a keyboard big enough to sit on. For these kids, it's just part of taking for granted that you can make a computer bigger and bigger but that doesn't mean that you can see it better."

At the MassCUE discussion, one currently popular position about computer literacy is underrepresented. This is the view that computer literacy should no longer be about the computer at all but rather about the application programs you can run on it. The arguments for this position are strong. One is grounded in practical, economic concerns. Entering today's workforce requires fluency with software. Word processors, spreadsheets, databases, Internet search engines, computer-aided design programs—these are the tools of contemporary trades. Learning to use these tools demands a new kind of craftsmanship, one that confers a competitive edge. Additionally, like all craftsmanship, there is a thin line between craft and artistry. These tools, artfully used, enable users to discover new solutions to old problems and to explore problems that were never previously envisaged.

Another argument for software fluency as an educational goal goes beyond such practicalities to a more philosophical point. The computer is a simulation machine. The world of simulation is the new stage for playing out our fantasies, both emotional and intellectual. The walk-through computer is its theater, its perfect icon. From this point of view, what children need to know is how to play on this new stage, how to sort out the complex relationship between the simulated and the "real," between representations of the world and the world itself. The "hands-on" manipulation of software may bring these heady issues down to earth. An eleven-year-old child who spends an afternoon manipulating images on Adobe *Photoshop,* creating landscapes that exist only within the computer, may use the software as an object-to-think-with for thinking through issues at the center of contemporary cultural debate. And yet it is often the case—too often the case—that experiences with simulation do not open up questions but close them down.

Simulation and Its Discontents

In the 1980s, the controversy in the world of computers and education was about whether computer literacy should be about programming. Would an emphasis on programming skills in the curriculum teach something important, or would it, as some feared in the parlance of the time, turn children into "linear thinkers"? Today, the debate about computers in education centers around the place of educational software and simulations in the curriculum.

"Your orgot is being eaten up," flashes the message on the screen. It is a rainy Sunday afternoon and I am with Tim, 13. We are playing *SimLife,* Tim's favorite computer game, which sets its users the task of creating a functioning ecosystem. "What's an orgot?" I ask Tim. He doesn't know. "I just ignore that," he says confidently. "You don't need to know that kind of stuff to play." I suppose I look unhappy, haunted by a lifetime habit of not proceeding to step two before I understand step one, because Tim tries to appease me by coming up with a working definition of orgot. "I think it is sort of like an organism. I never read that, but just from playing, I would say that's what it is."

A few minutes later the game informs us: "Your fig orgot moved to another species." I say nothing, but Tim reads my mind and shows compassion: "Don't let it bother you if you don't understand. I just say to myself that I probably won't be able to understand the whole game any time soon. So I just play." I begin to look through dictionaries in which orgot is not listed and finally find a reference to it embedded in the game itself, in a file called READ ME. The text apologizes for the fact that orgot has been given several and in some ways contradictory meanings in this version of *SimLife,* but one of them is close to organism. Tim was right—enough.

Tim's approach to *SimLife* is highly functional. He says he learned his style of play from video games: "Even though *SimLife's* not a video game, you can play it like one." By this he means that in *SimLife,* like video games, one learns from the process of play. You do not first read a rule book or get your terms straight. Tim is able to act on an intuitive sense of what will work without understanding the rules that underlie the game's behavior. His response to *SimLife*—comfort at play, without much understanding of the model that underlies the game—is precisely why educators worry that students may not be learning much when they use learning software.

Just as some teachers do not want to be "reduced" to instructing children in a computer "appliance," many resent providing instruction in a learning environment that often strikes them as an overblown video game. The question of simulation is posed from preschool through the college years. Why should four-year-olds manipulate virtual magnets to pick up virtual pins? Why should seven-year-olds add virtual ballast to virtual ships? Why should fifteen-year-olds pour virtual chemicals into virtual beakers? Why should eighteen-year-olds do virtual experiments in virtual physics laboratories? The answer to these questions is often: because the simulations are less expensive; because there are not enough science teachers. But these answers beg a large question: Are we using computer technology not because it teaches best but because we have lost the political will to fund education adequately?

Even at MIT, the effort to give students ready access to simulation tools has provoked an intense and long-lived debate. In the School of Architecture and Planning, for example, there was sharp disagreement about the impact of computer-aided design tools. Some faculty said that computers were useful insofar as they compensated for a lack of drawing skills; others complained that the results had a lower aesthetic value, making the architect more of an engineer and less of an artist. Some claimed that computers encouraged flexibility in design. Others complained that they made it easier for students to get lost in a multitude of options. Some faculty believed that computer-aided design was producing novel solutions to old problems. Others insisted that these solutions were novel and sterile. Most faculty agreed that the computer helped them generate more precise drawings, but many described a loss of attachment to their work. One put it this way:

> I can lose this piece of paper in the street and if [a day later] I walk on the street and see it, I'll know that I drew it. With a drawing that I do on the computer . . . I might not even know that it's mine.

Another architecture professor felt that simulation not only encourages detachment from one's work, but detachment from real life:

Students can look at the screen and work at it for a while without learning the topography of a site, without really getting it in their head as clearly as they would if they knew it in other ways, through traditional drawing for example. . . . When you draw a site, when you put in the contour lines and the trees, it becomes ingrained in your mind. You come to know the site in a way that is not possible with the computer.

In the physics department, the debate about simulation was even sharper. Only a small subset of real-world physics problems can be solved by purely mathematical, analytical techniques. Most require experimentation in which one conducts trials, evaluates results, and fits a curve through the resulting data. Not only does the computer make such inductive solutions easier, but as a practical matter, it also makes many of them possible for the first time. As one faculty member put it:

A student can take thousands of curves and develop a feeling for the data. Before the computer, nobody did that because it was too much work. Now, you can ask a question and say, "Let's try it." The machine does not distance students from the real, it brings them closer to it.

But Victor Weisskopf, an emeritus professor who had for many years been chair of MIT's physics department, provided a resonant slogan for the anticomputer group. When colleagues showed him their computer printouts, Weisskopf was fond of saying, "When you show me that result, the computer understands the answer, but I don't think you understand the answer." Physicists in the anticomputer camp speak reverently of the power of direct, physical experiences in their own introductions to science, of "learning Newton's laws by playing baseball." For one, simulation is the enemy of good science. "I like physical objects that I touch, smell, bite into," he said. "The idea of making a simulation . . . excuse me, but that's like masturbation."

There is general agreement that since you can't learn about the quantum world by playing baseball, only a computer simulation can provide visual intuitions about what it would look like to travel down a road at nearly the speed of light. But beyond that, simulations are controversial. The pro-simulation faculty stresses that computers make it possible to play with different parameters and see how systems react in real time, giving students an experience of "living physics," but the opposing camp thinks that using simulation when you could directly measure the real world is close to blasphemy. One puts it this way:

My students know more and more about computer reality, but less and less about the real world. And they no longer even really know about computer reality, because the simulations have become so complex that people don't build them any more. They just buy them and can't get beneath the surface. If the assumptions behind some simulation were flawed, my students wouldn't even know where or how to look for the problem. So I'm afraid that where we are going here is towards *Physics: The Movie.*

Readership in a Culture of Simulation

Of course, both sides of the debating faculty at MIT are right. Simulations, whether in a game like *SimLife* or in a physics laboratory or computer-aided-design application, do teach users how to think in an active way about complex phenomena as dynamic, evolving systems. And they also get people accustomed to manipulating a system whose core assumptions they may not understand and that may or may not be "true." Simulations enable us to abdicate authority to the simulation; they give us permission to accept the opacity of the model that plays itself out on our screens.

Writing in this journal ["Seductions of Sim: Policy as a Simulation Game," Spring 1994], Paul Starr has pointed out that this very abdication of authority (and acceptance of opacity) corresponds to the way simulations are sometimes used in the real worlds of politics, economics, and social planning. Perhaps screen simulations on our personal computers can be a form of consciousness-raising. Starr makes it clear that while it is easy to criticize such games as *SimCity* and *SimHealth* for their hidden assumptions, we tolerate opaque simulations in other spheres. Social policymakers regularly deal with complex systems that they seek to understand through computer models that are used as the basis for actions. Policymaking, says Starr, "inevitably re[lies] on imperfect models and simplifying assumptions that the media, the public, and even policymakers themselves generally don't understand." He adds, writing about Washington and the power of the Congressional Budget Office, America's "official simulator," "We shall be working and thinking in *SimCity* for a long time." So, simulation games are not just objects for thinking about the real world but also cause us to reflect on how the real world has itself become a simulation game.

The seduction of simulation invites several possible responses. One can accept simulations on their own terms, the stance that Tim encouraged me to take, the stance that Starr was encouraged to take by Washington colleagues who insisted that even if the models are wrong, he needed to use the official models to get anything done. This might be called simulation resignation. Or one can reject simulations to whatever degree possible, the position taken by the MIT physicists who saw them as a thoroughly destructive force in science education. This might be called simulation denial.

But one can imagine a third response. This would take the cultural pervasiveness of simulation as a challenge to develop a new social criticism. This new criticism would discriminate among simulations. It would take as its goal the development of simulations that help their users understand and challenge their model's built-in assumptions.

I think of this new criticism as the basis for a new class of skills: readership skills for the culture of simulation. On one level, high school sophomores playing *SimCity* for two hours may learn more about city planning than they would pick up from a textbook, but on another level they may not know how to think about what they are doing. When I interview a tenth grader named Marcia about *SimCity*, she boasts of her prowess and reels off her "top ten most useful rules of Sim." Among these, number six grabs my attention: "Raising taxes always leads to riots."

Marcia seems to have no language for discriminating between this rule of the game and the rules that operate in a "real" city. She has never programmed a computer. She has never constructed a simulation. She has no language for asking how one might write the game so that increased taxes led to increased productivity and social harmony. And she certainly does not see herself as someone who could change the rules. Like Tim confronted with the orgot, she does not know how to "read" a simulation. Marcia is like someone who can pronounce the words in a book but doesn't understand what they mean. She does not know how to measure, criticize, or judge what she is learning. We are back to the idea over which the MassCUE teacher stumbled when trying to describe the notion of an "appropriate" level at which to understand computers and the programs that animate them. When Oliver Strimpel talked about wanting to use the computer museum as a place to teach the power of a transparent understanding of the layers of the machine, he was talking about understanding the "naked" computer. As we face computers and operating systems of an increasingly dizzying size and complexity, this possibility feels so remote that it is easy to dismiss such yearnings as old-fashioned. But Marcia's situation—she is a fluent "user" but not a fluent thinker—re-poses the question in urgent terms. Marcia may not need to see the registers on her computer or the changing charges on a computer chip, but she needs to see something. She needs to be working with simulations that teach her about the nature of simulation itself, that teach her enough about how to build her own simulation that she becomes a literate "reader" of the new medium.

Increasingly, understanding the assumptions that underlie simulation is a key element of political power. People who understand the distortions imposed by simulations are in a position to call for more direct economic and political feedback, new kinds of representation, more channels of information. They may demand greater transparency in their simulations; they may demand that the games we play (particularly the ones we use to make real-life decisions) make their underlying models more accessible.

We come to written text with centuries-long habits of readership. At the very least, we have learned to begin with the journalist's traditional questions: who, what, when, where, why, and how. Who wrote these words, what is their message, why were they written, how are they situated in time and place, politically and socially? A central goal for computer education must now be to teach students to interrogate simulations in much the same spirit. The specific questions may be different but the intent is the same: to develop habits of readership appropriate to a culture of simulation.

Walt Whitman once wrote: "There was a child went forth every day. And the first object he look'd upon, that object he became." We make our technologies, our objects, but then the objects of our lives shape us in turn. Our new objects have scintillating, pulsating surfaces; they invite playful exploration; they are dynamic, seductive, and elusive. They encourage us to move away from reductive analysis as a model of understanding. It is not clear what we are becoming when we look upon them—or that we yet know how to see through them.

REFLECTING ON THE READING

1. How have the goals of computer education changed in the past two decades, according to Turkle? What questions does Turkle raise about these goals? Why is there uncertainty about the goals of computer education, in her view?

2. Why, according to Turkle, was the development of the Macintosh computer in 1984 significant? What changes did it help bring about in the way people thought about computers? How did the Macintosh influence the way computer users understood the term *transparent* when referring to computers? Why does

Turkle believe the way we understand this term is important? Do you agree? Explain.

3. What does Turkle mean by the "culture of simulation"? What is the role of computers in such a culture? What characterizes how people understand "reality" in such a culture? What are some of the implications she sees in the culture of simulation regarding how we use computers and how we should teach computer literacy? Why is Turkle concerned about some of these implications of the culture of simulation? Cite specific passages from her essay in your answer.

4. What is the nature of the disagreement among computer educators about what the focus of computer education should be, as Turkle describes it? How does the idea of an *algorithm* figure into this disagreement?

5. How does the "Walk-Through Computer" exhibit at the Boston Computer Museum illustrate the evolution of ideas about computer education? What was the original goal of that exhibit? How did that goal change in the 1990's? What do the feelings of local teachers about the exhibit indicate about how our thinking about computers has changed, according to Turkle? Do you think these changes are important? Why or why not?

6. What does the example of Tim and the program *SimLife* reveal about computers and how they are used in the culture of simulation, according to Turkle? Why does a situation like this one concern her? Do you share her concerns? Why or why not?

7. Why is the use of computer simulations controversial among faculty members at MIT? What might these disagreements reveal about how computers are influencing education and changing the way children learn?

8. In what sense does Turkle believe the use of computer simulations is an "abdication of authority" to computers? What are some implications of such an abdication in the way simulations are used by the government? What responses to this situation among computer educators does Turkle describe? What response does she herself propose? What does she present as the goal of computer education in the response she proposes to the culture of simulation?

9. Why does Turkle believe it is important to develop new "habits of readership appropriate to a culture of simulation"? How would these new ways of reading differ from traditional text-based reading skills? Do you think she is right that such new skills should be taught to students? Why or why not? What might your answer suggest about your own views of the role of computers in education?

Examining Rhetorical Strategies

1. Turkle is a respected academic who writes regularly on complex technical topics for specialized academic audiences. How would you characterize her writing style in this article? Do you think her writing is accessible to wider audiences? Why or why not? What specific aspects of her style do you find most effective? Most troublesome? Explain.

2. Assess Turkle's use of examples to support her arguments in this article. Identify two or three key examples that she offers in making her points. What kinds of

examples does she use? What pictures of computers and of people's beliefs about computers does she paint? Does she offer overt criticism or praise of the people she describes in her examples? Why or why not? Do you find her use of examples effective? Explain.

3. Turkle's essay is in many ways an indictment of the way our use of computers has evolved over the past few decades, especially in schools. Yet Turkle's own reputation has grown out of her work with the same computer technology she seems to criticize in this article. How would you characterize her attitudes toward computer technologies? Does she see computers as dangerous in themselves? Does she share the overt antitechnology views of critics like Sven Birkerts and Wendell Berry in Chapters 1 and 2 of this reader? Is she enthusiastic about the possibilities computers represent for learning? How do her views of technology in general, as they emerge in this essay, shape her argument about computer education? Cite specific passages from her essay in your answer.

4. In this essay, Turkle presents descriptions of various teachers, professors, and students who use computers. Who are these people? How would you describe them in terms of such factors as social class, ethnicity, or race? Does Turkle seem to be directly concerned with such factors in her essay? Why or why not, in your view? Do you think her argument about computer education in the "culture of simulation" applies to people from *all* social backgrounds? Or does it seem to apply only to people from a specific kind of social background? Explain. How did you react to her arguments about computer education? Do you think your reaction might relate in any way to your own social background? Explain.

5. Examine Turkle's ending to this essay. How would you characterize it? Do you find it hopeful? Concerned? Pessimistic? Explain. What effect do you think she achieves in her ending by using the quotation from the famous nineteenth-century American poet Walt Whitman? Were you familiar with Whitman and/or the quotation when you first read this essay? How did the quotation affect you? Did you find it effective? Why or why not?

6. In this essay Turkle expresses concern about how computers are used in schools, and she proposes important changes in computer education that she believes would address those concerns. On the basis of this article, what do you think are Turkle's ideas about education in general? What does she seem to believe about the general purposes of education? How, in her view, can computer education help achieve the goals of education as she sees them? How do her views of the purposes of education shape her argument about the uses of computers in schools? Do you agree with her? Why or why not? What does your answer reveal about your own beliefs about education?

Engaging the Issues

1. Write a conventional academic essay in which you explain Turkle's idea about what she calls the "culture of simulation" and its implications for education. In your essay, draw on your own experiences with technology and education—and on any other sources you find appropriate—to draw conclusions about Turkle's ideas.

2. In her essay, Turkle describes two main views about how to teach computer literacy to students: (1) teach students how computers work; (2) teach students how to use computer applications but not how the applications or the computers themselves actually work. Turkle offers a third view: teach students to be critical "readers" of computer technology and the "culture of simulation" they help create. In an essay intended for your classmates, argue for which of the three views of computer education that you think is right. Assume that your classmates are generally familiar with Turkle's ideas and with the technical arguments she makes. In your essay, summarize each of the three views Turkle discusses in her article, and explain why you support the view you believe is right. You might draw on your own experiences with computers and schools to help support your position.

3. Rewrite the essay you wrote for Question #2 above for a general audience that includes parents of school children. (You might think of your audience as residents of your own school district, for example.) Imagine that you are writing an open letter about computer education to such an audience.

4. If possible, play one of the computer games, such as *SimLife* or *SimCity,* that Turkle mentions in her article. Pay attention to how the game seems to encourage you to think about the situations it presents (such as building a city's infrastructure). Then write a review of the game for your classmates. In your review, describe how the game works and your experiences playing it, and discuss the way the game presents life situations. Identify problems or concerns you might have with the game. How might your experiences with these games influence your reaction to Turkle's arguments?

5. Find a teacher in a local school who teaches technology or computer literacy. (You might contact a teacher you had in your school for this assignment.) Interview that person about computer education in order to understand that person's views on what students should be taught about computers and how they should be taught to use computers. Give this person an opportunity to read Turkle's essay, and ask him or her for a response to it. Discuss it during your interview. After your interview, write a report for your classmates describing your interview, making sure to explain the teacher's ideas about computer education. Try to draw conclusions about Turkle's ideas on the basis of your conversations with the teacher.

6. Write an essay for your classmates about your own experiences with computer education in the schools you attended. In your essay, describe your experiences with computers and computer classes in school. Try to identify what seemed to be the primary purpose of the computer classes and assignments you had. Analyze those experiences using Turkle's descriptions of the three views of computer education. Which of those views seems to characterize the computer education you had? Draw conclusions about the usefulness of your computer education.

7. On the basis of the experiences you described in Question #6, write a letter to the superintendent of your school district proposing changes to computer education in that school district. In your letter, describe your own experiences with

computers in school and explain the problems you see with computer education in your district. Refer to Turkle's essay, if appropriate.

8. In a group of your classmates, compare the essays you wrote for Question #6 above. What similarities and differences emerge from your essays regarding how you learned about computers? What do your essays suggest about computer education? Additionally, examine how each of you recounted your experiences with computers in schools. What attitudes toward education and technology emerge from each of your essays?

9. Visit several sites on the World Wide Web designed by or for students. Examine these sites in terms of the picture of computer technology and computer education each seems to present. Write an analysis of these sites and try to draw conclusions about what they suggest about computer education.

10. Construct a Web site for your class based on Turkle's ideas about a critical computer literacy. What would you include on that site? How might it foster the kinds of reading skills that Turkle believes we should teach students in computer education classes?

FURTHERING YOUR INQUIRY

1. Write an essay intended for your classmates in which you present a general statement of principles about the uses of technology in education. In your essay, discuss what you believe are the primary purposes of education in general and discuss what you see as the appropriate role of technology in achieving those purposes. Draw on authors in this chapter (or other chapters in this book) where appropriate.

2. Write a conventional academic essay in which you analyze the views of education as they emerge from several (or all) of the essays in this chapter. What general themes about education emerge from these essays? What assumptions about the purposes of education do these authors share? How do they understand the role of literacy in education? What important differences in their views do you see? What conclusions can you draw from these readings regarding education?

   Alternatively, write an essay as described in this question focused on *technology* in education.

3. With a group of your classmates, monitor coverage by the news media (television, print, radio, and the Internet) of educational issues. Gather several reports from different news sources about important stories related to education, education reform, technology in education, and so on. After you have collected a sufficient number of stories, analyze the news coverage to illuminate how education and technology are presented. Is the coverage generally positive or negative? What specific issues tend to receive attention? How are teachers, students, schools, and administrators represented in the coverage? How is technology represented? What assumptions about the purposes of education seem to emerge in the coverage? What biases can you see in the coverage? What assumptions seem to be made about how Americans feel about education and technology?

Present the results of your analysis in an essay for an audience of your class-mates, drawing conclusions about the nature of press coverage of education and technology.

4. Construct a Web site on the basis of the research you did for Question #3 above. Create the Web site as a critical resource for general readers who might be concerned about education. Design your site to educate such readers about how you believe the press covers education, and advise them how to read or view press reports on education and where they can get reliable information.

5. Using the library, World Wide Web, and any other appropriate resources, investigate education as it is structured in a different culture. Choose a culture about which you know little. Try to find out how the schools and curriculum are managed in that culture. How are students and teachers generally regarded? What kinds of subject matter is presented in the curriculum? What kinds of activities and assignments characterize schooling in that culture. What are the roles of technology and literacy in education in that culture? Write a report on the basis of your research, and try to draw conclusions about the relationship of education to culture.

6. If possible, establish an Internet connection with students from a different state or country and begin a discussion with them about education and technology. Describe your own experiences with technology in education, and ask them to describe theirs. Raise questions about technology in education, and try to deter-mine their beliefs regarding the use of technology in education. On the basis of your discussions, reexamine your own views about technology in education. Have your views changed in any way as a result of your interactions with your Internet "pen pals"? Explain.

7. Write a conventional academic essay in which you discuss the idea of culture (or cultural background) as it emerges in the essays by Peter Rondinone, Fan Shen, and E. D. Hirsch. In your essay, define *culture* and discuss how each of these writers seems to understand culture's role in education, specifically literacy education. Identify any important similarities or differences you see in how these writers understand this concept. Discuss how their understanding of culture affects the way they present education in their respective essays.

8. Construct a dialogue among E. D. Hirsch, Paulo Freire, and Sherry Turkle about education reform, specifically the issue of literacy education. Pose a ques-tion you have about literacy education, and imagine how each might answer it. What agreements or disagreements might emerge in this group? What might they say to each other?

9. Write an essay in which you compare the educational experiences of Peter Rondinone and Emily Weiner. In your essay, discuss the circumstances of each writer's college experience, identifying what you see as important similarities and differences in their experiences. Examine how their backgrounds might have influenced these experiences. Draw conclusions about the nature of formal education and about the role of technology in education.

10. Write an essay in which you discuss Bigelow's critique of *Oregon Trail II* from the perspective that Hirsch provides in his essay. In your essay, explain Hirsch's

basic views about education and "cultural literacy," and summarize Bigelow's complaints about the educational computer game *Oregon Trail II*. Analyze the specific points of Bigelow's critique from Hirsch's point of view. How might we understand Bigelow's critique in the context of Hirsch's ideas about cultural literacy? Draw conclusions about the nature of education from your analysis.

11. Write a conventional academic essay in which you discuss the role of literacy in education. In your essay, examine how writing and reading are taught in school, based on your own experiences and on readings from this chapter (or other appropriate sources). Discuss what you see as the most important implications of how writing and reading are taught in schools. Propose changes in literacy instruction that you believe should be made.

CHAPTER 5

Writing Technologies and the Workplace

It is hard to imagine work without technology. Think of just about any kind of job, and almost immediately you can think of a tool or machine that is associated with that job. Some such associations are obvious. What would a truck driver be without a truck? An airline pilot without a jet? A software developer without a computer? Other kinds of work make less obvious uses of technology. For example, lawyers are valued for their knowledge of the law and rhetorical skills rather than their ability to use tools, yet lawyers could not do their work without a variety of commonplace technologies: pens, paper, paper clips, telephones, typewriters, copy machines, computers—and, of course, writing itself. Look at any aspect of modern society, and it quickly becomes clear that technology is integral to the ways in which we work.

If we examine work in this light, we tend to think of the technology we use in terms of specific tools that enable us to accomplish certain tasks or that make those tasks easier. A backhoe and a dump truck, for instance, both of which are enormously sophisticated machines that incorporate various technologies (such as combustion engines, electrical devices, and hydraulic systems), enable construction workers to excavate a foundation or build a road much more quickly and efficiently than they could with a pick and shovel. But technology also *shapes* the work we do and redefines the skills and knowledge we need to do that work. Think for a moment about those construction workers and the complicated, heavy machinery they use. At first glance, their machines—backhoes, trucks, pile drivers, cranes, and so on—enable them to do the same kind of work—for example, to build roads—better and faster than they could with the older, less sophisticated tools they once had to rely on, such as picks, shovels, wheel barrows, and manual pulleys. But in order to take advantage of the capabilities of these sophisticated modern machines, the workers must learn to use them, which is a job in itself. They must, for instance, be trained to operate a backhoe so that it can dig efficiently and safely; they must also learn to maintain the backhoe so that it continues to run properly, knowing when to oil the engine or grease the gears and knowing how to repair parts that break or wear out. In other words, to use these sophisticated machines requires that workers acquire specialized knowledge and develop particular skills that are unnecessary for the proper use of

344

less sophisticated tools like shovels and picks. Whereas in the past it may have been possible for a construction worker to begin working with a pick and shovel immediately after being hired and without any special training, the complex machines now used in construction may require lengthy and specialized training.

This example of construction work reveals that technology can also *create* work. Initially, technology was developed to facilitate the physical labor that was once done with rudimentary tools. But the development of new technology to do that labor led to the creation of new and different kinds of work, such as maintenance and training, which have now become commonplace and integral to modern industrialized society. Backhoes and dump trucks, for example, require maintenance and repairs—jobs that are done by specially trained technicians. In addition, the training of the workers who operate those machines involves yet other workers with different training and knowledge. The supervisors of such work must take on new roles as these jobs are created, which means that they must acquire new kinds of knowledge and skills as well. None of these jobs would exist without the heavy machines now used in construction.

You can look closer to home to find examples of this process of technology creating work. For instance, if you use a computer instead of a typewriter or pen and paper for writing, you must perform certain tasks that are unnecessary with those less sophisticated technologies. For one thing, you must learn to operate the computer and, more specifically, the word processing program that you use for your writing. Your old typewriter also required some training, and perhaps you even took a typing class at some point. But the operation of a typewriter is far less complicated than the operation of a computer, requiring less specialized knowledge. Maintaining a typewriter is much easier as well. Whereas your typewriter required you to periodically change the ribbon, computers require more complex tasks such as running antivirus programs, upgrading your software, and backing up (or copying) the files you create with the computer programs you use. In fact, until you learn a variety of special commands as well as how to use the keyboard (which is similar to a typewriter keyboard), you cannot even use the word processing software to write. In short, even on the scale of your own writing, the use of newer, more complex technology—the computer—to facilitate your work—writing—creates other tasks for you as well as for others with whom you may interact, such as computer consultants or salespeople.

All of this may seem obvious and perhaps not terribly important in terms of our broader investigation into literacy and technology. We tend to accept that as new technologies become available, we have to learn to use them because they seem to make our lives better. But as Chapters 1 and 2 show, literacy itself is a technology that can have profound implications not only for how we communicate and interact with one another but also for how we understand who we are and how we live. In the same way, the technologies we use to do work—including the technology of literacy—can significantly influence how we structure our jobs, our communities, and our lives. One compelling example of this kind of influence involves a man named Frederick Winslow Taylor, an engineer who lived in the United States in the late nineteenth and early twentieth centuries. Taylor is regarded as the founder of "systems engineering," a business philosophy in which scientific principles are applied to business management and production. While working in a metal-products factory as a young man, Taylor came to believe that the inefficiency he saw in the factory's production processes could be reduced or even eliminated by making adjustments in those processes on the basis of careful scientific studies of time and motion. For example, working as a consultant for a steel company in the 1890's, Taylor studied workers who used shovels to move various materials at the factory and determined the ideal load per shovel that would enable those workers to move materials most efficiently. If their work could be structured so that they routinely shoveled the ideal load, Taylor reasoned, then the work would be done more efficiently and cheaply. To accomplish this goal, Taylor suggested changes in the entire shoveling process, including supplying specialized tools (different shovels for different materials), constructing several shoveling rooms around the factory to save steps and therefore time, planning work in advance, hiring a staff to do such planning, and installing new technology (in this case, telephones) to improve communications among staff and workers. The result of these changes was substantial: the company needed only 140 men to do the work that had previously required more than four hundred, and although the workers' wages increased by 60 percent, the company's costs for moving materials at the factory were reduced by half. In effect, what Taylor accomplished was to adjust the way in which the work of shoveling was done at the steel company by applying specific technologies to complete the work in order to save time and money for the company. In the process, he changed the nature of the jobs done at that factory and created new kinds of work to facilitate the old.

Taylor's ideas, which he outlined in a book titled *The Principles of Scientific Management* (1911), influenced many industrialists, notably Henry Ford, who applied these ideas to his automobile-manufacturing production line. It is easy to appreciate the appeal of Taylor's principles for achieving efficiency in work, and their application to business and industry seems logical. What may be less obvious is the central role technology played in the application of his thinking. As Taylor's ideas became more widely applied, the role of technology in work shifted, and technology's importance increased. Taylor's time-and-motion studies of the shovelers at the steel company, for instance, focused on a specific kind of work that was done with a specific tool. According to Taylor's advice, the company modified the tool, created new kinds of work (planning and communications), and restructured its physical facility all for the purpose of accomplishing that specific kind of work with that specific tool. In addition, other tools—telephones, for example—were used to facilitate the work of the shovelers and the managers who helped plan the shoveling. These technologies were essential to the gains in efficiency that Taylor helped the steel company achieve. By the 1920's, these same principles were being employed with the more sophisticated technologies of industrial mass production at places like Ford's automobile plants. In each case, old technologies were altered, new ones were developed, and jobs were created, changed, or eliminated in the pursuit of production efficiency. In a sense, Taylor's "science" is a process of maximizing the use of technology to accomplish specific kinds of work, and one of its primary results is to reshape the nature of that work.

The consequences of Taylor's ideas extend beyond these changes in production and efficiency at places like steel factories and automobile plants. According to scholar Richard Ohmann, Taylor's applying the principles of scientific measurement to work "constituted a new kind of rationality, which treated, not just the worker, but his individual motions, as interchangeable parts of a process" (*English in America,*

1976, p. 268). In other words, Taylor's studies of work and the changes he helped foster in the uses of technology for doing work represented a new way of thinking—not just about work itself but about the people who did the work and their role in that work. As Ohmann points out, the application of Taylor's ideas in places like the steel plant and the automobile factory "meant further dependence on old and new knowledge—on a mode of thought that was orderly, experimental and, after a time, sufficiently abstract to be applied to a variety of situations." And that new way of thinking ultimately affected the nature of the work itself and, more importantly, the workers. According to Ohmann, "Scientific techniques of management required that the organization of work be withdrawn from the workers themselves and given over to specialized managers, an ever-increasing corps whose main work was thinking." In other words, as the principles of scientific management were implemented and as workers were assigned ever more specialized jobs with increasingly specialized technology, the workers had less and less responsibility for the larger enterprise in which they were involved. A production line worker at an automobile factory, for example, might perform one specific task, such as attaching the bumpers to the cars or operating a special welding tool, and have no involvement in other aspects of the manufacturing of a car; thus, that worker's specialized skill and knowledge would enable him or her to place bumpers on cars or weld metal efficiently but would qualify that worker to do little else.

Ohmann goes on to argue that American industry's growing need for specialized managers "whose main work was thinking" led to various developments in education, especially higher education, and in the teaching of writing and reading. The changes in work and the uses of technology in growing industries like steel and car manufacturing placed demands on schools to produce graduates with the reading, writing, and thinking skills that would enable them to become the "specialized managers" needed to help run the new mass-production factories. In this sense, the rise of industrialism and the influence of Taylor's principles of scientific management helped create a class of workers who were expert in the use of one technology (literacy) to manage another class of workers who used the emerging new technologies of mass production.

These developments in work reshaped American society in the twentieth century in ways that went far beyond the workplace and the classroom. Suburbs grew around large factories in the East and Midwest, and with the suburbs emerged a new kind of life-style that had never before existed in American society. As the automobile became affordable and widely available, it became a commonplace technology that facilitated the growth of those suburbs, which were designed in part with the automobile in mind. The automobile enabled workers to live at quite a distance from their workplaces and thus contributed to the restructuring of work in American society. The construction of the interstate highway system after World War II furthered this process. These developments are extremely complicated and were shaped by many other social, economic, and political factors that are not discussed here. But if you examine the evolution of lifestyles in the United States in the twentieth century, you will inevitably begin to see the integral role that technology played in shaping how Americans work and live.

But not everyone views these developments as "progress" or "improvement." Along with such monumental changes in how we work and live arise questions about the benefits and costs of these changes. Some critics question whether these developments have truly resulted in a better society. Ohmann, for one, argues that industrialization and the development of the technologies associated with it not only fostered inequality but also caused economic and political power imbalances in American society in the twentieth century. He writes:

> The Industrial Revolution both created *and* destroyed huge amounts of technology. The old technology spread skill and lore fairly evenly throughout society. The new [technology] demands a high concentration of special and theoretical knowledge, of the capacity to create more knowledge as needed, and of the managerial skill to bring this about. (p. 271)

For Ohmann, the greater affluence that Americans seemed to enjoy in the latter half of the twentieth century as a result of industrialization does not offset the loss of equality in American society as a whole. More recently, critics have complained about similar inequalities that have arisen in the wake of rapid new technological developments, especially those associated with the computer and the Internet. The great worldwide concern in 1999 over the so-called "Y2K bug" (which refers to the inability of computer programs to distinguish between the year 1900 and the year 2000) was accompanied by criticism of a society that has allowed itself to become too dependent upon technologies like the computer and that distributes those technologies unequally. The Y2K bug highlighted the profound influence that technology can have on human life and work. And while many observers took comfort in the fact that the Y2K bug did not lead to the disasters that some had predicted, the possibility of technology-related problems nevertheless may serve as a reminder that technology can shape our lives and work in ways that we may not anticipate or desire.

These concerns about the role of technology in the work we do in modern society are echoed in the reading selections in this chapter. Several of the authors look ahead and consider how new technologies may be reshaping our working lives and ponder the implications of the changes they see. Others look back to earlier times when other technologies—the typewriter, for instance—were changing the workplace and the lives of workers. In these readings we are asked to consider some of the implications of our uses of technology in the work we do, and in some cases we are given glimpses of those implications in the lives of individual people as they go about their jobs. Perhaps one or more of these readings will take you to an unfamiliar place—the business office of half a century ago, for example, or a telecommuter's "virtual" workplace—and may provide you with a new perspective on technology and work that may diverge from your own perspective. These readings may thus encourage you to reconsider your understanding of the role of technology in your own life.

In all of these selections, literacy emerges as an important concern. In some cases, the technologies in question are technologies for literacy or written communication, such as the typewriter or computer. In other cases, larger questions about the nature of work or the lives of workers highlight the importance of literacy in modern industrialized society. The kinds of work described or referred to in these readings require not only the ability to read and write but also specific ways of reading and writing. Moreover, the kinds of work described would, for the most part, not exist without literacy itself. In this sense, literacy may be the most important—and powerful—technology of all. Its effects extend into virtually every aspect of our work and our lives.

What Do You Do For a Living? Me? I Type Really Fast

CYNTHIA HOFFMAN

INTRODUCTION   How often has someone asked you what you do for a living? Or how often have you been asked what your parents do for a living? In a sense, such a question is one of the most basic anyone can ask you if he or she wishes to get to know you, since we tend to define ourselves by the work we do. But what does your answer really reveal about you?

In the following essay, writer Cynthia Hoffman poses that question, prompting us to examine why our work seems to be such an integral part of who we are. For Hoffman, the idea that our work defines us was instilled in her at an early age by her parents, both of whom were successful professionals whose careers seemed to determine their identities as people. But Hoffman learned that the relationship between the work and the person is not so straightforward. Despite a comfortable upbringing and a good education, Hoffman found that the skill that seemed to earn her the best living was the seemingly mundane skill of typing. Typing, however, enabled her to land only the kind of secretarial positions that didn't seem to qualify as a "career." In fact, Hoffman states quite unequivocally that typing is not a career. But what, then, *is* a career? And why should it matter whether one has a career or simply works for a living? Is there a difference between the two?

In telling her story about her work experiences as a typist, Hoffman raises the larger questions of how we value work in our culture and how our work helps define our identities as members of that culture. Hoffman's uneasiness about becoming a secretary reflects a broader cultural assumption that secretaries are somehow not equal to or not as important as, say, a lawyer (like Hoffman's mother) or a professor (like her father). Moreover, it reveals how deeply we tend to associate work with our sense of identity. In other words, if Hoffman works as a secretary, then she *is* a secretary. For Hoffman, that identity doesn't seem to match the expectations she developed as a result of her upbringing and her education, nor did that identity necessarily reflect who she is as a person in a broader sense. But in sharing her uneasiness with us, she is perhaps revealing our larger cultural uneasiness about how we understand and value work. Why is it that we seem to value some kinds of work more than others? Why do we describe some kinds of work as "jobs" and others as "careers" and still others as "vocations"? Hoffman's story suggests that there are no easy answers to such questions. Yet because work makes up such a significant part of our lives, it seems important that we address these questions and try to make sense of our beliefs about work.

In the same way that Hoffman's essay raises important questions about how we understand work, it also reveals how deeply technology can be part of our working lives. Technology in the form of a computer, which for Hoffman represented an improvement over the typewriter that she learned to use as a young girl, became the central component of her working life. Her ability to use the computer for typing enabled her to support herself. Paradoxically, that same technology and the work (typing) it enabled her to do so efficiently also led to serious health problems. Ultimately, her experiences prompted her to rethink some of her own beliefs about work and to appreciate an older technology for writing, the pen. In a larger sense, her experiences can help us see how thoroughly integrated into our work and our lives some technologies have become and to examine some of the unintended consequences of our dependence upon those technologies. It may be that, for better or worse, those technologies are as much a part of our identities as the work we do with them.

Cynthia Hoffman is a writer and a poet whose work has appeared in a variety of print and online publications. She has written a number of articles on aspects of contemporary culture for *Bad Subjects: Political Education for Everyday Life,* a journal devoted to progressive political and cultural issues, in which the following essay appeared in 1998.

REFLECTING BEFORE READING

1. Hoffman's essay raises a number of questions about the value of work and careers. As you prepare to read the essay, examine your own beliefs about work. How do you define a "career"? How do you define a "job"? Do you make a distinction between those two terms? If so, what is the difference between them? Why do you think people value some kinds of work more than other kinds? Do you see greater value in some kinds of work? Explain. As you read, consider how your beliefs about work might influence your reaction to Hoffman's essay.

2. Hoffman's essay was originally published in *Bad Subjects,* a journal published by an organization of the same name that, according to its Web site, "seeks to revitalize progressive politics in retreat. We think too many people on the left have taken their convictions for granted." How do you understand "the left" as a political category? As you read, try to determine whether Hoffman reveals anything about her own political beliefs in her article, which is ostensibly not about political issues. Jot down any statements she makes that seem to you to reveal those beliefs. Consider as well whether you think Hoffman wishes to present her political views in this essay.

Did you know that I've gained three ring sizes in the past four years without gaining any weight?

— Me, in response to Steven Rubio's comment that I was one of the fastest typists he knew.

C onsider the irony here, because I sure as hell am: here I am, sitting in a bookstore/cafe, eating a croissant and drinking a triple latte, putting pen to paper to write an article about typing fast. Imagine that. Before you know it, I'm going to admit to actually reading books printed on paper rather than reading electrons floating on the monitor of my computer.

But I digress, and I haven't even really begun.

As I approach 40, I find myself beginning to consider what I have versus what I thought I'd have, or more to the point, what I was raised to believe I was entitled to expect. I suppose this is also part and parcel of having left graduate school without finishing a degree and of suddenly finding myself having to explain to people what I am, or who I am, without the benefit of that wonderful short hand excuse for being not quite really employed: "I'm a graduate student."

I admit right up-front to having been raised with a sense of upper-middle class entitlement that went beyond the usual ballet classes and piano lessons: my parents were a college professor and the first female trial attorney in Sacramento County, California. As a result, I grew up believing that what I would ultimately choose to do for a living would, much as it did for my parents, define me: I am a college professor, I am an attorney crusading for social justice or rewriting the US Constitution in my own image of equality for all. These were the things I was taught to desire to be, as if saying "I am a lawyer" told the world what it needed to know about me but most importantly, as if that designation also told *me* what I most needed to know about myself as well. I was taught that what I did would define who I was. My parents, I believed at any rate, were the prototypes, evidence that if I chose my career carefully enough, saying what I did for a living would somehow denote what I cared about and what mattered to me. And since I was smart and destined to be well-educated, I was taught and eventually came to believe that I would be able to choose a career that would fulfill my every need.

Those piano lessons, by the way, play a part in my life even today: since I play piano I have a great keyboard carriage which helps me to . . . you guessed it . . . type really fast.

Yet, as I begin the arduous task of slowly removing evidence of higher education from my resume, having come to the conclusion that it hampers my job search to admit to having done extensive graduate work, I am struck by the fact that what I do for a living is "type really fast for lawyers." After years of feeling less than human for doing this work, but justifying it because it paid for graduate school; after years of quite obviously failing to be either emotionally or intellectually fulfilled by this work; and after finally facing that I was, in fact, the typist I was warned against becoming all those years ago by my professional mother who insisted that even the admission that I knew how to type would relegate me to the lifelong position of secretary (I can still hear the contempt in her voice when she said this), I am finding myself interviewing for jobs where people are asking me questions such as "all that graduate work . . . aren't you going to find this work rather. . . boring?" And I'm wondering how anyone can possibly believe that whatever the level of education of the applicant, anyone would find typing really fast interesting!

Typing fast is a job, not a career.

When my mother first uttered those anti-secretarial/anti-typist words of wisdom to me, I was ten, being taught the QWERTY keyboard on an old manual typewriter in an airless room off the auditorium at my middle school—along with every other latch-key-kid who was left at school prior to the beginning of first period. (Side note:

we weren't called latch-key-kids. . . that term didn't exist yet. I think what we mostly were was a pain in someone's ass.) I whole-heartedly agreed with her. Manual typewriters, to put it bluntly, sucked. I was determined never to use one again, and except to fool around on an old Royal relatively recently, I haven't. In fact, if the truth be told *I don't know how to type at all.* What I do know how to do, is use a computer keyboard and a mouse, which is remarkably different from typing. Ever try to type without knowing that carriage return needs to be hit at the end of every line? Not a pretty sight.

When I first went to college, I took an old Smith-Corona portable electric typewriter with me. I bet you know the kind I mean: portable because it came with a case that had a handle on it—rather like those first portable television sets that really weren't portable but were movable because they had a handle. Ever try carrying one of those typewriters through an airport? I was such a lousy typist my roommates used to volunteer to type my papers for me so I wouldn't keep them up all night. The first time I actually typed anything of any length I was using an old Kaypro computer, memorable for CPM (PIP anyone?), Wordstar 1 and floppy disks I could actually hear spinning. I think, somehow, the advent of computers made *typing* acceptable. The first time I left graduate school, knowing nothing that made me employable beyond Wordstar 1 and the QWERTY keyboard, that same mother who demonstrated contempt for the secretarial pool that made her job easier, made sure I learned to be a legal secretary saying: "You need a vocation beyond running a copy machine or waiting tables." Notice how the terms have shifted from who I will be to what I will do. We are no longer talking career: we are now talking vocation.

Unfortunately, it took my head ten more years and a serious round of disability caused by. . . typing really fast . . . to get there. In short, I had to discover that typing fast is damaging to more than the psyche in order for it to become something I could do as a job, and not as a career.

As I moved from my Kaypro to my PC to my Windows environment, as my tempo picked up, I discovered that typing fast for others, once they knew I could, became the expectation and not the surprise extra benefit. That was a deadly combination with my belief that what I did defined who I was. "Of course I can handle it" became my refrain. And I could, for whatever reason, type incredibly quickly (120 words per minute!) accurately and efficiently and since I'm a trained writer, I could edit what I was typing as well. It was my ability to do the job so well which created my problem. Since I'd been taught that what I did defined me, and since I hated what I did, trouble naturally ensued.

Flash forward a few years to a small law firm where I am the lead secretary, pretending that what I really am is a graduate student in order to make myself get up every morning and go to work so I can type really fast. In this particular job, I am expected to do most of the office's word processing as well as the general secretarial stuff I hate, in addition to keeping the court calendar for the entire office. As a result of the stress, I've stopped sleeping nights without anxiety medication, my eyes are going crazy from the computer screen and I am popping Motrin like a middle school teacher pops Tums. I eventually discover that my body isn't designed to accommodate typing for eight hours at a stretch under high pressure as well as typing for a few hours every night to meet my own personal needs. As a result, my shoulder freezes and I suddenly can't type any speed, anywhere, at all. And as a result of that, I lost an identity that I was never really happy with in the first place, but which nonetheless left me searching for who I was.

So, for the first time in my life, in spite of hassles with worker's compensation, dealing with a law office that was hostile to my going out on disability, and my own struggle to accept the fact that I was unable to work, even though I had come to hate not only my job, but myself for doing it, I had the time to discover who I was, outside of what I did for a living. Strange gift, disability.

Don't get me wrong here. I'm not Pollyanna. I hate being in pain and a frozen shoulder hurts like hell. I can't stand ultrasound or muscle stim and I hate physical therapy even though I know it eventually rewards me. But for nine months, since I couldn't type, fast or otherwise, I retrained myself to write by hand, by putting pen to paper and remembering what it was like to write when I was a teenager writing really bad angsty poetry and short stories about death. I took the time to retrain myself into thinking of myself as a writer, and came to believe that my words would wait for me, even if I was unable to write by hand anywhere near as quickly as I could think. I have come to like the way it feels to put a pen to paper, and find myself writing that way more often than not because it feels real to me in a way that blips on a screen have ceased to feel tangible.

Since I've returned to the working world, and continue to find employment because I type fast, I find myself wondering why the world values this skill which I think is so silly and which has become—as the opening of this article so clearly indicates—incidental to my own writing life. I understand that law offices appreciate it because it means more billable hours for them, but part of what I discovered during that long disability is that I am no longer willing to play that game with them.

I recently applied for a job at an office which, upon seeing my resume, redefined the job to fit my skills. They were rather stunned to discover that I was no longer interested in interviewing for the "new" job and in fact, walked out of the office apologizing for having taken their time, while simultaneously assuring them that should the earlier job become available again, I would be happy to discuss it with them.

The office where I am now set to begin work likes it that I type really fast, but seems equally interested in maintaining an office environment where if there is no work that needs to be done, makes it perfectly acceptable for me to read a book until there is some. They are also willing to buy me a trackball to replace that stinking mouse. In other words, yes, I type really fast, but since it is my skill, I have decided that I get to choose how it is marketed and how and to whom I sell it.

I may never understand why typing fast has more value in the world than teaching people to read and write; but I have finally come to accept that doing it for a living beats the hell out of waiting tables. And if I control the way I do it, it doesn't have to beat the hell out of my body at the same time.

If only I could figure out why my ring sizes keep growing.

REFLECTING ON THE READING

1. What is the irony that Hoffman refers to in the opening paragraph of her essay? Why does she say that she is thinking about this irony as she writes this essay?

2. At one point in this essay, Hoffman writes, "Typing fast is a job, not a career." What exactly does she mean by that statement? What does that statement suggest about her beliefs regarding work? Do you share those beliefs? Explain. Later in the essay she uses the term "vocation" to describe work that is distinct from a "career." What does she mean by *vocation* in this context? How does it relate to a *job?* What might these categories suggest about the value of work?

3. Hoffman writes that "I had to discover that typing fast is damaging to more than the psyche in order for it to become something I could do as a job, and not as a career." What does she mean by that statement? Why was this discovery important to her? What does it suggest about the nature of work and the relationship between work and one's identity?

4. According to Hoffman, her parents instilled in her the belief that what you do constitutes who you are. As a result, she is hesitant to call herself a secretary. Yet at one point in the essay, she describes herself as "a trained writer," even though her "job" is secretary. What does she mean by "trained writer" in this context? Is "writer" a *job,* in her view? Is it a *career? A vocation?* What might her use of the term *writer* suggest about her assumptions regarding writing?

5. Why does Hoffman call her disability a "strange gift"? What discovery does that disability lead her to make? Why is that discovery so important to her? What might this discovery reveal about Hoffman's own deepest values?

6. What advantages to writing with a pen and paper does Hoffman discover once she can no longer type? Why are these discoveries important to her sense of identity? What might they suggest about the role of technology in our work? What might they suggest about the technologies we use for writing?

7. At the end of this essay we learn that Hoffman is still typing for a living. What has changed about her work? What has changed about her attitudes toward her work? Do you agree that this change was important? Why or why not?

Examining Rhetorical Strategies

1. Why do you think Hoffman calls attention to the irony that she refers to in her opening paragraph? What do you think she accomplishes by highlighting this irony? In what ways might this irony introduce a key idea in her essay? Do you see other ironies in her story? Explain. Do you find her use of irony an effective strategy in this essay? Why or why not?

2. Why do you think Hoffman provides information about her "upper-middle class" upbringing? What does this information reveal about her? How does it relate to the main ideas she explores in this essay? Do you think Hoffman wishes to present her background in a positive light? Or does she wish to offer a more critical view of it? Explain, citing specific passages from her essay in your answer.

3. How would you describe Hoffman's voice in this essay? Early in the essay, she tells us that she is approaching forty years of age. Do you think she "sounds"

forty in this essay? Explain. How might her voice help her make her point in this essay?

4. Hoffman uses special terminology in this essay to refer to specific aspects of using typewriters or computers. For example, she mentions the QWERTY keyboard, a mouse, Kaypro, CPM, Wordstar, and Windows. What does her use of these terms suggest about her assumptions regarding her audience's knowledge of typewriter and computer technologies? Do you think these terms would be familiar to most readers? Were they familiar to you? How did Hoffman's use of these terms affect your reading of her essay?

5. Hoffman devotes much attention in her essay to the ideas of "jobs" and "careers"—that is, to work in general. Given what she describes in this essay, how would you characterize Hoffman's attitude toward work? What beliefs does she reveal about work and its relationship to our identities as people? Do you think she wishes to encourage her readers to consider these beliefs? Explain. Do you share them? Why or why not?

6. Examine the way Hoffman organizes her essay. For example, does she present a strictly chronological narrative? If not, how does she convey the passage of time in the essay? How does she provide necessary background information in her story? What advantages do you see to the way she has organized her essay? Would you describe her essay as well organized? Why or why not?

Engaging the Issues

1. Write a narrative essay for a general audience about your own work history. In your narrative, try to find a common thread that runs through your experiences, much as Hoffman does in her essay.

2. In a group of your classmates, share the essays you wrote for Question #1 above. As a group, discuss the kinds of work experiences that your group members describe in their essays. What do these experiences reveal about the nature of work? What might they reveal about your group members' attitudes toward work? What conclusions can you draw about the role of work in our lives in contemporary society?

3. Write a conventional academic essay for an audience of your classmates in which you discuss the role of technology in Hoffman's work life. In your essay, describe the technologies she has used in her work and the effects those technologies have had on her as a person and as a worker. Consider the relationship of technology to her identity. Try to draw conclusions about the role of technology in our lives and our work.

4. Write an essay for a general audience, such as the readers of a large-circulation publication like *USA Today,* in which you present your ideas about technology and work as they emerged in your conclusions to the essay you wrote for Question #3 above. In your essay, assume that your audience is not familiar with Hoffman's essay. Try to present your ideas about Hoffman's essay and your

conclusions about technology, work, and identity in a way that will be effective for a general audience.

5. Compare the essays you wrote for Questions #3 and #4 above. Write a rhetorical analysis in which you discuss the style and structure of each essay in terms of audience and purpose.

6. Rewrite the essay you wrote for Question #1 above as a Web site on the Internet. In creating your Web site, consider how you can use the technology of the Internet to tell the story of your working life. Include relevant links to other Web sites, if appropriate.

7. Write an essay for an audience of your classmates in which you compare the experiences of writing with a pen and paper to writing with a typewriter or computer.

8. Interview someone who is a secretary. Find out about the work that person does as a secretary, his or her training, the technologies he or she uses at work, and his or her attitudes about all these. Ask especially about the role of typing in that person's work. Ask as well about that person's own feelings about the job of secretary. Then write an essay for an audience of your classmates in which you report on your interview. In your essay, describe the person you interviewed and the nature of his or her job as a secretary. Try to convey a sense of the person's attitude about the work and about the use of technology in that work. Compare your findings to Hoffman's passage.

A Virtual Life

Maia Szalavitz

INTRODUCTION   By the end of 1999, an estimated twenty million Americans were "telecommuting" to work—that is, they worked from their homes using telephones, fax machines, and computers connected to the Internet to communicate and to complete their job-related tasks. Although that figure of twenty million represented a relatively small proportion of the total number of working Americans, it had grown steadily through the 1990's as the Internet became a more integral part of American culture and business. Indeed, telecommuting is possible because of the development of various communications technologies including fax machines, cellular phones, and, of course, powerful desktop computers that enable workers not only to connect to their companies' offices via the Internet but also to perform a wide range of sophisticated tasks in their own homes, from word and data processing to desktop and Web publishing. The emergence of these technologies has profoundly changed the way many Americans work. Telecommuters do not have to travel to their companies' offices each morning to do their work; they do not necessarily have to keep the traditional nine-to-five workday schedule, nor do they have to meet physically with colleagues, clients, or supervisors. Technologies like computers and the Internet enable them to restructure their workdays, their workplaces, and the way they actually go about fulfilling their responsibilities as employee rely telecommuting is as obvious an example as any of the profound impa at technologies can have on work.

Many economists and other business observers consider the emergence of telecommuting to reflect some of the benefits of the so-called Information Age, in which new technologies can make work more efficient and more flexible. Telecommuters, these observers point out, can balance their personal and family lives with their professional responsibilities more easily than workers who are constrained by traditional workday schedules and the need to be physically present at the offices of their employers. For example, workers who telecommute may have more flexibility in their schedules to take their children to school or to the doctor's office without taking time away from their work. Their use of online technologies means that they can work at any time of day, thus leaving them available to attend to their personal responsibilities or their families' needs whenever those needs might arise. Moreover, some observers have argued that workers who have such flexibility and autonomy may be more efficient and more content in their jobs, which benefits their employers. In short, according to these observers, technologies that enable telecommuting ultimately benefit both workers and employers and thus represent a positive development for the economy as a whole.

Writer Maia Szalavitz offers a different view of telecommuting. Szalavitz became a telecommuter in the 1990's when she left her job as a television producer. The nature of her work and the availability of computer technology as well as the Internet enable her to do her work and to manage other parts of her life from her home. On the surface at least, she seems to enjoy the advantages of flexibility and autonomy that telecommuting offers. But Szalavitz has learned that these advantages carried significant costs in her life. For her, the very same characteristic that is often identified as a benefit of telecommuting—the ability to work from one's home—becomes a liability. She has found that working exclusively from her home deprives her of the kind of contact with other people that was routine in her life before she began telecommuting. Moreover, her new, more isolated life affected her relationships with others. For Szalavitz, the computer that enables her to telecommute as a professional has also become the central feature of her private life. Her essay raises the question of whether that life is better as a result of the technology that changed it. In raising this question, Szalavitz reminds us that far-reaching technological and economic developments like the emergence of telecommuting can have unforeseen effects on individual lives; her essay may therefore give us cause to wonder whether these developments ultimately benefit our society.

Maia Szalavitz is a television producer and writer whose articles on political and cultural issues have appeared in a variety of publications including the *Washington Post*, the *Village Voice, Salon,* and the *New York Times*. Much of her work has focused on drug policy in the United States. She has authored "US: War On Drugs, War On Women," which appeared in *On the Issues: The Women's Progressive Quarterly* (1998), and coauthored *Recovery Options: The Complete Guide* (2000). She was also an associate producer and writer for

Moyers on Addiction: Close to Home, a PBS documentary that aired in 1998. The following article was originally published in the *New York Times Magazine* in 1996.

REFLECTING BEFORE READING

1. In the following article, Maia Szalavitz describes some of her experiences as a telecommuter—that is, someone who works from home by using technologies like computers and the Internet. As you prepare to read the article, think about your own experiences on the Internet. Have they been positive, negative, or both? What are your views of the Internet and its impact on your life and work? How might these views affect the way you respond to Szalavitz's article? If you have never been on the Internet, what impressions of it do you have? Are they generally favorable or unfavorable? What expectations for this article might your impressions of the Internet create for you?

2. This article was originally published in 1996. As you read, consider whether Szalavitz's views of the Internet and of telecommuting still seem valid today. Has anything changed significantly in the few years since her article was originally published that might call her views into question? Or do you think her views are still applicable today?

A fter too long on the Net, even a phone call can be a shock. My boyfriend's Liverpudlian accent suddenly becomes indecipherable after the clarity of his words on screen; a secretary's clipped tonality seems more rejecting than I'd imagined it would be. Time itself becomes fluid—hours become minutes, and alternately seconds stretch into days. Weekends, once a highlight of my week, are now just two ordinary days.

For the last three years, since I stopped working as a producer for Charlie Rose, I have done much of my work as a telecommuter. I submit articles and edit them via e-mail and communicate with colleagues on Internet mailing lists. My boyfriend lives in England, so much of our relationship is also computer-mediated.

If I desired, I could stay inside for weeks without wanting anything. I can order food, and manage my money, love and work. In fact, at times I have spent as long as three weeks alone at home, going out only to get mail and buy newspapers and groceries. I watched most of the blizzard of '96 on TV.

But after a while, life itself begins to feel unreal. I start to feel as though I've merged with my machines, taking data in, spitting them back out, just another node on the Net. Others online report the same symptoms. We start to feel an aversion to outside forms of socializing. It's like attending an A.A. meeting in a bar with everyone holding a half-sipped drink. We have become the Net naysayers' worst nightmare.

What first seemed like a luxury, crawling from bed to computer, not worrying about hair, and clothes and face, has become an evasion, a lack of discipline. And once you start replacing real human contact with cyberinteraction, coming back out of the cave can be quite difficult.

I find myself shyer, more circumspect, more anxious. Or, conversely, when suddenly confronted with real live humans, I get manic, speak too much, interrupt. I constantly worry if I'm dressed appropriately, that perhaps I've actually forgotten to put on leggings and walked outside in the T-shirt and underwear I sleep and live in.

At times, I turn on the television and just leave it to chatter in the background, something that I'd never done previously. The voices of the programs soothe me, but then I'm jarred by the commercials. I find myself sucked in by soap operas, or compulsively needing to keep up with the latest news and the weather. "Dateline," "Frontline," "Nightline," CNN, New York 1, every possible angle of every story over and over and over, even when they are of no possible use to me. Work moves from foreground to background. I decide to check my e-mail.

Online, I find myself attacking everyone in sight. I am irritable, and easily angered. I find everyone on my mailing list insensitive, believing that they've forgotten that there are people actually reading their invective. I don't realize that I'm projecting until after I've been embarrassed by someone who politely points out that I've flamed her for agreeing with me.

When I'm in this state, I fight with my boyfriend as well, misinterpreting his intentions because of the lack of emotional cues given by our typed dialogue. The fight takes hours, because the system keeps crashing. I say a line, then he does, then crash! And yet we keep on, doggedly.

I'd never realized how important daily routine is: dressing for work, sleeping normal hours. I'd never thought I relied so much on co-workers for company. I began to understand why long-term unemployment can be so insidious, why life without an externally supported daily plan can lead to higher rates of substance abuse, crime, suicide.

To counteract my life, I forced myself back into the real world. I call people, set up social engagements with the few remaining friends who haven't fled New York City. I try to at least get to the gym, so as to differentiate the weekend from the rest of my week. I arrange interviews for stories, doctor's appointments—anything to get me out of the house and connected with others.

But sometimes, just one engagement is too much. I meet a friend and her ripple of laughter is intolerable—the hum of conversation in the restaurant, overwhelming. I make my excuses and flee. I re-enter my apartment and run to the computer as though it were a sanctuary.

I click on the modem, the once grating sound of the connection now as pleasant as my favorite tune. I enter my password. The real world disappears.

<hr>

REFLECTING ON THE READING

1. What is Szalavitz's line of work? What do we learn about her working life in this essay? How does this information affect what happens later in her essay?

2. What advantages does Szalavitz see in being a telecommuter? What disadvantages does she see? What might her descriptions of what she considers the

advantages and disadvantages of telecommuting suggest about her own values regarding work and life?

3. In what sense has Szalavitz "merged with her machines," as she puts it, in her life as a telecommuter? What are the consequences of this "merging"? Why does Szalavitz consider these consequences negative? Do you agree with her? Why or why not?

4. Why does Szalavitz find it more difficult now to interact with other people? To what does she attribute this difficulty? Do you think she is right? Explain.

5. What is the primary difference between the "real world" and the online world, as Szalavitz sees it? What might this difference suggest about the role of technology in our lives? What might it suggest about what we value as people?

6. Why do you think Szalavitz returns to her computer when she is feeling overwhelmed by a social engagement? What might that indicate about her? About the role of technology in her life?

Examining Rhetorical Strategies

1. Assess Szalavitz's introduction to this essay. How does she introduce her subject? What does she emphasize in the opening paragraph? What background information does she provide? In what ways might this information influence readers as they learn more about her life as a telecommuter? Do you find her introduction effective? Why or why not?

2. This essay was originally published in the *New York Times Magazine,* a large-circulation publication that reaches a wide audience. What assumptions do you think Szalavitz makes about her audience's knowledge of the Internet and related technologies? Do you think most readers would have such knowledge? Do you think Szalavitz assumes that her readers would have a favorable attitude toward technologies like the Internet? Explain, citing specific passages from the essay to support your answer.

3. How would you characterize Szalavitz's voice in this essay? Cite specific features of her style—such as her word choice and sentence structure—that help create her voice. How did you respond to her voice? Did you find her voice in this essay appropriate for her subject matter? Explain. What might your response to Szalavitz's voice suggest about you as a reader?

4. Examine how Szalavitz organizes this essay. She is writing in the first person about her own experiences as a telecommuter. How does she present these experiences? Does she rely on chronological order to organize her experiences or does she organize her essay in some other way? Why do you think she has organized her essay in the way she has? What purposes might she accomplish by organizing her essay as she does?

5. Why do you think Szalavitz concludes her essay as she does? What does she seem to emphasize in her conclusion? Did you find her conclusion effective? Why or why not?

Engaging the Issues

1. Write a conventional academic essay in which you discuss Szalavitz's attitudes about technology and work. What role does technology play in her professional and personal life? What does she seem to value about technology? What reservations does she have about it? Cite specific passages from her article to support your discussion. Draw conclusions about what Szalavitz's article might have to say about the role of technology in our lives.

2. In a group of your classmates, share the essays you wrote for Question #1 above. Identify the key points each of your group members has made in his or her essay about Szalavitz's article, and try to find similarities and differences among your group members' essays. Discuss these similarities and differences and what they might indicate about how the members of your group read Szalavitz's essay. What might your discussion reveal about you as readers? How can you account for similarities and differences in the reactions your group had to Szalavitz's essay? What might you conclude from your discussion about the nature of reading?

3. If your work or school schedule allows for it, spend a weekend at home communicating with others exclusively through the Internet. Try to avoid all contact with other people except through online communications. Keep notes about your online encounters and discussions. What kinds of online experiences did you have? How might these experiences differ from or compare to your typical, everyday encounters with other people in your life? Did you enjoy the weekend? Why or why not? Did your experience lead you to share Szalavitz's feelings about her life as a telecommuter? What might your experiences indicate about the technology of the Internet and its role—or potential role—in peoples' lives?

    Now write an essay for an audience of your classmates about your weekend experience. In your essay, describe the kinds of online experiences you had during the weekend, and discuss your own feelings about the weekend. Try to address the questions listed above, and draw your own conclusions about the role of technology in peoples' professional and private lives. If appropriate, make comparisons to Szalavitz's experiences as a telecommuter.

4. Rewrite the essay you wrote for Question #3 above for a different audience— for example, readers of your local newspaper. In your rewrite, be sure to consider what your readers might know about telecommuting and about the Internet.

    Alternatively, rewrite the essay you wrote for Question #3 for an audience of people who telecommute—perhaps readers of a newsletter for telecommuters.

5. Compare the essays you wrote for Questions #3 and #4 above. Identify similarities and differences in the tone, style, voice, structure, and content of each essay. How did the different audiences and purposes for each seem to affect these aspects of your writing? Now write a brief essay in which you present your analysis. In your essay, be sure to cite specific passages to support your analysis.

6. Using your library, the Internet, or any other available resources, investigate the phenomenon of telecommuting. Try to find information about the extent of telecommuting and the nature of work done by most telecommuters. Try to find out also who telecommuters are: Do they tend to work in certain professions? Do they tend to represent specific racial, gender, or socioeconomic groups? If possible, interview people who telecommute—perhaps by contacting them through Internet discussion groups or Web sites. Also interview people at companies that allow their employees to telecommute. (If you have been a telecommuter, draw on your own experiences as well.) Try to find out how telecommuting emerged as a trend in business. Is it related to specific economic or technological developments?

   Now write a report for an audience of your classmates based on your research about telecommuting. In your report, describe the phenomenon of telecommuting and try to account for its emergence and growth. Discuss advantages, disadvantages, and potential implications of telecommuting for workers and for companies. Try to draw conclusions about telecommuting and about the role of technology in modern society.

7. Create a Web site based on the research you did for Question #6 above. Make your Web site a resource about telecommuting for visitors who may be telecommuters themselves or who may be seeking information about telecommuting. Be sure to indicate the purpose of your site for potential visitors.

8. Write an essay for a general audience (or some other audience you wish to address) in which you make an argument for or against telecommuting. In your essay, support your argument in ways that you think will be persuasive to the audience you are addressing.

Women Clerical Workers
and the Typewriter
The Writing Machine

MARGERY W. DAVIES

INTRODUCTION Historians often point to the development of specific technologies as they try to account for broader social, political, and economic developments in history. The printing press, for example, is cited by some historians as a factor in a number of major developments in European societies in the sixteenth and seventeenth centuries, as noted in the introduction to this reader. In recent years, the development of computer technologies, especially those associated with the Internet, is regularly invoked by scholars and other observers as a key factor in everything from changes in the way individuals gather information and communicate to the restructuring of the global economy. The closer we look at such developments, the more complicated they tend to become, suggesting that it is usually an oversimplification to identify a single technology as the sole cause of large-scale social and economic changes. Indeed, as scholars Lucien Febvre and Henri-Jean Martin contend in their history of printing, *The Coming of the Book,* the changes in European society that are usually associated with the development of the printing press may be more accurately accounted for by examining other factors, such as the emergence of the university as a key social and cultural institution during that time. Febvre and Martin believe that the printing press facilitated the emergence of universities as important institutions that restructured learning and knowledge during the Middle Ages, but they warn against assigning too much influence to that technology. Many contemporary scholars raise similar cautions in discussing the impact of computer technologies today.

Scholar Margery W. Davies is among those scholars who argue that the impact of technology should be understood in terms of the broader social, cultural, and economic contexts within which specific technologies emerge. The example that Davies offers to support this claim is that of the typewriter. As Davies suggests in the following article, some historians identify the typewriter as the central cause of important changes in American business in the twentieth century, particularly the substantial increase in the number of women who entered the American workforce after World War II. There is little doubt that the changes in American business practices were significant from the late nineteenth century through the postwar years of the mid-twentieth century. Women did indeed enter the workforce in unprecedented numbers, and the nature of the work available to them changed. Moreover, the business offices where so many women found work in those years underwent dramatic evolution as new business practices and new technologies reshaped the way companies organized their work and conducted their operations. The typewriter seems to have played a significant role in these changes. Davies acknowledges that role, but she also insists that the impact of the typewriter be placed in the context of the larger and even more dramatic economic changes that occurred in American society throughout the first half of the twentieth century. For Davies, to understand the impact of a technology like the typewriter on the American workplace requires a broad historical view.

Davies attempts to provide such a view in the article reprinted here. Like other authors in this chapter, she focuses on the different ways in which a specific technology—in this case the typewriter—affects the lives of workers. Her particular interest is women in the workplace, and she wishes to understand the effects of the typewriter on the nature of the office work women did as well as on their lives as women. Her account of the role of the typewriter can thus provide us with a picture of technology in the workplace that is complex and multilayered. Her focus on women further enriches her story, for she shows that even when we try to isolate a specific technology or group of workers, we inevitably confront the complexity of technology and of work and of their connection to larger social forces. It may be useful to read Davies' article in conjunction with the selection earlier in this chapter by Cynthia Hoffman, who also writes about the typewriter, though from a decidedly different perspective.

Davies provides a view that may complicate and challenge the perspective offered by Hoffman, and her take on capitalism, which emerges subtly in her article, may challenge you to reconsider your own views of work and technology in American society.

Margery W. Davies is the author of *Woman's Place Is at the Typewriter: Office Work and Office Workers, 1870–1930* (1982) and has served as an editor of *Radical America*, a journal devoted to social and political issues. The following article was published in 1988 in *Technology and Women's Voices: Keeping in Touch*, a collection of essays.

REFLECTING BEFORE READING

1. The title of the following article suggests that it focuses on the typewriter as a workplace technology and the women who used it. As you read, try to pay attention to the main ideas that Davies seems to be making in her article. To what extent is this article about technology? To what extent is it about something else?

2. The following article was originally published in a collection of scholarly essays intended primarily for academics who study technology and women's issues. As you read, try to identify specific features of the article that indicate its scholarly nature. How do these features affect you as a reader? What might your reaction to them suggest about your own expectations and experiences as a reader?

'Of the woman who took down his instructions in shorthand before typewriting them he knew absolutely nothing. To him she was merely a part of the typewriting machinery, and the glazed pigeon-hole might have been a great gulf dividing them, instead of what it was.'

(Ellen Ada Smith, 1898)

'Shortly before Mr Sholes's death a daughter-in-law remarked to him what a wonderful thing he had done for the world [in inventing the typewriter], and this was his . . . reply, "I don't know about the world, but I do feel that I have done something for the women who have always had to work so hard. It will enable them more easily to earn a living."'

(Heath 1944, *272*)

W hether or not Christopher Latham Sholes, often cited as the inventor of the typewriter, actually said this, many other writers since Sholes have said much the same thing. And they are all wrong—on all counts. Sholes was not the first person to invent the typewriter; scores of people before him had devised writing machines. Sholes's renown comes more from the fact that his machine was sold to the Remington Company, the first mass manufacturer of typewriters in the United States. Nor did the typewriter cause the employment of women in clerical work in the United States; women were drawn into the office because of the mushrooming demand for clerical labor occasioned by the expansion and consolidation of the capitalist economy at the end of the nineteenth century. In fact, those very structural changes in capitalism underlay the successful manufacture of the typewriter, for not until accounting, correspondence and record keeping increased along with governments and firms did the usefulness of a writing machine become self-evident.

Nonetheless, there are ways in which the typewriter affected the employment of women in offices. Because the typewriter was a new machine, it was 'sex-neutral' and did not have a history of being associated with men. In the absence of this association, women seeking work as typists did not face the obstacle that typing was 'men's work,' even though there were many who maintained that the office in general was not a suitable place for a woman. Although there is nothing intrinsic to the typewriter which dictates that it be operated hour after hour by the same person, it is true that typing fast and accurately are skills that take some time to develop. Thus the very existence of the machine helped to justify a division of labor within office work where some people did nothing but type all day long. As the work of typing came quite rapidly in the United States to be identified as 'women's work,' a larger and larger percentage of typists was female. The typewriter was a factor in the concurrent feminization and proletarianization of the clerical labor force.

Insofar as the typewriter was a facilitating factor in the employment of women in clerical work, it helped to move women out of work in the home and family and into work in the labor force. Given the feminization of clerical labor in general and, to an even greater extent, typing in particular, it is tempting to conjure up the image of women, cast together in large groups through their common work as typists, forming strong workplace bonds of communication, friendship and support—bonds which might grow into organizing campaigns, union drives and successful united efforts to wrest better wages and working conditions from employers. Up until the 1970s, such was seldom the case, even though attempts to organize office workers in the United States date back to the efforts of the Women's Trade Union League in the early twentieth century. Although there were many firms that had large typing pools, these pools were often divided and divided again into finely graduated hierarchies and small promotional steps which could often lead to a competitive rather than a cooperative climate. Furthermore, many clerical workers, even if they worked at large companies, were in relatively small working groups once they actually got to their desks in the departmental divisions and subdivisions. This was certainly true for private secretaries. Many clerical workers, in addition, worked in small companies and institutions. The small size of the actual clerical work unit, not to mention the competitiveness virtually inherent in a finely graduated promotional hierarchy, mitigated against the development of a coherent clerical class.

This is not to say, of course, that clerical workers did not form close personal ties or supportive communities in the workplace. There was clearly a lot of personal communication among women (and no doubt men) in the office. The evidence is in the strong memories that clerical workers have of their sister workers, in the frettings of office managers over how to cope with 'office gossip,' in the photographs and personal effects that office workers pin to their bulletin boards and put on their desk tops—a statement that they are people with personal lives that invites comment and interaction. But what is not at all clear is the role that the typewriter in particular played in the establishment or discouragement of such patterns of communication.

For it is conceivable that, had office work expanded in the absence of the typewriter or other business machines, the clerical labor force would have grown as well; only instead of an army of typists there would have been an army of copyists. Probably the most sensible argument is that the typewriter, like other technological inventions, was one part of complex structural developments in the United States that changed the face of the office and the sex of the office worker. To pluck the typewriter out of that context and to try to isolate its particular role in the development of communication among men and among women is not only a thankless but also an ill-conceived task. Although the typewriter did play a role in helping to determine the organization of office work, it seems important to remember that technology in no way operates in a vacuum. A successful technological innovation owes its very life to a specific historical situation, and while it in turn may have a great or a small effect on that social context and its development, it is the sociohistorical situation that must be understood first and foremost.[1]

The Impact of the Typewriter

It was capitalist expansion, not the typewriter, that drew women into the office workforce. As I have written in *Woman's Place Is at the Typewriter* (1982), it was the rapid expansion of capitalist firms and government agencies, accompanied by the growth of correspondence and record keeping, which led to a mounting demand for clerical labor. That demand was met, in part, by the availability of literate female labor. The economic instability of small farm and small business families and the decline of productive work in the home released women to the paid labor force and made the income they could earn more important. They found clerical work more desirable than other working-class jobs because of the higher wages it offered and the comparatively high status it enjoyed; few other jobs specifically requiring literacy were open to women. Meanwhile, literate males were being employed not only for the growing clerical field, but also for management and professional positions, which rapidly increased in number with late-nineteenth-century capitalist expansion. The first women known to work in offices in the United States were employed at the US Treasury in Washington to sort and trim bank notes during the Civil War, when male labor was siphoned off to the military.[2] Women also have been mentioned as copyists, stenographers and bookkeepers in the 1860s. They worked for substantially lower wages than men, another factor which no doubt encouraged some employers to hire them.[3] And when women started working in offices in large numbers, they did much more than type. By 1880, there were more than 4200 women working as bookkeepers, cashiers, and accountants and 2000 employed as stenographers and typists; the figures for 1890 are 27,772 and 21,270 respectively (Edwards 1943; Davies 1982, 178–9).

It is, then, important to understand that fundamental structural change (rather than the technological invention of the typewriter that was itself a product of that structural change) caused the employment of women in office work. Crediting the typewriter leads to a superficial explanation of the changes in women's labor force participation. Worse yet, crediting the typewriter can encourage the conclusion that a technological invention causes women's employment because said invention is particularly appropriate for women, a conclusion that is dangerously close to thinking that women are naturally suited to particular occupations. To argue that 'women's' work or 'men's' work are in some way ordained by nature is to confine women and men to a limited range of human activity. It is crucial to understand the historical specificity of gender-defined work, and to understand the root causes of that gender definition operating in each particular circumstance. Throwing all the typewriters out the window, not to mention the myriad other office machines that have followed closely in their wake, would not in and of itself change women's subordinate position in the office.

Nonetheless, it is easy to understand the sentiments of my friend who purposely refused to learn to type in high school because she didn't want to be pushed by circumstances into office work; or of the young women cited in a 1977 *US News and World Report* who are 'firmly convinced that if they learn to type they will be put behind a typewriter the rest of their lives' (Frank talk . . . 75).[4] From the earliest days of its commercial production in the United States, the typewriter was seen in association with women as well as with men. A photograph of one of Sholes's early machines shows his daughter at the keyboard and is annotated, 'Miss Sholes 1872. The first typist.'[5] Remington advertised its machine in *The Nation* of 15 December 1875, as an ideal 'Christmas present for a boy or girl. And the benevolent can, by the gift of a "Type-Writer" to a poor, deserving young woman, put her at once in the way of earning a good living as a copyist or corresponding clerk' (Current 1954, 86). The early typewriter stores had people demonstrating the machine for prospective customers; Mark Twain was influenced in his purchase by the 'type girl' who had typed fifty-seven words per minutes (Bliven 1954, 61).

There were plenty of men finding jobs as typists too; in fact, well into the twentieth century most of the people who won the speed typing contests were men. But 'stenographers and typists' was the clerical job category which was feminized the most quickly. Women were already 40 per cent of stenographers and typists in 1880 and over 63 per cent in 1890. After 1910 the absolute number of men in the category began to decline; by 1930 women constituted more than 95 per cent (Davies 1982, 178–9).

It is not really clear to me why the typewriter was operated by women (as well as by men) from its earliest days of commercial production. Possibly it was because the typewriter had not built up a history of being operated by men, and hence women who sought jobs as typists did not face the obstacle that they were trying to do 'men's work.' Possibly it was because female labor was cheaper than male. In any event, the tremendous surge in demand for clerical labor that was well underway by the end of the nineteenth century and continued on into the twentieth century brought hundreds of thousands of women into the labor force as office workers in general and as typists in particular.

The uses made of typewriters also had an impact on the reorganization of office work. The rapidly multiplying paperwork that accompanied capitalist expansion in the late nineteenth century prompted some firms to reorganize their offices. The small office where an owner or manager supervised a handful of clerks was superseded by the large office, which was divided up into a variety of functionally defined departments. This division of labor on a gross scale was accompanied by another division of labor on a finer scale within each department (Davies 1985, 8). Many clerical jobs were broken down into their composite units—there were billing clerks, receiving clerks, payroll clerks, file clerks, typists and so on. The existence of business machines, the first and most ubiquitous of which was the typewriter, helped to justify and entrench this finely tuned division of labor. For once a clerical worker had become proficient at operating a particular machine, it could be and was argued that the clerical worker should do nothing else. If a typist could consistently turn out sixty words per minute, why waste her time on filing or answering the phone? A skilled typist was likely to be kept in her job for as long as her employer could keep her there. As I have argued in *Woman's Place Is at the Typewriter,* this restriction of many clerical workers to one narrow job meant that they lost the capacity to understand how their own work fit into the overall work of their firm or institution, and hence the capacity to exercise much judgment or informed control over their work.

It should be emphasized that there was nothing inherent to the typewriter which compelled such an organization of clerical work. The typewriter, in fact, can be quite useful for people who operate it sporadically: the private secretary who spends a couple of hours a day typing correspondence or reports; the writer who alternates stretches of pounding the keyboard with long periods of staring into space. The organization of work is largely determined by the efforts of businessmen and scientific office managers to organize their clerical labor as profitably as possible, and not to make the 'inefficient' error of having a typist do work that a lower-paid file clerk could just as easily do.

The typewriter was thus a contributing factor in the entrance of women into the clerical labor force and in the mechanization of clerical work. These developments in turn affected communication among women. Grouped together in the workplace, women had a basis for communication that is different from their connections within the family and community. Women in the office talked to each other. Some of their conversation focused on their work—which letters had to be gotten out immediately, what to do about a mistake on a bill, etcetera. But much of their conversation was also personal (Feldberg and Glenn 1983). The writings of scientific managers of the office are full of descriptions of the amount of time wasted in office gossip and prescriptions for what to do about it. Clerical workers' own accounts of their work in popular magazines such as the *Ladies' Home Journal* contain countless references to wedding showers, return visits from former workers to show off their new babies, and so forth. And there are also complaints, particularly during the past twenty years, about the management not granting female office workers promotions when they merited them or about a man moving up the office hierarchy much more quickly than the women who trained him. Women clearly had a lot to say to each other, both about their home and personal lives and also about their work.

That women were gathered together as office workers and that there was much communication among them did not necessarily lead, however, to organization. There have been attempts to organize office workers into unions since early in the twentieth century, beginning with the efforts of the Women's Trade Union League (Feldberg 1980; Strom 1983). In 1939 *Business Week* started to issue annual warnings that clerical workers were ripe for organizing, warnings that had their obverse in the glowing predictions issued in the *American Federationist* by the presidents of the AFL clerical unions. But neither the warnings nor the predictions were the harbingers of widespread unionization among clerical workers.

Although the number of clerical workers has been mushrooming since the 1880s, these office workers have not always worked in large units such as giant typing pools. The extensive division of labor within firms and other bureaucratic organizations meant the actual work unit could be quite small. Furthermore, many office workers did not work for large organizations, but for a real estate office, small insurance agency, or the office of a relatively small manufacturing firm. Separated as they were from each other, it was often hard for large groups of clerical workers to see their common interest. The situation was only exacerbated by employers' efforts to get office workers to identify their interests with those of their bosses, efforts which worked particularly well with personal secretaries. The low pay and absence of substantial promotional opportunities for many clerical workers contributed to high turnover. When women left clerical jobs to return to the home it was in part because, in the absence of socialized child care, their family labor was crucial to the care of young children, and in part because the loss of dead-end office jobs did not seem like such a terrible thing. The ideology that woman's proper place was in the home with her family only served to strengthen the notion that women's work in the labor force was secondary. No matter that many single women, not to mention the widowed or divorced, remained in the labor force for all their 'working' lives. Many people, notably union leaders who did not put their greatest efforts into organizing clericals, seemed to believe that office workers' jobs weren't important to them and that consequently they were difficult to organize. This is not to belittle the efforts of those, such as the activists in the CIO United Office and Professional Workers of America, who did try to unionize office workers. But overall, clerical organizing was no match whatsoever to the successes among industrial workers.

Since the early 1970s there has been a new surge in clerical organizing, fueled in part by the principles and values of feminism. The rapid success of organizations such as 9 to 5: The National Association of Working Women, District 65 of the United Auto Workers, and District 925 of the Service Employees International Union attests to the growing ability of unions to attract clerical workers. It seems plausible that we are in the beginning years of a significant increase in unionization among clerical workers. As a group of office workers writes in *They Can't Run the Office Without Us: 60 Years of Clerical Work:*

> New issues have been raised that will not disappear, and the consciousness of women office workers has changed over the past few decades. Moreover, some of the obstacles to organizing office workers have receded or disappeared. The superior attitude of secretaries who thought they were better or more skilled or more middle class than factory workers is not nearly so common among clerical workers today. . . . As the Harvard University clerical workers said in one of their union drives: 'You can't eat prestige.' Indeed, given today's wages and working conditions, it is hard to understand the prestige or status once attached to white-collar work. (Massachusetts History Workshop 1985, 74)

Just as the typewriter was one facilitating factor in the entrance of women into the clerical labor force, so was it part of the mechanization of clerical work. Some have argued that the more clerical work is mechanized, the more sympathetic the clerical worker will be to unionism. As a writer in *The New Republic* (1938) described it:

> Tillie the Toiler, that independent pardon-my-gum stenog, is beginning to wonder. The changes in the old office during the past ten years have bewildered her and they are beginning to get on her nerves. It began when the company took over another factory, piling so much work on the office that an addition had to be built. Then the

office was divided up into filing, transcription and accounting departments, where the company installed telephone filing systems, dictaphones, calculators, billing machines and many other devices. Tillie was put on an assembly line where she does one small job in the business of producing a letter. And worse, Tillie's salary was stopped and she began to be paid by piece rate. As the company buys new machinery and learns to use the machinery already installed in her office more efficiently, the value of a union is growing on Tillie. Her friends are being laid off. Her work is being speeded up. Tillie is now, after ten years of preparation, beginning to join a union. (Stuart 1938, 70)

But the minute division of labor described here was not caused by mechanization; at most it was enabled by it. The decision to assign clerical workers to the repetitious execution of the same narrow task was made by management, not by machines. As Anne Machung also argues, it is people who decide how to organize work. The machines only make it possible for the owners and managers to hide their decisions behind the so-called 'technological imperatives' of certain office equipment. The only direct way in which the typewriter could be said to affect communication among women is that many typewriters operated at the same time in the same room make a lot of noise. A typist for an insurance company told Jean Tepperman (1976):

> 'One thing we were just talking about at work is noise pollution. It's very loud. And the machines are not easy to type on. It's like—especially for a machine that was designed to be typed on all day long—driving a big truck with standard, without automatic steering. It's very hard and it's very noisy. I can't hear anything when people talk to me. Everybody thinks their hearing is impaired.' (23)

Certainly women in large typing pools would have a hard time talking to each other while working at their machines. But even here the amount of communication is not dictated solely by the machine. Under the control of the people supervising the work are the decisions about how many scheduled breaks to allow, whether or not to stop typists from taking informal breaks, or whether or not to monitor trips to the bathroom (a well-known site for communication among office workers).

In analyzing the impact the typewriter has had on women clerical workers and communication among them, it is crucial always to bear in mind the historical situation which surrounds the typewriter at any given moment. For the very development of a commercially successful mechanical writing machine was dependent on changes in the political economy, just as it was those changes, and not the typewriter, that brought women into the clerical labor force. It is a mistake to isolate any particular technological invention from the social circumstances which produced it, for in doing so one generally misses the root causes of changes associated with technological innovation.

Notes

1. *The Writing Machine* by Michael Adler (1973) is the best-documented and most thoroughly researched history of the different machines that he considers can be proved to have been invented. He arbitrarily limits his book to 'unconventional' typewriters, thus eliminating coverage of the ones with which we are most familiar, the 'front-stroke, type bar machines with

four-row keyboards' (18). This is actually quite instructive for our purposes, since it provides examples of inventions that were devised at times or in places that were not favorable to the mass production—and hence the successful 'invention'—of the machine. He makes the very apt point that the nationality of the author has a strong influence on the claim of who invented the first typewriter: a French writer credits a Frenchman, an Italian claims the honor for a Giuseppe Ravizza, and US writers generally name Christopher Latham Sholes from Milwaukee, Wisconsin. Certainly both Bruce Bliven, Jr. (1954) and Richard N. Current (1954) name Sholes as the 'father' of the typewriter. Adler does such a thorough and careful job of demonstrating the large number of writing machines that were devised before and after the Sholes machine that it seems ridiculous to call Christopher Latham Sholes the 'father of the typewriter,' even though that label is still common. Adler's book does not appear to be very well-known. Even a careful writer such as Terry Abraham (1980) refers to Bliven's and Current's books as 'the two major works on the typewriter's history' (430). I had never seen this book referred to in writing about the office or business machines in the United States, and stumbled across it by chance in the stacks of Harvard's Widener Library. Other useful research sources are William G. LeDuc (1916); Frederic Heath (1944); and Richard Current (1947; 1954).

2. For more on these early Washington office workers, see the excellent article by Cindy Aron (1981).

3. See Davies (1982, 51–2). The US Treasury clerks were said to work for $900 a year, half the male wage; a New York merchant hired a woman for $500 a year to replace his $1800 a year male bookkeeper.

4. This *US News and World Report* article also mentions the growing status of male secretaries:

> Some of the most sought-after secretaries, in fact, are men. In some circles, they are status symbols once associated with secretaries who spoke with British or French accents. Frank Arnold, a 42-year-old Chicago secretary, reports: 'My employers always would offer me a job at a higher salary than they were paying female secretaries, and ask me not to mention my pay—something they could never get away with now.' (76)

5. It is unclear when this annotation was written, although it was probably later than in 1872. At that time the people who operated writing machines were called 'typewriters.'

References

Abraham, Terry. 1980. 'Charles Thurber: typewriter inventor.' *Technology and Culture* 21:3 (July), 430–4.

Adler, Michael H. 1973. *The Writing Machine*. London: Allen & Unwin.

Aron, Cindy S. 1981. '"To barter their souls for gold": female clerks in federal government offices, 1862–1890.' *Journal of American History* 67:4 (March), 835–53.

Bliven, Jr., Bruce. 1954. *The Wonderful Writing Machine*. New York: Random House.

Current, Richard N. 1947. 'The first newspaperman in Oshkosh.' *Wisconsin Magazine of History* 32:4 (June), 391–407.

Current, Richard N. 1954. *The Typewriter and the Men Who Made It*. Urbana: University of Illinois Press.

Davies, Margery W. 1982. *Woman's Place Is at the Typewriter: Office Work and Office Workers, 1870–1930*. Philadelphia: Temple University Press.

Davies, Margery W. 1985. 'Women and the office: a historical perspective.' *ILR Report* 23:1 (Fall), 7–10. Published by the New York State School of Industrial and Labor Relations.

Edwards, Alba M. 1943. *Comparative Occupation Statistics for the United States, 1870–1940.* Part of the Sixteenth Census of the United States: 1940. Washington: Government Printing Office.

Feldberg, Roslyn L. 1980. '"Union fever": organizing among clerical workers, 1900–1930.' *Radical America* 14:3. Reprinted in James R. Green, ed. 1983. *Workers' Struggles, Past and Present: A 'Radical America' Reader.* Philadelphia: Temple University Press, 151–67.

Feldberg, Roslyn L. and Evelyn Nakano Glenn. 1983. 'Incipient workplace democracy among United States clerical workers.' *Economic and Industrial Democracy* 4:1, 47–67.

'Frank talk from secretaries about their jobs and pay.' 1977. *US News and World Report* 82:25 (27 June), 75–6.

Heath, Frederic. 1944. 'The typewriter in Wisconsin.' *Wisconsin Magazine of History* 27:3 (March), 263–75.

Kearney, Paul M. 1951. 'Woman's great emancipator—the typewriter.' *Independent Woman* 30 (July), 192–3.

LeDuc, William G. 1916. 'The genesis of the typewriter.' *The Magazine of History* 22:3 (March), 83–7.

Massachusetts History Workshop. 1985. *They Can't Run the Office Without Us: 60 Years of Clerical Work.* Massachusetts History Workshop, 238 Pearl Street, Cambridge, MA 02139.

Smith, Ellen Ada. 1898. 'The typewriting clerk.' *Longman's Magazine* 31:185 (March), 431–46.

Strom, Sharon Hartman. 1983. 'Challenging "woman's place": feminism, the left and industrial unionism in the 1930s.' *Feminist Studies* 9:2, 359–86.

Stuart, Mal J. 1938. 'Robots in the office.' *The New Republic* (25 May), 70–2.

Tepperman, Jean. 1976. *Not Servants, Not Machines: Office Workers Speak Out!* Boston: Beacon Press.

REFLECTING ON THE READING

1. Who is Christopher Latham Sholes? Why does Davies mention him at the very beginning of this article? Why does she assert that he was wrong about the impact of the typewriter? What position does she take with respect to the development of the typewriter? Why is this position important to the point she makes in the rest of her article?

2. What effects did the typewriter have on women in the workplace, according to Davies? In what sense was the typewriter a factor in what Davies calls the "feminization and proletarianization of the clerical labor force"? Why did the increase in the number of women typists not lead to union organizing campaigns among women clerical workers, according to Davies? What point of view regarding labor and women does Davies imply in her discussion of the effects of the typewriter on women workers? Do you share her point of view? How might your answer to that question influence your reading of her article?

3. How does the growth in the use of the typewriter as an office machine illustrate Davies' point that "technology in no way operates in a vacuum"? Why is this an

important point for Davies' purposes in this article? Why is Davies resistant to the idea that the typewriter as a technology was the primary factor in the increase in the number of women in the clerical workforce? Do you agree with her? Why or why not?

4. According to Davies, what was the primary factor that drew women into the office workforce? Why is this an important point in her analysis of the typewriter? What does this point reveal about Davies' own perspective on economics?

5. What role did literacy play in the increase in the number of women entering the clerical workforce, in Davies' view? What might this role suggest about the relationship between literacy and work? Between literacy and gender?

6. What impact did the typewriter have on the way office work was organized, according to Davies? What were the implications of this reorganization for workers, especially women? What might the impact of the typewriter suggest about the role of technology in the workplace?

7. In what sense did the typewriter contribute to what Davies calls "the mechanization of clerical work"? Why was this an important development with respect to women clerical workers, as Davies sees it? What conclusions does Davies draw about the role of the typewriter in such developments?

Examining Rhetorical Strategies

1. Assess the way Davies begins this article. How does she position her argument in the article's opening paragraph? What opposition does she set up? What point of view does she highlight? What reaction did you have to her introduction? Were you engaged or taken aback by her rather blunt assertion that Sholes was wrong? Explain. What might your reaction to her introduction suggest about you as a reader? How might your reaction affect the way you read the rest of her article? Do you think Davies wished to provoke the kind of reaction that you had to her introduction? Why or why not?

2. What would you say is the main point Davies wishes to make in this article? Is her article primarily about the typewriter or something else, in your view? Support your answer with specific references to her article.

3. This article was originally published in a collection of scholarly essays about women and technology. The intended audience was a specialized one: primarily other scholars interested in technology and women's issues. In what ways do you think Davies addresses this audience? What features of her text suggest that it was written primarily for an academic audience? Do you think her essay is accessible to readers who are not academic specialists? Explain. Did you find her article accessible? What might your answer suggest about you as a reader?

4. Davies asserts early in her essay that the increase in clerical workers was related to the expansion of the capitalist economy in the United States at the end of the nineteenth century. Based on your reading of this essay, how would you characterize Davies' position regarding capitalism? Do you think she wishes to present a critical view of capitalism? Explain, citing specific passages from her article to support your answer.

5. How do the two epigraphs at the beginning of Davies' article function in her article? What purposes do you think Davies accomplishes with those epigraphs? In what ways do they help highlight or introduce ideas that are important to her article? How would the article be different if the epigraphs were not included? Did you find them effective? Why or why not? What might your reaction to them indicate about your expectations as a reader?

6. Examine Davies' use of evidence to support her assertions in this article. What kinds of evidence does she provide? Does she offer adequate support for her statements, in your view? Explain, citing specific passages from her article in your answer. What might her use of evidence suggest about the assumptions she makes about her readers?

Engaging the Issues

1. Write an essay for an audience of your classmates in which you discuss work and gender in modern American society. In your essay, present your own view about the problems facing women (or men) in the workplace and the ways in which prevailing attitudes about gender affect women (or men) in the workplace. Be sure to support your position by drawing on information you might gather about men and women in the workplace, on readings in this chapter, and on your own experiences.

2. Write the essay described in Question #1 above for a general audience—for example, readers of a large-circulation publication like *USA Today.*

3. Rewrite the essay described in Question #1 above specifically for an audience of the opposite sex. That is, if you are a woman, write your essay specifically for your male classmates; if you are a man, write for the women in your class.

4. In a group of your classmates (that includes both men and women, if possible), discuss the essays you wrote for Question #3 above. What do you notice about the ways in which men and women address each other in their essays? Can you identify significant similarities or differences in how men and women address each other? Are there noticeable similarities or differences among the men and women regarding work and technology? Discuss these similarities and differences. What conclusions can you draw about gender and work from your discussions?

5. Write an analysis of Davies' essay in which you discuss the effectiveness of her argument regarding technology and women workers. In your analysis, summarize the main points you believe she makes in her article and examine the way she supports those points, including the kinds of evidence she provides. Also consider the nature of her likely audience (academic readers; other scholars like her) and her apparent purpose. How effectively does she address her audience? How effectively do you think she achieves her purpose? Draw conclusions about the overall effectiveness of her essay.

6. Conduct a search of the World Wide Web for sites devoted to working women, issues related to women and work, or similar sites. Try to identify a variety of such sites (academic, business, government, nonprofit organizations). Explore

these sites, trying to identify their purposes and the audiences they hope to reach. Examine the kinds of information they contain and identify the distinguishing features of each. Then write a report on your findings for an audience of your classmates. In your report, describe the sites you found and explain what those sites contain and the purposes they seem to have. Focus especially on what the sites explicitly or implicitly convey about women, work, and technology. Compare the sites in terms of these issues and assess the effectiveness of each site.

7. Create a Web site instead of writing an analysis as described in Question #6 above. Design your Web site as a resource for information about women in the workplace. Offer critiques of the other sites you've identified and include appropriate links to those sites.

8. In a group of your classmates, compare the Web sites you created for Question #7 above. Discuss the features of each and especially examine the similarities and differences among the sites. Discuss the decisions each group member made about what to include in his or her site and how he or she organized the site. Examine the attitudes each site seems to convey about gender, work, and technology.

9. Try to find an Internet discussion group or listserv related to issues of gender and work, and follow the discussion for several days or weeks (if possible). What kinds of issues regarding gender and work emerge in the online discussion? How do the men and women in the discussion view these issues? Can you identify similarities or differences in the views of men and women regarding work and gender?

   Now write a report for an audience of your classmates about the online discussion you followed. In your report, be sure to describe the nature of the discussion group you joined and provide some information about the participants (if possible). Identify the key issues that emerged and any differences you detected in how the men and women in the discussion approached these issues. Discuss whether you think the online forum facilitated or inhibited discussion among men and women in any way. Try to draw conclusions about attitudes toward gender and work on the basis of your experiences with this discussion group.

The Myth of Cyber Inequality

ROBERT J. SAMUELSON

INTRODUCTION As advanced computer technologies proliferated in the 1980's and 1990's and began to reshape American business, education, and social life, some observers worried that the rapid increase in the use of these new technologies would contribute to inequalities in the American workplace. To put it simply, they worried that those who have computers and know how to use them would have a distinct advantage over those who do not. Employment and income statistics seemed to validate these concerns. For instance, in 1995 *Newsweek* reported that although only a third of all Americans owned a computer, 74 percent of Americans who earned more than $75,000 per year owned a computer. Moreover, by the mid-1990's, jobs involving computer technologies were among the fastest-growing and best-paying in the job market, and people with advanced computer skills were in high demand. Such figures seemed to suggest that computer technologies were causing disparities in the American job market and were helping to increase the gap between rich and poor. The term *cyber inequality* was coined to refer to this problem.

As the title of the following essay suggests, columnist Robert J. Samuelson doesn't believe that there is such a thing as cyber inequality. He doesn't deny that there is inequality in the American job market and that there are huge differences in the wages earned by Americans. But these differences, according to Samuelson, are not the result of the increasing use of computers or the development of ever more sophisticated computer technologies. Rather, Samuelson sees the problem of inequality in the American job market as a much bigger issue, related to many other social and economic factors. For Samuelson, who has written extensively about economic and financial matters, the use of computers in American society should be understood as one part of the complicated processes by which businesses expand and contract and compete in a global economy. Some Americans benefit from those complicated processes and some do not. Those who do not benefit, Samuelson suggests briefly, may be those from less advantaged backgrounds. In this sense, his essay encourages us to think about technology in the context of the complex workings of the American economy. How might technology shape the American job market? How might a person's access to technology influence that person's prospects in the job market? In what ways might the job market reflect broader inequalities in American society? These are large and complicated questions about which Samuelson's essay may provide some insight.

Robert J. Samuelson has been writing essays on economics and finance for *Newsweek* since 1984, when he joined the magazine's staff as a contributing editor. He also writes a biweekly column that appears in newspapers such as the *Los Angeles Times*, the *Boston Globe*, and the *Washington Post*. He has won much recognition for his writing, including such prestigious awards as the National Magazine Award and the John Hancock Award for Best Business and Financial Columnist. His book *The Good Life and Its Discontents: The American Dream in the Age of Entitlement 1945–1995* (1996) was widely praised and earned a spot on the *New York Times* best-seller list. The following essay appeared in *Newsweek* in 1995.

REFLECTING BEFORE READING

1. In his essay, Samuelson discusses inequality in American business. What does he mean by "inequality" in this essay? Do you think his understanding of this term is one that is shared by most Americans? How do you understand inequality?

2. Samuelson's essay was originally published in *Newsweek*, which has a very large and broad readership. As you read, consider how Samuelson addresses

his audience. In what specific ways do you think he writes for general readers rather than for economic or financial experts?

P erhaps within a decade, most Americans will have an e-mail address, just as most now have phone numbers. The computer will become (as it is already becoming) a democratic appliance that will increasingly resemble the kitchen stove. Almost everyone has a stove. But some of us make hamburgers, and others make fettucini. Computers are the same; they reveal differences more than create them. Once this becomes clear, the idea of cyber inequality will implode.

Cyber inequality is the notion that computers are helping splinter America economically. They seem one explanation for the sharp increase of wage inequality. Consider this oft-cited comparison: in 1979 a recent male college graduate earned about 30 percent more than his high-school counterpart; by 1993, the gap was 70 percent. The prevailing wisdom among economists is that, as computers have spread, the demand for workers who can use them has increased. Wages for those workers rise, while wages for the unskilled (who can't use them) fall.

What could be simpler: if the problem is no computer skills, then provide skills. Give the poor a tax credit for laptops, suggested Newt Gingrich. Although he retracted that proposal, he didn't disavow the impulse. "[T]here has to be a missionary spirit," he says, "that says to the poorest child in America, 'Internet's for you'." Vice President Al Gore gushes similarly about the Information Superhighway. Technology, if denied, is doom; if supplied, it is salvation.

Bunk. Cyber inequality is mostly a myth. Computers do not really explain widening wage inequalities. The more important cause is a profound change in the business climate, beginning in the 1970s. Economic optimism waned and competitive pressures intensified. Companies gradually overhauled the ways they pay, promote, hire and fire. Put simply they began treating their most valuable workers better and their least valuable workers worse.

Everyone knows the pressures that prompted this upheaval: harsh recessions, tougher competition and more corporate debt. Shrinking profit margins reflect the intensity of those pressures. In the 1950s and 1960s, profits before taxes averaged about 16 percent of corporate revenues: they dropped to 11 percent in the 1970s and 9 percent in the 1980s.

When profit margins were fat, companies routinely promoted and provided across-the-board pay increases. The idea was to offset inflation and give something extra. Many companies adopted elaborate "job evaluation" systems that graded jobs across different departments in an attempt to ensure "fairness." Jobs with similar responsibilities would be paid similarly. "The focus was on internal equity," says Paul Platten, a compensation expert with the Hay Group. Companies hired optimistically, because they expected higher profits from higher sales. Young and less skilled workers (the last hired) benefited.

Dropping profit margins devastated these practices. Across-the-board pay increases diminished. In a recent survey of 317 big companies, Bucks Consultants found that 90 percent paid only merit increases. "Job evaluation" systems have been de-emphasized. More money is funneled into pay arrangements aimed at rewarding good performance. In the Buck survey, 30 percent of companies used lump-sum merit increases and 15 percent used "gainsharing." New workers are hired more reluctantly, because companies fear bloating labor costs; entry-level salaries are suppressed. Now the last hired often suffer.

Computers are only incidental to this process. This does not mean they haven't changed the nature of work or eliminated some low-skilled jobs. They have. For example, the need for secretaries has dropped as more managers use computers. Between 1983 and 1993, the number of secretaries decreased by 14 percent. But this is an age-old process. New technologies have always destroyed and created jobs.

The issue is not whether some people have better computer skills and are rewarded for them; clearly, that happens. So what? Skills differences have always existed. The real question is whether computers have escalated those differences. By and large, the answer is no. Indeed, computers have spread—both at home and at work—precisely because more powerful microprocessors, memory chips and software have made them easier to use. Fewer generic computer skills are needed. As this happens, computers merely complement people's other skills.

Almost accidentally, economists are now confirming that a broader process is fostering inequality. Men laid off between 1960 and 1992 lost an average 20 percent of pay when they got new jobs, says a Census Board study. They didn't become less skilled, but they were thrust into a hard labor market. Two thirds of the increase of inequality does not reflect growing gaps between more and less educated workers (say college and high-school graduates), reports Gary Burtless of The Brookings Institute. Rather, it reflects bigger gaps among workers with similar educations (say, college graduates). Companies are tougher at all levels. Finally, Peter Gottschalk of Boston College and Robert Moffitt of Brown University find that people's earnings now fluctuate more from year to year than they used to; that's consistent with harsher hiring, firing and pay practices.

Contrary to Gingrich and Gore, the Internet is not the promised land. Sure, our economic and social well-being would improve if some of our worst workers had better skills; but the skills they need most are basic literacy and good work habits. With those, computer competence will come if needed. The infatuation with computers as a cause or cure of social distress is misplaced. Mostly, computers mirror who we are: a people of vast vitality, great ingenuity and manifest imperfections.

REFLECTING ON THE READING

1. In the opening paragraph of this essay, Samuelson describes the computer as "a democratic appliance that will increasingly resemble the kitchen stove." What does he mean by that description? In what sense is the computer "democratic"? Do you think Samuelson is correct when he writes in the same paragraph that computers "reveal differences rather than create them"? Why or why not? What does this suggest about Samuelson's assumptions about technology?

2. How does Samuelson define *cyber inequality?* Why does he call it a myth?

3. What does Samuelson mean by "wage inequalities"? Why is this an important issue? How does he establish that it is a problem? What profound change in American business helped cause this problem, according to Samuelson?

4. In Samuelson's view, what specific developments in American business most affect wages and hiring practices? In what ways are computers only "incidental" to these developments? What might this point suggest about Samuelson's assumptions regarding business and technology? Do you think those assumptions are valid? Explain.

5. Samuelson asserts that computers have not escalated differences in wages among American workers. What support does he offer for this assertion? Do you think he is right? Why or why not?

6. What does Samuelson believe low-wage workers need most in order to improve their employment opportunities? Do you agree with him? Why or why not?

Examining Rhetorical Strategies

1. In his opening paragraph, Samuelson compares the computer to a stove. He writes that although almost everyone has a stove, "some of us make hamburgers, and others make fettucini." What do you think this comparison of the computer and the stove is meant to suggest about computers? What does it reveal about Samuelson's own beliefs regarding technology in American society? Did you find this comparison effective? Why or why not?

2. Examine the evidence Samuelson offers to support his arguments in this essay. What kinds of evidence does he cite to support his claims? Do you think his evidence is convincing? Why or why not? Do you think he leaves out important factors in his argument? Explain.

3. Samuelson writes his essays for a very large general audience—that is, readers of *Newsweek,* which is a large-circulation national newsmagazine, and readers of major newspapers throughout the United States. Do you think this essay is appropriate for such an audience? What does he assume about his audience's knowledge of such issues as economics and business technology? For example, he writes, "Everyone knows the pressures that prompted this upheaval [in American business in the 1970's]: harsh recessions, tougher competition and more corporate debt." Do you think "everyone" does in fact know this? Who might know it? Who might be excluded from such knowledge? Do you think you are part of the audience for which Samuelson writes? Explain.

4. How would you characterize Samuelson's attitude toward technology in this essay? Do you think he is generally in favor of advances in technologies like computers? Does he see technology as a problem in any way? Do you think he wishes to present technology in a favorable or a critical way? Explain. What do you think he assumes about his readers' attitudes regarding technology? Cite specific passages from his essay to support your answer.

5 Describe Samuelson's tone in this essay. Cite specific phrases and sentences that you think help establish this tone. What effect do you think his tone might have on readers? What effect did it have on you? Do you think Samuelson intended such an effect? Explain.

6. Samuelson ends his essay with the following sentence: "Mostly, computers mirror who we are: a people of vast vitality, great ingenuity and manifest

imperfections." What do you think this statement reveals about Samuelson's views regarding American culture and American business? Do you agree with him? Why or why not? Do you think this statement is an appropriate conclusion to his essay? Explain.

Engaging the Issues

1. Based on your own knowledge of economics and your own experiences in the job market (or the experiences of people you know), write an essay in response to Samuelson focusing on the impact of technology on American workers. Use appropriate sources and your own experience to support your arguments. Write your essay for the same general audience for which Samuelson wrote his essay.

2. Write an analysis of Samuelson's arguments about computers and inequality. Focus on the kinds of evidence he uses to support his arguments and the kinds of claims he makes. In your analysis, consider the audience for which he was writing his essay. Try to draw conclusions about the effectiveness of his arguments for such an audience.

3. Do a search of the World Wide Web to find out about wages and incomes among American workers. Try to find information about how technology might have affected the job market in the years since Samuelson wrote his essay. Compare your findings with the figures he provides in his essay. Are there any differences? Has the situation changed significantly since he wrote his essay? Do your findings change your feelings about his essay? Explain.

4. In a group of your classmates, share your experiences with technology in the jobs you have had or the jobs held by people you know well (such as your parents or other relatives). Compare your respective experiences, trying to identify any similarities among them. Now consider Samuelson's article in light of your group's experiences. How do your experiences support or challenge Samuelson's arguments? What might they suggest about the role of technology in the American workplace?

5. Write an essay for an audience of your classmates describing your experiences with technology in the workplace. You may write about your experiences with technology in the workplace in general (in several jobs, for instance), or you might focus on a specific experience in one job. Or you might write about a situation in which you obtained a job because of your background with a specific technology or perhaps were denied a job because you lacked experience with a specific kind of technology. Describe your experience so that your readers can understand the situation you were in. Focus on how the technology involved might have influenced your work. For instance, did you need special skills for the job? Did technology somehow create opportunities for you or limit you in some way? Try to draw conclusions about technology and opportunity in the workplace based on the experience you describe.

   Compare your essay with the essays of several of your classmates. What similarities and differences emerge in the experiences all of you wrote about? How can you account for those similarities and differences? What conclusions might you draw about technology and inequality in the workplace? What conclusions can you draw about the American job market?

6. Visit a workplace near where you live and talk with workers there about the role of technology in their jobs. Try to interview several different people at different worksites, if possible. Or talk to friends or family members about their jobs. Ask them about their training with technology and the relationship between their knowledge of technologies—especially computers—and their own prospects in the job market. Have computers enhanced their prospects or worsened them? How has the rapid growth of computer technologies in the workplace affected their jobs and their lives? Now write a report for your classmates in which you present your findings. In your report, describe the people you spoke to and their places of work. Explain the kinds of jobs they do and the role of technology in their jobs. Present their views on the impact of technology on their working lives. Try to draw conclusions about the role of technology in the American workplace.

7. Create a Web site as a resource for people interested in learning more about the role of technology in the American job market.

8. Visit some sites on the Internet for job seekers and/or scan the job advertisements in your local newspaper. Examine the available jobs to see whether certain computer skills or knowledge of computer technology seem to be in demand in the job market. What kinds of "technology" jobs can you find? What kind of computer skills do they require? Also, try to find information about available jobs involving technology (such as computer programmers, consultants, technicians, and so on). Then write a report for your classmates on the basis of your research. In your report, describe the sources you consulted and discuss what you learned about the job market. Try to draw conclusions about technology in the job market.

9. Write a response to Samuelson drawing on the research you did for Question #8 above. Assume that your response will be published in *Newsweek.*

Interview with Robert Reich

DAVID S. BENNAHUM

INTRODUCTION   Turn to almost any newspaper or newsmagazine or watch any television news broadcast and you're likely to encounter discussion about the "new" global economy and the effects of technology on American business and economic life. *E-commerce,* a term coined in the 1990's to refer to business transacted through online media, has become almost as common in our economic lexicon as *stock market* or *Wall Street.* A study of news coverage of the Internet in 1999 indicated that major American newspapers mentioned *e-commerce* in 20,641 different news articles during that year alone, which suggests the high level of attention that Americans seem to be paying to the changing economy at the start of the new millennium. Few people seem to doubt that the American economy is in the midst of a profound restructuring, largely as a result of technological developments associated with computers and the Internet. Perhaps the most dramatic example of these changes was the stunning rise of online business during the December holiday season at the end of 1999. Sales figures from that period indicate that online holiday commerce increased by as much as 200 percent over the previous year. Such figures seemed to justify the large number of businesses that developed online services at the end of the 1990's and suggested the rapid pace of change in the way Americans engaged in commerce. But what these changes ultimately will mean—not only for the nation as a whole but for individual workers—is less clear. Will the nation and its workers be better off in this "new" economy? Is e-commerce good for all? How will the digital technologies that are changing the way Americans do business affect the lives of individual workers? In a larger sense, how *should* the nation in the best interests of its citizens address—and facilitate or resist—these economic and technological developments?

These are questions that have preoccupied former U.S. Secretary of Labor Robert Reich. Reich served as President Bill Clinton's labor secretary during the early 1990's, when the Internet was emerging as perhaps the most significant development to influence the American economy since the industrialization that occurred in the early twentieth century. As labor secretary, Reich was responsible for helping formulate American economic policy and for guiding presidential and governmental decisions about important economic developments, including the rise of e-commerce. As American businesses were becoming increasingly digital and global in ways that challenged traditional economic assumptions about how to conduct and control commerce, Reich was a key figure in helping the U.S. government decide how best to respond to these developments.

Reich is widely considered to be one of the most creative economic minds of our time, and his ideas have been influential as the American economy has experienced the changes described above. But although Reich is often credited with helping facilitate the global economy and promoting the preeminent role of the United States in that economy, he has also established himself as a thinker whose economic views are deeply shaped by his sense of social justice. In a 1998 article about the economic policies of the Clinton administration during the longest economic expansion in American history (an article he wrote after stepping down from his post as labor secretary), Reich argued for "a more inclusive, more equitable society, in which everyone has a fair chance of making it." He charged the government with ignoring the fact that "almost seven years of economic recovery has done remarkably little for people in the bottom half." The "real news," he went on, "is that the median wage—the take-home pay of the worker smack in the middle of the earnings ladder—is still less than it was before the last recession, adjusted for inflation. More people are in poverty. At the same time, the upper reaches of America have never had it so good" ("Broken Faith: Why We Need to Renew the Social Contract," *Nation*, Feb. 16, 1998). Such views, which emerge in the following interview as well, have sometimes sparked controversy within the government and among economists. But they have also gained Reich a wide audience, many of whom undoubtedly share his sense of caution about recent economic developments and his desire for an equitable society in which all members might share in the benefits of economic growth.

In the interview reprinted here, Reich probes some of the most pressing economic issues facing the United States in the new global economy. Although the interview was conducted in 1996, the issues Reich addresses remain at the center of economic policy discussions in the United States at the beginning of the new millennium: economic growth, equality, the role of technology, the role of education, the quality of life of workers in the new global economy. Indeed, in 2000, Reich was still making news by addressing these same issues in his distinctive way in his newspaper columns and on radio and television news programs. It is noteworthy that the following interview originally appeared in *MEME*, a newsletter distributed exclusively online. That fact underscores some of the technological changes affecting the American economy that Reich discusses in the interview. Moreover, it may implicitly highlight one of Reich's central concerns regarding the influence of technology on the American economy: fair access to the technologies that are reshaping the world within which Americans live and work.

Robert Reich is currently Distinguished University Professor at Brandeis University. He is a widely sought-after speaker and writer who has authored many articles and newspaper columns as well as two best-selling books, *The Work of Nations* and *Locked in the Cabinet*. He is a frequent guest on television news shows and appears regularly on *Marketplace*, a daily business news program on National Public Radio. The following interview, which was conducted while Reich was still secretary of labor, appeared in 1996 in *MEME*, an online newsletter edited by David Bennahum (whose writing appears in Chapters 1 and 3 of this book).

REFLECTING BEFORE READING

1. The following selection is an interview originally published in an online newsletter. As you read, pay attention to the format of the interview, which has become a popular form as online journals and newsletters have proliferated in recent years. Pay particular attention to the way Bennahum conducts the interview. In what ways is the interview format different from more conventional news or magazine articles that address the same kinds of issues? How is the experience of reading an interview such as this one different from reading other forms of news writing? What advantages or disadvantages do you see to this form? Why do you think it has become more popular as online media have grown?

2. In the following interview, Reich and Bennahum discuss important economic developments associated with new technologies in the 1990's. As you read, examine the views of technology that seem to emerge in Bennahum's questions and Reich's answers. How does each seem to view technology? Do you think their views are widely shared? Do *you* share them? Explain.

"Ultimately, we have to decide whether we are no more than an economy sharing a common currency in which the primary social glue binding us together is the business transactions we do with one another, or if we are still a society in which we have special obligations to one another as citizens."

— *Robert Reich, in* MEME *2.02.*

I n the first week of January, AT&T fired approximately 40,000 employees out of a total workforce of approximately 305,000 people. This came several months after AT&T shocked the world by announcing its intention to divide into three separate companies: a telecommunications service company (known as AT&T), an un-named second company based at Bell Labs which will build the hardware behind telephone networks, and a third company specializing in computers, to be named National Cash Register (NCR).

AT&T, one of the oldest, and arguably most successful, corporations in the United States, made this decision for several reasons. One, according to CEO Bob Allen, included making AT&T more competitive in the changing world of communications, a world where simply carrying telephone conversation is replaced by complex layers of "content"—from multimedia to video-conferencing to unknown digital network applications. Simultaneously, the U.S. Secretary of Labor, Robert Reich, made several pronouncements about the significance of these firings for the US economy at the start of the so-called Information Age. Reich used the term "electronic capitalism" in a New York Times op-ed to describe the changing nature of the world economy and work.

I managed to get the Secretary on the telephone for about a half-hour, and we discussed the implications of AT&T's actions and the changing nature of capitalism in the Information Age. What follows is a transcript of that conversation.

DAVID BENNAHUM: Mr. Secretary, I want to thank you for taking the time to speak to me today. I read your op-ed piece, and I'm hoping in this conversation to really sink our teeth into the nature of work in an era of electronic capitalism and the degree to which capitalism is changing, in a sense, because of, shall we say, the Information Age or the arrival of an economy based on information. Reading your Op-Ed, you had this phrase "electronic capitalism" and that it's replaced the gentlemanly investment system that we used to have before. So I'm wondering, maybe to begin with, if we can start by looking at what do you mean by "electronic capitalism"?

ROBERT REICH: A form of capitalism in which investment decisions are made with extraordinary rapidity. Money can be moved at the speed of an electronic impulse. And there are a wide range of alternative places to park money, not only inside the borders of one country, but literally around the globe. Capital has never been as mobile. In fact, it is hard to conceive of how it could be more mobile. People, however, are still rather immobile. In fact, two-wage-earner families are becoming the norm, and two wage-earners have a harder time moving from place to place and getting jobs than one wage-earner. It's also difficult for people to leave friends and family when they depend on friends and family as never before for baby-sitting, support, economic support, and even loneliness. And finally, it's become difficult for people to move because often much of their assets are tied up in their homes, in property values. The rich rely upon stocks and bonds. The middle-class relies upon their own home as their primary savings vehicle. But when the economy turns sour in a particular region because of a massive layoff, housing values begin to deteriorate. It's more difficult to afford to move to a place where jobs are growing and property values are, accordingly, soaring. So we have the paradoxical situation in which electronic capitalism is making financial capital ever more mobile, at precisely the same time as it has become ever more difficult for people to move, change jobs, and change locations. I ought to add one more point about the difficulty of shifting ground. New jobs often require new skills. Unlike the old days in which a machinist in one firm could leave that firm if necessary, and become a machinist in another firm, today the good jobs require skills, and it is not always easy to get new skills for a new job. Often one has to learn those new skills. So mobility from job to job, particularly good-paying jobs—well, actually all jobs—is somewhat less than it was in a mass production economy.

DB: Is the core behind all these problems the digitization of our economy, in a sense?

RR: To call it a problem I think makes a conceptual leap. It's a problem to the extent that there is a widening disjuncture between the extraordinary speed at which financial capital is moving and the difficulties that individuals and families have catching up. It means that many people who lose their jobs are left without easy access to a new job. Financial insecurity is rampant because job insecurity is endemic . . .

DB: Let me ask you this question then. If one of the fundamental powers of our nation used to be, in a sense, that it had some degree of control over its economy, to what degree does this mobile, sort of nomadic capital undermine the ability of nation-states to have a say in governing how their economy functions?

RR: Well, considerably. Not only the nation-states have less capacity because economic policy increasingly is determined by bond traders and investment capital moving around the world, but communities have even less capacity to determine their own fates. Entire communities are susceptible to sudden loss of jobs, or a decision by a major business to leave. Communities, states and nations are all being played off against other communities, states and nations in a giant bidding war which is undermining local tax bases at the same time as it penalizes the smaller businesses that have less bargaining leverage, because they can't get the same tax benefits. Now, what's the answer here? Surely not to immobilize financial capital. I think it would be a mistake to believe that the only solution lies in imposing draconian controls on the movement of capital. Part of the solution may be making it easier for people to gain mobility. In fact, that's one of the goals that we have set for ourselves, creating a reemployment system that is modeled on a very different premise than the old unemployment insurance system, which assumed that one would get one's job back again after a downturn, when the company was rehiring. The term "layoff" is a misnomer. It comes from a time in our history in which most job loss was temporary, people were "laid off" until they were back on the payrolls. But these days, 70 percent of the people who lose their jobs lose them permanently. A better term would be probably "castoff." Perhaps in addition to easing the transition from job to job, giving people better opportunities to get new skills, setting up a new digitized information system so that people can know what jobs are available and what skills underlie those jobs . . . By the way, that's all now being created, and we're moving on that as fast as we can. But besides that, we perhaps also need to create incentives for companies to upgrade employee skills, to bring workers on as partners in terms of profit-sharing and gain sharing, and if they are going to lay off people, do so in a way in which the company assumes more of the cost of retraining them and finding them new jobs paying comparable salaries.

DB: Can I ask you a question, though, about . . . As someone who grew up with computers, as part of that first generation of people to sort of get them as kids in the Seventies, for me it's something I'm very comfortable with. I sort of understand the machine. I sort of grew up with it, so there's no real barrier for me. I know that I'm very fortunate in that way. And I do, because of that knowledge and being with the machine, have this feeling (and I think it might be true) that they are enabling companies to be more efficient in the way they process information and organize themselves. So is it actually possible that the people being pushed out simply really won't be able to find work because literally we've made the work "more efficient" so there's simply not the need for human power that there used to be?

RR: I don't believe that. I believe, and my belief is based upon travels all around the country where I've seen technology creating new demands for new skills we hadn't even heard of years ago . . . The garage mechanics, for example, who understand the electronics underneath the hoods of new cars and can diagnose and repair those electronics, are earning $50,000 and $60,000. They are not garage mechanics in the traditional sense of the word. Cashiers who can use computers to control inventories become inventory managers and are much more valuable than the cashiers of old. Truck drivers, those who have computers in their cabs and time deliveries for precisely when the customers need them and also understand how to repair and install the machinery are more than truck drivers—they really are technicians.

DB: I can see that happening. But the counter-argument is made that, you know, there used to be a clerk and an inventory manager; now there is a clerk who does the inventory management. They get paid the same amount the clerk used to get paid, and one job has disappeared.

RR: What we know from the economy is that of the 8 million jobs created over the past three years, most of them paid better than the median wage. In fact, the most rapidly growing job categories are knowledge-intensive; I've called them "symbolic analysts." Why are they growing so quickly? Why are they paying so well? Because technology is generating all sorts of new possibilities. There's not a fixed number of jobs to be parceled out of which technology might be replacing one portion. Rather, technology generates its own new jobs. And although the routine jobs are being replaced very rapidly, higher-skilled jobs which utilize the technology for problem-solving are being created at an even more rapid clip. The problem is that many people don't have the right skills. We were a mass production economy in the 1950's. Our middle class was created through mass production industries. In fact, high volume mass production, stable mass production generated the sorts of jobs that were the doorways into the post-War middle class. But the new middle class is based on a completely different premise. Instead of high-volume, standardized, stable mass production, it is based upon the paradigm of continuous technological change. The only people who are thriving in this new economy are people who are becoming more valuable because they are utilizing the technology to generate greater and greater value and output. Professionals, top managers, technicians of all types are actually riding the wave of technology. The top 20 percent of income-earners in this country are doing exceedingly well. The top 5 percent are doing superbly well. The problem is that median wages are stagnating. They've been stagnating for 15 years. Even though the economy has grown, 97 percent of the growth in family income over the past fifteen years has gone to the top 20 percent of households—I should say household income. And half of that has gone to the top 5 percent. There's not a shortage of jobs. I mean, if you look at the employment picture, you'll see that (although I don't have December's figures) through November we had 15 straight months of unemployment lower than 6 percent, which many people said could not be achieved without igniting inflation. There's no inflation. There's no inflation in sight. The problem is that of the 115 million existing jobs, those already existing in 1993, they have split between a relatively few paying better and better, and a much larger number paying worse and worse. Technology and globalization have conspired to shift demand in favor of people with skills, the right education, and (I'll also add in) the right connections, and against people without these attributes.

DB: What do you mean by "right connections"?

RR: In the new . . . I mean, electronic capitalism places a great premium on being at the right place in the right time, with the right skills. One of the great benefits of going to an elite college (and by the way, this has always been a great benefit; it's probably more of a benefit now than ever before) is meeting people who are plugged in to the new economy, or more likely, whose parents and relatives are plugged in. It's those job connections. You know, my Uncle, my Father, my Mother, my Aunt, my Friend's Friend is in this industry, is doing that. Experience counts for so much, the first few jobs count for so much, that web of connections often in a university setting often is vitally important. There are also the connections that come from working in a dynamic sector of the economy. If you are deeply involved right now in the Internet in terms of products being generated on the Internet, chances are you're rubbing elbows in cyberspace with people who are doing some fascinating things. You have a greater likelihood of knowing what you need to learn over the next six months in order to get closer to the cutting edge.

DB: Does that tend to increase or accelerate the process of division between the top strata and the rest?

RR: Absolutely. Because the people who are in the middle of the income distribution, or below, are that much less likely to have that elite education or to be rubbing elbows in cyberspace. You mentioned a moment ago that you were a product of . . .

DB: Yeah, I'm one of those lucky people. I went to Harvard and work on cyberspace.

RR: But what I want to emphasize is, it's less generational than it is socio-economic. There are many people now who are middle-aged and who have become computer-literate, perhaps not computer nerds but computer-literate, because they have the tools to learn. But young people today who are 5, 6, 7, 8 years old, young teenagers today who are in homes without computers, who have no idea how to use them, what to do with them, how they can be tools for learning, those young people are at a serious disadvantage, even if they didn't face all the other barriers that they now face.

DB: The image of the Information Age that we used to have in the Fifties and Sixties was one of prosperity, and then in the Seventies and Eighties was one of prosperity mixed with technological wizardry, and that we'd have these high-scale jobs that at least would give us really high pay. But it was a very optimistic vision, I would say.

RR: Well, it's a vision that has come true for a segment of our population. But electronic capitalism also enables the most successful to secede from the rest of society. It is now possible for top level managers, professionals and technicians to communicate directly with their counterparts around the world to generate new products and services for other counterparts around the world without depending economically upon the productivity of lower-wage and less-skilled people.

DB: And in a sense, because of that, the moral link to the community has been severed, right?

RR: Exactly.

DB: I mean, you're no longer a part of a community, so you have no . . .

RR: Exactly. The word "community" right now is a very appealing . . . connotes very appealing images. But in reality, very few people live in socioeconomically diverse townships. In fact, we are, as a nation, segregating by income to a much larger extent than every before. Zip Code marketing has become the rage because marketers know that where we live has a lot to do with what we can afford to buy. And remember that the local tax base is still the major revenue source for schools, libraries, infrastructure, and many social services. It's not surprising, therefore, that we're seeing a wider and wider divergence between the public services available to those living in very wealthy suburbs and exurbs and people who are in working-class and poor towns.

DB: I was at AT&T, and what they're trying to build now is a whole framework for electronic commerce internationally and locally, where goods and services and jobs really know absolutely no borders, neither in this country nor outside of them. Does this process accelerate, then?

RR: Yes, it does. During the next few years, this country is going to be forced to do some very hard thinking about what it means to be a nation, and also what it means to be a community. The budget battle that's going on right now in Washington is just a small piece of that larger public discussion. Ultimately, we have to decide whether we are no more than an economy sharing a common currency in which the primary social glue binding us together is the business transactions we do with one another, or if we are still a society in which we have special obligations to one another as citizens.

DB: That's a pretty profound decision we have to make.

RR: Well, we'll make it one way or another, whether we know it and we make it consciously or if we don't know it and we make it implicitly.

DB: If you had one question to pose to Bob Allen, the CEO of AT&T right now, if you could be in a room with him, what would you ask him?

RR: Well, it's the same question I ask a number of CEO's these days, particularly from very profitable companies which are cutting back on their workers. What's the purpose of a corporation? Is it merely to maximize shareholder returns, or does a corporation also have special obligations to its employees and the communities in which they live? If it's only to maximize shareholder returns, then the burden of proof falls upon CEO's to show how meeting that goal is likely to improve the standard of living of all people in our society. To some extent, obviously, it does.

DB: Right. But at what cost?

RR: Yes, at what cost? Remember, corporations are creatures of law. They don't exist in Nature. We have decided to organize them in a certain way. It could be that in this era of electronic capitalism, we have to think creatively about a slightly different form of organization, which maximizes shareholder returns but also living standards for a much broader segment of our society.

DB: And that's the role of government and us as a community, to decide what . . .

RR: Well, ultimately, it's a social choice. Again, because corporations don't exist in a state of Nature, we need to make that choice consciously.

DB: Do you think the 30,000 folks who got laid off yesterday are going to be able to find satisfying, meaningful work?

RR: Some of them will. The Telecommunications sector of the economy is going to be growing very rapidly. Those who have the right combinations of education, skills and connections will do very well. But middle and lower level white collar supervisors and also blue and pink collar workers who don't have the right skills or who . . . well, maybe just who don't have the right skills, may find it far more difficult.

At this point we were cut off by Reich's press secretary because Reich had another appointment.

REFLECTING ON THE READING

1. What is the occasion for *MEME* editor David Bennahum's interview with Robert Reich? What events give rise to the interview? Why are these events important? How do they relate to the issues that Robert Reich addresses in the interview?

2. How does Reich define "electronic capitalism"? Why is this an important concept for him? What paradox has electronic capitalism given rise to, according to Reich? Does Bennahum consider this paradox a problem? Does Reich? Explain. Do you? Why or why not?

3. What effects has electronic capitalism had on communities and on individual workers, in Reich's view? Is Reich worried about these effects? How does he think they can be addressed? Do you think he's right? Why or why not?

4. What does Reich see as the impact of computer technologies on individual workers in the new electronic economy? Does he hold a generally positive or a generally skeptical view of technology and its effects on the economy and on

workers? How does he explain his position? Do you think his views are justified? Why or why not? Does Bennahum agree with Reich? Explain.

5. In what ways do new computer technologies, especially the Internet, contribute to economic inequality in the new economy, as Reich and Bennahum discuss it? How might this inequality be addressed, according to Reich? Do Reich and Bennahum seemed disturbed by these developments? Explain. Are you? What might your answer suggest about your own beliefs regarding the economy?

6. What does Reich see in the near future for the United States as these economic and technological developments continue to change American society? Is he concerned about the future? Why or why not? Do you think his views about the future are justified, based on his comments in this interview? Explain.

Examining Rhetorical Strategies

1. Assess the way *MEME* editor David Bennahum sets up his interview with Robert Reich. How do the events that Bennahum describes in his introductory note provide a context for the interview? What expectations does Bennahum's note establish for you as a reader? How does it influence the way you read the interview? Do you think Bennahum intended his note to affect readers in this way? Explain.

2. Discuss what you see as the advantages and disadvantages of the interview format for addressing issues such as the ones addressed by Bennahum and Reich in this interview. Do you think the interview format facilitates discussion of such complex issues in any noticeable way? Does it inhibit substantive examination of such issues? Explain. What might Bennahum accomplish by using the interview format that might be more difficult or impossible to accomplish in a conventional article format about Reich's views?

3. Describe the writing style in this interview. Do you think the writing "sounds" like an oral dialogue? Do you "hear" two different voices in the interview? Explain, citing specific passages from the interview to support your answer. In what specific ways does the writing in this interview differ from the writing of a more typical news article? Do you find the writing in this interview engaging? Why or why not? What might your answer to that question suggest about you as a reader?

4. Describe Bennahum's approach or strategy in this interview. What sort of persona does he establish through his questioning? Do you think he is a sympathetic interviewer, an aggressive or confrontational one, a passive one? Do his questions strike you as hard questions intended to challenge or provoke Reich? Explain, citing specific examples from the interview. Why do you think he would adopt the strategy he adopts in this interview? What purposes might his interview strategy accomplish? Also, how might Reich's status as an important member of the presidential cabinet have influenced Bennahum's strategy?

5. Assess how Bennahum presents Reich and Reich's views in this interview. Do you think Bennahum has edited this interview in a way that does justice to Reich and his views? Explain, citing specific passages from the interview to support your answer. How do Bennahum's questions, and especially his follow-up questions, influence the way Reich is portrayed in this piece? Do you think Bennahum intended that Reich be presented favorably? Why or why not?

6. Why do you think Bennahum describes the end of the interview as he does? What purpose might such an ending accomplish in terms of the interview format and in terms of the issues addressed? What does the ending seem to emphasize or call attention to? In what other ways might Bennahum have ended this piece? Did you find the ending appropriate and/or effective? Explain.

7. This interview appeared in *MEME,* an exclusively online publication. Its readers are likely to be well-educated, middle or upper-middle class professionals with access to computer technology and the Internet. How do you think such readers would read this interview? Do you think they would look favorably upon the opinions conveyed in this interview? Why or why not? How might readers of less-privileged socioeconomic standing react to this interview? How might unemployed readers react to it? Do you think Bennahum was mindful of such potential readers in the way he conducted and edited this interview? Explain.

Engaging the Issues

1. Write an essay for an audience of your classmates in which you describe the impact of recent economic developments on you, your family, or others you know. In your essay, focus on what you see as important developments in American business (such as the rise of the Internet and related technologies, the globalization of business, the downsizing of American businesses, or similar developments). Discuss those developments and describe how they have affected you or your family. You might describe the ways in which these developments have benefited or disadvantaged you or others you know. In a sense, tell the story of the recent changes in the American economy by telling the story of their impact on you or your family.

2. In a group of your classmates, share the essays you wrote for Question #1 above. What specific economic developments did you and your classmates focus your essays on? What impact did those developments have on you and on your classmates? What differences and similarities emerge in the impact of recent economic developments on you and your classmates? Try to draw conclusions about how larger economic developments might affect the lives of individual workers.

3. Using your library, the Internet, and any other appropriate sources, investigate the rise of the new digital economy that Reich and Bennahum discuss in this interview. If possible, interview experts (such as economics or business professors at

your school or local businesspeople or financial advisors) for their views on these developments. Then write a report for an audience of your classmates based on your research. In your report, describe the changes in American businesses as a result of the new digital technologies, documenting your discussion appropriately with your sources. Try to draw conclusions about the impact of these changes on American workers and American businesses. If appropriate, refer to the views Reich expresses in this interview.

4. Try to find someone who has been directly affected by the emergence of the new economy as a result of new digital technologies. For example, you might know someone who conducts an online business or someone who works for a company that has developed an online component to its business. Or perhaps you know someone who has lost a job as a result of recent economic changes. Interview this person about his or her experiences and views on recent technological and economic developments. Be sure to prepare for your interview by doing some background research on the nature of the business in which the person you are interviewing is involved. Prepare your questions carefully and take accurate notes (or, with the person's permission, use a tape recorder). Then write up the interview in a format similar to the one Bennahum used in his interview with Reich. Write your interview with a general audience in mind (such as readers of large-circulation publications such as *USA Today* or *Time* magazine).

   Alternatively, conduct your interview online via email. Then write it up as described above.

5. Rewrite the interview you conducted for Question #4 above as a conventional article (appropriate for a large-circulation publication such as *USA Today* or the *New York Times* or *Time* magazine).

6. Write a rhetorical analysis in which you compare the interview you wrote for Question #4 and the article you wrote for Question #5 above. In your analysis, discuss differences and similarities in the two texts, focusing on the form of the interview and the article. In what ways does each form enable you to accomplish or inhibit you from accomplishing specific goals as a writer? Try to draw conclusions about the nature of each form from a writer's perspective.

7. Write an editorial or an essay for the op-ed page of your local newspaper (or some other publication you are familiar with) based on the interview you conducted for Question #4 above. In your essay, draw on what you learned in your interview to offer your own perspective about the recent economic and technological developments experienced by American workers and businesses.

8. Search the Internet for business-related Web sites. Identify three or four such sites that are similar in terms of the products or services they provide. (For example, you might choose four different online retailers specializing in outdoor or recreational gear.) Explore these sites and how they are set up. Examine the kinds of products or services they provide and how they present these products and services to viewers of the sites. Examine, too, how commerce is actually conducted through the site. Look carefully at the assumptions these businesses seem to make about visitors to their sites. Then write a report in which you critique the sites you visited. In your report, describe the sites you selected and the

online services they offer and explain how you examined them. Analyze the sites in terms of their design, their services, and the assumptions they seem to make about visitors to the site and about online business in general. Try to draw conclusions about online commerce based on your research.

Alternatively, construct a web site to present the results of your analysis, including appropriate links, and structure your site in a way that you think will most effectively facilitate its purpose.

Literacy, Technology, and Monopoly Capital

RICHARD OHMANN

INTRODUCTION If you consider some of the technological developments that have occurred in your lifetime, you might reasonably conclude that these developments have, for the most part, improved your life. For example, consider just one effect of the desktop computer: its ability to create professional-looking resumes and other documents used in applying for a job. In the early 1980's, most people looking for employment relied on typewriters and professional printing services to create those documents. By the middle of the 1990's, computers and laser printers with advanced desktop publishing capabilities enabled just about anyone to create high-quality, professional-looking resumes as well as all sorts of other documents that previously only a professional printing service could create. To be able to create such documents seems to give job seekers more flexibility, more possibilities for finding employment, and more independence. In this sense, computers offer benefits to job seekers with access to them. Computers certainly seem to be a big improvement over the old typewriters that were once standard equipment for someone entering the job market.

Of course, to take advantage of the potential benefits of technologies like desktop computers, you need to have access to them. You also need to be able to use them properly and to have appropriate literacy skills in order to write the documents that you want to create with those computers. Without those skills, you may not be able to reap the benefits that computers promise. Similarly, how computers are used in the workplace may not result in benefits for all workers, especially for those with limited literacy and technology skills. In other words, whether or not computers will bring improvements to your life depends upon a variety of factors. Scholar Richard Ohmann believes that the most important of those factors have to do with the economic system within which we live and work. According to Ohmann, how computers and other technologies are used and who gets to use them are determined largely by the workings of capitalism. And since Ohmann believes that a capitalist economic system such as we have in the United States is inherently unfair, he is worried about how new technologies like computers may exacerbate that unfairness.

He explains his worries in the following essay, in which he examines what he sees as the roles played by literacy and technology in a capitalist economic system. Although you may disagree with Ohmann's left-wing political views, his essay encourages you to consider the complicated ways in which the development of a technology like the computer should be understood within the context of the economic system within which it is developed. He implicitly asks you to think about how technology may deepen the divisions among social classes that he believes are inherently a part of that economic system. Moreover, Ohmann sees literacy as the crucial piece of this whole puzzle, so he focuses our attention on how the use of new technologies like the computer relates to the value of reading and writing within our economic system. His concerns about computers, then, reflect broader concerns about litercy in a market economy and thus may offer insights into the connections among literacy, technology, and the workplace.

Richard Ohmann is a professor of English at Wesleyan University. He has written widely about the social, political, and economic aspects of literacy and of the teaching of English, and he has served as editor of the prestigious journal *College English*. Among his published works are many scholarly articles and several books including *English in America: A Radical View of the Profession* (1976) and *The Politics of Letters* (1987). The following essay was published in *College English* in 1985.

REFLECTING BEFORE READING

1. When Richard Ohmann wrote this essay in 1985, the Soviet Union still controlled much of Eastern Europe and Asia and supported other socialist and Marxist states, such as Cuba, around the world. Since that time, the Soviet Union has broken up into smaller nations, almost all of which now operate within capitalist economic systems, and few Marxist systems remain anywhere in the world. As you read Ohmann's essay, consider whether his arguments about capitalism ring true to you today, at a time when capitalism has become the dominant economic system in the world. Do you think Ohmann's arguments are still valid? Are they even more important today, given the dominance of capitalism in the world? Or are they outdated? Does he perhaps offer insight into some of the dangers of capitalism?

2. Ohmann's essay focuses on problems that he sees with a capitalist economic system. What exactly is capitalism? What are your opinions of capitalism? As you read, consider how your own perspective on economic issues might influence how you react to Ohmann's essay.

M y late, lamented colleague Vernon Dibble once told me this rule of thumb: if a title comprises three words or phrases in a series, and their order makes no difference, then the lecture or article will be nonsense. (Vernon used a stronger word than "nonsense," actually.) I hope to make some sense in this essay, although the three terms of my title could as well come in any sequence.[1] In fact, the five sections of the

---

[1] This essay is a revised talk, given at the Wyoming Conference on Freshman and Sophomore English, June, 1984. The theme of the conference was "Literacy in an Age of Technology," and my original title, implying a critique of that conceptualization, was "Literacy in an Age of Monopoly Capital."

essay might themselves be rearranged. They represent five pieces of what I take to be a Big Picture, so big that to fill it all in would require a fat volume which I do not plan to write. So I ask the courteous reader to bear with my somewhat fragmentary method, here, and with an argument that cannot be decisive, only suggestive.

It may help if I indicate where I am heading. I claim that exhortations about the need for "computer literacy" have much in common with longer-standing debates about literacy itself; that both kinds of discussion usually rest on a serious misconception of technology and its roles in history; and that we can best understand the issues that trouble us by situating them within the evolution of our present economic and social system—a very recent historical process, going back little more than a hundred years. The whole discussion presumes that questions of literacy and technology are inextricable from political questions of domination and equality.

1. History

The earliest citations for the word "literacy" in the OED [Oxford English Dictionary] come from the 1880s. The word "illiteracy," in the common modern sense, appears only a bit earlier. (Before that, it referred to lack of cultivation, or to ignorance.) The adjectives "literate" and "illiterate" have a much longer history; but again, before the late nineteenth-century they had a global, qualitative meaning—well-read and civilized, or the reverse—rather than indicating a line that divided those who could read and write from those who could not.

If this were 1850, we could not talk about literacy in the language we use now, nor with the same concepts. Of course people had been discussing for centuries the ability to read and write, and who should have it. But they did so without a mass noun that isolated that ability from other human practices and that referred to it as a measurable attribute of individuals, groups, or whole societies. That seems odd to me. Why did the concept and the term "literacy" come into play just when they did, toward the end of the last century?

We can get a hint by looking at the discourse within which writers (and doubtless speakers) began to use the words "literacy" and "illiteracy." One of the OED's earliest citations for "literacy" points us to *The New Princeton Review,* Nov., 1888.[2] The word turns up in an article by George R. Stetson, called "The Renaissance of Barbarism," which laments and analyzes the rise in crime—statistically documented—since mid-century. He sees this quite specifically as a class phenomenon. There has been a widening "separation of those who have, from those who have not, a complete control of their appetites and passions"; the latter, he calls "the brutalized class," and to them he attributes almost all "the outrageous, inhuman, and barbarous crimes." That is why, although "Education is more general, our literacy greatly increased," moral degeneracy is also on the rise—with immigrants and Negroes contributing far more than their share (336–7).

A companion article in the same issue, by James P. Munroe, ponders "The Education of the Masses." Munroe, like Stetson, worries about moral degeneration, idleness, and crime; like Stetson, he writes of these dangers in terms of class. There

---

[2] Actually, the OED says *December.* It had never occurred to me that the OED could be wrong about something.

is a "dangerous class," composed mainly of immigrants, which may easily contaminate the class next to it, "the so-called working class." (His theory of class interaction: "Below a certain stratum of the social structure, all populations have a tendency toward degeneration,—a tendency enormously increased by contact with classes upon a still lower plane.") Munroe's concern is to provide the right education for these "slowly-plodding millions, without fame, almost without identity. . . ."

In this context he, too, uses one of the new words. He does *not* advocate repeal of compulsory education laws: "Not for one moment would I advocate illiteracy," he writes, even though at the moment, "the evils of mal-education" are "perhaps greater . . . than those of illiteracy. . . ." His solution: take the children of the masses—who are "unfitted or indisposed" to educate their children—from the parents at age two or three, put them in "kindergartens," and train them "to habits of cleanliness, order, neatness, and punctuality." To offset the cost of such education, Munroe advocates the abolition of free high schools, whose "higher education" is wasted upon most of the lower classes (348–52 *passim*). I would note that Stetson also fixes upon education as a cause, and possible cure, for crime: a purely "intellectual" schooling has pushed out "religious and manual training," expanding literacy but not moral character (342–3).

I don't want to make these two articles bear too much weight, but I suggest that we think about the soil in which our main concept took root. The argument over education for poor people had been joined long before the 1880s, of course. What catches my attention is how easily the new idea slid into that discourse. For it was a top-down discourse from the start, and its participants almost invariably took the underlying question to be: how can we keep the lower orders docile? Thus, for instance, Bernard de Mandeville: "Going to School . . . is Idleness, and the longer Boys continue in this easy sort of Life, the more unfit they'll be when grown up for downright Labour. . . ." (180). And, on the other side, Adam Smith: "An instructed and intelligent people . . . are always more decent and orderly than an ignorant and stupid one" (269; see Altick for a useful treatment of this debate). Once the lower orders came to be seen as masses and classes, the term "literacy" offered a handy way to conceptualize an attribute of theirs, which might be manipulated in one direction or the other for the stability of the social order and the prosperity and security of the people who counted.

From these origins, the concept evolved naturally to serve purposes of social diagnosis and reform. One could *measure* literacy scientifically. The first study of illiteracy in the United States was published in 1870 (Leigh),[3] but it was not until World War I, when thirty percent of recruits were unable to take the written intelligence test, that a movement toward systematic literacy testing got underway (Resnick and Resnick 381–82). Literacy *tests* and census questions become evidence to fix the literacy *rate* of a society. After that, of course, we may thrill to periodic literacy *crises,* followed by back-to-basics movements. And international agencies may attack low literacy rates in third world countries with literacy campaigns designed to hasten modernization. (Modernization theory held that a literacy rate of forty percent was necessary for "takeoff" to occur.)

---

[3] Thanks to my colleague, Gerald Burns, for this reference. Burns also tells me that Horace Mann referred to the "stigma of illiteracy" as early as 1838, in his *Second Annual Report,* but I think this was the older usage of the term.

All of this—the analytic division of people into measurable quantities, the attempt to modify these quantities, the debate among professionals and political leaders over what's good for the poor—all this legacy still inheres in the discourse of literacy, even now, when almost everyone takes it for granted that literacy is a Good Thing, and when it would be hard to find a Mandeville to argue that the poor should be kept illiterate in order to keep them content.

2. Monopoly Capital

By coincidence—or maybe not—the term "literacy" came into use roughly at the beginning of the epoch of monopoly capital.[4] A word about the transformation I have in mind: in the mid- and late-nineteenth century, *competitive* capitalism ran its energetic course, building a huge industrial system with unparalleled speed. The familiar movement from farm and shop to factory, from country to city, can be expressed in any number of statistics. For instance, the value of manufactured goods increased seven-fold in the last four decades of the century, far outdistancing the value of farm products. The number of factories quadrupled, and the number of people working in them tripled. Profits were large, and most of them went into the building of more industrial capacity: industrial capital quadrupled just in the last three decades of the century, and the *rate* of capital formation reached the highest point before or since, in the 1890s. Production changed utterly, and businessmen were in command of the nation's future.

But as they raced ahead, making fortunes and transforming the society, they were experiencing painfully the contradictions of the system they had built. Every decade between 1870 and 1900 brought a major depression; crises of overproduction were apparently untamable. Within this volatile *system,* individual businesses led precarious existences; competition was fierce, and none of the legal or illegal attempts to restrain it worked. The rate of profit began to decline. And attempts on the part of businessmen to counter these dangers by reducing wages led to all but open class warfare in 1877, 1885, and the early 1890s. (These conflicts sponsored the discourse of dangerous classes, and what to do about them, to which I referred earlier; just as in England the Hyde Park riots provided an impetus for Arnold's *Culture and Anarchy.*) By concentrating their energies on production and on price competition, businessmen had built an empire, but one they could not govern, either as a class or individually—one whose anarchy led to great instability, killing risk, falling profits, and social rebellion.[5]

What emerged from this extended crisis—and partially resolved it—was the system I am calling monopoly capitalism. This is no time to characterize it in detail; it is, in any case, the ocean in which we now swim, as familiar to all of us as our bodies. I will mention only a few of its main features, as they bear on the themes of

---

[4] I follow Baran and Sweezy and many other Marxists in the use of this term and in my characterization of our economic system. Other terms—"advanced capitalism," "late capitalism," etc.—imply different theories of history, but point to the same social formation. Terminology aside, almost everyone agrees that a new stage of capitalism emerged around the turn of the century.

[5] Here and at the end of this section, I adapt the argument and some phrasing from Ohmann, 1981.

this essay. Please keep in mind that every aspect of monopoly capitalism was a response to the crisis of which I have spoken, and an effort to control and rationalize processes that felt—to businessmen as well as to most other people—chaotic and threatening. In fact, one might characterize monopoly capitalism by its powerful drive toward *planning*—its attempt to replace Adam Smith's invisible hand with the visible hand of management.

I take that phrase from Alfred D. Chandler's *The Visible Hand: The Managerial Revolution in American Business,* a classic study of monopoly capitalism's main institutional form, the giant corporation, which emerged in the last two decades of the nineteenth century. Where before, entrepreneurs had built factories and concentrated on getting out the goods, from the 1880s on, the impersonal corporation became dominant. Characteristically, it brought the entire economic process within its compass, from extraction of raw materials through manufacturing through distribution. Far too complex for the supervision of a single businessman (and his family), it brought into existence the modern table of organization, with divisions and subdivisions and layers of hired management. It attempted to coordinate every stage of making and selling, so as to eliminate uncertainty from the process. That project never succeeded entirely, of course, but it did establish an economic order that has proved supple enough through our century.

Before redirecting these large, pear-shaped thoughts toward technology and literacy, I want to mention two ways in which the new corporations carried out this design. First, monopoly capital took control of the labor process, far more precisely and intrusively than had been done before. It developed the approach that came to be known as scientific management, following that magical moment when Frederick Winslow Taylor, overseeing the work of a "Dutchman" named Schmidt, got him to move far more pigs of iron in a day than had previously been thought possible. Taylor analyzed labor into its minutest components, divided the process among various workers, and created the techniques which culminated in Ford's assembly line. He built on three principles: (1) dissociate the labor process from the vested skills and knowledge of workers; (2) separate conception from execution; and (3) reserve understanding for management, and use it to control each step of production. (As Studs Terkel's workers put it, one way and another, "a robot could do my job.") Harry Braverman, from whom I draw this understanding, sums up the role of management thus:

> to render conscious and systematic, the formerly unconscious tendency of capitalist production. It was to ensure that as craft declined, the worker would sink to the level of general and undifferentiated labor power, adaptable to a large range of simple tasks, while as science grew, it would be concentrated in the hands of management (120–21).

The second main movement of monopoly capital was to add control of *sales* to control of production. This was a change of great complexity and unevenness, working through the evolution of department stores, chain stores, mail order houses, the railroads, the telegraph, and the postal system, as well as the new corporate structure and its sales division. The outcome was a universal, national market, increasingly managed by the same corporations that produced the goods. To enter national markets successfully, they quickly developed a number of new practices: uniform packaging (as opposed to the barrel of anonymous pickles or crackers); brand names to help form habits of loyalty among buyers; trademarks to link a *second* sign to the product and enhance its aura; slogans, jingles, and cartoon characters to penetrate every buyer's mind. In short, they came to depend on advertising as a direct channel of instruction from manufacturer to customer. And piggy-back on the new advertising industry, there arose for the first time a national mass culture, whose main product was not the magazine, the newspaper, the radio or TV broadcast, but the *attention of the audience,* sold in blocks to advertisers. I assert that this characteristic feature of modern society and contemporary humanity—mass culture—derives from exactly the same forces that transformed labor. In fact, the two are obverse and reverse, in a social mode that had polarized work and leisure, production and consumption, worker and consumer.

3. Technology

Against this background, I will now marshal some reflections on technology—unsystematic, but I hope suggestive. First, as a kind of loosening-up exercise, I ask you to imagine some instances of the almost unimaginable.

a. Suppose that writing (a technology, as Walter Ong rightly insists) had been invented by slaves—say, in the Roman Empire—and for purposes of survival, resistance, and rebellion. How might they have devised a writing system to advance those purposes? Might it have been a shifting code, to preserve its secrets from masters? Might there have been a common form that could encode the different languages spoken by slaves? I don't know, but my guess is that writing would not have evolved as it did, had its inventors wanted it as an aid to solidarity and revolt.

b. What about printing? You may recall that when Raphael Hythloday, Thomas More's traveler, showed European books to the Utopians, they quickly re-invented printing and papermaking: their sole purpose was to make available thousands of copies of the Greek classics, so that all who wished might pursue wisdom and the study of nature. Shortly after More wrote, the English adapted printing to a different use, in the *Great Boke of Statutes:* organizing the laws for their more rational administration and enforcement.[6] Would the Utopians, with their purely humanistic and relatively egalitarian aims, have developed the technology of printing in ways different from those that served state power? Certainly the printing technology that served English radicals of the 1790s, with their plethora of small presses, pamphlets, and journals was sharply different from the technology developed for mass circulation magazines, with gigantic rotary presses and photoengraving, to address people as a mass audience rather than as participants in a common discourse. (The 1790s term, "corresponding societies," suggests a very different setting for technology than does our term, "mass communications.")

c. Suppose that wireless communication had evolved, not under the guidance and for the needs of the British Navy, the United Fruit Company, and commercial advertisers, but among women tinkering in their homes, sharing knowledge

---

[6] See Eisenstein (58–59) for some of the social consequences of this printing innovation. I'm suggesting that social purposes like this had an impact on the technology as well.

about domestic production, establishing networks of childcare and concern. Every receiver is in principle a transmitter as well. Might we have had electronic systems that actually merited the name "communication," rather than or in addition to *broadcasting?*

d. And what if the computer . . . ? I don't even know the right bizarre question to ask, but I do know that computers are an evolving technology like any other, shaped within particular social relations, and responsive to the needs of those with the power to direct that evolution. I will return to this subject shortly, for a mixture of anxiety and excitement about computers inevitably surrounds any discussion of literacy and technology today.

First, though, let me state the point of the in-some-ways absurd thought experiments I just asked you to conduct. Following Raymond Williams's helpful clarifications (10–14), I have meant to call into question technological determinism (the idea that, e.g., TV somehow got invented, and from that accident many consequences have inexorably followed), and also what Williams calls "symptomatic technology" (the idea that TV was invented on the margins of the social process, and was simply deployed by other forces that dictate the direction of society—so that it is a *symptom* of consumerism, mass culture, passivity, or whatever). This second view is close to what I might call "neutral technology"—the idea that every invention, still thought of as appearing independently, can be put to an infinite number of uses—humane and inhumane, tyrannical and democratic.

I agree with Williams that these views err in abstracting technology from society, sometimes in a way that makes it seem like a miraculous intervention in history. The history of radio and television, as told by Williams, or by Eric Barnouw in *Tube of Plenty,* reveals quite a different process. The technology developed over a century and more, in ways far from accidental. Those with the vision, the needs, the money, and the power gradually made it what they wanted—a mass medium. (I exaggerate only a bit.) Technology, one might say, is itself a social process; saturated with the power relations around it, continually reshaped according to some people's *intentions.* The point is borne out with respect to electric lighting, the telephone, the chemical industry, etc., in David Noble's fine study, *America by Design.* As a recent TV commercial aptly put it: "The future is being driven by technology, and Martin Marietta is masterminding it."

Perhaps I can make the point another way by entering a friendly objection to some characteristic formulations of Walter Ong, one of our most stimulating and learned writers on these matters. In *Interfaces of the Word,* for instance, he writes of "technological devices . . . which enable men to . . . shape, store, retrieve, and communicate knowledge in new ways" (44). Again, "writing and print and the computer enable the mind to constitute within itself . . . new ways of thinking. . . ." (46). And, "the alphabet or print or the computer enters the mind, producing new states of awareness there. . . . the computer actually releases more energy for new kinds of exploratory operations by the human mind itself . . ." (47). My objections are, first, to phrases like "the computer," as if it were one, stable device; second, to these phrases used as grammatical agents ("the computer enables the mind . . ."), implying that the technology somehow came before *someone's* intention to enable *some* minds to do *some* things; and third, to phrases like "man," "the mind," and "the human mind," in these contexts, suggesting that technologies interact with people or with "culture" in global, undifferentiated ways, rather than serving as an arena of inter-action among classes, races, and other groups of unequal power. Certainly Fr. Ong is no stranger to such ideas, and he may well agree with most of what I am saying. My point is just that technological determinism is a powerful ideology which tends to infiltrate our minds when we look the other way. I think we need to be on guard against it, when thinking about literacy or any other technology, including:

4. Computers

About which I know remarkably little—so that I may now air my prejudices with only slight interference from the facts.

We are told (in the language of technological determinism) that computers will transform the workplace and the home, not to mention the school, and that in antic-ipation of this change, we need to provide "computer literacy" for everyone, or at least for the young. Paul A. Strassmann, vice president for "strategic planning" at Xerox's Information Products Group, holds that we are now at the end of the Gutenberg era and "the beginning of the 'electronic display' era." Adults ignorant of computers will soon be as restricted as those who today are unable to read. Software will become the language of the future, and "the dominant intellectual asset" of the human race, so that an "understanding of software . . . will be a primary component of literacy in the electronic age" (116, 119). Many of those who worry about edu-cation see things the same way. The National Council of Teachers of Mathematics committed itself a few years ago to the proposition that "an essential outcome of con-temporary education is computer literacy." The National Science Foundation then funded a study to define computer literacy; its findings appeared in *Mathematics Teacher* (Johnson, et al.).[7] The article lists sixty-four objectives for computer education (including forty "core" objectives), ranging from a grasp of how computers work to familiarity with computer crime. The authors acknowledge that achievement of these objectives would require more than a single course. There is already a lot of pressure on schools to provide such education.

Behind such pressure, of course, is the fear of parents and students that computer literacy will be required for many or most good jobs in the future. People like Strassmann encourage that view. He predicts that almost 30 million people—roughly one-quarter of the workforce—will have "electronic workstations" by 1990, and use this means of communication about one-half the time they are at work (117). I don't know just what Strassmann has in mind, but one may perhaps allay one's anxiety *or* euphoria; in anticipating this revolution, by looking around oneself right now.

For example: in my own department of 23 full-time workers, only one has an electronic workstation, and is required to possess a small degree of computer lit-eracy. She is the junior secretary, and, at $10,000 a year, the worst paid of the 23. (I don't believe that the computer has improved her life or her temperament.) All the workers at my travel agency have electronic workstations, which have consid-erably routinized (and dehumanized) their work. So does the baggage agent at the airline. So does the teller at my bank. And I wonder if Strassmann's count included

---

[7] Thanks to Marilyn Frankenstein and Bob Rosen for pointing me to this and other articles on comput-ers, and to Rosen for helpfully reading a draft of this article.

the check-out clerks at my supermarket, with their recently installed, computerized scanners, which have reduced the skill required to an almost entirely manual one of the most repetitive kind. Or how about the young people behind the fast-food counter, whose computer keyboards no longer carry numbers and letters, but pictures of food items, so that the work could be done by someone who is both computer-illiterate and just plain illiterate? Predictions that 50 to 75 percent of jobs will be "computer-related" by 1990 sound intimidating, but how many of those jobs will call for even the slightest understanding of computers?[8]

I am suggesting that, seen from the side of production and work, the computer and its software are an intended and developing technology, carrying forward the deskilling and control of labor that goes back to F. W. Taylor and beyond, and that has been a main project of monopoly capital. As Taylor consciously sought to transfer all understanding of production to management and reduce the worker's role to that of a conduit for the transfer of commands into physical energy, engineers are shaping computers now so that those who work at them will be only keyboard operators. As Phil Kraft puts it, "all the skill is embodied in the machines"—in fact, that could be a definition of the term "user-friendly." ("Designing for idiots is the highest expression of the engineering art," in David Noble's words.)[9] In a special irony, engineers are programming some of their *own* skill into obsolescence, along with that of technicians, in the booming field of Computer-Assisted Design/Computer-Assisted Manufacture—"CAD/CAM." And predictably, there begin to be programs for *programming,* aimed at reducing the need for intelligent programmers even as schools and colleges scramble to train them.

Of course there will be more jobs in the computer field itself. But that doesn't amount to much, as against the deskilling that is underway (or indeed, against the number of jobs *eliminated* through computerization). It seems that a decade from now there will be only half a million or so additional jobs in this field, compared to 800,000 new jobs for janitors (Pincus 7). Furthermore, the field is layered into specialties, which will be dead ends for most people in them. Operators seldom become programmers; programmers seldom become systems analysts; analysts seldom become designers or computer scientists (Corson 35). Graduates of MIT will get the challenging jobs; community college grads will be technicians; those who do no more than acquire basic skills and computer literacy in high school will probably find their way to electronic workstations at McDonald's. I see every reason to expect that the computer revolution, like other revolutions from the top down, will indeed expand the minds and the freedom of an elite, meanwhile facilitating the degradation of labor and the stratification of the workforce that have been hallmarks of monopoly capitalism from its onset.[10]

After this brief look at production, an even briefer glance now at consumption, before I skip back to literacy. Microcomputers *will* be in the homes of most people, without question (some forecasts see them penetrating the home market almost as

---

[8] Corson (35) reports these predictions (by the U.S. Labor and Commerce Departments and by corporations like IBM) and discusses this question.

[9] Corson (35) is my source for both of these quotations.

[10] Pincus (7) reports Bureau of Labor statistics suggesting that however much high tech *gear* may be around, high tech *employment* may be no more important in 1995 than it is today [1985].

universally as television has done). And to judge from some of my friends who are buffs, hobbyists, and addicts, some people *will* have their horizons widened and their minds challenged. (Though I also forecast even more broken marriages from this cause than have resulted from TV football coverage.) But I remain skeptical about the import of the change. Apparently, eighty percent of home computers are used *exclusively* for games (Douglas Noble 42, another helpfully critical source). I bet many of them will fall into disuse, like other new toys. Yet the manufacturers are selling them hot and heavy, often appealing to the hopes and anxieties of parents in quite unscrupulous ways. Thus, a radio commercial that I often heard last year featured a dad saying to a mom that if they bought a personal computer it could change their daughter's whole life. To Mom's incredulity, Dad explained that their daughter would get an edge on other kids at school that could get her into a prestigious college, and that could even affect whom she might *marry!* Mom was convinced. This appeal to hope and anxiety calls to mind strongly the pitch of door-to-door encyclopedia salespeople, thirty years ago.

Seen from *this* side of the market, computers are a commodity, for which a mass market is being created in quite conventional ways. And their other main use in the home, besides recreation, most likely will be to facilitate the marketing of still *more* commodities, as computerized shopping becomes a reality. Thus our "age of technology" looks to me very much like the age of monopoly capital, with new channels of power through which the few try to control both the labor and the leisure of the many.

And the education? That is not my subject here; but a brief aside may be in order, to connect the instructional use of computers to my argument. Only two years ago, Stanley Pogrow lamented that schools were not responding well to the new "information economy." There were only 96,000 microcomputers in the schools, and they were not being used to improve learning for most students. He saw a high likelihood that in this decade, the dissatisfaction of parents and employers will go beyond "political activism" to *abandonment* of public schools, and to "environmental collapse" of a school system unable to adapt, with industry taking over this side of education (92–94). Two other specialists in this area—Tim O'Shea and John Self—are confident that computers will become standard furniture in classrooms, but pose the danger and the choices in this way:

> Computers will cause great changes in education. Already there are examination halls in American universities where rows of nervous students type answers to multiple-choice questions at computer consoles and anxiously await their grade. There are also experimental classrooms where young children happily and confidently command a computer to draw pictures or play music, and articulately explain their latest computer program. Motivated by cost-effectiveness and efficiency, educators may try to use computers to turn classrooms into human battery farms. But there is a possibility that computers will be used to enhance the educational process and equip each learner with an exciting medium for problem-solving and individual tuition. (1)

Most people I've asked agree that O'Shea and Self's first alternative is ascendant at the moment, with computers being used as little more than electronic workbooks and data banks. That the liberatory possibilities explored by O'Shea and Self lag behind may have something to do with the way that Pogrow's forecast is already proving to be wrong. There are now about 500,000 computers in American schools, many of them gifts or nearly so from the manufacturers and from other companies. The motives for such generosity are not hard to imagine. Apparently, business will take care that its needs are met without the "environmental collapse" of public schools, and one cannot expect those needs to include many of the liberatory classrooms mentioned by O'Shea and Self. This is the first area of public education to be so stimulated and directed by business. Most likely, the technology of classroom computers—especially software—will serve purposes I have already described.

Now, none of these developments is foreordained. The technology is malleable; it does have liberatory potential. Especially in education, we have something to say about whether that potential is realized. But its fate is not a technological question: it is a political one.

5. Literacy

I have stated my outlook on these themes in enough ways, now, that you will know whether you find it congenial or not. I will not develop it in detail, with respect to the prospects for literacy in the United States today, but will just reflect on some of its implications.

Plainly, from this perspective it is not helpful to think of literacy as an invariant, individual skill, or as a skill whose numerically measurable distribution across a society (as in "literacy rate") will tell us much of scholarly interest or human relevance. Literacy is an activity of social groups, and a necessary feature of some kinds of social organization. Like every other human activity or product, it embeds social relations within it. And these relations always include *conflict* as well as cooperation. Like language itself, literacy is an exchange between classes, races, the sexes, and so on. Simply recall the struggle over black English, or think on the continuing conflict over the CCCC [Conference on College Composition and Communication] statement, "Students' Right to Their Own Language," or the battle over generic male pronouns, for times when the political issues have spilled out into the open. But explicit or not, they are always there, in every classroom and in every conversation—just as broadcasting technology is an exchange which has up to now been resolved through control by the dominant classes, and participation by the subordinate classes in the form of Neilson [Nielsen] ratings and call-in shows.

That means that we can usefully distinguish between literacy-from-above and literacy-from-below.[11] From the 1790s to roughly the 1830s, popular literacy in England was broad and vigorous (among men, at least), as artisans and the new industrial working class taught one another to read, formed corresponding societies, drafted petitions, put out pamphlets and books, held meetings. *The Rights of Man* sold

---

[11] As does James Donald, whose discussion I found particularly helpful, both for its historical account and for its theoretical position, and I have drawn upon it here. Myron Tuman also offers a good discussion of literacy as cause and effect.

1.5 million copies by the time of Paine's death—equivalent to sales of 25 million in the United States today. This happened in a context where, as Donald puts it,

> what we now specify as politics, education, literacy, journalism and recreation were still bound inextricably together. Their division into separate institutions was one effect of the ruling bloc's new techniques of power. (56)

Those techniques won out, both in England and in the United States, as literacy was subsumed within state-run school systems. As we well know, the results here have been such as to provoke both patriotic self-congratulation and repeated literacy "crises" over the last 75 years—the latter meaning a periodic rediscovery by those at the top and their allies that after ten or twelve years of instruction in "English," very many citizens read and write badly.

But why should it be otherwise? Isn't the functional literacy rate just about what you'd expect, given how schooling relates to the needs and life chances of the working class? (Shouldn't we expect similar results in computer literacy, once people understand the false promises behind that movement?) Likewise, top-down literacy campaigns in "developing" countries have been almost universally failures. In Cuba, on the other hand, during the single year of 1961, 750,000 illiterate adults learned to read and write, leaving only 250,000 illiterates there; or about four percent of the population. I've suggested that a literacy rate is in itself mystifying; but you can sense the *kind* of literacy and the context that supported it by reading some of the letters that "students" wrote to Castro, as their final "exam."

> Dr. Fidel Castro Ruz
> Dear Comrade:
> I write this to let you know that now I know how to read and write thanks to our Socialist and democratic Revolution. That's why I'm writing to you, so that you can see with your own eyes. I take leave with a firm Revolutionary and democratic salute. I used to be illiterate
> *Patria o Muerte*
> Teaching, we shall triumph.

> Comrade Fidel Castro:
> I am very thankful because I know how to write and read. I would like you to send me the Follow-Up books to improve my knowledge more in the reading and in the writing. To be an educated people is to be free. (Kozol, "A New Look at the Literacy Campaign in Cuba" 358–59)

These peasants had learned to read and write in the context of a revolution, and with the aim of becoming full participants in it, not of passing from third grade into fourth or of meeting a college requirement. Their learning was saturated with politics, an activity of conscious liberation. Of course it did not happen spontaneously, and it *began* at the top in that Castro initiated the campaign. But he spoke for nearly all the people of Cuba when he articulated the goal of full literacy, and those people responded with energy because they saw the revolution as theirs, and literacy as contributing to it.

Cuba at that time had only 35,000 teachers, and they stayed in their classrooms teaching kids. The *brigadistas* who went out into the hills to live and work with peasant families were students, ninety percent of them between ten and nineteen years old, mainly from the cities. Over 100,000 volunteered after Castro's call, in spite of the distances they would travel from home, the crude shacks they would live in, and the strangeness of their task (after just ten days of training). "I knew nothing about reading" (said a woman who was 16 in 1961). "My first motive . . . was not to teach. It was to be part of a great struggle. It was my first chance to take a stand" (Kozol, *Children of the Revolution* 31). They learned to use a primer and a book of readings, which began, not with "See Jane run," but with key political terms; "OEA," Spanish acronym for the Organization of American States; "INRA," the National Institute of Agrarian Reform. From the first day, the project of literacy was for these *campesinos* connected to their needs and their situation in the world. As David Harman (an adult literacy worker in Israel) said to Kozol, the pedagogical theories and classroom techniques don't matter a lot: "None of it works . . . unless it is allied with something else. That 'something else' is what they did in Cuba. It is the promise of a better life for every man and woman in the land" (*Children of the Revolution* 77). The more recent literacy campaign in Nicaragua, which also offered "something else," used similar methods with similar results (Arnove).

Technique is less important than context and purpose in the teaching of literacy; and the *effects* of literacy cannot be isolated from the social relations and processes within which people become literate.

Enough. The age of computer technology will bring us some new tools and methods for teaching literacy. I hope we (or rather, those of us teachers who are on my side!) will manage to shape that technology to democratic forms.

But this age of technology, this age of computers, will change very little in the social relations—the *class* relations—of which literacy is an inextricable part. Monopoly capital will continue to saturate most classrooms, textbooks, student essays, and texts of all sorts. It will continue to require a high degree of literacy among elites, especially the professional-managerial class. It will continue to require a meager literacy or none from subordinate classes. And yet its spokesmen—the Simons and Newmans and Safires and blue ribbon commissions on education—will continue to kvetch at teachers and students, and to demand that all kids act out the morality play of literacy instruction, from which the moral drawn by most will be that in this meritocracy they do not merit much.

But then monopoly capital will *also* continue to generate resistance and rebellion, more at some times than at others. I hope many of us will find ways to take part in that resistance, even in our daily work. Apparently we must learn to fight mindless computer literacy programs, as we have sometimes fought mindless drills in grammar and usage. We should remember that most programmed instruction, in addition to being mindless, builds in imperatives other than ours and other than those of our students. Computerized testing is likely to be undemocratic, not because the computer is, but because it will help realize the impulse toward inequality that is implicit in all standardized testing. We should be critically analyzing the politics of all these tendencies, trying to comprehend them historically, and engaging our students in a discussion of literacy and technology that is both historical and political. It's worth trying to reconstitute literacy as a process of liberation—but also to remember that work for literacy is not in itself intrinsically liberating. The only way to have a democracy is to make one.

Works Cited

Altick, Richard D. *The English Common Reader: A Social History of the Mass Reading Public 1800–1900.* Chicago: U of Chicago P, 1957.

Arnove, Robert F. "The Nicaraguan National Literacy Crusade of 1980." *Comparative Education Review* 25 (1981): 244–60.

Baran, Paul A., and Paul M. Sweezy. *Monopoly Capital: An Essay on the American Economic and Social Order.* New York: Modern Reader Paperbacks, 1966.

Barnouw, Eric. *Tube of Plenty: The Evolution of American Television.* New York: Oxford UP, 1982.

Braverman, Harry, *Labor and Monopoly Capital: The Degradation of Work in the Twentieth Century.* New York: Monthly Review, 1974.

Chandler, Alfred D. *The Visible Hand: The Managerial Revolution in American Business.* Cambridge, MA: Harvard UP, 1977.

Corson, Ross. "Computer Revolution." *The Progressive* Sept. 1982: 32, 34–36.

Donald, James. "Language, Literacy and Schooling." *The State and Popular Culture 1,* a unit in the Open University course on popular culture. Milton Keynes: The Open University, 1982.

Eisenstein, Elizabeth L. "Some Conjectures About the Impact of Printing on Western Society and Thought: A Preliminary Report." *Literacy and Social Development in the West: A Reader.* Ed. Harvey J. Graff. Cambridge, Eng.: Cambridge UP, 1981: 53–68.

Johnson, David C., Ronald E. Anderson, Thomas P. Hansen, and Daniel L. Klassen. "Computer Literacy—What Is It?" *Mathematics Teacher* 73 (1980): 91–96.

Kozol, Jonathan. *Children of the Revolution: A Yankee Teacher in the Cuban Schools.* New York: Delacorte, 1978.

——. "A New Look at the Literacy Campaign in Cuba." *Harvard Educational Review* 48 (1978): 341–77.

Leigh, Edwin. "Illiteracy in the United States." *Annual Report of the Commissioner of Education,* 1870: 467–502.

Mandeville, Bernard de. "Essay on Charity and Charity Schools." *The Fable of the Bees.* 1723. London, 1795.

Munroe, James P. "The Education of the Masses." *The New Princeton Review* Nov. 1888: 346–54.

Noble, David. *America by Design: Science, Technology, and the Rise of Corporate Capitalism.* New York: Knopf, 1977.

Noble, Douglas. "The Underside of Computer Literacy." *Raritan* 3 (1984): 37–64.

Ohmann, Richard. "Where Did Mass Culture Come From? The Case of Magazines." *Berkshire Review* 16 (1981): 85–101.

Ong, Walter J. *Interfaces of the Word: Studies in the Evolution of Consciousness and Culture.* Ithaca: Cornell UP, 1977.

O'Shea, Tim, and John Self. *Learning and Teaching with Computers.* Englewood Cliffs, NJ: Prentice, 1984.

Pincus, Fred, "Students Being Groomed for Jobs That Won't Exist." *The Guardian* 9 May 1984: 7.

Pogrow, Stanley. *Education in the Computer Age: Issues of Policy, Practice and Reform.* Beverly Hills: Sage, 1983.

Resnick, Daniel P., and Lauren B. Resnick. "The Nature of Literacy: An Historical Exploration." *Harvard Educational Review* 47 (1977): 370–85.

Smith, Adam. *The Wealth of Nations,* 2 vols. London: J. M. Dent and Sons, 1910. Vol. 2.

Stetson, George R. "The Renaissance of Barbarism." *The New Princeton Review.* Nov. 1888: 336–345.

Strassmann, Paul A. "Information Systems and Literacy." *Literacy for Life: The Demand for Reading and Writing.* Ed. Richard W. Bailey and Robin Melanie Fosheim. New York: Modern Language Association, 1983. 115–24.

Tuman, Myron. "Words, Tools, and Technology." *College English* 45 (1983): 769–79.

Williams, Raymond. *Television: Technology and Cultural Form.* New York: Schocken, 1975.

REFLECTING ON THE READING

1. What lessons does Ohmann draw from the brief history of literacy that he provides in part 1 of his essay? How does he believe that ideas about literacy in the United States in the nineteenth century were related to concerns about immigrants and working-class people?

2. What does Ohmann mean by "monopoly capitalism"? What was the crisis that gave rise to it? What are the main features of monopoly capitalism that Ohmann describes? What effects did it have on labor and on sales processes, according to Ohmann? In what ways are the idea of monopoly capital and the related economic matters important to Ohmann's points about technology and literacy?

3. How does Ohmann understand *technology* in this essay? Does he use that term to refer primarily to computers or does it refer to other kinds of tools or machines as well? What does he mean when he writes that technology is not neutral but is "a social process"? Why is this an important point in Ohmann's analysis of the relationship between literacy and technology?

4. What does Ohmann mean by "technological determinism"? Why is he concerned about such a perspective on technology? Do you agree with his concerns? Why or why not?

5. In what ways does Ohmann believe that computers are contributing to what he calls the "deskilling" of work? What instances of this kind of "deskilling" does he offer? Are his concerns valid, in your view? Why or why not?

6. What does Ohmann mean when he says that literacy is not an individual skill but "an activity of social groups"? Why is this an important point for his argument about technologies like computers? What is the difference between "literacy-from-above" and "literacy-from-below"? What examples of each does he provide? What is his preference? Why?

7. Why does Ohmann believe that literacy is more important than technologies like the computer when it comes to the problems of inequality that he sees in our

capitalist economic system? Do you think he is right? Why or why not? What might your answer suggest about your own beliefs about literacy and work?

Examining Rhetorical Strategies

1. Ohmann begins this essay by explaining his title, and he asks his "courteous reader" to have some patience as he develops his argument. Whom do you think he imagines his "courteous reader" to be? In answering this question, consider the journal (*College English*) in which this essay was published as well as what he tells us about his essay in the first footnote. Also consider what he reveals about himself and those he seems to be addressing in his essay. Are you part of the audience he imagines for this essay? Do you think his essay is effective for a wider audience than the one for which he originally wrote this essay? Explain, citing specific passages in the essay to support your explanation.

2. How would you characterize Ohmann's voice in this essay? Do you think he sounds academic? Do you think he intends to? Explain. Did you find his voice effective? Why or why not? What might your reaction to his voice suggest about you as a reader?

3. Near the end of this essay, Ohmann writes that he hopes that "we (or rather, those of us teachers who are on my side!) will manage to shape that technology to democratic forms." Whom do you think he means when he refers to teachers on his "side"? How would you describe "his side"? In what ways do you think his essay reveals his "side"? Cite specific passages from his essay to support your answer. How do you think readers who disagree with him might react to such a reference to teachers "on my side"?

4. Assess the effectiveness of Ohmann's arguments about literacy and technology. He states clearly at the very beginning of his essay the main points he will make and he connects literacy directly to what he calls "our present economic and social system." In your view, does he argue these claims effectively? Why or why not? Identify specific passages in his essay to support your answer. How did you react to his arguments? Do you agree with his criticisms of capitalism? Why or why not? Do you think your own views of capitalism influence your assessment of the effectiveness of his essay? Explain.

5. At the beginning of his essay, Ohmann informs his readers that the five sections of his essay could be arranged in any order. Do you agree? Do you think the essay is carefully organized as it is? Does the effectiveness of his argument depend upon the order of the five sections, in your view? Explain. How might the way he organizes the essay enhance or weaken the effectiveness of his argument?

Engaging the Issues

1. Write an academic essay for an audience of your classmates in which you respond to Ohmann's concerns about technology and literacy within a capitalist economic system. Draw on your own experiences and your knowledge of

economics to argue in favor of or in opposition to the position Ohmann takes in his essay. In your essay, try to respond to Ohmann's key points. Draw conclusions about the validity of his argument.

2. Write a narrative essay in which you describe a work experience involving technology. For your narrative, select an experience in which technology was a key aspect of your job and either benefited you or limited you in some way. In your narrative, be sure to describe your experience so that your readers will understand the nature of your job and the technology you used. Try to tell your story so that you explore the role of technology in that job and its implications for you or for others.

3. In a group of your classmates, share the essays you wrote for Question #2 above. Compare the experiences all of you wrote about, and try to identify differences and similarities in those experiences. Discuss how technology was used in your workplaces. Try to identify some implications of those uses of technology. Was it beneficial in any way? To whom? How did it affect your work? Draw conclusions about the nature of technology in the workplace.

4. Write a conventional academic essay in which you explain capitalism and socialism. For your essay, you may need to consult sources, such as textbooks or appropriate sites on the Internet. Your essay should include some information about how capitalism and socialism developed. It should also include some discussion of technology in each system.

   Alternatively, write an essay in which you explain capitalism and socialism to a general audience—for example, readers of your hometown newspaper, most of whom are not likely to be professional economists or political scientists.

   Consider the differences between these two essays. How do those differences relate to the intended audience?

5. Find someone on your campus or in your community who is an exchange student from a country like the People's Republic of China that has an economic system different from the system in the United States (or someone from a country, such as Russia or Romania, that once had a Marxist economic system). Or use the Internet to establish an email connection with a person from such a country. Interview that person about the nature of the system within which that person lives (or lived previously). Ask him or her about how the economic system affected his or her life-style and work. If the person you are interviewing is an exchange students, ask him or her to compare his or her experiences in the United States to experiences in his or her home country.

6. Interview a manager or a person in charge of hiring at several businesses in your community. Ask about the literacy skills expected in an employee. Ask about how technology is used in his or her business and about how knowledge of technologies (such as computers) influences hiring decisions. Ask as well about how employees use reading and writing in their work. If possible, interview employees at each business. Once you have finished your interviews, write a report for an audience of your classmates in which you describe the businesses you visited and report on what you learned about literacy and technology in those businesses. Try to draw conclusions about literacy and technology in the workplace

based on your research. Try to draw conclusions as well about how literacy and technology function in a capitalist economic system.

7. Conduct interviews as described in Question #6 above. On the basis of what you learned from those interviews, write a letter to your local school board in which you discuss your views about the ways in which literacy and technology are addressed in the school curriculum. Propose changes to the curriculum that you think would help prepare students better for the kinds of challenges they will face in the workplace.

8. Find a listserv or Internet discussion group devoted to issues of economics, capitalism, socialism, or related issues. Follow the discussion on that listserv or discussion group for a week or two to get a sense of the views expressed by participants about technology and literacy in the workplace. Post your own questions about these issues, if appropriate. Then write a report for your classmates based on your experiences with the listserv or discussion group.

9. Write an essay for the editorial page of your local newspaper in which you express your own views about the role of technology and literacy in the American workplace. In your essay, draw on Ohmann's essay and on any other relevant resources to help you make your argument.

Sponsors of Literacy

Deborah Brandt

INTRODUCTION   We generally accept that literacy is not only central to the workings of modern society but also crucial for people to function effectively within society. The important place of reading and writing within conventional school programs, the many workplace literacy programs that emerged in the 1980's and 1990's as changes in the economy forced workers to seek new kinds of employment, the regular talk of the "literacy crisis" by legislators and other leaders—all these underscore the widespread view that literacy plays a central role in our lives as citizens and workers. Indeed, it seems a simple and straightforward principle: Literacy is essential in our modern, highly technological culture. But as many of the authors in this chapter and elsewhere in this book demonstrate, literacy is anything but simple or straightforward, particularly in an age of rapid change. And when it comes to the role of literacy in the work we do, the inherent complexity of literacy can become dramatically apparent.

Part of literacy researcher Deborah Brandt's intent in her studies is to explore that complexity in order to understand better the workings of literacy in the lives of individual people as each negotiates modern society. Like other scholars whose work is included in this book, Brandt acknowledges the importance of literacy in our lives, and her own research reinforces our collective sense that literacy remains a crucial part—perhaps *the* crucial part—of life in our increasingly technological economy. But Brandt is interested in pushing further into the complexity of literacy to see more clearly how reading and writing function in people's lives. Specifically, Brandt explores the various institutional and cultural influences that seem to shape an individual's literacy learning. Among those influences are institutions such as churches, unions, businesses, and nonprofit organizations, which tend to figure prominently in our lives in general. What Brandt reveals is that these institutions—along with a variety of other complicated and interrelated factors—can help determine how we read and write and how our uses of literacy can affect our prospects as workers and citizens. To understand these influences, Brandt introduces the concept of "sponsors of literacy" to refer to these institutions that shape our literacy learning and use. One of the most important such sponsors of literacy for many of the people Brandt studies is the business or institution where they work. In Brandt's view, looking carefully at the workplace as a sponsor of literacy can help illuminate the complex workings of writing and reading in the life of an individual as he or she tries to find a place in a changing economy.

Brandt's article is a report and analysis of her extensive studies of various people from different social and cultural backgrounds. To conduct her research, Brandt spends a great deal of time examining the specific role of literacy in the lives of the people she studied. In order to illustrate what she learns through her study, she provides detailed histories of several of these people, and she tries to make sense of their histories by looking at them from the perspective of the sponsors of literacy. Through these histories and Brandt's analysis of them, her article offers us a vivid picture of the specific workings of literacy in the day-to-day lives of very different people, all of whom face similar kinds of economic and social pressures. At the same time, her analysis of the sponsors of literacy provides a way to understand literacy in a broader sense. Her article may thus enable us to see how literacy functions in ways that are perhaps invisible when we examine literacy from our more conventional viewpoints.

Deborah Brandt is a professor of English at the University of Wisconsin at Madison and project head at the National Research Center on English Learning and Achievement. She has written widely on literacy and writing instruction and is the author of *Literacy as Involvement: The Acts of Writers, Readers, and Texts* (1990). The following article was originally published in 1999 in the journal *College Composition and Communication*.

REFLECTING BEFORE READING

1. In the following essay, Brandt presents her idea of the "sponsors of literacy," a concept she uses to refer to institutions and other entities that influence how we learn and use literacy. As you read, pay attention to how Brandt introduces this concept and how she uses it to make sense of the specific situations and incidents she describes. In what ways does this abstract concept enable Brandt to make her analyses of the people she studies and present her argument for understanding the role of literacy in contemporary society?

2. Brandt's article describes her research on literacy in the lives of various people she studied. As noted above, it was originally published in a specialized academic journal. As you read, look for features of her article that identify it as a scholarly article and as a research report. Consider, too, your own reaction to

these features: Do they enable you to follow her discussion more easily or do they inhibit your reading of her article in any way?

I n his sweeping history of adult learning in the United States, Joseph Kett describes the intellectual atmosphere available to young apprentices who worked in the small, decentralized print shops of antebellum America. Because printers also were the solicitors and editors of what they published, their workshops served as lively incubators for literacy and political discourse. By the mid-nineteenth century, however, this learning space was disrupted when the invention of the steam press reorganized the economy of the print industry. Steam presses were so expensive that they required capital outlays beyond the means of many printers. As a result, print jobs were outsourced, the processes of editing and printing were split, and, in tight competition, print apprentices became low-paid mechanics with no more access to the multi-skilled environment of the craft-shop (Kett 67–70). While this shift in working conditions may be evidence of the deskilling of workers induced by the Industrial Revolution (Nicholas and Nicholas), it also offers a site for reflecting upon the dynamic sources of literacy and literacy learning. The reading and writing skills of print apprentices in this period were the achievements not simply of teachers and learners nor of the discourse practices of the printer community. Rather, these skills existed fragilely, contingently within an economic moment. The pre-steam press economy enabled some of the most basic aspects of the apprentices' literacy, especially their access to material production and the public meaning or worth of their skills. Paradoxically, even as the steam-powered penny press made print more accessible (by making publishing more profitable), it brought an end to a particular form of literacy sponsorship and a drop in literate potential.

The apprentices' experience invites rumination upon literacy learning and teaching today. Literacy looms as one of the great engines of profit and competitive advantage in the 20th century: a lubricant for consumer desire; a means for integrating corporate markets; a foundation for the deployment of weapons and other technology; a raw material in the mass production of information. As ordinary citizens have been compelled into these economies, their reading and writing skills have grown sharply more central to the everyday trade of information and goods as well as to the pursuit of education, employment, civil rights, status. At the same time, people's literate skills have grown vulnerable to unprecedented turbulence in their economic value, as conditions, forms, and standards of literacy achievement seem to shift with almost every new generation of learners. How are we to understand the vicissitudes of individual literacy development in relationship to the large-scale economic forces that set the routes and determine the wordly worth of that literacy?

The field of writing studies has had much to say about individual literacy development. Especially in the last quarter of the 20th century, we have theorized, researched, critiqued, debated, and sometimes even managed to enhance the literate potentials of ordinary citizens as they have tried to cope with life as they find it. Less easily and certainly less steadily have we been able to relate what we see, study, and do to these larger contexts of profit making and competition. This even as we recognize that the most pressing issues we deal with—tightening associations between literate skill and social viability, the breakneck pace of change in communications technology, persistent inequities in access and reward—all relate to structural conditions in literacy's bigger picture. When economic forces are addressed in our work, they appear primarily as generalities: contexts, determinants, motivators, barriers, touchstones. But rarely are they systematically related to the local conditions and embodied moments of literacy learning that occupy so many of us on a daily basis.[1]

This essay does not presume to overcome the analytical failure completely. But it does offer a conceptual approach that begins to connect literacy as an individual development to literacy as an economic development, at least as the two have played out over the last ninety years or so. The approach is through what I call sponsors of literacy. Sponsors, as I have come to think of them, are any agents, local or distant, concrete or abstract, who enable, support, teach, model, as well as recruit, regulate, suppress, or withhold literacy—and gain advantage by it in some way. Just as the ages of radio and television accustom us to having programs *brought* to us by various commercial sponsors, it is useful to think about who or what underwrites occasions of literacy learning and use. Although the interests of the sponsor and the sponsored do not have to converge (and, in fact, may conflict) sponsors nevertheless set the terms for access to literacy and wield powerful incentives for compliance and loyalty. Sponsors are a tangible reminder that literacy learning throughout history has always required permission, sanction, assistance, coercion, or, at minimum, contact with existing trade routes. Sponsors are delivery systems for the economies of literacy, the means by which these forces present themselves to—and through—individual learners. They also represent the causes into which people's literacy usually gets recruited.[2]

For the last five years I have been tracing sponsors of literacy across the 20th century as they appear in the accounts of ordinary Americans recalling how they learned to write and read. The investigation is grounded in more than 100 in-depth interviews that I collected from a diverse group of people born roughly between 1900 and 1980. In the interviews, people explored in great detail their memories of learning to read and write across their lifetimes, focusing especially on the people, institutions, materials, and motivations involved in the process. The more I worked with these accounts, the more I came to realize that they were filled with references to sponsors, both explicit and latent, who appeared in formative roles at the scenes of literacy learning. Patterns of sponsorship became an illuminating site through which to track the different cultural attitudes people developed toward writing vs. reading as well as the ideological congestion faced by late-century literacy learners as their sponsors proliferated and diversified (see my essays on "Remembering Reading" and "Accumulating Literacy"). In this essay I set out a case for why the concept of sponsorship, is so richly suggestive for exploring economies of literacy and their effects. Then, through use of extended case examples, I demonstrate the practical application of this approach for interpreting current conditions of literacy teaching and learning, including persistent stratification of opportunity and escalating standards for literacy achievement. A final section addresses implications for the teaching of writing.

Sponsorship

Intuitively, *sponsors* seemed a fitting term for the figures who turned up most typically in people's memories of literacy learning: older relatives, teachers, priests, supervisors, military officers, editors, influential authors. Sponsors, as we ordinarily think of them, are powerful figures who bankroll events or smooth the way for initiates. Usually richer, more knowledgeable, and more entrenched than the sponsored, sponsors nevertheless enter a reciprocal relationship with those they underwrite. They lend their resources or credibility to the sponsored but also stand to gain benefits from their success, whether by direct repayment or, indirectly, by credit of association. *Sponsors* also proved an appealing term in my analysis because of all the commercial references that appeared in these 20th-century accounts—the magazines, peddled encyclopedias, essay contests, radio and television programs, toys, fan clubs, writing tools, and so on, from which so much experience with literacy was derived. As the 20th century turned the abilities to read and write into widely exploitable resources, commercial sponsorship abounded.

In whatever form, sponsors deliver the ideological freight that must be borne for access to what they have. Of course, the sponsored can be oblivious to or innovative with this ideological burden. Like Little Leaguers who wear the logo of a local insurance agency on their uniforms, not out of a concern for enhancing the agency's image but as a means for getting to play ball, people throughout history have acquired literacy pragmatically under the banner of others' causes. In the days before free, public schooling in England, Protestant Sunday Schools warily offered basic reading instruction to working-class families as part of evangelical duty. To the horror of many in the church sponsorship, these families insistently, sometimes riotously demanded of their Sunday Schools more instruction, including in writing and math, because it provided means for upward mobility.[3] Through the sponsorship of Baptist and Methodist ministries, African Americans in slavery taught each other to understand the Bible in subversively liberatory ways. Under a conservative regime, they developed forms of critical literacy that sustained religious, educational, and political movements both before and after emancipation (Cornelius). Most of the time, however, literacy takes its shape from the interests of its sponsors. And, as we will see below, obligations toward one's sponsors run deep, affecting what, why, and how people write and read.

The concept of sponsors helps to explain, then, a range of human relationships and ideological pressures that turn up at the scenes of literacy learning—from benign sharing between adults and youths, to euphemized coercions in schools and workplaces, to the most notorious impositions and deprivations by church or state. It also is a concept useful for tracking literacy's materiel: the things that accompany writing and reading and the ways they are manufactured and distributed. Sponsorship as a sociological term is even more broadly suggestive for thinking about economies of literacy development. Studies of patronage in Europe and *compradrazgo* in the Americas show how patron-client relationships in the past grew up around the need to manage scarce resources and promote political stability (Bourne; Lynch; Horstman and Kurtz). Pragmatic, instrumental, ambivalent, patron-client relationships integrated otherwise antagonistic social classes into relationships of mutual, albeit unequal dependencies. Loaning land, money, protection, and other favors allowed the politically powerful to extend their influence and justify their exploitation of clients. Clients traded their labor and deference for access to opportunities for themselves or their children and for leverage needed to improve their social standing. Especially under conquest in Latin America, *compradrazgo* reintegrated native societies badly fragmented by the diseases and other disruptions that followed foreign invasions. At the same time, this system was susceptible to its own stresses, especially when patrons became clients themselves of still more centralized or distant overlords, with all the shifts in loyalty and perspective that entailed (Horstman and Kurtz 13–14).

In raising this association with formal systems of patronage, I do not wish to overlook the very different economic, political, and educational systems within which U.S. literacy has developed. But where we find the sponsoring of literacy, it will be useful to look for its function within larger political and economic arenas. Literacy, like land, is a valued commodity in this economy, a key resource in gaining profit and edge. This value helps to explain, of course, the lengths people will go to secure literacy for themselves or their children. But it also explains why the powerful work so persistently to conscript and ration the powers of literacy. The competition to harness literacy, to manage, measure, teach, and exploit it, has intensified throughout the century. It is vital to pay attention to this development because it largely sets the terms for individuals' encounters with literacy. This competition shapes the incentives and barriers (including uneven distributions of opportunity) that greet literacy learners in any particular time and place. It is this competition that has made access to the right kinds of literacy sponsors so crucial for political and economic well being. And it also has spurred the rapid, complex changes that now make the pursuit of literacy feel so turbulent and precarious for so many.

In the next three sections. I trace the dynamics of literacy sponsorship through the life experiences of several individuals, showing how their opportunities for literacy learning emerge out of the jockeying and skirmishing for economic and political advantage going on among sponsors of literacy. Along the way, the analysis addresses three key issues: (1) how, despite ostensible democracy in educational chances, stratification of opportunity continues to organize access and reward in literacy learning; (2) how sponsors contribute to what is called "the literacy crisis," that is, the perceived gap between rising standards for achievement and people's ability to meet them; and (3) how encounters with literacy sponsors, especially as they are configured at the end of the 20th century, can be sites for the innovative rerouting of resources into projects of self-development and social change.

Sponsorship and Access

A focus on sponsorship can force a more explicit and substantive link between literacy learning and systems of opportunity and access. A statistical correlation between high literacy achievement and high socioeconomic, majority-race status routinely shows up in results of national tests of reading and writing performance.[4] These findings capture yet, in their shorthand way, obscure the unequal conditions of literacy sponsorship that lie behind differential outcomes in academic performance. Throughout their lives, affluent people from high-caste racial groups have multiple and redundant contacts with powerful literacy sponsors as a routine part of their economic and political privileges. Poor people and those from low-caste racial groups have less consistent, less politically secured access to literacy sponsors—especially to the ones that can grease their way to academic and economic success. Differences in their performances are often attributed to family background (namely education and income of parents) or to particular norms and values operating within different ethnic groups or social classes. But in either case, much more is usually at work.

As a study in contrasts in sponsorship patterns and access to literacy, consider the parallel experiences of Raymond Branch and Dora Lopez, both of whom were born in 1969 and, as young children, moved with their parents to the same, mid-sized university town in the midwest.[5] Both were still residing in this town at the time of our interviews in 1995, Raymond Branch, a European American, had been born in southern California, the son of a professor father and a real estate executive mother. He recalled that his first grade classroom in 1975 was hooked up to a mainframe computer at Stanford University and that, as a youngster, he enjoyed fooling around with computer programming in the company of "real users" at his father's science lab. This process was not interrupted much when, in the late 1970s, his family moved to the midwest. Raymond received his first personal computer as a Christmas present from his parents when he was twelve years old, and a modem the year after that. In the 1980s, computer hardware and software stores began popping up within a bicycle-ride's distance from where he lived. The stores were serving the university community and, increasingly, the high-tech industries that were becoming established in that vicinity. As an adolescent, Raymond spent his summers roaming these stores, sampling new computer games, making contact with founders of some of the first electronic bulletin boards in the nation, and continuing, through reading and other informal means, to develop his programming techniques. At the time of our interview he had graduated from the local university and was a successful freelance writer of software and software documentation, with clients in both the private sector and the university community.

Dora Lopez, a Mexican American, was born in the same year as Raymond Branch, 1969, in a Texas border town, where her grandparents, who worked as farm laborers, lived most of the year. When Dora was still a baby her family moved to the same midwest university town as had the family of Raymond Branch. Her father pursued an accounting degree at a local technical college and found work as a shipping and receiving clerk at the university. Her mother, who also attended technical college briefly, worked part-time in a bookstore. In the early 1970s, when the Lopez family made its move to the midwest, the Mexican-American population in the university town was barely one per cent. Dora recalled that the family had to drive seventy miles to a big city to find not only suitable groceries but also Spanish-language newspapers and magazines that carried information of concern and interest to them. (Only when reception was good could they catch Spanish-language radio programs coming from Chicago, 150 miles away.) During her adolescence, Dora Lopez undertook to teach herself how to read and write in Spanish, something, she said, that neither her brother nor her U.S.-born cousins knew how to do. Sometimes, with the help of her mother's employee discount at the bookstore, she sought out novels by South American and Mexican writers, and she practiced her written Spanish by corresponding with relatives in Colombia. She was exposed to computers for the first time at the age of thirteen when she worked as a teacher's aide in a federally-funded summer school program for the children of migrant workers. The computers were being used to help the children to be brought up to grade level in their reading and writing skills. When Dora was admitted to the same university that Raymond Branch attended, her father bought her a used word processing machine that a student had advertised for sale, on a bulletin board in the building where Mr. Lopez worked. At the time of our interview, Dora Lopez had transferred from the university to a technical college. She was working for a cleaning company, where she performed extra duties as a translator, communicating on her supervisor's behalf with the largely Latina cleaning staff. "I write in Spanish for him, what he needs to be translated, like job duties, what he expects them to do, and I write lists for him in English and Spanish," she explained.

In Raymond Branch's account of his early literacy learning we are able to see behind the scenes of his majority-race membership, male gender, and high-end socioeconomic family profile. There lies a thick and, to him, relatively accessible economy of institutional and commercial supports that cultivated and subsidized his acquisition of a powerful form of literacy. One might be tempted to say that Raymond Branch was born at the right time and lived in the right place—except that the experience of Dora Lopez troubles that thought. For Raymond Branch, a university town in the 1970s and 1980s provided an information-rich, resource-rich learning environment in which to pursue his literacy development, but for Dora Lopez, a female member of a culturally unsubsidized ethnic minority, the same town at the same time was information- and resource-poor. Interestingly, both young people were pursuing projects of self-initiated learning, Raymond Branch in computer programming and Dora Lopez in biliteracy. But she had to reach much further afield for the material and communicative systems needed to support her learning. Also, while Raymond Branch, as the son of an academic, was sponsored by some of the most powerful agents of the university (its laboratories, newest technologies, and most educated personnel), Dora Lopez was being sponsored by what her parents could pull from the peripheral service systems of the university (the mail room, the bookstore, the second-hand technology market). In these accounts we also can see how the development and eventual economic worth of Raymond Branch's literacy skills were underwritten by late-century transformations in communication technology that created a boomtown need for programmers and software writers. Dora Lopez's biliterate skills developed and paid off much further down the economic-reward ladder, in government-sponsored youth programs and commercial enterprises, that, in the 1990s, were absorbing surplus migrant workers into a low-wage, urban service economy.[6] Trackng patterns of literacy sponsorship, then, gets beyond SES shorthand to expose more fully how unequal literacy chances relate to systems of unequal subsidy and reward for literacy. These are the systems that deliver large-scale economic, historical, and political conditions to the scenes of small-scale literacy use and development.

This analysis of sponsorship forces us to consider not merely how one social group's literacy practices may differ from another's, but how everybody's literacy practices are operating in differential economies, which supply different access routes, different degrees of sponsoring power, and different scales of monetary worth to the practices in use. In fact, the interviews I conducted are filled with examples of how economic and political forces, some of them originating in quite distant corporate and government policies, affect people's day-to-day ability to seek out and practice literacy. As a telephone company employee, Janelle Hampton enjoyed a brief period in the early 1980s as a fraud investigator, pursuing inquiries and writing up reports of her efforts. But when the breakup of the telephone utility reorganized its workforce, the fraud division was moved two states away and she was returned to less interesting work as a data processor. When, as a seven-year-old in the mid-1970s, Yi Vong made his way with his family from Laos to rural Wisconsin as part of the first resettlement group of Hmong refugees after the Vietnam War, his school district—which had no ESL programming—placed him in a school for the blind and deaf, where he learned English on audio and visual language machines. When a meager retirement pension forced Peter Hardaway and his wife out of their house and into a trailer, the couple stopped receiving newspapers and magazines in order to avoid cluttering up the small space they had to share. An analysis of sponsorship systems of literacy would help educators everywhere to think through the effects that economic and political changes in their regions are having on various people's ability to write and read, their chances to sustain that ability, and their capacities to pass it along to others. Recession, relocation, immigration, technological change, government retreat all can—and do—condition the course by which literate potential develops.

Sponsorship and the Rise in Literacy Standards

As I have been attempting to argue, literacy as a resource becomes available to ordinary people largely through the mediations of more powerful sponsors. These sponsors are engaged in ceaseless processes of positioning and repositioning, seizing and relinquishing control over meanings and materials of literacy as part of their participation in economic and political competition. In the give and take of these struggles, forms of literacy and literacy learning take shape. This section examines more closely how forms of literacy are created out of competitions between institutions. It especially considers how this process relates to the rapid rise in literacy standards since World War II. Resnick and Resnick lay out the process by which the demand for literacy achievement has been escalating, from basic, largely rote competence to more complex analytical and interpretive skills. More and more people are now being expected to accomplish more and more things with reading and writing. As print and its spinoffs have entered virtually every sphere of life, people have grown increasingly dependent on their literacy skills for earning a living and exercising and protecting their civil rights. This section uses one extended case example to trace the role of institutional sponsorship in raising the literacy stakes. It also considers how one man used available forms of sponsorship to cope with this escalation in literacy demands.

The focus is on Dwayne Lowery, whose transition in the early 1970s from line worker in an automobile manufacturing plant to field representative for a major public employees union exemplified the major transition of the post-World War II economy—from a thing-making, thing-swapping society to an information-making, service-swapping society. In the process, Dwayne Lowery had to learn to read and write in ways that he had never done before. How his experiences with writing developed and how they were sponsored—and distressed—by institutional struggle will unfold in the following narrative.

A man of Eastern European ancestry, Dwayne Lowery was born in 1938 and raised in a semi-rural area in the upper midwest, the third of five children of a rubber worker father and a homemaker mother. Lowery recalled how, in his childhood home, his father's feisty union publications and left-leaning newspapers and radio shows helped to create a political climate in his household. "I was sixteen years old before I knew that goddamn Republicans was two words," he said. Despite this influence, Lowery said he shunned politics and newspaper reading as a young person, except to read the sports page. A diffident student, he graduated near the bottom of his class from a small high school in 1956 and, after a stint in the Army, went to work on the assembly line of a major automobile manufacturer. In the late

1960s, bored with the repetition of spraying primer paint on the right door checks of 57 cars an hour, Lowery traded in his night shift at the auto plant for a day job reading water meters in a municipal utility department. It was at that time, Lowery recalled, that he rediscovered newspapers, reading them in the early morning in his department's break room. He said:

> At the time I guess I got a little more interested in the state of things within the state. I started to get a little political at that time and got a little more information about local people. So I would buy [a metropolitan paper] and I would read that paper in the morning. It was a pretty conservative paper but I got some information.

At about the same time Lowery became active in a rapidly growing public employees union, and, in the early 1970s, he applied for and received a union-sponsored grant that allowed him to take off four months of work and travel to Washington, D.C. for training in union activity. Here is his extended account of that experience:

> When I got to school, then there was a lot of reading. I often felt bad. If I had read more [as a high-school student] it wouldn't have been so tough. But they pumped a lot of stuff at us to read. We lived in a hotel and we had to some extent homework we had to do and reading we had to do and not make written reports but make some presentation on our part of it. What they were trying to teach us, I believe, was regulations, systems, laws. In case anything in court came up along the way, we would know that. We did a lot of work on organizing, you know, learning how to negotiate contracts, contractual language, how to write it. Gross National Product, how that affected the Consumer Price Index. It was pretty much a crash course. It was pretty much crammed in. And I'm not sure we were all that well prepared when we got done, but it was interesting.

After a hands-on experience organizing sanitation workers in the west, Lowery returned home and was offered a full-time job as a field staff representative for the union, handling worker grievances and contract negotiations for a large, active local near his state capital. His initial writing and rhetorical activities corresponded with the heady days of the early 1970s when the union was growing in strength and influence, reflecting in part the exponential expansion in information workers and service providers within all branches of government. With practice, Lowery said he became "good at talking," "good at presenting the union side," "good at slicing chunks off the employer's case." Lowery observed that, in those years, the elected officials with whom he was negotiating often lacked the sophistication of their Washington-trained union counterparts. "They were part-time people," he said. "And they didn't know how to calculate. We got things in contracts that didn't cost them much at the time but were going to cost them a ton down the road." In time, though, even small municipal and county governments responded to the public employees' growing power by hiring specialized attorneys to represent them in grievance and contract negotiations. "Pretty soon," Lowery observed, "ninety percent of the people I was dealing with across the table were attorneys."

This move brought dramatic changes in the writing practices of union reps, and, in Lowery's estimation, a simultaneous waning of the power of workers and the power of his own literacy. "It used to be we got our way through muscle or through political connections," he said. "Now we had to get it through legalistic stuff. It was no longer just sit down and talk about it. Can we make a deal?" Instead, all activity became rendered in writing: the exhibit, the brief, the transcript, the letter, the appeal. Because briefs took longer to write, the wheels of justice took longer to turn. Delays in grievance hearings became routine, as lawyers and union reps alike asked hearing judges for extensions on their briefs. Things went, in Lowery's words, "from quick, competent justice to expensive and long term justice."

In the meantime, Lowery began spending up to 70 hours a week at work, sweating over the writing of briefs, which are typically fifteen to thirty-page documents laying out precedents, arguments, and evidence for a grievant's case. These documents were being forced by the new political economy in which Lowery's union was operating. He explained:

> When employers were represented by an attorney, you were going to have a written brief because the attorney needs to get paid. Well, what do you think if you were a union grievant and the attorney says, well, I'm going to write a brief and Dwayne Lowery says, well, I'm not going to. Does the worker somehow feel that their representation is less now?

To keep up with the new demands, Lowery occasionally traveled to major cities for two or three-day union-sponsored workshops on arbitration, new legislation, and communication skills. He also took short courses at a historic School for Workers at a nearby university. His writing instruction consisted mainly of reading the briefs of other field reps, especially those done by the college graduates who increasingly were being assigned to his district from union headquarters. Lowery said he kept a file drawer filled with other people's briefs from which he would borrow formats and phrasings. At the time of our interview in 1995, Dwayne Lowery had just taken an early and somewhat bitter retirement from the union, replaced by a recent graduate from a master's degree program in Industrial Relations. As a retiree, he was engaged in local Democratic party politics and was getting informal lessons in word processing at home from his wife.

Over a 20-year period. Lowery's adult writing took its character from a particular juncture in labor relations, when even small units of government began wielding (and, as a consequence, began spreading) a "legalistic" form of literacy in order to restore political dominance over public workers. This struggle for dominance shaped the kinds of literacy skills required of Lowery, the kinds of genres he learned and used, and the kinds of literate identity he developed. Lowery's rank-and-file experience and his talent for representing that experience around a bargaining table became increasingly peripheral to his ability to prepare documents that could compete in kind with those written by his formally-educated, professional adversaries. Face-to-face meetings became occasions mostly for a ritualistic exchange of texts, as arbitrators generally deferred decisions, reaching them in private, after solitary deliberation over complex sets of documents. What Dwayne Lowery was up against as a working adult in the second half of the 20th century was more than just living through a rising standard in literacy expectations or a generalized growth in professionalization, specialization, or documentary power—although certainly all of those things are, generically, true. Rather, these developments should be seen more specifically, as outcomes of ongoing transformations in the history of literacy as it has been wielded as part of economic and political conflict. These transformations become the arenas in which new standards of literacy develop. And for Dwayne Lowery—as well as many like him over the last 25 years—these are the arenas in which the worth of existing literate skills become degraded. A consummate debater and deal maker, Lowery saw his value to the union bureaucracy subside, as power shifted to younger, university-trained staffers whose literacy credentials better matched the specialized forms of escalating pressure coming from the other side.

In the broadest sense, the sponsorship of Dwayne Lowery's literacy experiences lies deep within the historical conditions of industrial relations in the 20th century and, more particularly, within the changing nature of work and labor struggle over the last several decades. Edward Stevens Jr. has observed the rise in this century of an "advanced contractarian society" (25) by which formal relationships of all kinds have come to rely on "a jungle of rules and regulations" (139). For labor, these conditions only intensified in the 1960s and 1970s when a flurry of federal and state civil rights legislation curtailed the previously unregulated hiring and firing power of management. These developments made the appeal to law as central as collective bargaining for extending employee rights (Heckscher 9). I mention this broader picture, first, because it relates to the forms of employer backlash that Lowery began experiencing by the early 1980s and, more important, because a history of unionism serves as a guide for a closer look at the sponsors of Lowery's literacy.

These resources begin with the influence of his father, whose membership in the United Rubber Workers during the ideologically potent 1930s and 1940s, grounded Lowery in class-conscious progressivism and its favorite literate form: the newspaper. On top of that, though, was a pragmatic philosophy of worker education that developed in the U.S. after the Depression as an anti-communist antidote to left-wing intellectual influences in unions. Lowery's parent union, in fact, had been a central force in refocusing worker education away from an earlier emphasis on broad critical study and toward discrete techniques for organizing and bargaining. Workers began to be trained in the discrete bodies of knowledge, written formats, and idioms associated with those strategies. Characteristic of this legacy, Lowery's crash course at the Washington-based training center in the early 1970s emphasized technical information, problem solving, and union-building skills and methods. The transformation in worker education from critical, humanistic study to problem-solving skills was also lived out at the school for workers where Lowery took short courses in the 1980s. Once a place where factory workers came to write and read about economics, sociology, and labor history, the school is now part of a university extension service offering workshops—often requested by management—on such topics as work restructuring, new technology, health and safety regulations, and joint labor-management cooperation.[7] Finally, in this inventory of Dwayne Lowery's literacy sponsors, we must add the latest incarnations shaping union practices: the attorneys and college-educated co-workers who carried into Lowery's workplace forms of legal discourse and "essayist literacy."[8]

What should we notice about this pattern of sponsorship? First, we can see from yet another angle how the course of an ordinary person's literacy learning—its occasions, materials, applications, potentials—follows the transformations going on within sponsoring institutions as those institutions fight for economic and ideological position.

As a result of wins, losses, or compromises, institutions undergo change, affecting the kinds of literacy they promulgate and the status that such literacy has in the larger society. So where, how, why, and what Lowery practiced as a writer—and what he didn't practice—took shape as part of the post-industrial jockeying going on over the last thirty years by labor, government, and industry. Yet there is more to be seen in this inventory of literacy sponsors. It exposes the deeply textured history that lies within the literacy practices of institutions and within any individual's literacy experiences. Accumulated layers of sponsoring influences—in families, workplaces, schools, memory—carry forms of literacy that have been shaped out of ideological and economic struggles of the past. This history, on the one hand, is a sustaining resource in the quest for literacy. It enables an older generation to pass its literacy resources onto another. Lowery's exposure to his father's newspaper-reading and supper-table political talk kindled his adult passion for news, debate, and for language that rendered relief and justice. This history also helps to create infrastructures of opportunity. Lowery found crucial supports for extending his adult literacy in the educational networks that unions established during the first half of the 20th century as they were consolidating into national powers. On the other hand, this layered history of sponsorship is also deeply conservative and can be maladaptive because it teaches forms of literacy that oftentimes are in the process of being overtaken by new political realities and by ascendent forms of literacy. The decsion to focus worker education on practical strategies of recruiting and bargaining—devised in the thick of Cold War patriotism and galloping expansion in union memberships—became, by the Reagan years, a fertile ground for new forms of management aggression and cooptation.

It is actually this lag or gap in sponsoring forms that we call the rising standard of literacy. The pace of change and the place of literacy in economic competition have both intensified enormously in the last half of the 20th century. It is as if the history of literacy is in fast forward. Where once the same sponsoring arrangements could maintain value across a generation or more, forms of literacy and their sponsors can now rise and recede many times within a single life span. Dwayne Lowery experienced profound changes in forms of union-based literacy not only between his father's time and his but between the time he joined the union and the time he left it, twenty-odd years later. This phenomenon is what makes today's literacy feel so advanced and, at the same time, so destabilized.

Sponsorship and Appropriation in Literacy Learning

We have seen how literacy sponsors affect literacy learning in two powerful ways. They help to organize and administer stratified systems of opportunity and access, and they raise the literacy stakes in struggles for competitive advantage. Sponsors enable and hinder literacy activity, often forcing the formation of new literacy requirements while decertifying older ones. A somewhat different dynamic of literacy sponsorship is treated here. It pertains to the potential of the sponsored to divert sponsors' resources toward ulterior projects, often projects of self-interest or self-development. Earlier I mentioned how Sunday School parishioners in England and African Americans in slavery appropriated church-sponsored literacy for economic and psychic survival. "Misappropriation" is always possible at the scene of literacy transmission, a reason for the tight ideological control that usually surrounds reading and writing instruction. The accounts that appear below are meant to shed light on the dynamics of appropriation, including the role of sponsoring agents in that process. They are also meant to suggest that diversionary tactics in literacy learning may be invited now by the sheer proliferation of literacy activity in contemporary life. The uses and networks of literacy crisscross through many domains, exposing people to multiple, often amalgamated sources of sponsoring powers, secular, religious, bureaucratic, commercial, technological. In other words, what is so destabilized about contemporary literacy today also makes it so available and potentially innovative, ripe for picking, one might say, for people suitably positioned. The rising level of schooling in the general population is also an inviting factor in this process. Almost everyone now has some sort of contact, for instance, with college educated people, whose movements through workplaces, justice systems, social service organizations, houses of worship, local government, extended families, or circles of friends spread dominant forms of literacy (whther wanted or not, helpful or not) into public and private spheres. Another condition favorable for appropriation is the deep hybridity of literacy practices extant in many settings. As we saw in Dwayne Lowery's case, workplaces, schools, families bring together multiple strands of the history of literacy in complex and influential forms. We need models of literacy that more astutely account for these kinds of multiple contacts, both in and out of school and across a lifetime. Such models could begin to grasp the significance of re-appropriation, which, for a number of reasons, is becoming a key requirement for literacy learning at the end of the 20th century.

The following discussion will consider two brief cases of literacy diversion. Both involve women working in subordinate positions as secretaries, in print-rich settings where better educated male supervisors were teaching them to read and write in certain ways to perform their clerical duties. However, as we will see shortly, strong loyalties outside the workplace prompted these two secretaries to lift these literate resources for use in other spheres. For one, Carol White, it was on behalf of her work as a Jehovah's Witness. For the other, Sarah Steele, it was on behalf of upward mobility for her lower middle-class family.

Before turning to their narratives, though, it will be wise to pay some attention to the economic moment in which they occur. Clerical work was the largest and fastest growing occupation for women in the 20th century. Like so much employment for women, it offered a mix of gender-defined constraints as well as avenues for economic independence and mobility. As a new information economy created an acute need for typists, stenographers, bookkeepers and other office workers, white, American-born women and, later, immigrant and minority women saw reason to pursue high school and business-college educations. Unlike male clerks of the 19th century, female secretaries in this century had little chance for advancement. However, office work represented a step up from the farm or the factory for women of the working class and served as a respectable occupation from which educated, middle-class women could await or avoid marriage (Anderson, Strom). In a study of clerical work through the first half of the 20th century, Christine Anderson estimated that secretaries might encounter up to 97 different genres in the course of doing dictation or transcription. They routinely had contact with an array of professionals, including lawyers, auditors, tax examiners, and other government overseers (52–53). By 1930, 30% of women office workers used machines other than typewriters

(Anderson 76) and, in contemporary offices, clerical workers have often been the first employees to learn to operate CRTs and personal computers and to teach others how to use them. Overall, the daily duties of 20th-century secretaries could serve handily as an index to the rise of complex administrative and accounting procedures, standardization of information, expanding communication, and developments in technological systems.

With that background, consider the experiences of Carol White and Sarah Steele. An Oneida, Carol White was born into a poor, single-parent household in 1940. She graduated from high school in 1960 and, between five maternity leaves and a divorce, worked continuously in a series of clerical positions in both the private and public sectors. One of her first secretarial jobs was with an urban firm that produced and disseminated Catholic missionary films. The vice-president with whom she worked most closely also spent much of his time producing a magazine for a national civic organization that he headed. She discussed how typing letters and magazine articles and occasionally proofreading for this man taught her rhetorical strategies in which she was keenly interested. She described the scene of transfer this way:

> [My boss] didn't just write to write. He wrote in a way to make his letters appealing. I would have to write what he was writing in this magazine too. I was completely enthralled. He would write about the people who were in this [organization] and the different works they were undertaking and people that died and people who were sick and about their personalities. And he wrote little anecdotes. Once in a while I made some suggestions too. He was a man who would listen to you.

The appealing and persuasive power of the anecdote became especially important to Carol White when she began doing door-to-door missionary work for the Jehovah's Witnesses, a pan-racial, millennialist religious faith. She now uses colorful anecdotes to prepare demonstrations that she performs with other women at weekly service meetings at their Kingdom Hall. These demonstrations, done in front of the congregation, take the form of skits designed to explore daily problems through Bible principles. Further, at the time of our interview, Carol White was working as a municipal revenue clerk and had recently enrolled in an on-the-job training seminar called Persuasive Communication, a two-day class offered free to public employees. Her motivation for taking the course stemmed from her desire to improve her evangelical work. She said she wanted to continue to develop speaking and writing skills that would be "appealing," "motivating," and "encouraging" to people she hoped to convert.

Sarah Steele, a woman of Welsh and German descent, was born in 1920 into a large, working-class family in a coal mining community in eastern Pennsylvania. In 1940, she graduated from a two-year commercial college. Married soon after, she worked as a secretary in a glass factory until becoming pregnant with the first of four children. In the 1960s, in part to help pay for her children's college educations, she returned to the labor force as a receptionist and bookkeeper in a law firm, where she stayed until her retirement in the late 1970s.

Sarah Steele described how, after joining the law firm, she began to model her household management on principles of budgeting that she was picking up from one of the attorneys with whom she worked most closely. "I learned cash flow from

Mr. B____," she said. "I would get all the bills and put a tape in the adding machine and he and I would sit down together to be sure there was going to be money ahead." She said that she began to replicate that process at home with household bills. "Before that," she observed, "I would just cook beans when I had to instead of meat." Sarah Steele also said she encountered the genre of the credit report during routine reading and typing on the job. She figured out what constituted a top rating, making sure her husband followed these steps in preparation for their financing a new car. She also remembered typing up documents connected to civil suits being brought against local businesses, teaching her, she said, which firms never to hire for home repairs. "It just changes the way you think," she observed about the reading and writing she did on her job. "You're not a pushover after you learn how business operates."

The dynamics of sponsorship alive in these narratives expose important elements of literacy appropriation, at least as it is practiced at the end of the 20th century. In a pattern now familiar from the earlier sections, we see how opportunities for literacy learning—this time for diversions of resources—open up in the clash between long-standing, residual forms of sponsorship and the new: between the lingering presence of literacy's conservative history and its pressure for change. So, here, two women—one Native American and both working-class—filch contemporary literacy resources (public relations techniques and accounting practices) from more educated, higher-status men. The women are emboldened in these acts by ulterior identities beyond the workplace: Carol White with faith and Sarah Steele with family. These affiliations hark back to the first sponsoring arrangements through which American women were gradually allowed to acquire literacy and education. Duties associated with religious faith and child rearing helped literacy to become, in Gloria Main's words, "a permissable feminine activity" (579). Interestingly, these roles, deeply sanctioned within the history of women's literacy—and operating beneath the newer permissible feminine activity of clerical work—become grounds for covert, innovative appropriation even as they reinforce traditional female identities.

Just as multiple identities contribute to the ideologically hybrid character of these literacy formations, so do institutional and material conditions. Carol White's account speaks to such hybridity. The missionary film company with the civic club vice president is a residual site for two of literacy's oldest campaigns—Christian conversion and civic participation—enhanced here by 20th-century advances in film and public relations techniques. This ideological reservoir proved a pleasing instructional site for Carol White, whose interests in literacy, throughout her life, have been primarily spiritual. So literacy appropriation draws upon, perhaps even depends upon, conservative forces in the history of literacy sponsorship that are always hovering at the scene of acts of learning. This history serves as both a sanctioning force and a reserve of ideological and material support.

At the same time, however, we see in these accounts how individual acts of appropriation can divert and subvert the course of literacy's history, how changes in individual literacy experiences relate to larger scale transformations. Carol White's redirection of personnel management techniques to the cause of the Jehovah's Witnesses is an almost ironic transformation in this regard. Once a principal sponsor in the initial spread of mass literacy, evangelism is here rejuvenated through late-literate corporate sciences of secular persuasion, fund-raising, and bureaucratic management that Carol White finds circulating in her contemporary workplaces. By the same token, through Sarah Steele, accounting practices associated with corporations are, in a sense, tracked into the house, rationalizing and standardizing even domestic practices. (Even though Sarah Steele did not own an adding machine, she penciled her budget figures onto adding-machine tape that she kept for that purpose.) Sarah Steele's act of appropriation in some sense explains how dominant forms of literacy migrate and penetrate into private spheres, including private consciousness. At the same time, though, she accomplishes a subversive diversion of literate power. Her efforts to move her family up in the middle class involved not merely contributing a second income but also, from her desk as a bookkeeper, reading her way into an understanding of middle-class economic power.

Teaching and the Dynamics of Sponsorship

It hardly seems necessary to point out to the readers of *CCC* [*College Composition and Communication*] that we haul a lot of freight for the opportunity to teach writing. Neither rich nor powerful enough to sponsor literacy on our own terms, we serve instead as conflicted brokers between literacy's buyers and sellers. At our most worthy, perhaps, we show the sellers how to beware and try to make sure these exchanges will be a little fairer, maybe, potentially, a little more mutually rewarding. This essay has offered a few working case studies that link patterns of sponsorship to processes of stratification, competition, and reappropriation. How much these dynamics can be generalized to classrooms is an ongoing empirical question.

I am sure that sponsors play even more influential roles at the scenes of literacy learning and use than this essay has explored. I have focused on some of the most tangible aspects—material supply, explicit teaching, institutional aegis. But the ideological pressure of sponsors affects many private aspects of writing processes as well as public aspects of finished texts. Where one's sponsors are multiple or even at odds, they can make writing maddening. Where they are absent, they make writing unlikely. Many of the cultural formations we associate with writing development—community practices, disciplinary traditions, technological potentials—can be appreciated as make-do responses to the economics of literacy, past and present. The history of literacy is a catalogue of obligatory relations. That this catalogue is so deeply conservative and, at the same time, so ruthlessly demanding of change is what fills contemporary literacy learning and teaching with their most paradoxical choices and outcomes.[9]

In bringing attention to economies of literacy learning I am not advocating that we prepare students more efficiently for the job markets they must enter. What I have tried to suggest is that as we assist and study individuals in pursuit of literacy, we also recognize how literacy is in pursuit of them. When this process stirs ambivalence, on their part or on ours, we need to be understanding.

Notes

1. Three of the keenest and most eloquent observers of economic impacts on writing teaching and learning have been Lester Faigley, Susan Miller, and Kurt Spellmeyer.

2. My debt to the writings of Pierre Bourdieu will be evident throughout this essay. Here and throughout I invoke his expansive notion of "economy," which is not restricted to literal and ostensible systems of money making but to the many spheres where people labor, invest, and exploit energies—their own and others'—to maximize advantage. See Bourdieu and Wacquant, especially 117-120 and Bourdieu, Chapter 7.

3. Thomas Laqueur (124) provides a vivid account of a street demonstration in Bolton, England, in 1934 by a "pro-writing" faction of Sunday School students and their teachers. This faction demanded that writing instruction continue to be provided on Sundays, something that opponents of secular instruction on the Sabbath were trying to reverse.

4. See, for instance, National Assessments of Educational Progress in reading and writing (Applebee et al.; and "Looking").

5. All names used in this essay are pseudonyms.

6. I am not suggesting that literacy that does not "pay off" in terms of prestige or monetary reward is less valuable. Dora Lopez's ability to read and write in Spanish was a source of great strength and pride, especially when she was able to teach it to her young child. The resource of Spanish literacy carried much of what Bourdieu calls cultural capital in her social and family circles. But I want to point out here how people who labor equally to acquire literacy do so under systems of unequal subsidy and unequal reward.

7. For useful accounts of this period in union history, see Heckscher; Nelson.

8. Marcia Farr associates "essayist literacy" with written genres esteemed in the academy and noted for their explicitness, exactness, reliance on reasons and evidence, and impersonal voice.

9. Lawrence Cremin makes similar points about education in general in his essay "The Cacophony of Teaching." He suggests that complex economic and social changes since World War Two, including the popularization of schooling and the penetration of mass media, have created "a far greater range and diversity of languages, competencies, values, personalities, and approaches to the world and to its educational opportunities" than at one time existed. The diversity most of interest to him (and me) resides not so much in the range of different ethnic groups there are in society but in the different cultural formulas by which people assemble their educational—or, I would say, literate—experience.

Works Cited

Anderson, Mary Christine. "Gender, Class, and Culture: Women Secretarial and Clerical Workers in the United States, 1925–1955." Diss. Ohio State U, 1986.

Applebee, Arthur N., Judith A. Langer, and Ida V.S. Mullis. *The Writing Report Card: Writing Achievement in American Schools.* Princeton: ETS, 1986.

Bourdieu, Pierre. *The Logic of Practice.* Trans. Richard Nice. Cambridge: Polity, 1990.

Bourdieu, Pierre and Loic J. D. Wacquant. *An Invitation to Reflexive Sociology.* Chicago: Chicago UP, 1992.

Bourne, J. M. *Patronage and Society in Nineteenth-Century England.* London: Edward Arnold, 1986.

Brandt, Deborah. "Remembering Reading, Remembering Writing." *CCC* 45 (1994): 459–79.

———. "Accumulating Literacy: Writing and Learning to Write in the 20th Century." *College English* 57 (1995): 649–68.

Cornelius, Janet Duitsman. *'When I Can Ready My Title Clear': Literacy, Slavery, and Religion in the Antebellum South.* Columbia: U of South Carolina, 1991.

Cremin, Lawrence. "The Cacophony of Teaching," *Popular Education and Its Discontents.* New York: Harper, 1990.

Faigley, Lester. "Veterans' Stories on the Porch." *History, Reflection and Narrative: The Professionalization of Composition. 1963–1983.* Eds. Beth Boehm, Debra Journet, and Mary Rosner. Norwood: Ablex, in press.

Farr, Marcia. "Essayist Literacy and Other Verbal Performances." *Written Communication* 8 (1993): 4–38.

Heckscher, Charles C. *The New Unionism: Employee Involvement in the Changing Corporation.* New York: Basic, 1988.

Horstman, Connie and Donald V. Kurtz. *Compradrazgo in Post-Conquest Middle America.* Milwaukee: Milwaukee-UW Center for Latin America, 1978.

Kett, Joseph F. *The Pursuit of Knowledge Under Difficulties: From Self Improvement to Adult Education in America 1750–1990.* Stanford: Stanford UP, 1994.

Laqueur, Thomas. *Religion and Respectability: Sunday Schools and Working Class Culture 1780–1850.* New Haven: Yale UP, 1976.

Looking at How Well Our Students Read. The 1992 National Assessment of Educational Progress in Reading. Washington: US Dept. of Education, Office of Educational Research and Improvement, Educational Resources Information Center, 1992.

Lynch, Joseph H. *Godparents and Kinship in Early Medieval Europe.* Princeton: Princeton UP, 1986.

Main, Gloria L. "An Inquiry Into When and Why Women Learned to Write in Colonial New England," *Journal of Social History* 24 (1991): 579–89.

Miller, Susan. *Textual Carnivals. The Politics of Composition.* Carbondale: Southern Illinois UP, 1991.

Nelson, Daniel, *American Rubber Workers & Organized Labor, 1900–1941.* Princeton: Princeton UP, 1988.

Nicholas, Stephen J, and Jacqueline M. Nicholas. "Male Literacy, 'Deskilling,' and the Industrial Revolution." *Journal of Interdisciplinary History* 23 (1992): 1–18.

Resnick, Daniel P., and Lauren B. Resnick. "The Nature of Literacy: A Historical Explanation." *Harvard Educational Review* 47 (1977): 370–85.

Spellmeyer, Kurt. "After Theory: From Textuality to Attunement With the World." *College English* 58 (1996): 893–913.

Stevens, Jr., Edward. *Literacy, Law, and Social Order.* DeKalb: Northern Illinois UP, 1987.

Strom, Sharon Hartman. *Beyond the Typewriter: Gender, Class, and the Origins of Modern American Office Work, 1900–1930.* Urbana: U of Illinois P, 1992.

REFLECTING ON THE READING

1. According to Brandt, how did the invention of the steam press change the printing industry in the nineteenth century? How did these changes affect apprentice workers in printing shops? What does the situation of these workers suggest about literacy and literacy learning, according to Brandt? In what way is the example of the nineteenth century print shop workers relevant today, in Brandt's view? What might this view suggest about the work of scholars who study literacy?

2. Why is literacy such an important element in the economic lives of people, in Brandt's view? What does she believe that she and other scholars should try to understand about the relationship between literacy and economics? What is missing from our scholarly understanding of the connection between literacy and economics, according to her?

3. What does Brandt mean by "sponsors of literacy"? What examples of such sponsors does Brandt provide? What effects do these sponsors have on the literacy of the people under their influence? Why is this concept important in Brandt's analysis of the relationship between literacy and the working lives of the people she studies? How did Brandt come to this realization about the importance of the idea of "sponsors" of literacy?

4. In what sense is literacy a "valued commodity," according to Brandt? What does such an understanding of literacy help explain, in Brandt's view? Do you agree with her? Why or why not?

5. What effects does a person's socioeconomic status have on his or her access to literacy sponsors, according to Brandt? How are these effects illustrated in the experiences of Raymond Branch and Dora Lopez? In Brandt's view, what do the literacy experiences of these two people reveal about access to literacy in American society? Do you agree with her conclusions on this point? Explain. What might your answer suggest about your own beliefs regarding American society?

6. In what sense had literacy standards risen in the United States in the twentieth century, according to Brandt? How does Brandt account for this rise? What effects has this rise in standards had on the lives of individual Americans, according to Brandt? How can Brandt's idea of sponsors of literacy help explain this rise, especially in the example of Dwayne Lowery? What might this change in literacy standards indicate about the role of literacy in the lives of Americans? About attitudes toward literacy?

7. What does Brandt mean by the "appropriation" of literacy on the part of individuals connected to specific literacy sponsors, such as churches or unions? Why does this appropriation occur? What purposes does it serve in the lives of people like those Brandt studied? Do you think Brandt sees this appropriation as a positive occurrence? Why or why not? Do you? Explain. What might this idea of the appropriation of literacy suggest about the nature of literacy and its role in people's lives in modern society?

8. What implications for teaching does Brandt see in her study of the sponsors of literacy? Do you find these implications appropriate? Explain.

Examining Rhetorical Strategies

1. Examine the way Brandt justifies her article and positions it with respect to other studies of literacy. What specifically is Brandt's concern as a literacy scholar in this article? What problem or omission—what she calls the "analytical failure"—in the available scholarship on literacy does she hope to address with this article? How does she propose to address this problem? Do you find her justification for her study convincing? Why or why not?

2. How would you describe Brandt's voice in this article? Given that her article was originally published in a specialized scholarly journal, would you describe her voice as "academic" or "scholarly"? Explain. Did you find her voice engaging? Why or why not? What might your reaction to her voice suggest about you as a reader?

3. Examine how Brandt addresses her audience in this article. Keep in mind that the article was originally published in *College Composition and Communication,* a specialized scholarly journal devoted to issues of literacy and literacy instruction. Whom do you think Brandt sees as the primary audience for her article? Who specifically is the "we" to whom she refers in the third paragraph of the article? Do you think her use of the first person ("we") excludes readers who are not among the specific audience she is addressing in her article? Explain.

4. Brandt explains early in this article that it emerged from her extensive research into the literacy of a number of people whose lives and work she studied. Why do you think she explains her article in this way? How might this explanation affect the way other scholars read her article? Do you think they would expect such an explanation? Why or why not? How did her explanation affect the way you read her article? Would you have read her anecdotes of the people she describes differently if she had not explained her research in this way? Explain.

5. Assess Brandt's use of the case histories of the people she describes in this article, such as Raymond Branch, Dora Lopez, and Dwayne Lowery. What kinds of information does Brandt tell us about these people? What picture of these people does she provide? Does she leave anything out of this picture, in your view? Explain. Do you think her descriptions of these people are effective in helping her make her arguments about sponsors of literacy? Why or why not?

6. Examine the way Brandt organizes this article. She indicates early on that she will discuss three key issues in her analysis of the "dynamics of literacy sponsorship." How do these three key issues provide structure to her article? In what ways does Brandt call attention to that structure? Do you think the way she organizes her article is effective? Explain. Does it enable her readers to follow her complex analysis more easily, in your view? Why or why not?

7. Analyze how Brandt's position as a scholar might shape her understanding of literacy and her conclusions about the importance of studies like hers. She holds a position as a professor at a large research university, a position in which she is expected to conduct studies such as she describes in this article. Do you think her study has wider usefulness beyond the relatively small community of scholars who are interested in and conduct such research? Explain. Do you think her position as a university researcher influences her sense of the importance of such research? Why or why not?

Engaging the Issues

1. Write an essay for an audience of your classmates in which you discuss the "sponsors of literacy," as Brandt defines that term, in your own life. In your essay, identify and describe what you consider to be the most important sponsors of literacy in your life and describe those sponsors and the role they seem to have played in your life. Try to identify the effects these sponsors have had

on your life in terms of your development as a literate person and your working life. Draw conclusions about the role of these sponsors in your life.

2. In a group of your classmates, share the essays you wrote for Question #1 above. Examine the various sponsors of literacy that each group member describes in his or her essay and discuss the role these sponsors played in the lives of your group members. Try to identify similarities or differences in these sponsors and their roles in your lives, and draw conclusions about the importance of sponsors of literacy in the lives of working people.

3. Write a conventional academic essay in which you discuss Brandt's understanding of literacy as it emerges from her article. In your essay, use specific references to her article to define literacy as she understands it. Explain her understanding of the role of literacy in the social, economic, and political systems of American society and in the lives of individual Americans. Discuss the implications of her view of literacy in terms of things like schooling and instruction in reading and writing. Offer your own assessment of Brandt's view. If appropriate, contrast her view with those of other authors you've read in this book.

4. Visit one or more businesses near your home and, with their permission, investigate the way literacy is used there. Observe the operations of the business or businesses to get a sense of the specific ways in which reading and writing are used by workers there. Interview employees and managers to learn about the kinds of writing and reading they do and to get their views about the expectations for literacy skills that characterize that business. Try to get a sense of their backgrounds in terms of schooling and training. Find out if writing and reading play a role in the hiring process there and whether the company has a literacy or training program of any kind. Then write a report on the basis of your research about the role of literacy in the business (or businesses) you visited. In your report, describe the business you observed and how you gathered your information. Describe in detail the specific kinds of writing and reading done in that business and explore the implications of those uses of literacy for workers. Try to draw conclusions about the importance of literacy in that workplace.

5. On the basis of your research for Question #4 above, write a letter to your local school board in which you express your views about the kinds of literacy instruction you believe students should have in order to be prepared for workplaces like the one you studied. In your letter, refer to your research, to Brandt's article, or to any other appropriate sources of information in order to support your proposal.

6. On the basis of the research you did for Question #4 above (or on the basis of library or Internet research you have done), create a pamphlet intended for high school students about the importance of literacy in the workplace. Include information that you believe will help readers of the pamphlet understand the role of literacy in their futures as workers and provide appropriate advice for them.

   Alternatively, create a Web site instead of a pamphlet as described here.

7. If possible, gather job applications from several different employers near your home. Focus on employers with entry-level jobs for which high school or college

students might apply (for example, fast-food restaurants or grocery stores). With a group of your classmates, examine these applications to see what they seem to expect of potential employees in terms of literacy skills. Discuss the applications and try to draw conclusions about what they indicate regarding literacy and work.

FURTHERING YOUR INQUIRY

1. Drawing on several of the reading selections in this chapter (and on other appropriate resources as well as on your own experiences), write an essay for an audience of your classmates in which you present your views on literacy and technology in the workplace. In your essay, identify a main idea that emerges for you from your reading. This main idea could be a question that you had after reading several selections, a problem you see with literacy or technology as they relate to the workplace, a concern you have about recent developments regarding literacy and technology in the workplace, or something similar. Develop this idea, offering your analysis of the problem or question or concern you have, and use your sources to complete that analysis. Draw your own conclusions about the future in terms of literacy and technology in the workplace.

2. Write a dialogue about technology in the workplace among Margery Davies, Robert Samuelson, Robert Reich, and Richard Ohmann. Present yourself as the moderator of the discussion, and in that role, pose one or more questions about technology in the workplace and the implications of specific developments such as the rise of the Internet for workers. Imagine how each of these writers might respond to your questions and to each other.

3. Write a conventional academic essay in which you analyze the personal experience of Cynthia Hoffman or Maia Szalavitz from the perspective of Richard Ohmann or Robert Reich. How would Ohmann or Reich explain Hoffman's or Szalavitz's work situations? What might Ohmann or Reich emphasize or conclude about Hoffman's or Szalavitz's work situations? Be sure to summarize the ideas of Ohmann or Reich in your essay and explain how those ideas might help us understand a situation such as Hoffman's or Szalavitz's.

4. Write an essay in which you compare the writing styles of Margery Davies, Richard Ohmann, and Deborah Brandt. All these writers are academic writers whose essays were originally intended for academic audiences. How are these writers similar in terms of the specific features of their style? In what ways are they different? Assess the effectiveness of their styles and their voices as writers, in your own view, and discuss the appropriateness of each for nonacademic audiences. Be sure to cite specific passages from each selection to illustrate your analysis.

5. Working with a group of your classmates, create a Web site devoted to issues of literacy and technology in the workplace. As a group, decide upon the audience you hope to reach and the purpose you want your Web site to have. Then design the site with that audience and purpose in mind. (You might begin with

the work of some of the authors in this chapter and the Web sites they have on the Internet.)

6. On the basis of the readings in this chapter, write an essay for the editorial page of your local newspaper (or a similar publication) in which you discuss your concerns about an important recent development involving literacy and technology in the workplace (for example, the passage of a law related to literacy or technology or the development of a new workplace technology). Draw on any readings in this chapter that you find appropriate in making your point in your essay.

7. Using any appropriate readings from this chapter and other sources you have found in your library or on the Internet, write a report on the state of technology in the workplace today. In your report, identify what you consider to be important technological and economic developments in recent years and discuss the implications of these developments for workers and consumers. You might focus your report on one such development or on several. Draw on your own experiences or those of people you know, if appropriate. Draw conclusions about the future in terms of technology and work.

8. Write a conventional academic essay in which you discuss the connections you see between Samuelson's view of inequality in the American job market and the work experiences described by Cynthia Hoffman and Maia Szalavitz in their essays in this chapter. In your essay, explain Samuelson's views regarding inequalities in American life and the role of technology in those inequalities. Discuss how his views might help explain the experiences Hoffman and Szalavitz describe. Or discuss how the essays by Hoffman and Szalavitz call Samuelson's argument into question.

9. Investigate workplace literacy programs, using your library and the Internet as well as any other relevant resources available to you, such as local officials who are involved in workplace literacy programs. If possible, interview workers who are enrolled in or have completed such programs for their views about their experiences and about the role of literacy in the workplace. Then write a report for your classmates about your research. In your report, discuss what you learned about workplace literacy programs and draw conclusions about their importance or about problems you see with them.

10. On the basis of the research you did for Question #9 above, write an editorial for your local newspaper in which you express your views about workplace literacy programs. In your editorial, discuss your findings from your research on workplace literacy programs and propose any changes you think are needed in such programs.

CHAPTER 6

The Power of the Written Word

In the opening scene of George Orwell's *1984,* Winston Smith, the novel's main character, slips into an alcove of the main room of his home and secretly writes in his diary. Smith must conceal his writing because, in the totalitarian society in which he lives, such acts of writing, if discovered, could be punished by imprisonment or even execution. In the society that Orwell created in *1984,* the state exercises absolute control over writing and reading—and over all media. Books, newspapers, magazines, and written records of any kind are strictly controlled. Language itself is managed by the state and is the primary tool by which the state maintains its power over its citizens. In this kind of society, Winston Smith's diary is not only illegal; it is also a means of resistance and subversion.

Orwell published his famous novel in 1949. The frightening world he described did not come to pass in 1984 in quite the form he imagined, but his depiction of literacy as a political tool and a potential means to control information, knowledge, and even thought itself is perhaps all the more frightening because it often seems so true to life. Indeed, some critics have pointed out that Orwell based his novel on events that occurred in Russia after the Russian Revolution and the establishment of the Soviet Union. Rigid control of writing and reading and the media was a characteristic of life in the Soviet Union that its critics often decried. But if the Soviet state used literacy as a means of maintaining its power, it surely isn't the only example of such uses of literacy.

Consider, for instance, the press accounts of events that took place in Eastern Europe after the fall of the Berlin Wall in 1989. In the months following the collapse of the Wall, nations in that region, such as Romania and Czechoslovakia, which were formerly within the orbit of the Soviet Union, struggled to overthrow their own totalitarian governments. Often, a focal point in those struggles was control of newspapers as well as television and radio stations, and sometimes gun battles were waged at newspaper offices or television studios. In many such instances, the new government moved quickly to take control of the media, often establishing strict censorship laws. Such blatant state-sponsored censorship is not limited to nations in such dire circumstances, however. Censorship exists in some form in every nation. One often-cited example is Iran, whose monarchy was overthrown in the late 1970's and replaced with an Islamic government headed by the Iranian spiritual leader Ayatollah Khomeini. Khomeini's government and its supporters exercised tight and often brutal control over all media and over printed materials used in schools and other public institutions. The famed journalist Walter Cronkite, in his preface to a special commemorative edition of Orwell's *1984*, described Iran as "Orwellian" and referred to Khomeini as "Big Brother," the name of the totalitarian leader in Orwell's novel. In Cronkite's view, the efforts of Iran's revolutionary government to control the media were the real-life equivalent of the frightening authoritarian rule that Orwell depicted in his novel.

More recently, we have witnessed the ongoing efforts of the People's Republic of China in the wake of the protests at Tiananmen Square in 1994 to suppress the publication of what it considered to be subversive ideas. One of the activities that eventually led to the protests in Tiananmen Square was the posting of political writings by ordinary citizens on a public wall in Beijing. After the bloody suppression of those protests, the Chinese government was quick to remove from the Square what it considered to be treasonous writings and to prevent anyone from posting similar writings in public places. Such governmental efforts to control writing can extend outside national borders as well. Perhaps the most spectacular such example in the late twentieth century was that of writer Salman Rushdie, a British citizen whose novel *The Satanic Verses* was declared blasphemous by Khomeini. Khomeini decreed a *fatwa*, or execution order, against Rushdie in 1989, and for the next decade Rushdie, an internationally acclaimed novelist, lived in secrecy, fearing the assassins who might carry out the *fatwa*. It wasn't until 1998 that leaders of Iran lifted Khomeini's decree. Rushdie's case is a chilling example of the fact that writing can literally be dangerous. And his example is perhaps even more disturbing in view of the dozens of journalists around the world who are assassinated each year for writing stories that one or another political group deems "subversive"—thirty-four such assassinations in 1999 alone, according to the Committee to Protect Journalists.

These and countless similar examples suggest quite dramatically that literacy is a gravely serious political matter. And we need not look outside the United States to find instances of political struggles over writing and reading. If you attended elementary or secondary school in the United States, it's quite possible that you have been directly affected by attempts to censor specific materials in your school. Each year hundreds of attempts to censor books and other kinds of texts or visual materials are mounted in the United States. In 1998 alone, the American Library Association tracked more than five hundred instances of efforts to ban works like Maya Angelou's *I Know Why the Caged Bird Sings* and Mark Twain's *The Adventures of Huckleberry Finn*. It is almost certain that there were many more such efforts that never came to the ALA's attention. Sometimes these efforts are well publicized and lead to public battles that are waged in school board hearings, in direct mail campaigns, and in the media. But often such efforts are less visible, occurring in curriculum committee meetings or school board meetings, where decisions are quietly made about what students should read—and what they shouldn't—and about the writing that students should—or should not—be allowed to do in their classes. In these ways, the writing and reading done in schools is quietly but directly controlled. School administrators also exercise more obvious control over student publications, sometimes censoring articles in the school newspaper or even canceling the publication of student writing altogether. Such censorship efforts are entirely legal: In several landmark decisions in the last three decades, the United States Supreme Court has upheld the right of school administrators to censor student publications. All these efforts suggest the extent to which the reading and writing that you do may be subject to strict control by various authorities.

Why?

"Literacy," writes teacher and critic Elspeth Stuckey, "is an economic and social regulation" (*The Violence of Literacy,* 1991, p. 19). In other words, literacy can be a means of controlling our social and economic lives. Because writing and reading are directly or indirectly involved in just about every significant social or economic activity in which we engage as members of the society we live in, writing and reading are central to how our society functions. Thus, how we read and write and the kinds of reading and writing we do—or are allowed to do—can have a profound impact on that society. Literacy, to a great extent, *shapes* society and, perhaps more important, our roles within it. Think, for example, of the many texts you read and wrote as part of your social studies classes in middle school or high school. Those texts not only provide information about the history of the United States or other nations: they also present images and ideas about what the United States stands for and about who you are as a citizen of the United States. The reading and writing you do in such classes is thus an important part of the complex process by which you come to understand yourself as a citizen and learn the conventional beliefs and behaviors we associate with being Americans. In this sense, literacy directly shapes the role you play in society and your attitudes about society. It is no surprise, then, that great effort is often expended on controlling the writing and reading that students or citizens do.

Obviously, if literacy helps shape our understanding of ourselves and our roles in the society we inhabit, it can also provide access to ideas that question or challenge or even threaten that understanding. You do not have to live in a totalitarian state to have had the experience of gaining a new understanding of yourself or your situation in life through reading or writing. But if that new understanding relates to a situation of power and control, it can itself become a powerful tool for resistance or change. It has been said that when Abraham Lincoln met Harriet Beecher Stowe, the author of the famous novel *Uncle Tom's Cabin,* which depicted the harsh lives of slaves in the American South prior to the Civil War, he said, "So this is the lady who started the war." Whether he spoke those exact words or not, Lincoln's comment highlights the enormous influence that Stowe's book had on American attitudes about slavery. In a sense, the ideas and events about which she wrote shaped the way Americans thought about themselves and thus influenced the history of an entire nation. Perhaps a recognition of that kind of "power of the pen" motivated the slave states to ban literacy among slaves. In his famous autobiography, Frederick Douglass tells the story of how he became literate while he was still a slave. Learning to read, which was a crime for slaves in many states before the Civil War, deeply influenced how Douglass understood his position as a slave and his relationship to his white owners. "The more I read," he wrote, "the more I was led to abhor and detest my enslavers." It isn't hard to see how dangerous such reading could seem from the perspective of the slaveholders, whose power was directly threatened by the spread of the ideas that Douglass encountered in his reading and recorded in his own writing.

The extensive and frightening state-sponsored censorship efforts that we have witnessed in the past hundred years, such as those referred to earlier in the former Soviet Union or in Iran, underscore the power of literacy that Douglass invokes in his compelling autobiography. But stories such as Douglass' also reveal the potential power of literacy to dramatically affect individual lives. Part of what Douglass gained through literacy was not only access to ideas about freedom but also a new perspective on himself as a black man and as a human being. Reading and writing became tools for transforming his understanding of himself and his potential role as a citizen of the United States. After becoming literate, he was no longer just a slave. He could—and did—imagine new roles for himself in the society that enslaved him, and he subsequently struggled to change that society so that those roles could be realized by other black Americans. Writing was, not incidentally, one of the primary tools by which Douglass engaged in that struggle as he worked for the abolition of slavery in the United States. His books and articles became important weapons in the fight for equality for African Americans. If control of literacy was a means by which the governments of the slave states maintained domination over black people, literacy was also a means by which Black Americans—from Douglass to Martin Luther King, Jr., to Malcolm X to Maya Angelou—have resisted and overcome that domination.

The writers in this chapter understand that complex and sometimes paradoxical power of literacy. Several of them tell stories of the crucial role literacy played in shaping their identities as members of a community or culture. These stories reveal the power of literacy—for good or ill—as it emerges in individual lives. But the reading selections also explore the power of literacy in a broader sense. They reveal how literacy was one means by which groups of people exercised domination over others. They reveal, too, that the writing of history itself can be understood as an exercise of power. In Orwell's novel *1984,* the government controls the history books, regularly rewriting them so that they are in accord with the doctrines and ideology that the state wishes to promote. Such blatant state-supported "revisions" of history were known to occur in totalitarian states such as the former Soviet Union, but some critics argue that the same kind of control of history, though perhaps less overt, occurs in democratic nations, including the United States. The intense public debates that occurred in the United States in the 1990's over the national guidelines for teaching history that were released by the U.S. Department of Education remind us that the stories we write about ourselves matter deeply and have political power. In this same vein, the selections in this chapter provide examples of how writing can—intentionally or not—affect what we know and what we believe about ourselves and the society we inhabit—and they help us understand what we mean when we talk about the "power of the pen."

These issues of power and control regarding literacy have become increasingly complicated by the development of new technologies for literacy and communications in the last several decades. Accordingly, this chapter also explores the ways in which emerging digital technologies may be reshaping the proverbial power of the written word. Technologies like email can represent new and potentially revolutionary ways to wield that power. In this sense, such technologies may profoundly change the way we understand and participate in our world. Furthermore, these technologies are challenging our very notions of reading and writing in ways that raise difficult questions about who controls the writing and reading that we can do in the electronic media.

Together, these readings demonstrate some of the many ways in which writing can constitute power. They suggest that literacy is not only a political tool but that it is integral to our political and cultural identities. And they may encourage you to reexamine your sense of the formidable, sometimes frightening and ambiguous, power of literacy in your own life.

From Silence to Words

Writing as Struggle

MIN-ZHAN LU

INTRODUCTION Writers—and especially student writers—often complain about how difficult it can be to write. The late *New York Times* sports columnist Red Smith was quoted as saying that writing is easy: you just open a vein and bleed onto the paper. Smith's sentiment is one that most writers would probably agree with. It describes the *struggle* that writers often seem to engage in as they create a text. It says what writers often seem to feel: that writing is hard work. For scholar and teacher Min-zhan Lu, however, the struggle that is writing involves more than the hard work required to produce an effective text: her struggle with writing was played out in the midst of a much larger political and cultural struggle at a time of enormous change in her native China. Her essay about how she learned to read and write is really a story of the complex and powerful role writing can play in our lives within the context of the societies in which we live.

Lu was a student in China during the 1950's, when the government of Mao Tse-tung solidified its control of that country and established a Marxist system of government. As Lu tells us in her essay, the education she experienced in Chinese schools was shaped by the government's Marxist ideology, which conflicted with the values Lu learned in her parents' household. This conflict was most pronounced in the ways in which she was expected to read and write in school. In telling the story of that conflict and her struggle to overcome it, Lu presents us with a picture of the political and cultural nature of writing and how literacy can be used as a means of cultivating certain values regarding oneself and one's culture. Like all students, Lu often struggled to meet her teachers' expectations, but in her case that struggle challenged not only the ways of writing and reading she learned at home but also her very sense of herself as a member of society. For her, writing in school wasn't just a matter of completing assignments: it was a matter of confronting who she was and how she fit into— or didn't fit into—China's Marxist society. And that could be a potentially dangerous matter.

Lu's story makes it clear that writing and reading were taught in Chinese schools in an overtly political way: literacy was a means of conveying and reinforcing a particular ideology—in this case, a Marxist one. Some education critics argue that the same is also true of literacy education in the United States and in other Western countries whose governments are ostensibly free and democratic. They charge that writing and reading are taught in ways that reinforce a capitalist ideology (rather than a Marxist one). Such arguments suggest that if literacy is indeed political and cultural, it is always so, whether we acknowledge it as such or not. In other words, the ways in which writing and reading are taught in American schools reflect the American political system and American culture just as literacy instruction in Chinese schools reflects the politics and culture of that nation. Indeed, Lu's reference near the end of her essay to her own daughter, who was educated in American schools, suggests that her daughter is experiencing some of the same kinds of conflict between literacy learned at home and literacy learned at school that Lu experienced as a student in Chinese schools. In short, Lu's story suggests that writing is always a political and cultural struggle, even if that struggle is not always obvious.

Min-zhan Lu is an Endowment Professor of the Humanities at Drake University, where she has taught since 1989. She has written widely for professional journals on pedagogy, feminist and postcolonial theory, and the teaching of nonmainstream students, and she is co-author of *Representing the 'Other': Basic Writers and the Teaching of Basic Writing* (1999). Several of her essays have been cited for awards, including the Mina P. Shaughnessy Award from the National Council of Teachers of English. The following essay was originally published in 1987 in *College English*, a professional journal for college teachers of English.

REFLECTING BEFORE READING

1. Much of the story Min-zhan Lu tells in the following essay is set in the People's Republic of China during the Cultural Revolution. At that time, the great Chinese leader Mao Tse-tung ruled China's Marxist political and economic system. As you prepare to read this essay, recall what you know about China's modern history and especially about the Cultural Revolution and Mao Tse-tung's rule. What do you know about the society in which Min-zhan Lu grew up? What do you know about the Cultural Revolution and its effect on Chinese society? As you read, consider how your knowledge (or lack of knowledge) about China's history might influence the way you respond to Lu's story.

2. In the title of her essay and in the essay itself, Min-zhan Lu describes writing as "struggle." What does that description mean to you? What do you think she wishes to convey to her readers through her use of this term? As you prepare to read her essay, consider whether you view writing as a struggle, and if so, what kind of struggle it is for you. As you read, be aware of how Lu defines *struggle* in this context and whether her understanding of writing as struggle matches your own.

Imagine that you enter a parlor. You come late. When you arrive, others have long preceded you, and they are engaged in a heated discussion. . . . You listen for a while, until you decide that you have caught the tenor of the argument; then you put in your oar. Someone answers; you answer him; another comes to your defense; another aligns himself against you, to either the embarrassment or gratification of your opponent, depending upon the quality of your ally's assistance. However, the discussion is interminable. The hour grows late, you must depart. And you do depart, with the discussion still vigorously in progress.

—*Kenneth Burke,* The Philosophy of Literary Form

Men are not built in silence, but in word, in work, in action-reflection.

—*Paulo Freire,* Pedagogy of the Oppressed

M y mother withdrew into silence two months before she died. A few nights before she fell silent, she told me she regretted the way she had raised me and my sisters. I knew she was referring to the way we had been brought up in the midst of two conflicting worlds—the world of home, dominated by the ideology of the Western humanistic tradition, and the world of a society dominated by Mao Tsetung's Marxism. My mother had devoted her life to our education, an education she knew had made us suffer political persecution during the Cultural Revolution. I wanted to find a way to convince her that, in spite of the persecution, I had benefited from the education she had worked so hard to give me. But I was silent. My understanding of my education was so dominated by memories of confusion and frustration that I was unable to reflect on what I could have gained from it.

This paper is my attempt to fill up that silence with words, words I didn't have then, words that I have since come to by reflecting on my earlier experience as a student in China and on my recent experience as a composition teacher in the United States. For in spite of the frustration and confusion I experienced growing up caught between two conflicting worlds, the conflict ultimately helped me to grow as a reader and writer. Constantly having to switch back and forth between the discourse of home and that of school made me sensitive and self-conscious about the struggle I experienced every time I tried to read, write, or think in either discourse. Eventually, it led me to search for constructive uses for such struggle.

From early childhood, I had identified the differences between home and the outside world by the different languages I used in each. My parents had wanted my sisters and me to get the best education they could conceive of—Cambridge. They had hired a live-in tutor, a Scot, to make us bilingual. I learned to speak English with my parents, my tutor, and my sisters. I was allowed to speak Shanghai dialect only with the servants. When I was four (the year after the Communist Revolution of 1949), my parents sent me to a local private school where I learned to speak, read, and write in a new language—Standard Chinese, the official written language of New China.

In those days I moved from home to school, from English to Standard Chinese to Shanghai dialect, with no apparent friction. I spoke each language with those who spoke the language. All seemed quite "natural"—servants spoke only Shanghai dialect because they were servants; teachers spoke Standard Chinese because they were teachers; languages had different words because they were different languages. I thought of English as my family language, comparable to the many strange dialects I didn't speak but had often heard some of my classmates speak with their families. While I was happy to have a special family language, until second grade I didn't feel that my family language was any different than some of my classmates' family dialects.

My second grade homeroom teacher was a young graduate from a missionary school. When she found out I spoke English, she began to practice her English on me. One day she used English when asking me to run an errand for her. As I turned to close the door behind me, I noticed the puzzled faces of my classmates. I had the same sensation I had often experienced when some stranger in a crowd would turn on hearing me speak English. I was more intensely pleased on this occasion, however, because suddenly I felt that my family language had been singled out from the family languages of my classmates. Since we were not allowed to speak any dialect other than Standard Chinese in the classroom, having my teacher speak English to me in class made English an official language of the classroom. I began to take pride in my ability to speak it.

This incident confirmed in my mind what my parents had always told me about the importance of English to one's life. Time and again they had told me of how my paternal grandfather, who was well versed in classic Chinese, kept losing good-paying jobs because he couldn't speak English. My grandmother reminisced constantly about how she had slaved and saved to send my father to a first-rate missionary school. And we were made to understand that it was my father's fluent English that had opened the door to his success. Even though my family had always stressed the importance of English for my future, I used to complain bitterly about the extra English lessons we had to take after school. It was only after my homeroom teacher had "sanctified" English that I began to connect English with my education. I became a much more eager student in my tutorials.

What I learned from my tutorials seemed to enhance and reinforce what I was learning in my classroom. In those days each word had one meaning. One day I would be making a sentence at school: "The national flag of China is red." The next day I would recite at home, "My love is like a red, red rose." There seemed to be an agreement between the Chinese "red" and the English "red," and both corresponded to the patch of color printed next to the word. "Love" was my love for my mother at home and my love for my "motherland" at school; both "loves" meant how I felt about my mother. Having two loads of homework forced me to develop a quick memory for words and a sensitivity to form and style. What I learned in one language carried over to the other. I made sentences such as, "I saw a red, red rose among the green leaves," with both the English lyric and the classic Chinese lyric—red flower among green leaves—running through my mind, and I was praised by both teacher and tutor for being a good student.

Although my elementary schooling took place during the fifties, I was almost oblivious to the great political and social changes happening around me. Years later, I read in my history and political philosophy textbooks that the fifties were a time when "China was making a transition from a semi-feudal, semi-capitalist, and semi-colonial country into a socialist country," a period in which "the Proletarians were breaking into the educational territory dominated by Bourgeois Intellectuals." While people all over the country were being officially classified into Proletarians, Petty-bourgeois, National-bourgeois, Poor-peasants, and Intellectuals, and were trying to adjust to their new social identities, my parents were allowed to continue the upper middle-class life they had established before the 1949 Revolution because of my father's affiliation with British firms. I had always felt that my family was different from the families of my classmates, but I didn't perceive society's view of my family until the summer vacation before I entered high school.

First, my aunt was caught by her colleagues talking to her husband over the phone in English. Because of it, she was criticized and almost labeled a Rightist. (This was the year of the Anti-Rightist movement, a movement in which the Intellectuals became the target of the "socialist class-struggle.") I had heard others telling my mother that she was foolish to teach us English when Russian had replaced English as the "official" foreign language. I had also learned at school that the American and British Imperialists were the arch-enemies of New China. Yet I had made no connection between the arch-enemies and the English our family spoke. What happened to my aunt forced the connection on me. I began to see my parents' choice of a family language as an anti-Revolutionary act and was alarmed that I had participated in such an act. From then on, I took care not to use English outside home and to conceal my knowledge of English from my new classmates.

Certain words began to play important roles in my new life at the junior high. On the first day of school, we were handed forms to fill out with our parents' class, job, and income. Being one of the few people not employed by the government, my father had never been officially classified. Since he was a medical doctor, he told me to put him down as an Intellectual. My homeroom teacher called me into the office a couple of days afterwards and told me that my father couldn't be an Intellectual if his income far exceeded that of a Capitalist. He also told me that since my father worked for Foreign Imperialists, my father should be classified as an Imperialist Lackey. The teacher looked nonplussed when I told him that my father couldn't be an Imperialist Lackey because he was a medical doctor. But I could tell from the way he took notes on my form that my father's job had put me in an unfavorable position in his eyes.

The Standard Chinese term "class" was not a new word for me. Since first grade, I had been taught sentences such as, "The Working class are the masters of New China." I had always known that it was good to be a worker, but until then, I had never felt threatened for not being one. That fall, "class" began to take on a new meaning for me. I noticed a group of Working-class students and teachers at school. I was made to understand that because of my class background, I was excluded from that group.

Another word that became important was "consciousness." One of the slogans posted in the school building read, "Turn our students into future Proletarians with socialist consciousness and education!" For several weeks we studied this slogan in our political philosophy course, a subject I had never had in elementary school. I still remember the definition of "socialist consciousness" that we were repeatedly tested on through the years: "Socialist consciousness is a person's political soul. It is the consciousness of the Proletarians represented by Marxist Mao Tse-tung thought. It takes expression in one's action, language, and lifestyle. It is the task of every Chinese student to grow up into a Proletarian with a socialist consciousness so that he can serve the people and the motherland." To make the abstract concept accessible to us, our teacher pointed out that the immediate task for students from Working-class families was to strengthen their socialist consciousnesses. For those of us who were from other class backgrounds, the task was to turn ourselves into Workers with socialist consciousnesses. The teacher never explained exactly how we were supposed to "turn" into Workers. Instead, we were given samples of the ritualistic annual plans we had to write at the beginning of each term. In these plans, we performed "self-criticism" on our consciousnesses and made vows to turn ourselves into Workers with socialist consciousnesses. The teacher's division between those who did and those who didn't have a socialist consciousness led me to reify the notion of "consciousness" into a thing one possesses. I equated this intangible "thing" with a concrete way of dressing, speaking, and writing. For instance, I never doubted that my political philosophy teacher had a socialist consciousness because she was from a steelworker's family (she announced this the first day of class) and was a Party member who wore grey cadre suits and talked like a philosophy textbook. I noticed other things about her. She had beautiful eyes and spoke Standard Chinese with such a pure accent that I thought she should be a film star. But I was embarrassed that I had noticed things that ought not to have been associated with her. I blamed my observation on my Bourgeois consciousness.

At the same time, the way reading and writing were taught through memorization and imitation also encouraged me to reduce concepts and ideas to simple definitions. In literature and political philosophy classes, we were taught a large number of quotations from Marx, Lenin, and Mao Tse-tung. Each concept that appeared in these quotations came with a definition. We were required to memorize the definitions of the words along with the quotations. Every time I memorized a definition, I felt I had learned a word: "The national red flag symbolizes the blood shed by Revolutionary ancestors for our socialist cause"; "New China rises like a red sun over the eastern horizon." As I memorized these sentences, I reduced their metaphors to dictionary meanings: "red" meant "Revolution" and "red sun" meant "New China" in the "language" of the Working class. I learned mechanically but eagerly. I soon became quite fluent in this new language.

As school began to define me as a political subject, my parents tried to build up my resistance to the "communist poisoning" by exposing me to the "great books"—novels by Charles Dickens, Nathaniel Hawthorne, Emily Brontë, Jane Austen, and writers from around the turn of the century. My parents implied that these writers represented how I, their child, should read and write. My parents replaced the word "Bourgeois" with the word "cultured." They reminded me that I was in school only to learn math and science. I needed to pass the other courses to stay in school, but I was not to let the "Red doctrines" corrupt my mind. Gone were the days when I could innocently write. "I saw the red, red rose among the green leaves," collapsing, as I did, English and Chinese cultural traditions. "Red" came to mean Revolution at school, "the Commies" at home, and adultery in *The Scarlet Letter.* Since I took these symbols and metaphors as meanings natural to people of the same class, I abandoned my earlier definitions of English and Standard Chinese as the language of home and the language of school. I now defined English as the language of the Bourgeois and Standard Chinese as the language of the Working class. I thought of the language of the Working class as someone else's language and the language of the Bourgeois as my language. But I also believed that, although the language of the Bourgeois was my real language, I could and would adopt the language of the Working class when I was at school. I began to put on and take off my Working class language in the same way I put on and took off my school clothes to avoid being criticized for wearing Bourgeois clothes.

In my literature classes, I learned the Working-class formula for reading. Each work in the textbook had a short "Author's Biography": "X X X, born in 19— in the province of X X, is from a Worker's family. He joined the Revolution in 19—. He is a Revolutionary realist with a passionate love for the Party and Chinese Revolution. His work expresses the thoughts and emotions of the masses and sings praise to the prosperous socialist construction on all fronts of China." The teacher used the "Author's Biography" as a yardstick to measure the texts. We were taught to locate details in the texts that illustrated these summaries, such as words that expressed Workers' thoughts and emotions or events that illustrated the Workers' lives.

I learned a formula for Working-class writing in the composition classes. We were given sample essays and told to imitate them. The theme was always about how the collective taught the individual a lesson. I would write papers about labor-learning experiences or school-cleaning days, depending on the occasion of the collective activity closest to the assignment. To make each paper look different, I dressed it up with details about the date, the weather, the environment, or the appearance of the Master-worker who had taught me "the lesson." But as I became more and more fluent in the generic voice of the Working-class Student, I also became more and more self-conscious about the language we used at home.

For instance, in senior high we began to have English classes ("to study English for the Revolution," as the slogan on the cover of the textbook said), and I was given my first Chinese-English dictionary. There I discovered the English version of the term "class-struggle." (The Chinese characters for a school "class" and for a social "class" are different.) I had often used the English word "class" at home in sentences such as, "So and so has class," but I had not connected this sense of "class" with "class-struggle." Once the connection was made, I heard a second layer of meaning every time someone at home said a person had "class." The expression began to mean the person had the style and sophistication characteristic of the Bourgeoisie. The word lost its innocence. I was uneasy about hearing that second layer of meaning because I was sure my parents did not hear the word that way. I felt that therefore I should not be hearing it that way either. Hearing the second layer of meaning made me wonder if I was losing my English.

My suspicion deepened when I noticed myself unconsciously merging and switching between the "reading" of home and the "reading" of school. Once I had to write a report on *The Revolutionary Family,* a book about an illiterate woman's awakening and growth as a Revolutionary through the deaths of her husband and all her children for the cause of the Revolution. In one scene the woman deliberated over whether or not she should encourage her youngest son to join the Revolution. Her memory of her husband's death made her afraid to encourage her son. Yet she also remembered her earlier married life and the first time her husband tried to explain the meaning of the Revolution to her. These memories made her feel she should encourage her son to continue the cause his father had begun.

I was moved by this scene. "Moved" was a word my mother and sisters used a lot when we discussed books. Our favorite moments in novels were moments of what I would now call internal conflict, moments which we said "moved" us. I remember that we were "moved" by Jane Eyre when she was torn between her sense of ethics, which compelled her to leave the man she loved, and her impulse to stay with the only man who had ever loved her. We were also moved by Agnes in *David Copperfield* because of the way she restrained her love for David so that he could live happily with the woman he loved. My standard method of doing a book report was to model it on the review by the Publishing Bureau and to dress it up with detailed quotations from the book. The review of *The Revolutionary Family* emphasized the woman's Revolutionary spirit. I decided to use the scene that had moved me to illustrate this point. I wrote the report the night before it was due. When I had finished, I realized I couldn't possibly hand it in.

Instead of illustrating her Revolutionary spirit, I had dwelled on her internal conflict, which could be seen as a moment of weak sentimentality that I should never
have emphasized in a Revolutionary heroine. I wrote another report, taking care
to illustrate the grandeur of her Revolutionary spirit by expanding on a quotation
in which she decided that if the life of her son could change the lives of millions
of sons, she should not begrudge his life for the cause of Revolution. I handed in
my second version but kept the first in my desk.

I never showed it to anyone. I could never show it to people outside my family,
because it had deviated so much from the reading enacted by the jacket review.
Neither could I show it to my mother or sisters, because I was ashamed to have been
so moved by such a "Revolutionary" book. My parents would have been shocked to
learn that I could like such a book in the same way they liked Dickens. Writing this
book report increased my fear that I was losing the command over both the "language of home" and the "language of school" that I had worked so hard to gain. I
tried to remind myself that, if I could still tell when my reading or writing sounded
incorrect, then I had retained my command over both languages. Yet I could no
longer be confident of my command over either language because I had discovered
that when I was not careful—or even when I was—my reading and writing often surprised me with its impurity. To prevent such impurity, I became very suspicious of
my thoughts when I read or wrote. I was always asking myself why I was using this
word, how I was using it, always afraid that I wasn't reading or writing correctly.
What confused and frustrated me most was that I could not figure out why I was no
longer able to read or write correctly without such painful deliberation.

I continued to read only because reading allowed me to keep my thoughts and
confusion private. I hoped that somehow, if I watched myself carefully, I would figure
out from the way I read whether I had really mastered the "languages." But writing
became a dreadful chore. When I tried to keep a diary, I was so afraid that the voice
of school might slip in that I could only list my daily activities. When I wrote for
school, I worried that my Bourgeois sensibilities would betray me.

The more suspicious I became about the way I read and wrote, the more guilty
I felt for losing the spontaneity with which I had learned to "use" these "languages."
Writing the book report made me feel that my reading and writing in the "language"
of either home or school could not be free of the interference of the other. But I was
unable to acknowledge, grasp, or grapple with what I was experiencing, for both my
parents and my teachers had suggested that, if I were a good student, such interference would and should not take place. I assumed that once I had "acquired" a discourse, I could simply switch it on and off every time I read and wrote as I would
some electronic tool. Furthermore, I expected my readings and writings to come out
in their correct forms whenever I switched the proper discourse on. I still regarded
the discourse of home as natural and the discourse of school alien, but I never had
doubted before that I could acquire both and switch them on and off according to the
occasion.

When my experience in writing conflicted with what I thought should happen
when I used each discourse, I rejected my experience because it contradicted what
my parents and teachers had taught me. I shied away from writing to avoid what I
assumed I should not experience. But trying to avoid what should not happen did not
keep it from recurring whenever I had to write. Eventually my confusion and frustration over these recurring experiences compelled me to search for an explanation:

how and why had I failed to learn what my parents and teachers had worked so hard to teach me?

I now think of the internal scene for my reading and writing about *The Revolutionary Family* as a heated discussion between myself, the voices of home, and those of school. The review on the back of the book, the sample student papers I came across in my composition classes, my philosophy teacher—these I heard as voices of one group. My parents and my home readings were the voices of an opposing group. But the conversation between these opposing voices in the internal scene of my writing was not as polite and respectful as the parlor scene Kenneth Burke has portrayed (see epigraph). Rather, these voices struggled to dominate the discussion, constantly incorporating, dismissing, or suppressing the arguments of each other, like the battles between the hegemonic and counterhegemonic forces described in Raymond Williams' *Marxism and Literature* (108–14).

When I read *The Revolutionary Family* and wrote the first version of my report, I began with a quotation from the review. The voices of both home and school answered, clamoring to be heard. I tried to listen to one group and turn a deaf ear to the other. Both persisted. I negotiated my way through these conflicting voices, now agreeing with one, now agreeing with the other. I formed a reading out of my interaction with both. Yet I was afraid to have done so because both home and school had implied that I should speak in unison with only one of these groups and stand away from the discussion rather than participate in it.

My teachers and parents had persistently called my attention to the intensity of the discussion taking place on the external social scene. The story of my grandfather's failure and my father's success had from my early childhood made me aware of the conflict between Western and traditional Chinese cultures. My political education at school added another dimension to the conflict: the war of Marxist-Maoism against them both. Yet when my parents and teachers called my attention to the conflict, they stressed the anxiety of having to live through China's transformation from a semi-feudal, semi-capitalist, and semi-colonial society to a socialist one. Acquiring the discourse of the dominant group was, to them, a means of seeking alliance with that group and thus of surviving the whirlpool of cultural currents around them. As a result, they modeled their pedagogical practices on this utilitarian view of language. Being the eager student, I adopted this view of language as a tool for survival. It came to dominate my understanding of the discussion on the social and historical scene and to restrict my ability to participate in that discussion.

To begin with, the metaphor of language as a tool for survival led me to be passive in my use of discourse, to be a bystander in the discussion. In Burke's "parlor," everyone is involved in the discussion. As it goes on through history, what we call "communal discourses"—arguments specific to particular political, social, economic, ethnic, sexual, and family groups—form, re-form and transform. To use a discourse in such a scene is to participate in the argument and to contribute to the formation of the discourse. But when I was growing up, I could not take on the burden of such an active role in the discussion. For both home and school presented the existent conventions of the discourse each taught me as absolute laws for my action. They turned verbal action into a tool, a set of conventions produced and shaped prior to and outside of my own verbal acts. Because I saw language as a tool, I separated the process of producing the tool from the process of using it. The tool was made by someone else and was then acquired and used by me. How the others made it before

I acquired it determined and guaranteed what it produced when I used it. I imagined that the more experienced and powerful members of the community were the ones responsible for making the tool. They were the ones who participated in the discussion and fought with opponents. When I used what they made, their labor and accomplishments would ensure the quality of my reading and writing. By using it, I could survive the heated discussion. When my immediate experience in writing the book report suggested that knowing the conventions of school did not guarantee the form and content of my report, when it suggested that I had to write the report with the work and responsibility I had assigned to those who wrote book reviews in the Publishing Bureau, I thought I had lost the tool I had earlier acquired.

Another reason I could not take up an active role in the argument was that my parents and teachers contrived to provide a scene free of conflict for practicing my various languages. It was as if their experience had made them aware of the conflict between their discourse and other discourses and of the struggle involved in reproducing the conventions of any discourse on a scene where more than one discourse exists. They seemed convinced that such conflict and struggle would overwhelm someone still learning the discourse. Home and school each contrived a purified space where only one discourse was spoken and heard. In their choice of textbooks, in the way they spoke, and in the way they required me to speak, each jealously silenced any voice that threatened to break the unison of the scene. The homogeneity of home and of school implied that only one discourse could and should be relevant in each place. It led me to believe I should leave behind, turn a deaf ear to, or forget the discourse of the other when I crossed the boundary dividing them. I expected myself to set down one discourse whenever I took up another just as I would take off or put on a particular set of clothes for school or home.

Despite my parents' and teachers' attempts to keep home and school discrete, the internal conflict between the two discourses continued whenever I read or wrote. Although I tried to suppress the voice of one discourse in the name of the other, having to speak aloud in the voice I had just silenced each time I crossed the boundary kept both voices active in my mind. Every "I think . . ." from the voice of home or school brought forth a "However . . ." or a "But . . ." from the voice of the opponents. To identify with the voice of home or school, I had to negotiate through the conflicting voices of both by restating, taking back, qualifying my thoughts. I was unconsciously doing so when I did my book report. But I could not use the interaction comfortably and constructively. Both my parents and my teachers had implied that my job was to prevent that interaction from happening. My sense of having failed to accomplish what they had taught silenced me.

To use the interaction between the discourses of home and school constructively, I would have to have seen reading or writing as a process in which I worked my way towards a stance through a dialectical process of identification and division. To identify with an ally, I would have to have grasped the distance between where he or she stood and where I was positioning myself. In taking a stance against an opponent, I would have to have grasped where my stance identified with the stance of my allies. Teetering along the "wavering line of pressure and counter-pressure" from both allies and opponents, I might have worked my way towards a stance of my own (Burke, *A Rhetoric of Motives* 23). Moreover, I would have to have understood that the voices in my mind, like the participants in the parlor scene, were in constant flux. As I came into contact with new and different groups of people or read different books, voices entered and left. Each time I read or wrote, the stance I negotiated out of these voices would always be at some distance from the stances I worked out in my previous and my later readings or writings.

I could not conceive such a form of action for myself because I saw reading and writing as an expression of an established stance. In delineating the conventions of a discourse, my parents and teachers had synthesized the stance they saw as typical for a representative member of the community. Burke calls this the stance of a "god" or the "prototype"; Williams calls it the "official" or "possible" stance of the community. Through the metaphor of the survival tool, my parents and teachers had led me to assume I could automatically reproduce the official stance of the discourse I used. Therefore, when I did my book report on *The Revolutionary Family,* I expected my knowledge of the official stance set by the book review to ensure the actual stance of my report. As it happened, I began by trying to take the official stance of the review. Other voices interrupted. I answered back. In the process, I worked out a stance approximate but not identical to the official stance I began with. Yet the experience of having to labor to realize my knowledge of the official stance or to prevent myself from wandering away from it frustrated and confused me. For even though I had been actually reading and writing in a Burkean scene, I was afraid to participate actively in the discussion. I assumed it was my role to survive by staying out of it.

Not long ago, my daughter told me that it bothered her to hear her friend "talk wrong." Having come to the United States from China with little English, my daughter has become sensitive to the way English, as spoken by her teachers, operates. As a result, she has amazed her teachers with her success in picking up the language and in adapting to life at school. Her concern to speak the English taught in the classroom "correctly" makes her uncomfortable when she hears people using "ain't" or double negatives, which her teacher considers "improper." I see in her the me that had eagerly learned and used the discourse of the Working class at school. Yet while I was torn between the two conflicting worlds of school and home, she moves with seeming ease from the conversations she hears over the dinner table to her teacher's words in the classroom. My husband and I are proud of the good work she does at school. We are glad she is spared the kinds of conflict between home and school I experienced at her age. Yet as we watch her becoming more and more fluent in the language of the classroom, we wonder if, by enabling her to "survive" school, her very fluency will silence her when the scene of her reading and writing expands beyond that of the composition classroom.

For when I listen to my daughter, to students, and to some composition teachers talking about the teaching and learning of writing, I am often alarmed by the degree to which the metaphor of a survival tool dominates their understanding of language as it once dominated my own. I am especially concerned with the way some composition classes focus on turning the classroom into a monological scene for the students' reading and writing. Most of our students live in a world similar to my daughter's, somewhere between the purified world of the classroom and the complex world of my adolescence. When composition classes encourage these students to ignore those voices that seem irrelevant to the purified world of the classroom, most students are often able to do so without much struggle. Some of them are so adept at doing it that the whole process has for them become automatic.

However, beyond the classroom and beyond the limited range of these students' immediate lives lies a much more complex and dynamic social and historical scene. To help these students become actors in such a scene, perhaps we need to call their attention to voices that may seem irrelevant to the discourse we teach rather than encourage them to shut them out. For example, we might intentionally complicate the classroom scene by bringing into it discourses that stand at varying distances from the one we teach. We might encourage students to explore ways of practicing the conventions of the discourse they are learning by negotiating through these conflicting voices. We could also encourage them to see themselves as responsible for forming or transforming as well as preserving the discourse they are learning.

As I think about what we might do to complicate the external and internal scenes of our students' writing, I hear my parents and teachers saying: "Not now. Keep them from the wrangle of the marketplace until they have acquired the discourse and are skilled at using it." And I answer: "Don't teach them to 'survive' the whirlpool of crosscurrents by avoiding it. Use the classroom to moderate the currents. Moderate the currents, but teach them from the beginning to struggle." When I think of the ways in which the teaching of reading and writing as classroom activities can frustrate the development of students, I am almost grateful for the overwhelming complexity of the circumstances in which I grew up. For it was this complexity that kept me from losing sight of the effort and choice involved in reading or writing with and through a discourse.

Works Cited

Burke, Kenneth. *The Philosophy of Literary Form: Studies in Symbolic Action.* 2nd ed. Baton Rouge: Louisiana State UP, 1967.

———. *A Rhetoric of Motives.* Berkeley: U of California P, 1969.

Freire, Paulo. *Pedagogy of the Oppressed.* Trans. M. B. Ramos. New York: Continuum, 1970.

Williams, Raymond. *Marxism and Literature.* New York: Oxford UP, 1977.

REFLECTING ON THE READING

1. What does Lu tell us is the reason that she is writing this essay? What is the *struggle* she associates with her own writing about her life? Why has she been silent until now?

2. At several points in this essay (beginning with the second paragraph), Lu refers to the "discourse of home and that of school." What does she mean by the *discourse* of home and the *discourse* of school? What are the differences between these two discourses, as Lu describes them? In what sense does she "switch back and forth" between them, as she writes? How does this "switching" become a problem for her?

3. What kind of family background does Lu describe? In what ways does her family background become a problem for her in Communist China? How is language, especially English, related to those problems? What might her situation

suggest about the relationship between language and identity? About the political nature of language and literacy?

4. What particular words become important ones for Lu as she grows up in Communist China? Why are these words important ones? What might her experiences with such words tell us about the role of language in a culture and in shaping one's sense of identity as a member of that culture?

5. In what ways does school help define Lu as a "political subject"? How are reading and writing taught in the school she attends, as she describes them? How does her education compare with what she is taught at home? What strategies does Lu develop to deal with the differences between her learning at home and at school? Do you think *all* students develop such strategies, even in less dramatic circumstances than what Lu experienced? Explain.

6. At one point in her essay, Lu writes that her reading and writing often surprise her with "its impurity." What does she mean by that term in this instance? Why is the "impurity" of her writing a problem for her at that time in her life? In what ways does this problem make writing a "dreadful chore" for her? What does this problem suggest about the political nature of writing and reading?

7. Why is the writing of a book report on *The Revolutionary Family* such a difficult yet important event for Lu? What does she believe it reveals about the conflict she is experiencing between home and school? What two views of language does Lu believe are at the heart of that conflict? What does Lu learn about writing and reading—and *discourse*—through this experience?

8. Why is Lu concerned about the idea of writing as a "survival tool" when it comes to the teaching of composition? How does she believe her own experiences challenge that idea about writing? What alternative to this view of writing does she suggest? Do you think her concerns are justified, based on her story? Why or why not?

9. What does the experience of Lu's daughter suggest about the nature of schooling and specifically the teaching of literacy? In what ways are Lu's experiences and her daughter's different? In what ways are they similar? What might their experiences suggest about literacy?

Examining Rhetorical Strategies

1. Evaluate Lu's voice in this essay. How does she present herself as a writer and a person in this essay? How would you describe the identity or persona that she creates in this essay? Do you find her voice a credible one in this essay? Why or why not? Are you sympathetic to her? What might your answer to that question suggest about you as a reader?

2. How does Lu characterize the Chinese Communists and the Communist system under which she grew up? Do you think she tries to present an objective view of the Communists, or does she wish to present a more overtly critical or sympathetic one? Why? How does her characterization of the Communists fit in with

what you see as her main purpose in this essay? Explain, citing specific passages from the text to support your answer.

3. This essay was originally published in a professional academic journal intended for college teachers of English. In what ways do you think Lu addresses readers of such a journal? What assumptions does she make about them in terms of their knowledge of and interest in language, culture, politics, and writing? Cite specific passages from her essay to support your answer. Do you think Lu's essay would be appropriate for a less-specialized and more-general audience—for example, for readers of a large-circulation general interest newsmagazine or newspaper such as the *New York Times?* Explain.

4. Assess Lu's use of anecdotes to tell her story and to support her points about the political role of writing and reading in her life. What kinds of anecdotes does she include in her essay? What picture of writing and reading do these anecdotes provide? What do they reveal about Lu's own beliefs about writing and reading and its political uses? Do you find these anecdotes effective? Why or why not? What might your reaction to them indicate about your own attitudes toward writing and reading?

5. Examine how Lu "reads" her own experiences as a student in Communist China. In discussing those experiences, and especially the experience of writing the report about *The Revolutionary Family,* Lu draws on the theoretical ideas of Kenneth Burke to analyze and explain the difficulties she had in completing her school writing and reading assignments. How effectively does she explain her difficulties, in your view? How do Burke's ideas help her explain her own experiences with writing and reading? What advantages do you think Lu can gain by referring to Burke's theories? How might such references affect her original audience for this essay? How did it affect you?

6. What do you think Lu accomplishes with her reference to her daughter near the end of her essay? What key ideas do you think she emphasizes by discussing her daughter's situation in American schools? What might that brief discussion of her daughter reveal about Lu as a person, a writer, and a scholar? Do you think she wishes to reveal these things? Explain. What effect did her reference to her daughter have on you as a reader? Do you think Lu intended to provoke such an effect in her readers? Why or why not?

Engaging the Issues

1. Write an essay for an audience of your classmates in which you describe an especially difficult experience you had as a reader or a writer. The experience you describe may be related to school or may have occurred in some other setting. In your essay, tell the story of that experience in a way that will enable your readers to understand why the writing or reading was so difficult for you in that instance.

2. In a group of your classmates, share the essays you wrote for Question #1 above. Compare the experiences each of you chose to write about, and try to identify similarities and differences in those experiences. What was the source

of difficulty in writing or reading that each of you experienced? Was that difficulty connected to "language" in the way that Lu's was? Was it related to your cultural background in any way? What might your collective experiences suggest about the nature of writing and reading and about the role of literacy in your life?

3. Select one of the scenes in Lu's essay in which she tells one of her experiences with writing and reading as a student in China or as a parent in the United States, and examine that scene in terms of what it reveals about Lu as a reader and a writer and the ways in which writing and reading figure into her life. Write an analysis for an audience of your classmates in which you explain the scene and discuss the way Lu uses that scene to reveal the political nature of writing and reading as she experiences it in her life. In your analysis, draw conclusions about the effectiveness of the scene in conveying Lu's ideas about writing as "struggle."

4. Write an analysis of the essay you wrote for Question #1 above in which you try to explain the experience you describe in that essay, as Lu does in her essay. What accounts for the difficulties with writing or reading that you experienced? What might your experience suggest about literacy and its importance in your life?

5. Using your library, the World Wide Web, or any other appropriate resource, find out more about Kenneth Burke and his theories. If possible, check out some of his books from your library and locate some articles that explain his ideas. What is Burke's view of language and literacy? How might his views explain some of the complexities of literacy? Why is he considered an important theorist?

   Now, write a report for your classmates about Burke's ideas regarding language and literacy. In your report, explain Burke's ideas as clearly as you can and provide your readers with a sense of Burke's importance as a theorist.

   Alternatively, using what you've learned from your research on Burke, write an analysis of the essay you wrote for Question #1 above. In your analysis, apply Burke's ideas to your own experience of difficulty with writing and reading in order to explain that experience, much as Lu does in her essay.

6. Lu's essay reveals that people learn to read and write in ways that reflect the cultural and political circumstances in which they live. Using your library, the World Wide Web, or any other resources available to you, investigate the cultural aspects of literacy. In what ways are reading and writing linked to one's cultural background? How might the teaching of writing and reading relate to the political circumstances under which one lives? Try to find out what researchers and scholars have learned about the cultural nature of literacy and about the difficulties of learning to write and read in a culture different from the one into which a person was born. Then write a report for your classmates based on your research.

7. Visit a writing center, literacy center, or similar service on your campus or in your community where people from other countries go for help with their reading and writing. Try to arrange to talk with some of those people about the difficulties they experience with their writing and reading. What common

difficulties do they seem to have? What do they do to overcome those difficulties? In what ways might their difficulties be connected to the specific culture from which they come?

Now write a report for your classmates on what you learned from your visits to the writing or literacy center. In your report, describe the center you visited and the people to which you spoke. Describe as well the kinds of writing and reading difficulties they experience. Draw conclusions about the relationship of literacy to one's cultural background.

8. Based on your research for Question #7 above, construct a site on the World Wide Web for readers interested in learning more about the connections between literacy and culture. Include links to other Web sites that you find useful. Be sure to identify the purpose of your site.

Nobody Mean More to Me Than You and the Future Life of Willie Jordan

JUNE JORDAN

INTRODUCTION   Is the old adage "The pen is mightier than the sword" true? If so, is it true for everyone? In other words, does the power of writing extend equally to all people, no matter what the circumstances in which they are writing? Or can the "pen" overcome the "sword" only for certain groups of people in certain situations? In a sense, teacher and writer June Jordan asks these questions, but she casts them in a particular light: She wants to ask what role race might play when one takes up the pen against the sword.

History provides us many examples of the power of the pen—or the press. One of the most spectacular is Thomas Paine's *Common Sense*. Paine, an American colonist who supported the independence of the thirteen American colonies from England, published *Common Sense* early in 1776, approximately six months before the Declaration of Independence was adopted by representatives of the colonies. In that pamphlet, Paine expounded his philosophical principles for American independence from England. His ideas struck a chord with American readers at an uncertain and turbulent time. Within a few months *Common Sense* sold 120,000 copies at a time when the population of the colonies numbered about 2.5 million people. (Some estimates place total sales of the pamphlet at 500,000.) More important, *Common Sense* was credited with helping establish a consensus among the often fractious colonists for a declaration of freedom from England. It was also widely cited among supporters of the French Revolution two decades later. In short, Paine's brief published statement of his principles of freedom can be said to have helped shape the course of history by influencing the ideas of those fighting oppression—a dramatic example of the power of the pen.

June Jordan's essay offers a less-influential but no less-dramatic example of the efforts of a group of people to use writing in their own search for justice against oppression. In her essay, she tells the story of her students' attempts to help publicize an apparent case of police brutality against a Black man. For Jordan's students at the State University of New York at Stony Brook, one of whom was the brother of the man who was killed by the police, the incident was a reflection of the oppressive conditions in which they lived. They used her English class as an opportunity to fight those conditions. But the ending to their story was not the victorious ending of Thomas Paine's story. In the case of Jordan's students, writing did not seem to bring them the power to overcome injustice that Paine's writing seemed to have.

In telling this story, Jordan thus complicates the picture of the power of the pen that Thomas Paine's story describes. Significantly, Jordan and most of her students are Black, and they decide to emphasize that fact in the letters they write about the killing of Reggie Jordan, the man who was shot by the police. That decision has important—and dismaying—consequences in their quest for justice. Jordan's essay also raises difficult questions about the extent to which sociocultural factors such as race can enhance or limit the power a writer can enjoy. Moreover, Jordan highlights the way in which nonmainstream versions of Standard English, such as Black English, can further disempower writers and speakers who may already lack power. In this way Jordan encourages us to reconsider our attitudes about "standard" language and suggests that the conventional wisdom about the power of the pen may be too simplistic to account for the complex ways in which literacy works in our world.

June Jordan is a professor of African American studies at the University of California at Berkeley. She is a widely acclaimed poet and essayist and is the recipient of many prestigious awards, including the Lila Wallace Reader's Digest Writers Award and the PEN Center USA West Freedom to Write Award. Among her many books are *June Jordan's Poetry for the People: A Revolutionary Blueprint* (1995), *Civil Wars: Selected Essays 1963–1980* (1995), *Technical Difficulties: New Political Essays and Writings* (1992), and *On Call: New Political Essays* (1985). The following essay first appeared in the *Harvard Educational Review* in 1988.

REFLECTING BEFORE READING

1. In her essay, June Jordan focuses attention on Black English, a nonmainstream version of standard English. What do you know about Black English, which has also been called "Ebonics"? Have you had any experience with it, either as a speaker of it yourself or as someone who has encountered other speakers of it? How have your own experiences shaped your attitudes toward it? As you read, consider how your understanding of and attitudes toward Black English might influence the way you respond to Jordan's essay.

2. Race is a central issue in Jordan's essay. As you read, consider the ways in which she discusses race and whether you think she addresses her essay to readers of a particular racial background. For instance, do you think she is writing specifically to Black readers? To a mixed audience? How might your own racial background affect your reaction to her essay?

Black English[1] is not exactly a linguistic buffalo; as children, most of the thirty-five million Afro-Americans living here depend on this language for our discovery of the world. But then we approach our maturity inside a larger social body that will not support our efforts to become anything other than the clones of those who are neither our mothers nor our fathers. We begin to grow up in a house where every true mirror shows us the face of somebody who does not belong there, whose walk and whose talk will never look or sound "right," because that house was meant to shelter a family that is alien and hostile to us. As we learn our way around this environment, either we hide our original word habits, or we completely surrender our own voice, hoping to please those who will never respect anyone different from themselves: Black English is not exactly a linguistic buffalo, but we should understand its status as an endangered species, as a perishing, irreplaceable system of community intelligence, or we should expect its extinction, and, along with that, the extinguishing of much that constitutes our own proud, and singular, identity.

What we casually call "English," less and less defers to England and its "gentlemen." "English" is no longer a specific matter of geography or an element of class privilege; more than thirty-three countries use this tool as a means of "intranational communication."[2] Countries as disparate as Zimbabwe and Malaysia, or Israel and Uganda, use it as their non-native currency of convenience. Obviously, this tool, this "English," cannot function inside thirty-three discrete societies on the basis of rules and values absolutely determined somewhere else, in a thirty-fourth other country, for example.

In addition to that staggering congeries of non-native users of English, there are five countries, or 333,746,000 people, for whom this thing called "English" serves as a native tongue.[2] Approximately 10 percent of these native speakers of "English" are Afro-American citizens of the U.S.A. I cite these numbers and varieties of human beings dependent on "English" in order, quickly, to suggest how strange and how tenuous is any concept of "Standard English." Obviously, numerous forms of English now operate inside a natural, an uncontrollable, continuum of development. I would suppose "the standard" for English in Malaysia is not the same as "the standard" in Zimbabwe. I know that standard forms of English for Black people in this country do not copy that of Whites. And, in fact, the structural differences between these two kinds of English have intensified, becoming more Black, or less White, despite the expected homogenizing effects of television[3] and other mass media.

Nonetheless, White standards of English persist, supreme and unquestioned, in these United States. Despite our multi-lingual population, and despite the deepening Black and White cleavage within that conglomerate, White standards control our official and popular judgments of verbal proficiency and correct, or incorrect, language skills, including speech. In contrast to India, where at least fourteen languages co-exist as legitimate Indian languages, in contrast to Nicaragua, where all citizens are legally entitled to formal school instruction in their regional or tribal languages,

---

[1] Black English aphorisms crafted by Monica Morris, a junior at S.U.N.Y., Stony Brook, October, 1984.

[2] *English Is Spreading, But What Is English?* A presentation by Professor S. N. Sridhar, Department of Linguistics, S.U.N.Y., Stony Brook, April 9, 1985: Dean's Convocation Among the Disciplines.

[3] *New York Times,* March 15, 1985, Section One, p. 14; Report on Study by Linguists at the University of Pennsylvania.

compulsory education in America compels accommodation to exclusively White forms of "English." White English, in America, is "Standard English."

This story begins two years ago. I was teaching a new course, "In Search of the Invisible Black Woman," and my rather large class seemed evenly divided among young Black women and men. Five or six White students also sat in attendance. With unexpected speed and enthusiasm we had moved through historical narration of the 19th century to literature by and about Black women, in the 20th. I then assigned the first forty pages of Alice Walker's *The Color Purple,* and I came, eagerly, to class that morning:

"So!" I exclaimed, aloud. "What did you think?" How did you like it?"

The students studied their hands, or the floor. There was no response. The tense, resistant feeling in the room fairly astounded me.

At last, one student, a young woman still not meeting my eyes, muttered something in my direction:

"What did you say?" I prompted her.

"Why she have them talk so funny. It don't sound right."

"You mean the language?"

Another student lifted his head: "It don't look right, neither. I couldn't hardly read it."

At this, several students dumped on the book. Just about unanimously, their criticisms targeted the language. I listened to what they wanted to say and silently marvelled at the similarities between their casual speech patterns and Alice Walker's written version of Black English.

But I decided against pointing to these identical traits of syntax, I wanted not to make them self-conscious about their own spoken language—not while they clearly felt it was "wrong." Instead I decided to swallow my astonishment. Here was a negative Black reaction to a prize-winning accomplishment of Black literature that White readers across the country had selected as a best seller. Black rejection was aimed at the one irreducibly Black element of Walker's work: the language—Celie's Black English. I wrote the opening lines of *The Color Purple* on the blackboard and asked the students to help me translate these sentences into Standard English:

You better not never tell nobody but God. It'd kill your mommy.

Dear God,

I am fourteen years old. I have always been a good girl. Maybe you can give me a sign letting me know what is happening to me.

Last spring after Little Lucious come I heard them fussing. He was pulling on her arm. She say it too soon, Fonso. I aint well. Finally he leave her alone. A week go by, he pulling on her arm again. She say, Naw, I ain't gonna. Can't you see I'm already half dead, an all of the children.[4]

Our process of translation exploded with hilarity and even hysterical, shocked laughter: The Black writer, Alice Walker, knew what she was doing! If rudimentary criteria for good fiction include the manipulation of language so that the syntax and

---

[4] Alice Walker, *The Color Purple* (New York: Harcourt Brace Jovanovich, 1982), p. 11.

diction of sentences will tell you the identity of speakers, the probable age and sex and class of speakers, and even the locale—urban/rural/southern/western—then Walker had written, perfectly. This is the translation into Standard English that our class produced:

> *Absolutely, one should never confide in anybody besides God. Your secrets could prove devastating to your mother.*

> Dear God,

> I am fourteen years old. I have always been good. But now, could you help me to understand what is happening to me?
> Last spring, after my little brother, Lucious, was born, I heard my parents fighting. My father kept pulling at my mother's arm. But she told him, "It's too soon for sex, Alfonso. I am still not feeling well." Finally, my father left her alone. A week went by, and then he began bothering my mother, again: Pulling her arm. She told him, "No, I won't! Can't you see I'm already exhausted from all of these children?"

(Our favorite line was "It's too soon for sex, Alfonso.")

Once we could stop laughing, once we could stop our exponentially wild improvisations on the theme of Translated Black English, the students pushed to explain their own negative first reactions to their spoken language on the printed page. I thought it was probably akin to the shock of seeing yourself in a photograph for the first time. Most of the students had never before seen a written facsimile of the way they talk. None of the students had ever learned how to read and write their own verbal system of communication: Black English. Alternatively, this fact began to baffle or else bemuse and then infuriate my students. Why not? Was it too late? Could they learn how to do it, now? And, ultimately, the final test question, the one testing my sincerity: Could I reach them? Because I had never taught anyone Black English and, as far as I knew, no one, anywhere in the United States, had ever offered such a course, the best I could say was "I'll try."

He looked like a wrestler.

He sat dead center in the packed room and, every time our eyes met, he quickly nodded his head as though anxious to reassure, and encourage me.

Short, with strikingly broad shoulders and long arms, he spoke with a surprisingly high, soft voice that matched the soft bright movement of his eyes. His name was Willie Jordan. He would have seemed even more unlikely in the context of Contemporary Women's Poetry, except that ten or twelve other Black men were taking the course, as well. Still, Willie was conspicuous. His extreme fitness, the muscular density of his presence underscored the riveted, gentle attention that he gave to anything anyone said. Generally, he did not join the loud and rowdy dialogue flying back and forth, but there could be no doubt about his interest in our discussions. And, when he stood to present an argument he'd prepared, overnight, that nervous smile of his vanished and an irregular stammering replaced it, as he spoke with visceral sincerity, word by word.

That was how I met Willie Jordan. It was in between "In Search of the Invisible Black Women" and "The Art of Black English." I was waiting for departmental approval and I supposed that Willie might be, so to speak, killing time until he, too, could study Black English. But Willie really did want to explore contemporary women's poetry and, to that end, volunteered for extra research and never missed a class.

Towards the end of that semester, Willie approached me for an independent study project on South Africa. It would commence the next semester. I thought Willie's writing needed the kind of improvement only intense practice will yield. I knew his intelligence was outstanding. But he'd wholeheartedly opted for "Standard English" at a rather late age, and the results were stilted and frequently polysyllabic, simply for the sake of having more syllables. Willie's unnatural formality of language seemed to me consistent with the formality of his research into South African apartheid. As he projected his studies, he would have little time, indeed, for newspapers. Instead, more than 90 percent of his research would mean saturation in strictly historical, if not archival, material. I was certainly interested. It would be tricky to guide him into a more confident and spontaneous relationship both with language and apartheid. It was going to be wonderful to see what happened when he could catch up with himself, entirely, and talk back to the world.

September, 1984: Breezy fall weather and much excitement! My class, "The Art of Black English," was full to the limit of the fire laws. And in Independent Study, Willie Jordan showed up weekly, fifteen minutes early for each of our sessions. I was pretty happy to be teaching, altogether!

I remember an early class when a young brother, replete with his ever-present porkpie hat, raised his hand and then told us that most of what he'd heard was "all right" except it was "too clean." "The brothers on the street," he continued, "they mix it up more. Like 'fuck' and 'motherfuck.' Or like 'shit.'" He waited. I waited. Then all of us laughed a good while, and we got into a brawl about "correct" and "realistic" Black English that led to Rule 1.

Rule 1: *Black English is about a whole lot more than mothafuckin.*

As a criterion, we decided, "realistic" could take you anywhere you want to go. Artful places. Angry places. Eloquent and sweetalkin places. Polemical places. Church. And the local Bar & Grill. We were checking out a language, not a mood or a scene or one guy's forgettable mouthing off.

It was hard. For most of the students, learning Black English required a fallback to patterns and rhythms of speech that many of their parents had beaten out of them. I mean *beaten*. And, in a majority of cases, correct Black English could be achieved only by striving for incorrect Standard English, something they were still pushing at, quite uncertainly. This state of affairs led to Rule 2.

Rule 2: *If it's wrong in Standard English it's probably right in Black English, or, at least, you're hot.*

It was hard. Roommates and family members ridiculed their studies, or remained incredulous, "You *studying* that shit? At school?" But we were beginning to feel the companionship of pioneers. And we decided that we needed another rule that would establish each one of us as equally important to our success. This was Rule 3.

Rule 3: *If it don't sound like something that come out somebody mouth then it don't sound right. If it don't sound right then it ain't hardly right. Period.*

This rule produced two weeks of compositions in which the students agonizingly tried to spell the sound of the Black English sentence they wanted to convey. But Black English is, preeminently, an oral/spoken means of communication. *And spelling don't talk.* So we needed Rule 4.

Rule 4: *Forget about the spelling. Let the syntax carry you.*

Once we arrived at Rule 4 we started to fly, because syntax, the structure of an idea, leads you to the world view of the speaker and reveals her values. The syntax of a sentence equals the structure of your consciousness. If we insisted that the language of Black English adheres to a distinctive Black syntax, then we were postulating a profound difference between White and Black people, *per se*. Was it a difference to prize or to obliterate?

There are three qualities of Black English—the presence of life, voice, and clarity—that intensify to a distinctive Black value system that we became excited about and self-consciously tried to maintain.

1. Black English has been produced by a pre-technocratic, if not anti-technological, culture. More, our culture has been constantly threatened by annihilation or, at least, the swallowed blurring of assimilation. Therefore, our language is a system constructed by people constantly needing to insist that we exist, that we are present. Our language devolves from a culture that abhors all abstraction, or anything tending to obscure or delete the fact of the human being who is here and now/the truth of the person who is speaking or listening. Consequently, *there is no passive voice construction possible in Black English.* For example, you cannot say, "Black English is being eliminated." You must say, instead, "White people eliminating Black English." The assumption of the presence of life governs all of Black English. Therefore, overwhelmingly, *all action takes place in the language of the present indicative.* And every sentence assumes the living and active participation of at least two human beings, the speaker and the listener.

2. A primary consequence of the person-centered values of Black English is the delivery of voice. If you speak or write Black English, your ideas will necessarily possess that otherwise elusive attribute, *voice.*

3. One main benefit following from the person-centered values of Black English is that of *clarity.* If your idea, your sentence, assumes the presence of at least two living and active people, you will make it understandable, because the motivation behind every sentence is the wish to say something real to somebody real.

As the weeks piled up, translation from Standard English into Black English or vice versa occupied a hefty part of our course work.

Standard English (hereafter S.E.): "In considering the idea of studying Black English those questioned suggested—"

(What's the subject? Where's the person? Is anybody alive in here, in that idea?)

Black English (hereafter B.E.): "I been asking people what you think about somebody studying Black English and they answer me like this:"

But there were interesting limits. You cannot "translate" instances of Standard English preoccupied with abstraction or with nothing/nobody evidently alive, into Black English. That would warp the language into uses antithetical to the guiding perspective of its community of users. Rather you must first change those Standard English sentences, themselves, into ideas consistent with the person-centered assumptions of Black English.

Guidelines for Black English

1. Minimal number of words for every idea: This is the source for the aphoristic and/or poetic force of the language; eliminate every possible word.

2. Clarity: If the sentence is not clear it's not Black English.

3. Eliminate use of the verb *to be* whenever possible. This leads to the deployment of more descriptive and, therefore, more precise verbs.

4. Use *be* or *been* only when you want to describe a chronic, ongoing state of things.

    He *be* at the office, by 9. (He is always at the office by 9.)

    He *been* with her since forever.

5. Zero copula: Always eliminate the verb *to be* whenever it would combine with another verb, in Standard English.

    S.E.: She is going out with him.

    B.E.: She going out with him.

6. Eliminate *do* as in:

    S.E.: What do you think? What do you want?

    B.E.: What you think? What you want?

Rules number 3, 4, 5, and 6 provide for the use of the minimal number of verbs per idea and, therefore, greater accuracy in the choice of verb.

7. In general, if you wish to say something really positive, try to formulate the idea using emphatic negative structure.

    S.E.: He's fabulous.

    B.E.: He bad.

8. Use double or triple negatives for dramatic emphasis.

    S.E.: Tina Turner sings out of this world.

    B.E.: Ain nobody sing like Tina.

9. Never use the *ed* suffix to indicate the past tense of a verb.

    S.E.: She closed the door.

    B.E.: She close the door. Or, she have close the door.

10. Regardless of intentional verb time, only use the third person singular, present indicative, for use of the verb *to have*, as an auxiliary.

    S.E.: He had his wallet then he lost it.

    B.E.: He have him wallet then he lose it.

    S.E.: We had seen that movie.

    B.E.: We seen that movie. Or, we have see that movie.

11. Observe a minimal inflection of verbs. Particularly, never change from the first person singular forms to the third person singular.

S.E.: Present Tense Forms: He goes to the store.

B.E.: He go to the store.

S.E.: Past Tense Forms: He went to the store.

B.E.: He go to the store. Or, he gone to the store. Or, he been to the store.

12. The possessive case scarcely ever appears in Black English. Never use an apostrophe ('s) construction. If you wander into a possessive case component of an idea, then keep logically consistent: *ours, his, theirs, mines.* But, most likely, if you bump into such a component, you have wandered outside the underlying world view of Black English.

S.E.: He will take their car tomorrow.

B.E.: He taking they car tomorrow.

13. Plurality: Logical consistency, continued: If the modifier indicates plurality then the noun remains in the singular case.

S.E.: He ate twelve doughnuts.

B.E.: He eat twelve doughnut.

S.E.: She has many books.

B.E.: She have many book.

14. Listen for, or invent, special Black English forms of the past tense, such as: "He losted it. That what she felted." If they are clear and readily understood, then use them.

15. Do not hesitate to play with words, sometimes inventing them: e.g. "astropotomous" means huge like a hippo plus astronomical and, therefore, signifies real big.

16. In Black English, unless you keenly want to underscore the past tense nature of an action, stay in the present tense and rely on the overall context of your ideas for the conveyance of time and sequence.

17. Never use the suffix *-ly* form of an adverb in Black English.

S.E.: The rain came down rather quickly.

B.E.: The rain come down pretty quick.

18. Never use the indefinite article *an* in Black English.

S.E.: He wanted to ride an elephant.

B.E.: He wanted to ride him a elephant.

19. Invariant syntax: in correct Black English it is possible to formulate an imperative, an interrogative, and a simple declarative idea with the same syntax:

B.E.: You going to the store?

You going to the store.

You going to the store!

Where was Willie Jordan? We'd reached the mid-term of the semester. Students had formulated Black English guidelines, by consensus, and they were now writing with remarkable beauty, purpose, and enjoyment:

I ain hardly speakin for everybody but myself so understan that.

—Kim Parks

Samples from student writings:

Janie have a great big ole hole inside her. Tea Cake the only thing that fit that hole. . . .

That pear tree beautiful to Janie, especial when bees fiddlin with the blossomin pear there growin large and lovely. But personal speakin, the love she get from starin at that tree ain the love what starin back at her in them relationship. (Monica Morris)

Love a big theme in, *They Eye Was Watching God.* Love show people new corners inside theyself. It pull out good stuff and stuff back bad stuff . . . Joe worship the doing uh his own hand and need other people to worship him too. But he ain't think about Janie that she a person and ought to live like anybody common do. Queen life not for Janie. (Monica Morris)

In both life and writin, Black womens have varietous experience of love that be cold like a iceberg or fiery like a inferno. Passion got for the other partner involve, man or women, seem as shallow, ankle-deep water or the most profoundest abyss. (Constance Evans)

Family love another bond that ain't never break under no pressure. (Constance Evans)

You know it really cold/When the friend you/Always get out the fire/Act like they don't know you/When you in the beat. (Constance Evans)

Big classroom discussion bout love at this time. I never take no class where us have any long arguin for and against for two or three day. New to me and great. I find the class time talkin a million time more interestin than detail bout the book. (Kathy Esseks)

As these examples suggest, Black English no longer limited the students, in any way. In fact, one of them, Philip Garfield, would shortly "translate" a pivotal scene from Ibsen's *A Doll's House,* as his final term paper.

NORA: I didn't gived no shit. I thinked you a asshole back then, too, you make it so hard for me save mines husband life.

KROGSTAD: Girl, it clear you ain't any idea what you done. You done exact what I once done, and I losed my reputation over it.

NORA: You asks me believe you once act brave save you wife life?

KROGSTAD: Law care less why you done it.

NORA: Law must suck.

KROGSTAD: Suck or no, if I wants, judge screw you wid dis paper.

NORA: No way, man. (Philip Garfield)

But where was Willie? Compulsively punctual, and always thoroughly prepared with neat typed compositions, he had disappeared. He failed to show up for our regularly scheduled conference, and I received neither a note nor a phone call of explanation. A whole week went by. I wondered if Willie had finally been captured by the extremely current happenings in South Africa: passage of a new constitution that did not enfranchise the Black majority, and militant Black South African reaction to that affront. I wondered if he'd been hurt, somewhere. I wondered if the serious workload of weekly readings and writings had overwhelmed him and changed his mind about independent study. Where was Willie Jordan?

One week after the first conference that Willie missed, he called: "Hello, Professor Jordan? This is Willie. I'm sorry I wasn't there last week. But something has come up and I'm pretty upset. I'm sorry but I really can't deal right now."

I asked Willie to drop by my office and just let me see that he was okay. He agreed to do that. When I saw him I knew something hideous had happened. Something had hurt him and scared him to the marrow. He was all agitated and stammering and terse and incoherent. At last, his sadly jumbled account let me surmise, as follows: Brooklyn police had murdered his unarmed, twenty-five-year-old brother, Reggie Jordan. Neither Willie nor his elderly parents knew what to do about it. Nobody from the press was interested. His folks had no money. Police ran his family around and around, to no point. And Reggie was really dead. And Willie wanted to fight, but he felt helpless.

With Willie's permission I began to try to secure legal counsel for the Jordan family. Unfortunately, Black victims of police violence are truly numerous, while the resources available to prosecute their killers are truly scarce. A friend of mine at the Center for Constitutional Rights estimated that just the preparatory costs for bringing the cops into court normally approaches $180,000. Unless the execution of Reggie Jordan became a major community cause for organizing and protest, his murder would simply become a statistical item.

Again, with Willie's permission, I contacted every newspaper and media person I could think of. But the Bastone feature article in *The Village Voice* was the only result from that canvassing.

Again, with Willie's permission, I presented the case to my class in Black English. We had talked about the politics of language. We had talked about love and sex and child abuse and men and women. But the murder of Reggie Jordan broke like a hurricane across the room.

There are few "issues" as endemic to Black life as police violence. Most of the students knew and respected and liked Jordan. Many of them came from the very neighborhood where the murder had occurred. All of the students had known somebody close to them who had been killed by police, or had known frightening moments of gratuitous confrontation with the cops. They wanted to do everything at once to avenge death. Number One: They decided to compose a personal statement of condolence to Willie Jordan and his family, written in black English. Number Two: They decided to compose individual messages to the police, in Black English. These should be prefaced by an explanatory paragraph composed by the entire group. Number Three: These individual messages, with their lead paragraph, should be sent to *Newsday*.

The morning after we agreed on these objectives, one of the young women students appeared with an unidentified visitor, who sat through the class, smiling in a peculiar, comfortable way.

Now we had to make more tactical decisions. Because we wanted the messages published, and because we thought it imperative that our outrage be known by the police, the tactical question was this: Should the opening, group paragraph be written in Black English or Standard English?

I have seldom been privy to a discussion with so much heart at the dead beat of it. I will never forget the eloquence, the sudden haltings of speech, the fierce struggle against tears, the furious throwaway, and useless explosions that this question elicited.

That one question contained several others, each of them extraordinarily painful to even contemplate. How best to serve the memory of Reggie Jordan? Should we use the language of the killer—Standard English—in order to make our ideas acceptable to those controlling the killers? But wouldn't what we had to say be rejected, summarily, if we said it in our own language, the language of the victim, Reggie Jordan? But if we sought to express ourselves by abandoning our language wouldn't that mean our suicide on top of Reggie's murder? But if we expressed ourselves in our own language wouldn't that be suicidal to the wish to communicate with those who, evidently, did not give a damn about us/Reggie/police violence in the Black community?

At the end of one of the longest, most difficult hours of my own life, the students voted, unanimously, to preface their individual messages with a paragraph composed in the language of Reggie Jordan. *"At least we don't give up nothing else. At least we stick to the truth: Be who we been. And stay all the way with Reggie."*

It was heartbreaking to proceed, from that point. Everyone in the room realized that our decision in favor of Black English had doomed our writings, even as the distinctive reality of our Black lives always has doomed our efforts to "be who we been" in this country.

I went to the blackboard and took down this paragraph dictated by the class:

YOU COPS!

WE THE BROTHER AND SISTER OF WILLIE JORDAN, A FELLOW STONY BROOK STUDENT WHO THE BROTHER OF THE DEAD REGGIE JORDAN. REGGIE, LIKE MANY BROTHER AND SISTER, HE A VICTIM OF BRUTAL RACIST POLICE, OCTOBER 25, 1984. US APPALL, FED UP, BECAUSE THAT ANOTHER SENSELESS DEATH WHAT OCCUR IN OUR COMMUNITY. THIS WHAT WE FEEL, THIS, FROM OUR HEART, FOR WE AIN'T STAYIN' SILENT NO MORE.

With the completion of this introduction, nobody said anything. I asked for comments. At this invitation, the unidentified visitor, a young Black man, ceaselessly smiling, raised his hand. He was, it so happens, a rookie cop. He had just joined the force in September and, he said, he thought he should clarify a few things. So he came forward and sprawled easily into a posture of barroom, or fire-side, nostalgia:

"See," Officer Charles enlightened us, "Most times when you out on the street and something come down you do one of two things. Over-react or under-react. Now, if you under-react then you can get yourself kilt. And if you over-react then maybe you kill somebody. Fortunately it's about nine times out of ten and you will over-react. So the brother got kilt. And I'm sorry about that, believe me. But what you have to understand is what kilt him: Over-reaction. That's all. Now you talk about Black people and White police but see, now, I'm a cop myself. And (big smile) I'm Black. And just a couple months ago I was on the other side. But it's the same for me. You a cop, you the ultimate authority: the Ultimate Authority. And you on the street, most of the time you can only do one of two things: over-react or under-react. That's all it is with the brother. Over-reaction. Didn't have nothing to do with race."

That morning Officer Charles had the good fortune to escape without being boiled alive. But barely. And I remember the pride of his smile when I read about the fate of Black policemen and other collaborators, in South Africa. I remember him, and I remember the shock and palpable feeling of shame that filled the room. It was as though that foolish, and deadly, young man had just relieved himself of his foolish, and deadly, explanation, face to face with the grief of Reggie Jordan's father and Reggie Jordan's mother. Class ended quietly. I copied the paragraph from the blackboard, collected the individual messages and left to type them up.

Newsday rejected the piece.

The Village Voice could not find room in their "Letters" section to print the individual messages from the students to the police.

None of the TV news reporters picked up the story.

Nobody raised $180,000 to prosecute the murder of Reggie Jordan.

Reggie Jordan is really dead.

I asked Willie Jordan to write an essay pulling together everything important to him from that semester. He was still deeply beside himself with frustration and amazement and loss. This is what he wrote, unedited, and in its entirety:

> Throughout the course of this semester I have been researching the effects of oppression and exploitation along racial lines in South Africa and its neighboring countries. I have become aware of South African police brutalization of native Africans beyond the extent of the law, even though the laws themselves are catalyst affliction upon Black men, women and children. Many Africans die each year as a result of the deliberate use of police force to protect the white power structure.

> Social control agents in South Africa, such as policemen, are also used to force compliance among citizens through both overt and covert tactics. It is not uncommon to find bold-faced coercion and cold-blooded killings of Blacks by South African police for undetermined and/or inadequate reasons. Perhaps the truth is that the only reasons for this heinous treatment of Blacks rests in racial differences. We should also understand that what is conveyed through the media is not always accurate and may sometimes be construed as the tip of the iceberg at best.

> I recently received a painful reminder that racism, poverty, and the abuse of power are global problems which are by no means unique to South Africa. On October 25, 1984 at approximately 3:00 p.m. my brother, Mr. Reginald Jordan, was shot and killed by two New York City policemen from the 75th precinct in the East New York section of Brooklyn. His life ended at the age of twenty-five. Even up to this current point in time the Police Department has failed to provide my family, which consists of five brothers, eight sisters, and two parents, with a plausible reason for Reggie's death. Out of the many stories that were given to my family by the Police

Department, not one of them seems to hold water. In fact, I honestly believe that the Police Department's assessment of my brother's murder is nothing short of ABSOLUTE BULLSHIT, and thus far no evidence had been produced to alter perception of the situation.

Furthermore, I believe that one of three cases may have occurred in this incident. First, Reggie's death may have been the desired outcome of the police officer's action, in which case the killing was premeditated. Or, it was a case of mistaken identity, which clarifies the fact that the two officers who killed my brother and their commanding parties are all grossly incompetent. Or, both of the above cases are correct, i.e., Reggie's murderers intended to kill him and the Police Department behaved insubordinately.

Part of the argument of the officers who shot Reggie was that he had attacked one of them and took his gun. This was their major claim. They also said that only one of them had actually shot Reggie. The facts, however, speak for themselves. According to the Death Certificate and autopsy report, Reggie was shot eight times from point-blank range. The Doctor who performed the autopsy told me himself that two bullets entered the side of my brother's head, four bullets were sprayed into his back, and two bullets struck him in the back of his legs. It is obvious that unnecessary force was used by the police and that it is extremely difficult to shoot someone in his back when he is attacking or approaching you.

After experiencing a situation like this and researching South Africa I believe that to a large degree, justice may only exist as rhetoric. I find it difficult to talk of true justice when the oppression of my people both at home and abroad attests to the fact that inequality and injustice are serious problems whereby Blacks and Third World people are perpetually short-changed by society. Something has to be done about the way in which this world is set up. Although it is a difficult task, we do have the power to make a change.

—Willie J. Jordan, Jr.

EGL 487, Section 58, November 14, 1984

It is my privilege to dedicate this book to the future life of Willie J. Jordan, Jr., August 8, 1985.

REFLECTING ON THE READING

1. What does Jordan mean when she writes that Black English is "not exactly a linguistic buffalo"? Why is this point an important one for her argument in this essay?

2. How do Jordan's students react to Alice Walker's novel *The Color Purple?* How do they explain this reaction? What significance does Jordan see in her students' reaction to the novel? What is her response to their comments about the novel? Do you think her response was an appropriate one? Explain.

3. Why does Jordan decide to teach her students Black English? Do you think it is a good idea for her to do so? Why or why not? What might your answer to this question suggest about your own beliefs regarding language and schooling?

4. Why does Jordan agree to help Willie Jordan with his independent research project? What does she hope to accomplish by helping him with this project? What might her decision to help him say about her as a teacher?

5. What are the most important differences between Black English and Standard English, as Jordan describes these two versions of the language in her essay? Why are these differences important? What might they reveal about the language and about the people who use them? Why is *syntax,* specifically, important in understanding these differences, according to Jordan? What does she mean when she writes that "syntax . . . leads you to the world view of the speaker and reveals her values"? (If necessary, look up definitions of *syntax* in your dictionary and/or in a grammar handbook.)

6. What is the reaction of Jordan's class to the news of the death of Willie's brother? Why do they choose the course of action they do? What might their course of action have to do with language and/or literacy? What might it reveal about the relationship between literacy and race?

7. Why was the decision to write to the police and to the press in Black English so difficult for the students in Jordan's class? Why does Jordan say that the students' decision "doomed" their writing? Do you agree with that assessment? Why or why not?

8. What is the result of the efforts of Jordan's students to publicize the case of Reggie Jordan? Why do you think their efforts turn out as they do? What might these results suggest about language and literacy in American society?

Examining Rhetorical Strategies

1. Note Jordan's use of the first person in this essay. In the first paragraph, for instance, she writes that "Afro-Americans living here depend upon this language for our discovery of the world." And later in that same paragraph she writes that "we should understand its [Black English's] status as an endangered species." Who is the *we* in this passage? Is Jordan referring to the same groups in the first instance ("our") as she is in the second ("we")? If these references in the first person are to different groups, who are these groups? What is their relationship to each other? What does Jordan's use of first person say about *her* identity as the writer of this passage? Which group or groups does she identify herself with? How does that identification affect her credibility with you as a reader?

2. Jordan introduces this essay, which tells the story of her experiences with the students in one of her English classes, with a discussion of Black English and other varieties of English that differ from Standard English. Her "story" doesn't begin until the fifth paragraph of the essay. Why do you think she begins her essay in this way? What purposes does this background information on Standard English and Black English serve in her narrative? How does it influence the way you read the story she tells of her students and of Willie Jordan?

3. Analyze Jordan's description of Willie Jordan when she first introduces him in her essay. How does she describe him? What characteristics does she emphasize about him? Why do you think she emphasizes these specific characteristics? How do they influence your reaction to him? Do you think June Jordan intended such a reaction? Explain. How might your own racial background have affected the way you reacted to her description of Willie? Do you think June Jordan expected White readers and Black readers to react differently to him? Why or why not? Cite specific passages from the essay to support your answer.

4. In her relating the events that occurred as her class studies Black English, Jordan describes many distinctive features of Black English and points out differences between Black English and Standard English. Examine the passages in which she describes Black English and Standard English. What kinds of differences between these two versions of the English language does she tend to emphasize? How does her emphasis on these differences influence the views of the two versions of English that she is describing? Do you think her discussion of these differences includes criticism or support for one or both of these versions of English? Explain, citing specific passages in the text to support your answer. How might her comparisons of these versions of the language serve her larger argument in this essay?

5. Note the examples of Black English that Jordan includes in her essay. What do these examples reveal about Black English? What do they seem to emphasize about Black English and about users of Black English? Do you think these examples are effective in helping reinforce Jordan's points about Black English? Explain.

6. Early in this essay, Jordan tells us that among the students in her course "In Search of the Invisible Black Woman" were five or six White students. She never refers again in this essay specifically to those White students, though she does devote a great deal of space in the essay to descriptions of the students in her class. Why do you think she mentions these few White students early in her essay? Why do you think she doesn't refer to them again after she first mentions them? Do you think this was intentional on her part? What purpose might it serve for her to mention the White students once and not refer to them again? How did you react to her mention of these students? What might your reaction suggest about you as a reader and as a person?

7. Whom do you think Jordan imagined as the audience for this essay? Do you think she was writing to a largely Black audience, a White audience, or a mixed audience? Explain. In what ways do you think the essay addresses the racial background of its potential readers? Cite specific passages from the essay to support your answer.

8. Assess the effectiveness of Jordan's ending to this essay. In what ways might it be appropriate to end the piece with Willie's essay? What points that June Jordan raises in her essay does her ending reinforce? Do you think it is significant that she doesn't end the essay with an example of Black English? Why or why not? How did you react to this ending? What might your reaction reveal about your own expectations as a reader? What might it reveal about you as a person?

Engaging the Issues —————————————————————————————

1. Write an essay for an audience of your classmates in which you analyze June Jordan's views about language and literacy, as those views emerge in this essay. In your analysis, be sure to discuss the role of race in her understanding of language and literacy. Cite specific passages from her essay to support your analysis, and try to draw conclusions about the relationship of language and racial or cultural background.

2. Write an essay for an audience of your classmates about an experience you have had in which writing was part of your efforts to deal with a difficult situation. For example, perhaps you had to write a letter to a teacher, principal, or employer about some trouble you were in. Or perhaps you had to write a letter as part of a court case or legal suit in which you (or someone you know) were involved. Or you might have written a letter to a local newspaper about a problem or event in your town. In your essay, tell the story of that experience in a way that will enable your readers to understand what happened and how writing played an important role in the experience.

3. In a group of your classmates, share the essays you wrote for Question #2. Compare the experiences about which members of your group wrote. What kinds of experiences did each of you describe? In what ways were these experiences similar or different? What role did writing play in each experience? What might these experiences suggest about the role of writing in situations of conflict or problems?

4. Compare how you typically speak in your home or community to the ways in which you are expected to speak at school, at work, or in formal settings like courtrooms or city council meetings. What differences or similarities can you identify? Do you use a different language in these different settings? Explain. Try to draw conclusions about the relationship between language use and power based on your own experience.

5. Rewrite the essay you wrote for Question #2 above in the language you use in your home or neighborhood.

6. Rewrite the essay you write for Question #1 above in the language you use in your home or neighborhood.

7. Using your library, the World Wide Web, or any other appropriate sources, examine prevailing attitudes as they emerge in controversies about Black English or some other nonmainstream version of English. Find articles, essays, or scholarly studies written about these controversies (such as the Oakland, California, School Board's decision to declare Ebonics a language in the mid-1990's). Try to determine whether there is any consensus about these versions of English among linguists or other language or literacy experts. Then write a report for your classmates on the basis of your research, drawing your own conclusions about the status of nonmainstream versions of English.

8. On the basis of the research you conducted for Question #7 above, write a letter to your local newspaper expressing your views about standards for written English that should be used in schools or other public settings.

9. Write a conventional academic essay in which you discuss why the letter written by June Jordan's students was not published by *Newsday,* the *Village Voice,* or any of the other publications to which they submitted their letter. In your essay, address the larger issues of race and power and how they relate to literacy. Refer to similar situations of the "power of the pen" that you may know about, and draw conclusions about how that "power" functioned in the situation Jordan describes in her essay.

Learning to Read

MALCOLM X

INTRODUCTION   If literacy is inherently political, as many scholars believe, few examples of that view are more compelling than that of Malcolm X. In this famous excerpt from his autobiography, Malcolm describes how he took it upon himself to improve his reading and writing abilities while serving a prison term for robbery. A young man in his early twenties at the time, Malcolm imposed upon himself a rigorous course of study that, as he himself writes, few college students could match. In reading, he says, he found freedom, and his commitment to expanding his knowledge resulted in remarkably sustained and extensive reading that continued, he tells us, long after he left prison and became an internationally known activist for African American civil rights. But Malcolm X was not someone who simply loved to read, a voracious bookworm who indulged in reading for its own pleasures. For him, reading was integral to the political activism that earned him such notoriety. As he writes in the following passage, "You will never catch me with a free fifteen minutes in which I'm not studying something I feel might be able to help the black man." From such a perspective, reading is not escape or enjoyment but a form of political action.

In a sense, Malcolm X's story of teaching himself to read and write while he was incarcerated is a version of a familiar American tale: the determined individual who overcomes great adversity to educate himself and eventually achieve greatness. We have many such tales, which often underscore the important role of literacy and learning in earning success. Two notable ones are Abraham Lincoln studying by candlelight in a humble cabin and Frederick Douglass secretly teaching himself to read while he was still a slave. Both went on from these difficult beginnings to become great leaders. So did Malcolm X. Born in Omaha, Nebraska, in 1925, he was only six years old when his father, a minister, was murdered by Whites. At age fifteen he dropped out of school and turned to street crime. But while serving his prison sentence, he discovered Islam, and he emerged from prison dedicated to the cause of civil rights for African Americans. The extensive and focused reading he did while in prison was instrumental in his transformation and in shaping his strident views about race.

Those views made him controversial among Blacks as well as Whites. In the following passage from his autobiography, his descriptions of his reading contain some of the strong sentiments about race for which he was sometimes criticized and vilified. But later in his autobiography (not reprinted here), we learn that the pilgrimage he made to the Middle East in 1964 as part of his practice of Islam profoundly reshaped his perspective on race. He writes, "In the past, yes, I have made sweeping indictments of all white people. I will never be guilty of that again—as I know now that some white people are truly sincere, that some truly are capable of being brotherly toward a black man." His evolving views about race and religion led in 1964 to his leaving the Nation of Islam, to which he had devoted much of his adult life. He took the name of El-Hajj Malik al-Shabazz and subsequently founded the Muslim Mosque and the Organization of Afro-American Unity. But in the minds of many Americans, he continued to be associated with the angry antiwhite sentiments he had so often expressed in his writing and in the many speeches he gave. He was assassinated in 1965, and his death remains the subject of speculation and controversy even today.

It may be that Malcolm X's words, both written and spoken, represented a threat to those who didn't share his beliefs. His story thus underscores the power of literacy to transform a life as well as to wage a political struggle on behalf of others. It may reveal, too, the risks associated with that power.

REFLECTING BEFORE READING

1. Malcolm X is one of the most important—and controversial—African American leaders of the twentieth century. What do you know about him? What opinion, if any, do you hold of him and his work as a political activist? As you read, consider how your knowledge of him and your views of him might influence your reaction to this passage.

2. The following passage from Malcolm X's autobiography is ostensibly about how he improves his reading and writing abilities and the importance of reading in his life. But in a sense, the passage is about more than that. As you read, consider how literacy relates to Malcolm X's role as an activist for African Americans and his vision of himself and his work. What role does literacy play in his life? What might his experience say about literacy? What might he be saying about the connection between literacy and power?

I t was because of my letters that I happened to stumble upon starting to acquire some kind of a homemade education.

I became increasingly frustrated at not being able to express what I wanted to convey in letters that I wrote, especially those to Mr. Elijah Muhammad. In the street, I had been the most articulate hustler out there—I had commanded attention when I said something. But now, trying to write simple English, I not only wasn't articulate, I wasn't even functional. How would I sound writing in slang, the way I would *say* it, something such as, "Look, daddy, let me pull your coat about a cat, Elijah Muhammad—"

Many who today hear me somewhere in person, or on television, or those who read something I've said, will think I went to school far beyond the eighth grade. This impression is due entirely to my prison studies.

It had really begun back in the Charlestown Prison, when Bimbi first made me feel envy of his stock of knowledge. Bimbi had always taken charge of any conversations he was in, and I had tried to emulate him. But every book I picked up had few sentences which didn't contain anywhere from one to nearly all of the words that might as well have been in Chinese. When I just skipped those words, of course, I really ended up with little idea of what the book said. So I had come to the Norfolk Prison Colony still going through only book-reading motions. Pretty soon, I would have quit even these motions, unless I had received the motivation that I did.

I saw that the best thing I could do was get hold of a dictionary—to study, to learn some words. I was lucky enough to reason also that I should try to improve my penmanship. It was sad. I couldn't even write in a straight line. It was both ideas together that moved me to request a dictionary along with some tablets and pencils from the Norfolk Prison Colony school.

I spent two days just riffling uncertainly through the dictionary's pages. I'd never realized so many words existed! I didn't know *which* words I needed to learn. Finally, just to start some kind of action, I began copying.

In my slow, painstaking, ragged handwriting, I copied into my tablet everything printed on that first page, down to the punctuation marks.

I believe it took me a day. Then, aloud, I read back, to myself, everything I'd written on the tablet. Over and over, aloud, to myself, I read my own handwriting.

I woke up the next morning, thinking about those words—immensely proud to realize that not only had I written so much at one time, but I'd written words that I never knew were in the world. Moreover, with a little effort, I also could remember what many of these words meant. I reviewed the words whose meanings I didn't remember. Funny thing, from the dictionary first page right now, that "aardvark" springs to my mind. The dictionary had a picture of it, a long-tailed, long-eared, burrowing African mammal, which lives off termites caught by sticking out its tongue as an anteater does for ants.

I was so fascinated that I went on—I copied the dictionary's next page. And the same experience came when I studied that. With every succeeding page, I also learned of people and places and events from history. Actually the dictionary is like a miniature encyclopedia. Finally the dictionary's A section had filled a whole tablet—and I went on into the B's. That was the way I started copying what eventually became the entire dictionary. It went a lot faster after so much practice helped me to pick up handwriting speed. Between what I wrote in my tablet, and writing letters, during the rest of my time in prison I would guess I wrote a million words.

I suppose it was inevitable that as my word-base broadened, I could for the first time pick up a book and read and now begin to understand what the book was saying. Anyone who has read a great deal can imagine the new world that opened. Let me tell you something: from then until I left that prison, in every free moment I had, if I was not reading in the library, I was reading on my bunk. You couldn't have gotten me out of books with a wedge. Between Mr. Muhammad's teachings, my correspondence, my visitors, ... and my reading of books, months passed without my even thinking about being imprisoned. In fact, up to then, I never had been so truly free in my life.

The Norfolk Prison Colony's library was in the school building. A variety of classes was taught there by instructors who came from such places as Harvard and Boston universities. The weekly debates between inmate teams were also held in the school building. You would be astonished to know how worked up convict debaters and audiences would get over subjects like "Should Babies Be Fed Milk?"

Available on the prison library's shelves were books on just about every general subject. Much of the big private collection that Parkhurst had willed to the prison was still in crates and boxes in the back of the library—thousands of old books. Some of them looked ancient: covers faded, old-time parchment-looking binding. Parkhurst . . . seemed to have been principally interested in history and religion. He had the money and the special interest to have a lot of books that you wouldn't have in a general circulation. Any college library would have been lucky to get that collection.

As you can imagine, especially in a prison where there was heavy emphasis on rehabilitation, an inmate was smiled upon if he demonstrated an unusually intense interest in books. There was a sizable number of well-read inmates, especially the popular debaters. Some were said by many to be practically walking encyclopedias. They were almost celebrities. No university would ask any student to devour literature as I did when this new world opened to me, of being able to read and *understand.*

I read more in my room than in the library itself. An inmate who was known to read a lot could check out more than the permitted maximum number of books. I preferred reading in the total isolation of my own room.

When I had progressed to really serious reading, every night at about ten P.M. I would be outraged with the "lights out." It always seemed to catch me right in the middle of something engrossing.

Fortunately, right outside my door was a corridor light that cast a glow into my room. The glow was enough to read by, once my eyes adjusted to it. So when "lights out" came, I would sit on the floor where I could continue reading in that glow.

At one-hour intervals the night guards paced past every room. Each time I heard the approaching footsteps, I jumped into bed and feigned sleep. And as soon as the guard passed, I got back out of bed onto the floor area of that light-glow, where I would read for another fifty-eight minutes—until the guard approached again. That went on until three or four every morning. Three or four hours of sleep a night was enough for me. Often in the years in the streets I had slept less than that.

The teachings of Mr. Muhammad stressed how history had been "whitened"—when white men had written history books, the black man simply had been left out. Mr. Muhammad couldn't have said anything that would have struck me much harder. I had never forgotten how when my class, me and all of those whites, had studied seventh-grade United States history back in Mason, the history of the Negro had been covered in one paragraph, and the teacher had gotten a big laugh with his joke, "Negroes' feet are so big that when they walk, they leave a hole in the ground."

This is one reason why Mr. Muhammad's teachings spread so swiftly all over the United States, among *all* Negroes, whether or not they became followers of Mr. Muhammad. The teachings ring true—to every Negro. You can hardly show me a black adult in America—or a white one, for that matter—who knows from the history books anything like the truth about the black man's role. In my own case, once I heard of the "glorious history of the black man," I took special pains to hunt in the library for books that would inform me on details about black history.

I can remember accurately the very first set of books that really impressed me. I have since bought that set of books and I have it at home for my children to read as they grow up. It's called *Wonders of the World*. It's full of pictures of archeological finds, statues that depict, usually, non-European people.

I found books like Will Durant's *Story of Civilization*. I read H. G. Wells' *Outline of History*. *Souls of Black Folk* by W. E. B. Du Bois gave me a glimpse into the black people's history before they came to this country. Carter G. Woodson's *Negro History* opened my eyes about black empires before the black slave was brought to the United States, and the early Negro struggles for freedom.

J. A. Rogers' three volumes of *Sex and Race* told about race-mixing before Christ's time; and Aesop being a black man who told fables; about Egypt's Pharaohs; about the great Coptic Christian Empires; about Ethiopia, the earth's oldest continuous black civilization, as China is the oldest continuous civilization.

Mr. Muhammad's teaching about how the white man had been created led me to *Findings In Genetics* by Gregor Mendel. (The dictionary's G section was where I had learned what "genetics" meant.) I really studied this book by the Austrian monk. Reading it over and over, especially certain sections, helped me to understand that if you started with a black man, a white man could be produced; but starting with a white man, you never could produce a black man—because the white chromosome is recessive. And since no one disputes that there was but one Original Man, the conclusion is clear.

During the last year or so, in the *New York Times,* Arnold Toynbee used the word "bleached" in describing the white man. His words were: "White (i.e., bleached) human beings of North European origin. . . ." Toynbee also referred to the European geographic area as only a peninsula of Asia. He said there is no such thing as Europe. And if you look at the globe, you will see for yourself that America is only an extension of Asia. (But at the same time Toynbee is among those who have helped to bleach history. He has written that Africa was the only continent that produced no history. He won't write that again. Every day now, the truth is coming to light.)

I never will forget how shocked I was when I began reading about slavery's total horror. It made such an impact upon me that it later became one of my favorite subjects when I became a minister of Mr. Muhammad's. The world's most monstrous crime, the sin and the blood on the white man's hands, are almost impossible to believe. Books like the one by Frederick Olmsted opened my eyes to the horrors suffered when the slave was landed in the United States. The European woman, Fanny Kemble, who had married a Southern white slaveowner, described how human beings were degraded. Of course I read *Uncle Tom's Cabin*. In fact, I believe that's the only novel I have ever read since I started serious reading.

Parkhurst's collection also contained some bound pamphlets of the Abolitionist Anti-Slavery Society of New England. I read descriptions of atrocities, saw those illustrations of black slave women tied up and flogged with whips; of black mothers watching their babies being dragged off, never to be seen by their mothers again; of dogs after slaves, and of the fugitive slave catchers, evil white men with whips and clubs and chains and guns. I read about the slave preacher Nat Turner, who put the fear of God into the white slavemaster. Nat Turner wasn't going around preaching pie-in-the-sky and "non-violent" freedom for the black man. There in Virginia one night in 1831, Nat and seven other slaves started out at his master's home and through the night they went from one plantation "big house" to the next, killing, until by the next morning 57 white people were dead and Nat had about 70 slaves following him. White people, terrified for their lives, fled from their homes, locked themselves up in public buildings, hid in the woods, and some even left the state. A small army of soldiers took two months to catch and hang Nat Turner. Somewhere I have read where Nat Turner's example is said to have inspired John Brown to invade Virginia and attack Harpers Ferry nearly thirty years later, with thirteen white men and five Negroes.

I read Herodotus, "the father of History," or, rather, I read about him. And I read the histories of various nations, which opened my eyes gradually, then wider and wider, to how the whole world's white men had indeed acted like devils, pillaging and raping and bleeding and draining the whole world's non-white people. I remember, for instance, books such as Will Durant's *The Story of Oriental Civilization,* and Mahatma Gandhi's accounts of the struggle to drive the British out of India.

Book after book showed me how the white man had brought upon the world's black, brown, red, and yellow peoples every variety of the suffering of exploitation. I saw how since the sixteenth century, the so-called "Christian trader" white man began to ply the seas in his lust for Asian and African empires, and plunder, and power. I read, I saw, how the white man never has gone among the non-white peoples bearing the Cross in the true manner and spirit of Christ's teachings—meek, humble, and Christlike.

I perceived, as I read, how the collective white man had been actually nothing but a piratical opportunist who used Faustian machinations to make his own Christianity his initial wedge in criminal conquests. First, always "religiously," he branded "heathen" and "pagan" labels upon ancient non-white cultures and civilizations. The stage thus set, he then turned upon his non-white victims his weapons of war.

I read how, entering India—half a *billion* deeply religious brown people—the British white man, by 1759, through promises, trickery, and manipulations, controlled much of India through Great Britain's East India Company. The parasitical British administration kept tentacling out to half of the sub-continent. In 1857, some of the desperate people of India finally mutinied—and, excepting the African slave trade, nowhere has history recorded any more unnecessary bestial and ruthless human carnage than the British suppression of the non-white Indian people.

Over 115 million African blacks—close to the 1930's population of the United States—were murdered or enslaved during the slave trade. And I read how when the slave market was glutted, the cannibalistic white powers of Europe next carved up, as their colonies, the richest areas of the black continent. And Europe's chancelleries for the next century played a chess game of naked exploitation and power from Cape Horn to Cairo.

Ten guards and the warden couldn't have torn me out of those books. Not even Elijah Muhammad could have been more eloquent than those books were in providing indisputable proof that the collective white man had acted like a devil in virtually every contact he had with the world's collective non-white man. I listen today to the radio, and watch television, and read the headlines about the collective white man's fear and tension concerning China. When the white man professes ignorance about why the Chinese hate him so, my mind can't help flashing back to what I read, there in prison, about how the blood forebears of this same white man raped China at a time when China was trusting and helpless. Those original white "Christian traders" sent into China millions of pounds of opium. By 1839, so many of the Chinese were addicts that China's desperate government destroyed twenty thousand chests of opium. The first Opium War was promptly declared by the white man. Imagine! Declaring *war* upon someone who objects to being narcotized! The Chinese were severely beaten, with Chinese-invented gunpowder.

The Treaty of Nanking made China pay the British white man for the destroyed opium; forced open China's major ports to British trade; forced China to abandon Hong Kong; fixed China's import tariffs so low that cheap British articles soon flooded in, maiming China's industrial development.

After a second Opium War, the Tientsin Treaties legalized the ravaging opium trade, legalized a British-French-American control of China's customs. China tried delaying that Treaty's ratification; Peking was looted and burned.

"Kill the foreign white devils!" was the 1901 Chinese war cry in the Boxer Rebellion. Losing again, this time the Chinese were driven from Peking's choicest areas. The vicious, arrogant white man put up the famous signs, "Chinese and dogs not allowed."

Red China after World War II closed its doors to the Western white world. Massive Chinese agricultural, scientific, and industrial efforts are described in a book that *Life* magazine recently published. Some observers inside Red China have reported that the world never has known such a hate-white campaign as is now going on in this non-white country where, present birth-rates continuing, in fifty more years Chinese will be half the earth's population. And it seems that some Chinese chickens will soon come home to roost, with China's recent successful nuclear tests.

Let us face reality. We can see in the United Nations a new world order being shaped, along color lines—an alliance among the non-white nations. America's U.N. Ambassador Adlai Stevenson complained not long ago that in the United Nations "a skin game" was being played. He was right. He was facing reality. A "skin game" *is* being played. But Ambassador Stevenson sounded like Jesse James accusing the marshal of carrying a gun. Because who in the world's history ever has played a worse "skin game" than the white man?

Mr. Muhammad, to whom I was writing daily, had no idea of what a new world had opened up to me through my efforts to document his teachings in books.

When I discovered philosophy, I tried to touch all the landmarks of philosophical development. Gradually, I read most of the old philosophers, Occidental and Oriental. The Oriental philosophers were the ones I came to prefer; finally, my impression was that most Occidental philosophy had largely been borrowed from the Oriental thinkers. Socrates, for instance, traveled in Egypt. Some sources even say that Socrates was initiated into some of the Egyptian mysteries. Obviously Socrates got some of his wisdom among the East's wise men.

I have often reflected upon the new vistas that reading opened to me. I knew right there in prison that reading had changed forever the course of my life. As I see it today, the ability to read awoke inside me some long dormant craving to be mentally alive. I certainly wasn't seeking any degree, the way a college confers a status symbol upon its students. My homemade education gave me, with every additional book that I read, a little bit more sensitivity to the deafness, dumbness, and blindness that was afflicting the black race in America. Not long ago, an English writer telephoned me from London, asking questions. One was, "What's your alma mater?" I told him, "Books." You will never catch me with a free fifteen minutes in which I'm not studying something I feel might be able to help the black man.

Yesterday I spoke in London, and both ways on the plane across the Atlantic I was studying a document about how the United Nations proposes to insure the human rights of the oppressed minorities of the world. The American black man is the world's most shameful case of minority oppression. What makes the black man think of himself as only an internal United States issue is just a catch-phrase, two words, "civil rights." How is the black man going to get "civil rights" before first he wins his *human* rights? If the American black man will start thinking about his *human* rights, and then start thinking of himself as part of one of the world's great peoples, he will see he has a case for the United Nations.

I can't think of a better case! Four hundred years of black blood and sweat invested here in America, and the white man still has the black man begging for what every immigrant fresh off the ship can take for granted the minute he walks down the gangplank.

But I'm digressing. I told the Englishman that my alma mater was books, a good library. Every time I catch a plane, I have with me a book that I want to read—and that's a lot of books these days. If I weren't out here every day battling the white man, I could spend the rest of my life reading, just satisfying my curiosity—because you can hardly mention anything I'm not curious about. I don't think anybody ever got more out of going to prison than I did. In fact, prison enabled me to study far more intensively than I would have if my life had gone differently and I had attended some college. I imagine that one of the biggest troubles with colleges is there are too many distractions, too much panty-raiding, fraternities, and boola-boola and all of that. Where else but in a prison could I have attacked my ignorance by being able to study intensely sometimes as much as fifteen hours a day?

REFLECTING ON THE READING

1. What motivates Malcolm X to try to improve his reading, writing, and speaking abilities? How does he go about doing so? What enables him to sustain his studies? What do you think his description of how he improved his literacy skills reveals about him as a person? What does it reveal about our cultural values regarding literacy?

2. What does Malcolm X mean when he writes that his extensive reading made him feel truly free even while he is still in prison? What does that statement reveal about his beliefs about literacy?

3. What role does reading play in Malcolm X's understanding of his heritage as an African American? How does reading influence his views about his race and about the White race? What might his experience with the books he read suggest about the relationship between literacy and racial or cultural identity?

4. What kinds of books does Malcolm X read once he has improved his literacy abilities? What does he learn from these books? Do you think the conclusions

he draws from these books are valid? Why or why not? Cite specific passages from the text to support your answer.

5. What does Malcolm X believe is the purpose of his extensive reading? In what ways has it benefited him? Do you think his views about reading are widely shared? Explain. Do you share his views? What might your answer suggest about your beliefs regarding literacy?

Examining Rhetorical Strategies

1. Examine how Malcolm X tells the story of how he improves his literacy skills. What kinds of information does he provide? What kinds of events or incidents does he include? What does he emphasize in this story? What do you think he leaves out? Does his story of his literacy learning seem unusual or unique to you? Does it seem familiar in any way? Explain. Do you think he wished to present it as unusual or unique? If so, why? What might his story suggest about literacy and about how one learns to become literate? Do you think Malcolm X intended to suggest this? Explain.

2. Based on this passage, how would you characterize Malcolm X's attitudes toward literacy and learning in general? What beliefs about literacy does he hold? What beliefs about education does he hold? Do you think Malcolm X assumes that his readers share his views about literacy and learning? Do you share those views? Why or why not? How might your own beliefs about literacy and learning have influenced your reaction to this passage?

3. How would you describe Malcolm X's voice in this passage? What features make his voice distinctive—or not distinctive—in your view? Cite specific passages from the text to support your answer. Did you find his voice compelling? Why or why not? What might your reaction to his voice suggest about you as a reader? How might your reaction relate to your attitudes toward Malcolm X?

4. Malcolm X published his autobiography, from which this passage is taken, in 1965, a time of widespread activism among African Americans and great racial tension in the United States. He himself was a highly visible and controversial figure in the struggle for civil rights at that time. Many people, both supporters of his and enemies of his, would find his book of intense interest. Assess the way he seems to address his readers in this passage. What audience do you think he imagined for his writing? Do you think he expected that many of his readers would be sympathetic to him while many would be hostile? Explain. Do you think he wished to provoke a strong reaction to his writing on the part of his readers? Explain, citing specific passages from the text in your answer. How might White and Black readers react differently to his story? Do you think Malcolm X was aware of those potential differences? Why or why not?

5. Examine the references that Malcolm X makes to the specific books he reads while in prison. What kinds of books does he mention? Why does he mention these specific books in this passage? How do you think he expected readers to react to these references? What effect did these references have on you as a reader? Do you find them effective evidence to support Malcolm X's point? Why or why not?

Engaging the Issues

1. Write an essay for an audience of your classmates in which you describe an experience you had as a reader that was especially important to you and perhaps changed you in some way. You might focus your essay on a specific book you read that deeply affected you. Or you might focus on an experience involving a book or some other text (a poem, an article, a letter) that was somehow important in your life. In your essay, tell the story of your experience in a way that will enable your readers to understand the significance of the experience to your life.

2. In a group of your classmates, share the essays you wrote for Question #1 above. What kinds of experiences did you each write about? What similarities and differences emerge from those essays? What views of literacy seem to emerge from them? How might your respective views of literacy and its role in your lives relate to your racial, ethnic, gender, or social class background? Based on your discussions, try to draw conclusions about the role literacy can play in our lives.

3. Write an essay in which you discuss the kinds of reading you have been asked to do in school. In your essay, describe the books and other materials that you were assigned to read as a student in middle and high school and describe, too, how those materials were treated by your teachers. How much choice did you have in the materials you were asked to read? What seemed to be the purpose of the specific books and related materials that you were assigned to read? Compare your experiences as a reader to those of Malcolm X. Were the books you were asked to read similar or different in any way from the books he reads while he is in prison? Did the books and related materials you were asked to read have the kind of effect on you that the books he reads have on him? Why or why not? Try to draw conclusions about how reading might influence a person's life.

4. On the basis of the experiences you described in Question #3 above, write a letter to the superintendent of your local school district in which you express your views about how reading should be taught to students in your district. In your letter, describe the kinds of reading materials to which you believe students should be exposed and explain your choices. You might refer to your own experiences or to other accounts, such as Malcolm X's, in discussing the teaching of reading in schools.

5. Consider the ways in which new technologies for literacy might affect the kinds of experiences with reading that Malcolm X describes in this passage. Do you think his experiences with books and reading in general, as he describes them in this passage, would have been similar or different in any way if he had had access to technologies like the World Wide Web? Do you think that *books* specifically play a special role in the experiences he describes in a way that newer literacy technologies could not? Write an essay for your classmates in which you discuss this issue. In your essay, try to imagine how the *technologies* for literacy might shape the experiences of readers—like Malcolm X and like yourself. Address the question of whether new literacy technologies—such as the computer technologies associated with the Internet and

online communications—might represent a different "power of the pen" than was experienced by Malcolm X.

6. Using your library and the World Wide Web, investigate the life of Malcolm X. Locate some books and articles about him and visit several Web sites devoted to his life. Assess the kinds of information about Malcolm X and the perspectives on his life that emerge from the various sources you consulted. What information about him seems widely available? What kinds of views about him did you encounter? Did you detect any differences in the media that your sources used? In other words, were the books and articles about Malcolm X different from the Web sites you found in the ways they seemed to characterize Malcolm X?

On the basis of this research, write a report for your classmates. In your report, describe the kinds of sources you consulted and discuss the kinds of information contained in them. Analyze the perspective that these sources seem to have on Malcolm X. Draw conclusions about how the medium of the source might affect the nature of the information or the perspective of that source. (For example, discuss differences between printed books and organization Web pages as sources of information about a controversial figure like Malcolm X.)

Alternatively, create a Web site on the basis of your research. Be sure to identify the purpose of your Web site, and include appropriate links to other sites, including those you analyzed for this assignment.

7. Write a conventional academic essay in which you discuss the differences and similarities in the experiences of Malcolm X and June Jordan with respect to literacy. In your essay, describe the role literacy played in their personal lives and their public lives as activists for Black rights. Take into account the different circumstances within which each writer lived and relate those circumstances to the power of literacy in their lives.

Forbidden Reading

ALBERTO MANGUEL

INTRODUCTION The history of reading, author Alberto Manguel tells us in the following passage, "is lit by a seemingly endless line of censors' bonfires." Manguel goes on to list the names of some of those censors, and his list—brief though it may be—makes it clear that efforts to control what people read are not isolated or unique to a particular time or place. Censorship, Manguel suggests, seems to be a universal urge.

The question is, Why? Manguel provides a variety of answers, all somehow related to a sense of reading's power to convey ideas that someone has determined ought to be suppressed. The examples of censorship that Manguel provides reveal that this supposed power of reading often seems to clash with other kinds of power: political, religious, moral. Some of these examples are familiar ones. The public book burnings instigated by the Nazi Party in Germany during the 1930's, for instance, are often cited as dramatic and frightening efforts to exercise political control and to suppress any ideas that might challenge that control. There are other such examples from throughout history, as Manguel indicates. And recent history reveals quite clearly that conflicts over the distribution or suppression of reading materials continue to be common in the United States and throughout the world. Perhaps the most well-publicized such conflicts in recent years involve the selection of science and history textbooks for use in American public schools. High-profile controversies over specific textbooks in Texas, California, and several other states in the 1990's indicate that controlling what we read remains a matter of intense public debate.

But it would be a mistake to think of censorship—or, more generally, the control of writing and reading—only in terms of these highly visible controversies. For the control of reading and writing can take many forms that are more subtle but perhaps no less effective than publicized efforts to ban books. In his essay, Manguel tells of the experiences of Mrs. Gosse, the mother of English writer Edmund Gosse, who in her childhood in the early nineteenth century was forbidden from reading novels or stories of the kind that most children read. Manguel describes the powerful long-term effects of that policy on Mrs. Gosse's own imagination and on her son's childhood. The example of Gosse reminds us that the many efforts by parents, teachers, and others to control what children read can perhaps influence those children in far-reaching ways that we never see. And Manguel reminds us that controlling what one reads is not the only form of censorship: *how* one reads can also be controlled or at least influenced. To understand the importance of that insight, you might think about how your teachers have presented the textbooks and other books that they have assigned as reading in your classes. How were you taught to read those texts? Whose opinions about them were considered "right"? Were you ever encouraged to question the ideas presented in a textbook? Were you ever told that your understanding of an idea contained in those textbooks was wrong? In these seemingly small ways, your reading may have been controlled, even if it wasn't censored. In this sense, Manguel might help us see how complex a matter reading is—and how subtle and powerful the efforts to control it can be.

Alberto Manguel is an internationally acclaimed writer, editor, and translator who is currently the Markin-Flanagan distinguished writer at the University of Calgary in Canada. Among the many short story anthologies he has edited or coedited are *By the Light of the Glow-Worm Lamp: Three Centuries of Reflections on Nature* (1998), *The Ark in the Garden: Fables for Our Times* (1998), and *The Second Gates of Paradise: The Anthology of Erotic Short Fiction* (1997). He has translated many novels and volumes of stories and is author of the novel *News From a Foreign Country Came*. The following essay appears in his book *A History of Reading* (1996), for which he received the prestigious French Medici Prize.

REFLECTING BEFORE READING

1. As Alberto Manguel demonstrates in the following essay, censorship—along with other efforts to control reading—is an old practice, extending back in time to the earliest civilizations. As you prepare to read, consider what you know about censorship and recall any experiences you might have had with censorship or similar efforts to control your reading or writing. What are your

own feelings about censorship? Are there any circumstances under which you think reading materials should be controlled or banned? Keep you own views about censorship in mind as you read Manguel's essay.

2. Many of the authors in this chapter—and in this reader—refer to the "power" of reading or the "power" of literacy. Not all of them, however, understand those phrases in the same way. As you read, consider what Manguel means by the "power" of reading. How does his idea about that power compare to the ideas of other authors you've read?

I n 1660, Charles II of England, son of the king who had so unfortunately consulted Virgil's oracle, known to his subjects as the Merrie Monarch for his love of pleasure and loathing of business, decreed that the Council for Foreign Plantations should instruct natives, servants and slaves of the British colonies in the precepts of Christianity. Dr. Johnson, who from the vantage point of the following century admired the king, said that "he had the merit of endeavouring to do what he thought was for the salvation of the souls of his subjects, till he lost a great empire."[1] The historian Macaulay,[2] who from a distance of two centuries did not, argued that for Charles "the love of God, the love of country, the love of family, the love of friends, were phrases of the same sort, delicate and convenient synonyms for the love of self."[3]

It isn't clear why Charles issued this decree in the first year of his reign, except that he imagined it to be a way of laying out new grounds for religious tolerance, which Parliament opposed. Charles, who in spite of his pro-Catholic tendencies proclaimed himself loyal to the Protestant faith, believed (as far as he believed anything) that, as Luther had taught, the salvation of the soul depended on each individual's ability to read God's word for himself or herself.[4] But British slave-owners were not convinced. They feared the very idea of a "literate black population" who might find dangerous revolutionary ideas in books. They did not believe those who argued that a literacy restricted to the Bible would strengthen the bonds of society; they realized that if slaves could read the Bible, they could also read abolitionist tracts, and that even in the Scriptures the slaves might find inflammatory notions of revolt and freedom.[5] The opposition to Charles's decree was strongest in the American colonies, and strongest of all in South Carolina, where, a century later, strict laws were proclaimed forbidding all blacks, whether slaves or free men, to be taught to read. These laws were in effect until well into the mid-nineteenth century.

For centuries, Afro-American slaves learned to read against extraordinary odds, risking their lives in a process that, because of the difficulties set in their way, sometimes took several years. The accounts of their learning are many and heroic. Ninety-year-old Belle Myers Carothers—interviewed by the Federal Writers' Project, a commission set up in the 1930s to record, among other things, the personal narratives of former slaves—recalled that she had learned her letters while looking after the plantation owner's baby, who was playing with alphabet blocks. The owner, seeing what she was doing, kicked her with his boots. Myers persisted, secretly studying the child's letters as well as a few words in a speller she had found. One day, she said, "I found a hymn book . . . and spelled out 'When I Can Read My Title Clear'. I was so happy when I saw that I could really read, that I ran around telling all the other slaves."[6] Leonard Black's master once found him with a book and whipped him so severely "that he overcame my thirst for knowledge, and I relinquished its pursuit until after I absconded".[7] Doc Daniel Dowdy recalled that "the first time you was caught trying to read or write you was whipped with a cow-hide, the next time with a cat-o-nine-tails and the third time they cut the first joint off your forefinger."[8] Throughout the South, it was common for plantation owners to hang any slave who tried to teach the others how to spell.[9]

Under these circumstances, slaves who wanted to be literate were forced to find devious methods of learning, either from other slaves or from sympathetic white teachers, or by inventing devices that allowed them to study unobserved. The American writer Frederick Douglass, who was born into slavery and became one of the most eloquent abolitionists of his day, as well as founder of several political journals, recalled in his autobiography: "The frequent hearing of my mistress reading the Bible aloud . . . awakened my curiosity in respect to this *mystery* of reading, and roused in me the desire to learn. Up to this time I had known nothing whatever of this wonderful art, and my ignorance and inexperience of what it could do for me, as well as my confidence in my mistress, emboldened me to ask her to teach me to read. . . . In an incredibly short time, by her kind assistance, I had mastered the alphabet and could spell words of three or four letters. . . . [My master] forbade her to give me any further instruction . . . [but] the determination which he expressed to keep me in ignorance only rendered me the more resolute to seek intelligence. In learning to read, therefore, I am not sure that I do not owe quite as much to the opposition of my master as to the kindly assistance of my amiable mistress."[10] Thomas Johnson, a slave who later became a well-known missionary preacher in England, explained that he had learned to read by studying the letters in a Bible he had stolen. Since his master read aloud a chapter from the New Testament every night, Johnson would coax him to read the same chapter over and over, until he knew it by heart and was able to find the same words on the printed page. Also, when the master's son was studying, Johnson would suggest that the boy read part of his lesson out loud. "Lor's over me," Johnson would say to encourage him, "read that again," which the boy often did, believing that Johnson was admiring his performance. Through repetition, he learned enough to be able to read the newspapers by the time the Civil War broke out, and later set up a school of his own to teach others to read.[11]

Learning to read was, for slaves, not an immediate passport to freedom but rather a way of gaining access to one of the powerful instruments of their oppressors: the book. The slave-owners (like dictators, tyrants, absolute monarchs and other illicit holders of power) were strong believers in the power of the written word. They knew, far better than some readers, that reading is a strength that requires barely a few first words to become overwhelming. Someone able to read one sentence is able to read all; more important, that reader has now the possibility of reflecting upon the sentence, of acting upon it, of giving it a meaning. "You can play dumb with a sentence," said the Austrian playwright Peter Handke. "Assert yourself with the sentence against other sentences. Name everything that gets in your way and move it out of the way. Familiarize yourself with all objects. Make all objects into a sentence with the sentence. You can make all objects into your sentence. With this sentence, all objects belong to you. With this sentence, all objects are yours."[12] For all these reasons, reading had to be forbidden.

As centuries of dictators have known, an illiterate crowd is easiest to rule; since the craft of reading cannot be untaught once it has been acquired, the second-best recourse is to limit its scope. Therefore, like no other human creation, books have been the bane of dictatorships. Absolute power requires that all reading be official reading; instead of whole libraries of opinions, the ruler's word should suffice. Books, wrote Voltaire in a satirical pamphlet called "Concerning the Horrible Danger of Reading", "dissipate ignorance, the custodian and safeguard of well-policed states".[13] Censorship, therefore, in some form or another, is the corollary of all power, and the history of reading is lit by a seemingly endless line of censors' bonfires, from the earliest papyrus scrolls to the books of our time. The works of Protagoras were burned in 411 BC in Athens. In the year 213 BC the Chinese emperor Shih Huang-ti tried to put an end to reading by burning all the books in his realm. In 168 BC, the Jewish Library in Jerusalem was deliberately destroyed during the Maccabean uprising. In the first century AD, Augustus exiled the poets Cornelius Gallus and Ovid and banned their works. The emperor Caligula ordered that all books by Homer, Virgil and Livy be burned (but his edict was not carried out). In 303, Diocletian condemned all Christian books to the fire. And these were only the beginning. The young Goethe, witnessing the burning of a book in Frankfurt, felt that he was attending an execution. "To see an inanimate object being punished," he wrote, "is in and of itself something truly terrible."[14] The illusion cherished by those who burn books is that, in doing so, they are able to cancel history and abolish the past. On May 10, 1933, in Berlin, as the cameras rolled, propaganda minister Paul Joseph Goebbels spoke during the burning of more than twenty thousand books, in front of a cheering crowd of more than one hundred thousand people: "Tonight you do well to throw in the fire these obscenities from the past. This is a powerful, huge and symbolic action that will tell the entire world that the old spirit is dead. From these ashes will rise the phoenix of the new spirit." A twelve-year-old boy, Hans Pauker, later head of the Leo Baeck Institute for Jewish Studies in London, was present at the burning, and recalled that, as the books were thrown into the flames, speeches were made to add solemnity to the occasion.[15] "Against the exaggeration of unconscious urges based on destructive analysis of the psyche, for the nobility of the human soul, I commit to the flames the works of Sigmund Freud," one of the censors would declaim before burning Freud's books. Steinbeck, Marx, Zola, Hemingway, Einstein, Proust, H.G. Wells, Heinrich and Thomas Mann, Jack London, Bertolt Brecht and hundreds of others received the homage of similar epitaphs.

In 1872, a little over two centuries after Charles II's optimistic decree, Anthony Comstock—a descendant of the old colonialists who had objected to their sovereign's educating urges—founded in New York the Society for the Suppression of Vice, the first effective censorship board in the United States. All things considered, Comstock would have preferred that reading had never been invented ("Our father Adam could not read in Paradise," he once affirmed), but since it had, he was determined to regulate its use. Comstock saw himself as a reader's reader, who knew what was good literature and what was bad, and did everything in his power to impose his views on others. "As for me," he wrote in his journal a year before the society's founding, "I am resolved that I will not in God's strength yield to other people's opinion but will if I feel and believe I am right stand firm. Jesus was never moved from the path of duty, however hard, by public opinion. Why should I be?"[16]

Anthony Comstock was born in New Canaan, Connecticut, on March 7, 1844. He was a hefty man, and in the course of his censoring career he many times used his size to defeat his opponents physically. One of his contemporaries described him in these terms: "Standing about five feet in his shoes, he carries his two hundred and ten pounds of muscle and bone so well that you would judge him to weigh not over a hundred and eighty. His Atlas shoulders of enormous girth, surmounted by a bull-like neck, are in keeping with a biceps and a calf of exceptional size and iron solidarity. His legs are short, and remind one somewhat of tree trunks."[17]

Comstock was in his twenties when he arrived in New York with $3.45 in his pocket. He found a job as a dry-goods salesman and was soon able to save the $500 necessary to buy a little house in Brooklyn. A few years later, he met the daughter of a Presbyterian minister, ten years his elder, and married her. In New York, Comstock discovered much that he found objectionable. In 1868, after a friend told him how he had been "led astray and corrupted and diseased" by a certain book (the title of this powerful work has not come down to us), Comstock bought a copy at the store and then, accompanied by a policeman, had the shopkeeper arrested and the stock seized. The success of his first raid was such that he decided to continue, regularly causing the arrest of small publishers and printers of titillating material.

With the assistance of friends in the YMCA, who supplied him with $8,500, Comstock was able to set up the society for which he became famous. Two years before his death, he told an interviewer in New York, "In the forty-one years I have been here, I have convicted persons enough to fill a passenger train of sixty-one coaches, sixty coaches containing sixty passengers each and the sixty-first almost full. I have destroyed 160 tons of obscene literature."[18]

Comstock's fervour was also responsible for at least fifteen suicides. After he had a former Irish surgeon, William Haynes, thrown in prison "for publishing 165 different kinds of lewd literature", Haynes killed himself. Shortly afterwards, Comstock was about to catch the Brooklyn ferry (he later recalled) when "a Voice" told him to proceed to Haynes's house. He arrived as the widow was unloading the printing-plates of the forbidden books from a delivery wagon. With great agility Comstock leapt onto the wagoner's seat and rushed the wagon to the YMCA, where the plates were destroyed.[19]

What books did Comstock read? He was an unwitting follower of Oscar Wilde's facetious advice: "I never read a book I must review; it prejudices you so." Sometimes, however, he dipped into the books before destroying them, and was aghast at what he read. He found the literature of France and Italy "little better than histories of brothels and prostitutes in these lust-crazed nations. How often are found in these villainous stories, heroines, lovely, excellent, cultivated, wealthy, and charming in every way, who have for their lovers married men; or, after marriage, lovers flock about the charming young wife, enjoying privileges belonging only to the husband!" Even the classics were not above reproach, "Take, for instance, a well-known book written by Boccaccio," he wrote in his book, *Traps for the Young*. The book was so filthy that he would do anything "to prevent this, like a wild beast, from breaking loose and destroying the youth of the country."[20] Balzac, Rabelais, Walt Whitman, Bernard Shaw and Tolstoy were among his victims. Comstock's everyday reading was, he said, the Bible.

Comstock's methods were savage but superficial. He lacked the perception and patience of more sophisticated censors, who will mine a text with excruciating care in search of buried messages. In 1981, for instance, the military junta led by General Pinochet banned *Don Quixote* in Chile, because the general believed (quite rightly) that it contained a plea for individual freedom and an attack on conventional authority.

Comstock's censoring limited itself to placing suspect works, in a rage of abuse, on a catalogue of the damned. His access to books was also limited; he could only chase them as they appeared in public, by which time many had escaped into the hands of eager readers. The Catholic Church was far ahead of him. In 1559, the Sacred Congregation of the Roman Inquisition had published the first *Index of Forbidden Books*—a list of books that the Church considered dangerous to the faith and morals of Roman Catholics. The *Index,* which included books censored in advance of publication as well as immoral books already published, was never intended as a complete catalogue of all the books banned by the Church. When it was abandoned in June 1966, however, it contained—among hundreds of theological works—hundreds of others by secular writers from Voltaire and Diderot to Colette and Graham Greene. No doubt Comstock would have found such a list useful.

"Art is not above morals. Morals stand first," Comstock wrote. "Law ranks next as the defender of public morals. Art only comes in conflict with the law when its tendency is obscene, lewd or indecent." This led the *New York World* to ask, in an editorial, "Has it really been determined that there is nothing wholesome in art unless it has clothes on?"[21] Comstock's definition of immoral art, like that of all censors, begs the question. Comstock died in 1915. Two years later, the American essayist H.L. Mencken defined Comstock's crusade as "the new Puritanism", . . . "not ascetic but militant. Its aim is not to lift up saints but to knock down sinners."[22]

Comstock's conviction was that what he called "immoral literature" perverted the minds of the young, who should busy themselves with higher spiritual matters. This concern is ancient, and not exclusive to the West. In fifteenth-century China, a collection of tales from the Ming Dynasty known as *Stories Old and New* was so successful that it had to be placed in the Chinese index so as not to distract young scholars from the study of Confucius.[23] In the Western world, a milder form of this obsession has expressed itself in a general fear of fiction—at least since the days of Plato, who banned poets from his ideal republic. Madame Bovary's mother-in-law argued that novels were poisoning Emma's soul, and convinced her son to stop Emma's subscription to a book-lender, plunging her further into the swamp of boredom.[24] The mother of the English writer Edmund Gosse would allow no novels of any kind, religious or secular, to enter the house. As a very small child, in the early 1800s, she had amused herself and her brothers by reading and making up stories, until her Calvinist governess found out and lectured her severely, telling her that her pleasures were wicked. "From that time forth," wrote Mrs. Gosse in her diary, "I considered that to invent a story of any kind was a sin." But "the longing to invent stories grew with violence; everything I heard or read became food for my distemper. The simplicity of truth was not sufficient for me; I must needs embroider imagination upon it, and the folly, vanity and wickedness which disgraced my heart are more than I am able to express. Even now, tho' watched, prayed and striven against, this is still the sin that most easily besets me. It has hindered my prayers and prevented my improvement, and therefore has humbled me very much."[25] This she wrote at the age of twenty-nine.

In this belief she brought up her son. "Never in all my early childhood, did anyone address to me the affecting preamble, 'Once upon a time!' I was told about missionaries, but never about pirates; I was familiar with humming-birds, but I had never heard of fairies," Gosse remembered. "They desired to make me truthful; the tendency was to make me positive and sceptical. Had they wrapped me in the soft folds of supernatural fancy, my mind might have been longer content to follow their traditions in an unquestioning spirit."[26] The parents who took the Hawkins County Public Schools to court in Tennessee in 1980 had obviously not read Gosse's claim. They argued that an entire elementary school series, which included *Cinderella, Goldilocks* and *The Wizard of Oz,* violated their fundamentalist religious beliefs.[27]

Authoritarian readers who prevent others from learning to read, fanatical readers who decide what can and what cannot be read, stoical readers who refuse to read for pleasure and demand only the retelling of facts that they themselves hold to be true: all these attempt to limit the reader's vast and diverse powers. But censors can also work in different ways, without need of fire or courts of law. They can reinterpret books to render them serviceable only to themselves, for the sake of justifying their autocratic rights.

In 1967, when I was in my fifth year of high school, a military coup took place in Argentina, led by General Jorge Rafael Videla. What followed was a wave of human-rights abuses such as the country had never seen before. The army's excuse was that it was fighting a war against terrorists; as General Videla defined it, "a terrorist is not just someone with a gun or bomb, but also someone who spreads ideas that are contrary to Western and Christian civilization."[28] Among the thousands kidnapped and tortured was a priest, Father Orlando Virgilio Yorio. One day, Father Yorio's interrogator told him that his reading of the Gospel was false. "You interpreted Christ's doctrine in too literal a way," said the man. "Christ spoke of the poor, but when he spoke of the poor he spoke of the poor in spirit and you interpreted this in a literal way and went to live, literally, with poor people. In Argentina those who are poor in spirit are the rich and in the future you must spend your time helping the rich, who are those who really need spiritual help."[29]

Thus, not all the reader's powers are enlightening. The same act that can bring a text into being, draw out its revelations, multiply its meanings, mirror in it the past, the present and the possibilities of the future, can also destroy or attempt to destroy the living page. Every reader makes up readings, which is not the same as lying; but every reader can also lie, wilfully declaring the text subservient to a doctrine, to an arbitrary law, to a private advantage, to the rights of slaveowners or the authority of tyrants.

Notes

1. James Boswell, *The Life of Samuel Johnson,* ed. John Wain (London, 1973).

2. T.B. Macaulay, *The History of England,* 5 vols. (London, 1849–61).

3. Charles was nevertheless viewed as a worthy king by most of his subjects, who believed that his small vices corrected his greater ones. John Aubrey tells of a certain Arise Evans who "had a fungous Nose, and said it was revealed to him, that the King's Hand would Cure him: And at the first coming of King Charles II into St. James's Park, he kiss'd the King's Hand, and rubbed his Nose with it; which disturbed the King, but Cured him": John Aubrey, *Miscellanies, in Three Prose Works,* ed. John Buchanan-Brown (Oxford, 1972).

4. Antonia Fraser, *Royal Charles: Charles II and the Restoration* (London, 1979).

5. Janet Duitsman Cornelius, *When I Can Read My Title Clear: Literacy, Slavery, and Religion in the Antebellum South* (Columbia, S.C., 1991).

6. Quoted ibid.

7. Ibid.

8. Ibid.

9. Ibid.

10. Frederick Douglass, *The Life and Times of Frederick Douglass* (Hartford, Conn., 1881).

11. Quoted in Duitsman Cornelius, *When I Can Read My Title Clear.*

12. Peter Handke, *Kaspar* (Frankfurt-am-Main, 1967).

13. Voltaire, "De l'Horrible Danger de la Lecture", in *Mémoires, Suivis de Mélanges divers et precédés de "Voltaire Démiurge" par Paul Souday* (Paris, 1927).

14. Johann Wolfgang von Goethe, *Dichtung und Wahrheit* (Stuttgart, 1986), IV:I.

15. Margaret Horsfield, "The Burning Books" on "Ideas", CBC Radio Toronto, broadcast Apr. 23, 1990.

16. Quoted in Heywood Broun & Margaret Leech, *Anthony Comstock: Roundsman of the Lord* (New York, 1927).

17. Charles Gallaudet Trumbull, *Anthony Comstock, Fighter* (New York, 1913).

18. Quoted in Broun & Leech, *Anthony Comstock.*

19. Ibid.

20. Ibid.

21. Ibid.

22. H.L. Mencken, "Puritanism as a Literary Force", in *A Book of Prefaces* (New York, 1917).

23. Jacques Dars, Introduction to *En Mouchant la chandelle* (Paris, 1986).

24. Gustave Flaubert, *Madame Bovary,* II 7 (Paris, 1857).

25. Edmund Gosse, *Father and Son* (London, 1907).

26. Ibid.

27. Joan DelFattore, *What Johnny Shouldn't Read: Textbook Censorship in America* (New Haven & London, 1992).

28. Quoted from *The Times* of London, Jan. 4, 1978, reprinted in Nick Caistor's Foreword to *Nunca Más: A Report by Argentina's National Commission on Disappeared People* (London, 1986).

29. In *Nunca Más.*

REFLECTING ON THE READING

1. What fears did slaveowners have about allowing slaves to read? What might their fears suggest about literacy? Why, according to Manguel, is reading such a powerful tool?

2. Why, in Manguel's view, do rulers resort to censorship of books and other reading materials? Do you think his explanation is right? Why or why not? What

does his perspective on the motivations for censorship suggest to you about the relationship between literacy and political power?

3. Who was Anthony Comstock? What does the story of Anthony Comstock reveal about censorship efforts and about reading in general? Why does Manguel believe that Comstock is a significant figure in history? Do you agree with him? Why or why not?

4. What does Manguel mean by the phrase "the fear of fiction"? What examples of that fear does he provide? What are the implications of that fear, according to Manguel? Do you think Manguel is right about this fear? Explain.

5. How was Mrs. Gosse affected by her governess' rule that no novels were to be allowed in their home? What does the example of Mrs. Gosse reveal about efforts to keep children from reading specific books?

6. What does Manguel mean when he writes that "not all the reader's powers are enlightening"? Why, as Manguel sees it, is this an important insight? What might it suggest about literacy?

Examining Rhetorical Strategies

1. Examine the way Manguel begins this essay. Why do you think he focuses on Charles II in his introductory paragraphs? What historical perspectives on King Charles II of England does he present in the opening paragraphs? What do these perspectives indicate about Charles II? Why do you think Manguel presents these different perspectives on Charles II? In what ways might this introduction be appropriate for this essay? Did you find the introduction effective? Why or why not? What might your reaction to it indicate about your expectations as a reader?

2. Assess Manguel's use of anecdotes in this essay. What kinds of historical incidents does he include? What common themes do you see in these anecdotes? Do you think these anecdotes provide effective support for Manguel's ideas about reading and censorship? Explain. Do you think he leaves anything out in his accounts of the history of censorship?

3. In recounting past incidents of book burning and other forms of censorship, Manguel mentions a number of authors and books by name. Examine the authors and books he mentions. How might you describe these specific authors and books? What do you think Manguel wishes to suggest by mentioning them? What might these names and titles suggest about Manguel's' own views regarding reading and books? Did you recognize the names and titles he mentions? What reaction did you have to them? Do you think he hoped to elicit the kind of reaction you had? Explain. What might your reaction to these names and titles indicate about you as a reader?

4. What sort of audience do you think Manguel imagined for this essay? On the basis of this essay, try to characterize that audience. What does Manguel assume his readers know about books, history, knowledge, and culture? What does he seem to assume about their beliefs regarding such matters? Do you think he

imagined an audience that shares his own views about these matters? Explain. Are you the kind of reader Manguel imagined for this essay? Why or why not?

5. Manguel provides many historical examples of censorship efforts in this essay, but he spends more time on the story of Anthony Comstock and the Society for the Suppression of Vice than on any other example he cites. Why do you think he devotes so much of his attention to Comstock? How does he present Comstock? Does his characterization of Comstock seem fair to you? Why or why not? What purposes does this extended example of censorship serve for Manguel? Do you think Manguel makes effective use of the example of Comstock in this essay? Explain.

6. How would you characterize the tone of this essay? Do you think Manguel is being critical in his essay? Of whom? Explain, citing specific passages from the text to support your answer.

7. Analyze the effectiveness of Manguel's reference to himself and his own experiences, which appear at the end of this essay. What effect does his use of the first person and his reference to his own experiences have on you as a reader? Did it influence how you feel about him as a writer and as an authority about the topic of censorship? Why or why not? Do you think Manguel intended this effect? Explain.

Engaging the Issues

1. Recall a time when you were forbidden from reading or perhaps were encouraged not to read something, and write an essay for an audience of your classmates in which you tell the story of that incident. (If this has never happened to you, perhaps you might recall such an incident involving someone you know.) In your essay, describe the situation in a way that will enable your readers to understand what happened and why. What were the circumstances surrounding the incident? Who tried to prevent you or discourage you from reading? What authority did that person have in that situation? What book or text were you reading or trying to read? Why did the person not want you to read it? What was your reaction?

2. Write an essay as described in Question #1 but focusing on writing. In other words, describe an experience in which you were encouraged *not* to write something or found yourself in trouble for something you *did* write. In your essay, try to answer the same kinds of questions about your writing that you answered in Question #1 about reading.

3. In a group of your classmates, share the essays you wrote for Questions #1 or #2 above. What kinds of experiences did your group write about? Who were the authorities in the experiences you and your classmates described? Why was reading or writing an issue in those circumstances? Identify similarities or differences in your respective experiences and discuss what those similarities or differences might suggest about literacy and censorship.

4. Write an editorial essay for your school or community newspaper in which you present your views about censorship and about the relationship between literacy and freedom in general. In your essay, draw on Manguel's essay and any other appropriate sources to support your views.

5. Access the World Wide Web and search for sites related to freedom of speech issues. Examine several such sites to determine what kinds of arguments they present in favor of greater freedom of speech or in favor of greater restrictions on speech in certain situations (such as on the Internet). What common arguments did you encounter in your examination of these Web sites? Which arguments do you find effective? Why? What conclusions can you draw about literacy, power, and technology based on your research?

   Now write a brief essay for your classmates in which you present the results of your research.

6. Rewrite the essay you wrote for Question #5 above for a general audience (such as readers of a large-circulation newspaper like the *New York Times*, the *Washington Post*, or *USA Today*).

7. Using the library, World Wide Web, and any other appropriate resources, learn what you can about recent censorship efforts or similar controversies involving writing, reading, or visual media. Focus your research on a specific situation. For example, you might focus on efforts to control the reading and writing that students do in schools (such as efforts to ban particular books from a school's curriculum). Or you might focus on controversies surrounding the display of unorthodox art in a public museum or the publication of a controversial book (such as Salman Rushdie's *The Satanic Verses*). Try to find out as much as you can about the situation you are looking into. On the basis of your research, write a conventional academic research paper presenting what you learned.

   Alternatively, construct a Web site based on your research. Construct your site in a way that makes it suitable for a general audience.

8. At the end of his essay, Manguel writes "Every reader makes up readings, which is not the same as lying; but every reader can also lie, wilfully declaring the text subservient to a doctrine, to an arbitrary law, to a private advantage, to the rights of slaveowners or the authority of tyrants." Write a conventional academic essay in which you discuss this statement. What does Manguel mean? What is he saying about reading and about the meaning of a text? Do you agree with him? Why or why not? In your essay try to address these questions in a way that presents your own perspective on what it means to read a text.

   Alternatively, write an essay about an incident in which you were involved that had to do with a disagreement about the meaning of a text. For example, you might write about a heated discussion about a book or poem that took place in an English class you took. Or you might write about an incident involving a religious or political document. Try to relate that incident in a way that highlights the nature of the disagreement and what it might reveal about reading and meaning.

Head Chief

ROBERT M. UTLEY

INTRODUCTION When White Europeans began to settle in North America on lands occupied by Native American peoples, two starkly different cultures came into often violent contact. Europeans and Native Americans lived in very different ways and understood themselves and their worlds very differently as well. Their respective dress, food, language, technologies, and customs diverged in sometimes dramatic ways. But there was another significant difference between these peoples that is sometimes overlooked: Europeans brought with them alphabetic literacy, whereas Native Americans had no written versions of their languages. It is true that Native Americans used pictographs and other symbols painted on rocks and weapons and the like, but their written communication systems were nothing like the alphabetic literacy of the Europeans. Although scholars have investigated the differences between oral cultures and literate ones (as several of the selections in Chapters 1 and 2 of this reader indicate), these scholars often focus on how literacy affects cognition or the way a society functions or organizes itself. In other words, in such investigations scholars tend to focus on the relationship between literacy and thought or social customs. But as the readings in this chapter suggest, literacy can also be a political tool wielded for the purposes of acquiring or maintaining power. The conflicts between White Europeans and Native Americans prior to 1900 provide compelling and sometimes unsettling examples of that power of literacy.

In the following passage, historian Robert M. Utley presents one such example. Utley describes a brief moment in the long and painful history of conflict between Whites and Native Americans in the American West during the nineteenth century. In the 1860's, after the Civil War ended and the United States entered a period usually called "Reconstruction," the federal government also turned its attention to settling the West. For three centuries, White settlement had inexorably pushed west, and as a consequence, Native American communities were forced off their traditional lands. In the process, their cultures were often destroyed. By the end of the Civil War, only relatively remote areas of the far west remained unsettled by Whites and under the control of Native American tribes. But as White settlement pushed rapidly west in the 1860's, conflicts, often bloody and vicious, between Whites and Native Americans intensified. In 1867, the U.S. government embarked on an effort to negotiate a wide-ranging settlement with various Native American tribes living in what are now parts of Colorado, Kansas, Nebraska, South Dakota, Montana, and Wyoming. Leaders of many of these tribes "signed" what came to be called the Fort Laramie Treaty, or the Treaty of 1868—in effect agreeing to give up most of their traditional lands in exchange for material assistance (in the form of supplies and food) and a promise that Whites would stay out of lands in the far west (in what is now western Wyoming, Montana, Utah, and Idaho).

However, the great Sioux leader Sitting Bull, who was actively resisting white expansion into these regions, would have no part of such an agreement. Sitting Bull believed the Whites had already ventured much too far into Indian lands, and he especially resented the construction of roads, railroads, and forts in these areas. As he waged war against White settlers who entered his tribe's traditional lands, he amassed a huge following. Other bands of Native Americans joined him until he came to be recognized as the nominal leader of many Indians living north of Kansas. As we learn in the following passage, Sitting Bull had no interest in negotiating with the Whites, though he agreed to meet with representatives, such as the Jesuit priest Pierre-Jean De Smet. But such meetings and similar councils in which treaties were "signed" reveal the very different ways that Whites and Native Americans understood what it meant to negotiate. Moreover, those meetings demonstrate the role of literacy in the conflicts between Native Americans and Whites. For a Native American leader like Sitting Bull, a council was an opportunity to present grievances or make demands and to negotiate some kind of settlement about those griev-ances or demands; all of this was accomplished through oral speeches, which carried great force in Native American communities. For White negotiators, however, spoken words were virtually meaningless in such settings; only when a decision or agreement was put in written form did it have any meaning to them. From their perspective, writing carried the force of law. In the following passage, Utley provides a vivid example of the implications of that crucial dif-ference. In doing so, he helps us see the complicated ways that literacy can function as a powerful means of political and legal control, even when some of those involved cannot write or read.

Robert M. Utley is a widely respected historian of the American West. A former chief historian of the National Park service, Utley has written more than ten histories of the West, including *The Last Days of the Sioux Nation* (1963), *Cavalier in Buckskin: George Armstrong Custer and the Western Military Frontier* (1988), and *A Life Wild and Perilous: Mountain Men and the Paths to the Pacific* (1997). The following passage is taken from his biography of Sitting Bull, *The Lance and the Shield: The Life and Times of Sitting Bull* (1993).

REFLECTING BEFORE READING

1. Sitting Bull is perhaps the most famous Native American leader of the nine-teenth century. What do you know about him? What opinion do you have of him? As you read, consider how your sense of who Sitting Bull was agrees with—or does not agree with—the picture Utley paints of him. Consider, too, how your opinion of Sitting Bull—and of the actions of the U.S. government in the nineteenth century against Native Americans—might influence your reac-tion to Utley's description of Sitting Bull and the Treaty of 1868.

2. Although the following passage is not overtly about literacy, literacy plays a key role in the conflict between the U.S. government and the Native American people that Utley refers to in the passage. As you read, pay attention to the role of writing in the situation that Utley describes. In what sense is writing "power" in this context?

A s the officials of the Indian Office well knew, the Jesuit missionary Pierre-Jean De Smet enjoyed unrivaled credibility with many of the tribes of the American West. Where no other white man dared venture, the beloved Black Robe found welcome. Secure in the righteousness of his faith, trusting to God's protection, he went fearlessly among even the most remote groups, speaking kindly and gently, urging universal peace, and calling on them to embrace the Christian God. Few could resist his charm and grace, and few found grounds for dispute in the principles he espoused.

The Sioux, regardless of faction, proved as receptive as other tribes. They too professed to want universal peace. After all, it was an ideal proclaimed by the White Buffalo Woman herself—although within the Lakota confederation and with the admonition to war ruthlessly on all enemies. Peace could be had readily, therefore, if the whites and the enemy tribes simply cleared out of lands claimed by the Sioux.

Nor did the priest's theology trouble the Sioux, so long as it did not undermine the elaborate body of belief and ritual that centered on *Wakantanka*. A crucifix might provide as much protection as a sacred bundle, the holy waters of baptism match the *wakan* powers of a sacred stone.

As had occurred often in the past, in 1867 the Indian Office enlisted Father De Smet in the latest peace movement. This shift in policy sprang from the bitter and costly Indian wars of 1864–65 and from the moral indignation of easterners over the butchery at Sand Creek. It sprang also from a fresh surge of the westward movement that dramatized the continuing need, from the white viewpoint, for a solution to the "Indian problem."

The end of the Civil War released the enormous national energies generated by the war for a renewed assault on the economic potential of the western territories. Emigrants by the thousands moved west, seeking fortune or adventure in the new towns and cities, the newly opened mines, the unfenced grasslands awaiting cattle and sheep, the prairie sod inviting the plow, and all the related opportunities of a booming frontier. Up the Platte Road, crowded with stagecoaches and wagon trains, advanced the rails of the Union Pacific, aiming for a meeting with the Central Pacific building east from California. To the south, the Kansas Pacific struck up the Smoky Hill toward Denver. As never before, white people crowded into the Indian hunting grounds, aggravating the problems that had always divided the two races.

To government theorists, a better solution to the problems than war seemed attainable. If only the Indians were treated kindly and fairly, ran the argument, a just settlement responsive to the needs of both sides could be worked out. From such thinking grew the comprehensive peace effort of 1867–68. It focused on the central Plains, where the conflict of interests and peoples was most acute. But conflict troubled the upper Missouri too, and in addition the Indians there were linked by tribal kinship to those opposing the whites farther south. Thus the upper Missouri Lakotas found themselves on the margins of the peace offensive, and the particular concern of the Jesuit Black Robe from St. Louis.

Aside from making peace, the main purpose of the peace commission of 1867–68 was to clear all Indians away from the principal overland travel routes— the Platte Road and Union Pacific Railway, the Smoky Hill Trail and Kansas Pacific Railway, and the Santa Fe Trail. Two huge reservations, one north of Nebraska and the other south of Kansas, would be set aside for all the tribes of the Great Plains. In October 1867, in the Medicine Lodge treaties, the negotiators persuaded the southern Plains tribes to promise to settle on the reservation south of Kansas, in the Indian Territory.

In 1868 the peace commission turned to the northern Plains, where the central issue was not Sitting Bull's remote guerrilla war against Forts Buford and Stevenson but Red Cloud's headline-grabbing war against Forts Phil Kearny and C. F. Smith. With the government now ready to give up the Bozeman Trail in exchange for peace, the Oglala and Miniconjou chiefs gathered at Fort Laramie to touch the pen. Red Cloud had won his war.

It remained, however, to persuade the upper Missouri Lakotas to sign the Fort Laramie Treaty. Leaders of the peace faction presented no problem, but leaders of the war faction had to be coaxed into council before there could even be talk of signing. To carry out this mission, the commissioners looked to Father De Smet.

Even as the missionary prepared for the dangerous journey to the warring camps, Sitting Bull kept his eye fixed on the hated forts, ignoring the vaporous talk of peace that always drifted through the Lakota villages. Well aware that commissioners wanted to meet with him and his fellow chiefs, he answered, in May 1868, with a war expedition.

Sitting Bull led his warriors first to the favorite objective, Fort Buford. At the fort's hay field they found two civilian laborers loading a wagon with hay. The military patrol sent to search for them that night discovered both bodies, "horribly mutilated, stripped of clothing, scalped, and pierced and pinned to the ground with 27 barbed arrows." The feathers identified the arrows as Hunkpapa.[1]

From Fort Buford, the war party rode down to Fort Stevenson but, finding the garrison alert, headed northeast to Fort Totten, on Devils Lake. En route the warriors cut down two mail riders, then ran off with four mules from the Totten herd. On May 24 they seized two replacement mail riders sent out from Fort Stevenson. Sitting Bull judged them to be mixed bloods, so he spared their lives. After relieving them of their clothing, arms, horses, and other equipment, he instructed them to serve notice on the army commanders that he, Black Moon, Four Horns, and Red Horn did not intend to meet with the peace commissioners but rather would keep on killing white men until all left the Indian country.[2]

Hostility toward white people, however, did not demand rudeness toward so revered a white person as Father De Smet. The chiefs had known of his plan to visit them for nearly a year. Through Running Antelope, Bear's Rib, and other chiefs along the Missouri, trader Charles Galpin had been putting out feelers all winter. His wife Matilda, Eagle Woman, offspring of a Hunkpapa–Two Kettle union, helped give Galpin high credibility with the Sioux. Without compromising their grievances or their demands, therefore, the militants could extend traditional Lakota hospitality, listen politely, and utter sentiments calculated to please the Black Robe.

Sitting Bull had been home from the raid against Forts Buford, Stevenson, and Totten for only a few days when Father De Smet's entourage approached. The Hunkpapa village lay on the south side of the Yellowstone River a few miles above the mouth of the Powder. It consisted of about six hundred lodges of several bands, including those of Black Moon, Four Horns, and Red Horn. Among the war chiefs were Sitting Bull, Gall, and No Neck.

De Smet had organized his expedition at Fort Rice, where the local Sioux, fearful for his scalp, had looked on the journey incredulously. The party consisted of about eighty Lakota and Yanktonai tribesmen, including such prominent chiefs as Running Antelope, Two Bears, and Bear's Rib. Charles and Matilda Galpin went along as interpreters.[3]

On June 19, 1868, amid great excitement, the Black Robe entered the Hunkpapa village. Four Horns had dispatched scores of colorfully painted and clothed warriors to meet the procession in the valley of the Powder. As the cavalcade advanced on the village, the entire population turned out to shout greetings and participate in the welcome. De Smet's "standard of peace," displaying an image of the Virgin Mary surrounded by gilt stars, floated in the vanguard as the parade drew up at Sitting Bull's lodge in the center of the village.

Rigid security measures betrayed the apprehension of the tribal leadership for the guests' safety. During the march from Powder River, twenty *akicita* had surrounded the Black Robe and his party. At the village, as throngs of people pressed in from all sides, Black Moon ordered the *akicita* to disperse the crowd, and Sitting Bull had the priest's baggage carried into his own tipi. *Akicita* escorted De Smet and the Galpins into the lodge, brought food and water, and stood guard outside while they rested. Others tended the horses. At sundown Sitting Bull, Black Moon, Four Horns, and No Neck entered the tipi. De Smet awoke from a nap to find Sitting Bull crouched beside him.

Galpin translated as Sitting Bull spoke, and De Smet later set it down in Jesuitical language scarcely faithful to the Hunkpapa idiom. Even so, the meaning remains clear:

> Black-robe, I hardly sustain myself beneath the weight of white men's blood that I have shed. The whites provoked the war: their injustices, their indignities to our families, the cruel, unheard of and wholly unprovoked massacre at Fort Lyon [Sand Creek, in Colorado] . . . shook all the veins which bind and support me. I rose, tomahawk in hand, and I have done all the hurt to the whites that I could. To-day thou art amongst us, and in thy presence my arms stretch to the ground as if dead. I will listen to thy good words, and as bad as I have been to the whites, just so good am I ready to become toward them.[4]

And doubtless he was, with the usual caveats about complete white withdrawal from Lakota country.

The council took place the next day, June 20, Ten tipis had been joined to form a single huge council lodge. De Smet's banner had been hoisted in the center, near buffalo robes spread on the ground as seats. At noon *akicita* ushered the priest and the Galpins to the robes and seated them facing Black Moon and Four Horns, the principal spiritual and political leaders of the village. Behind them, the lodge partly uncovered to expose the interior, five hundred tribesmen had arranged themselves according to the several bands composing the village. In their front, behind Black Moon and Four Horns, sat the war chiefs—Sitting Bull, White Gut, No Neck, and Gall. Pressing the warriors from the rear, with order imposed by *akicita,* the old men, women, and children formed a dense mass of absorbed spectators.

Four Horns opened the council by lighting his pipe. After extending it to the sky, the earth, and the four directions, he handed it to Father De Smet. From him, with each taking several puffs, it descended from chief to chief in order of rank. Black Moon then invited Father De Smet to speak.

As the priest stood, complete silence prevailed. He had come only as an advisor, De Smet said, to urge the Sioux to meet with the Great Father's commissioners at Fort Rice and "end this cruel and unfortunate bloodshed." What he asked "beseeched"—was a Christian forgiveness and forbearance alien to the concept of vengeance so deeply embedded in the Lakota way—"to bury all your bitterness toward the whites, forget the past, and accept the hand of peace which is extended to you." Gesturing toward his flag, he declared that he would leave this "holy emblem of peace" in the possession of the chiefs, "a token of my sincerity and good wisdom for the welfare of the Sioux Nation."

After passing the pipe once again, Black Moon responded. Conceding the Black Robe's words to be "good and full of truth and meaning," he nevertheless chronicled the "many sores in our bosoms to be healed." There were the forts, the travel routes, the slaughtered buffalo and other game, the ravaged stands of timber, and all over the land red spots on the ground that were not from slain buffalo but from humans, red and white, killed by one another. "We have been cruelly treated and often treacherously deceived." He hoped these were all things of the past, and "we will try and forget them from this day."

Repeating the pipe ritual, Sitting Bull, as tribal war chief, spoke on behalf of the warriors. His speech was clearly inferior to Black Moon's. It seemed designed less to convey his true feelings than to ingratiate himself with the Black Robe. After invoking the aid of the Great Spirit, he conceded that for four years he had led his warriors in "bad deeds," but only because "they pushed me forward." Now he welcomed the Black Robe and hoped he succeeded in his quest for peace. Hunkpapa emissaries would return with De Smet to meet with the white commissioners. Whatever they agreed in council, Sitting Bull concluded, "I will accept and remain hereafter a friend of the whites."

After shaking hands with Father De Smet and both Charles and Matilda Galpin—the latter a mark of high respect for Eagle Woman—Sitting Bull returned to his seat. No sooner had he sat down, however, than he sprang up and said he had forgotten a few things. He then poured out an afterthought that all but wiped out his formal speech. He wanted all to know that he did not propose to sell any part of his country; that the whites must quit cutting his timber along the Missouri River; and that the forts of the white soldiers must be abandoned, "as there was no greater source of grievance to his people."

Whereupon, as De Smet noted, "with cheers from all, he resumed his seat."[5]

Once again De Smet and the Galpins slept in Sitting Bull's lodge, with all the chiefs present and *akicita* outside. At daybreak on June 21 the caravan began the return journey to Fort Rice. Sitting Bull and a contingent of *akicita* rode escort as far as Powder River, where he delivered a brief address recalling the pledges made the day before, then shook hands and turned back.

That neither Four Horns nor Black Moon, still less the war leader Sitting Bull, intended to go to Fort Rice reveals that they regarded the prospects for peace on acceptable terms as not likely. To accommodate the respected Black Robe, however, they sent a delegation of lesser chiefs headed by Gall.

Patiently waiting at Fort Rice were the three commissioners designated to carry the Fort Laramie Treaty to the upper Missouri Lakotas. On July 2 Hunkpapas,

Blackfeet, and Yanktonais assembled for the council and heard the treaty read. The agenda called for each chief to make a speech, then sign the treaty already negotiated with the Lakotas at Fort Laramie. The proceedings dramatized the fantasy world in which Indian treaties were concocted.

Gall (identified as Man-that-Goes-in-the-Middle) spoke first. His speech contained no hint of an understanding that the commissioners expected him simply to sign a document that had already been worked out, no hint even that he fathomed the nature of a treaty. "The whites ruin our country," he declared. "If we make peace, the military posts on this river must be removed and the steamboats stopped from coming up here."[6]

Having set his own conditions for a treaty, Gall sat patiently while twenty other chiefs made their speeches. Then, with the treaty laid on the table, he marched to the front and touched the pen. Of all the Indians who signed at Fort Rice on July 2, Gall's mark appeared first.

The treaty that Gall had so innocently signed addressed no fundamental grievances of the Hunkpapas. The government had agreed to abandon the Bozeman Trail forts, a matter of interest to the Hunkpapas but hardly vital. Altogether ignored were the detested forts on the upper Missouri, the steamboats, and whites in general. In blustering language, Gall had asserted that all must go or there could be no peace. Yet he signed a treaty of peace that said nothing about any.

Though silent on Hunkpapa complaints, the Fort Laramie Treaty spelled out provisions of breathtaking portent for all the Lakotas. Obscured by technical jargon that even white officials had trouble understanding was a sweeping blueprint for the future of the Sioux that no chief who signed could have even dimly comprehended.

The treaty created a "Great Sioux Reservation"—all of what later became the state of South Dakota lying west of the Missouri River. Except along the northern fringes, this was not even part of the traditional Hunkpapa range. There the government would establish an agency, issue clothing and rations for thirty years, build schools and educate the Indians, and teach them how to support themselves by farming.

Since Red Cloud's war had been fought over the Bozeman Trail, the treaty contained a vaguely worded article labeling as "unceded Indian territory" the Powder River country west of the Great Sioux Reservation as far as the summit of the Bighorn Mountains. By inference at least, Indians who wished to live by the chase rather than by government dole might continue to reside in this tract. That neatly postponed a dispute over going to the reservation, but white officials confidently looked to the day when the extinction of the buffalo would eliminate the issue.

At that point another article would govern. It bound the signatories to "relinquish all right to occupy permanently the territory outside their reservation as herein defined." That, at least in the legal framework of the white people, shrank Lakota domain to the limits of the Great Sioux Reservation. On the reservation, moreover, railroads and wagon roads could be constructed only after damages had been assessed—a backhanded way of opening even the reservation to the hated travel routes.[7]

All these legalisms were bewildering enough to white officials. Gall can hardly be reproached for not perceiving that he had bound the Hunkpapas not only to end their war against the whites but ultimately to settle on and remain on a reservation, there to give up the chase, obey the dictates of a white agent, dress like white people, live like white people, and learn to farm like white people.

Sitting Bull probably had less understanding of the treaty than Gall, or even interest in its contents. That in only a few years it would be cited as proof of his broken promises and justification for war against him would have struck him as nonsense. But government officials could read the treaty and find evidence that he had promised not to make war on whites or other Indians, not to oppose a railroad up the Yellowstone River, and ultimately even to live within the confines of the Great Sioux Reservation. He of course had agreed to nothing, and the proposition that Running Antelope, Bear's Rib, or even Gall could agree to on his behalf would have struck him as still greater nonsense.

Testifying to Sitting Bull's view of the De Smet mission, less than two months after Gall signed the treaty, Sitting Bull led another devastating raid on Fort Buford. With 150 yipping warriors, he bore down on the fort's beef herd, made off with 250 head, and left three soldiers dead and three grievously wounded.[8]

Notes

1. Lt. Cornelius Cusick to Post Adjutant Fort Buford, May 14, 1868, RG 393, Fort Buford LR (but mislabeled Fort Sumner, N.M., box 1), NARA.

2. Col. Philippe Régis de Trobriand to Gen. A. H. Terry, Fort Stevenson, May 30, 1868, RG 393, Department of Dakota LR, box 4, NARA. See also Capt. George W. Hill to AAG Department of Dakota, Fort Totten, May 23, 1868, ibid., box 3.

3. Three sources document the De Smet mission, a journal kept by Galpin and two accounts De Smet wrote based on the Galpin journal: Rev. Louis Pfaller, ed., "The Galpin Journal: Dramatic Record of an Odyssey of Peace," *Montana the Magazine of Western History* 18 (April 1968): 2–23; Hiram M. Chittenden and Alfred T. Richardson, eds., *Life, Letters, and Travels of Father Pierre-Jean De Smet, S.J., 1801–1873*, 4 vols. (New York: Francis P. Harper, 1905), vol. 3, pp. 899–922; and "Statement of the Rev. P.J. De Smet, S.J., of his Reception by and Council with the Hostile Uncpapa Indians," *Papers Relating to Talks and Councils Held with the Indians in Dakota and Montana Territories in the Years 1866–1869* (Washington, D.C.: Government Printing Office, 1910), 108–13. The Rev. Pfaller, who worked out De Smet's route both in the documents and on the ground, identified the probable location of the village as on Powder River about a dozen miles above its mouth. However, De Smet wrote that the eighteen Hunkpapas who returned with his scouts said that the village was on the Yellowstone above the Powder. Later he places his first meeting with a large welcoming delegation on the Powder about eight miles above its mouth. This delegation then escorted him to the village about twelve miles distant. The sources do not indicate whether this was exclusively a Hunkpapa village or included other Lakota tribes as well. The implication is Hunkpapa, since no other chiefs are named. If so, the five to six thousand people De Smet estimated as living there is excessive.

Late in life Matilda Galpin gave her account of the mission to Frances C. Holley, a Bismarck resident. She portrayed the Indians as planning to kill De Smet's party and represented their intent as a threat throughout the entire stay in the village. If so, no hint of the danger creeps into the contemporary accounts of either De Smet or Charles Galpin. Frances C. Holley, *Once Their Home: or, Our Legacy from the Dahkotahs* (Chicago: Donohue & Henneberry, 1892), 303–11.

An excellent biographical sketch of Matilda Galpin, also known as Eagle Woman, is John S. Gray, "The Story of Mrs. Picotte-Galpin, a Sioux Heroine," *Montana the Magazine of Western History* 36 (Spring 1986): 2–21; (Summer 1986): 2–21.

4. Chittenden and Richardson, *Life, Letters, and Travels of Father Pierre-Jean De Smet*, vol. 3, p. 912.

5. *Papers Relating to Talks and Councils,* 111.

6. "Council of the Indian Peace Commission with the Various Bands of Sioux Indians at Fort Rice, Dakt. T., July 2, 1868," *Papers Relating to Talks and Councils,* 95.

7. The text of the treaty is in Charles J. Kappler, comp., *Indian Affairs: Laws and Treaties,* 2 vols. (Washington, D.C.: Government Printing Office, 1904), vol. 2, pp. 998–1007.

8. Capt. C. D. Dickey to AAAG Middle District, Fort Buford, August 21, 1868, RG 393, Department of Dakota LR, box 4, NARA. Details of unsuccessful attempts to recover the cattle appear in subsequent correspondence in the same source. For a lengthy analysis of the military situation on the upper Missouri at this time, see Col. Philippe Régis de Trobriand to AAG Department of Dakota, Fort Stevenson, September 6, 1868, ibid. Same to same, September 22, 1868, ibid., links Sitting Bull to the Fort Buford raid through a rifle he had taken from one of the mail carriers the previous May, which was seized in association with some of the cattle run off from Fort Buford.

REFLECTING ON THE READING

1. Who is Pierre-Jean De Smet (whom the Indians called "Black Robe")? Why is he important in the "signing" of the treaty of 1868? How do the Indians who know him feel about him? What might their view of him suggest about their values?

2. According to Utley, what is the purpose of the U.S. government peace commission of 1867–1868? Why do Sitting Bull and his allies object to the peace commission's treaty that some Indian tribes signed at Fort Laramie in 1868?

3. Why, according to Utley, is Father De Smet's request that the Indians forgive the Whites and end their war against the Whites unrealistic? What does his request suggest about his values and his understanding of the Indians' values?

4. How does Sitting Bull treat Father De Smet when he visits Sitting Bull's village? What does Sitting Bull say at the council he holds with Father De Smet? What might Sitting Bull's speeches at that council suggest about him as a person and as a leader?

5. According to Utley, what is Gall's understanding of the Fort Laramie Treaty when he attends the council at Fort Rice? What does Gall believe he is doing when he "touched the pen" at that council? In what ways do the Whites' understanding of the treaty that Gall "signed" differ from the Indians' understanding of it? What might these differences suggest about the cultural attitudes between white Americans and Native Americans concerning negotiation and governing? What does this incident suggest about the nature of literacy and its relationship to political power?

6. What do the terms of the Fort Laramie Treaty mean for the Sioux people? How does the specific wording of the Fort Laramie Treaty eventually influence the government's actions against Sitting Bull? What might this situation suggest about writing as a legal or political tool?

Examining Rhetorical Strategies

1. Assess the way Utley tells the story of the effort to convince Sitting Bull and his allies to sign the Treaty of 1868. What scenes or events does he emphasize?

What purposes might those scenes or events serve for Utley? What do you think is missing from the story, if anything? Do you find his telling of this story effective? Why or why not? What might your answer to that question indicate about your expectations as a reader of historical narratives?

2. How does Utley present Sitting Bull in this passage? How do you think Utley wishes his readers to feel about Sitting Bull? Do you think he presents Sitting Bull as a sympathetic figure? Explain, citing specific passages from the text to support your answer. How did you react to Utley's characterization of Sitting Bull?

3. What picture of Native Americans does Utley paint in this passage? What information or descriptions does he offer to characterize the Native Americans of the time, specifically the members of Sitting Bull's village? Do you think he tries to paint a sympathetic picture, a critical picture, an objective one—or something else altogether? Explain, citing specific passages from the text to support your answer.

4. How would you characterize Utley's voice in this passage? What features of his text help create his voice? Do you think his voice is appropriate for his subject matter? Is it the kind of voice you expect in a history text? Explain.

5. Assess the way Utley ends this passage. Why do you think he chooses to end it with the specific details of the attack on Fort Buford? What does this ending emphasize? Do you think it is an appropriate ending for this passage? Why or why not?

6. This passage is from a best-selling book that was published by a large commercial publisher. As such, we can assume it was read by a large and diverse audience. Do you think Utley intended his history of Sitting Bull for such a general audience? Explain, supporting your answer with specific references to this passage. Do you think he includes Native American readers among his audience? What assumptions do you think Utley makes about his readers' attitudes regarding the U.S. government's actions against Native Americans in Sitting Bull's day? Do you think these assumptions are fair ones? Why or why not?

Engaging the Issues

1. Write an essay discussing the role of writing in the incidents that Utley describes in this passage. In your essay, describe how writing functions in the conflict between the U.S. government, the White settlers, and the Native Americans in the American West in the nineteenth century. In what sense might you describe writing as "power" in this context? What might these events suggest about the political and cultural nature of literacy? (Consult additional sources, if necessary.)

2. Using your library or another appropriate resource, try to locate the text of the Fort Laramie Treaty (or a similar treaty from that time period). Read all or part of it carefully in order to understand its terms as fully as you can. Then write a synopsis of the main points of the treaty in less-formal prose. After you have finished your synopsis, compare its language to the language of the original treaty. What differences or similarities can you identify? What are the primary features of each text in terms of style? What might account for these differences? What

conclusions can you draw about writing style and specialized forms of writing such as treaties or other legal documents? (Note: If you are unable to locate the Fort Laramie Treaty or a similar treaty, you can do this exercise with any available legal document.)

3. Write an essay for an audience of your classmates in which you describe an experience you have had with cultural differences. For example, you might describe a situation in which you were traveling in a region you had never visited before where you encountered an unfamiliar local custom. If possible, choose an incident that somehow involved language or literacy. In your essay, try to describe your experience in a way that will enable your readers to understand the situation and how the local cultural practices or expectations were different from your own.

4. In a group of your classmates, compare the essays you wrote for Question #3 above. Discuss the various situations described in your essays and what they might suggest about cultural difference. What conclusions can you draw about such differences? How might problems associated with such differences be addressed? Try to focus your discussion on language or literacy, if possible.

5. If possible, visit the office of one of your local legislators (for example, a town council member or a state legislator). Speak to him or her about the role of writing in the work he or she does as a legislator. Ask questions about how bills and laws are drafted, how the language of a bill is determined, and why specific kinds of language are used. If possible, examine some examples of drafts of such bills or similar legal texts.

    Now write a report for your classmates about what you learned on your visit with your legislator. In your report, describe how writing is used in the work of the legislator you interviewed and discuss what you learned about legal writing in general. If possible, include examples of such writing in your report. Draw conclusions about the nature of such writing and its role in American society.

6. Using your library, the World Wide Web, and any other appropriate sources, investigate the legal or political practices of Native American peoples at the time of the Fort Laramie Treaty (or prior to that time period). Through your research, learn what you can about how Native American tribes governed themselves, about the role of public speeches in their systems of government, and the beliefs and values that influenced their systems of government. (Keep in mind that Native American peoples generally had no written form of their language.) Present the results of your research in a conventional academic paper.

7. Write an essay for an audience of your classmates in which you present your view of the conflict between the U.S. government and the Native American peoples in the American West during the nineteenth century. In your essay, be sure to support your position, drawing on Utley's text or any other sources you deem appropriate.

8. In a group of your classmates, share the essays you wrote for Question #7 above. Debate your respective positions on the conflict between the U.S. government and Native Americans in the nineteenth century. Try to identify the basic views each of you has about this conflict and about the larger matters of cultural difference and political power.

Misperspectives on Literacy

A Critique of an Anglocentric Bias in Histories of American Literacy

JAMIE CANDELARIA GREENE

INTRODUCTION In the early 1990's, the U.S. Department of Education commissioned several professional organizations of historians and educators to create national guidelines for the teaching of history in American schools. Because history—or "social studies"—is such a central component of the curriculum in American education, the task of the panel seemed important and straightforward. But when the National Center for History in the Schools at UCLA released the guidelines in 1994, it created a storm of controversy. Many observers were unhappy with the panel's recommendations for the specific content of the history curriculum. For example, one recommendation suggested that students should learn about the destructive impact of Christopher Columbus' explorations of North America on some Native American cultures. Some critics charged that such recommendations represented a critical view of American society and reflected an overt political bias. Others charged that the guidelines were not political enough, arguing that the presentation of American history to students should be *more* critical. Panel members defended their recommendations as broad and general enough to allow for teachers and schools to make their own choices about how best to present events like Columbus' exploration of America to their students.

Given the importance that American schools seem to place on the teaching of history, it is perhaps not surprising that the panel's guidelines sparked such intense debate. But it is revealing that the debate itself was not always about the recommendations for teaching specific content or historical events like Columbus' arrival in the New World; rather, the debate was often about the writing of history itself: how it is done and *who* gets to do it. Is history about "facts" or about "perspectives"? No clear consensus emerged from the debate about the guidelines for teaching history, but the intensity of the debate seems to underscore the important role that our histories play in shaping our sense of who we are; it underscores as well the political nature of the writing of history. In that sense, history as we understand it represents another aspect of the power of literacy.

Jamie Candelaria Greene agrees that our histories carry great importance. In the following article, she focuses on a particular history—the history of literacy in North America—to reveal that our conventional histories can have significant omissions. In this case, Greene shows that histories of the development of literacy in North America tend to exclude the important and extensive role played by Spanish-speaking peoples who settled much of the New World well before the arrival of people from northern Europe. To ignore the contribution of these Spanish peoples to the development of literacy, Greene argues, is to present a "misperspective" on literacy. But Greene's article goes beyond describing the role of Spanish peoples in the history of literacy in North America. She also suggests that the histories we write are shaped by our own biases and cultural perspectives. In this case, historians of literacy focus attention on White Europeans in their accounts of the development of literacy in North America, in effect "erasing" from history the Spanish peoples and those from other cultures who contributed to that development. As the intense debates about the national history guidelines suggest, Greene's concerns about such bias in our written histories can extend to other aspects of our past.

Greene also reminds us of the crucial link between history and literacy. She helps us see that when we write a history, we write ourselves into existence. Literacy thus becomes a way to create ourselves and our place in the world. And Greene shows us that such an idea is not merely abstract. Her example of the case of Eliseo Baca demonstrates that the histories we write and the written records we keep to document our past *matter* in our individual lives.

Jamie Candelaria Greene is a special education teacher and consultant who has worked for various institutions in California including the Northern California Access Project and the National University in Sacramento. The following article first appeared in the scholarly journal *Written Communication* in 1994.

1. The following article was originally written for a specialized scholarly journal about literacy and written communication. As you read, try to identify the features of the article that distinguish it as "scholarly" (such as its style, organization, use of evidence, references, and so on) and consider how those features affect your reading of the article. Do they make it easier or more difficult for you to follow? Explain. What might your reaction to those features indicate about you as a reader?

2. Greene's argument in the following article has to do with how histories are written. As you prepare to read the article, consider your own understanding of history. For example, do you see history as a straightforward description of certain "important" events or people? Do you see it as a "story"? Who do you believe is responsible for the histories available to us? Consider how your own understanding of history might influence your reaction to Greene's argument.

The Literal Erasing of History

Eliseo Baca, a 12th-generation New Mexican, was perplexed. For years he had been researching his family tree, identifying ancestors who had settled in this region as far back as 1598. He was now, however, at an impasse. He could not locate records naming the person who represented the one missing link of a family chain going back to the 1500s. Efforts were made to examine lists of births, deaths, and marriage certificates, as well as other documents that had been dutifully recorded and meticulously kept by the early New Mexican clergy. The person's name, however, remained elusive. Then one day, while reviewing records of a more recent ancestor, he came across new information. Within minutes, he was gazing upon the name of his 18th-century ancestor. He was ecstatic. His family history was now complete.

A mystery remained, however. Why had it been so difficult to find the name in the first place? In particular, why did the parental name not appear on the baptismal record? We do know that in certain small towns, many babies were baptized and given a name but were listed as being "of unknown parents"—*de padres no conocidos.* Since the parental names often appear in subsequent records, one conclusion is that at the time of the birth the parents were in disfavor, and so their names were withheld from the baptismal record of the child.[1] In such a case, unless the parental names existed on later records of the descendant (such as on prenuptial investigations or marriage certificates), and unless efforts were made to search for these other records, parental identities would be lost forever. Thus when a name is omitted from any historical record an individual becomes at risk of being omitted from history itself.

The decision to include or not to include names, dates, and other facts in historical records is a powerful one. These written accounts shape our perceptions of the past and are used as a base to determine the policies and practices of tomorrow. Freire (1970) emphasized the importance of being an active participant in the historical process (p. 145). Without a complete and accurate knowledge of the past, an active participation is jeopardized. This article explores the incompleteness of the American historical process, one that is based on perceptions that are particularly acute in the widely accepted accounts of literacy in North America.

The Erasing of North American Literacy History

In the United States, histories—written under headings such as *The New World, Early America, The Colonies,* and *North America*—supposedly offer a base on which to predicate the study of the American historical process. But how complete are these histories? Are they the truth—but not the whole truth? The subject of this article is a case in point. The arguments and historical data on North American written literacy presented by Graff (1982), Kaestle (1985), and de Castell and Luke (1983) persuasively argue that a consideration of literacy from a historical perspective is necessary to better understand literacy issues. Indeed, these articles were selected for reprinting in a popular literacy anthology, *Perspectives on Literacy* (Kintgen, Kroll, & Rose, 1988), to provide readers with "the requisite background" on the history of literacy "for informed and intelligent discussion of the many issues surrounding the question of literacy today" (p. xi [all subsequent references to these articles are to the Kintgen et al. volume]). Certainly, these authors do provide us with valuable information on the subject of literacy. Graff substantiates the correlation of literacy with one's place in the social structure. Kaestle traces the progression of oral to written culture. De Castell and Luke address the subjective and the social dimensions of literacy development. However, to consider literacy only from the perspective of those authors would result in a flawed historical perspective, not on the basis of the data they include, but rather on the basis of what they do not include.

De Castell and Luke in "Defining Literacy in North American Schools" begin with the premise that "in the European Protestant educational tradition on which the public schools of the New World were first based, commonality of religious belief was central to literacy instruction" (pp. 159-160). Clearly, when the authors write *North American Schools* in their title, they are not referring to *all* literacy (or schools) in "that of the northernmost continent of the western hemisphere" (*Oxford American Dictionary*, 1990, p. 454). Their entire study of North America and the New World is based on data referring only to the area of the present-day northeastern United States and Canada, excluding, for example, Mexico. Their historical account is further limited by considering only those literacy events that occurred after the 16th century.

Kaestle, in "History of Literacy and Readers," also discusses literacy in America from 1600 to 1900. He is much more careful in identifying the ethnic and geographical sources of his study. By citing the "*British* Colonies" for example, he does not leave the reader to wonder whether "Colonies" means Dutch, Spanish, or all established American colonies. However, because Kaestle does not acknowledge the presence of written literacy outside his similarly narrow range of geographical study and period, his reader is left with the same impression of early American literacy that de Castell and Luke give us.

In "The Legacies of Literacy," Graff goes further in limiting the history of American literacy. He uses Lockridge's (1974) *Literacy in New England* as a base for his chart on sources of literacy in North America. His exclusion of Spanish literacy results in throwing off dates for document availability in North America and in Europe by typically a century (see Table 1).

Ironically, all four authors stress the importance of the historical dimension of literacy development. Yet in a nation as diverse as the United States this message gets lost because of their narrow view of American history based on one geographical area, ethnic group, and time frame. These authors are sending out clear, if unintended, messages as to *what* they feel constitutes "literacy" and *which groups* they feel are worthy of study as "literates." As a result, the reader is unwittingly presented with incomplete research and is left to assume a similarly narrow perspective on what went into the making of our country's literacy heritage. By describing types of literacy used by Hispanics in the 16th and 17th centuries, I hope that at least part of this historical gap will be narrowed.

Oral and written literacies were prevalent in North America long before the arrival of the Europeans. Kaestle (1985) acknowledges the early syllabic writing systems of the Aztecs and the Mayans. The subject of early Native American literacy is a voluminous study in its own right, as is citing the many other contributions to North American literacy made by immigrants from throughout the world. I am limiting my comparison to (a) the early history of written literacy use (of the Roman alphabet) in New Spain (see Figure 1)[2] between the years 1513 and 1650 by people who, regardless of race, lived in the "manner of Spaniards" (Weber, 1992, p.8); and (b) the uses of literacy in that part of New Spain that is now part of the coterminous (48-state) United States. In limiting my study accordingly, I recognize that I am presenting just one other small part of a truly ethnically diverse study.

The Introduction of the Roman Alphabet into the United States

In the 15th and 16th centuries, Spanish explorers led the way in the exploration of the Americas. From the arrival of Columbus in 1492, there was a constant need for written information, including navigational charts, maps, descriptions of lands sighted, and native peoples encountered. The explorations propelled the start of a transatlantic exchange of written communiques regarding laws, customs, and practices in the New World.

TABLE 1

Sources for the Historical Study of Literacy in North America and Europe

Source	Measure of Literacy	Population	Country of Availability	Years of Availability	Additional Variables
Census	Questions: read and write, read/write, signature/mark (Canada 1851, 1861 only)	Entire "adult" population (in theory): ages variable (e.g., over 20 years, 15 years, 10 years)	Canada, United States	Manuscripts: 19th century	Age, sex, occupation, birthplace, religion, marital status, family size and structure, residence, economic data
Wills	Signature/mark	20%–50% of adult males dying; 2%–5% of adult females dying	Canada, United States, England, France, etc.	Canada from 18th century on, United States from 1660 on, others from 16th–17th century on	Occupation, charity, family size, residence, estate, sex
Deeds	Signature/mark	5%–85% of living land-owning adult males; 1% or less of females	Canada, United States	18th century on	Occupation, residence, value of land, type of sale
Inventories	Book ownership	25%–60% of adult males dying; 3%–10% of adult females dying	Canada, United States, England, France, etc.	17th–18th century on (quantity varies by country and date)	Same as wills
Depositions	Signature/mark	Uncertain: potentially more select than wills, potentially wider; women sometimes included	Canada, United States, England, Europe	17th–18th century on (use and survival varies)	Potentially age, occupation, sex, birthplace, residence

(continued)

TABLE 1 (*continued*)

Sources for the Historical Study of Literacy in North America and Europe

Source	Measure of Literacy	Population	Country of Availability	Years of Availability	Additional Variables
Marriage records	Signature/mark	Nearly all (80%+) young men and women marrying (in England)	England, France, North America	From 1754 in England; 1650 in France	Occupation, age, sex, parents' name and occupation, residence (religion–North America)
Catechetical examination records	Reading, memorization, comprehension, writing examinations	Unclear, but seems very wide	Sweden, Finland	After 1620	Occupation, age, tax status, residence, parents' name and status, family size, migration, periodic improvement
Petitions	Signature/mark	Uncertain, potentially very select; males only in most cases	Canada, United State, England, Europe	18th century on	Occupation or station, sex, residence, political or social views
Military recruit records	Signature/mark or question on reading and writing	Conscripts or recruits (males only)	Europe, esp. France	19th century	Occupation, health, age, residence, education
Criminal records	Questions: read, read well, etc.	All arrested	Canada, United States, England	19th century	Occupation, age, sex, religion, birthplace, residence, marital status, moral habits, criminal data

(*continued*)

TABLE 1 (continued)

Sources for the Historical Study of Literacy in North America and Europe

Source	Measure of Literacy	Population	Country of Availability	Years of Availability	Additional Variables
Business records	Signature/mark	1. All employees 2. Customers	Canada, United States, England, Europe	19th–20th century	1. Occupation, wages 2. Consumptions level, residence, credit
Library/mechanics institute records	Books borrowed	Members or borrowers	Canada, United States, England	Late 18th–early 19th century	Names of volumes borrowed, society membership
Applications (land, job, pension, etc.)	Signature/mark	All applicants	Canada, United States, England, Europe	19th–20th century	Occupation, residence, family, career history, etc.
Aggregate data sources[a]	Questions or direct tests	Varies greatly	Canada, United States, England, Europe	19th–20th century	Any or all of the above

[a] Censuses, education surveys, statistical society reports, social surveys, government commissions, prison and jail records, etc. Source: Graff, *The Literacy Myth*, 325–327. This is a modified and greatly expanded version of Table A in Lockridge, *Literacy in New England*. From "The Legacies of Literacy" by H. Graff, 1992, *Journal of Communication*, 32(1), p. 14. Copyright 1982 by *Journal of Communication*. Adapted with permission.

NORTH AMERICA

NEW SPAIN

NEW SPAIN IN NORTH AMERICA
CIRCA 1598

Figure 1

Written literacy was introduced into the present-day United States by the year 1513, when Ponce de Leon recorded his arrival in Florida. From then on, there are records of administrative, military, civil, and ecclesiastical documents, bringing us bountiful evidence that written literacy was present in the 16th-century United States. During this time, most records pertain to the Spanish settlements in the present-day states of Florida, New Mexico, Georgia, Texas, Arizona, Louisiana, and South Carolina, although there are also records about the areas of California, Missouri, Mississippi, Kansas, Arkansas, Alabama, and Nebraska and Labrador (Natella, 1980).

In the Americas, the Spanish were responsible for many literacy firsts (again, in the context of using the Roman alphabet). Some of the literacy firsts in the United States are the following:

- The first recordings of births, deaths, and marriages, dating back at least as early as 1565, when St. Augustine (the first permanent European community in the United States) and St. Augustine Cathedral (the first cathedral) were founded. Actual documents which date back from 1594 are at the Cathedral of St. Augustine, Florida (Otis, 1952, p. 42).

- The first basic reading grammar text, written in Georgia in 1568 (Otis, 1952, p. 41).

- The first theatrical works, written and performed in 1598 in New Mexico. One was written by Captain Marcos Farfan de los Godos and the other play was entitled *Los Moros y Los Christianos* (Munilla, 1963; Natella, 1980).
- The first schools. By 1600, the Dominicans and the Franciscans (mostly university graduates) had established schools, most notably in Florida, New Mexico, and Georgia. Options for higher education in North America proper included the University of Mexico, which was established in 1551, and Santo Domingo, a college that was raised to the rank of University in 1538. Encarnacion, one of at least six women's colleges established between the years 1530 and 1600, offered three distinct schools: the *Escuela de Derecho* (School of Law), the *Escuela de Parbulos* (School for Children), and the *Escuela Normal de Profesoras* (Normal School for Women Professors) (Barth, 1950, p. 100). Mission documents of the time make references to schools and infirmaries (Bolton, 1921, p. 178; Hallenbeck, 1926; Lockhart & Otte, 1976).
- The first written musical compositions (including the *alabado,* a religious ballad) and the first music education based on European musical forms, all present by 1600. New Mexico's first music teacher, Fray Cristobal de Quinones, a man who was well trained in letters and in the arts, is credited with bringing the first organ into the United States, which would have been sometime in the late 1500s (New Mexico Writers' Project, 1945).
- The first maps, more notably made by those scribes, priests, and explorers traveling through the area mentioned earlier, such as the Coronado and Oñate parties. These 16th-century maps, covering the North American continent, were necessary not only for their own use but for that of the governments in Mexico City and Spain.[3]
- The first petitions, commissions, edicts, inventories, contracts, and ledgers (beginning in 1513). In the 16th century, these items were just some of the documents required by the Spanish government to explore or settle an area.[4]
- The first European signature artifact. This is dated April 16, 1605 and is signed by Governor Juan de Oñate at what is now El Morro National Monument, New Mexico.
- The first written translations of books into an Indian language (Timucuan). Father Pareja, a Franciscan, did these translations in Georgia between 1612 and 1627 (Góngora, 1975, p. 161; Otis, 1952, p. 41).
- The first scientific journals. During the 1540 expedition of Coronado, in which areas from Kansas to California were explored, detailed journals were maintained regarding the flora and fauna from Kansas to California. Geographic and geological journals were also kept (Udall, 1987).

These examples of literacy firsts clearly challenge the histories of literacy put forth by Graff, de Castell and Luke, and Kaestle. Of these authors, the earliest documentation of U.S. literacy is given to us by Kaestle. He cites Lockridge's study of New England wills "from 1640 to 1800" (p. 109). In Graff's chart of "Sources for the Historical Study of Literacy in North America and Europe" (p. 84), an even later first date is cited: 1660—120 years after Coronado's scientific journals of Kansas were penned and 60 years after schools in New Mexico, Florida, and Georgia had been established. One is left to wonder, at what date, if ever, do historians begin to include Hispanic literacy into their account?

In their depth and scope, these examples of literacy firsts also challenge the authors' implied premise that the history of U.S. literacy followed the same "westward manifestation" path as its government. It clearly did not. Indeed, the introduction of written literacy into the United States did not "manifest westward" from the east. As early as the 16th century, the use of the Roman alphabet was established by southerners heading north.

Literacy in Spanish Colonial Society

When asked "What role did written literacy play in the Spanish colonial society in the U.S.?", Walter Brem, head of Public Services of the University of California at Berkeley's Bancroft Library, explained that the Spanish Americans provided a wealth of historical data for future scholars. New Spain was a documenting bureaucracy, he added, evidenced by the sharp decline of government records kept by officials after the Spanish government was no longer in power—more notably in the southwestern United States (W. Brem, personal communication, November 1991).

The northernmost reaches of the Spanish Empire relied heavily on written literacy to maintain the form and function of its society and government. In New Spain, this documentation process began before *anyone* went *anywhere*. Petitions, contracts, and appointments to explore and settle new areas not only specified what was to be taken for the journey but also what kind of administrative government settlers would have once they got there.

Documents related to New Mexican settlements provide us with typical examples of this process. In the contract of September 25, 1596 between Don Pedro Ponce de Leon (not to be confused with Juan) and the king for the exploration of New Mexico, the Spanish monarch required that Ponce de Leon supply certain provisions. These included

> 12,000 reales worth of drugs or the cure of the sick . . . 2,000 reales worth of articles for barter and gifts to the Indians . . . 2,000 head of cattle for breeding, 5,000 wool-bearing sheep . . . [and] 2,600 reales of paper. (Natella, 1980, p. 58)

This latter provision for paper clearly assumes that writing materials would be needed and used.[5]

As far as determining what kind of administrative hierarchy would be used once the settlement was founded, one need not have looked any further than the colonizers' written contracts and titles and in Spanish law books.

In granting the title of *Adelantado* (in this case, governor) to Don Juan de Oñate, King Philip stated,

> You shall have and receive the salary, rights, and other things owing and pertaining to the said office of governor, and, by this, my letter, I command my councillors, justices, regidores (city councillors), gentlemen, squires, officials . . . of all the cities, towns, and villages of the said province of New Mexico . . . [to] receive you and hold

you as my governor. . . . They shall not place or allow to be placed any obstacle or impediment against you in it or any part of it; for I by this writing receive and have received you into the use and exercise of it, and I give you the power and authority to make use of it [this writing] in case that you shall not be received in it [the office] by them or any one of them. Given at Villalpando, February 7, 1602. I, THE KING. (Natella, 1980, p. 72)

The power of the governor and a description of municipalities were clearly spelled out in Law 2, Title 7, Book 4, of the *Recopilacion de Las Indias,* which was Ordinance No. 43 of Philip II. As with the preceding quotation, note the special importance given to the function of writing:

> The land, province, and place having been elected in which a new settlement is to be made, . . . the governor in whose district it may be or confined shall declare whether the pueblo which is to be settled must be a city, villa, or place, and in conformity with what he shall declare shall be formed the council, government, and officials thereof; so that if it should be a metropolitan city, it shall have a judge, . . . who shall exercise jurisdiction *in solidum;* and jointly with the town council (*regimiento*), shall have the administration of the city; two or three officials of the royal treasury; twelve councilmen (*regidores*); . . . one attorney-general (procurador general); . . . one notary of the council; two notaries public; one of mines and registers; one public crier; one exchange broker; and if a diocese or suffragan, eight councilmen, and the other perpetual officials; for the villas and places, an alcalde ordinario; four councilmen; one alguacil (constable); one notary of the council and a notary public; and one mayordomo. (Hall, 1885, p. 7)

Some of the richest literacy events took place during and after expeditions. In 1537, Alvar Nuñez Cabeza de Vaca sailed to Spain to hand-deliver to the King his own written account of his famous walk from Florida to Culiacan, a town less than 50 miles from the Gulf of California. These documents included a map of the area he journeyed through and references to the North American buffalo (Bolton, 1949; Munilla, 1963). Coronado had three official chroniclers, one royal notary, and several letter couriers on his 1540 expedition into the United States (Bolton, 1949, p. 72). One example of the many records kept was a muster roll, listing names, descriptions, and equipment of all accompanying 336 soldiers. Additional data are given regarding Indians, priests, and others in the party, including three women: "Francisca de Hozes (the wife of the shoemaker), Maria Maldonado (who became the expedition's nurse), and the native wife of Lope Caballero" (Udall, 1987, p. 73). In his own journal, Coronado makes note of the written accounting system used by the Indians of the area. He writes that they "painted in their own way, as they are accustomed to do, what they had thus given" to those of the Coronado party, "and that through these paintings and reckonings" they had been paid by order of the viceroy "much to their satisfaction, and that nothing was owed them" (Bolton, 1949, p. 58). Due to the importance of conserving paper, a style of shorthand developed. This printing style can be seen today by reading the hand-carved 1605 inscription of Juan de Oñate at El Morro National Monument, New Mexico.

Literacy also played an important part in the private lives of the Spanish colonists. Lockhart and Otte (1976) write that

From the examples that have been coming to light one can deduce that letter-writing among private individuals was a well-established custom in both Spain and the Indies (America). . . . Correspondents acknowledge previous letters, complain of lack of mail, speak of the cheapness of paper and ink, and in other ways betray that it was customary to write letters to absent relatives and friends. (pp. ix–x)

In the 16th century, literature and printed matter played an important role in Spanish society in general as is pointed out in the following excerpt:

> The period between 1500 and 1660, known as "The Golden Age," was the Spanish manifestation of the European Renaissance. It was an age of literary giants such as Lope de Vega, Tirso de Molina, Luis de Gongora, Francisco de Quevedo, and Miguel de Cervantes. It was the age of the mystics, the picaresque novel, and books of chivalry. Like Elizabethan England, it was an age when literary creativity ran the gamut of all social classes, was practiced by many, and was enjoyed by most. The mass appeal of literature stimulated book production for over a hundred and fifty years. With the exception of England, Spain was the only country in Western Europe where the number of titles in the vernacular surpassed those in Latin. Printed ecclesiastical texts, and particularly popular literature, began to appear during the fifteenth century and, during the following two centuries, reached prodigious proportions. (Rodríguez-Buckingham, quoted in Garner, 1985, p. 40)

It is only natural to assume that a similar demand for written material would be replicated in the Spanish New World. It was. Records indicate that Esteban Martin was printing in Mexico City in 1537. From 1539 to 1579, Mexico's presses printed over 100 titles, and the number of copies per title varied "from a few hundred to several thousand" (Rodríguez-Buckingham, quoted in Garner, 1985, p. 43). According to Rodríguez-Buckingham, printing presses were responsible for printing literary works, papal bulls, standard contracts for power of attorney, public notices, registration forms for departing ships, and Indian, Latin, and Spanish language grammar and prayer books. Before bringing their own printing presses to northern New Spain, missionaries and settlers took along such publications from Spain or southern New Spain.

This information clearly shows that a sophisticated use of the Roman alphabet was taking place in North America when, as an uncle of mine would say, "Plymouth Rock was still a pebble."

The Catholic Church and Spanish Law in the Fostering of Literacy

The Role of the Mission and of Women Under Civil Law

In 1493, Pope Alexander VI issued a bull:

> For the purposes of overthrowing heathenism, and advancing the Roman Catholic Religion (the crown of Castille was to be granted the) whole of the vast domain then discovered, or to be discovered, between the north and south poles, or so much thereof as was not considered in the possession of any Christian power. (Hall, 1885, p. 2)

Hence a written proclamation was to set the wheels in motion for the Roman Catholic Church and the Spanish state to explore and settle the New World together. As a result, priests and other university-trained religious came to the New World to open missions. The development of literacy skills, both oral and written, consumed a large part of their work. For their own training, Franciscan colleges of the 16th century used dictionaries and grammars of Indian languages which had been written by some of the first missionaries. There are a number of references to mission schools being in place by the late 1500s in the United States from Florida to New Mexico (Beers, 1979; Hallenbeck, 1926; Lummis, 1929). Munilla (1963) writes that by 1630 New Mexico had 50 monks and that

> twenty-five missions had been founded to serve ninety villages and there were some 600 neophytes (converts). Every mission had its own school and workshops in which the Indians learned to read and write, sing and play musical instruments, and practice different arts and crafts. (p. 23)

From the beginning, the Franciscan Order played a critical role in determining not only *what* was going to be taught in the Spanish colonies but *who* was going to be taught. This influence is evidenced by the writings of Fray Juan Zumárraga who was the first bishop of Mexico. Zumárraga, a Franciscan, held the firm conviction that American Indians and girls were to be educated on the same par with that of Spanish boys. He maintained for example, that every provincial capital and principal pueblo have schools for girls (Barth, 1950, p. 95). Empress Isabella, herself a Franciscan of the Third Order,[6] worked closely with the bishop to assure that Indian and Spanish females would be provided educational opportunities. She did this in a number of ways. First, she arranged for a number of interested women teachers and supervisors to be sent from Castile to set up schools. She then saw to it that a number of royal *cedulas,* or mandates, were written to grant financial assistance to these schools. Last, but not least, Doña Isabella provided funding for girls' schools and women's colleges herself (Barth, 1950, p. 97).[7] Thus, in the beginning of Spanish dominion in North America, the Spanish Crown sent a strong message that the education of girls and of Indians was expected to occur.

At this point, it is important to note the rights of women under Spanish law in general. If property rights may be considered the litmus test for determining women's legal power, then women living under the civil law of 16th- and 17th-century New Spain fared much better than their New England sisters. Under Spanish law, community property was recognized. Property acquired during the marriage belonged to both spouses and property acquired before the marriage belonged only to that individual. Should the marriage have dissolved, the property would have been divided equally (Schmidt, 1851). Although it was still basically a patriarchal system, the women of New Spain did have both property and power. Historians make it *very* clear, for example, that it was thanks to the generosity of Doña Beatríz in sharing *her* wealth that her husband Coronado had such a well-outfitted expedition. The money and property that she had inherited was hers to do with as she pleased (Bolton, 1949). (In terms of women having administrative power, the account of "Fidalgo d'Elvas," originally published in 1557, tells us that Doña Isabella remained in charge of the government in Cuba when her husband, Hernando de Soto, left to explore Florida in 1539. Historically, it is also important to remember that when Pope

Alexander joined forces with "the Crown of Castille," he was referring to Queen Isabella of Castille and *her* heirs, not to her husband King Ferdinand of Aragon.)

Contrast the description given above with the following comments regarding common law in New England:

> In one way or another, everything women owned before marriage became their husbands' afterwards. A significant result of this social policy was the inability of femes covert (married women) to contract. No agreement a woman made could be enforced against her because she owned nothing the court could seize to meet a judgment. Even a woman's contract to provide services was unenforceable. According to common law rules, a woman's services belonged to her husband. They could not be given to another unless he consented. (Salmon, 1986, p. 41)

In addition, laws pertaining to inheritance tended to be more generous to widows and daughters. The property rights of women, of which leading Southwest historian Herbert Bolton (1921) makes particular salute to, can be used as an additional reason to cite the need and use for literacy skills in New Spain, particularly for women. Although oral contracts were recognized, the form and structure of the Spanish government and society encouraged written literacy.

A Closing Note

Let us return now to Mr. Baca's search for his 18th-century ancestor. The omission of his name from official records meant that an American lineage of 400 years could not be formally established. Written documents not only provided the *name* of the man, they also provided the socially recognized *evidence* that the man existed. In effect, this is the historical equivalent of determining that the tree really did fall in the woods because someone saw it fall.

What lesson can U.S. educators, particularly those interested in literacy development, cull from this tale of omission? Educators may recognize and appropriately respond to the sad irony that our nation's Hispanic students, whose Indian and Spanish ancestors brought literacy to the Americas in the first place (e.g., the Roman alphabet), should now find themselves representing a group at "high risk" academically, particularly in the area of literacy skills.[8] Although an actual rate of literacy for the entire population of Hispanics in pre-17th-century America is not available, an abundance of historical evidence of their written literacy practice is. Those documents strongly suggest that their demand for written literacy was comparable to, if not higher than, that of other ethnic groups arriving in North America after 1600. Historical records left by Hispanics, such as letters, maps, documents, and literature, are excluded from mainstream academic charts and tables, which are used to describe which ethnic groups brought literacy to North America and when. That omission invariably has formed the historical premise on which pedagogical dialogue concerning the low literacy rates among U.S. Hispanics is implicitly based: that Hispanics in North America presumably had no history of literacy until Anglo-Saxon arrivals to the Americas opened their eyes and ears to the Roman alphabet and to an enlightened world of literacy. Thus premised, educators would have little cause to consider that over the past 300 years there could arguably have been a *decline* in

Hispanic literacy rates when compared to rate gains made by those of other ethnic groups coming to the United States. Unfortunately, however, accounts such as those given by Graff, de Castell and Luke, and Kaestle, which effectively erase the history of Hispanic literacy in North America by ignoring it, deny the importance of such a significant heritage.

Notes

1. Bernardo Gallegos (1992) posits that young Plains Indian captives, who had been purchased and raised as servants until adulthood, would also have been identified in baptismal records as having "parents unknown" (p. 13).

2. This map represents the areas claimed for the Crown by Spanish explorers or settlers.

3. Maps were also of critical use to those newer settlers, some of whom would come from the eastern United States some 200 years later.

4. Such requirements are heavily evidenced by the documents we have regarding the more noted explorations and settlements of Juan Ponce de Leon, Panfilo de Narvaez, and Hernando de Soto (who moved inland from the southeast) and Francisco Vasquez de Coronado and Juan de Oñate (who traveled inland from the southwest).

5. In this contract, King Philip further stipulated that none of the items listed were to be "touched" until they had arrived at the settlement, implying that additional supplies were expected to be obtained for the journey over.

6. The Third Order is a branch of the Franciscan Order which extends membership to lay people.

7. One example of Queen Isabella's grants included half of the large and small unclaimed cattle of New Spain and New Galacia; to be used for schools serving Indian and Spanish girls. The other half was to go to designated boys' schools (Barth, 1950, p. 97).

8. As indicated by the results of the National Assessment of Educational Progress (Hakuta, 1986).

References

Barth, P. J. (1950). *Franciscan education and the social order in Spanish North America (1502–1821)*. Chicago: n.p.

Beers, H. P. (1979). *Spanish and Mexican records of the American Southwest.* Tucson: University of Arizona Press.

Bolton, H. E. (1921). *The Spanish borderlands: A chronicle of Old Florida and the Southwest.* New Haven, CT: Yale University Press.

Bolton, H. E. (1949). *Coronado: Knight of pueblos and plains.* Albuquerque: Whittlesey.

de Castell, S., & Luke, A. (1983). Defining literacy in North American schools: Social and historical conditions and consequences. *Journal of Curriculum Studies, 15,* 373–389. Reprinted in E. R. Kintgen, B. M. Kroll, & M. Rose (Eds.), *Perspectives on literacy.* Carbondale and Edwardsville: Southern Illinois University Press, 1988.

"Fidalgo d'Elvas" [Gentleman of Elvas]. (1557). *The discovery of Florida.* Berkeley: Bancroft Library Collection, University of California.

Freire, P. (1970). *Pedagogy of the oppressed.* New York: Seabury Press.

Gallegos, B. (1992). *Literacy, education, and society in New Mexico, 1693–1821.* Albuquerque: University of New Mexico Press.

Garner, R. (Ed.). (1985). *Iberian colonies, New World societies: Essays in memory of Charles Gibson.* Private printing.

Góngora, M. (1975). *Studies in the colonial history of Spanish America.* Cambridge: Cambridge University Press.

Graff, H. J. (1982). The legacies of literacy. *Journal of Communication, 32*(1), 12–26. Reprinted in E. R. Kintgen, B. M. Kroll, & M. Rose (Eds.), *Perspectives on literacy.* Carbondale and Edwardsville: Southern Illinois University Press, 1988.

Hakuta, K. (1986, April). Societal and policy contexts of research with language minority students. In C. Underwood (Ed.), *Schooling language minority youth, Volume 2: Proceedings of the Linguistic Minority Project Conference,* Berkeley, CA.

Hall, F. (1885). *The laws of Mexico: A compilation and treatise relating to real properly, mines, water rights, personal rights, contracts and inheritances.* San Francisco: A. L. Bancroft & Company.

Hallenbeck, C. (1926). *Spanish missions of the old Southwest.* New York: Doubleday, Page & Company; Harcourt Brace.

Kaestle, C. (1985). The history of literacy and the history of readers. *Review of Research in Education, 12,* 11–53. Reprinted in E. R. Kintgen, B, Kroll, & M. Rose (Eds.), *Perspectives on literacy.* Carbondale and Edwardsville: Southern Illinois University Press, 1988.

Kintgen, E. R., Kroll, B., & Rose, M. (Eds.). (1988). *Perspectives on literacy.* Carbondale and Edwardsville: Southern Illinois University Press.

Lockhart, J., & Otte, E. (1976). *Letters and people of the Spanish Indies: The sixteenth century.* London: Cambridge University Press.

Lockridge, K. A. (1974). *Literacy in colonial New England: An enquiry into the social context of literacy in the early modern west.* New York: Norton.

Lummis, C. (1929). *The Spanish pioneers and the California missions.* Chicago: A. C. McClurg & Company.

Munilla, O. G. (1963). *Spain's share in the history of the United States of America.* Madrid: Publicaciones Españolas.

Natella, A. (1980). *The Spanish in America, 1513–1979: A chronology and fact book.* Dobbs Ferry, NY: Oceana.

New Mexico Writers Project. (1945). *New Mexico.* Albuquerque: University of New Mexico Press.

Otis, R. R. (1952?). *First settlement of the United States by Catholic Spain.* Jacksonville (?), FL: Georgia Historical Society.

Oxford American dictionary. (1990). E. Ehrlich (Ed.). New York: Oxford University Press.

Rodríguez-Buckingham, A. (n.d.). *The first forty years of the book industry in sixteenth-century Mexico.* Reprinted in R. Garner (Ed.), *Iberian colonies, New World societies: Essays in memory of Charles Gibson,* private printing, 1985.

Salmon, M. (1986). *Women and the law of property in early America.* Chapel Hill: University of North Carolina Press.

Schmidt, G. (1851). *The civil law of Spain and Mexico.* New Orleans: Thomas Rea. (UC Berkeley Bancroft Library Collection)

Udall, S. L. (1987). *To the inland empire.* New York: Doubleday.

Weber, D. J. (1992). *The Spanish frontier in North America.* New Haven, CT and London: Yale University Press.

1. Why does Greene believe that it is important for people like Eliseo Baca to be able to locate written records of their ancestors? What does Eliseo Baca's experience with researching his ancestry suggest about the importance of written record keeping, according to Greene? How do such records affect us, as Greene sees it? Do you think she is right? Why or why not?

2. According to Greene, what is missing from the histories of literacy that she discusses in this article? Why does she believe these histories present a "flawed historical perspective"? What is her stated purpose in reviewing these histories? How does she justify this purpose? Do you think her purpose is an important one? Explain.

3. According to Greene, when was written literacy introduced into the United States? Why is this fact important, as Greene sees it? How does it relate to her criticisms of conventional histories of literacy?

4. What literacy "firsts" does Greene say were accomplished by Spanish peoples in North America? Why are these "firsts" significant, according to Greene? Do you think she is right? Why or why not?

5. What roles did literacy play in Spanish colonies in North America? What examples of these roles does Greene provide? What do these examples suggest about the importance of literacy among Spanish peoples in North America in the fifteenth and sixteenth centuries?

6. Why, according to Greene, was literacy important to the Catholic missionaries and other church officials who helped establish Spanish settlements in North America in the fifteenth and sixteenth centuries? What might the uses of literacy among these church officials suggest about the political and religious importance of literacy?

7. What lesson should educators learn from the story of Eliseo Baca, according to Greene? Is this a valid lesson, in your view? Explain.

Examining Rhetorical Strategies

1. Assess the effectiveness of Greene's introduction. How does she use the anecdote about Eliseo Baca? What purposes might she accomplish by including this anecdote? How does it influence your reading of the rest of the essay? Do you think Greene intended that this anecdote would influence readers in this way? Explain.

2. Which histories of literacy does Greene choose to review in her article? What justification does she offer for her choice of these particular histories? Do you find her justification convincing? Why or why not? How might your knowledge of this subject matter have influenced your answer to that question?

3. Evaluate Greene's use of charts and maps in this article. What purpose do these charts and maps serve? How do they relate to Greene's argument

about histories of literacy? What information do they present to readers? Why do you think Greene presents this information in charts or maps rather than including it in the body of her article? Did you find her use of these features of her article effective? Why or why not?

4. Greene wrote this article for a very specific and specialized audience of scholars interested in literacy. In what ways do you think she addresses this audience? What does she assume about their knowledge of her subject matter? Do you think her article is also suitable for a more general audience? Explain, citing specific passages in the article to support your answer.

5. How does Greene build her argument about histories of literacy? Note, for example, the order in which she presents her information and her specific points about the history of literacy. Why do you think she organizes the article in this way? How might her decisions about how to organize her article relate to her audience and to the kind of scholarly article she writes? Also, what kinds of evidence does she present to support her arguments? Do you think this evidence would be convincing to her audience? Explain. Was it convincing to you? Why or why not? What might your answer to that question reveal about your own background as a reader?

6. How would you characterize the tone of this article? Do you find it critical, even-handed, objective? Explain, citing specific passages from the text to support your answer. Do you think Greene presents her criticisms of other scholars fairly in this article? Why or why not? Would you characterize her approach in this article as biased in any way? Explain.

Engaging the Issues

1. Write a conventional academic essay in which you analyze the effectiveness of Greene's article on the basis of the argument she makes. In your essay, identify the main argument Greene makes and explain her criticisms of other literacy histories. Discuss how she develops her argument and assess her use of evidence to support her points. Be sure to make reference to her audience and the journal for which she wrote the article. Draw conclusions about the overall effectiveness of her article.

2. Find one of the articles by Graff, Kaestle, or de Castell and Luke that Greene refers to in her article. (You can find the bibliographic information about these articles among the "References" at the end of the article.) Read the article you have chosen, and write a brief summary of it. Then assess Greene's treatment of that article. What specific criticisms does Greene make of the article? On the basis of your reading of the article, do you think her characterization of the article is fair? Why or why not? How might your own understanding or familiarity with this subject matter have affected your assessment of Greene's criticisms? Present the results of your analysis to your classmates in a brief informal essay.

3. In this article, Greene argues that the histories we write and the written records we keep are important in shaping our sense of who we are. Do you agree? In an essay for an audience of your classmates, present your own perspective on the writing of history. In your essay, you might consider such issues as who writes the histories we read and why. You might also draw on Greene's article or on any other appropriate sources to help support your argument. In addition, you might refer to controversies, such as the presentation of Columbus in school history books, to illustrate your position.

4. In a group of your classmates, compare the essays you wrote for Question #3 above. Identify the various perspectives each of you presented in your essays and discuss them. Are there opposing viewpoints on some issues? If so, what are the points of contention? What might your group's discussion suggest about the writing of history and its importance?

5. Find one of your old history textbooks from middle school or high school (or borrow one from a friend, relative, or the library). Read about a period of history or a specific event in which you are especially interested. How is that period or event presented? What is emphasized? Is anything left out, in your view? Do you see any bias in the way that period or event is described in the book? Present the results of your analysis in a report to your classmates. In your report, try to draw conclusions based on your analysis about the writing of history.

6. Choose a time period or event in history that especially interests you, and search the World Wide Web for sites related to that period or event. (You might focus on the same period or event about which you wrote for Question #5 above.) Select several sites that you've located and compare their treatment of a specific event or period in history. Try to identify the group sponsoring the Web site. For example, is it a site for a professional organization, a university history course, a political organization, or something else? What similarities or differences do you see in how these sites present information about the period or event? Are these similarities or differences related in any way to the organization or person sponsoring the Web site?

   Now compare the results of your research with those of other members of your class and discuss your respective findings. Were there any important similarities or differences in what each of you found? What conclusions can you draw about the way history is written? Consider how the technologies of the Internet and the World Wide Web might affect the writing of history.

7. Using your library, the World Wide Web, or other appropriate sources, investigate how oral cultures preserve their history. For example, as we learned in the previous reading selection by Robert Utley about Sitting Bull, Native American peoples generally had no written version of their languages. How do such cultures preserve their history? Find out what you can about the way they create oral histories and how those histories are preserved in their culture. Then consider how these oral methods might differ from the written histories of your own culture. What conclusions might you draw about the relationship of history and literacy?

Copyright in the Digital Age

Karen Coyle

INTRODUCTION   You may not often think about the fact that most of the words you read in your daily life are copyrighted: from the morning newspaper to the advertisement fliers in the day's mail to the novel you curl up with before you go to sleep to this book that you are reading right now. All these written words are "protected" by laws that make them the "property" of someone or some organization or business. Copyright laws give persons the right to keep or sell their written words and to prevent others from doing so without permission. For instance, the reading selections in this book are protected by copyright laws and therefore could not be reprinted in this book without the permission of the person or organization that "owns" the copyright to them. To gain that permission usually requires the payment of a fee. Indeed, the fact that published texts are bought and sold in this way makes copyright law of such great interest to so many people: writers, publishers, booksellers, advertisers, software developers, corporate managers, educators, librarians, and many, many others. The sale of written texts can be lucrative. And where there is money, there is also power.

Historians of literacy and the law tell us that copyright laws as we know them today were generally established after the development of the printing press. The printing press created the possibility of mass distribution of written texts that had not previously been possible with older technologies, and thus various business interests emerged with the publishing industry. In some cases, copyright laws were implemented primarily as a means of maintaining control over ideas and information. For example, laws developed in England during the sixteenth and seventeenth centuries gave the Crown control of most commercial publishing. Under such laws, royal censors were able to prevent publication and distribution of materials they deemed critical of the Crown or obscene in some way. Still, individual authors and publishers made money, and as publishing developed into a large and complex business, more people had interest in copyright laws to protect potential earnings.

The history of these laws reveals the central role that technology has played not only in the development of copyright laws but also in the emergence of the very idea that one's words could be bought and sold and thus should be protected. The printing press helped give rise to the idea of *author*—one who can "own" his or her written words. The new digital technologies that were developed in the latter part of the twentieth century may be having a similar impact today. As Karen Coyle suggests in the following selection, the digital technologies we use today are challenging existing copyright laws as well as the principles on which those laws are based. Coyle helps us see that the special capabilities of these new technologies change the way in which published material is created, distributed, and used. A written text that is put in digital form can easily be copied and distributed to millions of people in a way that a published book cannot. Thus it can be "published" without a publisher. Existing copyright laws were written for technologies without these capabilities.

According to Coyle, those with financial interest in publishing worry that such capabilities can undermine their "ownership" of published materials—and thus compromise their economic and political power. So they have an interest in changing copyright laws in order to preserve their rights as "owners" of such materials. But Coyle worries that changes in copyright laws that would seem to protect conventional copyright holders might also compromise our collective freedom of access to information.

You may think that these are arcane legal issues for lawyers, legislators, and librarians to worry about. But as Coyle tries to demonstrate in her text, these issues can have a significant impact on your own access to ideas and information as well. Copyright laws, she reminds us, help determine what information we can acquire and how (or whether) we can use it. Moreover, these laws help determine who has access to the power of literacy and the new technologies for literacy. As a result, copyright laws play an important role in your life, even if you aren't aware of it. In this sense, Coyle's concerns about seemingly minor changes in copyright laws relate to much larger questions about freedom of speech in the new digital age and about the power of literacy in the context of new technologies.

Karen Coyle is a librarian who works in database development on the staff of the California Digital Library, which is part of the University of California library system. She has been active not only in developing digital systems for libraries but also in addressing complex legal issues that have emerged with the development of new technologies in libraries. She is chair of the Berkeley chapter of Computer Professionals for Social Responsibility and has spoken widely about intellectual property and copyright issues. She is also the author of *Coyle's Information Highway Handbook* (1998), which was on *Library Journal's* list of "The Year's Best Professional Reading" in 1998. The following selection is the text of a talk she gave at the San Francisco Public Library in 1996.

REFLECTING BEFORE READING

1. In the following selection, Karen Coyle focuses on copyright laws and the impact that changes in such laws might have in the context of new digital media. What do you know about copyright law? Have you ever considered how it affects you in your work and your everyday life? As you read the text of Coyle's talk, consider how the specific laws she discusses might affect you. Think about whether the changes in those laws that are occurring because of new technologies might benefit you or compromise you in any way.

2. The following text is a written version of a speech that Karen Coyle delivered in 1996. As you read, consider the features of the text that might indicate that it was originally given as a speech. Consider, too, how the text might be different if it had been written originally to be published rather than spoken.

The U.S. Constitution gives Congress the power to "promote the progress of science and useful arts, by securing for limited times to authors and inventors the exclusive right to the respective writings and discoveries."

That simple phrase is represented today by hundreds of pages of law and thousands of pages of legal cases. It isn't a simple world.

Copyright law first developed at a time when copies were relatively hard to make. You needed a printing press, and you had to reset all of the type for the work. Early in US history, at a point where English law seemed totally irrelevant to us since we'd just broken away from it, publishers in this country imported British books and reprinted them here without giving anything back to the British copyright holder.

But it just wasn't within the power of the average person to make copies.

The advent of the photocopy machine (Xerox) began the modern age in copyright, throwing things into disarray. Then came home sound tape recording, video recording, and now—the biggest threat of all to copyright—the computer—the ultimate copying machine.

The change from hard copy to digitized materials is really much greater than just a change in the method of copying. Up until now, there has always been a physical object that could be referred to. Something you could hold in your hand.

And up until now, most copies were degraded forms of the original. Photocopies are of a lower quality than a printed book or article (though that technology is getting better). Home sound recordings are inferior to professionally produced ones. And of course video tapes of TV programs are abysmal. So they aren't really great rivals for the originals.

Now we have digital information, information stored on a computer. That information can be copied exactly, with no loss of quality, with the touch of a few keys. Add the Internet to the mix, and you have a situation where in the information can be copied and sent to thousands of other people with those same few keystrokes.

Let me tell you, the holders of copyrights are very upset about this.

Copyright Holders

Let's first clarify who we are talking about here. Who are the copyright holders who have a stake in this? Because most of us, when we hear about copyright, we think of authors. (As an aside, we should really think of authors, song writers, playwrights, artists)

In fact, most copyrights today are held by corporations. In order to get your work published, you sign the "rights" over to the publisher. If you are a famous author, the contract you sign gives you a nice percentage of the sales and lets you make money off any new editions or reprints of your work. If you are a regular, non-famous author, the contract essentially gives you a small percentage of the sales and you lose any rights to any future use of the work—or else you don't get published. Many digital compilations of works that were originally issued in print, like the many online databases of journal articles, are not returning any money to the original authors.

So when we talk about copyright we need to remember that we aren't talking about authors vs. Readers. We're talking about the interests of corporations versus the interests of the public.

Enter the Information Highway

One of the misconceptions that people have about the Internet when they first get onto it (or before they do) is that it contains all of the information in the world.

That it is, in essence, this library [San Francisco Public Library]—digitized. The opposite is true.

There is very little intersection between the content of the Internet and the content of your local public library. The library consists mainly of commercially published works. Works that are protected by copyright. These works are revenue for their publishers, that is they are sold. There is profit to be made. Place any one of these works on the Internet and it is instantly available, for free, to some tens of millions of people. Because there is not, as yet, a way to charge people for the documents they access over the Internet, and there is no way to keep them from making copies of digital documents once they have received them.

After all, the Internet was designed so that researchers and academics could quickly and cheaply share information. It was never intended to be used to sell information. And I'm not even sure that we can use computer networks to sell information in the way that we sell books or CDs. We no longer have a physical object that we can call our product. Something very fundamental has changed.

The New Copyright Law

But those who make their profits off of intellectual property very much want to make use of this new technology of computer networks. To them, it promises great wealth. So one of the primary goals that was included when the Clinton administration announced its program called the "National Information Infrastructure" was the development of ways to protect intellectual property.

First I need to remind you that the information infrastructure planning is taking place in the Department of Commerce. The information infrastructure is not an education project, it is not a logical outgrowth of the Library of Congress—it is business, and purely business for the Clinton administration. And for the business interests of our country. And in their mind, the Internet as it exists today, with billions and billions of bytes of information, tens of millions of users—is irrelevant because there is no place for for-profit activities.

Commissioner Bruce Lehman, head of the National Telecommunications and Information Administration, goes around giving speeches in which he tells people that unless we find a way to protect intellectual property on the Internet, there will be no content worth accessing.

This seems absurd on the surface, but in some ways he is right. The current content of the Internet is a portion of the total output of intellectual property in this country, and not a representative portion. It still reflects its academic beginnings in many ways. And being non-profit, it has government information, lots of non-profit organizations, the works of interesting but somewhat quirky individuals, etc. But waiting in the wings we have folks like Disney, Time/Warner, Viacom—with all of their films, music, and programming. And these are the people the Department of Commerce is designed to serve.

So the first thing that the DoC did was work on some changes to the copyright law aimed at protecting intellectual property in the digital, networked environment. After some study, they came out with a draft paper that stated that there was really very little that had to be changed in the copyright law. The main thing they did was add a short phrase to define the making of a copy to include "transmission."

17 U.S.C. 106(3) "(3) to distribute copies or phonorecords of the copyrighted work to the public by sale or other transfer of ownership property, or by rental, lease or lending, or by transmission.

"To 'transmit' a reproduction is to distribute it by any device or process whereby a copy or phonorecord of the work is fixed beyond the place from which it was sent." (NII Copyright Protection Act of 1995–S.1284)

This looks innocent enough. But what it comes down to is that every time you access information on another computer, that is every time you browse a Web page, that you follow a link, the information is being transmitted to your computer. So every access would be an act of making a copy under the copyright law.

In addition, the report interprets some case law as implying that if you have a document stored on your own hard drive, it is "transmitted" when you then view it on your own screen.

This is an incredible grab of power for the copyright holders. In the hard copy world, once they have sold a physical object, say a book, it is out of their control. The owner of a book can show it to others, sell it to a used book store, or lend it out. The object belongs to the buyer. If that were a digital document, each of these transactions would be a "transmission," and would, by law, be part of the rights of the copyright holder—that is that it wouldn't be legal without payment or the permission of the copyright holder.

Understand that this also eliminates library lending of digital information objects, since there is no lending that does not make a copy.

In between the draft report, called the green paper, and the final report, called the white paper, the DoC held a series of four public hearings where interested parties could give their input. They announced these "public" hearings in the Federal Register (which we all read daily, right), and held them in four cities: NY, Los Angeles, Chicago and Washington D.C. That covers everybody, doesn't it?

No one stood up at these hearings as a simple member of the public. A librarian or two testified at each session, arguing for the public interest. But most of those giving testimony were members of law firms representing the interests of the corporations that hold the copyrights. I'm going to share with you some quotes from those hearings, because I think it will help you understand the tenor of the discussion.

The Money Connection

". . . the United States copyright industries are one of the healthiest and fastest growing sectors of the American economy. In 1991 the core copyright industries accounted for over $20 billion in revenues, 3.6 percent of the gross domestic product. In recent years those industries have grown at close to three times the rate of the economy as a whole."

- 5% of all U.S. employment
- $40 billion in foreign sales

George Vradenberg/Fox, Inc.

What was obvious from the caliber of the speakers was made even more clear by some. As Vradenberg points out here, intellectual property is big business. It's also one of the few businesses, other than computing, where we are running a healthy balance of trade. After all, how many French TV shows do we watch? (Not even on cable!) The whole world is awash in American cultural products.

Content, Content, Content

> ". . . people don't buy wires and digital and head ends and all of the technology in its arcane form. What they buy and subscribe to and want to have come into their home is programming that they want to see, when they want to see it."
>
> *Jack Valenti/Motion Picture Association of America*

The success of the information highway depends on content. Though Valenti is talking about entertainment as content, we should remember that this is also true of information content. People aren't going to purchase equipment and pay monthly fees unless the system gives them what they need. The current emphasis on ISDN vs. Fiber to the home ignores the fact that we don't currently have a clue as to what will be traveling over those wires.

Protection of Intellectual Property

> ". . . I also very strongly agree with the report's statement that the potential of the NII [National Information Infrastructure] will not be realized if the information and entertainment products protectable by intellectual property laws are not protected effectively when disseminated on the NII . . ."
>
> *Priscilla Walter/law firm of Gardner, Carton & Douglas, Chicago*

This sentiment was reiterated by a large number of the speakers—the need for some kind of protection of their products as an essential element of the NII. As I've said, this does ignore the fact that a huge information system has developed without any of that protection. These people really don't think that the Internet has any substance at all. Perhaps they don't even know that I was able to download every word they said at those hearings—I, who normally wouldn't be privy to this kind of discussion.

And note that she is the first to use the words "entertainment products." Really, that's what it's all about—that's the real market. A new vehicle to bring entertainment into the home. She's not concerned about everyone in the country having instantaneous access to every bill in Congress. Of course, that's not her business.

Browsing

One of the issues that was discussed often was "browsing." If even viewing a document on a screen constitutes the making of a copy, how will people browse?

> "But I think that we want to make clear though that when you have public access that does not mean free access. . . . And I don't think that, given the nature of our

products, magazines, newspapers, that browsing should be something that would be fair use."

William Barlow, Times-Mirror

His first statement is very interesting—public access does not mean free access. Is his concern that his company won't get paid, or is he concerned that some people will get access to the information for free?

Libraries lend books for free, but the publishers have gotten their legal payment for those books. But I get the impression that in the digital age, even if libraries had infinite budgets and paid for every patron's use, this guy still wouldn't be happy, because someone is getting something for free. I begin to wonder if the discussion here is really about copyright.

Online materials, like all other materials, are copyrighted simply by the fact of their existence. You may know that for something to be copyrighted, it does not have to be registered with the Copyright Office, nor does it have to have the little "c" in a circle on it. The mere fact that you wrote it, and you can prove that you wrote it, is enough.

Fair Use

But this guy isn't suggesting that his materials be copyrighted—because they already are. What he's suggesting is that there shouldn't be "fair use." That no one should be allowed to even look at his "products" without paying. The issue instead is really about greater control of digital works, and this quote is a perfect example of that.

In the hardcopy world, even with magazines and newspapers, which is Mr. Barlow's line of work, we have a concept of "fair use." Fair use, in a nutshell, because it's a very complex topic and I'm not knowledgeable enough to go beyond the nutshell level, allows a person to make a copy of a portion of [a] work for personal or educational use.

> "Without this privilege to use copyrighted materials, copyright would not serve its constitutional purpose 'to promote the progress of Science and Useful Arts.' Fair use thus limits the copyright owner's monopoly by reserving to others the right to make reasonable uses of copyrighted materials without the specific consent of the author."
>
> *[The copyright primer for Librarians and Educators]*

Fair use is the other side of the copyright equation—it's the side that says that the public has a right to read and review intellectual property; to quote from it; to make copies of portions for personal and educational use. But what this copyright grab (as Pam Samuelson called it in her Wired magazine article) is about is control of use of the products, not just the copying.

Control of Use

LEHMAN: ". . . you know, the digital technology permits you to cut off a given user if you wanted to."

BARLOW: "That would be right. We'd like to have that control."

If a book is in the library, the publisher cannot "cut off a user." The publisher has lost control over that work. What Barlow has said here means essentially that the publishers and corporations could decide who gets to have information.

If you think this is unlikely, let me tell you a story. You might know that the online information system called Lexis/Nexis gives special discounts to educational institutions for access, since it's otherwise quite pricey. When their system reaches a certain point of load (or overload), they are able to tweak it so that the higher paying corporate customers get faster service, and the discount educational customers get slower service. A little over a year ago, one of our CSU [California State University] campuses was getting a lot of complaints from the students when the Lexis/Nexis system was terribly slow. The students didn't understand that it wasn't something that the library could fix. Tired of giving the explanation over and over, the library placed a sign on the Lexis/Nexis terminal explaining the situation.

Now I didn't see the wording of that sign, but Mead, the parent company, found the sign to be "critical" of their service, and cut off the CSU's access to the system. After what I presume was an amount of closed-door cow-towing to Mead, access was restored a few weeks later.

I'm sure you can grasp what this means for intellectual freedom in the digital age. You can criticize a book that you find on the library shelf, and it will still be there. But digital resources can be withdrawn.

Pay Per View

But there's more. If you accept that each "viewing" is a transmission, and each transmission makes a copy, then you can reasonably conclude that the copyright holder should get paid "per viewing"—meaning that if you access the same document twice, you may be asked to pay twice. And sure enough, one of the questions discussed at the hearings was how users might be required to pay for works.

> "Per user is a hard copy business. . . You don't care how many times . . . they use it. . . . The motion picture business is based on per use licensing. . . . You go in to see a movie a second time you pay a second ticket."
>
> *Lorin Brennan, American Film Marketing Association*

I think this concept points out some of the real problems we are having in terms of reconciling different interests in the digital world. We have had very different ways of paying for different kinds of products, like performance rights. Until looking into this area, I wasn't really aware of "performance rights", which are [an] important part of copyright law and pertain to performed intellectual property like songs, plays, etc.

But this speaker is wrong about "per user" and "per use." Neither really exists. For example, you sell a magazine to a user, who can read it over and over. But the magazine world knows darn well that each copy is read by more than one user. They do polls and use these figures when negotiating with advertisers rather than the number of copies they print. Even for movies, you can rent a video and cram as many people as you want around your TV set.

And we have never paid for each and every use of anything, except perhaps live performances. And in spite of this, the intellectual property industries seem to be doing just fine. These folks are asking to be paid for uses in the digital world that are far beyond the uses they can charge for in the analog world. Though they claim that they are merely trying to "maintain" their current set of rights, they are actually trying to tack on a number of rights that they have never had. And all of these rights would restrict the public's access to these materials.

Libraries Under Assault

This isn't, though, the worst of the bad news, I'm afraid. The worst, to me, is that libraries are being portrayed as part of the problem.

> "Similarly, there is not and should not be a "private" or "personal" use exemption from copyright as such (. . .). It must be recalled, after all, that disseminating printed and electronic works to individual consumers for their "personal" or "private" use is precisely the business authors and publishers are about."

> "Unauthorized digital 'Lending'—a clear misnomer—to patrons at remote locations will destroy publishers. Their entire business model is to provide readers with content to read. A digitized version of a book that can be electronically provided to anyone anywhere under the label "library lending" directly competes with both conventional and new authorized forms of publishing. . ."

> *Position Paper on Libraries, Copyright and the Electronic Environment of the*
> *International Publishers Copyright Council (IPPC)*

This statement from International Publisher's Association reveals their interest in having the copyright holder have control over every single use of an item. And it implies that the library, insinuating itself between the reader [and the] publisher, is really stepping on the publisher's business.

Information Wants to Be . . .

There's also a strong backlash against the "free information" movement on the Internet. You know the expression "information wants to be free."

> "West commends the Working Group's timely recognition that a strong and continuing education program at every education level is necessary to reverse the present and growing attitude of many citizens that works should be free for the taking in the electronic environment."

> *James Schatz/West Publishing*

Of course, the fact is that there is a rather large body of free information, such as government information, a lot of academic information, information coming out from non-profits or public service areas. Clearly, that information is just giving users mistaken ideas.

And of course, some people get those ideas from libraries.

"We're concerned about the use of metaphors for the NII such as information high-way, digital library or universal service, that imply that all of the information available might be free."

Edward Massie, CEO, Commerce Clearing House

This speaker seems to think that we should quit even talking about libraries, since the mere concept gives people the wrong idea. And I love his inclusion here of universal service. Obviously, he doesn't want to be required to provide his service in an affordable and equitable way to all members of our society. It's clear that to these people, there is no place for libraries in the digital age.

Libraries and the Third Wave

The digital age then follows perfectly the Tofflerian vision of the "Third Wave" where we function entirely as individuals, with no need for institutions mediating between us and the rest of the world. Note that in Toffler's book "Third Wave" he mentions libraries only once, and in an example of second wave institutions.

Where Are We Now?

It's true that there have been some tensions between publishers and libraries in the past—mostly with publishers of higher end academic journals, which libraries share through Inter-Library Loan because they can't afford copies. This then makes the prices of these journals go up, more libraries drop their subscriptions . . . etc. But there's never been, to my knowledge, any evidence that libraries cut into the business of book publishers. And some books are published almost entirely for the library market, like the more expensive reference books.

Remember that everything that libraries do in terms of lending and disseminating information is within the scope of the copyright law. What's happening today is an overt assault on the idea that we should be providing universal access to information.

What's happening today is that we have moved abruptly from the Jeffersonian ideal of an educated public, and have truly entered the information age. Because, as it has been said, information is the Product of the 90's.

REFLECTING ON THE READING

1. According to Coyle, why is the computer, among the various communications technologies, the biggest threat to the principle of copyright? What specific features of the computer make it such a threat to copyright? How does it differ from other technologies that might affect copyright, such as the Xerox machine? Why are these differences important when it comes to copyright?

2. Who holds most of the copyrights to published works today? Why is this fact significant for Coyle's point in this talk? What might it suggest about the relationship between literacy technologies like computers and the economy? Why are copyright holders so interested in the Internet and its potential implications for publishing? Do you think their interest is justified? Explain.

3. According to Coyle, what is the fundamental change in how published works are distributed and controlled that has been brought on by the Internet? What are the implications of this change for the distribution of published works?

4. What is the National Information Infrastructure? According to Coyle, why is it significant that this project is taking place in the U.S. Department of Commerce? What does that suggest about the U.S. government's views about copyright? Why does Coyle believe that we should be concerned about this development in copyright law? Do you share her concern? Why or why not?

5. Why is the addition of the word "transmission" to existing copyright law so important, in Coyle's view? What are the implications of that single word to the copyright law? In what sense would such a change represent a "grab of power," as Coyle sees it? Who would have such power? Do you agree with Coyle that such a development is worrisome? Explain.

6. Why were the Congressional hearings on the National Information Infrastructure so important, in Coyle's view? Who testified at those hearings? What views were expressed at those hearings by those who testified? Why is Coyle concerned about those views?

7. What is the "fair use" of copyrighted materials? What does Coyle mean when she describes fair use as "the other side of the copyright equation"? Why is this such an important principle, according to Coyle? How would this principle be changed if the National Information Infrastructure is implemented? What would be the implications of this change for libraries and others who benefit from the principle of fair use? How might such a change affect you? Do you think this would be a good change? Explain.

8. What does the story of the shutting down of the Lexis/Nexis database at the California State University campuses reveal about the control of information, according to Coyle? What does this incident reveal about the nature of digital technology and freedom of information? Why does Coyle believe that the incident is about intellectual freedom? Do you agree with her? Why or why not?

9. Why, according to Coyle, are libraries threatened by the National Information Infrastructure initiative? How is this threat different from similar threats in the past, as Coyle sees it? Why does Coyle call this threat "an overt assault on the idea that we should be providing universal access to information"? Do you agree with her? Explain.

Examining Rhetorical Strategies

1. Assess the way Coyle introduces this talk. Why do you think she begins with a quotation from the U.S. Constitution? What effect might such a quotation have on her audience, which was primarily composed of librarians like her? Do you think the opening paragraphs of her talk effectively introduce her subject? Why or why not? Do you think the paragraphs establish her own point of view clearly? Explain.

2. How would you characterize Coyle's voice in this talk? What specific features distinguish her voice? Find specific passages in the text that illustrate those

features. Do you find her voice credible, engaging, effective? Why or why not? Do you think her voice in this piece has anything to do with the fact that the piece was originally written to be delivered as a speech rather than published as a text? Explain, citing specific passages in the text to support your answer.

3. Coyle originally delivered this talk to an audience of other librarians. In what ways do you think she addressed her talk specifically to that audience? If you did not know that this talk had been addressed to that audience, would you be able to tell from her text that she was addressing other librarians? Explain, citing specific passages in the text to support your answer. Do you think a more general audience—that is, an audience that was not composed of librarians but people who were not specialists in library work—would find her talk accessible and engaging? Why or why not? Did you find it accessible and engaging? Why or why not? What might your reaction to her talk suggest about you as a reader?

4. Assess Coyle's use of quotations from the Congressional hearings on copyright law. Whom does she quote? What interests do the people she quotes from the hearings have in copyright law? What is the nature of the quotations she includes in her talk? Coyle tells us that she includes these quotations to give us a sense of the "tenor of the discussion." What was the "tenor" of the discussion that Coyle wishes to convey in these quotes? Do you think she accomplished that goal? Explain.

5. Coyle argues in this talk that new developments in copyright law represent a significant threat to libraries and to the idea of free access to information. What assumptions do you think she makes about such matters as freedom of information and similar principles that we tend to associate with living in the United States? How might her assumptions influence her characterization of recent developments in copyright law such as the National Information Infrastructure? Do you think her characterization of such developments is fair? Why or why not? How might your own assumptions about free speech, free information, commerce, and related matters affect your reaction to Coyle's argument?

Engaging the Issues

1. Write an essay in which you discuss how copyright law affects you. In your essay, consider how you use copyrighted materials in your everyday life, at your job, and/or in school. Examine the role technologies such as printed books, copy machines, and computers have in your uses of such materials. Consider, too, how some of the changes in copyright law described by Coyle might affect your own uses of copyrighted materials. Discuss whether you think these changes would be beneficial or detrimental to you and others.

2. In a group of your classmates, compare the essays you wrote for Question #1 above. Try to identify similarities and differences in how copyright laws seem to affect each of you. How might you account for such similarities or differences? For example, can you account for these similarities and differences on the basis

of your socioeconomic backgrounds? Based on your discussions, try to draw conclusions about how copyright laws—and changes in them—might affect different segments of society.

3. Write a conventional academic essay in which you discuss the idea that copyright is power. In your essay, draw on Coyle's talk and on any other appropriate sources to support your discussion and to illustrate ways in which you think copyright laws might reveal the "power of the pen." In your discussion, consider economic and political as well as legal aspects of copyright. Draw conclusions about the relationship between the power associated with copyright and the development of new technologies.

4. Interview a librarian at your local library about copyright laws and related matters such as those that Coyle brings up in her talk. Ask him or her about the importance and implications of copyright laws for the people who use that library. Also ask about the impact of new digital technologies on that library and its patrons. You might share your copy of Coyle's talk with the person you interview in order to get his or her reaction to it. Report on your interview to your classmates. In your report, discuss how your interview might support, challenge, or complicate the views that Coyle expresses in her talk.

5. Using your library, the World Wide Web, and any other appropriate resources, investigate the National Information Infrastructure to see whether it has been implemented in the time since Coyle delivered her talk in 1996. Try to find out about other important developments regarding copyright laws with respect to digital media. Then write a report for your classmates about copyright laws in the digital age. In your report, describe important developments that have occurred in recent years, including the passage of new laws or the establishment of initiatives like the National Information Infrastructure. Explain some of the implications of these developments. Try to determine whether Karen Coyle's concerns about copyright are valid ones.

6. On the basis of your research for Questions #4 and #5 above, write an editorial for your local newspaper about recent developments in copyright laws, especially regarding digital materials. In your essay, briefly describe these recent developments and their implications. Explain why readers of the newspaper should be aware of and/or concerned about such developments. Offer your own views about what the government as well as private citizens should do about this issue.

7. Using your library and the World Wide Web, locate several newspaper or newsmagazine articles about the National Information Infrastructure and specifically about the Congressional Hearings on the NII. Review those articles to get a sense of how those hearings and the NII in general were covered by the press. What did press reports emphasize about the NII hearings? Did they express concerns similar to those that Coyle expresses in her talk? Write a report for your classmates about what you found in your review of the press coverage of the NII. In your report, be sure to explain the NII and describe the kinds of newspaper and magazine articles you reviewed. Describe as well the nature of the coverage as reflected in those articles, and try to draw conclusions about that coverage.

8. On the basis of the research you did for Question #7 above, write a letter to the editor of one of the newspapers or newsmagazines that covered the National Information Infrastructure hearings. In your letter, express your views about the nature of the paper's or magazine's coverage.

FURTHERING YOUR INQUIRY

1. Write a conventional academic essay in which you discuss the political nature of literacy. In your essay, draw on several of the readings in this chapter—or on other appropriate sources—to illustrate and support your analysis.

2. Write an essay for a general audience (for example, readers of a large-circulation publication such as *USA Today*) titled "The Power of Literacy." In your essay, present your perspective on the idea that literacy constitutes power. Draw on any readings in this chapter or on related sources to support your discussion. Use whatever approach and style you deem appropriate for your audience.

3. Write an essay in which you compare the role of literacy in the lives of Min-zhan Lu and Malcolm X. In your essay, identify similarities and differences in the ways in which reading and writing shaped their lives. Try to draw conclusions about the "power" of literacy in individual lives.

4. Investigate the current status of copyright laws as they apply to digital media. What laws have been passed in recent years that affect copyright for such media? What important legal cases have been presented in court in recent years that have influenced copyright law? On the basis of your research, write a report about copyright laws as they apply to digital media. In your report try to draw conclusions about how new technologies are influencing not only laws related to copyright but also the basic principles of "ownership" of texts. Discuss how copyright laws and the changes made to them in recent years reflect the "power" of literacy.

5. Interview several people who come from different cultural backgrounds about their histories as readers and writers and the role of literacy in their lives. (If you are unable to find people to interview, try to find several written accounts of literacy, such as those by Min-zhan Lu and Malcolm X.) Ask your interviewees about how they learned to read and write. Find out about how writing and reading were used in their homes. Try to identify any special features of their literacy histories that seem unique to them or somehow connected to their cultural backgrounds. After you have completed your interviews, write a report about the interviews you conducted. In your report, describe each of the people you interviewed, making sure to identify their cultural backgrounds as clearly and as accurately as you can. Describe, too, their histories as literate persons. Compare their histories in an effort to determine how their experiences as readers and writers might have been different. Draw conclusions about the relationship between literacy and culture.

6. Using the World Wide Web or your library, try to find an example of social or political activism that interests or concerns you. For example, you might learn about a letter-writing campaign to oppose a specific law. Or you might find a

Web site devoted to publicizing some social problem or legal injustice. Once you locate such an example, find out as much as you can about the circumstances. If possible, talk to some of the people involved (or contact them via email). Carefully examine the role literacy played in this case. Then write a report for your classmates on this case of activism. In your report, describe the circumstances and provide background about the case. Describe, too, the uses of literacy in this case. Try to draw conclusions about the "power" of literacy on the basis of this case.

Alternatively, write an essay in which you describe your own experiences in activism as described in this question. In your essay, address the role that literacy played in your experience.

7. Construct a Web site for a social, political, environmental, or other cause that you believe is important. Try to create a site that is intended to help further that cause. As you are designing your site, visit other such sites to determine what features they include and how they seem to further the cause they support. Consider the audience you hope to reach and design your site accordingly. Consider the potential legal or ethical issues related to the kinds of material you wish to include on your site.

8. In a group of your classmates, compare the Web sites you created for Question #7 above. What features distinguish each site? What similarities and differences emerge among the various sites? How effectively does each site accomplish its apparent purpose? Try to draw conclusions about the potential "power" of such sites on the basis of your discussion.

9. Write an essay in which you discuss differences among technologies for literacy—the printing press, the computer, pen and paper—as tools for political action. In your essay, draw on readings from this chapter or elsewhere in this reader—or any other appropriate sources you find—to support and illustrate your analysis. Cite specific instances in which the technologies you are describing were used specifically for social or political purposes.

10. Write an essay in which you compare and/or contrast the way in which two or more authors in this chapter define the "power" of literacy. In your essay, try to draw conclusions about what we mean by the "power" of literacy.

CHAPTER 7

Futures

In its very first issue of the year 2000, the newsmagazine *Newsweek* includes a special report titled "The 21st Century: A User's Guide." The beginning of a new year typically invites reflection, prompting people to ponder the previous year's events and wonder about the future. But the turn of the calendar to the year 2000—which marked the end of a year, a decade, a century, and a millennium—was obviously special, and musings about the future like the *Newsweek* report proliferated as people turned their attention to the meaning of that seemingly momentous date. Like so many such reports, the one in *Newsweek* sounds a hopeful and excited note about what lies ahead in the new century. The authors promise that their report covers "what we can expect. What we can look forward to. What we should worry about." And they confidently proclaim, "The good news is that, in our judgment, the 'look forwards' greatly outweigh the 'worry abouts.'" Although they acknowledge "some darkish clouds" on the horizon, they anticipate a very bright future in which we can expect "perfect" organ transplants; "nanobiology"—an emerging field in which tiny medical devices and drugs will be used to cure "a number of nasty disorders"; new techniques to "rewire our brains to repair individual deficiencies"; computers to do just about anything; cars that will be "so smart that they'll drive us"; and more. Not surprisingly, with such a vision of the future, the *Newsweek* writers declare themselves "optimistic."

You need not look too closely at *Newsweek*'s special report to realize that technology lies at the center of this vision for the future. Of the twenty-two separate articles that comprise the report, only a few do not focus on some sort of technology, and even those that ostensibly address other topics often indirectly deal with technology (for example, a story about expected business developments in the twenty-first century refers to technology companies and technological developments that might influence commerce). In short, to these writers, the future *is* technology. Their hopes, their wishes, their predictions, and their expectations all rest on their faith in technology. For them, there is little question but that life will be better because of technology. We ourselves will be better through the uses of technologies that will overcome human limitations.

This vision of a better world, of progress through technological developments, is widely shared. In describing their optimistic picture of what lies ahead for us, the *Newsweek* writers reflect a deep American faith in progress. And as we saw in the first chapter of this reader, such a vision is not new. Americans—as well as other peoples— have long hitched their dreams of a better life to the chariot of technology. But although the belief that technology will provide us a better future seems common- sensical to many people, defining exactly what we mean by a "better" life is another matter. Well-known journalist James Reston, Jr., has pointed out that our definitions of progress differ. He offers a list of things by which we tend to measure progress: "Human happiness. Greater comfort. Faster speed in transportation and communi- cation. Reduction in human suffering. Dazzling technology. Longer life span." Then he adds, "Measuring such things is difficult, partly because there seems to be no objective standard. . . . How do we balance any one of these positive abstractions against regression? Against poverty, AIDS, the scourge of drugs, environmental dis- aster, the impoverishment of family life?" (*How We Want to Live,* 1998, pp. 3–4). Reston suggests that our deep confidence in the technologies we create to make our lives better may not be enough to answer such hard questions.

Perhaps because of the difficulties of defining what progress means and of deter- mining what kind of future we really want, the turn of the calendar to 2000 brought with it anxiety as well as excitement. The great deal of attention paid to the "Y2K bug" as 1999 came to an end may have been as much a reflection of this anxiety as it was a practical need to address a technical problem. The "Y2K bug" refers to a glitch in computer programs in which dates are designated by the last two digits of the year—so that 1999 would be designated "99" and 2000 would be "00." This use of two digits rather than four to designate dates was intended to save space in com- puter codes. But if computer systems confused the years 1900 and 2000, both of which appear as "00" in program codes, a host of problems could result, from minor mistakes on credit card bills to the possible failure of entire electrical power grids and communications systems. The potentially catastrophic nature of these problems prompted governments, businesses, public and private institutions, and private citi- zens around the world to try to correct the computer codes before January 1, 2000, or prepare for the worst. Billions of dollars were spent to "fix" the Y2K problem, and computer programmers devoted countless hours to it. In the end, serious problems of the kind that some had predicted did not occur, perhaps because so much money and effort had been put into correcting the Y2K bug. But despite the fact that Y2K did not result in catastrophe, it did cause much worrying and prompt many people to reflect on their uses of—and dependence upon—technology. For some, Y2K indi- cated a need to rethink our enthusiasm for technology and to re-examine our basic values regarding life-style. It suggested that the future, with its promise of even more astonishing technological developments, may not be as bright as the *Newsweek* report would have us believe.

Whatever your own sense of the future—whether optimistic or otherwise—the impulse to look ahead and anticipate what is to come is an old one. Among the arti- cles included in that *Newsweek* report is one that describes some of the predictions that people made as 1899 turned into 1900. The writer of that article, John Leland, reviews some of those predictions and provides a sense of the general expectations that people at that time had about the twentieth century. If today we see technology as the means to a better life in the twenty-first century, Leland suggests that our predecessors in 1900 had an even rosier view of what technology would do for us in the twentieth century. They put their faith in technological developments like aluminum as a building material and cameras and telephones as communications tools, and they envisioned an easier, safer, and more efficient life-style as a result of these technologies. Some of their predictions came to be; others did not. But what is noteworthy is that our collective faith in technology and progress seems to be a constant. One hundred years has not weakened it. Like our forbears in 1900, we seem to look ahead to the future with excitement.

It seems worthwhile to ask whether that excitement is warranted—or whether the many warnings we hear about the future should be heeded. The readings in this chapter provide an opportunity to reflect on what may lie ahead and to consider whether our excitement and our anxieties about the future are justified. Some of the writers whose essays appear in this chapter share the optimism of the *Newsweek* reporters and look ahead with great anticipation to the technological advances they envision in the years to come. But the tone of other selections in this chapter is more measured and serves to remind us that the changes we are facing now and those we can expect to face in the years ahead are complex and at times uncertain. In these readings you will encounter some of the warnings that were sounded as the 1990's turned into 2000, and you will glimpse some of the specific hopes and fears of writers who have carefully examined important aspects of our lives. The year 2000 prompted many to wonder what we can expect and hope for in the new century. These readings may encourage you to ask what we *should* hope for.

In these selections, three central issues emerge. As always, technology is a key issue. Some of the authors in this chapter will ask you to imagine new technologies that could change your life and perhaps make it easier or more comfortable. But others will insist that you ask hard questions about the uses of such technologies. What might be lost in technological developments that seem at first glance to improve our lives? How might such developments reflect—or diverge from—what we most deeply value about ourselves and each other? How should we monitor such developments? How should we shape the technologies that shape us? Every generation must confront such questions. But these questions seem especially important now as technology becomes ever more integral to our lives and capable of things once believed impossible.

These questions inevitably lead to the second issue that runs through this chapter: the larger problem of who we are and what we want. Throughout these reading selections, questions about ourselves are always being asked, implicitly or explicitly. When we ask ourselves whether a specific technology is good for us or how we ought to use it, we are at some level asking about who we are as individuals, as members of communities and societies, as inhabitants of the earth. We are, in effect, confronting our own sense of identity and our deepest values about what is most important to us as human beings. As we imagine the future and explore how we should try to shape it, these values inevitably influence our decisions. In this sense, the authors in this chapter encourage you to consider how your view of yourself might shape your sense of the future.

Finally, literacy somehow figures into all of this questioning and examining, and it is perhaps the most complex of the issues addressed in this chapter. Some of the authors address writing or reading directly, pondering how literacy might change as technology continues to develop. Others examine the important role literacy plays in individual lives as technology shapes those lives. It is perhaps noteworthy that the Y2K bug was at heart a concern about written text—in this case, specific numbers hidden within lines of computer code. And it is not surprising that the year 2000 generated so much other writing, including some of the selections in this chapter. Writing, it seems clear, remains a most important technology in human life, perhaps even more so as we prepare for a future that we can only try to imagine.

Christmas Unplugged

AMY BRUCKMAN

INTRODUCTION One of the ways in which we measure progress is by examining how we spend our time. We use "timesaving" devices or techniques in our work and in our everyday lives, and we seem to look constantly for ways to "free up" our time. If we find ways to do something in ten minutes that once took an hour, we generally consider that to be progress. If we save time by traveling from New York to London in three hours—which the Concorde jet enables us to do—instead of a week—which is how long the trip takes by sea—then we have made progress. Faster and quicker are thought to be better. Just what we might mean by "saving time" in these ways is not always clear, however, even though we rarely seem to wonder about the benefits of doing something faster or sooner. Moreover, what we might actually do with the time we save—with our "free" or "extra" time—is not necessarily a straightforward matter. If you save time, what will you do with it? What *should* you do with it?

In one sense, researcher Amy Bruckman poses that question in the following essay. At a time of year when many people reflect on their lives—the Christmas and New Year's holidays—Bruckman finds herself feeling oddly disconnected from her daily work routine because she has disconnected herself from the Internet. As a result, she seems to have "extra" time on her hands—time that she is unsure how to use. It may be accurate to say that Bruckman has not "saved" or "gained" time; rather, she seems to have found herself in a situation in which she has to use her time differently. In short, by deciding to take a vacation from her work—and from the Internet that has become such an important part of her professional and personal life—Bruckman is confronting the question of how to spend her time.

In doing so, Bruckman raises other questions that seem especially relevant at the beginning of a new century and a new millennium that promise to be deeply shaped by technology. Her essay reminds us that technology is not only a means by which we "save" time: it is also integral to how we spend our time. For Bruckman, the Internet—which she calls "the Net" or "the network"—has become central to her life to such an extent that her physical location almost does not matter. As long as she has her computer and a way to connect it to the Internet, she can "be" wherever she wants to be: in her "office," with a friend in Hawaii, or in the midst of a casual discussion with other movie buffs. In this way, technology seems to alter time, for she can "be" any of those "places" at any time she chooses. Many observers view this feature of the technology of the Internet as "progress," as a way to control or conquer time. But Bruckman is not so sure. And in sharing with us her worries about how she spends her time, she may be giving us a glimpse of some of the challenges we will face in the years ahead as more people make use of the Internet and related technologies as extensively as Bruckman does.

It is fitting (and maybe a little ironic) that Bruckman is raising these questions and highlighting these worries about technology and time and—ultimately—about how we will live our lives, because she is in a sense a technology pioneer. As a researcher at the Massachusetts Institute of Technology in the early 1990's, Bruckman was among the first researchers and scholars to look seriously at how people were using the technologies of cyberspace and what the implications of their uses of the Internet might be. Her study, "Gender Swapping on the Internet," published in 1993, was among the first such studies to examine issues of gender and identity among participants in Internet discussion groups and MUD's (online text-based games in which participants create virtual characters). Since that time she has continued to study identity in cyberspace and has also helped develop online learning environments, including MOOSE Crossing, which is designed to help children develop reading, writing, and programming skills. Bruckman is currently an assistant professor in the College of Computing at the Georgia Institute of Technology, where she helped establish the Electronic Learning Communities, which supports research on computer-based networks. She continues to write about social and educational interactions in cyberspace for such publications as *Technology Review*, where the following essay was published in 1995. Her obvious commitment to computer technologies and her experience with online environments as a researcher make her misgivings about our uses of technology all the more compelling.

REFLECTING BEFORE READING

1. As you prepare to read Bruckman's essay, think about how you usually spend your time. Do you purposely set aside time for yourself when you are not working? Why or why not? In what ways might technology affect how you spend your time? For example, when you go on vacation or take a break from work, do you intentionally avoid devices like the telephone or the computer? Do you use such devices in your "free" time? What do your uses of time reveal about your own values?

2. Note the title of Bruckman's essay: "Christmas Unplugged." What does that title suggest to you? What expectations does it establish regarding the content of Bruckman's essay? Do you think Bruckman intended to establish those expectations with that title? Explain. What do the terms *Christmas* and *unplugged* suggest to you? How might your understanding of those terms influence your reading of Bruckman's essay?

I f I had a network link, I'd be home now.

From my chaise lounge on the terrace of my parents' Miami Beach apartment, I see a grid of four-lane roads with palm-treed median strips, yachts moored on the inland waterway, a golf course, and a dozen tall white condominiums. The hum of traffic is punctuated by the soft thunk of racquets striking tennis balls somewhere below. The temperature is in the 70s and a breeze blows through my toes. I am a long way from Boston. If I had a net link, I'd know exactly how far.

I'd know the weather forecast for Miami, and, if I cared, for Boston too. Just about anything you might like to know is out there on the worldwide computer network—the Net—if you know where to look.

It's Christmas day in Miami, but I'm not sure it would really be Christmas or I would really be in Miami if I were plugged into the Net. I would be in my virtual office, a "room" in the text-based virtual reality environment where I do most of my work. I have a desk there, piled with things to do, and a fish tank—just like my "real" office. Except that the virtual fish don't need to be fed—they're just a program I created one day while procrastinating from real work. My virtual office is just some data on a computer housed at MIT that I can tap into from anywhere, but it is a place to me. When I log onto the network, I am there.

And I would be there right now, if not for a difficult choice I made two days ago. I was packed for my trip south and had called a cab. I had the important things: airline ticket, wallet, bathing suit. I stood in the hall staring at a padded gray bag, the one containing my Macintosh Powerbook computer. I grabbed the bag, double-locked the door, and started to walk down the hall. I stopped. I went back, opened the door, and put down the gray bag. I stood in the doorway, feeling foolish. The taxi honked. The honk gave me courage: I locked up again, leaving my computer—my office—behind.

A vacation should be about escaping from routines; going somewhere else provides a new perspective. But when I travel with my Powerbook, I bring many of my routines with me. I can readily gain access to all my familiar tools for finding information. It's as if I never left. And that's the problem. Had I brought my Powerbook, I would not have written this essay (for which I am using a pencil). Instead, I would have logged onto the network and entered its seductive, engrossing world. By now I would have read the newswire and Miss Manners' column, answered a dozen questions from friends and colleagues, and possibly posted my thoughts on a movie I saw last night to a public discussion group. It would be as if I never left home.

The network destroys a sense of time as well as place. Daily and seasonal rhythms are subtle at best. As morning turns to evening, I am more likely to bump into my friends in Hawaii, less likely to encounter my friends in England. In the summer, things quiet down. April 1st is the only real network holiday—don't believe anything you read that day! Beyond that, life on the net proceeds at an even, unpunctuated pace. There are no holiday decorations on the Net.

On my flight down here I saw a young boy carrying a sleek black bag on his shoulder. He held it naturally, but with a hint of importance. It took me a moment to see the logo: it contained his Nintendo Game Boy. His generation sees nothing remarkable about traveling at all times with a computer. It is already possible to connect to the network from a palm-sized computer with a cellular link. As computers get smaller and cheaper, we will lose even the excuse of the weight of that black bag or the cost of losing it.

The network is becoming an important part of the lives of a broader segment of the population. Its spread presents a worrisome challenge: is it ever possible for us to take uninterrupted time off any more? The new technologies of connectedness are pushing people to blend their many roles into one: personal mail is mixed with professional correspondence, and work crises arrive on a cellular phone during leisure time. If our colleagues and competitors have made themselves perpetually available, we feel all the more pressure to do the same, lest we be left behind. One of my colleagues deliberately vacations in places so remote that getting a Net connection is almost impossible—it's the only way she can get a real break, and, for a little while at least, be a carefree newlywed instead of a world-renowned researcher. But such exotic locales are getting harder and harder to find.

I love the network and the people and places I find there. But sometimes I find it important to disconnect—to leave the cellular phone and the beeper in a desk drawer, leave that padded gray bag at home. To be out of touch, not for hours but for days. To leave behind routines, both virtual and real.

REFLECTING ON THE READING

1. What does Bruckman mean when she writes that if she had a network connection, she'd be "home"? Why isn't she home as she writes this essay? Why doesn't she have a network connection at this point? What is the significance of her lack of such a connection? What does it suggest about the role of technology in her life?

2. Why was Bruckman's decision to leave her computer at home a difficult one for her? What might the fact that she had difficulty making that decision suggest about her? About the role of technology in her life? Do you think she made the right decision? Why or why not? What might your answer suggest about your own view of technology?

3. Bruckman tells us that she wouldn't have written this essay if she had brought her computer with her on her vacation. Why? What difference would the presence of the computer have made with respect to the writing of this essay? What might that suggest about the role of technology in how we spend our time? In our writing?

4. In what sense does "the network destroy a sense of time as well as place," according to Bruckman?

5. What challenge does the Internet present as it becomes a more important part of people's lives? Why does Bruckman find this challenge "worrisome"? What might Bruckman's worry suggest about her own values? Do you share her worry about the Internet? Why or why not?

Examining Rhetorical Strategies

1. Examine the way Bruckman begins her essay. Why do you think she includes such a detailed description of her physical surroundings in her second paragraph? What important ideas or themes might these details highlight or introduce in her essay? Assess the effectiveness of her abrupt opening sentence. In what ways might that sentence set the tone and help establish the focus of the essay? Do you find the way she begins her essay effective? Why or why not?

2. Why do you think Bruckman chose the Christmas holiday as the occasion for her essay about how she uses her time? In what ways might that particular holiday serve her purposes in terms of the points she makes in this essay? What

associations do we make with Christmas that might serve her purposes in this sense? Would another holiday—Thanksgiving or the Fourth of July, for example—work as well, given her topic in this essay? Why or why not?

3. How would you describe the tone of Bruckman's essay? What features of her text—for example, word choice and sentence structure—help create this tone? Did you find the tone appropriate for the point Bruckman makes in the essay? Explain. Did you find her tone effective? Why or why not?

4. Analyze the paragraphs in which Bruckman describes her decision to leave her computer at home during her vacation. What details does she use to convey the difficulty of her decision? Why do you think Bruckman describes her decision in such detail? What purpose does this description serve in her essay? What does it seem to highlight or emphasize? Did you find this description vivid? Why or why not?

5. Why do you think Bruckman ends her essay as she does? What does she seem to emphasize or call attention to in her ending? Do you think Bruckman means to sound a hopeful note with her ending? A somber one? A pessimistic one? Explain. What might this ending suggest to you about technology and human life? Do you think Bruckman intended for her ending to suggest anything about technology? Explain.

6. Whom do you think Bruckman imagined as her audience for this essay? The essay was originally published in a journal called *Technology Review,* which is addressed to readers interested in issues related to technology and society. What do you think Bruckman assumes about those readers in terms of their knowledge of technology and their attitudes about technology? How do you think such readers might react to Bruckman's essay? Do you think they would be sympathetic to her points about technology? Explain. Do you think Bruckman expected them to be sympathetic? Do you think her essay would be suitable for a wider audience? Why or why not? Cite specific passages from her essay to support your answer.

Engaging the Issues

1. Write an essay for an audience of your classmates in which you describe how technology figures into the way you spend your time. Your essay might focus on a specific incident or time period—as Bruckman's essay does—or it may deal more generally with your uses of time and technology in your life. In your essay, try to convey a sense of how you typically spend your time; make distinctions between work and "free time." Explore how technology shapes your use of time and whether it influences what you consider your free time.

2. In a group of your classmates, share the essays you wrote for Question #1 above. Examine how each of you spends time and how technology affects your uses of time. More important, try to determine what each of you means by "free" time or "saving" time. Are there differences or similarities in how members of your group understand these terms? What might your discussion reveal about people's beliefs about time? About people's uses of technology?

3. Drawing on Bruckman's essay, the essay you wrote for Question #1 above, and any other relevant sources, write an essay for a general audience (such as readers of a large-circulation publication like *Time* magazine or *USA Today*) in which you discuss your thoughts about how we spend time in our society. In your essay, be sure to address the issue of technology and how it affects the way we spend time. Also, look ahead to the future and discuss what you see as possible developments and implications related to the way we use time and our technologies for saving time.

4. With a group of your classmates, create a brochure for a specific group of people (for example, students at your school) that offers information and advice about saving time. In your brochure, describe some of the techniques or habits that readers might adopt to save time, and discuss the specific technologies that they might use to save time. Be sure to make references to specific circumstances or situations that might affect the group of readers you are targeting (for example, the physical layout of your campus or the public transportation system there).

   Alternatively, create a Web site instead of a brochure. Target your Web site to the same audience you targeted for the brochure.

5. Write a rhetorical analysis of the brochure (or Web site) your group created for Question #4 above. In your analysis, examine the information and advice contained in the brochure as well as the design and layout of the brochure. Assess its effectiveness in terms of its intended audience and its purpose. Also, discuss your assumptions about technology and time as well as the intended audience that seem to have shaped the brochure.

6. Write a conventional academic essay in which you discuss our ideas about time and how those ideas relate to our uses of specific technologies (such as clocks, computers, and so on). Address what you see as our basic cultural assumptions about time and how we use it, and analyze the role of technology in how we spend time and how we think about time. Try to draw conclusions about how these assumptions might affect our uses of time in the future as new technologies are developed.

7. Using your library, the Internet, and any other appropriate resources, examine the ideas about time and technology in a culture different from your own. If possible, try to speak to someone (or communicate with someone via the Internet) from that culture to learn more about how that person thinks about time and the role of technology in his or her life. Then write a report for an audience of your classmates in which you present the results of your research. In your report, describe the culture you examined and how people in that culture seem to understand the relationship between time and technology. Draw comparisons between that culture and your own.

8. For one week, keep a careful record of how you spend your time. Make what you think are important distinctions among various uses of your time, such as "work," "play," "sleep," "meals," and so on. Pay particular attention to the technologies you use. After a week, analyze the records you kept to see exactly how you spent your time. Try to draw conclusions about how technologies influence the way you spend time. Then write a report for an audience of your classmates about how you use your time, drawing on your records to support conclusions about our uses of time.

9. Compare and discuss your findings from Question #8 above with those of your classmates. What differences and similarities emerge? How can you account for these differences and similarities? What might your discussion suggest about how we spend time and about the role of technology in our uses of time?

It's T-Day, as in Traditions

ELLEN GOODMAN

INTRODUCTION   National holidays are occasions for commemorating the past. They are also occasions to take stock of the present and look ahead to the future. Public officials often use holidays such as the Fourth of July or Memorial Day to remind us of the contributions or sacrifices of people who came before us and sometimes to exhort us to consider how we ourselves might contribute to our society today. But Thanksgiving is a holiday on which we rarely hear such exhortations. Instead, as essayist Ellen Goodman points out in the following essay, Thanksgiving has become less a national holiday than a celebration of family. Like Goodman, we tend to associate Thanksgiving with family reunions and dinners rather than public gatherings and speeches.

Goodman's description of her family's preparations for their annual Thanksgiving dinner may strike you as familiar. She provides a vivid picture of the food and the activities that make Thanksgiving what it is in her home—a picture that is at once distinctive and yet typical of the way many Americans celebrate Thanksgiving. What may be less familiar is Goodman's description of her family's Thanksgiving book, a well-used binder full of information and thoughts recorded each year at Thanksgiving dinner. This book carries the significance of Goodman's family's holiday tradition. For Goodman, the Thanksgiving book is a serious responsibility, and the opportunity to write in it each year is a reminder of the importance of the holiday traditions her family keeps and the connections her family members maintain. As she writes in the book each year, Goodman is as acutely mindful of the future as she is of her family's past.

Family traditions like Goodman's family's Thanksgiving book can perhaps be seen not only as attempts to preserve what we value about our past and our present lives but also as expressions of hope that what we value will remain. They are perhaps reflections of our anxiety as well: the worry that the future may mean the loss of some of the things we most value. In this sense, Goodman's seriousness about her family's Thanksgiving book seems appropriate, and it may cause you to consider the meaning of our own family and cultural traditions. As we wonder about what the future will bring, with its apparent promise of technological advances and progress, Goodman urges us to remember what we most value about our lives today.

In Goodman's family, writing is the means by which the past is preserved and carried into the future. Although your family may not construct its own written history in the form of a book as Goodman's family does, her essay is an implicit reminder that history itself owes its existence to writing. The technology of writing makes it possible for Goodman's family to record thoughts, feelings, information, and descriptions of events for family members in the future—just as writing makes possible *any* history. In this way, Goodman's essay may suggest that whatever else the future will bring, writing will somehow be at the center of what we preserve from the past and what we create for our new present. And yet Goodman's references to the technologies of email and telephones raise questions about the technologies we will use in the years ahead to preserve our personal and collective histories. What role might writing play in our efforts to maintain our traditions? How might technology—which enables us to preserve and carry on those traditions—also change those traditions in the years to come? It seems fitting that Goodman uses writing—in the form of an essay—to encourage us to ponder such questions.

Ellen Goodman is a syndicated columnist for the *Boston Globe* who writes about politics, society, and culture. She is the author of six books including *Close to Home* (1979), *Making Sense* (1989), and *Value Judgments* (1993). Among the many awards she has won for her writing are the Pulitzer Prize (1980) and the Hubert H. Humphrey Civil Rights Award (1988).

REFLECTING BEFORE READING

1. Goodman's essay describes an important Thanksgiving tradition in her family. As you prepare to read her essay, think about the traditions you have participated in for Thanksgiving. What roles do such traditions play in your own life? How do your experiences compare to Goodman's? How might your own sense of Thanksgiving and the traditions you associate with it shape your reading of Goodman's essay?

2. In one sense, Goodman's essay is as much about writing as it is about Thanksgiving. As you read, pay attention to her references to writing and the view of writing that she conveys. Do you think her view of writing is a common one? How might her family's Thanksgiving celebrations be different without writing? Consider, too, the role that technologies play in holiday traditions like Thanksgiving.

We have been on countdown to T-Day. The paper and pen, those basic kitchen utensils with which we map out this feast, are set upon the table. Lists must be made, Post-its must be posted, attention must be paid.

I reach up to the kitchen shelf for the duly designated Thanksgiving book in search of guidance to family feasts past. A small, navy notebook with gravy stains and mysterious cranberry-colored splotches has been stashed away since last November. It sits somewhere between "The Joy of Cooking" and a book stuffed with yellowing recipes that someone, someday, surely will make.

I brush the cover and open the pages in search of tips: which pies were eaten last year, how many pans of stuffing and pounds of turkey were devoured, did we run out of white wine or red?

This small book has become my family's archeological record of Thanksgiving. Along with entries about potatoes, sweet and not, there are seating lists, culinary hits and flops, portion control and portions out of control. It's as close as we come to a family bible.

On Thursday, it will be exactly 10 years since this book and this holiday moved one door and one generation down the street and into our home. The tradition was delivered into our ambivalent hands, an unmistakable rite of passage, incontrovertible proof that we had come of age.

My aunt handed it over with pleasure and reservations. Could we be trusted with the stuff and stuffing of this inheritance?

In fact, over a decade, our original vow to be culinary conservatives has been stretched if not broken. Chestnuts have crept into the stuffing. Sautéed apples and onions now sit beside the dreaded green bean casserole. Pecan pie has appeared, along with a son-in-law, next to the lemon chiffon.

Even the book has changed. My aunt's fine hand managed to fit a whole year's worth of information on a single page. She saved paper and empty pages for posterity as if we would all live to celebrate a hundred holidays between these covers.

Her profligate heirs scrawl across the white space, passing the book around for comments and updates. We demand after-dinner notes as payment for dessert.

But for all our modern, postmodern, ways, we have taken our inheritance seriously. Around our dining room with its mongrel collection of chairs, dishes, generations, and eating prejudices, we assemble the people we collectively call family. We have become the home that our family goes to when they go "home for the holidays."

Our house was eight years old in 1863 when Abraham Lincoln proclaimed this "day of Thanksgiving and Praise." The force behind that Civil War declaration was Josepha Hale, editor of the powerful Godey's Lady's Book. She crusaded for the Union, for "the renewed pledge of love and loyalty to the Constitution of the United States."

The Pilgrims had given thanks for bountiful harvest; Lincoln declared thanks for the Union.

But today's feast is less about national union than family reunion. Americans don't worry about a fractured nation; we worry about splintered families. We take the United States for granted and give thanks for each other.

In the years since I became the keeper of the Thanksgiving book I have learned just how fragile family connection can be. How easily it can break off.

Most of our grown children have left home; they are exports from their native Pilgrim state. The cousins connect by phone and e-mail, talking across borders, oceans, and time zones, keeping in touch without touching.

Now my generation provides their roots. We are not just a sandwich generation, stuffed between growing kids and aging parents. We are also the link, the open line, the cord. We stay in place, and, in so doing, keep their place.

Today I am much more conscious of how much work—not hard work, but daily work—my elders did to keep family together. This is the message given to us between the binders of a small blue book: It's our turn.

So today we'll be up by dawn, chopping onions and stuffing turkey by breakfast. Sometime between the potatoes and the pie, I will insist that everyone write in the Thanksgiving "bible."

There are only a few pages left for this millennium. Next year we will begin a new book. We promise. It is, after all, our turn.

1. Why does Goodman describe pen and paper as "basic kitchen utensils"? What might this description suggest about the role of writing in her family life? What might it suggest about her view of writing in general?

2. In what sense is Goodman's family's Thanksgiving book an "archaeological record"? What might this description suggest about Goodman's values regarding her family life? Do you share those values? Explain.

3. Why do you think Goodman describes herself as "ambivalent" upon receiving the family Thanksgiving book? What might that description indicate about her attitudes toward the book and the tradition it represents? What might it suggest about her sense of herself?

4. What has changed in the years since Goodman received the Thanksgiving book? What do these changes suggest about family? About time? About tradition? Do you think Goodman sees these changes as positive ones? Explain, citing specific passages from her essay to support your answer.

5. At one point in her essay, Goodman mentions that family members communicate with each other throughout the year using email and telephones. Does Goodman see these forms of communication as positive or otherwise? Explain. How do they relate—if at all—to the family's Thanksgiving book? What might Goodman's references to these technologies suggest about her view of technology in general? Do you share her view? Why or why not?

6. What do we learn about the history of the Thanksgiving holiday in this essay? What significance does Goodman see in that history? In what sense is the tradition of Thanksgiving "fragile" for Goodman? Do you agree with her? Why or why not?

Examining Rhetorical Strategies

1. Examine Goodman's introduction in this essay. What central ideas or themes does she introduce in her opening paragraphs? What assumptions does she seem to make about her readers' attitudes toward Thanksgiving? Do you think her introduction is surprising in any way? Explain. Did you find it effective? Why or why not?

2. In a sense, this essay is as much about writing as it is about Thanksgiving. Examine Goodman's references to writing, books, and related matters. What picture of writing as an activity does she present in this essay? What does she seem to value about writing? Do you think she assumes her readers share her view of writing, as presented in this essay? Explain. Do *you* share her view? Why or why not?

3. Examine Goodman's treatment of the idea of *family* in her essay. What image of family does she present? Is it a positive image? How does she convey this image? Identify specific words and phrases in her essay that help convey her

idea of family. Do you think she assumes that most readers will share her overall view of family? Explain, citing specific passages from her essay to support your answer.

4. Ellen Goodman is considered one of the preeminent essayists writing today. Based on this essay, what do you think accounts for her reputation as a writer? What features of this essay do you think readers might find appealing? What did you find appealing about her writing? What might your answer to that question suggest about you as a reader?

Engaging the Issues

1. Write an essay for an audience of your classmates in which you describe the role of writing in your own family life. Your essay might focus on a special artifact that has something to do with writing—such as the Thanksgiving book that Goodman describes in her essay. Or it may focus on some activity or tradition in your family that somehow involves writing or on a particular event that involved writing, such as an important letter or document. Whatever you choose to describe in your essay, describe it in such a way that your readers will understand the significance of the artifact (or activity or event) and the role that writing played in your family life.

2. In a group of your classmates, share the essays you wrote for Question #1 above. Examine the different ways in which writing seems to have played a role in your respective family lives and discuss these roles, identifying any important similarities and differences among them. Discuss as well what the essays might suggest about the importance of writing in maintaining social and cultural institutions and in preserving traditions.

3. Write a conventional academic essay in which you compare Goodman's essay to the essay by Amy Bruckman that appears earlier in this chapter. In your essay, summarize their essays and describe what you see as the most important features of each. Focus your analysis on how each writer presents the holiday about which she is writing and develops her themes through her depiction of that holiday. Compare as well the writing styles of each writer and any other aspects of the essays that seem important to your analysis. Draw conclusions about the effectiveness of each essay.

4. Write an essay for a general audience in which you discuss what you see as the future of an important American tradition in the twenty-first century. For your essay, you may choose to focus on a holiday tradition—as Goodman does in her essay—or some other American tradition, such as an annual sporting event, a political practice, or cultural events like summer picnics or festivals. In your essay, describe this tradition as you understand it and discuss its significance in American culture. Try to address how changes in technology might affect this tradition and anticipate what those changes might mean in the future. If appropriate, address the role of writing in this tradition. Draw your own conclusions about the future of this tradition.

5. Write a brief history of Thanksgiving as you have experienced it in your life. In your history, describe the traditions or activities that you think define that holiday for you, and refer to any important moments from past Thanksgiving celebrations.

6. Share the history you wrote for Question #5 above with someone who has been part of your Thanksgiving history—for example, a family member or close friend with whom you have celebrated Thanksgiving throughout the years. Ask that person to read your history and decide whether he or she thinks it accurately reflects Thanksgiving as he or she has experienced it. Identify aspects of your history about which there may be disagreement, confusion, or uncertainty, and discuss those aspects in an effort to understand the disagreement, confusion, or uncertainty. Then consider what this discussion might suggest about the issue of *accuracy* in written histories (or memories) of important personal or family events. Also consider the role of writing in preserving memories.

7. Create a Web site about an important tradition in your family that you hope will continue in the years ahead. If possible, invite family members to help you design and construct the site.

In Search of the Poetry in Technology
An Amiable Debate between Paul Jones and Betty Adcock

INTRODUCTION   Given the remarkable pace of technological change in the last two decades of the twentieth century, it is not surprising that so many writers, critics, political leaders, and others turned their attention to debating the proper role of technology in our lives as the 1990's turned into 2000. Many of these commentators urged us to wonder—and worry—about what technology might have in store for us in the coming years. Indeed, this reader includes several selections—including the following one—in which the writers do just that.

What makes the following debate between Paul Jones and Betty Adcock different from other discussions about technology and progress is the perspective each participant brings to the issues of technology and progress. Jones and Adcock are poets, and they examine questions about our uses of technology explicitly through their poets' eyes. Like some of the other writers in this reader—and like so many writers who addressed these issues in the 1990s—Jones and Adcock express concerns about technological change and about the impact of technological progress on human life as well as on the natural world. They ask us to consider carefully what role technology should have in our lives and what kind of future we should strive to create. Although each offers different answers to these questions about technology and progress, both poets approach such questions in a similar way. Neither is concerned about specific technological developments; rather, they are concerned about general trends in technology and its impact on our lives. More important, they wish to examine our assumptions about technology and the values we hold as human beings who inhabit a natural world. Despite their obvious disagreements, together they urge us to examine how we understand ourselves as inhabitants of that world and how we understand our past and our present. They also ask us to identify our most basic values as human beings as we imagine the future that we will create with new technologies.

In reading this exchange between Jones and Adcock, you will quickly notice that they not only see the world through poets' eyes but also present their arguments with poets' voices. Many of the writers in this book make sophisticated arguments about complex matters such as technology and progress. But Adcock and Jones weave poetry into their arguments. They use lines from poems to bolster their specific points as deftly as a scientist might use statistical data or a philosopher might use logic. To read their exchange, then, is to encounter a distinctive way of engaging in thoughtful, considered debate. And it may challenge you to reexamine your own expectations about what constitutes a persuasive argument, even as it encourages you to think in new and complicated ways about technology and human life.

Paul Jones is on the faculties of the School of Journalism and Mass Communication and the School of Information and Library Science at the University of North Carolina, where he also directs the UNC MetaLab, which develops and studies networked media and digital libraries. His poems have appeared in *Southern Poetry Review, American Literary Review,* and the *Georgia Review.* He is also coauthor of *The Web Server Book* (1995) and editor of the Internet Poetry Archives, published by the University of North Carolina Press. Betty Adcock is Kenan Writer-in-Residence at Meredith College in Raleigh, North Carolina. She has written four books of poetry and has had poems published in more than twenty anthologies and in Internet journals. The following dialogue appeared in 1998 in *Educom Review* (now called *Educause Review*), a journal devoted to education and technology.

REFLECTING BEFORE READING

1. In the following article, poets Paul Jones and Betty Adcock repeatedly refer to specific poems and use poetry in general for making their respective arguments about technology. As you read, pay attention to how they use poetry in their discussion. Examine the references they make to specific poems. What do you think they are trying to accomplish with these references to poetry? What might their uses of poetry indicate about their own understanding of the world and how to engage in discussions of complex issues like technological progress? Consider as well your own response to their uses of poetry. Do you enjoy poetry? Do you read it regularly? How might your own experiences with poetry and your feelings about it influence your reading of this article?

2. In this debate, Adcock and Jones present two very different views of the role of technology in our lives. As you read, try to identify the basic values that each poet seems to bring to this debate. What do they most value about human life and culture? About the world we live in? About language and literacy? Do they share any important values? If so, describe them. How do their respective values seem to shape the specific arguments that each poet makes about technology and progress?

JONES: In Keats' long poem, "Lamia," the shape-shifting rainbow creature, by assuming the body of a lovely young woman, has brought love and joy to a young man who abandoned philosophy to live with her in a magical hut. But as the young man and Lamia call their friends to a wedding feast, trouble arrives in the form of the young man's teacher, a philosopher-scientist, who unmasks the Lamia much as science had unmasked the rainbow as merely broken light. Lamia, who was exotic and illusionary, is revealed to be known "in the dull catalogue of common things." She shrieks, resumes her supernatural serpent-like form, and flies off. The young man dies. There is something in this tale like the unmasking of the imagination and something of the pain that Keats and other Romantics felt in the face of logical positivism, the force that was then driving science.

What do we feel today as we face a similar revolution of thinking about the world? What do we face losing and what might we gain? When *Educom Review* asked me to think about these changes from a poet's viewpoint, it was obvious that I could only see the picture from one side. So I invited Betty Adcock, Kenan Professor of Poetry at Meredith College, to join me in a dialogue/discussion/argument about information technology and what it means to our worlds. Actually Betty and I have been having very spirited discussions along these lines for several years now with each of us defending our personal utopias and fighting to fend off our personal dystopic versions of the future. I sent Betty these initial two paragraphs to start our discussion for this article. Our (on paper) discussion follows.

Poem: Time After Time

An Australian sound engineer has developed a unique way of clearing the hiss and clatter out of vintage jazz recordings. —Associated Press

Time: it does things
out there among the galaxies.
Clatter and hiss? Perhaps.
That's one metaphor for distance

which is time. And our remembering?
There's less and less,
the dissonance of now and then
no longer audible when
mechanics cancels difference.

So out with the scritch of decades,
the sizzle and scar of error,
remembrance's waver, susurrus
of mortality, dust-riff, and blues-ether.

We will turn them into us,
our sound loud as a spotlight,
bright as an electronic toy,
cleansed of those troublesome sixty years
and that old distortion: joy.

by Betty Adcock
(This poem first appeared in the Georgia Review.)

ADCOCK: We might look more than one way at your use of the Keats poem to introduce our argument. Your note about the romantic poets' reaction to, for instance,
the discovery that the rainbow is "only broken light" is correct, and such discoveries did take much magic out of the world. They were, however, discoveries of science. Our concern here is with technology. And though science uses
high technology today, and the latter has depended on science throughout its
existence, the two are not the same thing.

Neil Postman, in his excellent book Technopoly, begins with the statement
that C.P. Snow was wrong in his claim that the two warring cultures were science
and art, or science and the humanities. The arts and humanities have no quarrel with science; the war is between technology and everything else.

In a beautiful essay titled "Standing by Words," the poet and farmer
Wendell Berry quotes one of technology's priests, Buckminster Fuller, to illustrate bad writing and, since we think in language, bad thinking. In a typically ver-
bose passage, Fuller elaborates his theme of technological destiny, beginning with
men making "fish catching and carving tools," through "outrigger canoes," and
"the taming and breeding" of animals.

"Next," says Fuller, "they developed oxen, then horse-drawn vehicles, then
horseless vehicles, then ships in the sky. Then employing rocketry and packaging up the essential life-supporting environmental constituents of the biosphere
they made sorties away from their mothership Earth and finally ferried over to
their Sun-orbiting companion, the Moon." What is wrong with this passage?
Aside from poor construction, this self-serving little history assumes there is no
essential difference between the move from simple tools to outrigger canoes and
the move from horse to horseless carriage, as if this did not involve qualitative
difference. Fuller gets from the horseless carriage to packing up the biosphere for
outer space as if there were nothing in between, nothing else worth noting, and
no difference in kind between technologies. As Berry notes, Fuller proposes that
we have ahead of us only the next "breakthrough," which, now that we have progressed to spaceships, is not work for individuals and real communities but for
governments and corporations. I would add that this is as true for computers as
for spaceships, despite the endless rhetoric about electronic democracy. Berry
says, and I agree absolutely, "Value and technology can meet only on the
ground of restraint."

The scientists and philosophers addressed by Keats in "Lamia" were
involved with discovery, which Robinson Jeffers, a scientist and a poet, has
called "a form of worship." The means had not yet been found to break the
prism of the air that held the rainbow. Only technology could punch holes in the
ozone with a chosen application of knowledge (not knowledge or discovery
itself). Perhaps Keats was a prophet as well, not unusual for poets, intuiting
where science would sell itself.

The Encyclopedia of Poetry and Poetics opens its definition of romanticism
this way: "F.L. Lucas, in 'The Decline and Fall of the Romantic Ideal,' (1948)
counted 11,396 definitions of romanticism." I won't go further with that except
to say that I have not seen anything more romantic, more exotic or illusionary
in whatever romantic sense, than technophile predictions for the computer's role
in the glorious future we are happily slouching toward. We remain unaware of
the form we have taken as destroyer not only of ourselves (that we have always
done . . . the 100 Years' War was no new thing) but of nature, our very being

and context. We send to extinction all species in our way. And that is a new thing. The power to do that is new, though we have not changed, we have as little control over ourselves as ever, murdering the planet while waxing rhapsodic over the technological feat of looking for live microbes on Mars. Our new technologies, married to governments and global corporations, are past reason. The destructive versions of "edu-tainment" they send throughout the education system are opiates, pure and simple. In a Technopoly, as Postman points out, the technology controls the culture, though there is an illusion that things are otherwise.

Nature is not something one nods to. It is the ground of existence. Only a computer company would have had the sheer brass to run an ad like the one I saw recently in the New York Times. There are three drawings in the ad. One is of a tree with the caption, "A deciduous plant native to the North Temperate Zones. Foliage may cause cooling of the earth's surface." A second drawing depicts a horse with a caption reading, "A mammal of the genus equus . . ." and so on. Then we see a computer resting on the meadow with the horse and tree: "The HP Network ScanJet 5. Converts paper-based information into electronic data . . ." and it goes on in this jargon. Beneath all, in large caps, runs the headline: BUILT BY ENGINEERS. The intent, obviously, is to make the reader imagine that the two living entities and the machine are somehow the same, that there is a true connection between natural things and high technology, and then that God must be an engineer . . . Bill Gates perhaps? Or that engineers are all gods.

The Greeks had a word for what is happening in that tasteless and pathetically transparent ad. Their word applies to the activities of the computer industry generally: Where hubris is, tragedy is not far behind. Today's tragedies aren't very different, metaphorically, from the Greek idea: the most gifted and privileged among us, heroes whose eyes are only on speed, volume, innovation and profit, are bringing about vast losses we will someday see as tragic.

Computers and all their elaborations have a place, so long as they stay in the toolshed where they belong. Limited, as reasonable aids for medicine, real science and records storage, they're valuable. But the culture our tools are creating for us is not worth the jeopardized quality of civic life, of literary heritage, of real time, and of participation in the natural world.

The Web and Internet are more aptly named than their creators knew. Robinson Jeffers' powerful poem "The Purse-Seine" will show why. I recommend it to you.

JONES: Betty, Technology, I argue, is the way that we extend ourselves into the world. This is what makes humans human—our sophisticated tool-making and tool-creating. With technology we probe, extend ourselves, explore, discover and even destroy the mysteries that our world presents us. Technology and science are much more closely related than you would have us believe as they constitute a continuum from conception through application. Detaching the insight from the applications may be fine for certain university projects, but not so within the sphere in which most of us live our lives. A prism might explain a rainbow, create lovely baubles, and even small delights, but it is also one of the keys to my own—and your own—corrected sight, what allows us to read and move through the world. The Internet might be no more to some than a piece of cut crystal, a way to make a fake rainbow or a fake personality, but to many it is and will be a tool that creates new jobs, new learning, new relationships and new cultures.

Yes, Keats—and the other Romantics—are more complex than my simplified introductory might indicate. The ambivalence of Keats toward the philosopher-scientist and toward the Lamia is the point. Any intelligent person would share his attraction and his caution. Still, I would submit that many more have died of ignorance than from an overload of information. In fact, I challenge you to list three instances of death by information overload. I can, on the other hand, cite many examples of easily available electronic information saving people's lives and more examples of the Net improving our ways of living. As Dickinson might write: "There is no frigate like the Net." Yet the Net, like the book of Dickinson's era, is not so exotic; it is commonplace and utilitarian. Useful is the word here. But useful as a transport, a ship set into seas of discovery. In this I agree with Stephen Vincent Benet:

> Say neither in their way,
> "It is a deadly magic and accursed"
> not "it is blest" but only
> "It is here."

More exotic and illusionary than the Internet are the voices of cottage-industry Cassandras, who, like Neil Postman and Kirkpatrick Sales, make a living out of the exploitation of our own Romantic attachments to the past and our fear of tackling the ambivalent future. They, and you in your opening salvo, confuse the technologies with which we have become comfortable with a utopic past. Each scientific discovery, each technological advance was unsettling and disturbing. Books, your friends and your friends' friends, are often credited and blamed for the Reformation and the 100 Years' War. I notice that there is no call for a return to stone carving from any of you or to the extremely elitist and tedious world of the hand-transcribed scrolls.

You may nod to nature, as if it were yours and only yours to understand and defend, but an acknowledgment that nature is dangerous is only the beginning. Humans were rarely at one with nature; they were and are more likely at war with nature (and usually losing at that). Anyone who landscapes a flood plain or puts rip-rap along a creek bed should be aware of that. Simulations of weather systems won't replace weather (nor are they intended to). A CD-ROM of a bird call is a passage toward the natural, but no one would claim it was the natural any more than an Audubon painting can claim to replace an egret or a hawk.

Coming back to Benet and to Keats, "It is here" and we must face it as the scientist faced the Lamia as he revealed her nature as common and a part of daily life. We need not embrace all of it, but we must not ignore it.

Artichokes

On long stalks they make a masculine bouquet,
head-heavy bunch nodding over my shoulder,
disinterested planets, older versions of quiet
camp fires where men circled the round coals,
where thorny silence was a way to speak.

Once at home, they are stone mothers
covered in green scale of lichen, the weight
carried in the womb, firm seasonal bud,
private and pollenless, that blessing on all
lips come round to confirm the feeling we reach

when we hold the green world in one fist,
one perfect globe unstemmed. Each thick
fleshed rose, each tight petalled breast,
a thing no one can know without the trick
of slow steaming, of softening the spikes.

So we meet in hunger, ripe to taste
the other in this meal as we shred
the leaves free, work toward the delicate
secretive hair, peel it apart,
devour the old cliche, the tender heart.

by Paul Jones

Selected Readings

Adcock, Betty. *Beholdings.* Baton Rouge: LSU Press, 1988.

——. *The Difficult Wheel.* Baton Rouge: LSU Press, 1995.

——. *Nettles.* Baton Rouge: LSU Press, 1983.

——. *Walking Out.* Baton Rouge: LSU Press, 1975.

Benet, Stephen Vincent. *John Brown's Body.* New York: Holt, Rinehart and Winston, 1968.

Berry, Wendell. "Standing by Words."

Fuller, R. Buckminster. *Humans in Universe.* New York: Mouton, 1983.

Jeffers, Robinson. *Rock and Hawk: A Selection of Shorter Poems.* Edited by Robert Hass.

Jones, Paul. *What the Welsh and Chinese Have in Common.* Carrboro, NC: NC Writers' Network, 1980. Also at http://sunsite.unc.edu/pjones/poetry/

——, Doug Matthews, Jonathan Magid, Donald Ball and Michael Hammel. *The UNIX Web Server Book,* 2nd Edition. Research Triangle Park, NC: Ventana, 1997.

Keats, John. *Selected Poems and Letters.* Edited by Douglass Bush. Cambridge, MA: Riverside Press, 1959.

Logan, Robert. *Alphabet Effect: The Impact of the Phonetic Alphabet on the Development of Western Civilization.* William Morrow, 1986.

McLuhan, Marshall. *Understanding Media: The Extensions of Man.* Boston: MIT Press, 1994.

Pool, Ithiel de Sola. *Forecasting the Telephone: A Retrospective Technology.* Norwood, NJ: ABLEX Pub., 1983.

Postman, Neil. *Technopoly: The Surrender of Culture to Technology.* New York: Knopf, 1992.

Preminger, Alex, editor. *Encyclopedia of Poetry and Poetics.* Princeton, NJ: Princeton University Press, 1965.

Snow, C.P. *Two Cultures and the Scientific Revolution.* Cambridge, England: Cambridge University Press, 1993.

The Purse-Seine
by Robinson Jeffers

Our sardine fishermen work at night in the dark of the moon;
    daylight or moonlight
They could not tell where to spread the net, unable to see the
    phosphorescence of the shoals of fish.
They work northward from Monterey, coasting Santa Cruz; off
    New Year's Point or off Pigeon Point
The look-out man will see some lakes of milk-color light on the
    sea's night-purple; he points and the helmsman
Turns the dark prow, the motorboat circles the gleaming shoal
    and drifts out her seine-net. They close the circle
And purse the bottom of the net, then with great labor haul it in.

                I cannot tell you
How beautiful the scene is, and a little terrible, then, when the
    crowded fish
Know they are caught, and wildly beat from one wall to the
    other of their closing destiny the phosphorescent
Water to a pool of flame, each beautiful slender body sheeted
    with flame, like a live rocket
A comet's tail wake of clear yellow flame; while outside the
    narrowing
Floats and cordage of the net great sea-lions come up to watch,
    sighing in the dark; the vast walls of night
Stand erect to the stars.

        Lately I was looking from a night mountain-top
On a wide city, the colored splendor, galaxies of light: how could
    I help but recall the seine-net
Gathering the luminous fish? I cannot tell you how beautiful
    the city appeared, and a little terrible.
I thought, We have geared the machines and locked all together
    into interdependence; we have built the great cities; now
There is no escape. We have gathered vast populations incapable
    of free survival, insulated

From the strong earth, each person in himself helpless, on all
    dependent. The circle is closed, and the net
Is being hauled in. They hardly feel the cords drawing, yet they
    shine already. The inevitable mass-disasters
Will not come in our time nor in our children's, but we and our
    children
Must watch the net draw narrower, government take all powers
    —or revolution, and the new government
Take more than all, add to kept bodies kept souls—or anarchy,
    the mass-disasters.

>   These things are Progress;
> Do you marvel our verse is troubled or frowning, while it keeps
>   its reason? Or it lets go, lets the mood flow
> In the manner of the recent young men into mere hysteria, splin-
>   tered gleams, crackled laughter. But they are quite wrong.
> There is no reason for amazement: surely one always knew that
>   cultures decay, and life's end is death.

REFLECTING ON THE READING

1. What is the occasion for this exchange between Jones and Adcock? What is the primary purpose of their exchange? What key issues are they asked to address in their exchange? Why are they, specifically, asked to engage in this discussion? Do you think they bring a special perspective to these issues that others don't have? Explain.

2. What is the distinction that Adcock makes between science and technology? Why is this distinction important in her argument about technological progress? Does Jones agree with this distinction? Explain.

3. Why does Adcock describe those who are enthusiastic about new technology (whom she calls "technophiles") as romantic? What does she mean by "romantic" in this context? What does her use of this term in this passage indicate about her own values regarding technology and human life? Do you agree with her? Why or why not?

4. What does Adcock mean when she writes that nature is "the ground of existence"? How does her view of nature differ from Jones'? What, according to Adcock, are we losing as a result of technological progress, especially with respect to computer technologies? Do you think she is right? Explain. What might your answer indicate about your own views regarding technology and progress?

5. In what sense is technology an extension of humans into the world, according to Jones? How does technology serve human existence, in Jones' view? How does his view of the relationship between technology and human beings differ from Adcock's? Do you agree with him? Why or why not?

6. What complaint does Jones make about Adcock's view of the technology? In what sense does Adcock confuse technology and the past, according to Jones? Do you think this is a valid criticism of Adcock's position? Explain. What vision of technology and the past does Jones present in place of Adcock's view?

Examining Rhetorical Strategies

1. Examine Jones' introduction to this article. How does he explain the discussion that he and Adcock engage in for *Educom Review* magazine? What does he seem to emphasize in his explanation? What background information does he provide

about this discussion? How does that background information influence your expectations for the article? Do you think he intended to provoke a reaction such as yours? Explain. Notice, too, his reference to John Keats' poem "Lamia." What purposes do Jones' references to that poem serve in this introduction? What expectations do you think his references to this poem establish for the rest of the article?

2. As noted in the introduction to this selection, this article was originally published in a journal called *Educom Review,* which focuses on technology and educational issues. Based on Jones' introduction and on your reading of the discussion between him and Adcock, what kind of audience do you think Jones was addressing? What assumptions do he and Adcock seem to make about their readers' understanding of technology? What assumptions do they seem to make about their readers' knowledge and understanding of poetry? How do you think readers would react to the information that Adcock and Jones are poets? Do you think Adcock and Jones intended such a reaction? Explain. What effect did the information that Adcock and Jones are poets have on you as a reader?

3. Throughout this article, both Adcock and Jones use references to specific poems and poetry in general to support their respective arguments about technology and progress. Examine their use of poetry in this light. In what ways do they use poetry as "evidence" to support their claims? Do you think they distinguish between poetry and other kinds of evidence in their arguments? Explain. How persuasive did you find their use of poetry in their arguments about technology? Do you think they might have made more convincing arguments by using other kinds of strategies or evidence? Explain. What might your answers to these questions suggest about you as a reader? How might your own feelings about poetry have influenced your responses to these questions? In your answer, note especially the references to the poems "Lamia" and "The Purse-Seine."

4. Examine the way in which Jones and Adcock present their respective visions of poets and poetry in this article. What view of poets does each of them have? What distinguishes poets from other people, such as scientists, in their view? Identify any important similarities or differences you see in the way each views poets. Do you share the view of poets of either Adcock or Jones or both? Explain. Cite specific passages from the article to support your answer.

5. Examine the writing style of Adcock and Jones. Describe what you see as the key features that distinguish each writer's style, citing specific words, phrases, or sentences from the article to support your answer. Identify any similarities or differences that you see in their respective writing styles. Which writer's style do you find more appealing? Which do you find more effective? Why? What might your response to their respective styles indicate about you as a reader?

6. Compare the way each writer ends his or her section of this article. Both use references to poetry in their conclusions, but they do so in different ways. Explain the strategy each seems to employ in his or her conclusion. What do you think each tries to emphasize with his or her reference to a specific poem? Which ending did you find more effective? Why?

Engaging the Issues ————————————————————————————

1. Write a poem expressing your view of technology and progress.

2. Write an essay for an audience of your classmates in which you express your view of technology and progress.

3. Write a rhetorical analysis of the poem you wrote for Question #1 above and the essay you wrote for Question #2 above. In your analysis, examine each piece of writing in terms of the arguments it makes or the ideas it expresses. Discuss similarities and differences in terms of the style and structure of each piece of writing and assess the effectiveness of each piece in conveying your ideas or arguments. Be sure to address the matter of audience in your analysis and how different readers might respond to each piece of writing. Draw conclusions about the uses of genres like poetry and nonfiction prose for addressing important social issues like progress and the uses of technology in modern society.

4. Write a rhetorical analysis of the discussion between Jones and Adcock focusing on the argumentative strategies of each participant. In your analysis, summarize the position of each and describe the specific strategies each uses to make his or her argument about technology. Pay particular attention to the way each participant uses poetry in making her or his argument. Draw conclusions about the effectiveness of their respective strategies.

5. Write your own contribution to the discussion between Jones and Adcock. In your response, address the main issues that they raise and present your perspective on those issues. Try to support your arguments effectively. Assume your audience for your text is the same as the audience for which Jones and Adcock wrote their article.

6. In a group of three or four of your classmates, write a discussion similar to the one Adcock and Jones have in this reading selection. Your discussion should focus on the same general issues of technology and progress that Adcock and Jones address in their article. Have each member of your group write his or her own part of the discussion. Decide among yourselves how you will share your texts and whether you will provide opportunities for revision after sharing them. Be sure to arrange to have all the texts put together in one complete article.

7. If possible, go online to a chat room or an email discussion listserv and have a discussion with several of your classmates about the issues addressed by Adcock and Jones in their article. Allow the discussion to continue until each classmate has had a chance to present his or her view of these issues and to respond to other classmates. Then, as a group, examine the online discussion. (If possible, print out a transcript of the discussion.) What do you notice about how each classmate engaged in the discussion? About the strategies each used to present his or her position? What main ideas emerged from the discussion? Identify any key similarities or differences in the positions taken by each classmate. Draw conclusions about the nature of the online medium for conducting such debates, and contrast it with the more conventional format of the print article, such as the one by Jones and Adcock. How does an online medium such as a chat room

differ from a conventional print medium, such as a magazine article or newspaper editorial, when it comes to presenting an argument or exchanging points of view? What advantages and disadvantages do you see with each medium?

Beyond the Information Revolution

PETER F. DRUCKER

INTRODUCTION You have probably heard some version of the aphorism that the key to the future lies in the past. As we anticipate the years ahead, it seems natural to look to the past for lessons we might learn. And there is no shortage of scholars and others to remind us of important historical developments that seem to offer insight into our present circumstances. (Indeed, some of those scholars are included in this reader.) If we are in the midst of a revolution sparked by the computer, the Internet, and related technological developments, as many observers claim, then it would make sense to examine previous revolutions that might help us understand where we are headed. Renowned social scientist Peter F. Drucker invites us to do so in the following article.

Drucker unequivocally accepts the notion that we are in the midst of a revolution at the start of a new century, a revolution that has been called the Information Revolution. But Drucker believes that it is not information that is at the heart of this revolution; rather, it is commerce—or more accurately, *e-commerce*. In Drucker's view, the Internet is revolutionizing how we distribute goods and services and even employment, and in this way, the Internet is having a far-reaching social, economic, and political impact throughout the world. The Internet, Drucker asserts, is unprecedented. But the kinds of sweeping changes that the Internet is causing are not. And that fact becomes clear if we look at previous technological revolutions. Specifically, Drucker directs our attention to the Industrial Revolution in the nineteenth century. Technology, he shows us, drove that revolution, too—most importantly, the technology of the railroad. The railroad enabled a redistribution of goods and services that completely changed not only how people conducted business but also how they lived their lives and how they understood their world. As he puts it, with the railroad, "humanity mastered distance." The Internet, Drucker believes, is having a similar impact today. He asserts that with the Internet, humanity has *eliminated* distance. The changes he foresees as a result of the special qualities of the Internet are as profound as those brought on by the railroad and the Industrial Revolution—perhaps more so.

Whether or not Drucker—or others who share his views—will turn out to be right remains to be seen, of course. Drucker himself has written that anyone who tries to predict the specific consequences of the Information Revolution will be "dead wrong." But his analysis of the Information Revolution and specifically of the role of the Internet raises many questions about what we might expect in the coming decades. As we embrace the latest technologies such as those that make the Internet possible, we may wish to consider the broad social changes that these technologies might help create. Our daily use of the

Internet to purchase a book or send a message to a friend may seem unremarkable, but Drucker reminds us that these seemingly insignificant activities, taken together, may constitute part of a vast social upheaval. In this sense, by clicking the mouse on your computer, you may be participating in a revolution.

Peter F. Drucker is the Clarke Professor of Social Science and Management at the Claremont Graduate School. Born in 1909, he is widely considered one of the most influential thinkers on business management, politics, and economics of the latter half of the twentieth century. He has been a consultant for some of the world's largest companies, for universities and other nonprofit organizations, and for a number of national governments, including the United States' and Canada's. In 1997, *Forbes* magazine called him one of "the youngest-thinking people in America." He has authored thirty books, including two novels, an autobiography entitled *Adventures of a Bystander* (1979), and influential works on social, political, and economic issues such as *The End of Economic Man: The Origins of Totalitarianism* (1939), *The Age of Discontinuity* (1969), and *Managing in a Time of Great Change* (1995). The following article was published in the *Atlantic Monthly* in 1999.

REFLECTING BEFORE READING

1. Much of Drucker's discussion in the following article focuses on developments that are associated with the Industrial Revolution. What do you know about the Industrial Revolution? As you read, pay attention to Drucker's portrayal of the Industrial Revolution, and determine whether the view he presents matches your own understanding of it. Also consider how your knowledge of the Industrial Revolution might influence your reading of Drucker's article and the vision of the future he presents.

2. Drucker's many books and articles have focused on business management, politics, and economics, often in specialized ways. The following article, however, was published in the *Atlantic Monthly* for a much more general though well-educated audience. As you read, note how Drucker discusses economic and business matters. What does he assume his audience knows about such matters? Consider whether his discussion is suitable for readers who do not possess specialized knowledge of economics and business.

T he truly revolutionary impact of the Information Revolution is just beginning to be felt. But it is not "information" that fuels this impact. It is not "artificial intelligence." It is not the effect of computers and data processing on decision-making, policymaking, or strategy. It is something that practically no one foresaw or, indeed, even talked about ten or fifteen years ago: *e-commerce*—that is, the explosive emergence of the Internet as a major, perhaps eventually *the* major, worldwide distribution channel for goods, for services, and surprisingly, for managerial and professional jobs. This is profoundly changing economies, markets, and industry structures; products and services and their flow; consumer segmentation, consumer values, and consumer behavior; jobs and labor markets. But the impact may be even greater on societies and politics and, above all, on the way we see the world and ourselves in it.

At the same time, new and unexpected industries will no doubt emerge, and fast. One is already here: biotechnology. And another: fish farming. Within the next fifty years fish farming may change us from hunters and gatherers on the seas into "marine pastoralists"—just as a similar innovation some 10,000 years ago changed our ancestors from hunters and gatherers on the land into agriculturists and pastoralists.

It is likely that other new technologies will appear suddenly, leading to major new industries. What they may be is impossible even to guess at. But it is highly probable—indeed, nearly certain—that they will emerge, and fairly soon. And it is nearly certain that few of them—and few industries based on them—will come out of computer and information technology. Like biotechnology and fish farming, each will emerge from its own unique and unexpected technology.

Of course, these are only predictions. But they are made on the assumption that the Information Revolution will evolve as several earlier technology-based "revolutions" have evolved over the past 500 years, since Gutenberg's printing revolution, around 1455. In particular the assumption is that the Information Revolution will be like the Industrial Revolution of the late eighteenth and early nineteenth centuries. And that is indeed exactly how the Information Revolution has been during its first fifty years.

The Railroad

The Information Revolution is now at the point at which the Industrial Revolution was in the early 1820s, about forty years after James Watt's improved steam engine (first installed in 1776) was first applied, in 1785, to an industrial operation—the spinning of cotton. And the steam engine was to the first Industrial Revolution what the computer has been to the Information Revolution—its trigger, but above all its symbol. Almost everybody today believes that nothing in economic history has ever moved as fast as, or had a greater impact than, the Information Revolution. But the Industrial Revolution moved at least fast in the same time span, and had probably an equal impact if not a greater one. In short order it mechanized the great majority of manufacturing processes, beginning with the production of the most important industrial commodity of the eighteenth and early nineteenth centuries: textiles. Moore's Law asserts that the price of the Information Revolution's basic element, the microchip, drops by 50 percent every eighteen months. The same was true of the products whose manufacture was mechanized by the first Industrial Revolution. The price of cotton textiles fell by 90 percent in the fifty years spanning the start of the eighteenth century. The production of cotton textiles increased at least 150-fold in Britain alone in the same period. And although textiles were the most visible product of its early years, the Industrial Revolution mechanized the production of practically all other major goods, such as paper, glass, leather, and bricks. Its impact was by no means confined to consumer goods. The production of iron and ironware—for example, wire—became mechanized and steam-driven as fast as did that of textiles, with the same effects on cost, price, and output. By the end of the Napoleonic Wars the making of guns was steam-driven throughout Europe; cannons were made ten to twenty times as fast as before, and their cost dropped by more than two thirds. By that time Eli Whitney had similarly mechanized the manufacture of muskets in America and had created the first mass-production industry.

These forty or fifty years gave rise to the factory and the "working class." Both were still so few in number in the mid-1820s, even in England, as to be statistically insignificant. But psychologically they had come to dominate (and soon would politically also). Before there were factories in America, Alexander Hamilton foresaw an industrialized country in his 1791 *Report on Manufactures.* A decade later, in 1803, a French economist, Jean-Baptiste Say, saw that the Industrial Revolution had changed economics by creating the "entrepreneur."

The social consequences went far beyond factory and working class. As the historian Paul Johnson has pointed out, in *A History of the American People* (1997), it was the explosive growth of the steam-engine-based textile industry that revived slavery. Considered to be practically dead by the Founders of the American Republic, slavery roared back to life as the cotton gin—soon steam-driven—created a huge demand for low-cost labor and made breeding slaves America's most profitable industry for some decades.

The Industrial Revolution also had a great impact on the family. The nuclear family had long been the unit of production. On the farm and in the artisan's workshop husband, wife, and children worked together. The factory, almost for the first time in history, took worker and work out of the home and moved them into the workplace, leaving family members behind—whether spouses of adult factory workers or, especially in the early stages, parents of child factory workers.

Indeed, the "crisis of the family" did not begin after the Second World War. It began with the Industrial Revolution—and was in fact a stock concern of those who opposed the Industrial Revolution and the factory system. (The best description of the divorce of work and family, and of its effect on both, is probably Charles Dickens's 1854 novel *Hard Times.*)

But despite all these effects, the Industrial Revolution in its first half century only mechanized the production of goods that had been in existence all along. It tremendously increased output and tremendously decreased cost. It created both consumers and consumer products. But the products themselves had been around all along. And products made in the new factories differed from traditional products only in that they were uniform, with fewer defects than existed in products made by any but the top craftsmen of earlier periods.

There was only one important exception, one new product, in those first fifty years: the steamboat, first made practical by Robert Fulton in 1807. It had little impact until thirty or forty years later. In fact, until almost the end of the nineteenth century more freight was carried on the world's oceans by sailing vessels than by steamships.

Then, in 1829, came the railroad, a product truly without precedent, and it forever changed economy, society, and politics.

In retrospect it is difficult to imagine why the invention of the railroad took so long. Rails to move carts had been around in coal mines for a very long time. What could be more obvious than to put a steam engine on a cart to drive it, rather than have it pushed by people or pulled by horses? But the railroad did not emerge from the cart in the mines. It was developed quite independently. And it was not intended to carry freight. On the contrary, for a long time it was seen only as a way to carry people. Railroads became freight carriers thirty years later, in America. (In fact, as late as the 1870s and 1880s the British engineers who were hired to build the railroads of newly Westernized Japan designed them to carry passengers—and to this day Japanese railroads are not equipped to carry freight.) But until the first railroad actually began to operate, it was virtually unanticipated.

Within five years, however, the Western world was engulfed by the biggest boom history had ever seen—the railroad boom. Punctuated by the most spectacular busts in economic history, the boom continued in Europe for thirty years, until the late 1850s, by which time most of today's major railroads had been built. In the United States it continued for another thirty years, and in outlying areas—Argentina, Brazil, Asian Russia, China—until the First World War.

The railroad was the truly revolutionary element of the Industrial Revolution, for not only did it create a new economic dimension but also it rapidly changed what I would call the *mental geography*. For the first time in history human beings had true mobility. For the first time the horizons of ordinary people expanded. Contemporaries immediately realized that a fundamental change in mentality had occurred. (A good account of this can be found in what is surely the best portrayal of the Industrial Revolution's society in transition, George Eliot's 1871 novel *Middlemarch*.) As the great French historian Fernand Braudel pointed out in his last major work, *The Identity of France* (1986), it was the railroad that made France into one nation and one culture. It had previously been a congeries of self-contained regions, held together only politically. And the role of the railroad in creating the American West is, of course, a commonplace in U.S. history.

Routinization

Like the Industrial Revolution two centuries ago, the Information Revolution so far—that is, since the first computers, in the mid-1940s—has only transformed processes that were here all along. In fact, the real impact of the Information Revolution has not been in the form of "information" at all. Almost none of the effects of information envisaged forty years ago have actually happened. For instance, there has been practically no change in the way major decisions are made in business or government. But the Information Revolution has routinized traditional *processes* in an untold number of areas.

The software for tuning a piano converts a process that traditionally took three hours into one that takes twenty minutes. There is software for payrolls, for inventory control, for delivery schedules, and for all the other routine processes of a business. Drawing the inside arrangements of a major building (heating, water supply, sewerage, and so on) such as a prison or a hospital formerly took, say, twenty-five highly skilled draftsmen up to fifty days; now there is a program that enables one draftsman to do the job in a couple of days, at a tiny fraction of the cost. There is software to help people do their tax returns and software that teaches hospital residents how to take out a gall bladder. The people who now speculate in the stock market online do exactly what their predecessors in the 1920s did while spending hours each day in a brokerage office. The processes have not been changed at all. They have been routinized, step by step, with a tremendous saving in time and, often, in cost.

The psychological impact of the Information Revolution, like that of the Industrial Revolution, has been enormous. It has perhaps been greatest on the way in which young children learn. Beginning at age four (and often earlier), children now rapidly develop computer skills, soon surpassing their elders; computers are their toys and their learning tools. Fifty years hence we may well conclude that there was no "crisis of American education" in the closing years of the twentieth century—there was only a growing incongruence between the way twentieth-century schools taught and the way late-twentieth-century children learned. Something similar happened in the sixteenth-century university, a hundred years after the invention of the printing press and movable type.

But as to the way we work, the Information Revolution has so far simply routinized what was done all along. The only exception is the CD-ROM, invented around twenty years ago to present operas, university courses, a writer's oeuvre, in an entirely new way. Like the steamboat, the CD-ROM has not immediately caught on.

The Meaning of E-commerce

E-commerce is to the Information Revolution what the railroad was to the Industrial Revolution—a totally new, totally unprecedented, totally unexpected development. And like the railroad 170 years ago, e-commerce is creating a new and distinct boom, rapidly changing the economy, society, and polities.

One example: A mid-sized company in America's industrial Midwest, founded in the 1920s and now run by the grandchildren of the founder, used to have some 60 percent of the market in inexpensive dinnerware for fast-food eateries, school and office cafeterias, and hospitals within a hundred-mile radius of its factory. China is heavy and breaks easily, so cheap china is traditionally sold within a small area. Almost overnight this company lost more than half of its market. One of its customers, a hospital cafeteria where someone went "surfing" on the Internet, discovered a European manufacturer that offered china of apparently better quality at a lower price and shipped cheaply by air. Within a few months the main customers in the area shifted to the European supplier. Few of them, it seems, realize—let alone care—that the stuff comes from Europe.

In the new mental geography created by the railroad, humanity mastered distance. In the mental geography of e-commerce, distance has been eliminated. There is only one economy and only one market.

One consequence of this is that every business must become globally competitive, even if it manufactures or sells only within a local or regional market. The competition is not local anymore—in fact, it knows no boundaries. Every company has to become transnational in the way it is run. Yet the traditional multinational may well become obsolete. It manufactures and distributes in a number of distinct geographies, in which it is a *local* company. But in e-commerce there are neither local companies nor distinct geographies. Where to manufacture, where to sell, and how to sell will remain important business decisions. But in another twenty years they may no longer determine what a company does, how it does it, and where it does it.

At the same time, it is not yet clear what kinds of goods and services will be bought and sold through e-commerce and what kinds will turn out to be unsuitable for it. This has been true whenever a new distribution channel has arisen. Why, for instance, did the railroad change both the mental and the economic geography of the West, whereas the steamboat—with its equal impact on world trade and passenger traffic—did neither? Why was there no "steamboat boom"?

Equally unclear has been the impact of more-recent changes in distribution channels—in the shift, for instance, from the local grocery store to the supermarket, from the individual supermarket to the supermarket chain, and from the supermarket chain to Wal-Mart and other discount chains. It is already clear that the shift to e-commerce will be just as eclectic and unexpected.

Here are a few examples. Twenty-five years ago it was generally believed that within a few decades the printed word would be dispatched electronically to individual subscribers' computer screens. Subscribers would then either read text on their computer screens or download it and print it out. This was the assumption that underlay the CD-ROM. Thus any number of newspapers and magazines, by no means only in the United States, established themselves online; few, so far, have become gold mines. But anyone who twenty years ago predicted the business of Amazon.com and barnesandnoble.com—that is, that books would be sold on the Internet but delivered in their heavy, printed form—would have been laughed off the podium. Yet Amazon.com and barnesandnoble.com are in exactly that business, and they are in it worldwide. The first order for the U.S. edition of my most recent book, *Management Challenges for the 21st Century* (1999), came to Amazon.com, and it came from Argentina.

Another example: Ten years ago one of the world's leading automobile companies made a thorough study of the expected impact on automobile sales of the then emerging Internet. It concluded that the Internet would become a major distribution channel for used cars, but that customers would still want to see new cars, to touch them, to test-drive them. In actuality, at least so far, most used cars are still being bought not over the Internet but in a dealer's lot. However, as many as half of all new cars sold (excluding luxury cars) may now actually be "bought" over the Internet. Dealers only deliver cars that customers have chosen well before they enter the dealership. What does this mean for the future of the local automobile dealership, the twentieth century's most profitable small business?

Another example: Traders in the American stock-market boom of 1998 and 1999 increasingly buy and sell online. But investors seem to be shifting away from buying electronically. The major U.S. investment vehicle is mutual funds. And whereas almost half of all mutual funds a few years ago were bought electronically, it is estimated that the figure will drop to 35 percent next year and to 20 percent by 2005. This is the opposite of what "everybody expected" ten or fifteen years ago.

The fastest-growing e-commerce in the United States is in an area where there was no "commerce" until now—in jobs for professionals and managers. Almost half of the world's largest companies now recruit through Web sites, and some two and a half million managerial and professional people (two thirds of them not even engineers or computer professionals) have their résumés on the Internet and solicit job offers over it. The result is a completely new labor market.

This illustrates another important effect of e-commerce. New distribution channels change who the customers are. They change not only *how* customers buy but also *what* they buy. They change consumer behavior, savings patterns, industry structure—in short, the entire economy. This is what is now happening, and not only in the United States but increasingly in the rest of the developed world, and in a good many emerging countries, including mainland China.

Luther, Machiavelli, and the Salmon

The railroad made the Industrial Revolution accomplished fact. What had been revolution became establishment. And the boom it triggered lasted almost a hundred years. The technology of the steam engine did not end with the railroad. It led in the 1880s and 1890s to the steam turbine, and in the 1920s and 1930s to the last magnificent American steam locomotives, so beloved by railroad buffs. But the technology centered on the steam engine and in manufacturing operations ceased to be central. Instead the dynamics of the technology shifted to totally new industries that emerged almost immediately after the railroad was invented, not one of which had anything to do with steam or steam engines. The electric telegraph and photography were first, in the 1830s, followed soon thereafter by optics and farm equipment. The new and different fertilizer industry, which began in the late 1830s, in short order transformed agriculture. Public health became a major and central growth industry, with quarantine, vaccination, the supply of pure water, and sewers, which for the first time in history made the city a more healthful habitat than the countryside. At the same time came the first anesthetics.

With these major new technologies came major new social institutions: the modern postal service, the daily paper, investment banking, and commercial banking, to name just a few. Not one of them had much to do with the steam engine or with the technology of the Industrial Revolution in general. It was these new industries and institutions that by 1850 had come to dominate the industrial and economic landscape of the developed countries.

This is very similar to what happened in the printing revolution—the first of the technological revolutions that created the modern world. In the fifty years after 1455, when Gutenberg had perfected the printing press and movable type he had been working on for years, the printing revolution swept Europe and completely changed its economy and its psychology. But the books printed during the first fifty years, the ones called incunabula, contained largely the same texts that monks, in their scriptoria, had for centuries laboriously copied by hand: religious tracts and whatever remained of the writings of antiquity. Some 7,000 titles were published in those first fifty years, in 35,000 editions. At least 6,700 of these were traditional titles. In other words, in its first fifty years printing made available—and increasingly cheap—traditional information and communication products. But then, some sixty years after Gutenberg, came Luther's German Bible—thousands and thousands of copies sold almost immediately at an unbelievably low price. With Luther's Bible the new printing technology ushered in a new society. It ushered in Protestantism, which conquered half of Europe and, within another twenty years, forced the

Catholic Church to reform itself in the other half. Luther used the new medium of print deliberately to restore religion to the center of individual life and of society. And this unleashed a century and a half of religious reform, religious revolt, religious wars.

At the very same time, however, that Luther used print with the avowed intention of restoring Christianity, Machiavelli wrote and published *The Prince* (1513), the first Western book in more than a thousand years that contained not one biblical quotation and no reference to the writers of antiquity. In no time at all *The Prince* became the "other best seller" of the sixteenth century, and its most notorious but also most influential book. In short order there was a wealth of purely secular works, what we today call literature: novels and books in science, history, politics, and, soon, economics. It was not long before the first purely secular art form arose, in England—the modern theater. Brand-new social institutions also arose: the Jesuit order, the Spanish infantry, the first modern navy, and, finally, the sovereign national state. In other words, the printing revolution followed the same trajectory as did the Industrial Revolution, which began 300 years later, and as does the Information Revolution today.

What the new industries and institutions will be, no one can say yet. No one in the 1520s anticipated secular literature, let alone the secular theater. No one in the 1820s anticipated the electric telegraph, or public health, or photography.

The one thing (to say it again) that is highly probable, if not nearly certain, is that the next twenty years will see the emergence of a number of new industries. At the same time, it is nearly certain that few of them will come out of information technology, the computer, data processing, or the Internet. This is indicated by all historical precedents. But it is true also of the new industries that are already rapidly emerging. Biotechnology, as mentioned, is already here. So is fish farming.

Twenty-five years ago salmon was a delicacy. The typical convention dinner gave a choice between chicken and beef. Today salmon is a commodity, and is the other choice on the convention menu. Most salmon today is not caught at sea or in a river but grown on a fish farm. The same is increasingly true of trout. Soon, apparently, it will be true of a number of other fish. Flounder, for instance, which is to seafood what pork is to meat, is just going into oceanic mass production. This will no doubt lead to the genetic development of new and different fish, just as the domestication of sheep, cows, and chickens led to the development of new breeds among them.

But probably a dozen or so technologies are at the stage where biotechnology was twenty-five years ago—that is, ready to emerge.

There is also a *service* waiting to be born: insurance against the risks of foreign-exchange exposure. Now that every business is part of the global economy, such insurance is as badly needed as was insurance against physical risks (fire, flood) in the early stages of the Industrial Revolution, when traditional insurance emerged. All the knowledge needed for foreign-exchange insurance is available; only the institution itself is still lacking.

The next two or three decades are likely to see even greater technological change than has occurred in the decades since the emergence of the computer, and also even greater change in industry structures, in the economic landscape, and probably in the social landscape as well.

The Gentleman Versus the Technologist

The new industries that emerged after the railroad owed little technologically to the steam engine or to the Industrial Revolution in general. They were not its "children after the flesh"—but they were its "children after the spirit." They were possible only because of the mind-set that the Industrial Revolution had created and the skills it had developed. This was a mind-set that accepted—indeed, eagerly welcomed—invention and innovation. It was a mind-set that accepted, and eagerly welcomed, new products and new services.

It also created the social values that made possible the new industries. Above all, it created the "technologist." Social and financial success long eluded the first major American technologist, Eli Whitney, whose cotton gin, in 1793, was as central to the triumph of the Industrial Revolution as was the steam engine. But a generation later the technologist—still self-taught—had become the American folk hero and was both socially accepted and financially rewarded. Samuel Morse, the inventor of the telegraph, may have been the first example; Thomas Edison became the most prominent. In Europe the "businessman" long remained a social inferior, but the university-trained engineer had by 1830 or 1840 become a respected "professional."

By the 1850s England was losing its predominance and beginning to be overtaken as an industrial economy, first by the United States and then by Germany. It is generally accepted that neither economics nor technology was the major reason. The main cause was social. Economically, and especially financially, England remained the great power until the First World War. Technologically it held its own throughout the nineteenth century. Synthetic dyestuffs, the first products of the modern chemical industry, were invented in England, and so was the steam turbine. But England did not accept the technologist socially. He never became a "gentleman." The English built first-rate engineering schools in India but almost none at home. No other country so honored the "scientist"—and, indeed, Britain retained leadership in physics throughout the nineteenth century, from James Clerk Maxwell and Michael Faraday all the way to Ernest Rutherford. But the technologist remained a "tradesman." (Dickens, for instance, showed open contempt for the upstart ironmaster in his 1853 novel *Bleak House*.)

Nor did England develop the venture capitalist, who has the means and the mentality to finance the unexpected and unproved. A French invention, first portrayed in Balzac's monumental *La Comédie humaine*, in the 1840s, the venture capitalist was institutionalized in the United States by J. P. Morgan and, simultaneously, in Germany and Japan by the universal bank. But England, although it invented and developed the commercial bank to finance trade, had no institution to finance industry until two German refugees, S. G. Warburg and Henry Grunfeld, started an entrepreneurial bank in London, just before the Second World War.

Bribing the Knowledge Worker

What might be needed to prevent the United States from becoming the England of the twenty-first century? I am convinced that a drastic change in the social mind-set is required—just as leadership in the industrial economy after the railroad required the drastic change from "tradesman" to "technologist" or "engineer."

What we call the Information Revolution is actually a Knowledge Revolution. What has made it possible to routinize processes is not machinery; the computer is only the trigger. Software is the reorganization of traditional work, based on centuries of experience, through the application of knowledge and especially of systematic, logical analysis. The key is not electronics; it is cognitive science. This means that the key to maintaining leadership in the economy and the technology that are about to emerge is likely to be the social position of knowledge professionals and social acceptance of their values. For them to remain traditional "employees" and be treated as such would be tantamount to England's treating its technologists as tradesmen—and likely to have similar consequences.

Today, however, we are trying to straddle the fence—to maintain the traditional mind-set, in which capital is the key resource and the financier is the boss, while bribing knowledge workers to be content to remain employees by giving them bonuses and stock options. But this, if it can work at all, can work only as long as the emerging industries enjoy a stock-market boom, as the Internet companies have been doing. The next major industries are likely to behave far more like traditional industries—that is, to grow slowly, painfully, laboriously.

The early industries of the Industrial Revolution—cotton textiles, iron, the railroads—were boom industries that created millionaires overnight, like Balzac's venture bankers and like Dickens's ironmaster, who in a few years grew from a lowly domestic servant into a "captain of industry." The industries that emerged after 1830 also created millionaires. But they took twenty years to do so, and it was twenty years of hard work, of struggle, of disappointments and failures, of thrift. This is likely to be true of the industries that will emerge from now on. It is already true of biotechnology.

Bribing the knowledge workers on whom these industries depend will therefore simply not work. The key knowledge workers in these businesses will surely continue to expect to share financially in the fruits of their labor. But the financial fruits are likely to take much longer to ripen, if they ripen at all. And then, probably within ten years or so, running a business with (short-term) "shareholder value" as its first—if not its only—goal and justification will have become counterproductive. Increasingly, performance in these new knowledge-based industries will come to depend on running the institution so as to attract, hold, and motivate knowledge workers. When this can no longer be done by satisfying knowledge workers' greed, as we are now trying to do, it will have to be done by satisfying their values, and by giving them social recognition and social power. It will have to be done by turning them from subordinates into fellow executives, and from employees, however well paid, into partners.

REFLECTING ON THE READING

1. In what ways is the Information Revolution similar to the Industrial Revolution, according to Drucker? In what ways is the computer like the steam engine, in Drucker's view? Why is this comparison between the Information Revolution

and the Industrial Revolution important in Drucker's discussion of the future? What might it suggest about Drucker's perspective on technology and change?

2. What were the major social consequences of the Industrial Revolution, in Drucker's view? Why are these consequences important in considering the impact of the computer in the late twentieth century and now in the twenty-first century?

3. In what sense was the railroad "truly revolutionary," as Drucker describes it? What might this description suggest about Drucker's view of technology and its role in human life and in the structure of human societies? Refer to specific passages from his article in your answer.

4. In what sense is the term *the Information Revolution* a misnomer, according to Drucker? What has been the real impact of the computer, in his view? Do you think he is right? Explain.

5. Why does Drucker believe that e-commerce is the most important development associated with the Information Revolution? In what sense is e-commerce unprecedented and unexpected, as he sees it? What impact has it had on the way people live and work, in his view? What remains unclear about the effects it will have in the future? Do you think this uncertainty worries Drucker? Explain. Does it worry you? Why or why not?

6. In what sense did the printing revolution help create the modern world, according to Drucker? Why does he consider the development of the printing press to be an important one? What effects did that development have on European society? What importance does the printing revolution have for our own future, in Drucker's view? Do you agree with him? Why or why not?

7. In what way did the Industrial Revolution lead to a new mind-set among Americans, according to Drucker? Why was this mind-set important, in his view? What impact did it have on American society and on its economy? Why does Drucker believe the development of this mind-set in the United States is important for us today?

8. In Drucker's view, why is the social position of "knowledge workers" the key to economic and technological leadership in the future? What changes will have to be made in American business in order to maintain that leadership? Do you think Drucker expects such changes to occur? Why or why not?

Examining Rhetorical Strategies

1. Analyze Drucker's method of building his argument about his vision of the future. What key points does he make in presenting his vision of the future? What kinds of evidence does he provide? How does he use the past in anticipating the future? What do you think his way of making his argument suggests about his assumptions regarding his audience? Did you find his discussion convincing? Why or why not?

2. What vision of technology does Drucker present in this article? He devotes his discussion of the future largely to various technologies—like the computer and

the railroad—and the changes in human societies that those technologies seem to have brought on. Do you think he presents a view of technology that is positive, negative, or neutral? Explain, citing specific passages from his article to support your answer. How does his view of technology shape the predictions he makes for the future? Does it encourage him to emphasize certain kinds of developments while ignoring others? Explain.

3. Assess Drucker's use of examples to support his analyses and predictions. What kinds of examples does he use in his discussion? What do these examples suggest about what he seems to value regarding technology and human life? What is missing in these examples, in your view? Did you find his use of examples effective? Why or why not? Cite specific passages from his text to support your answer.

4. Drucker discusses broad social and economic changes brought on by the Industrial Revolution and the Information Revolution, including the rise of the working class and the emergence of millionaires. But he does not directly address issues such as inequality in wage earnings or some of the many social problems that are often associated with the Industrial Revolution. Nor does he discuss such problems as they might emerge in the Information Revolution. Do you think Drucker intentionally omits discussion of such problems? Why or why not? What purpose would be served by addressing such issues in his article? How might addressing such issues change his discussion of the future? How might it affect his presentation of technology in this article?

5. This article was originally published in the *Atlantic Monthly,* a magazine about social, political, and cultural issues read largely by educated middle-class and upper-middle class readers. Do you think such readers would generally find Drucker's analysis of the past and vision of the future appealing or convincing? Why or why not? Do you think they would generally agree with his assumptions about technology? Explain. How might readers with a different socioeconomic background—for example, a low-income background—react to Drucker's article? Do you think Drucker took such readers into account in his article? Explain.

Engaging the Issues

1. Write an essay for an audience of your classmates in which you offer your own vision of the future in response to Drucker's article. In your essay, address what you see as the key points that Drucker raises and the main features of his vision of the future as shaped by e-commerce. Offer your own perspective on these points, drawing on your own experiences and on any other relevant sources.

2. In a group of your classmates, share the essays you wrote for Question #1 above. Discuss your respective responses to Drucker's vision of the future, identifying important similarities and differences. Consider what values regarding technology and human life seem to be reflected in the respective visions of the future offered by the members of your group.

3. In a response to Drucker's article, one reader complained to the *Atlantic Monthly* that "Peter Drucker glosses over the tremendous social instability unleashed by industrialization. . . . If e-commerce is as revolutionary as Drucker claims, social dislocations will follow. At a minimum, the income gap between rich and poor will widen as low-skilled individuals find themselves unable to survive in an information-based economy" (John Quinterno, Jr., "Letters," *Atlantic Monthly,* February 2000, p. 13). Write an essay in which you develop this criticism of Drucker's article. In your essay, describe the major changes that Drucker foresees and discuss other social and economic implications of the Information Revolution that you believe Drucker ignores or neglects to discuss. If necessary, draw on other sources to support your critique of Drucker's article.

   Alternatively, write an essay defending Drucker's article against the criticism described above.

4. Using your library, the Internet, and any other available resources, investigate e-commerce. Find out what economists, businesspeople, and others mean by that term and locate articles or Web sites in which e-commerce and its implications are discussed. Visit Web sites of businesses to see what kinds of products and services are available online and how those might differ from traditional products and services. If possible, interview several people involved with e-commerce (for example, a friend or relative who might work for a company that engages in online business). Then write a report for an audience of your classmates about the phenomenon of e-commerce. In your report, define e-commerce based on the research you did and describe its key features. Discuss the implications of e-commerce. Offer your own perspective on these developments and on what e-commerce is likely to mean for us in the future.

   Alternatively, construct a Web site about e-commerce on the basis of your research.

5. On the basis of your research for Question #4 above, write an essay for the editorial page of your local newspaper in which you offer your view of e-commerce and its implications for the future. In your essay, offer your assessment of the impact that e-commerce has had on our lives and discuss your vision of or worries about what e-commerce might mean in the future.

6. Write a letter to the superintendent of your local school district in which you discuss what you see as the implications of the developments that Peter Drucker discusses in his article. Address what these implications might mean for schools, and propose changes in the curriculum that you believe schools should be making in order to prepare students for the e-commerce of the future.

7. Using your library and the Internet, investigate the life and work of Peter Drucker. Find out about Drucker's main contributions to business, economics, and politics, and discuss the impact his ideas have had on others involved in those matters. Then write a report about Drucker for an audience of your classmates.

   Alternatively, construct a Web site that is a resource on Drucker's life and work. Be sure to consider audience and purpose in designing your site.

Public Life in the Electropolis

*A Dialogue on Virtual Communities with Mark Slouka,
Howard Rheingold, and William Mitchell*

INTRODUCTION In 1995, *FEED* magazine, a respected online journal devoted to politics, culture, and technology, invited several prominent thinkers to engage in a discussion about online culture. The discussion took place in three parts, the last of which focuses on "virtual communities," a term that refers to the various social groups that form through interactions in Internet discussion groups, chat rooms, and similar online media. Specifically, the participants in the discussion take up the issue of what the growth of virtual communities might mean for our society as we conduct more and more of our affairs in the "electropolis" of online forums that are devoted to public debate and conversation. In this sense, the *FEED* dialogue is especially fitting, because it represents the very same kind of online discussion that the participants—Mark Slouka, Howard Rheingold, and William Mitchell—examine in their comments. In fact, *FEED*, as an online journal where such discussions routinely take place, represents one kind of virtual community that may become increasingly common in the near future.

The idea of virtual communities has preoccupied many observers since the very beginnings of the Internet. ARPANET, the computer network that was the precursor to the Internet, was developed in the late 1960's and early 1970's by the U.S. Department of Defense primarily to enable researchers to share information and conduct data analyses even when they were in different physical locations. But even in its earliest form, the network quickly became a medium through which researchers did more than collaborate on their projects: They also kept in touch with one another informally, asked each other for advice about professional and personal matters unrelated to their research, shared jokes, and interacted socially, much as they might if they had been neighbors or colleagues at the same research facility. In other words, they used the electronic network to create and maintain communities—in some cases, communities comprised of people who would never physically meet one another. Such virtual communities are now a common feature of the Internet.

The rapid proliferation of these virtual communities during the 1990's as the Internet expanded has raised many complex questions, not only about the nature of these communities but also about what they might mean for our future personal and public lives. As the *FEED* editor suggests in the introduction to the following dialogue, the very idea of *community* is difficult to define precisely. Just what constitutes a community? Is a community a group of people who share a space—a physical location such as a neighborhood or a "virtual" space such as an online chat room? Or is it comprised of people who share interests or expertise or specific characteristics? We speak of the "African American community," for example, or the "academic community" or the "scientific community" to refer to people who share characteristics or professions or who engage in similar activities, even though these people may not even know one another or live in the same part of the world. Is a virtual community different in any significant way from these "real" communities? Does the nature of communication on the Internet—with its speed and capacity to connect many people in many different places—change the way communities form and the way members of communities interact with one another? And if so, what might these changes mean for our "real" life communities and how they operate?

These are not simply questions for technophiles and scholars to ponder. They are questions that speak directly to the kind of life we will have in the future. The Internet is now a fixture of contemporary industrialized society that has begun to influence the ways in which we do business, conduct our personal lives, do our work, and participate in political processes—as several writers in this book demonstrate. Moreover, as the Internet becomes more accessible and more fully integrated into contemporary society, more people will spend more time online, presumably as part of virtual communities that will become increasingly important in their lives. Thus, how we think about virtual communities and how we structure them and participate in them may have a profound impact on the kind of world we will create for ourselves in the coming years. And as the participants in the *FEED* dialogue remind us, there are potentially as many problems ahead as there are benefits.

The three participants in the *FEED* dialogue are especially well qualified to address the topic of virtual communities. William Mitchell is a professor of architecture and media arts and sciences and Dean of the School of Architecture and Planning at the Massachusetts Institute of Technology. He studies computer-aided design, imaging, and architecture and is the author of numerous books on computer-related topics including *The Reconfigured Eye: Visual Truth in the Post-Photographic Era* (1992) and *City of Bits: Space, Place, and the Infobahn* (1995). Mark Slouka is a writer whose short stories and articles have appeared in various publications including *Harper's*. He is the author of *War of the Worlds: Cyberspace and the High-Tech Assault on Reality* (1995). Howard Rheingold brings to this discussion a great deal of experience with writing and technology. He has been editor of *The Whole Earth Review* and *The Millennium Whole Earth Catalog* (1994) and was a founder and editor of *HotWired* magazine. He has written a number of books about computer technology, notably *Virtual Reality* (1991).

REFLECTING BEFORE READING

1. The following selection is a dialogue in which three influential writers are asked to offer their views about virtual communities. As you read, be aware of the format of the dialogue, which has become an increasingly common format for public discussions as the Internet has expanded in recent years. What does this format enable the participants to do, if anything, that would be difficult or impossible to do in another format (for example, a conventional feature article in which their views were summarized by a single writer)? What advantages or disadvantages do you see to this format? How does it affect your own engagement with the topic, if at all?

2. What do you know about virtual communities? Have you participated in any such communities? As you read, consider how your own knowledge about or experiences with virtual communities might influence your reaction to this dialogue.

FEED EDITOR: Mark [Slouka] offers a provocative distinction between positive and negative uses for virtual communities: "the transmission of data [vs.] the transmission of experience." His line in the sand points to the promise of new technologies. This of course isn't the first time we've had to tease the benefits of new technology out of the hype: radio and TV are just two examples. We've also seen how difficult it is to wrest the benefits from these technologies once in play. TV created a nation of couch potatoes, each passively absorbing images created and filtered by media conglomerates. By now, it's a tired statistic that the average American spends far more of her leisure time watching TV than reading. Virtual communities are offered up as an antidote: now we can reclaim democracy, vent our opinions about the OJ trial, and circumvent Op-Ed page editors, not to mention obtain tons of useful information. Consensus seems to be, from both dialog readers and participants, that virtual communities are a step up from the boob-tube. So let's consider some of the more subtle aspects of hanging out in virtual communities: Do they really engender deeper, more informed conversations far from the distraction of pundits? Or do members trade serious reflection on an issue for postable prose, do-it-yourself sound bites?

And finally—we've spent a great deal of time here speculating on the future of online culture, the social possibilities unleashed by the new technologies of the information revolution. But as Tim Burke and other readers point out, "community" is often more of a state of mind than anything else. However much our virtual communities may be shaped by their underlying hardware, they are also profoundly shaped by us—the citizens and the cybernauts. So let's end on a note of activism: what can we do to make the electropolis as meaningful, lively, and diverse as its real-world predecessor? How do we ensure that virtual communities do not become yet another platform for an atomized world, where everyone lives in her own cube and connects to the Outside only through video-phone and e-mail? As millions of Americans jet into cyberspace, how do we make sure the virtual community remains a useful community-building "tool"—as Howard [Rheingold] puts it—and not an enveloping surrogate life?

WILLIAM MITCHELL: How does digital telecommunications technology become a useful community-building tool? How do we avoid the downsides?

I doubt that it's very useful to try to answer these questions at some high level of abstraction. But they become interesting when we consider the options that may face us in concrete, specific contexts.

Take the case of MIT, for example. (It's a very immediate and pressing one for me.) One possible future for us is to go virtual in a dramatic and sweeping way. We could sell all that valuable real estate along the Charles River, put the proceeds into endowment, and rent whatever laboratory and office space we still needed at some lower-cost location out along Route 128. We could (pretty soon) use high-bandwidth, two-way, multimedia telecommunications to deliver lectures, seminars, and even one-to-one discussions with professors to homes, workplaces, and classrooms throughout the world. Our student body would be dispersed and international, and so would our faculty—since they could conduct their research, deliver their teaching from pretty much anywhere. Essentially, MIT would become a research and education brokering service operating internationally to connect teachers to students and researchers to each other and to their sponsors. We would probably end up merging with some giant telecommunications conglomerate, much as movie and recording studios have done. Of course we would jealously protect the historic MIT name and logo, and zealously defend our intellectual property.

This could be a pretty good business, and I have no doubt that we will quite soon see some businesses flourishing along essentially these lines (and scaring the pants off established educational institutions in the process). But, as we'd probably all feel, something very important would be lost if we were to go that way. What, precisely, is that?

Well, consider what's particularly valuable about MIT. It is, of course, the special—indeed, unique—character of the community that it supports. Students compete to be admitted to that community, and their parents are prepared to pay a great deal to keep them in it for some years, because its attractions cannot be duplicated elsewhere. Similarly, outstanding faculty members can be recruited largely because the intellectual advantages of participating in the MIT community seem compelling. This all depends on the density and intensity of face-to-face interactions made possible by concentrating the whole enterprise on one small patch of ground. If you inhabit that patch of ground, you just get more stimulating and important intellectual interactions per day than you can in most other places. If MIT were to go virtual, the special character of the community—on which everything depends—would quickly be lost. It's a bad option.

But consider, now, the possibility of using advanced digital telecommunications to extend and enrich, rather than to replace that physically-based community. MIT might, for example, begin to offer electronically delivered ongoing educational services to alumni. This would be a return to the medieval idea of a university as a lifelong community of scholars, but would usefully adapt to the circumstance that senior members of the community now disperse widely into the world rather than remain for life behind college walls. In a similar way, immediate electronic connections to MIT might be offered to the most promising young mathematicians and scientists among high school seniors. This model could be elaborated endlessly, but I think the basic idea is now clear; selectively and critically augment the physically-based community with electronic links, rather than use electronics for wholesale replacement of face-to-face contact by telecommunication.

Now generalize this approach to other contexts and types of communities. I like Stacy's* notion that Echo provides some additional connections that extend and enrich New York's social and cultural life. I like the way that Seniornet breaks down the physical isolation that affects so many older members of our communities. I like the way that the Big Sky Telegraph (and some emergent similar efforts in the Australian outback) begins to weld tiny, isolated communities into a larger whole that provides greater diversity and wider social, intellectual, and economic opportunity. I like the proposal to create "Virtual Ireland"—a promising way to preserve and strengthen the culture of an emigrant people. These things have all emerged in response to very real human needs and desires in particular contexts, and I think they are very successful for that reason.

---

* Stacy Horn is the author of *Cyberville: Clicks, Culture, and the Creation of an Online Town* (1998) and founder of Echo, a virtual salon in New York City (www.echonyc.com).

You can always construct arguments that, by taking a wider view, we could find better ways to deal with these needs. For example, it might make more sense to resist a social system that systematically isolates its older members, rather than to create a technological palliative for that isolation. It's always prudent to raise and debate this sort of point before looking for a technological fix. (Mark could, no doubt, develop that point eloquently.) And we certainly have to consider the sometimes-subtle second-order effects that introducing a new technology can have. (Who could forget the lesson of the automobile!) But I think we will find, with increasing frequency, that telecommunications infrastructure is one of the most practical and effective community building tools we now have. When we find that deploying this infrastructure in some context can really make a positive difference in people's lives, we ought to go for it.

MARK SLOUKA: Will virtual communities help us "reclaim democracy, vent our opinions about the OJ trial, and circumvent Op-Ed newspaper editors" etc? Clearly, there's something very powerful (and potentially very positive) about a technology that allows millions of people to share ideas and allows them to side-step the occasionally ignorant or biased "filters" like magazine Op-Ed editors. My concern (a viable one, to judge by the mass of stuff online), is that the Net will privilege "venting" over debate and knee jerk speed over reflection. There's a very real chance that what the net will produce is not "tons of useful information," but virtual mountains of babble among which the occasionally useful tidbit of information (the kind not available in the local library), will be as easy to find as a nickel in a landfill.

At some point, we may have to ask ourselves a few unpleasant questions. Do we truly need another, even more egalitarian outlet for our ideas? Is anyone truly being shut out of the debate in this country? After all, there are currently thousands (probably tens of thousands) of outlets available—newspapers, magazines, journals, of all descriptions and political persuasions. To publish (even for the semi-literate or decidedly wacky) is simply not that tough. True, breaking onto the New York Times Op-Ed page or into The New Yorker may require a level of accommodation to the powers that be that many may find restricting, but there are other outlets. And for those who would argue that these other outlets are often marginal and do not let us enter the national debate, well, most are a whole lot less marginal than the newsgroups and BBS's* on which we can post our thoughts on the Net.

In short, the apparent egalitarianism on the net, while appealing, hides the unpleasant fact that some filtering is probably necessary; that not everyone who can tap on a keyboard has something interesting or useful to say. Sounds elitist, I know. But consider that Howard, Stacy, Bill and I are here only because the folks at FEED selected us to be here, because we, in turn, had done or written something which suggested that we had something to offer. Does that mean there aren't a hundred other people out there whose thoughts aren't potentially equally useful, or more so? Not at all. It simply means that in order to survive (and to be readable), FEED has to make certain choices. Not unlike The New Yorker after all.

---

* BBS refers to online bulletin boards.

Another unsettling thought regarding the "tons of useful information" comment. Do we, after all need tons of useful information? Don't we already have available to us more information than we possibly know what to do with? The New York Times worries continually (I notice again this morning) about the "information have nots." Is it a lack of information that gives young black men in south-central LA the life expectancy of front-line grunts during the Vietnam War, or that separates my bright (Anglo) six-year-old who reads on a fourth grade level from the equally bright (Chicano) six year-old a mile away who doesn't read at all? Is our scandalous infant mortality rate due to a lack of information? No, no, and no again. We're drowning in information (and drowning just the same). It seems to me that before buying into the Newt-like notion of information as the panacea for all that ails us, the New York Times might do better to worry about the "food have-nots," or the "education have-nots," or the "immmunization have-nots." The lap-tops can wait. As Neil Postman has pointed out so well (and I'm entirely with him on this one), there are very few problems we face that arise from a lack of information. We know what ails us; we're just not doing anything about it.

Let me end on a note of skepticism. "What can we do to make the electropolis as meaningful, lively, and diverse as its real-world predecessor?" In my opinion, not a damn thing. The real world is not susceptible to duplication; it's a problem no amount of bandwidth can compensate for. "How do we ensure that virtual communities do not become yet another platform for an atomized world, where everyone lives in her own cube," etc? At the risk of sounding glib, by turning off the machine whenever possible. By denying it the allegiance it demands. By recognizing that today (as Kevin Kelly* has put it), we already "inhabit a terrain of simulacra," and that the trend is toward ever-more pervasive and sophisticated simulations; by asserting, in the face of that trend, the value of the unmediated moment, and reacquainting ourselves with the aura of the real.

HOWARD RHEINGOLD: Teasing the benefits of new technology out of the hype is definitely a task at hand. I think it's deeper than that. Every technology changes us and changes the world around us, and those changes usually don't become evident for years or decades after the technologies are first deployed. We don't have any vocabulary for discussing the fine points of technology effects that are NOT beneficial. The only behavior that comes to hand, once you see beyond the hype or even experience the horrors that naive technological optimism ignores (Bhopal, Chernobyl, etc), is the extreme one of rejection. I think we are a world of people who have never learned to see the shades of gray. The virtual world is one area where we better crank up our ability to discriminate.

Sad commentary, isn't it? Making inane conversation with another human, faraway, insulated by wires and screens and ASCII, is better than being a total zombie. At least there is the chance that you might go beyond inane conversation. How much further than inane conversation is possible? How much of the important parts of real communities are authentic in cyberspace, and how much is cruel, even dangerous, illusion? I don't know. I don't think enough people have looked closely enough or long enough to know.

---

*Kevin Kelly is executive editor of *Wired* magazine.

Again, we're mesmerized by the tool and need to pull back from a tight focus to a long shot on the task that people are using the tool to accomplish. So what are people trying to accomplish? Some of them seem to be genuinely reaching out to each other. So what do you do when you reach out and find other people in the cyber-realm? What then, in your real life? I think that's where we are now. As more and more people rush into online discourse, we need to focus on what this actually does to affect our real lives, and whether those affects are beneficial. The only thing I am willing to bet on now is that the truth is neither in the realm of black nor in the realm of white, but in the shades of gray.

This dialogue is a start. But discussions at this level need to be repeated for many more people.

I've experienced enough real community through online discourse to know that in some instances, the tool can be used to enhance authentic community. But I don't have a magical belief that just because people are using computer conferencing software they are going to have the interest or the patience to work through the long, arduous, often painful process of community-building out in the world of bodies.

Words have great power. I started using the term "virtual community" in the nineteen eighties, in order to convince people that online discourse is not the sole province of antisocial geeks who can't handle face to face conversation. Now I find myself fighting the magical belief, or the perception of the magical belief, that adding computers will create "electronic democracy" or that virtual worlds are going to solve the problems we have in the nonvirtual world. I think talking about online conversation as a tool, which then leaves an opening for talking about what it is you are building with the tool, and how the building is designed, and how the design might affect human life [is crucial].

I was one of those who were caught up in enthusiasm for the democratizing potential inherent in many-to-many communication. When hundreds of millions of people can have the technological power on their desktops that only the Pentagon could afford twenty years ago, the potential is still significant. I still believe that potential can be realized, but not through unthinking enthusiasm. The time is right for looking cautiously, skeptically, but not pessimistically, at what people manage to actually accomplish with the tools of many-to-many communication over the coming years.

REFLECTING ON THE READING

1. Define *electropolis* as you understand it from this dialogue. What specifically do these writers mean by that term? Why do you think they use this term rather than a more established one?

2. What virtual future does Mitchell imagine in his portion of this dialogue? What characteristics of this future does he illustrate with his example of MIT? What would be lost in such a future, according to Mitchell? Do you agree with him? Why or why not?

3. What model of community does Mitchell advocate? What is the role of technology in that community? What advantages does Mitchell see to such a model as opposed to a strictly virtual community?

4. What concerns Slouka about online communities? What does he mean when he writes that "some filtering is probably necessary" when it comes to online discussions and information? Do you think he is right? Why or why not?

5. What role does Slouka propose for the electropolis? How does his vision of the relationship between online communities and real-world communities differ from Mitchell's? What general view of technology does Slouka convey in his comments about online technologies? Do you share the "note of skepticism" he offers in his final paragraph? Explain.

6. What does Rheingold mean when he writes, "The virtual world is one area where we better crank up our ability to discriminate"? What does this statement suggest about how human beings tend to view technology? What problems does Rheingold see with that tendency?

7. Is Rheingold opposed to online communities? Explain. Are you? What might your answer suggest about your own view of technology and your values as a human being?

Examining Rhetorical Strategies

1. Examine how the *FEED* editor introduces this dialogue. What is highlighted in the introduction? How does the introduction help establish the focus of the dialogue that follows? How effective do you think the introduction is in setting up the dialogue? Do you think you would have been more or less engaged in the dialogue without the editor's introduction? Explain.

2. Describe the voice of each of the three participants in this dialogue. Do you think each participant has a distinctive voice in this dialogue? Do you think these participants sound like writers or like participants in an oral discussion? Explain. Identify specific characteristics of each writer's style that contributes to his voice. Which of these writers do you find most appealing? What might your response suggest about you as a reader?

3. Compare how each participant in this dialogue constructs his main argument about virtual communities. What main argument does each make? What kind of support for his argument does each writer offer? Do you think these three writers take similar approaches in making their arguments? Explain. What might their methods of making their arguments suggest about the kind of audience they were addressing in this dialogue?

4. At one point, Howard Rheingold states, "This dialogue is a start. But discussions at this level need to be repeated for many more people." What do you think that statement suggests about who Rheingold assumed is the audience for this dialogue? Do you think that all three of these writers assumed a narrow, specialized audience for this dialogue? Explain. Whom would you expect to read this dialogue in an online journal such as *FEED?* How do you think a more general audience might respond to their arguments?

5. Comment on the order in which the participants "speak" in this dialogue. Does it matter in what order their comments appear? Why or why not? What difference, if any, do you think it would have made if Slouka or Rheingold "spoke" first? Do you think the editors intended this order for a specific purpose? Explain.

Engaging the Issues

1. Write your own contribution to this dialogue to be added after Rheingold's.

2. Using your library, the Internet, and any other relevant resources, investigate the idea of virtual communities. Find out how writers like Howard Rheingold define virtual communities. Look into the various kinds of virtual communities that have emerged on the Internet and the role they play in people's lives. Then write a conventional academic paper in which you report on the results of your research. In your paper, define *virtual community* and summarize the key points that emerged from the sources you consulted. Identify the advantages and disadvantages of virtual communities. Draw conclusions about what role these communities might play in the future.

3. Write a rhetorical analysis in which you compare the effectiveness of the arguments that each of the participants in this debate makes. In your essay, summarize the main argument of each writer and describe the way in which each supports his argument. Discuss which argument you found most effective and why. Be sure to consider the issue of audience in your analysis.

4. If you have been part of a virtual community, write an essay for an audience of your classmates in which you describe your experiences in that community. In your essay, describe the nature of the virtual community you were part of and the kinds of experiences you had as part of it. Discuss the role of the community in your life and the impact it had on important aspects of your personal life or your work. Compare your experiences as part of a virtual community to your experiences in "real" communities that you are a part of. Draw conclusions about virtual communities on the basis of your experiences.

5. In a group of your classmates, share the essays you wrote for Question #4 above. Compare the experiences about which each of you wrote and discuss what those experiences might suggest about virtual communities. Discuss, too, how your experiences might support or challenge the arguments of Mitchell, Slouka, and Rheingold in the *FEED* dialogue.

6. Write an essay for the editorial page of your local newspaper expressing your views about the rise of virtual communities and the role of technologies in our social lives. In your essay, discuss the implications of such technologies for the future.

FURTHERING YOUR INQUIRY

1. Write an essay for an audience of your classmates in which you express your expectations, hopes, and worries about the future. In your essay, draw on one

or more of the readings in this chapter (and on any other appropriate sources) to help you present your vision of the future. Discuss especially your expectations and concerns regarding technology and/or literacy. Propose measures that can be taken to avoid the problems you foresee with technology in the years ahead.

2. Rewrite the essay you wrote for Question #1 above for a different audience. For example, write your essay for readers of an online magazine such as *HotWired* that focuses on technology or for an audience that you assume will be skeptical about technology.

3. Write a conventional academic essay in which you compare the visions of the future presented by two or more writers in this chapter. For example, you might compare the respective visions of Betty Adcock, Peter Drucker, and Howard Rheingold, each of whom offers a somewhat different vision for the future. In your essay, summarize the vision of each writer and explain each writer's view of technology. Try to identify what you see as the basic values of each writer regarding human life and culture. Identify similarities and differences among the writers and draw conclusions about which vision you find most compelling.

4. Write a conventional academic essay in which you discuss the views of technology of two or more writers in this chapter. In your essay, summarize the view of technology of each writer you selected, identifying what you see as the key assumptions each writer makes about technology. Discuss the role that each writer sees for technology in human life. Identify key points of agreement or disagreement among the writers you selected and offer your own view of technology in comparison to the views of the writers you selected.

5. Write an essay entitled "A Day in My Life in 2010."

6. In a group of your classmates, compare the essays you wrote for Question #5 above. Look for important similarities and differences in how each of you envisions your life in the year 2010. Discuss how technology is portrayed in your respective essays and the role you each expect it to play in your future lives. Draw conclusions about the values you and your classmates hold regarding technology and human life.

7. Create a Web site in which you present your vision of the future. Be sure to design your site with a specific audience in mind, and make the purpose of your site clear to that audience.

8. Write an essay for a general audience (such as readers of a large-circulation publication like *USA Today*) in which you make an argument for or against a specific technology that you believe will have a significant impact on how we live in the next ten to twenty years. In your essay, explain why you selected the technology about which you are writing, and discuss its role in our lives as you see it. Propose specific measures that you believe should be taken by governments or individuals with respect to this technology.

Credits

Index of Authors and Titles